民初議員列傳——附民初政黨及議會史

中華民國珍貴史料

佐藤三郎
井上一葉

編著

BIOGRAPHIES OF MEMBERS

OF THE

UPPER AND LOWER HOUSES IN CHINA.

FIRST EDITION.

參議院議長　王家襄先生題辭

衆議院議長　湯化龍先生題辭

北京寫眞通信社　佐藤三郎編輯

民國之精華　第壹輯

北京寫眞通信社刊行

Edited by Peking Photo Agency.

旁搜博采
含英咀華

中華民國五年秋
湯化龍題

緒言

本書以民國之精華命名。以蒐集民國現代之俊傑爲
主。然尤以參衆兩院議員諸君。爲中華民國五族億兆
代表之英俊。而翼贊共和建設之偉人也。本書之第一
輯記載兩院議員諸君列傳。萃秀於一冊。流芳於萬年。
蓋云亞東出版界未有之盛舉。而蒐集資料編纂記事。
似易而實難。迫於時日。而編輯者本欲早爲成就。然一
時蒐集未全。兩院議員之列傳未及三分之二。殊深歉
仄。且議會史篇內。亦未克並列漢英二文。有負諸君之
厚望。完全之刊以俟他日。謹書數語以代叙言。

丙辰初冬 編輯者識

民國之精華

中華民國議會史（日文）

中華民國議員列傳

第壹輯目次

四

中華民國議會史

第壹章 最初の民意機關

一 上海代表會

明治四十四年十一月十二日（宣統二年九月二十二日）江蘇都督府代表雷奮、沈恩孚、浙江都督府代表姚桐豫、高爾登は武昌、南昌、福州、廣州、長沙、雲南、安慶、桂林、太原、貴陽、成都、西安、濟南、天津、開封、奉天、吉林、齊々哈爾、蘭州、迪化各地の都督府若くは諮議局に宛、通電を發して、伍廷芳、温宗堯二氏を臨時政府の組織に付き會議すべきことの公認を求めたり。越て十五日、雷奮に加るに滬軍都督府代表袁希洛、朱葆康、俞寰澄、福建都督府代表林長民、潘祖彝は上海に在る江蘇教育總會の一室に會して、本會を各省都督府代表聯合會と名づけ雷、林二名は假規則を起草し、文書並に庶務會計は敎育總會書記汪伯軒に囑託する事とせり。

十七日、鎮江都督府代表馬良、陶遜來り加り、沈は蘇州都督府の廣東來電を披露して曰く『武昌都督代表亦た各省に通電して代表の派遣を求む、武昌と上海、其の所謂各省代表聯合會と關係あるや否やを問ム』と。因て相議して『上海は交通便利なるが故に、各省代表會は此地に相會せん事を希望す、倘し同意せば則ち代表を上海に特派されたし』との旨を武昌の黎都督元洪、黄總司令宛與打電したり。

二十日、山東都督府代表謝鴻燾、雷光宇、湖南都督府代表宋教仁來り會す。

是等上海到着の各代表は其の代表せる各省をして黎黄宛發電して『武昌を中央軍政府、鄂軍都督府を中央政務執行處とする事を承認し、並に中央政府の名義を以て各代表の推定せる伍廷芳、温宗堯を民國外交總長及び副長と爲す事の承認』をば請求せしめたり。二十一日、江西都督府代表王照、陳宧、查徐鎮。二十三日、浙江都督府代表湯爾和、湖北都督府代表居正、陶鳳集、來着す。居正は『湖北都督府既に各省に通電して全權委員を武昌に特派し、以て臨時政府を組織すべきを請求したり。予の上海に來れる實は在上海の各省代表を武昌に迎へんが爲なりと云ふ。因て各省都督へ通電して全權委員を武昌へ向け上海を出發當日再議すべきを議決し、其の旨各省都督へ通報したり。而して二十五日出發當日再議の結果、各省代表は一人以上を上海に留め、武昌に赴きし者は臨時政府組織の事を議し、上海殘留者は聲氣聯絡以て其の後援を爲す事に改めたり。此日袁世凱宛打電して曰く『各省代表は一律に共和國體を承認す、請ふ再び君主立憲を持す勿れ』と。

二 漢口會議

十一月三十日、後七時漢口會議は開かる。此日上海より來着せるは僅に潘祖彝、謝鴻燾、雷光宇の三代表のみ。之に湖南都督府代表譚人鳳、鄒代藩、湖北都督府代表孫發緒、時象晉、胡瑛、王正廷の六名を加へ、譚人鳳年長者の故を以て、臨時議長に推さる。胡瑛、潘祖彝の各報告あり。次で（一）臨時議長は黎都督に面し、上海代表會の議決が鄂軍政府を中央軍政府と公認せる

事を逃べ、黎元洪に大都督の名義を以て中央政務を執行すべき事を請ひ(二)清軍々統馮國璋に停戰條項を回答せしむ(三)孫、王、潘を推して代表會議事細則を起草せしむる事を議決したり。

十二月一日、上海より雷奮、袁希洛、馬君武、陳陶怡來り、新に安徽都督府代表王竹懷、許冠堯來り會し、二日廣西都督府代表張其鍠來着す。而して譚人鳳を議長に、孫發緒を書記に公舉したり。此日(一)袁世凱にして共和政體に贊成せば臨時大總統に公舉すべし(二)袁希洛、阮銑崧を南京に派して停戰の事を商議せしむ(三)先づ臨時政府組織大綱を規定すべしとの三大事項を議決したり。

三日、新に直隸諮議局代表谷鍾秀、河南諮議局代表黃可權、浙江都督府代表湯爾和、陳時夏、陳毅、黃群、安徽都督府代表趙斌、來着し。雷奮、馬君武、王正廷が起草せる中華民國臨時政府組織大綱を議決したり。附則共に四章、二十一ヶ條にして『臨時大總統は各省都督府代表之を選舉し、一省一票を限り、投票數の三分の二以上の得票を當選とし、全國統治、海陸軍統率權並に外交專使特派權、臨時中央審判所設立權を有す。參議院は各都督府特派員にて組織し、議員各省三人にして一省一表決權とし、前揭の同意、臨時政府豫算、出納檢査、稅法幣制公債發行、暫行法律、大總統提出案等の議決及ひ同諮詢案の回答を爲す。普通會は過半數の所決、議決は大總統發布し行政各部執行す。大總統は十日內に再議請求權あるも全員三分の二仍は前議を固執すれば發布せざる能はず。議長は互選にして、參議院未成立以前は各省都督代表會之を代理し、表決權每省一票に限る。行政は外交、內務、財政、軍務、交通の五部に分ち、部長一人、部員の編制權限は部長規定し、大總統の批准を經べし。臨時政府成立後六ヶ月以內に大總統は國民議會を召集し、其の召集法は參議院議決す。本大綱施行期限は民國憲法成立の日を以て止む』此の正文に署名したる代表は(湖北)孫發緒、時象晉、胡瑛、王正廷(山東)謝鴻燾、雷光宇、(福建)潘祖彝(湖南)譚人鳳、鄒代藩(安徽)趙斌、王竹懷、許冠堯(廣西)張其鍠(浙江)陳毅、陳時夏、湯爾和、黃群(江蘇)馬君武、雷奮、陳陶怡(直隸)谷鍾秀(河南)黃可權なり。

四日『臨時政府を南京に設け、臨時大總統選舉會を開くこと。各省代表七日內に南京に集合すること。十省以上の代表南京着直に選舉會を開くこと』と議決す。五日、四川都督府代表周本本、來着す。此日密電を上海の伍廷芳に發し、武昌に來りて淸內閣派遣道の特使と和平會商することを求め、胡瑛、王正廷の二名之が副使たることを議決す。又た『滿洲政府の推倒、共和政體の主張、舊皇室禮遇、人道主義を以て滿人を待つ』との四大綱を議決す。六日、淸內閣の停戰條件たる『三日停戰、十五日繼續。北軍兵を南に向けず、南軍兵を北に向けず。北方居住各省人代表と和平會商することを議し、黎或は代表と大局を討論し、以上の南軍は秦晉及び北方土匪を加へざるを得ず』と改むべきを主張す。又た此日『上海聯合會は大元帥副元帥を討論せしと聞く。黎大都督より上海都督に取消方の請求を乞ふ』と議決す。此日上海の伍廷芳は武昌に來らずとの報告あり。在漢口の各省代表は八日出發して南京に赴くことゝなれり。

の代表とし、北方居住各省人代表を選派して南軍各代表と會議せしむ。唐紹儀を總理の代表とし、北方居住各省人代表を選派して南軍各代表と會議せしむ。唐紹儀を總理の代表とし、『北方居住各省人代表資格を否認す。停戰三日、續停十五日。民軍淸軍兩々相攻めず。區域方向を以て南北軍と稱するを得ず。停戰三日、續停十五日。民軍淸軍兩々相攻めず。』

三 上海聯合會

上海にては十一月二十六日（奉天）吳景濂、劉興甲（吉林）趙學臣。二十七日（直隷）谷鍾秀（河南）黃可權の各諮議局代表來着し、谷、黃は漢口に赴き、吳、劉は留りて連日舊の如く會議す。十二月一日宋敎仁、林長民、居正、陶鳳集、吳景濂、趙學臣等の連名にて各都督府諮議局宛、通電を發して曰く『漢陽守を失し武昌仍ほ力守す。各省代表の多數は武昌に赴きしも軍務緊急恐らく開議し難く、現に漢陽の失に阻まれす。臨時政府組織の議決は漢陽の失に因るに因すと、先づ上海に之を準備す。各代表到らば開議進行共に矢つて懈らす。南京の大勢動搖せず、諸公の力持を望む。聞く漢陽の失は軍權軍令の不統一に因すと、此の際に懲り自ら病痛の所在を知る、以て諸公の鑒戒を乞ふ。將に臨時政府成立すべく、軍事の部署、軍權の作用、以後全國民の用命に待ちて眞の自由を無窮に求め得べし、鑒察を祈る』と。

十二月三日、湖南都督府代表廖名搢、劉揆一來着す。此日直隷諮議局保安會より來電あり、曰く『資政院は佛國借款九千萬佛郞を議決す。力阻を望む』と。因て議して伍廷芳をして國民に向け國民不承諾の意思を通告せしむ。

四日、宋敎仁代理歐陽振聲、江蘇都督程德全、浙江都督湯壽潛、上海都督陳其美、及び章炳麟、章駕時、蔡元培、王一亭、黃中央、趙竹君、顧忠琛、袁錫範の諸志士新に出席す。而して大元帥、副元帥の投票を行ひ、漢陽の敗南京に赴くべく議決したり。

將黃興を大元帥に起義の首領黎元洪を副元帥に舉げ、南京を臨時政府所在地とすることを議決したり。馬良、王昭、居正を使て此事を黃興に報告せしめ、又た湯、程、陳の三都督名儀を以て其の旨黎元洪に打電して曰く『前に臨時政府を武昌に擬定せしも、南京は克復し、武昌は軍務緊し、援鄂の師、北伐の師、急ぎ其の統一者を需む。因て同人公議して新に南京に改む。黃君を大元帥に、閣下を副元帥とす、藉て以て大局の動搖を免れむ。武昌行代表の上海歸還を待ち、南京に同行して正式に發表し、有ゆる編制、力を併せて準備せむ。事機緊急、權宜に從はざるを得ず』と。

元帥當選當時の黃興先生

五日、彭丙一、胡子笈、田桐、翟梓百、鈕惕生、成國屏た出席し、上海代表聯合會規則を議定す、曰く『各都督府代表にて組織し、民國に歸せざる省及び藩屬亦た代表を派し、都督府設置後改派追任共に可とす。目的は臨時政府組織會議。正副首領は大副元帥として記名投票。各都督出席して表決選舉權は會員同樣。臨時政府組織は大元帥主持して本會議に提案す。議決權は每省三に限り、三人以上の派遣者あるものは一人を公選すべし、但し討議發言權は咸な有す。會長一人互選。本會は臨時政府組織事務完了當日を以て解散す』等計十一ヶ條なり。

六日（江西）吳鐵城。九日（江西）林子超新著、連日の會議無事。十日黎元洪より打電通知し來れる漢口代表會議決案報告を披露し、在上海代表は十一日南京に赴くべく議決したり。

三十一日、陽暦元旦より陰暦を廃し、中華民國元年正月一日とする事を議
定す。此日呂志伊、宋教仁、居正の提議にて臨時政府組織大綱中に副總統の
新設及び大副元帥の削除等を討議し、其の一部は討論終結し、俟は新年に讓
りたり。

明治四十五年(民國元年)正月元日、孫文上海より南京南。各省代表は新總
統府に集り、後十時臨時大總統受職式を行ふ。

大總統誓詞

満洲専制政府を傾覆し、中華民國を鞏固にし、
民生の幸福を圖るとの國民の公意。文實に之に遵
ひ國に忠に衆の務に服すべし。専制政府倒れて國
内變亂なく、民國を世界に卓立して列強公認する
に至らば、文當に臨時大總統の職を解くべし、謹
んで國民に誓ふ。

孫大總統宣言書

中華民國締造の始にして文不才を以て臨時大總
統の任に腐り、夙夜戒めて國民の望に副ふ無きを
懼るるものなり。夫れ中國に於ける専制政治の毒は二百餘年來甚だ滋し、一
旦國民の力を以て踏して之を去る、事を起して數旬に過ぎず、飢に十餘行
省を光復し、歴史あつてより以來成功の未だ此の如く速かなるあらざる也。
國民は内ち統一の機關なく、外か對待の主體なきを以て建設の事、緩なる
を容さず、是を以て臨時政府組織の責を以て相屬す。功を推し能を讓るの
觀念を容れず、務に服し責を盡すの觀念
より言へば、文敢て辭せざる所なり。是れ黽勉を用ゐて國民の後に從ひ、

南京代表會議長景耀月先生

能く専制の流毒を掃ひ、確に共和を定め、普ねく民生を利し、以て革命の
宗旨を達し、國民の志願を完ふするの端は今日に在り、敢て肝膽を披瀝し
て國民に告げむ。

國家の本は人民に在り、漢満蒙回藏諸地を合せて一國とす、以上諸族を合
せて一人とするは是を民族の統一と曰ふ。武漢義を起して十餘省獨立す、
所謂獨立とは満清より脱離して各省と聯合するものにして、蒙古西藏の意
亦た同じく、此行動既に一決して岐趨なく、樞機は中央に成り、經緯は四
至に周きは是を領土の統一と曰ふ。血鐘一た
び鳴つて義旗四に起り、擁甲帶戈の士十餘省
に遍く、編制一ならず號令一ならずと雖も、目
的の在る所同じからざる無く、共同の目的を
以て共同の行動を爲す、整齊劃一夫れ豈に難
からんや、是を軍政の統一と曰ふ。國家の副
員遼闊にして各省自ら其の風氣宜しき所あり、
前に清廷は中央集權の法を强て之を行ひ、以
て其の僞立憲の術を逞ぐ、今日は各省聯合し
て互に自治を謀り、此後行政は中央政府と各省との關係調劑宜しきを得ん
事を期して、大綱旣に擧げ條目自ら擧る、是を内政の統一と曰ふ。満清時代
は立憲の名に藉りて欲げ實を行ひ、雜損苛細にして民生を安せず、此後
國家の經費を民に取るや、必ず理財學理に合するを期して、尤も社會の組
識を改良し、人民をして生の樂を知らしむるに在り、是を財政の統一と曰
ふ。以上の數者は政務の方針と爲す、此を持して進行し、庶ば大過なら
ひ。革命主義は吾儕の倡言して萬口の喩を同ふする所と爲す、前後屢々起

り屢々躓くと雖、外人其の用心に蜜みざる無し。八月以來義旗颯發するや

諸友邦は平和の望を抱き、中立の態度を持して新聞及び輿論常に同情を表

す、隣誼篤良深く謝するに足る。臨時政府成立後、文明國が盡すべき義務

を盡して其の亨くべき權利を受けむ。滿淸時代に於ける辱國の擧措、排外

の心理悉く一洗し、平和主義を以て友邦と益々親睦を增進し、中國をして

國際社會に重きをなさしめ、且つ將に世界をして大同の循序に漸進せしめ

む、對外方針實に是に在り。夫れ民國新たに建つ外交內政の百緒繁生す、

文何人を顧みて而して克んや。然り臨時政府は革命時代の政府なり。十餘

年來より今日に至る、革命に從事する者、皆な誠摯純深の精神を以て、其

の遇ふ所の艱難に勝へたり、即ち今後の艱難は遠く前日に逾ゆるあるも、此

革命の精神を保たば一往阻なく必すや中華民國の基礎をして大地に樹立せ

む。然らば臨時政府の職務始て盡き、吾人始めて國民に罪なきを告げ得べ

き也。今ま我國民と初めて相見ゆるの日、腹心を披布す、我四萬々同胞之

を鑒みよ。

景　議　長　致　詞

中華民國建設元年元月元旦、民國第一期大總統孫文任に莅む。燕、遼・

魯、豫、湘、鄂、秦、晉、蘇、浙、皖、贛、閩、粤、蜀、滇、桂の公民代

表等、迎迓祝頌して之に辭を致す、曰く。

澳の曾孫政を失し、東胡內侵して淫虐猾夏帝制自ら爲すもの三百年、我皇

漢の慈孫は呻吟して深く佛蘭西、亞米利加合衆國人平等の制を熱慕し、群

謀衆策を用ひ、仰で視、俯して割し、虐政を傾覆して人權の恢復を思ひ、

洒ち頭を斷ち胸を裂き、群起號召して血を流し義を建て、佛米人共和の戰

史を續け、今天下を三分して其の二を克復す。是を以て民國を建立し、政

府を期成し、民主を揀選し、總統を推置す、僉な能く共和を尊重して民意

を宣達す。公の賢は禹域を光

復して河翔を克定し、漢滿蒙回藏を擧げて自由を蘴すべし。公の賢は禹域を光

亦た公の賢は軌度情徵、漢滿蒙回藏の信に投じ、衆庶の屬する所、群謀僉な同じ

く飢に兼符を協へ、歡忻して擁戴すべし。我國民久しく鈴制に困しみ、疾

首蹙額して民主を望むを知るを要す。況や今まにして當に公が軒車の任に

蒞むや、蒼白は枕に挟けられ、子女は額を加へ香を焚き、彗を擁して感激涕

泗する者は何ぞや。自由を拚舞して民權を致重するを以て也。故に四百兆

國民の大阿を付し、二億里山河の大命を寄せて吝まず、國民の公に委托す

るもの亦た旣に重き哉。公や翼々として憲に違ふ毋れ、輿意を拂ふ毋れ、

威福に任する毋れ、專斷を崇ぶ毋れ、非德に眠む毋れ、非才を任する毋れ

凡て我國民は忠を矢ひ信を矢ひ、至誠以て軒轅を愛戴せざるあらんや。金

天烈祖七十二代の君、實に斯の言を聞す。代表等國民委托の重を受け、敢

て意を盡さず、謹んで大總統の璽綬を致す。公伸くば號を發し令を旋せ、

崇んで符信と爲すべし、欽念する哉。

五　代行參議院

正月三日、臨時副總統選舉會を開く、出席十七省三十名にして、徐紹顧之

か監選員たり。投票の結果、黎元洪全會一致にて當選す。同日臨時會を開き中

央行政各部及び權限案を議決す。次で大總統出席し國務員の任命を發表して

正月二日、景耀月病て代理議長を辭し、湯議長は浙に歸り王副議長は浙に

留る。即ち改選を行ひて趙士北、馬君武は正副議長に當選したり。此日議し

て嗣後代表會を以て參議院の事を行ふことゝなれり。

多歎の同意を得たり。陸軍は黃興。海軍は黃鍾英。外交は王寵惠。司法は伍廷芳。財政は陳錦濤。內務は程德全。敎育は蔡元培。實業は張謇。交通は湯壽潛なり。

五日、鄂、慸、閩、澳、粵、桂の六代表は、臨時政府組織大綱に修正案を提出し。湘、慸、浙、滇、秦の五省代表は、同大綱に人民の權利義務の一章追加案を提出し。景耀月、張一膈、呂志伊、王有蘭、馬君武の五審査員附託となる。此日參議院假議事規則計參十二條を議決す。

八日、軍需公債規則計參十二條を議決す。其の額一億元、國家收入の鏠糧を抵當とし、利子年八分、無記名債券一枚百元、英貨九磅の計算、用途は臨時軍資及び治安保衛費にして、一月二十八日先づ上海より募集し、陸續各省各埠に及ぼし、內外人均しく購ひ得べしと。

九日華僑特派議員案討議。此日和議決裂の傾向ありとし、馬君武、陶鳳集を推し、作戰計畫を陸軍部に質問せしむ。

十日、參議院事務假規則十二箇條、同守衛規則四箇條を議定し、尚は曆本製定頒布、國旗制定の二案を議決したり。

十一日、湖北代表居正は內務次長就職の故を以て代表名義を取消す。十二日、政府の招兵を制限し、軍隊を整頓し、並に憲兵を編成して地方の治安を保つべく獻議したり。同日、法制局職制案八箇條を議決す、局長には宋敎仁任せられたり。十三日、大總統より國旗案の再議を求め來り承認す。時功玖、王有蘭を本院書記錄任に推定す。

十五日 議長指名にて劉成禺、湯漪、王正廷は議事細則起草員となる。本院事務員聘定前は議員に於て各事務を分擔する事に決し。庶務は王正廷、湯漪、林森。會計は馬君武、時功玖、歐陽振聲。糾察は趙士北、王有蘭、潘祖彝を互選したり。

十六日、黎副總統對靄淸銀行借欵案を議し、中央政府の借欵として額一百萬磅、其の抵當並に訂約法等は原案を可決す。十七日湯漪案の行政官は參議員を兼職すべからずとの議を可決す。當時馬良、景耀月、呂志伊等の議員は參議次官の職に就きたるを以てなり。十八日、趙玉鈺は山西陝西兩省の危急狀況を報告し、其の維持法に關する討論を求む。即ち大總統に質問し、黎及び和議代表に通告する事等を議決す。又た各省に通電を發して參議院議員の特派を催促し、一月二十八日を限りて着院するやふ、其の日を以て正式に參議院を成立開會せしむべしと議決したり。

十九日、王正廷は作戰計畫質問案を提出し周代表の總統責任問題。張伯烈の軍隊統一の動議。以上を一括して咨文を備へ、趙士北、王正廷、陳承澤を總統府に特派質問せしむ。

臨時大總統孫文先生

二十日陳承澤は前記質問の次第を報告す。二十二日、和議條件計四箇條の緊急案は大總統より提出され、之が討議中、大總統は改めて和議條件計五箇條を提出す。即ち前案は撤回され、後案は全會一致にて可決す。要に曰く『清帝退位す。袁は其の旨北京駐在各國公使に照會し、民國政府に電知すべし。或は上海駐在領事轉達亦た可なり。同時に袁は政見を宣布して絕對に共和主義に贊成すべし。孫は外交圈或は領事圈の通知を受け、清帝退位後絕對に辭職す。參議院は袁を臨時大總統に擧ぐる事。袁は當選後參議院所定の憲法を守る事を誓

ひて其事權を接受し能はズ」と。二十五日、大總統の和議條件草案を報告し、

清皇室優待條件は追て公認に補ひとせり。湯漁は政府既に本院に緊急會議を

要求し得、緊急案亦た追認を許さずと主張して可決す。

二十六日、夜、臨時會議を開き、正式大會の準備を議し、林森、淩文淵を

其の委員とせり。二十七日、彭允彝は代表と參議員との權限規定に關する動

議を提出し。湯漁案第三條の『代表は參議員を代理して同省參議員着院日を

限とす』の一項を可決す。同時に大總統より緊急諮詢案提出さる、曰く『停

戰期滿つ、主戰が抑も停戰延期か』と。日程を變更して本案を討議し全會一

致にて主戰に決す。

第二章　南京參議院

明治四十五年（民國元年）一月二十八日前十一時、正式開院式を舉行す。

出席議員代表共十七省參十一人にして、臨時大總統各部總次長列席す。

大總統頌詞

中華民國既に建ち、參議機關正式に成立す、文誠に忻喜慶慰し、謹で中

懷の希望を掬して諸參議に告ぐ。革命の事、破壞難く、建設尤も難しと言

ふ。仁人志士任俠勇夫、隱奧中に苦心焦慮し、危難に際して、元を喪ひ匢

を斷つ、其の艱難苦誠に思ひ及ばざる所の者あり。一旦機の成熟するや

悠然發して洪波の危堤を決し、一瀉千里なる如く、禦がんど欲すと雖も、

得べからず。後に於て其の事を思ふ、難きに似て易き也。建設の事は然ら

ず。一議を建つも贊成者前に居れば則ち反對者後に在り。一法を立つる今

日見て利とするも明日見て弊とす。其の得るや五族の人福を受け、其の失ふや五族の人

所は未曾有の制なり。況や議する所は國家無窮の基、立つる今

禍を受く。嗚呼破壞の難は各省の志士之を先にし建設の難は今日以後諸君

と文と共に黽勉仔肩し、敢て推謝せざる所の者なり。矧んや北虜未だ滅せ

ず、戰雲方に急にして立法事業は戎機と相待ちて用を爲す、破壞建設の二

難、畢に茲に萃る、諸君子勉めよや。各々心を盡し智を竭し、以て民國の

始基を奠し、以て我族の先烈を揚げむ事、則ち文一人の頭顱する所なるの

みならず、四萬々人實に之に嘉賴するもの也。

議長の答辭

維れ大中華民國共和の政は、既に三權の制度を成し、第一期議院を立て

開院の大禮を舉行す。大總統孫は辰に及び院に蒞み、辭を設けて祝頌希

望する所あり、議員等聆餘に侍し實に深く欽贊せざるもの無し。專制方に

烈しきや天下口を箝し、婦寺以て徵を察す可く、巫配以て謗を監す可し。

道路目を以てし、天下口を箝す可し、蓋し順風に呼べば四遠に達し易く、聲疾を加ふるに非ず、

勢の激するを以て也。民の口を防ぐは川より甚だし、川崩潰せば人

を傷く必ず多し。般鑒遙古に非ず、成訓具さに史冊に在り、前例欹く者に

非ず、これ唯清專制の政が倏忽として遂に亡ぶる所以なり。今ま幸に革命

の功を奏し、民國既に建ち三權を奠し議院を設け、四百餘州の庶民代議今

ま茲に集り、滿清政府時代狂呼して氣盡し力爭して支へ未だ得し者を一旦に得たり、懺忓流涕如何ぞや。議員等閭閻

の間に起ち、國民の意を宣達す、誠に空漏の議、坐言の誚を免がれざるを

知る。然り大總統及び行政諸公に議を建て辭を陳べ、遺を拾ひ闕を補ひ、

上下の隔閡を疎通し、朝野の意思を溝通し、自ら一日の力を盡して以て諸

士大夫諸言し依違皇として云ひ庶衆之を率ひ、一夫臂を振り

て天下響應す、蓋し順風に呼べば四遠に達し易く、聲疾を加ふるに非ず、

に棄てらる。士大夫諸言し依違皇として云ひ庶衆之を率ひ、一夫臂を振り

烈しきや天下口を箝し、婦寺以て徵を察す可く、巫配以て謗を監す可し。専制方に

望する所あり、議員等聆餘に侍し實に深く欽贊せざるもの無し。専制方に

公の後に隨はんど欲す。方今民國幼稚なり、樹立つて未だ固まらず、誠に群公の行政、須らく一朝の設を以て百年の長計を以てすべし。萬機周ねきこと難く天職は恭重なり、是を以て棉弱を擄らず、婚火を以て日月の光を增すべく共に危を謀つて群つて大計を策せんと欲す。奧亡任あり痼瘵切に懷ひて中邊を俯仰す、意は周備を求め、民命を出納して國の喉舌とならむ。れ議員等引て任務と爲す、願くは行政群公と共に之を勵めむ。

一月二十九日開議、出席十三省二十六人。正副議長の選舉を行ひ、林森は議長に、陳陶怡は副議長に當選す。湯漪が提議せる代表の代理參議員權限案討論未終結の第二第三條は一括して、其の權限參議員と同一なるも、長期職員被選舉權無しと決定す。三十日、政府は民國臨時組織法案を提出す。三十一日、抽籤法にて參議員席次を決定す。此日參議院は政府提出の民國臨時組織法案計五十五箇條に對し『憲法の發案權は應に國會の專有に歸すべき者、而して國會未召集前は本院を唯一立法機關とす。故に該法は本院に於て編纂すべき者、今さ遽に法制局より編纂するは越權なり。參考資料と稱するも本院の必要とする所に非ず』との主旨を以て、該案を政府に還付したり。

二月六日、各部審查員の選舉を行ふ。財政に李肇甫、潘祖蔭、歐陽振聲、揚廷棟、文群、殷汝驪、時功玖。法律に王有蘭、彭允彝、谷鍾秀、凌文淵、王正廷、趙士北、平剛、湯漪、熊成章。外交に陳陶怡、張繼、張伯烈、劉彦、錢樹芬。請願に李磐、劉懋賞、劉成禺、趙成鈺、鄧家彥當選したり。臨時約法案は審議會に附し、大綱討究後、特別審查會に附すとの劉彦の動議可成す。

臨時大總統袁世凱先生

七日より臨時約法大綱草案の審議會を開きて、李肇甫は其の議長に推選せられたり。

十二日、時功玖提議の一省一都督案一讀會を經て特別審查會附託となり、平剛、谷鍾秀、殷汝驪、潘祖蔭、錢樹芬、其の委員となる。此日政府委員出席して和議案を討論し、三日內約に依りて清皇遜位せざれば優待條件を取消すべしと議決したるが、此の日を以て清皇退位の上論は下りたり。

十四日、前日大總統提出の辭職薦舉案を討論したる結果『十五日孫文の辭職式を行ふ事。同日新總統選舉會を開く事』を議決し。李肇甫の提議にて臨時政府地點を北京とするに多數決定す。十五日孫大總統は臨時政府地點問題の再議を參議院に要求し、趙士北は先づ臨時大總統の選舉會を開くべしとの動議を提出し、日程を變更し、臨時大總統の選舉を行ひ全會一致にて袁世凱當選す。之を袁に電告し、次で討議の結果、前大總統孫文に咨文を具して、新總統受任前の民國政務は仍は貴院の結果を李審議長報告して應に討論に入らむとす。

十六日、谷鍾秀提出の北方各省統治權引繼法案を討論可決す。此日午後臨時約法案は特別審查會附託となり、李肇甫、鄧家彥、熊成章、錢樹芬、谷鍾秀、殷汝驪、歐陽振聲、張繼、湯漪の九名、本案特別審查員となりたり。十九日、黎元洪か副總統及び大元帥の辭職電報を披露し。二十日改めて臨時副

總統の選擧會を開き、全會一致を以て再び黎元洪を副總統に擧定したり。二十二日、參議院法編訂起草委員九名。二十三日、議事細則修正傍聽規則起草員三名等を決定したり。三月六日、政府提出の袁總統受職統一政府組織法案を討議し『參議院は袁總統が北京にて就職するを允す。三月六日、袁總統は電報を以て參議院に宣誓す。參議院は宣誓電報接受後電報を以て其の受職を承認す。袁總統受職後國務總理各國務員の姓名を參議院に電告して同意を求ひべし。國務總理各國務員任命後南京にて臨時政府事務を引繼ぐべし。孫總統は事務引繼後解職す』と議決す。

三月八日、臨時約法計七章五十六箇條の三讀會を終りて議決確定し、其の翌日前大總統の名を以て發布したり。此日袁は北京にて受職式を行ひ、袁は參議院が總統受職統一政府組織法と同時に議定通告せる宣誓文を取りて朗讀し即日之を參議院に電告す。

大總統宣誓辭

民國建設の端を造り、凡百治を待つ。世凱深く能力を竭して共和の精神を發揚し、專制の瑕疵を滌蕩するを願ふ。國民の願望に依り、國家を安全鞏固の域に達せしめ、五大民族同じく利を樂むに臻るを俾ふ。凡そ茲の志願は牢に履んで偽る勿れ、國會を召集して第一期大總統選定の日を俟ちて世凱は即ち解職を行ふべし。謹んで誠悃を攄して誓て同胞に告ぐ。

三月九日參議院は袁總統一政府組織法第三條により左の祝辭文を議決して哀に電告す。

(前略)共和端を肇めて群治理を待つ。公の才望を仰ぎ、大阿畢路の藍縷を以てす。孫公旣に其の先を開きて光を揚ぐ、我公宜しく其の後を善くすべし。四百兆の同胞公意の託する所、二億里の山河大命の寄する所なり。苟も隕越淪胥ありて之に隨ふ、況んや軍輿以來四民業を輟めて滿目瘡痍し、六師暴露し、九府實竭す、危を轉じて安と爲すは公の敷設を勞するなり。本院が國民を代表し、尤も孳々敦勉せざるを得ざるは隨時約法七章五十六條にして、倫は憲法に比してそれ之を守らざるべからず。謹んで輿情に逆ふ勿れ、專斷に鄰るを守れ、非德に狃るを勿れ、非才を登す勿れ。凡そ我共和國五大民族は至誠以て愛敬せざるあらんや、皇天宮土實に之を憑す。謹んで大總統の蟬綬を致し、公の令出で〻惟だ行ふを俾ふ。崇んで符信を爲す、欽念する哉。

十五日、各常任委員の補缺を行ひて、財政に席聘臣、黃樹中。法律に張耀曾。外交に劉星楠、吳景濂。請願に曾彥、常選す。副議長の補缺に王正廷當選す。十九日、女子參政請願案の第二讀會を開き、審查會報告通り否決す。華比銀行借款案(百萬磅)を議し、少しく修正を加へて可決す、李肇甫は四國借款團との契約訂結法に付き提案方を請求するの動議を出して可決す。二十二日夜臨時會議を開く。袁大總統提出の四國借款一千萬磅案を討議す。副總長王正廷、議長席に就く。二讀會に移りて湯濟は舊議の五百萬磅說を唱へしも、成立せず。李肇甫は豫め借款用途の報告を求め、並に力めて折衝を請ふ又た四國借歟條件質問の答電催促の旨とも本案通告文に附記すべしと主張して成立せず。斯くて本案は三讀會を經て九對十六の多數にて可決せり。二十七日、漢冶萍否決書を袁大總統に向け發送す。二十九日、國務總理唐紹儀出席して、各國務員の同意を求む。外交に陸徵祥。內務に趙秉鈞。陸軍に段祺瑞海軍に劉冠雄。財政に熊希齡。司法に王寵惠。教育に蔡元培。農林に宋敎仁工商に陳其美は同意多數なりしも交通の梁如浩は不同意者多數にて通過せず。因て交通は唐總理兼任して四月一日引繼を行ひたり。四月一日午後、

唐紹儀内閣閣員

孫大總統の解職式を行ふ。二日袁大總統は臨時政府北京移轉案を提出し、討議の上無記名投票にて六對二十票の大多數にて北京移轉を可決す。五日参院は七日より十五日間休會し、各參議院議員は休會期間中北京へ集合して改めて開議すべしと議決したり。六日、唐總理は交通總長に施肇基任命の同意を求めて通過す。是にて南京臨時参議院は終を告げたり。

臨時約法正文

第一章　總綱

第一條　中華民國は中華人民にて組織す

第二條　中華民國の主權は國民全體に屬す

第三條　中華民國の領土は二十二行省、内外蒙古、西藏、青海とす

第四條　中華民國は参議院、臨時大總統、國務員、法院を以て其統治權を行使す

第五條　中華民國は一律平等にして種族、階級、宗教の區別なし

第二章　人民

第六條　人民は左記各項の自由權を享有するを得

一、人民の身體は法律に依るに非ざれば逮捕、拘禁、審問、處罰するを得ず。

二、人民の家宅は法律に依るに非ざれば侵入或は搜索するを得ず。

三、人民は財産を保有し營業するの自由を有す。

四、人民は言論著作刊行及集會結社の自由を有す。

五、人民は書信秘密の自由を有す。

六、人民は居住、遷徙の自由を有す。

七、人民は信教の自由を有す。

第七條　人民は議會に請願するの權を有す。

第八條　人民は行政官署に陳訴するの權を有す。

第九條　人民は法院に訴訟し其の審判を受るの權を有す。

第十條　人民は官吏の違法にて權利を損害せる行爲に對し平政院に陳訴するの權を有す。

第十一條　人民は任官試驗に應ずるの權を有す。

第十二條　人民は選舉權及被選舉權を有す。

第十三條　人民は法律に依り納稅の義務を有す。

第十四條　人民は法律に依り兵役に服するの義務を有す。

第十五條　本章に載せたる人民の權利は公益を増進し治安を維持する爲め或は非常緊急に必要と認むる時法律に依り之を制限するを得。

第三章　參議院

第十六條　中華民國の立法權は參議院を以て之を行ふ。

第十七條　參議院は第十八條に定めたる各地方より選派せる參議員を以て之を組織す。

第十八條　參議院は各行省、內蒙古、外蒙古、西藏より各五人を選派し青海より一人を選派し、其の選舉方法は各地方自ら之を定め、參議院會議の時各參議員は一表決權を有す。

第十九條　參議院の職權は左の如し。

一、一切の法律案を議決す、

二、臨時政府の豫算決算を議決す。

三、全國の稅法兵制及度量衡の準則を議決す。

四、公債の募集及國庫にて負擔する契約を議決す。

五、第三十四條、第三十五條及第四十條の事件に承諾す。

六、臨時政府の諮詢事件に覆答す。

七、人民の請願を受理す。

八、法律及其の他の事件に關する意見を以て政府に建議するを得。

九、質問書を國務員に提出し並に其の出席復答を求むる事を得。

十、臨時政府に諮詢し官吏の納賄違法事件を查辦するを得。

十一、參議院は臨時大總統に對し謀叛の行爲ありと認むる時總員五分の四以上の出席を得、出席員三分の二以上の可決を以て之を彈劾するを得。

十二、參議員は國務員に對し失職或は違法と認むる時總員四分の三以上の出席を得、出席員三分の二以上の可決を以て之を彈劾するを得。

第二十條　參議院は自ら集會、開會、閉會するを得。

第二十一條　參議院の會議は之を公開すべし仙國務員の要求或は參議員出席者過半數の可決あれば之を秘密にするを得。

第二十二條　參議院の議決事件は咨して臨時大總統より公布施行す。

第二十三條　臨時大總統は參議院議決事件に對し若し否認する時咨達後十日內に理由を聲明し院に咨し覆議せしむるを得但し若し參議院は覆議事件に對し若し來會議員三分の二以上が仍ほ前議を執る時は第二十二條に照して辦理す。

第二十四條　參議院の議長は參議員より記名投票法を用ゐて之を互選し滿投票總數の半數なる得票者を以て當選とす。

第二十五條　參議院の參議員は院內に於て院外に對し責任を負はず。

第二十六條　參議院の參議員は現行犯及內亂外患に關する犯罪を除くの外會期中本院の許可を得るに非ざれば逮捕するを得ず。

第二十七條　參議院法は參議院自ら之を定む。

第二十八條　參議院は國會成立の日を以て解散し其の職權は國會にて之を行ふ。

第四章　臨時大總統

第二十九條　臨時大總統副總統は參議院にて之を選舉し總員四分の三以上の出席あり滿投票總數三分の二以上の得票者を當選とす。

第三十條　臨時大總統は臨時政府を代表し政務を總攬し法律を公布す。

第三十一條　臨時大總統は法律を執行する爲め或は法律の委任に基き命令を發布するを得並に之を發布せしむるを得。

第三十二條　臨時大總統は全國の陸海軍隊を統帥す。

第三十三條　臨時大總統は官制官規を制定するを得るを得但し須く參議院の同意を得ざるべからず。

第三十四條　臨時大總統は文武職員を任免するを得但し國務員及外交大使公使を任命するは須く參議院の同意を得ざるべからず。

第三十五條　臨時大總統は參議院の同意を經て宣戰講和及條約を締結することを得。

第三十六條　臨時大總統は法律に依り戒嚴を宣告する事を得。

第三十七條　臨時大總統は全國を代表して外國の大使公使を接受す。

第三十八條　臨時大總統は法律案を參議院に提出するを得。

第三十九條　臨時大總統は勳章並に其の他の榮典を頒給するを得。

第四十條　臨時大總統は大赦、特赦、減刑、復權を宣告するを得但し大赦は須く參議院の同意を經べし。

第四十一條　臨時大總統は參議院の彈劾を受けたる後最高法院全院の審判官より九人を互選し特別法廷を組織して之を審判す。

第四十二條　臨時副總統は臨時大總統事故に依りて職を去り或は事を視る能はざる時代つて其の職權を行ふ。

　　第五章　國務員

第四十三條　國務總理及各部總長は皆な國務員と稱す。

第四十四條　國務員は臨時大總統を輔佐し總べて其の責任者爲す。

第四十五條　國務員は臨時大總統が法律を提出し法律を公布し或は命令を發布する時之に副署すべし。

第四十六條　國務員及其の委員は參議院に出席し及び發言するを得。

第四十七條　國務員は參議院の彈劾を受けたる後臨時大總統其の職を免ずべし但し參議院に交し一回覆議せしむるを得。

　　第六章　法院

第四十八條　法院は臨時大總統及司法總長の分別して任命せる法官を以て之を組織し法院の編制及法官の資格は法律を以て之を定む。

第四十九條　法院は法律に依り民事訴訟及刑事訴訟を判定す但し行政訴訟及其の他の特別訴訟に關しては別に法律を以て之を定む。

第五十條　法院の審判は之を公開すべし但し安寧秩序を妨害すと認むるものあれば之を秘密にする事を得。

第五十一條　法院は獨立にして審判は上級官廳の干涉を受けず。

第五十二條　法官は獨立にして審判は上級官廳の干涉を受けず。

第五十三條　法官在任中減俸或は轉職するを得ず法律に依り刑罰の宣告或は免職すべき懲戒處分を受くるに非ざれば解職するを得ず懲戒の條規は法律を以て之を定む。

　　第七條　附　則

第五十三條　本約法施行後十箇月內を限り臨時大總統より國會を召集す其の國會の組織及選擧法は參議院にて之を定む。

第五十四條　中華民國の憲法は國會にて選定す憲法を施行せざる以前に於ては本約法の効力は憲法と同じ。

第五十五條　本約法は參議院の參議員三分の二以上或は臨時大總統の提議に依り參議員五分の四以上出席し出席員四分の三以上の可決を經て之を增修するを得。

第五十六條　本約法は公布の日より施行す臨時政府組織大綱は本約法施行の日に廢止す。

中華民國議會史

第參章　北京臨時參議院

明治四十五年（民國元年）四月二十九日前十時、開院式を行ふ。出席議員七十名にして南京參議院議長なりし林森主席に就き、袁大總統唐國務總理各部總次長其の他出席す。

　袁大總統の宣言

世凱忝くも五大族の推舉を承け、夙夜勝ゆる能はざるを恐る。謹んで誠悃を掬し敬んで我國民に告ぐ。志氣高遠なる者にありては、世凱任に蒞むに伊に始るを以て宏大なる議は以て聞聽を一新するあらむも然り時を審にし勢を度り未だ以て此に語るを敢てせざることを諒すべき也。古今國を立るの道は、惟だ紀綱を整飾し法度を修明し、強弱をして相安せしめ、內外をして相繫がらしめ、國基を鞏固にすべし。爭は宇內に存じ乃ち國基を鞏固にすべし。爭は宇內に存じ乃ち兵事擾攘し、四民業を失ひ、公私交も困むこと既に極度に達す。而して士卒多くは服從の義に昧く、人民は公共の益を知る能し。空談者は理想に偏し、私を營む者多くは權利を年す。此に循つて變せずんば必ずや紀綱廢墜して法度蕩然たるべく、引て人民の生命財產を保障すべからざるに至らむ。尚ほ復た侈言

北京臨時參議院開院式

舖張を敢てせん乎、世凱向に銳進主義を持し難きを懼れて保守するに甘せず、自ら數十年の苦心經營に居ることは當に諸君の共に見て共に諒する所なり。但し現に改革の後に值すべし、遂に當に秩序を維持して、用を利し生を厚ふすべし。建設は穩健より入手し、措置は實事を以て歸結とす。譬へば巨室を營造するや、須らく基礎を將りて愼重に測量し、工を擇び料を選びて、層々穩實に處々堅實にし、徒らに外觀を侈にして虛事粉飾すべからざるが如し。然る後は廣廈落成して方に能く久しきを歷て敝へざる也。倘し孟浪の涼草を以て之に出づ、恐くば牆壁未だ立たず、而して傾覆之に隨はん、其の損失何ぞ言ふに勝へ可けんや。是を以て必ずや根本を完固にして再び急起直追を行ふべく、則ち觀成つて左券を操る可し矣。百廢の興るは要するに財政に在り。去歲度支豫算、收入は支出に敷せずして二千六百余萬兩の歲入を虧ぎたり。半年以來工商荒癈して入稅は銳減し外債暫らく償ふに能はず。近く以て政治を改良する、必ず須らく外資を輸入せざるべからず。故に先づ財政の大綱を整頓し、財政の信用を增加すべく定む。每年に還付すべき借欵賠欵元利約五千萬兩あり、賠欵は多く關稅を以て抵當と作し、亦た厘金を以て抵當と作す者あり、賠

欵は關稅及び鹽稅を以て抵當と作す。速に條約國と加稅を商議して一面に厘金を廢し、及び輸出稅を減少すべし。每年海關常入額四千四百萬兩より六千萬兩に增加せば、前項の外債に抵支して餘あり。鐵道及び他項の借欵に至りては別に鐵道及び他項の收入を以て償還不足す、則ち鹽稅より支出補墳すべし。尙は各省の地方外債總額約一千餘萬兩あり。又た去冬庚子（北清事變）賠欵未拂額一千二百餘萬兩あり、均しく新政府に歸入す、即ち大借欵項中より速に償還すべし。建設の行政費、即ち應に迅速に豫算を成立して以て大借欵支用の標準を定むべし。目前先づ短期國庫債券を發行して急需を濟ひ、本項の國庫債劵は將來大借欵より返還すべし。此事極めて重要にして此を合て他法の財政信用を恢復すべき無し。新法に倣つて鹽稅を整理せば鹽稅五千萬兩を增すべし。田賦を整理し、胥役の積弊を剗り、人民の負擔を輕くすること、未だ升科の地を經ず、專門の人才を搜集して新に從つて測量し、稅則を酌定し國弊を改良し、圖法を劃一することは財政最要の關鍵と爲す、即ち必ず迅速に實行すべし。我國財政專門の人員尙は少なく、又た經驗に乏し、將來庶政具に擧げんとす、亦た須らく異材を借用し、以て先導に資して顧問に備へざるべからず。民國成立す、宜しく實業を以て先務と爲すが故に農林工商部を分設し、以て協助提倡の義を盡すべし。凡そ學校生徒は尤も實業を重んじて國本を培ふを宜しとす。吾國の實業は尙ほ幼稚時代に在り。質を以て言へば中華は實に農國にして開墾、森林、牧畜、漁業、茶、桑の富を地に藏して未だ關かざるを憂と爲す也。深く我國民に望むは、常に不足に處して誇張自滿するこ

議長吳景濂先生

るの菁華多し、願くば我國民空中に生活を討むる無く須らく脚底下に想を著けざるべからず。即ち礦產を以て言へば急は須らく礦務規則を改めて、民の便に從ひ、力めて寬大を主として進展に利せしむべからず。且つ商法と度量衡とを亦た應に迅速に妥訂すべし。近日軍隊複雜にして、其の數が常額に逾ゆること幾倍なり、消耗巨きに過ぎて國圉何ぞ此に堪へんや、已に財政陸軍兩部に收束の實行を飭したり。方に人民の信敎は自由にして凡そ各敎を擧げて均しく一視大同、毫も偏倚無し。其の信敎と否とを論せず亦た其の何敎も信仰するに論なく、均しく須らく互に相尊重して、悉く猜嫌を泯し、幸福を享くる贇ふべし。我國民の習慣積重して急切に大同に趨き難く、敎育尙は未だ普及せずして改革尙は疑沮多く、軍人は精神訓練缺乏す、當に本原を探るべし。法律亦た未だ完備せずして法權仍は多くは放棄され、交通未だ暢達する能はずして風氣畫一を期し難し、均しく正に國務員と時に隨つて審商し、力めて進行を求めむ。邇來外人の我に對する態度は皆な和平中正にして贊助の誠を示すに似たり、固と世界の文明に徵し更に友邦の睦誼に感す、凡そ我國民努めて當に深く此義を明にし、誠を開き公を布きて邦交を鞏固ならしむべきを重すべし。凡その從前締結せる條約は均しく切實に遵守し、其の旣に締結して未だ辦せざる事は迅速に處理すべし。數千百年專制の後より一躍して共和に踏むや、吾國民の色然り喜ぶに宜しき也、然かも世凱深く以て吾國の未だ進步せざ

と勿れ。深く望むは公誠を以て推與し、互に相猜忌すること勿れ。四億萬の心、惟だ一心にして國は乃ち強し。此次特任せる國務總理唐君と各部總長は皆な一時變を濟ふの才なり、世凱正に資衡して相共に大局を支持するに任すべし。顧みて國民深く之を信じ之を賛助せよ。

　　參議院の致辭

稚れ中華民國元年四月二十九日は、即ち統一政府成立して、參議院が北京に移れる開會の第一日とす。臨時大總統袁世凱躬ら落みて宣言す、本院は國民を代表して之に辯を致すべし。曰く國の大地に於ける各々其の體を殊にするも惟だ至著に止る。曰く民繁に主として我中華民國の基を肇び。武漢義を起して南北統一を定るに底り、今や統一政府成立して大總統躬ら本院に蒞みて宣言せらる。凡そ我五族同胞たるもの厥の成を贊觀せざるもの罔し。惟だ四千餘年の古國を摶挽して秦政以來十二朝專制の錮習、及び輓近時代社會傳染の惡風を廓淸せんとす、假令へ足を敏にすると雖も乃ち大に難し。望むらくは大總統及び執政諸君、其の人を用ゆる各々其の才に當り、政を行ふや先務とする所を急にし、即ち公意を乘り、輿情を察するに忠ならば、民國の前途、庶幾ば咎あらむ。本院は國民を代表し、言は尽さざるを得ざる者にして、當に內政は廢弛し、外交は困阨し、民庶は窮蹙し、軍士は慨援する事にして、政府は萬難を排し、萬險を冒すべし。苟も國に利あらん者は、措施の時に或は權を以て變を濟ふものと雖も、本院亦當んで賛助し、其の成功を期せざる靡し。否ざれば則ち苟且の策、補苴の術形式徒らに具りて精神坐ながら亡びん、本院職司の在る所、萬一、同流自ら陷つて國民に辜負する能はず、行政立法機關相切磋伊に始まる。共に斯言を失ふ。

五月一日後一時開會、出席議員七十五名にして南京參議院時代の議長林森辭職し、副議長は缺員の儘なりしを以て、谷鍾秀舉げられて臨時主席となり、抽籤法にて各議員の席次を定む。此日正副議長の選擧を行ひ、吳景濓四十六票にて議長に、湯化龍四十四票にて副議長に當選す。又た各部審査員の員數を討議して法制二十一名、財政二十三名は汪榮寶の提議の如く、請願懲罰各九名、庶政十一名は谷鍾秀の提議の如く多數を以て通過し、請願懲罰各五月二日前九時開會して、各委員の選擧を行ふ。谷鍾秀大多數を以て全院委員長に當選し、其の他の各委員當選者は左の如し。

法政委員　秦瑞玠、汪榮寶、那彥圖、湯化龍、阮慶瀾、張耀曾、陳鴻鈞、劉興甲、彭允彝、王振垚、陳承澤、周樹標、熊成章、顧視高、籍忠寅、谷鍾秀、劉星楠、張伯烈、平剛、陳時夏、時功玖。

財政委員　陳景南、李榘、席聘臣、阿穆爾靈圭、金鼎勳、楊策、殷汝驪、盧信、盧士模、劉積學、杜贇、楊廷棟、黃樹中、逄世鈺、王樹聲、潘祖彝、歐陽振聲、孫鐘、周珏、郭同、李國珍、李肇甫、林森。

庶政委員　丁世嶧、李素、宋汝梅、劉彥、李乘恕、鄭萬瞻、曾有翼、谷芝瑞、貫桑諾爾布、何裕康、劉懋賞、劉盥訓。

請願委員　高家驥、王文慶、劉懋賞、孫孝宗、曾彥、曾有瀾、王盦潤、吳鈞、椶楚克蘇隆。

懲罰委員　薛珠、彭占元、王赤卿、景志傳、田駿豐、博迪蘇、祺誠武、段宇清、李述膺。

五月三日前九時各部委員會を開きて委員長を互選し、張耀曾は法制委員長に殷汝驪は財政委員長に鄭萬瞻は庶政委員長に、曾彥は請願委員長に、彭占元は懲罰委員長に各々當選したり。

五月四日前九時特別會議を開き、議長指名により、湯化龍、谷鍾秀、汪榮

實、張耀曾、段宇清の五名は參議院議事細則起草員に舉げられたり。七日全

院委員會を開き國會組織及び選擧法大綱案を審議したり。十三日前九時本會

議を開き、國務員の政見發表あり。此日出席議員八十七名にして、國總理

唐紹儀、財政總長熊希齡、陸軍總長段祺瑞、教育總長蔡元培、農林總長宋教

仁、海軍總長劉冠雄、司法總長王寵惠、交通總長施肇基、工商總長署理王正

廷出席す。唐總理の發表せる政見左の如し。

前次、紹儀等大總統に隨ひ、恭しく貴院を詣む

時、大總統より政見の宣示を蒙り、財政、實業

軍事、法律、外交の諸端、均しく己に包括擧示

されたり。尤も諄々たりし者は、曰く建設は穩

健より入手し、措置は實事を以て歸結と爲すと

の言なり。紹儀等自ら常に大總統の政見に本づ

きて措施の方を爲すべし。此の建設の肇始に當

りて經緯萬端なり、紹儀等任を國務に當

夙夕以て負荷に克たざるを懼る。審に現狀を度

るに至難且つ鉅し惟だ其の先後緩急を分別して後ち措施根據する所あるな

り。謹んで其の愚を布きて諸君の敎を俟つ。我國土宇廣大にして二十二行

省と蒙古西藏の諸邊地と舊習相承け、未だ一旦にし難困難し化除し、一種

の制度にて統治する能はざる也。然かも軍民分治は黎副總統前に主張し、

大總統後に賛成す、紹儀等之を按ずるに東西各國省な此法を持して治行の

道と爲し因て強盛の域に進む、我中華民國自ら常に引いて導師とすべし。

紹儀等軍民分治の意に本づき、漸次行政の實を擧げて、時に因り勢に因り

全院委員長谷鍾秀先生

地に因り、宜しきに合する地方制度を布かんと擬す。軍與以來、各處增兵

して勢力を廣め、軍務繁多復難なるを免かれず。此に循つて變ずんば、獨

り人民の負擔加はるのみならず、地方の秩序亦た其の安寧を保つ無し。現に

既に參謀部陸軍部に於て善後の方法を籌劃し、務めて全國の形勢を按じ、

軍政を統一し、精銳を簡選して、加ふるに訓練を以てし、紀律を整飭して

勁旅と成すべ倘ひ倘稍の虛應を致さずして國防の鞏固ならむことを期す。

外人の我に對する態度は皆な保守和平を以て宗旨とす。宜しく深く各友邦

の懇誠を感謝すべし。今後益々睦誼を敦ふし、

誠を推して相與に東亞和平の局を維持せむ。從

前淸廷が訂結せる各項の條約契約、自ら應に切

實に履行して信用を彰かにすべし。法律を改良し、

獨立司法制度を建設し、敎育を普及し、幣制を

統一し、金融機關を整頓し實業を振興し、交通

を發達せしむる等の事は、亦た當に漸進主義を

以て次第に施行すべし。目下尤も緊急と爲す者

は財政なり。前年度歲入二千九百餘萬と稱する

も、軍與以來今に至る七簡月、各地に於て消耗せる費額飢に之に數倍す。

現に全國統一すと雖も。農は野に廢し、工は肆に荒び、商買は途に滯り、

求めて政府規畫の用に敷せんとするも汒然取る所無し。租稅、公債、金融

等の事、皆な財政關係の最要なる者、又た綏は急を濟はず。故に己むを得

ず、惟だ外債を輸入して以て急需を救はんと擬す。迄に財政總長と各國銀行

團と力を竭して以て磋商を經たるも、尙ほ未だ正確の解決に達せず、成議ある

を俟ちて再び貴決議に提出せむ。外債借入條件に付ては、則ち政府は必ず

院の議決を求めたり。而して参議院は政府が不免換券を立つる方法を付せず
べく、中央に請ふて速に各省一律に通用せしむべしとの電請に依據して参議
軍次長蔣作賓が南京陸軍部軍用鈔票三百萬圓を將り、暫らく不免換券と作す
して、同時に國民損所収の款を不免換券準備金と爲すべしとの電報、並に陸
務總理及び財政總長は、南京留守黃興より不免換券は目前救急の最要方法に
出の不免換券案を討議して、議案と成さずして否決す。之より先六月九日國
す。六月四日秘密會記事略す、此日陸海軍旗式案を可決す。十四日大總統提
方の負擔にして、漢口市場興築以外に使用すべからず、漢口地方税を抵當と
利率年五分、期限二十五年にして六年後より還付し始め、借款の實は全く地
七日漢口市場建築借欵案を議決す。總額二百五十萬磅、約九三五乃至九四、
十四日の本會議に於て國旗統一案を可決す。連日の會議記事を畧す。二十
五大民族の幸福、實に攸賴する焉。
織及び選擧法を速に議定し、國會をして早く成を觀るを得せしめば、我が
て其の端は國會に在り、國會開かれずんば基址固からから、貴院將に國會組
して急を救ふの亦た繼ぎ難き也。紹儀等の切望する所は、共和の精神にし
整理の筓を籌畫して次第に勵行すべし。否ざれば則ち急は已む時無く、而
りで運轉の樞紐と爲すべし。則ち租税、貨幣、銀行、實行等の事は、方に
活機を見る能はず。目前の方法としては何ほ應に國民損、國庫券等の事あ
に屬せしむべし。然かも僅に外債をのみ恃みては。仍は我國の財政恢復の
後の支出預算を編製し、必ず節約主義を守りて、支出各省な正當の用途
能く繼を爲すべし。既に財政部より結果以前の支出決算を編製し、規定以
以て目前の急需を救ふにありと雖も、又た必ず自ら切實の預備ありて方に
正當にして權利損害あるに至らざるを確信す。然り外債借入を籌る、固と

且つ案其の者の形式亦た完備せずこの理由を以て、之を議案と爲さずして還
付するに至りたるもの也。
六月十九日國務院官制修正案を議決す。二十八日参議院議事細則修正案を
議決す。二十九日特別會議を開き、國務總理陸徵祥任命同意案の投票を行ひ
出席議員八十四名にして、七十四票の同意を以て通過す。七月二日郵便權收
回案を議決す。十一日國務院秘書顧官制案、法制局官制修正案を議決す。其
の前後して各部各局の官制修正案は議定されたり。十五日、議員盧士模は
張耀曾、歐陽振聲、陳鴻鈞、王鑫潤、李肇甫、周珏、彭允彝、胡璧城、曹玉
德等各議員を贊成者として、國務總理陸徵祥が参議院に來りて政見を發表せ
ざる理由の質問書を提出したり。其の文に曰く、
唐總理辭職以來、國家は無政府の地位に陷り內閣は無政の現象に陷り、人
心惶々として全國震動す。今ま陸總理は大總統より任命されて参議院を通
過し、全國人民歡迎鼓舞すること大旱に雲霓を望むが如し。此の如く歡迎
する所以は總理の名詞に非ず、實に其の政策に在る也。果して國利民福を
以て前提とし、能く唐總理の上を凌す乎、內ち共和の基礎を穩固ならしめ
外か列強をして早く承認せしむる乎に在りて、受職以來二週日を越すも尙
は参議院に赴きて政見を宣布せずとは意はざりし所なり。當に危急存亡の
秋、一刻千金の時なるに新總理は二週日內一も表見する所無し。再三思維
して切に言を爲すの已むを得ざる者あり。武漢起義以來、君主を民主に變
じ、專制を共和に變ず、種々の政策均しく變更すべからず。蓋し君主
に適する者民主に適せず、專制に適する者共和の早く
宣布すべき理由の一なり。兵燹の警電時に耳に聞へ、經濟の困難到る處省
な然り、軍隊如何んか統一し、財政如何んか統一し、軍民分治如何んか解

決する、重要問題一にして足らず、之れ政見の早く宣布すべき理由の二な
り。蒙古は獨立を宣告し、英人は兵を片馬に進め、日本は兵を滿洲に增し
借款問題又た未だ解決せず、生死存亡此の一擧に在り、對付方針を豫定せ
ざるべからず、之れ政策の早く宣布すべき理由の三なり。之を總ぶるに此一
髮千鈞の時に當り、國務院は行政の最高機關とす、總理一日政見を宣布せ
ずんば、即ち全國の政治は一日驚濤駭浪の中に在り。總理は何を以て今日
に至るも尚ほ未だ院に赴きて政見を發表し、天下人民をして總理の立國方
針を曉然たらしめ、以て飢渴の望を牽せざるかを質問す。

七月十九日、國務總理陸徵祥は參議院本會議に臨み、政見を發表し、同時
に各國務員擬任案の提出理由を說明したり。曰く、
徵祥今日始て貴院に到り諸君子と相見へ、亦た諸君子と直接事を理す、非
常に欣幸とす。徵祥や二十年間外國に在りて歸國し、又た是れ一番の新氣
象に遭遇するもの、其の外本國に在ること二十年。然り中國人の外國に在
る者、貴賓、商家、學生、勞働者等、皆な輿に周旋せざる無く、徵祥は極
めて本國人を歡ぶが故に廚役に命ずる獻立書迄自ら作るの煩を爲したり。
此次本國に歸來じ諸君子に望む所は徵祥が外國に在りて本國人を周旋した
る如く、徵祥を待遇せられん事なり。而して徵祥は花酒に耽溺するを欲せ
ず、官界に運動するを欲せず、又た親戚あるも交際せず、己が繰故ある人
を引用せず錢を借ることを肯せず、交際場中極めて冷淡なる所以なり。此
次花酒耽溺を願はず、官場運動を願はず、己人を引用せず、借錢を肯せざ
るこご依然たるも呼んで極めて大切なる事體を處理せしめらること、徵祥
淸夜自ら思つて今日は實に生平最も欣樂の一日と爲す也。今日徵祥が貴院
に臨むは國務員擬任案提出の理由を說明せんが爲にして、當日徵祥大總統

の厚意を得、貴院諸君の推愛を蒙る、勉めて擔任せざるを得ず。受職の後
ち各國務員相繼で辭し、大總統と再三商量して之を挽留せしも能はず。己
むなく熊蔡宋王四君の辭職を准し、農工商長陳其美、交通總長施肇基二名
飢に其の官を免せらる。而して大總統と商議の上、內務に章宗祥、教育に
は舊の儘とし財政に周自齊、司法に章宗祥、教育に孫毓筠、農林に王人文
工商に沈秉堃、交通に胡維德を任命し、外交總長の一席は尚ほ相當の人な
きを以て暫らく徵祥兼任せんとす。(下略)

斯くて新總理の政見を聞かんとして期待したる參議院は滿場呆然たるもの
あり。其の翌十九日、國務員擬任案の投票を行ひ、出席議員投票者九十八名
にして、周自齊六十三票、章宗祥六十票、孫毓筠八十七票、王人文七十七票
沈秉堃六十一票、胡維德六十二票の不同意にて悉く否認されたり。次で二十
五日陸軍總長段祺瑞出席して國務員新擬任案を提出し、翌二十六日之が投票
を行ふ。出席議員投票者九十一名にして、財政の周學熙五十四票、司法の許
世英七十票、教育の范源濂七十票、農林の陳振先五十七票、交通の朱啓鈐四
十七票の同意にて、工商の蔣作賓のみ同意四十四に對し四十七票の不
同意にて否認さる。依て三十一日、工商總長に劉揆一任命の同意を求め、八
月二日海軍總長劉冠雄出席して其の理由を說明し、投票數八十一、不同意三
十六票に對し同意四十五票を以て承認されたり。此日國會組織法案、參議院
議員選擧區表を議決し。三日蒙古優待條件案を議決す。九日參議院議員、
各省覆選擧法案を議決し。十四日蒙古優待條件案を提議す。二十日劉成禹は張
振武、方維殺害の政府違法事件を提議す。歐陽振聲は昨十九日飢に張
國務員に翌日出席答復すべきを求むる事を提議して
多數可決す。二十日張伯烈等に對して政府より文書を以て前件の回答ありた

る事を披露したり。

陳景南は陸軍總理及び段陸軍總長の出席を求むる事を提議して可決し、二十三

日段祺瑞のみ出席辨明す。二十八日國務總理陸軍總長彈劾案議事日程に上り

前九時四十五分開議したるも、出席議員八十六名にして總員四分の三に及ず

して彈劾案は議せらるゝに至らざりし。九月十二日起草委員提出の軍人が政

十三日大總統より梁如浩の外交總長擬任案提出あり、十六日代理總理趙秉

鈞出席して其の理由を説明し、投票數七十五

不同意二十七票に對し四十七票の同意にて梁

如浩の外交總長任命案通過したり。廿四日國

慶紀念日案を可決し、武昌起義の日即ち陽曆

十月十日を國慶日とし、南京政府成立の日即

ち陽曆正月一日、及び北京共和宣布南北統一

の日即ち陽曆二月十二日を紀念日とする事と

なれり。此日趙秉鈞を國務總理に任命するの

の同意案を議して無記名投票を行ひ、在席者

七十一名にして同意者六十九票の大多數にて通過したり。十月三日趙國務總

理の政見發表演説あり。曰く、

現在民國初て成り、百度更新し、總理の一席は尤も繁重と爲す、鄙人自ら

維れ譾陋にして任に勝へ難きを恐るゝも、既に大總統より提出し、又た諸

君の同意を荷ふ、聰勉事に從ざる能はず。然かも委託に負かざらん事を期

するに過ずして、未だ作し到り能ふ可きや否やを識らざる也。大政方針は

皆て大總統より政綱八ヶ條を提出されて、業に宣言を經たる宏規遠矩、當

國務總理趙秉鈞先生

に我國民一般の心理共に盼む所の者なり。現在の臨時政府は時に限りあり、

鄙人敬んで此意に本づき先づ入手政策を將りて略ぼ宣布すべし。國家ある

必ず政治あり、內政あれば即ち外交あり、內政日に進步あれば外交亦た隨

つて轉移すること一定の至理なり。鄙人は對內政策に現狀維持主義を採り

對外政策に和平親睦を取るものなり。現在の大局を表面より觀れば地方の

秩序尙ほ未だ恢復せず、盜賊橫行して水旱疊ね有し、民其の生に聊せずし

て甚だ危險と爲すも、其の實は皆な生計問題にして業無き遊民太だ多く、

饑寒迫る所、甘じて匪と爲るに非ざる也。治安の計

は應に治標を先にすべし。治標の方法は先づ警察を

改良し、軍隊を變通し、以て之れを鎭懾して其の政

て匪たらしめず、然る後ち再び其の本を治するを要

す。治本の方法は必ず須らく實業を興し、工藝を勸

め磺を開き、路を修せざるべからず。用人既に多け

れば、生計活動し、自然に人の匪たるもの無し。現

狀維持の方法として、盜は則ち之れを捕へ、匪は則ち之れ

得る事にして、盜は則ち之れを捕へ、匪は則ち之れ

を劉し、饑は則ち之れを撫し、先づ四民をして業に復せしめなば、地方は

自然に安靖にして各國人民の我が境內に居る者、我が其の身命財產を保ち

て毫も危險無きを確信し、僅に秩序の恢復を算して中華民國眞に成立する

と算するに足るべし。鄙人の現狀維持を重ずる所以、實に對內對外の事應

に然るが故なり。若し專ら改革を論せば、此次の改革其の成の速なること歷

史上未曾有にして、武昌起義より今に至る一載を經て秩序未だ十分恢復せ

ざるも復た究めて好きに屬する者其の多數に居り、統一機關完全ならざる

も二十二行省命を中央に聽かざる無し。庫倫の獨立は實に邊邊の地方民智

開けずして諸多の誤解あるによるもの、極端の反對に非ることを斷言すべ

し前代の改革は武力を以て取る、尚ほ且つ

十年數十年なるも内地に於て統一する能は

ざるも。此次は純乎道德を以て解決す、數

月にして定まり、規模粗ぼ具る。專制より

一躍して共和となる、損失鉅しと雖も常に

代價を作るもの、亦是れ樂觀す。金融滯

塞して生計の艱難なるは今に始らず、水旱

の災、盜賊の出沒、何の時か之れなからむ

破壞の後ち建設の初め、之を平時に較べて

甚だしきとなすのみ。我國の地は大きく物

は博し、漸次富强に進むと決して難事に非

ず、甚だ願ふ所は諸君と共に之を圖らむ事

なり。此時財政困難にして一時周轉開かざ

るものあり、借償して僅に補助し能ふべし

借償本と慮るに足らず、但だ方法如何を看

るべし。借償必ず先が預め還償の方法が、

債務の累しき所と爲さるや否やを論るを要

す。則ち借ざるに危險なり。以て急

切に處理すべきものは（一）鹽法を整頓すること（二）稅務を釐通すること

（三）幣制を改良すること（四）銀行を擴充すること（五）紙幣を發行すること

（六）會計檢査院を速設する事なり。會計檢査の役は、獨り收入を愼しむの

みならず、並に且つ其の支出を謹ましめ、祇

だ用は其の當を得て、事は虛廢せざるを要

す。鉅償を借るも國民に對して亦た愧なきを覺ゆ

之れ郡人の十分に注重する者なり。此時先づ

鹽務稅務の兩項より著手して增收あらば皆な

民間の間接負擔なれども仍は休養の意たるを

失はざるなり。粗漫の政見、大略此の如く、

各部總長均しく同意を表したり、並に望む所

は、諸君時に隨つて匡正以て共濟を圖られん

事にして、民國の幸甚だしきと共に郡人の幸

甚し。

演說後、阮慶瀾は質問して曰く。本員病に

より河南省に歸り、道すがら河南省の情形を

見しに、巡防尚は未だ裁撤せず、警政亦た疏

敗し、行政機關仍は未だ組織を改めず、司法

機關仍は刑訊仍を用ゐ、之を舊時に較べ、全く

未だ改良されずして眞に共和の狀態無し』と。

趙總理之に答て曰く『貴議員所說の河南の情

形は、郡人も河南人にして亦た深く之を知

危險あり、郡人の志、先づ自己の財政を整頓するに在る所以なり。以て急

現に南陽一帶土匪出沒す、曾て兩營を派したるも、魯山地方山多くして、繫

てば處々の山間に散じて、兵士頗る之に苦む。然り地方の秩序を維持するは

北京參議院閉院當日紀念撮影

全く地方官に人を得るに在り、官若し其の人を得ずんば甚だ危險とす。此事當に地方官吏を選ぶべく責むべし、一に其の人を得ば地方の秩序尙ほ恢復すべからざる無し』と。次で葉顯揚は『總理は庫倫の獨立は大患無しとの意見を發表されたり。本員は庫倫獨立は既に內外蒙古を動かして民國の統一と影響ありと爲すもの也。政府宜しく速に法を設け、或は兵力を用ひ、或は感情を聯絡して取消さしむるか、然らずんば恐らくは內外蒙古相安んずる能はず』と。趙總理は是れ兵事に關すと雖も別の手續あり、秘密會議の時答辯すべしと答へ。次で張伯烈は國務總理は一切の政策を發表して外交は內政よりすとあり。惟だ今日の民國が最も注意すべき者は、財政問題にして、人常に欵なきが故に種々の事業均しく辦ずる能はずと云ふも財政上の計畫は錢無き時と雖も亦た預め規定せざる可からず。假令ば貨幣の本位は當に如何んか規定する、金融機關は當に如何んか改良する、錢無き時に於ても辦すべき者なり』と。趙總理は『貴議員の所說、甚だ欽佩す、鄙人當に財政總長と之を商定すべし』と答へたり。此日楊廷變請願の鐵路政策條陳を討論採擇せり。

十月十八日廣東地稅抵當の外債借入案を議決承認し、三十日の常會に於て五厘息英金一千萬磅借欵契約を討議承認す。十一月四日民國元年八月分概算案及び追加案を議決す。十五日大總統より梁如浩の外交總長を免じ、陸徵祥を外交總長に任ずるの同意請求案は提出され、同日の常會に於て投票數七十五、同意七十二票の大多數にて陸徵祥案は通過したり。十二月二十三日六釐公債案を議決したり。

之より先、正式國會議員の選擧は開始され、參議院議員の選擧運動其の他各方に散ずるもの多く、爲に本會議は議員の定數を缺きて流會に次ぐに流會を以てし民國二年の一月は二十七日、二月は三日の各一日を開會せるのみ、三月は三日、十四日二十四日二十六日の四日開會し、四月は七日の一日開會せしのみ。三月二十六日に於て鐵道公司條例修正案、省議會臨時法案、行政執行法案を議決し、四月七日西藏選擧國會議員變通處理案、西藏第一期國會議員選擧施行法案、中國銀行則例案を議決す。四月八日を期して正式國會開院すると共に、臨時參議院は閉會したり。

終りに北京臨時參議院議員として、南北統一後、國家建設の大業を翼贊したる氏名は下の如し。(直隷)谷鍾秀、谷芝瑞、王振垚、李榘、籍忠寅(奉天)吳景濂、孫孝宗、李秉恕、劉興甲、曾有翼(吉林)王樹聲、金鼎勳、揚策、李芳、何裕康(黑龍江)高家驥、薛珠、王赤鄉、關文鐸、戰雲霽、喜山(江蘇)汪榮寶、秦瑞玠、楊廷棟、張鶴第、王嘉賓、王立廷、張家鎭、江辛(安徽)俞道暄、曾玉德、胡璧城(江西)李國珍、陳鴻鈞、曾有瀾、郭同、盧士摸、吳寶田(浙江)殷汝驪、周珏、王文慶、王家襄、陳時夏(福建)林森、潘祖彝、鄭祖蔭、陳承澤、李兆年、建賢基、林翰、周[illegible]、劉崇祐、林輅存(湖北)鄭萬膽、湯化龍、張伯烈、時功玖、劉成禺(湖南)覃振、歐陽振聲、彭允彝、劉彥、陳家鼎(山東)劉星楠、彭占元、丁世嶧、周樹標、侯延爽(河南)陳景南、孫鐘、阮慶瀾、杜潛、劉積學(山西)宋汝梅、張聯魁、李素、劉盥訓、劉懋賞、黃雨潤(陝西)趙世鈺、景志傳、李述膺、茹欲可、陳同熙(甘肅)宋振聲、吳鈞、王鑫潤、田駿豐、秦望瀾、魏承耀(新疆)劉熔、蔣擧淸(四川)黃樹中、熊成章、李肇甫、劉聲元、鄧鎔、楊芬(廣東)盧信、徐傅霖、司徒穎、梁孝肅、楊永泰(廣西)劉崛、曾彥、鄧家彥、黃宏憲、蒙啓勳、陳太龍、李拔超、虢政(雲南)張耀曾、顧視高、段宇淸、席聘臣、張華瀾(貴州)平剛、文崇高、姚華、陳國祥、劉顯治、陳廷策(蒙古)阿穆爾靈圭、那彥圖、祺誠武、鄂多臺、博迪蘇、達賚、熙凌河、德色賴託布、葉顯揚、金承昌、張樹桐(青海)唐古色の百三十五名なるが、其の中林森、潘祖彝、陳承澤、林

翰、黄樹中、平剛、文崇高の七名は民選議員着院と同時に中途辞職し、孫孝

宗、薛珠、揚廷棟、王嘉賓、鄭祖蔭、劉懋賞、田駿豐、秦望瀾、熊成章、劉

嗣、曾彥、鄧家彥、裴啓勳、阿穆爾靈圭、那

彥圖の十五名は病氣其の他の事故を以て開期中前後して辞職し、盧七摚は元年十二月三日病死す、喜山、王立廷、張家鎮、吳賀田、林輅存、魏承耀、熊政の七名は補缺として中途より着院したる者なり。

第四章　第一次正式國會

一　正式國會の成立

民國二年一月十日、臨時大總統袁世凱は左の申令を發したり、曰く

正式國會召集の期は約法に照して十ヶ月を以て限りとす、民國元年八月業に將に國會組織法選び參議院衆議院議員選舉各法を公布施行したり。民國正式國會は共和建設の關する所にして、本大總統躬ら我國政府附託の重を承け、迅に國務總理内務總長を偪し、國會準備事務局及び各參議院議員選舉監督、衆議院議員選舉總監督、選舉監督等に令し、速に準備すべく、並に兩院議員選舉期日を制定

して進行するを俟ひたり。約法を施行してより現に十ヶ月にして期限に

届く、國務總理内務總長が國會準備事務局の報告により言ふ所によれば衆議院議員覆選舉は具報せる延期各省を除き、餘は民國二年一月十日に於て令に遵つて舉行し、參議院議員選舉亦た將に次第に令に遵つて舉行すとあり。本大總統は我中華民國締造の艱難に當り、夙夜兢々として未だ臨時期内なる故を以て稍も暇逸せざるなり。茲に幸に國會議員法の如く選出せらる、亟に應に約法に照して召集令を下す。民

第一大國會開院式當日

國二年一月十日正式國會召集令發布の日より三月以内に當選の參議院議員及び衆議院議員均しく北京に集り、兩院は各總議員過半數の到著を俟ちて即ち同時に開會すべし。國會開會の準備事項に關しては應に國務總理内務總長より國會準備事務局に督飭して速に籌備を完全せしめよ。共和政治の良否は政府固と完全の責任あり、而して尤も正式國會を以て範框と爲す、德を一にし心を一にし共に盛業を圖れよ。これ則ち本大總統が我滇滿蒙回藏の五大民族を代表して馨香禱祝以て之を求むる所の者なり、此に令す。

而して再び三月十九日臨時大總統令を下し

て、四月八日を以て正式國會の開院式を行ふべき旨を發布したり。

正式國會は北京臨時參議院に於て議決したる國會組織法案に準備して組織

されたるもの、即ち参衆兩議院を以て構成す。参議院は各省議會に於て毎省

十名、蒙古選舉會に於て二十七名、西藏選舉會に於

十三名、中央學會より八名、華僑選舉會に於て六名、計二百七十四名の議員

當選者を以て組織す。衆議院は各地人民より復選法により選出し、人口の比

例により、直隷四十六名、江蘇四十名、浙江三十八名、江西四川は各三十五

名、山東三十三名、河南三十二名、廣東三十名、山西二十八名、湖南安徽は

各二十七名、湖北二十六名、福建二十四名、雲南二十二名、陝西二十一名、

廣西十九名、奉天十六名、甘肅十六名、貴州十三名、吉林、黑龍江、新疆の

各十名、蒙古の二十七名、西藏の十名、青海の三名、計五百九十六名の議員

當選者を以て組織す。参議院議員の任期は六年にして二年毎に其の三分の一

を改選し、衆議院議員の任期は三年なり。

四月八日前十時、衆議院議事堂に於て正式國會第一次開院式を行ふ。参議

院議員百七十九名、衆議院議員五百〇三名、出席し、臨時大總統袁世凱代理梁

士詒及び國務總理趙秉鈞、並に陸徵祥、段祺瑞、劉冠雄、許世英、陳振先、朱啓

鈐等の各部總長、國會準備局長施愚、副長顧鼇等列席したり。十一時振鈴を

以て開會し、同時に禁衛軍に於て禮砲百〇八發を放ちたり。顧鼇開會を宣し

施愚の報告あり、最年長議員楊瓊を臨時主席とす。林長民代つて開會辭の

禮を行ひて式を終ゆ。兩院の開會辭に曰く、

中華民國二年四月八日、我正式國會第一次開會の辰とす。参議院衆議院

議員禮堂に集り盛典を舉げ謹んで詞を爲す。視聽は天よりし、默して下

民を定む。億兆與るあるは天下の權輿によるもの今人よりせず。帝制久

しく斁れて民意を拂ひ、付託の重き乃ち多士に及ぶ。衆の好み衆の惡む

多士に赴き、衆の志し衆の口、多士之を表す。張弛緊縱、天下の輕とな

り、緩急疾徐、天下の樞となる。與か廢か安か危か、禍福これ共にし、功

罪これ屬す、能く懼れなからんや。嗚呼邦を興すこと多難なり。惕惕蝦

を蒙る、茲に締造に當りて我顧ヶ伸べん。願は我一國其の中權を制

し、願くば我五族其の黨偏を正さむ。大種暢雨、農は先づ穀を首とし、

工は其の業を樂み、商は其の慶を安んじて、政は舉らざるなく、隙は宣

べざるなく、章皇發越す。吾言の洋々として逖聽遠慕す、四鄰我と感し

み、舊邦の新たなる命は悠久疆りなからむ。凡百の君子孰れか敢て之を忽

荒せんや。

袁總統の頌詞に曰く、

中華民國二年四月八日、我中華民國第一次國會は正式に成立したり。こ

れ實に四千餘年の歷史上莫大の光榮にして、四萬々人億萬年の幸福なり。

世凱亦た國民の一分子なり、當に諸子と同じく深く慶幸す。念ふに我共

和民國は四萬々人民の心理によりて繼造せらるゝ所にして、正式國會亦

た四萬々の人民心理の結合する所なれば、則ち國家の主權は當然民國全

體に歸すべし。但 民國成立より今に至る一年、所謂國民直接委任の機

關は事實上尚未だ完備せず。今日の國會諸議員は國民直接の選擧によ

りて即ち國民の實體藉りて以て統治權の運用

を表し亦た賴つて以て圓滿に進行すべし。諸君子は皆な時を識るの俊傑

なれば、必ずや能く各々讜論を紓して國の爲に謀るに忠なるべく、中華

民國の邦基益々鞏固を加へ、五大民族の幸福日に增進を見るべし。同心

協力以て強大なる民國を造成し、五色國旗をして常に神州大陸に照耀せ

しむる事は、則ち世凱と諸君子と企踵する所の者なり。謹んで頌を致し

て日々中華民國萬歳、民國々會萬々歳。

斯くて開院式後、日を經るも、參衆兩院共正式會議を開くに至らず、逐次豫備會を開きて協商の末參衆兩院共に廿四日より本會議を開く事に決定したり

二 參議院

四月二十四日開會、楊瑳臨時主席として討議し、翌二十五日議長副議長の選舉を行ふ事となり、出席者二百二名にして張繼百二十九票にて議長に、王正廷百二十七票にて副議長に常選したり、張繼の挨拶に曰く、

參議院議長王家襄

中華民國第一次國會參議院議長に常選し、自ら無德無才を慚づ、認つて諸君の推舉を辱み、實に此重任に勝ゆ能ざるを恐る。願くば諸公と心を盡し力を竭くし以て此最高立法機關を維持して穩固の地位に居らしめ、以て中華民國をして強大の國家として全球に立たしめば、方に能く四萬々同胞委托の重に負かん。願くば諸公と共に之を勉めん。

王正廷の挨拶に曰く、

吾國々會第一次成立す、誠に數千年の創舉なり。之を世界各國に考へ、代議制を有する者甚だ多し、然れども優劣等しからず、蓋し人民程度の齊

しからざるに因るなり。吾國今ま飫に代議制あり、精力を竭盡して國利民福を謀らざるべからず。諸公思想學術に於て正廷に勝るや百倍なることと多言を庸ゆる無し、願くば諸公共に指導せよ。

尚は全院委員長に林森常選す。後ち張繼職を辭し、王家襄擧げられて議長となる。而して開期中參議院に於て議決したる案件は左の如し。

案由	提出者或移付者	提付院議日期	議決日期
議院法	起草委員會	二年六月九日	二年九月十一日
兩院議員旅費表	起草委員會	二年八月廿二日	二年十月廿四日
參議院議事細則	起草委員會	二年六月十一日	二年十月十三日
參議院議長副議長	預備會提出	二年四月廿四日	二年四月廿四日
參議院委員會規則	起草委員會	二年八月六日	二年十月十三日
參議院互選規則	起草委員會	二年八月八日	二年九月廿三日
參議院秘書廳組織規則	起草委員會	二年八月廿日	二年九月十日
參議院警衛處規則	起草委員會	二年八月廿日	二年九月十日
參議院警衛處辦事規則	起草委員會	二年八月廿日	二年九月十日
參議院旁聽規則	起草委員會	二年五月三日	二年六月十三日
憲法起草委員互選細則	起草委員會	二年六月廿三日	二年六月廿五日

議案	提出者		
國會議員內亂外患罪逮捕法	衆議院提出	二年九月五日	二年九月五日
戒嚴法施行法	議員陸宗輿提出	二年九月八日	二年九月廿三日
浦信鐵鎔借欵合同	大總統提出衆議院移付	二年十月二十日	二年十月十九日
政府速將本年預算提交國會議決	議員袁嘉穀提出	二年八月六日	二年八月十三日
政府為國務總理求同意以任命熊希齡	大總統提移付衆議院	二年七月三十日	二年七月三十日
政府等為為國務員求同意以任命孫寶琦等	大總統提出衆議院移付	二年九月十一日	二年九月十一日
政府以禁炉公約求同意	大總統提出衆議院移付	二年十月二十日	二年十月二十日
衆議院以先行議定開統正式選舉方法求同意	衆議院提出	二年九月八日	二年九月八日
資辦河南芳違法溺職都督張鎮	議員段世垣提出	二年七月二日	二年七月十六日
查辦湖北夏口民政長夏職	議員鄭江灝提出	二年八月六日	二年八月十五日
美國承認民國美容謝	議員朱兆莘提出	二年六月廿三日	二年六月廿三日
建議應先派專使赴美容謝	議員黎尚雯提出	二年六月三十日	二年六月三十日
建議涉廢約停運還遠印烟約法	議員蔣義明提出	二年八月六日	二年八月十五日
建議與英國嚴重交規畫國民銀行	議員陳銘鑑提出	二年九月廿三日	二年九月廿三日
建議請政府勿事株連南方亂事飭定	議員陳銘鑑提出	二年九月廿三日	二年九月廿三日

三 衆議院

四月二十四日開會。當分臨時參議院時代の議事及び傍聽細則を準用する事に決定す。議長互選規則を討議して二十五日無記名投票に決し、二十六日互選會を開きたるも湯化龍吳景濂何れも過半數に滿たず、二十八日決選投票を行ひたるも決せず、三十日再び決選投票を試み、出席議員五百四十一人にして湯化龍二百七十九票にて議長に常選す。五月一日副議長の互選を行ひ、出席議員五百三十三人にして陳國祥二百六十九票にて當選したり。湯化龍の誓詞に曰く、

中華民國第一次衆議院議長に化龍適ま其の乏を承く、自ら維れ德は薄く能は鮮し、深く懍惶を用ゆ。國步方に新まり、憲政未だ熟せずして法度立たず、疾苦猶ほ塗る。飢に身を立定の地に献じ、正に忠を同胞に效するの日、就職の始に當りて敢て我議員諸君に宣誓し、我全體國民に宣誓す。誓つて曰く民憲成らずんば敢て國本焉んで立たんや、繼ぐに今より憲政を懸けて鵠とす、凡そ斯の軌に合す、誠を瀝して票を扶けん。其の道に背き軌を易くる若くんば視力至る所、努めて之を擴廓せん。敢て偏倚する閧く、亦た恆慮する閧く、心を同ふして共に濟ふことを矢ふ。以て鞠を出でて享を履まむ、凡そ諸の言ム所、生に在りて變ずる無し。

陳國祥の誓詞に曰く、

國祥親を以て躬ら立法府に廁す、復た選擧せられて衆議院副議長と爲る。望は輕ふして任は重く、我議長湯先生を佐けて其の職を舉る克ざるを懼る。惟だ誠を失つて宣誓するあり、冀くば同人の助を獲て、以て力を我新造の共和國に盡さんのみ。誓つて曰く、國體初て變じ、百廢舉るを待

つ。民視民聽は惟だ此國會にあり。國會能く其の議政の實を舉ぐ、民國始て其の無疆の基を奠むべし。同心協力して以て湯公を輔けて吾責を盡し、吾邦本を鞏くせざる所の者あらば、凡そ我國民共に之を舉げ得べし、忠を秉つて渝らず、敢て天下に告ぐ。

尚は全院委員長には張耀曾當選したり。而して開期中衆議院に於て議決したる案件は左の如し。

議案題目	提出者	可決或否決
關於蒙古事件中俄協約咨請同意案	大總統	可決
中華民國二年一月至六月預算案	大總統	可決
浦信鐵路五釐借欵案	大總統	否決
中央學會選舉資格諮詢案	大總統	否決
擬訂民事訴訟印紙暫行規則諮詢案	大總統	可決
契稅法案	大總統	可決
擬任施肇基爲駐美公使咨請同意案	大總統	否決
行政執行法第七條修正案	大總統	否決
預戒法案	大總統	可決

議案題目	提出者	可決或否決
擬任熊希齡爲國務總理咨請同意案	大總統	可決
禁烟公約咨請同意案	大總統	可決
擬任孫寶琦爲外交總長朱啟鈐爲內務總長梁啟超爲司法總長汪大燮爲教育總長張謇爲工商總長周自齊爲交通總長咨請同意案	大總統	可決
衆議院議長副議長互選規則案	本院	可決
憲法起草委員衆議院選舉規則案	本院	可決
議院法案	參議院	可決
衆議院規則案	參議院	可決
國會組織法第二條又參議院議員選舉法第五章修正案	本院	否決
咨請政府查辦奉天北路洮南各縣官吏違法案	本院	可決
關於內亂罪之嫌疑者應歸大理院審判建議案	本院	可決
兩院議員旅費表案	參議院	可決
南方亂事已平請政府迅卽宣告解嚴建議案	本院	可決
對於豫楚兩省勦辦白匪善後事宜建議案	本院	可決
關於蒙古事件中俄協約建議案	本院	可決

四　憲法起草委員會

二年六月三十日及び七月二日、参衆兩院に於て選出せる憲法起草委員並に候補委員左の如し。

参議院選出委員　湯濟、金永昌、楊永泰、張我華、蔣舉情、朱兆莘、金兆莘、宋淵源、向乃祺、金鼎勳、蔣曾澳、石德純、趙世鈺、王用賓、呂志伊、王盍潤、車林桑多布、高家驤、段世垣、饒應銘、王家襄、丁世嶧、王厇、藍公武、曹玉霖、陸宗輿、阿穆爾靈圭、陳銘鑑、解樹強、陳善

同上補缺委員　盧天游、劉積學、田永正、程瑩度、楊福州、徐鋭心、楊渡、袁嘉穀、劉映奎、楊增炳、齊忠甲、籍忠寅、姚華、李燮、辛漢鵬、吳宗慈

衆議院選出委員　何㷍、張耀曾、黃璟、李肇甫、伍朝樞、易宗夔、黃雲鵬、陳景南、格、祐輔成、王紹鑒、劉恩、澤咸、徐秀、彭允彝、史、鈞、孫潤宇、孫鐘、李芳、楊銘源、谷頒秀、汪榮寶、劉崇祐、李國珍、王敬芳、汪彭年、李慶芳、孟森、張國溶、夏同龢、王印川

同上補缺委員　襄政、黃贊元、陳發檀、馬小進、劉彥、駱繼漢、陳鴻鈞、

衆議院議長湯化龍先生

谷芝瑞、林萬里、沈河清、孫洪伊、李景龢、楊廷棟、范熙壬、虞熾懺、梅光遠、曾有翼、蕭湘。

六月十九日互選の結果、委員長に湯濟理事に蔣舉清、楊銘源、黃雲鵬、王家襄、夏同和、楊永泰常選したり。二十二日會場を天壇に定め又た張耀曾、汪榮寶、黃雲鵬、汪孫鐘を憲法大綱起草委員とし、八月二日より引

衆議兩院全院委員長張耀贊先生

継ぎ大綱に付き討議を爲したり。九月十三日参衆兩院合會より憲法中總統選舉法に關する一部分を先に起草すべしとの要求を報告して、議事日程を變更して、大總統選舉法を討議し、汪榮寶、伍朝樞、何㷍を其の起草委員としたり。而して十五日起草案大綱を議し、十六日多少の修正を加へて該案を通過したり。二十日既に議定せる憲法大綱に依り民國憲法全文を起草する事とし、其の委員に張耀曾、丁世嶧、黃雲鵬、孫鐘、李慶芳を指定したり。同委員會理事王家襄が参議院議長と爲りしを以て、其の補缺として、李國珍多數にて理事に當選したり。

十月十四日より前起草委員に於て分擔起草せる憲法草案全文計十一章百十三ヶ條を開議し、二十日より二十五日迄連日討議して多少の修正を加へ、十月三十日三讀會を經て憲法會議に提交する事としたり。此日委員孟森辭職の

補鋏として馬小進出席す。十一月一日天壇祈年殿西側の休息室に於て談話會を開き、憲法草案各條文の説明書を起草する事とし、各自分擔して之に當る事となれるが、其の氏名は左の如し。

湯漪、張耀曾、左慶芳、何雯、汪榮寶、孫鍾、劉崇祐、吳宗慈、汪彭年、黃雲鵬、向乃祺、聶政、藍公武、楊永泰、楊銘源、朱兆莘、黃贊元、陳景南、楊蓁、黃璋、程瑩度、解樹強、李國珍、馬小進。

斯くて大總統が國民黨員の兩 議員證書刺奪の命令を出すべき風聞あるを以て委員湯漪は憲法起草案理由書未だ盡く脱稿せざるものあるも一日を遲らせば終に永く提出の日無きを慮り、理由書を付せすして十一月三日憲法草案全文を憲法 に送付したり。而して十一月四日は大總統 より國民黨員の議員資格を取消されたる為 本會委員資格をも消滅するに至りたるは、湯漪、蔣翥清、楊永泰、楊銘源、高家驥、蔣曾燠、宋淵源、田永正、向乃祺、段世垣、盧天游、谷鍾秀、朱兆莘、張耀曾、陳景南、黃元、孫潤宇、陳發檀、馬小進、伍朝樞、聶政、易宗夔、張我華、褚輔成、劉恩格の二十八名にして、餘の三十二名にては法定人數に足らざるを以て開

第六條　中華民國人民の住居は法律に依るに非れば侵入或は搜索を受けず

第七條　中華民國人民通信の秘密は法律に依るに非れば侵犯を受けず

第八條　中華民國人民は住居及び職業を選擇する自由を有し法律に依るに非れば制限を受けず

第九條　中華民國人民は集會結社の自由ありて法律に依るに非れば制限を受けず

第十條　中華民國人民は言論著作及び刊行の自由あり法律に依るに非れば制限を受けず

第十一條　中華民國人民は信仰宗教の自由ありて法律に依るは非れば制限を受けず

第十二條　中華民國人民の財産所有權は侵犯を受けず

但し公益上必要の處分は法律の定むる所に依る

第十三條　中華民國人民は法律に依りて法院に訴訟するの權あり

第十四條　中華民國人民は法律に依りて請願及び陳訴の權あり

第十五條　中華民國人民は法律に依りて選擧及び被選擧權あり

第十六條　中華民國人民は法律に依りて公職に從事するの權あり

第十七條　中華民國人民は法律に依りて租稅を納むるの義務あり

第十八條　中華民國人民は法律に依りて兵役に服するの義務あり

第十九條　中華民國人民は法律に依りて初等教育を受くるの義務あり

國民教育は孔子の道を以て修身の大本と爲す

第四章　國　會

第廿條　中華民國の立法權は國會より之を行ふ

第廿一條　國會は參議院衆議院を以て之を構成す

第廿二條　參議院は法定の最高級地方議會及び其他選擧團體選出の議員を以て之を組織す

第廿三條　參議院は各選擧區の人々を比例したる議員を以て之を組織す

第廿四條　兩院議員の選擧は法律を以て之を定む

第廿五條　何人に論なく同時に兩院議員たるを得ず

第廿六條　兩院議員は文武官吏を兼任するを得ず

但し國務員は此限に在らず

第廿七條　兩院議員の資格は各院自ら之を審査するを得

第廿八條　參議院議員の任期は六年にして二年每に三分の一を改選す

第廿九條　衆議院議員の任期は三年とす

第三十條　兩院各議長副議長一人を設け兩院議員より之を互選す

第卅一條　國會は自ら集會開會閉會を行ふ

但し臨時會は大總統より之を召集す

第卅二條　國會の常會は每年三月一日に於て開會す

第卅三條　國會の常會會期は四ヶ月とす

但し之を延長することを得

第卅四條　國會臨時會の膜集は左記事情の一ある時に於て之を行ふ

一、兩院議員各三分一以上の請求

二、國會委員會の請求

三、政府の認めて必要とする時

第卅五條　國會の開會閉會は兩院同時に之を行ふ

一院停會の時は他院同時に休會す

衆議院解散の時は參議院同時に休會す

第卅六條　國會の議事は兩院各別に之を行ふ

第卅七條　兩院各議員總數の過半數の列席あるに非れば開議するを得ず

第卅八條　兩院の議事は列席議員過半數の同意を以て之を決し可否同數は決を議長に取る

第卅九條　國會の議定は兩院の一致を以て之を成す

第四十條　兩院の議事は之を公開す、但し政府の請求或は院議に依り之を秘密にするを得

第四十一條　衆議院が大總統副總統に謀叛の行爲あるを認むる時は議員總數三分二以上の列席列席員三分二以上の同意を以て之を彈劾す

第四十二條　衆議院が國務員の違法行爲あるを認むる時は列席員三分の二以上の同意を以て之を彈劾す

第四十三條　衆議院は國務員に對し不信任の決議を爲すを得

第四十四條　參議院は彈劾されし大總統副總統及國務員を審判す
前項審判は列席員三分二以上の同意を以てするに非ざれば有罪或は違法と

者草起文正案草法憲

判決するを得ず
大總統副總統の有罪を判決せる時は應に其職を黜し其罪の處刑は最高法院により之を定む

國務員の違法を判決せる時は應に其の職を黜し並に其の公權を奪ふ若し餘罪あれば法院に付して之を審判す

第四十五條　兩院各々政府に建議することを得

第四十六條　兩院各々國民の請願を受理することを得

第四十七條　兩院議員は國務員に質問書を提出し、或は其の議院に出席を請求して質問することを得

第四十八條　兩院議員院内の言論及表決は院外に對して責任を負はず

第四十九條　兩院議員は現行犯を除き各本院或は國會委員會の許可を得るに非ざれば逮捕或は監視するを得ず
兩院議員現行犯に因りて逮捕さるゝ時は政府應に即ち理由を將りて各本院或は國會委員會に報告すべし

第五章　國會委員

第五十條　兩院議員の歲費及び其他の公費は法律を以て之を定む

第五十一條　國會委員會は毎年國會常會閉會前に於て兩院より各議院內に於

て二十名の委員を選出して之を組織す

第五十二條　國會委員會の議事に委員總數三分二以上の列席、列席員三分二

以上の同意を以て之を決す

第五十三條　國會委員會は國會閉會期內に於て各本條所定の職權行使を除き

諸願並に建議及び質問を受理す

第五十四條　國會委員會は須らく經過事由を將りて國會開會の始に於て之を

報告すべし

　　第六章　大　總　統

第五十五條　中華民國の行政權は大總統により國務員の贊襄を以て之を行ふ

第五十六條　中華民國の人民にして完全に公權を享有し年滿四十歲以上並に

國內に滿十年以上住居する者は選舉されて大總統となるを得

第五十七條　大總統は國會議員より組織せる總統選舉會にて之を選舉す

前項選舉は選舉人總數三分二以上の列席を以て無記名投票にて之を行

ふ得票投票人數四分三に滿つる者を當選とす但し二回投票し得票投票人數の

半に過ぎる者を以て當選と爲す

第五十八條　大總統任期五年とす若し再選さるれば一回連任するを得、大總統

滿期前三ケ月前國會議員は須らく自ら集會を行ひ總統選舉會を組織し次任

大總統の選舉を行ふ

第五十九條　大總統就職の時須らく左記の宣誓を爲すべし

余誓つて至誠を以て憲法を遵守し大總統の職務を執行す謹んで誓ふ

第六十條　大總統缺位の時は副總統繼任し本任大總統期滿の日に至つて止む

大總統事故に因り職務を執行する能はざる時副總統之を代理す副總統同時

に缺位の時は國務院より其職權を攝行し同時に國會議員三ケ月內に於て自

ら集會を行ひ總統選舉會を組織し次任大總統の選舉を行ふ

第六十一條　大總統は應に滿期の日に於て解職すべし若し期に屆き次期大總

統尚ほ未だ選出されず或は選出後尚ほ未だ職に就かず次期副總統亦た代理

する能はざる時は國務院より其の職權を攝行す

第六十二條　副總統の選舉は大總統選舉法の規定に依り大總統の選舉と共に

之を行ふ但し副總統缺位の時は應に之を補選すべし

第六十三條　大總統は法律を公布し並に其の執行を監督確保す

第六十四條　大總統は法律を執行し或は法律の委任に依り命令を發布するを

得

第六十五條　大總統は公共の治安を維持し非常の災患を防禦する爲め時機緊

急にして國會を召集する能はざる時は國會委員會の議決を經て國務員連帶

責任を以て法律と同等の效力ある敎令を發布することを得

第六十六條　大總統は文武官吏を任免す

但し憲法及び法律に特別規定ある者は其の規定に依る

第六十七條　大總統は民國陸海軍大元帥として陸海軍を統率す

陸海軍の編制は法律を以て之を定む

第六十八條　大總統は外國に對し民國の代表と爲す

第六十九條　大總統は國會の同意を經て宣戰するを得但し外國の攻擊を防禦

する時は宣戰後に於て國會の追認を請求すべし。

第七十條　大總統は條約を締結す但し媾和及び立法事項に關係の條約に國會

の同意を經るに非ざれば效力を生せず

第七十一條　大總統は法律に依り戒嚴を宣告するを得、但し國會或は國會委員會の認めて戒嚴の必要なしと爲す時は應に即ち解嚴の宣告を爲すべし

第七十二條　大總統は榮典を頒與す

第七十三條　大總統は最高法院の同意を經て免刑減刑及び復權を宣告するを得、但し彈劾事件の判決に對しては國會の同意を經るに非れば復權の宣告を爲すを得ず

第七十四條　大總統は衆議院或は參議院の會議を停止するを得、但し每會期停會二回を超ゆるを得ず每會期停會期間十日を超ゆるを得ず

第七十五條　大總統は參議院列席議員三分二以上の同意を經て衆議院を解散することを得い　但し同一會期第二回の解散を爲すを得ず

大總統衆議院を解散したる時は應に即ち選擧を行ひ五個月內に於て期を定めて開會を繼續すべし

第七十六條　大總統は叛逆罪を除く外解職後に非れば刑事上の訴追を受けず

第七章　國務院

第七十七條　大總統副總統の歲俸は法律を以て之を定む

第七十八條　國務院は國務員を以て之を組織す

第七十九條　國務總理及び各部總長は均しく國務員と爲す

第八十條　國務總理の任命は須らく衆議院の同意を經べし　國務總理が國會閉會期內に於て缺位ある時は大總統は國會委員會の同意を

中華民國議會史

國務總理熊希齡先生

經て署理の任命を爲すことを得

第八十一條　國務員は大總統を贊襄し衆議院に對し責任を負ふ大總統の發する命令及び其の他國務關係の文書は國務員の副署を經るに非れば效力を生せず

第八十二條　國務員が不信任決議を受けし時は大總統は第七十五條の規定に依り衆議院を解散するに非れば應に即ち國務員の職を免ずべし

第八十三條　國務員は兩院に於て列席及び發言するを得、但し政府提案を說明する時は委員を以て代理せしむるを得

前項委員は大總統より之を任命す

第八章　法院

第八十四條　中華民國の司法權は法院より之を行ふ

第八十五條　法院の編制及び法官の資格は法律を以て之を定む

第八十六條　法院は法律に依り民事刑事行政及び其の他一切の訴訟を受理す、但し憲法及び法律に特別の規定ある者は此限にあらず

第八十七條　法院の審判は之を公開す、但し公安を妨害し或は風化に關係する者は之を秘密にするを得

第八十八條　法官は獨立して審判し何人に論なく之に干涉するを得ず

第八十九條　法官在院中は法律に依るに非れば減俸停職或は轉職するを得ず

法官在任中刑罰の宣告或は懲戒處分を受くるに非れば免職するを得ず、但し法院編制及び法官資格改定の時は此限に在らず

法官の懲戒處分は法律を以て之を定む

第九章　法　律

第九十條　兩院議員及政府各法律を提出するを得、但し一院の否決を經る者は同一會期に於て再び提出するを得ず

第九十一條　國會議定の法律案は大總統須らく中部送達後十五日內に於て之を公布すべし

第九十二條　國會議定の法律案を大總統若し否認する時は公布期間內に於て理由を聲明して覆議を請求するを得、若し兩院各列席員三分の二以上仍は前議を執るある時に即ち之を公布すべし

未だ覆議の請求を經ざる法律案公布期限を逾れば即ち成つて法律と爲す、但し公布期限が國會閉會或は衆議院解散後に在る者は此限に在らず

第九十三條　法律は法律を以てするに非ざれば之を變更し或は廢止するを得ず

第十章　會　計

第九十四條　法律が憲法と抵觸する者は無効とす

第九十五條　新に租稅を課し及び稅率を變更することは法律を以て之を定む

第九十六條　現行租稅未だ法律の變更を經ざる者は舊に仍つて徵收す

第九十七條　國債の募集及び國庫の負擔を增加する契約締結は須らく國會の議定を經べし

第九十八條　國家の歲出歲入は每年政府より豫算案を編成し國會開會後十五日內先づ衆議院に提出すべし。

參議院が衆議院議決の豫算案に對し修正或は否決の時は須らく衆議院の同意を求むべし、若し同意を得ざれば原議決案を即ち成立せしめて豫算と爲

第九十九條　政府は特別事業に因り豫算案內に年限を豫定して繼續費を設くるを得

第百條　政府は豫め不足或は豫算未だ及はざる所に備ゆる爲め豫算案內預備費を設くるを得

預備費の支出は須く次會期に於て衆議院の追認を請求すべし

第百一條　左記各項の支出は政府の同意を經るに非れば國會は之を廢除し或は削除するを得ず

一、法律上國家の義務に屬する者

二、條約の股行に必要なる所の者

三、法律の規定に必要なる所の者

四、繼續費

第百二條　國會は豫算案に對し歲出の增加を爲し得ず

第百三條　會計年度開始豫算未だ成立せざる時は政府は每月前年度の豫算十二分の一に依り施行す

第百四條　對外戰爭或は內亂裁定の爲め國會を召集する能はざる時は政府は國會委員會の議決を經て財政の緊急處分を爲すを得、但し須らく次期國會開會後七日內に於て衆議院の追認を請求すべし

第百五條　國家歲出の支出命令は須らく先づ審計院の核准を經べし

第百六條　國家歲出歲入の決算案は每年審計院の審定を經て政府より國會に報告し衆議院が決算に對し否認せし時は國務員は應に其の責を負ふべし

第百七條　審計院は參議院選舉の審計員を以て之を組織す。審計員任期九年にして三年每に三分の一を改選す

審計員の選擧及職任は法律を以て之を定む

第百八條　審計院々長一人を設く審計員より之を互選す

審計院々長は決算報告に關し兩院に列席及び發言し得

第十一章　憲法の修正及び解決

第百九條　國會は憲法修正の發議を爲し得

前項發議は兩院各々列席員三分二以上の同意あるに非れば成立するを得ず

兩院議員は各本院議員總額四分の一以上の連署あるに非ざれば憲法修正の提議を爲すを得ず

第百十條　憲法の修正は憲法會議により之を行ふ

第百十一條　國體は修正の議題を爲すを得ず

第百十二條　憲法に疑義ある時は憲法會議より之を解釋す

第百十三條　憲法會議は國會議員より之を組織す

前項會議は總員三分の二以上の列席あるに非れば開議するを得ず列席員四分の三以上の同意あるに非れば議決するを得ず

以上

五　兩院聯合會及憲法會議

二年九月十二日參衆兩院聯合會を開き、參議院議長王家襄主席に就き、出席參議院議員二百〇四名、衆議院議員四百五十九名なり。大總統選擧法案先議の事を議し、李鍾秀、李慶芳、黃群は憲法中總統選擧の一部の起草方を兩院聯合會より憲法起草委員會に委托し、五日間内に起草完成附議せしむと

參衆兩院全院委員長丁世嶧先生

提議せしが、出席議員四分の三以上の贊成にて通過す。又た此の日聯合憲法會議事起草委員として楊廷棟、韓玉辰、王源瀚籍忠寅、王湘、胡璧城、李景龢、黃燮鑫、蒲殿俊の九名を主席より指定したり。

九月十七日より前記委員の起草せる憲法會議規則案を討議し、十七、十九、二十二、二十四、二十六日の數回に上りしも、二十六日始めて初讀會を開きて審議統選擧法案は十九日の日程に付す事となり、十月一日より憲法會議を開きて、二日、二讀會、三日流會、四日三讀會、五日之を公布したり。大總統選擧法の全文左の如し。

第一條　中華民國人にして完全なる公權を享有し、滿四十歲以上にして且國内に居住する事滿十年以上なる者は大總統に選擧せらるゝ事を得

第二條　大總統は國會議員に依りて組織せられたる選擧會に於て之を選擧す

前條の選擧は選擧人總數三分の二以上出席し無記名投票を以て之を行ひ投票人數の四分の三以上の得票ある者を以て當選とす、但一回投票するも當選人無き時は第二回の得票比較的多數のものに就て之を決選し其の得票投票人物の過半數なる者を以て當選とす

第三條　大總統の任期は五年とし、再選せられたる場合は一回に限り連任する事を得

大總統の任期滿了三箇月前に國會議員は自ら集會を行ひ總統選擧會を組

織して次期大總統の選擧を行ふべし

第四條　大總統は其就職の時に於て須く左の宣誓を行ふべし

余は至誠を以て憲法を恪守し大總統の職務を行ふべき事を謹誓す

第五條　大總統缺位となれる場合には副總統之を繼任し本任大總統の任期
滿了の日を以て止む

大總統故障ありて職務を執行する能はざる時は副總統之を代理す

副總統同時に缺位となれる場合には國務員にて其の職を攝行し同時に國
會議員は三箇月內に自ら集會を行ひ總統選擧會を組織して次期大總統の
選擧を行ふ

第六條　大總統の任期滿了して解職せられし場合に若し次期大總統未だ選
出せられざるか或は選出後未だ就職せず次期副總統亦代理する能はざる
時は國務院にて其の職務を攝す

第七條　副總統の選擧は大總統の選擧と同時に之を行ふ但副總統缺位とな
れる場合には之を補擧すべし

附則　大總統の職權は憲法制定以前に於ては暫く臨時約法の臨時大總統に
關する規定に依る

六　大總統選擧會

前記憲法會議に於て議定せる大總統選擧法に依り十月六日大總統選擧會を
開く、參衆兩議院員の列席せる者計七百〇三名にして袁世凱五百七十票を以て
中華民國大總統に當選す。翌七日の副總統の選擧を行ひ參衆兩院議員の列席
せる者計七百十九人にして黎元洪六百十一票の多數を以て中華民國副總統に
當選したり。

大總統袁世凱は乃ち詞を黨禍に藉りて十一月四日大總統令を下して國民黨
の解散を命じ、同時に國民黨に籍を有する參衆兩院員三百九十餘名の議員資
格を取消したり。是に於てか國會は憲法會議開催の法定人數を缺くに至り、
憲法の議定は遂に中止さるに至れり。斯くして袁大總統は二年十二月二十
九日政治會議なるものを組織して、中央政務最高諮詢機關とす。而して政治
會議が、三年一月に於て約法增修案及び約法附屬の重要法案を議決すべき約
法會議組織條件を議了するに及び、一月十日、大總統令を以て國會乃ち參衆
兩議院に對し無期停會を命じたり。是に於て、か、飽に氣息奄々たりし民國議
會は一時全く滅亡の否運に遭遇したり。

七　國會の停止

第五章　國會停止中

三年一月二十六日、袁大總統は約法會議組織條例を公布し、三月十八日、其
の開院式を舉行す。而して民國元年南京臨時參議院に於て議定し、爾來公布施
行し來れる臨時約法に修正を加へ、五月一日之を公布したり、所謂新約法是れ
なり。其の重大なる修改條項は略ぼ左の如し。

一、舊約法の『中華民國は參議院、臨時大總統、國務員、法院を以て其の
統治權を行使す』とあるを。『大總統は國の元首にして統治權を總攬す』
と改む。

二、舊『中華民國の立法權は參議院を以て之を行ふ』とあるを。新『立法
は人民選擧の議員を以て立法院を組織し之を行ふ』と改む。

三、舊『參議院は自ら召集、開會、閉會を行ふことを得』とあるを。新『大

總統は立法院を召集し、開會、停會、閉會を宣言す」と改む。

四、舊『臨時大總統は全國海陸軍を統師す』とあるを。新『大總統は陸海軍大元師と爲し、全國陸海軍を統率し、大總統は陸海軍の編制及び兵額を定む』と改む。

五、舊『臨時大總統は官制と官僚を制定し、又は文武職員を任免することを得、但し參議院の議決又は同意を要す』とあるを。新『大總統は官制官規を制定し、又は文武職員を任免することを得』と改め、又た『條約を締結し、但し領土變更或は人民負擔額増加の條款は立法府の同意を經へし』と改む。

六、舊『臨時大總統は參議院の同意を經て宣戰講和及び條約を締結するを得』とあるを。新『大總統は開戰講和を宣告す』と改め、又新『大總統は陸海軍の編制及び兵額を定む』と改む。

七、舊『國務總理及び各部總長は均しく國務員と稱し、國務員は臨時大總統を補佐して其の責を負ふ』とあるを。新『行政は大總統を以て首長と爲し、國務卿一人や。行政事務は外交、內務、財政、陸軍、海軍、司法

教育、農商、交通の各部を置きて之を分掌す』と改む。

八、舊『國務員が參議院の彈劾を受けたる後、臨時大總統應に其の職を解くへし』とあるを。新『國務卿各部總長が違法行爲ありし時は肅政廳の糺彈及び平政院の審理を受く』と改む。

九、舊約法に無き一條項、即ち『大總統は國民の全體に帶して責任を負ふ』

との條項を新約法に増加したり。

新約法公布後、約法會議は參政院の組織法を議決し、六月二十日其の開院式を舉行す。斯くて參政院は大總統の諮詢機關として新約法に定めたる立法の事を代行する事となれり。八月十八日參政院通常會議に於て參政梁士詒は大總統選舉法修正建議案を提出して二年十月四日式國會議に決定公布したる大總統選舉法に根本的修改を試みたり。即ち大總統の任期五年を十年とし。一同連任を單に留任する事を得と改め。參衆兩議院員組織の選舉會に於て選舉する事を、參政院參政及び立法院議員各五十名を以て組織せる選舉會に於てすと改め又た大總統は次期大總統候補者三名を嘉禾金匱に親書し國璽を鈐して金匱に密藏し、選舉會は此三名と現任大總統以外を投票するを得ずどの條項を追加し。十二月二十四日參政院の議決によりて公布したり。

四年八月憲法顧問米人グードナウ博士が北京の亞細亞日報紙上に於て立憲君主論を發表するや。旋て參政院參政楊度は孫毓筠、嚴復、劉師培、李燮和等と商きて八月十五日籌安會を組織して帝政を主張し國體變更の運動を開始するに至れり。之より先、七月一日袁大總統は參政院に命じて民國憲法起草委員の推擧を求め、三日參政院は同起草委員十名を選舉したり。而して九月一日を以て參政院に代行立法會議を開く事となり、又た國民會議々員選舉期日及び準備期限令を公布したり。然るに一面に於ては一部各都督鎮守使が前後相繼ぎて大總統宛國體變更の諸願電報を發し來り、又た一面に於ては所謂民意の迎合電報陸

政治會議所全員之寫眞

續として代行立法院に到來して國體の變更を請ふあり。參政院は九月中旬第

二次第二次に分けて國體變更請願書三十三通を政府に送致す。而して九月二

十四日全國請願聯合會なるものの開催され『國民會議を俟たずして別に機關を

設けて國體變更に對する民意を徵求すべし』この第三次請願書は代行立法院

に致さる。依て九月十八日代行立法院は前記第三請願書を討議し、國民代表

大會組織法を起草する事とし、十月六日之を議定し、八日公布したり。

斯くて國民代表大會は十二月十日全國各縣各一人、蒙古三十三人、西藏十

二人、八旗二十四人、回敎徒四人、中央選擧會百十人、會計一千九百九十二

名の選擧を終り、各々該省各省に於て國體變更に關する投票を爲さしめ、十

一日代行立法院は之が開票の結果を、國民代表全體一致して君主立憲に贊成

し並に袁世凱を推戴して皇帝と爲すとありと報告し、勘進表を奉る。十二日

袁世凱は申令を發して皇帝推戴を受け、十四日參政院に帝國憲法起草員の選

定を命じ、十六日民國五年內に立法院召集の令を發したり。

之より先、袁を中心とせる國體變更問題進行するや、爲に國內の禍亂を激

成せん事を慮り、日本を始め英露佛伊各國相繼で其の延期を勸告する所あり

たり。果然、雲南將軍唐繼堯、巡按使任可澄は蔡鍔等と會商せる結果、十二

月二十四日袁世凱宛帝政取消しと帝政首唱者の嚴罰を要求せる最後通牒を發

し、二十六日唐繼堯、蔡鍔の名を以て正式に雲南の獨立を宣言したり。五年

一月二十七日貴州また獨立し、天下之に響應して鼎沸の狀あり。袁は乃ち二

月二十三日登極延期の申令を發布し、二十八日國民會議々員復選當選者を以

て立法院の復選常選議員とし、五月一日を以て是等立法議員を召集すべしと

の申令を發したり。然かも三月七日廣西亦た獨立し、廣東四川の形勢亦た日

に廹みて、各地の帝制反對の氣勢益々熾烈なるを以て、三月二十一日袁は帝

制の取消を宣布したり。

四月七日廣東亦た獨立し、十九日雲貴兩廣の獨立四省の獨立を各省將軍巡按使に

宛、袁世凱の帝政樹立皇帝登極の計畫を以て約法上の謀判罪を以て論じ、四

年十二月十三日以降、大總統の資格は當然消滅すとの宣言書を電致し。各地

亦た響應して袁の退位を求めて止まず。此時局混亂紛糾の最中に於て袁世凱

は腎臟炎に罹りて五月末一度び危篤を他にられ、六月四日病勢頓に激變し、

六日前三時袁は徐世昌、段祺瑞、王士珍を枕邊に招き『予や國民附託の重任

を受けて大權を總攬し、本より帝制の思想なく、一時の昏瞶迷惑、途に今日

の惡劇を演成するに至る。復た何をか言はんや。是れは唯

だ予が畢生の懺悔のみ。而して此國家多難の時に當り、民國の政務は約法に

照らし、黎副總統に代行せしめ、卿等同心之を輔佐し、斷じて國家をして滅

亡せしむる勿れ』と遺言し。前十時四十分溘然薨去す。其の計一度傳りて、

西南各省に蹶起せる護國軍は均しく戈を收め兵を息む。翌七日副總統黎元洪

は大總統を繼任し、即日(一)責任內閣を尊重し、速に憲

法を制定す(三)金融界を救濟する爲め資金を求め兌換を開くべしとの三政見

を發表したり。而して舊約法の復活、舊國會召集に付ては、所謂南北兩派間

の主張に多少の異論ありしも、途に六月二十八日袁の靈柩を河南に送るや、

其の翌日左の如き黎大總統の申令を以て解決したり。曰く

共和國體は首として、民意を重んず。民意の貴なる所は、厥れ惟だ憲法

にあり。憲法の成る、專ら國會に待つ。我中華民國々會は三年一月十日

より停止し、以後時を越ゆる兩載に及ぶも未だ召復せず。以て開國五年

に至るも憲法未だ定まらざる也。大本立たずしては庶政進行するに由な

し。亟に國會を召集し、速に憲法を定め、以て民志に協へ、而して國本を

固くすべし。憲法未だ定らざる以前は、仍ほ中華民國元年三月十一日公布の臨時約法を遵行し、憲法成立に至つて止む。其の二年十月五日宣布の大總統選擧法は憲法の一部に係るに依り、仍ほ有效とす。

茲に臨時約法第五十三條に依り、續いて國會の召集を行ひ、定めて本年八月一日より繼續開會す。

第六章　第二次國會

一　開　院　式

民國三年五月一日以後の各條約は均しく繼續して有效とすべし。其の餘の法令は、明令を以て廢止するものゝ外は一切舊に依る。

同時に立法院國民會議に關する各法は裁撤されたり。

撤消され參政院及び平政院所屬の憲政廳は裁撤されたり。

又た襄に袁世凱によりて取消されたる國民黨員の參衆兩議員資格悉く復活したるは無論なり。之より先、上海に集合したる參衆兩院議員三百餘名は、舊約法の國會自から召集開院を行ふを得ざるに依り七月十日を期して上海に於て國會を開かんとしつゝありしも、旣に其の要なく、る事となれり。

在上海兩院議員は陸續北上入京す

民國五年八月一日前十時、第二次國會の開院式を擧行す。此日召集に應じて出席せる參議院議員百三十九名、衆議院議員多三百十八名、參議院議長王家襄議長席に就く。大總統黎元洪臨場し、國務總理段祺瑞及び程璧光、陳錦濤、許世英、范源濂、張國淦の各總長、國務院祕書長徐樹錚列席したり。王議長開院を宣す、其の詞に曰く

大總統黎元洪先生

於鑠國會、晦に遭ひ時に休す、誰か屬階を爲す。茲に三秋、紫色の蛙聲。皇佑神宇廓除經營之譬ふる種々、咋死して今生す。一人の禍、胤を閉ぢ明を鋼す。多士の貴、善謀乃ち成る。國に憲章あり、我則ち之を卒ひん。國に輿論あり、我則ち之を擇ばん。程贓制用、我を節目せん。內治外交、我之を約束せん。各々言責を盡し、或は偏頗あるなけん。茲に綿々たる國會斯の年億萬なり。

天地否否、危基將に頹れんとして狂流時に砥す。

黎大總統乃ち頌詞を致す。曰く

天我華を佑け、政局肇めて新なり、經綸萬端宜しく我意を叩くべし。議會の諸君子は國民の選擧する所、其の民生國計を籌るに熱せり。方今時

局艱危、正に賢豪の補救に頼る、望らくば諸君子心を一にし、德を一に
し、黨なく偏なく、法治を以て指歸と爲し、憲政の基礎を立てん事を。
國運の隆昌と政象の清明とは皆な指歸と爲し、惟だ至誠を竭して諸君子の是れ頼るなり。元洪不敏にし
て恭しく重寄を膺く、惟だ至誠を竭して諸君子の後に從ひ、冀くば家邦
を造ることあらひ。躬ら盛會に蒞みて歡欣に堪へず、謹で一言を貢して
民國議會の祝を爲す也。
次で國旗に對する鞠躬の禮あり。新大總統は再び立ちて宜誓の辭を致す、
曰く『予は至誠を以て憲法を遵守し、大總統の職務を執行すべし、謹んで誓
ふ』と。斯くて奏樂聲裡開院式を終へたり。

二　參　議　院

議長　王家襄
副議長　王正廷

八月十六日㕣院委員長、二十一日常任委員の選擧を行ひ、其の結果左の如
し。(得票順)

全院委員長　趙世鈺
法制委員　張我華、楊永泰、盛時、蔣擧淸、宋淵源、劉瀉、許榮、李
英銓、王鑫潤、楊崇山、張聯魁、陳祖烈、盧天游、劉映奎、潘江、何
海濤、賈济川、彭建標、李槃、蘇毓芳、蔡國忱、程瑩度、謝書林、王
用賓、吳遹炬　以上二十五名

財政委員　丁象謙、金兆棪、童杭時、高仲和、陳善、孫乃祥、王觀銘、
李誠膺、焦易堂、王鳳翥、揭曰訓、蔣義朋、鄒樹聲、萬鴻圖、鄭林泉、
楊繩組、雷煥猷、楊擇、周擇、張瑞璣、王靖方、高家驥、賓應昌、范

振緒、祺誠武　以上二十五名
內務委員　王人文、陳煥南、彭介石、富元、蕭文彬、鄭江灝、
徐承錦、苗雨潤、班廷獻、王鴻龐　以上十一名
外交委員　朱念祖、盧信、李自芳、湯漪、秦錫圭、劉積學、趙運琪、
劉成禺、廉炳華、藍公武、朱兆莘　以上十一名
軍事委員　張漢、韓玉辰、居正、曾彥、陶遜、金鼎勳、劉丕元、劉星
楠、李溶、馬良駟、大陸坊　以上十一名
交通委員　李茂之、楊鴈洲、黎尚雯、婁鴻聲、梁士模、潘祖彝、段硯
田、蕭輝錦、周學源、溫雄飛、黃錫銓　以上十一名
教育委員　李文治、金永昌、吳景鴻、符鼎升、姚乘、陳銘鑑、蔡突靈、
王變聲、齊忠甲、郝瀯、岳雲鵵　以上十一名
實業委員　張翀泉、王湘、馬伯瑤、馬君武、戢恭、江浩、張光煒、李
漢丞、馬蔭棠、佈霖、楊渡　以上十一名
預算委員　向乃祺、張烈、李紹白、吳湘、劉先旭、何十果、張杜蘭、
吳文瀚、黃紹侃、張北墻、盧式楷、張金鑑、安朋東、李燿忠、榮厚
龔煥辰、孔憲端、黃樹棻、周擇南、王洪身、肅承涓、黃佩蘭、金德鏧、
姚翰鄉、周廷勛、田永正、蔣曾煥、陳敬棠、黃宏憲、辛漢、解樹强、
閻光耀、襲善達、陳光燾、趙學臣、朱甲昌、色旺端魯布、札希土噸、
蔣報和、胡璧城、范樵、劉新桂、唐仰攖、丁世嶧、王立廷　以上四
十五人

決算委員　彭邦棟、黃元操、宋梓、梁培、謝持、文登灜、董昆灜、何
多才、高蔭藻、謝樹瑰、傅階、魏鴻翼、張嚕、籍忠寅、周震鱗、布爾
格特、鄂博噶台、虔仲阿旺益喜、嘳拉增、陸宗輿、哈特爾、札噶謝雅、

十五人

曹汝霖、劉彭壽、萬實成、張爵森、馬雅麟、以上二十七名

請願委員　李兆鴻、李兆年、王試功、王文序、毛印相、宋國忠、鄭際

平、吳作棻、楊登瀛、郭相維、郭椿森、

趙成恩、梁登瀛、趙時欽、劉正墅、

龔玉嵐、袁嘉毅、謝鵬翰、祺克坦、方墅

徽、劉懋賞、阿穆爾靈圭、車林桑都布、

德色賴托布、以上二十五名

懲罰委員　林森、汪律本、王法勤、呂志

伊、石德鎔、李國定、王泩清、鄂多台、熙

凌阿、鄭斗南、趙鯨　以上十一名

三　衆議院

八月十六日全院委員長、二十一日各委員會委員長の互

員の選舉を行ひ、二十四日各委員會委員長の互

選を行ひ、其の結果汪の如し。(得票順)

議　長　湯化龍

副議長　陳國祥

全院委員長　彭允彝

法典委員長　蕭春榮

理事　秦廣禮、徐闌墅、呂復、駱繼漢、

揚銘源、葉夏聲

委員　羅永紹、石潤金、陶保晉、時功玖、易次乾、王侃、曾幹楨、

王槙、常恒芳、王廷弼、丁象、呂泮林、胡兆沂、張瑞賁、朱文劭、李

第二次國會開院式

之翰、黃汝瀛、王烈、禹瀛、朱騰芬、

芳、何雯、潘學海、張樹桐、孫鏡清、周慶恩、郭光麟、張知競、周

豫算委員長　褚輔成

理事　張伯烈、李肇甫、王樞、周珏、

王葆真、馬驤、王傑、

委員　文祥、張大義、鍾才宏、李積芳、

陳承箕、謝翔元、張翠、俞鳳韶、張宏銓、

樹、陳九韶、王有蘭、金詒厚、張宏銓、

乘文、陳蓉光、彭學沛、茅祖權、趙金

堂、莫德惠、汪秉忠、許楨材、林伯和、

克希克圖、姜毓英、邱冠棻、白逾桓、

魏毅、劉振生、吳汝澄、耿春宴、于均

生、錢崇墫、于洪起、康愼徽、文篤周、

賴慶暉、梁文淵、淩毅、唐玠、郭自修、

劉萬里、鄭懋修、熊成章、唐理淮、周

嘉坦、張傳保、蔣鳳梧、周克昌、葛莊、

王永錫、曾有翼、張瑾雯、王汝圻、張樹

森、易宗夔、慶經、高枬、姚文耡、董

繼昌、張敬之、閻鴻舉、陳發檀、羅繝

決算委員長　鄭懷辰

理事　歐陽振聲、溫世霖、劉澤龍、杜

委員　黃象熙、詹詢元、陳家鼎、覃壽公、曾有瀾、丁儁宣、黃肇河、

士珍、林長民、王敬芳、陳義

王多輔、陳有青、張國俊、張雅南、李錡、田桐、金秉理、馬文煥、

蔣宗周、王錫泉、韓蕃、石璜、金溶熙、吳源、杜潛、李克明、陳耀

先、方鎮東、段大信、李保邦、孫世杰、王安富、鄭化國、楊詩浙、熊兆

潤、管象賾、余棨、黃賓銘、于元芳、王默軒、蒲殿俊、張萬齡、朱

家訓、袁景熙、周大烈、龔政、呂金鏞、王篤成、歐陽成、秦肅三、恒

鈞、賀廷桂、張鶴弟、孫熾昌、翁恩裕、陳經鎔、嚴天駿、陳

治安、唐寶鍔、梅光遠、胡汝麟、梁仲則、徐兆瑋、查季華、陳繩虬、楊夢弼

內務委員長　羅　家　衡

理事　王謝家、曹振懋、王蔭棠、周澤苞、張浩、朱溥恩

委員　張書元、陳時銓、范殿棟、郟克莊、程鐸、楊榮春、楊

時傑、侯元熿、湯松年、曹瀛、狄樓海、李舍芳、盧鍾嶽、孫正宇、

外交委員長　汪　彭　年

理事　史澤咸、孫潤宇、邵瑞彭

委員　劉彥、李變陽、郭同、張益芳、陳恩格、劉冠三、徐傅霖、畢

恩和布林、楊肇基、耿兆棟、劉栽甫、鄭人康

維垣、賀昇平、石瑛、張治祥、張善與、李夢彪、梁系登、胡源匯、

江椿、馬小進

財政委員長　陳　鴻　鈞

理事　王源瀚、年琳、鄒魯、劉奇瑤

委員　張大昕、魏肇文、李蒜年、陳變樞、由宗龍、歐陽鈞、孟昭漢、

張嗣良、童啟曾、張則川、王雙岐、彭允彝、黃序鏞、郭廣恩、郭涵、

王之簽、全承新、李載庠、周維濚、江瑔、江維、高增融、

郭寶慈、李為綸、廖希賢、凌文淵、劉志詹、劉鴻慶、黃雲鵬、

軍政委員長　吳　宗　慈

理事　方曙、楊式震

委員　李根源、劉景烈、楊大實、居覺、胡祖舜、楊振洲、杜凱之、

楊樹璜、趙舒、焦子靜、黃增耆、王國祐、凌鉞、吳日法、裴廷藩、

熙鈺、郭人漳、劉棨棠

教育委員長　張　華　瀾

理事　黃攻素、陳瓢宸、李揩綮、李執中

委員　鄧元、于思波、岳秀夫、李秉恕、張官雲、高登鯉、高旭、葉

成玉、丁濟生、裴清源、彭運斌、周澤、黃耕雲、李元亮、王兆離、

饒芙裳

實業委員長　李　有　忱

理事　蔡匯東、周學燻、胡鄂公

委員　陳祖基、黃荃、徐清和、周廷弼、蔡汝霖、邵仲康、夏寅官、

王鴻賓、李國珍、閻與可、程崇信、石鳳岐、劉祖堯、歐陽沂、瞿啟甲

白常潔、任曜埰

交通委員長　陳　策

理事　賀贊元、徐象先、劉盥訓、段雄、王紹鳌

委員　杜凱元、陳允中、仇玉珽、王文璨、盛際光、賈鳴梧、丁超五、

邱國翰、陳鴻疇、段維新、黃汝鑑

金鑫、恩華、劉治洲、陳子斌、李景濂、陳嘉會、董增儒、葉顯楊、

精願委員長　王　乃　昌

理事　趙炳麟、楊士鵬、鄒繼龍、陳士髦、張相文

委員　覃振、沈河清、辛際唐、劉英、田稔、汪建剛、吳壽田、張士

才、闞文鐸、王吉言、傅夢豪、廖宗北、王廣瀚、林鴻超、蕭鳳藏、周
祖瀾、竷邅、穆郁、杜師業、張坤、劉緯、董毓梅、韓臚雲、齋耀璠、
張國溶、李景泉、張昇雲、王恩博、崔懷瀨、陳垣、黃霄九

懲戒委員長　曹玉德

理事　杭辛齊、劉峰一、楊廷棟、黃慜鑫

委員　李壎、盧元弼、李春榮、連賢基、樂山、魏丹書、茹欲立、祁
連元、焉泮春、姚守先、田美峰、曾銘、陳邦彝、康佩珩、王玉琦、
朱繼之

院內審計委員長　虞廷愷

理事　彭占元、彭施滌

委員　羅永慶、石銘、王恒、陳純修、朱觀亥、寸品昇、彭漢遺、鮑
喜、王定國、壯華、趙良辰、王弐、尚鎮圭、譚煥文、張則林、邵長
銘、劉畢沂、楊士聰

四　國務員

八月二十一日眾議院に於て大總統提出の國務總理段祺瑞追認案を議す。副
議長陳國祥議長席に就き、政府委員禮樹は同案提出の理由を說明して曰く、
段君を國務總理に特任する命令を發表したる當時は國會未だ開かれず、今
ま兩院正式に開會したるを以て約法第三十四條に依り眾議院に咨り同意を
經るものなり。民國二年段君臨時總理たりし時、豐富なる經驗を以て政治
を運用し、賴つて以て國家の治安を維持せり。帝制發生の後、段君は第一
に辭職して帶位勳等を受けず。雲南事成るや民國の再設に關し、實に功勞
あり。故に國務總理に特任し。今日眾議院に附議して其の同意を求むる所

圖國務總理段祺瑞先生

以てなり。云々。

對する百八十七の大多數を以て段祺瑞の國務總理任命を追認したり。
出席議員四百四十四人にして、投票の結果、四百〇七票の大多數の同意を以
て可決せられたり。嗣で二十三日參議院に於て本問題を附議し、是亦た六に

段國務總理略傳　　段祺瑞字は芝泉、安徽省合肥縣人にして本年五十二
歲なり。少にして偉儻大志あり、天下を以て己が任とす。時に李鴻章權要
の位置を占め、淮泗の士人贪緣以て身を立つ。段は支那の現勢に鑑みて強

兵の要を思ひ前
清光緒十一年北
洋武備學堂に入
學して兵學を修
め、十五年北洋
大臣李鴻章より
選拔派遣されて
獨逸に赴き、ク
ルップ兵器廠に
在りて造砲用砲の理法を研究し、後ち各地の要塞を參觀して見學し十六年
歸國す。時適ま袁世凱新站に於て、新建陸軍を創練するあり、二十一年十
月砲兵第一營を統帥す。二十二年本營兵學堂監督を兼充す。二十四年袁世
凱の奏獎により同知を以て選用され、並に知府銜を加へる。二十五年、
新建陸軍が武衛右軍と改めらる〜に及び、功を以て知府補用に進み、全軍
各學堂總辦に任せらる。二十七年東山省土匪勦辦の功を以て三品銜を以て
られ、後ち袁が直隸總督兼北洋大臣となるや、北洋陸軍參謀長に任じ、道

四二

海軍總長程璧光先生

員を獎せられ二品衘を加へらる。二十八年十一月清政府に於て練兵處を設くるや、軍參司正使に任じ、副都統衘を賞せらる。三十年三月、常備軍第三鎭翼長と爲る。三十一年正月、第四鎭統制官に任じ、八月改めて第六鎭統制官と爲る。旋て南北兩軍の大演習を擧行するや、北軍總統官に任ず、

年二月陸軍部より派せられて陸軍各學堂を督理す。二月袁の奏請により副都統記名を以て、九月鑲黃旗漢軍副統に補せらる。三十四年五月陸軍第六鎭統制官に充り、九月陸軍遊學卒業生試驗委員長に任ず。宣統元年十一月第二鎭統制官に任ず。二年十一月江北提督に署せらる。三年八月武昌義を起すや、第二軍々統に任じ、後ち馮國璋に代りて第一軍々統に任ず。時漢陽已に陷り南北和議の事あり。段乃ち意を決して全國の將師を聯合し、連名を以て清廷の退讓を逼る。旣に共和を宣布して民國成立するや、陸軍部正首領に任じ、五月陸軍總長に任せらる。又た國務總理を代理し、陸軍上將を以て清延の退讓を逼る。勳一位に叙し、二等嘉禾章を予へ、後ち改めて一等嘉禾章を給せらる。二年十月黎元洪北上するや、湖北都督に任じ、三年二月復た

三鎭統制官に署せられ、北洋武備各學堂監督を兼ぬ。二月福建汀州鎭總兵に補せられ、旋て行營軍官學堂督辦に充る。三十三年正月第一日に及べり。

九月一日午後一時乘議院開會。議長湯化龍より、大總統の國務總理段祺瑞の陸軍總長兼任同意請求の咨文を報告し、秘書長の朗讀畢るや又た其の他の文件を報告し、新舊議員七人は抽籤にて席次を定め、某山東選出議員は縣知事に任じ辭職したるにより法に依りて表決し、更に議員の七日以上休眼請求者を允許し、直ちに同日の議事日程第一案（唐紹儀を特任して外交總長と爲し、陳錦濤を財政總長と爲し、程壁光を海軍總長と爲し、范源濂を敎育總長と爲し、許世英を交通總長と爲し、孫洪伊を內務總長と爲し、張耀曾を司法總長と爲し、谷鍾秀を農商總長と爲す同意咨請案を開議することを宣告す、又昨日國務總理に補任せる段總理に陸軍總長を兼任せしむる可否の咨文に接到す、王謝家は孫洪伊辭職の事は審查中にして未だ同時に投票されたしと報告し、決定せざれば、先づ之を決定して然る後投票すべしと云ふ。議長は議事日程を變更し陸軍總長を加入して同時に投票する事を表決に付し、贊成者大多數にて通過せり。張伯烈は孫、張、谷三君の態度何は不明なり、究竟其の國務院に在る職は抑も本院に在るの事實をして民國復活の時に出現せしむるは實に三君に愛あるに非ず、本員は張、孫、谷三君の同意票は暫く緩投せんことの勳議を提起すと云ひ、議長は其の說を以て表決に付せるに贊成少數にて否決

河南都督に任じ、四月陸軍總長の本任に歸り、六月建威上將を授けられ將軍府事務を兼管す。四年夏、病に因りて其の職を固辭し、西山に隱退して病を養ふこと一年。五年四月袁世凱の懇請により出で、國務卿に任じ、六月黎元洪大總統を繼任して後ち、國務總理に任じ、陸軍總長を兼任して今

四四

され、遂に同時に投票を行ふに決定し、復た國務總理段祺瑞より各閣員任命の理由及び各閣員の履歴を説明す。

牢琳、郭涵、梅光遠氏等八人を擬定して監察員と爲し、無記名連記法を以て投票することとなし、先づ監察員より投票し、次で各議員より順次に投票し舉

る。議長は只今在場者四百五十六人にして投票せるものは四百五十五票なり、なれば百票を以て過半數と爲すと云ひ、無効たる九票を除きて唐紹儀は同意

察員は票數及び名刺を檢定す、議長は合計四百五十五票、名刺四百五十五枚にして數目相符せりと云ふ。時已に散會の時刻に達したるも、議長は今日若

し結果を報告せざれば二三日間遅るべし、故に何時に到るを論ぜんや今日は必す報告するを要す、諸君は自由に退席する勿れと云ひ、監察員乃ち之を開票

す。議長は無効票一枚にして、次で投票の結果を報告し、唐紹儀は同意票三百七十六を得、陳錦濤は三百九十一を得、程璧光は二百七十六を得、張耀曾は三百五十七を得、孫洪伊は三百四十五を得、范源濂は四百三十九を得、許世英は二百八十四を得、谷鍾秀は二百七十七を得、段祺瑞は四百三十二を得、均しく過半數にて通過せりと云ふ。一同拍手す。

九月四日午後參議院開會。議長王家襄主席として大總統提出、衆議院移交の國務員同意案を議す。首め段總理より各國務員の履歴を説明し、「政府一日も正式に成立する能はざれば、即ち各國務員は観望主義を持し、心を盡し事に任することに能はず、此次全體國務員の政治經驗を閲して退す。深く貴院の同意を望む」と。又議長より閉門の同意を宣告して人數を檢査し、且つ無記名連記點唱投票を布し、並に金鼎勛、金兆枬等八人を指

定して監票員と爲し、先づ此等監票員より投票したる後各議員より順次に投票秘書より順次に點唱して票數を檢查せるに凡そ百九十八にして在場人數百九十八と相符合したるより、議長は投票の結果を報告し、在場人數百九十八なれば百票を以て過半數と爲すと云ひ、無効たる九票を除きて、全體通過せりと宣し、一同拍手す。

陳財政總長略傳　陳錦濤字は瀾生、廣東省南海縣人にして本年四十六歳なり。幼にし

て聰穎學を好み、…二書院を卒業して曾て同書院の教師となり、又た北洋大學教員と爲る。旋りて米國に留學し、エール大學に入り卒業歸國して廣東學務處參議と爲る。後ち再び米國に留學して法博士の學位を受け、歸國して留學生試驗に應じて第一等の成績を以て、命を奉じて米國に赴き印刷の事を視學し、歸國後、印刷局長に任じ、大清銀行副監督となれり。辛亥の歳、第一軍革命の軍起りて、袁世凱が濟内閣の總理大臣となるや、財政部大臣に任せんとしたるも就かずし

財政總長陳錦濤先生

て南下す。旋て臨時大總統孫文より任せられて臨時政府財政部總長に任じ、九月引續きて、新內閣の財政總長として國會の同意を經て、在任以て今日に及びたり。

南北統一後、野に下り、民國三年審計院長に任せられて、米國駐在財政委員と爲る。民國五年六月周自齋の後を襲ふて財政部總長に任じたり。

張司法總長略傳　張耀曾字は鎔西、雲南省大理府の人にして本年三十二歲の少壯政治家なり。人と爲り精明强幹なり。曾て北京大學校に入りて學び、未だ卒業するに及ばずして日本に留學し、第一高等學校を經て帝國大學法科に入りて修業す。時適ま第一革命の事起る。雲南より選ばれて南京臨時參議院議員と爲り、並に中國同盟會院內總幹事に任じ、同盟會本部評議員長を兼ねたり。參議院が北京に移るや、依然引續きて北京臨時參議院議員と爲る、仍は同盟會院內總幹事に任ず。同盟會が統一共和黨と合併して國民黨を組織するや、其の政務研究會々長に推さる。

民國二年正式國會成立するや、衆議院議員に常選し、全院委員長に舉げられ、仍は國民黨院內總幹事に任じたり。又た憲法起草委員會委員に舉げられ、仍は國民黨院內總幹事に任じたり。國會解散後、再び日本に留學して、帝國大學を卒業し、歸國して北京大學法科教授に任ず。帝政問題起りてより、南下して、第三革命の舉義に干預し軍務院の要職を占めて功勞あり。五年六月袁氏死して黎元洪大總統を繼任し舊約法を恢復して責任內閣組織の事あるに及び、出でゝ司法總長に任じ遂に今日に及びたり。

孫內務總長略傳　孫洪伊字は伯蘭、直隷省天津縣人にして本年四十五歲なり。幼より書を好み、長じて博く群籍を讀み、尤も心を民治主義に留む。前清光緒甲午以後、國勢の凌夷を目睹して國民教育の必要を悟り、教育の振興を以て己が任とし乃ち私產を捐して鄉里に學校を創立したり。

順直諮議局成立するや、諮議局議員に常選す。各省諮議局聯合會請願團の有力者として奔走盡力し、又た同志と憲友會を組織したり。第一革命に際しては、南北の統一に盡瘁し、更に共和建設討論會を組織し、旋て民主黨に改めたり。民國元年正式國會成立に際し、衆議院議員に常選す。民主黨が他黨と合併して進步黨を組織するや其の政務部々長に任じたり。嵩安會發起されて帝制問題起るや、上海に走りて同志と興に之に反對し、雲南貴州相機で義を舉ぐるや遙に相響應し、袁世凱死して黎元洪大總統を繼任するに

及び、新內閣の敎育總長に擬せられ、後ち改めて內務總長に任せらるゝ。十一月事を以て其の職を免せられたり。

程海軍總長略傳　程璧光字は玉堂、廣東省香山縣人にして本年六十歲なり。曾て英國に留學して海軍學校を卒業し、鎮遠の副艦長たりし事あり。日淸戰役後一年、孫逸仙等と廣東に於て革命の事を起して敗れ、孫逸仙の弟之に死し、程は南洋に走りて商業を營みたり。後に李鴻章の保薦によりて歸國し、巡洋艦海容の艦長に任じたり。海軍部の設けらるゝに及び司令長に任じ、江南船澳總辦、艦隊統領等の職に歴充したり。英國皇帝戴冠式に際し、旗艦海

折を卒ゐて英國に赴きて賀を致し、民國五年六月、新內閣組織の事あるや、海軍部總長に任じ、九月國會の同意を經て、遂に今日に及びたり

許交通總長略傳　許世英字は靜仁、安徽省秋浦縣人にして本年四十三歳なり。資性穎敏にして頭腦明晰、並に幹濟の才に富む。曾て萬國監獄改良會中國代表として、歐米十餘ヶ國を歷遊して各國の司法制度を視察攻究し蓋し中華民國司法界に於て傑出せる新人材なり。民國元年大理院長に任じ、旋て榮轉して司法總長と爲る。

其の後も、奉天民政長、福建巡按使等の地力要職に歷充し、五年六月黎元洪大總統を繼任して、新內閣組織の事あるや、始め內務總長に任じ、後ち交通總長に轉じ、九月國會の同意を經て、遂に今日に及べり。

谷農商總長略傳　谷鍾秀字は九峰、直隸省定縣の人にして本年四十三歳なり。乘性聰頴にして人と爲り精明、然り幹濟の才に富む。少時桐城吳汝綸先生に從つて古文及び經史の學を修め、文名時に喧傳さる。朝獻に應じて知縣に補用さる、時適な保定高等師範學校開校するあり、遂に同校の歷史及び倫理科敎員に任ず。後ち一年官費を以て日本に留學し、早稻田大學に入り

交通總長許世英先生

て修業すること四ヶ年、浙江巡撫增韞より聘せられて其の幕に入り新政を裏理したり。第一革命常時、直隸諮議局より、推されて南下し、臨時政府組織の事に干豫し、南京臨時參議院議員となり、全院委員長に擧げられたり。民國二年正式國會成立するや、衆議院議員に當選す。國會停止後、上海に走りて、正誼雜誌を創立發刊して民論を鼓吹し、籌安會發起されて帝政の勸進を爲すや、共和維持會を創設して之に反對す。又た中華新報を創刊して極力帝制に反對し、岑春煊、梁啓超、李根源、鈕永建等と討袁の策を圖る。袁死して黎出づるや、南方代表として北京に抵りて善後事宜及び約法の恢復を商議し、新內閣成立するに及び、其の農商總長に任せられ、九月國會の同意を經て遂に現在に及べり。

以　上

（丙辰初冬民國之精華監修隈南內藤順太郎著）

中華民國議員列傳

王家襄　字幼山　歳四十五

選擧地　浙江省
籍貫　浙江省紹興縣　　參議院議長
住址　北京西城草帽胡同

君天資聰慧。秉性篤厚。攻究名法。前清光緒壬寅迄甲辰。留學日本。畢業於東京警視廳特設警察專科。歸國後。充本省巡警參議。紹興府巡警總理嗣辦理浙江高等巡警學堂。兼任教習。並擔任浙江官私立各法學校教授。宣統元年被選浙江諮議局議員。旋由吉林省調吉。總司警政。光復後。被選爲臨時參議院議員。正式國會成立。被選爲參議院議員。迭次被擧爲憲法起草委員會理事。參議院議長。憲法會議議長。大總統選擧會主席。國會解散後。被任參政院參政。頗抱消極主義。在院中不願所建白。迨帝制議起。各省紛紛請願到院。孫楊梁諸參政力主受理。君竭力反對。遂藉詞。請暇南旋。疊次函電辭職。至黎總統繼任。專電相招。始抵京。竭力陳情。恢復約法。重開國會。及國會復活。仍就爲參議院議長。

君天資聰慧にして、秉性篤厚、人と爲り精明強幹なり。弱冠儒を乘て法律を學ぶ。前清光緒壬寅甲辰間日本に留學し、東京警視廳附屬警察專科を卒業して歸國す。浙江省巡警參議、紹興府巡警總理に任じ、嗣で浙江高等巡警學堂を創設して教習に任じ、同時に浙江官私立各法學校教授に任じたり。宣統元年浙江諮議局議員に選ばれ、二年正式國會參議院議員に選ばる。第一革命後、臨時參議院議員に選ばれ、吉林省より聘せられて同省の警政を總監したり。旋て員に當選し、擧げられて憲法起草委員會理事、參議院議員、憲法會議議長、大總統選擧會主席ど爲る。國會解散後、參政院參政に任せらる、頗る消極主義を持して帝制請願書受理に反對し、後ち事に託して請暇歸鄉し、屢々辭職を云ふ。黎總統繼任するや、招電によりて上京し約法の恢復及び國會の復活に力を盡し、國會再び開院するに至り、仍ち參議院議長の職に就きたり。

民國之精華　（傳記）　王家襄先生

Mr. Wang Chia hsiang, otherwise known as Yu shan, forty five years of age, is a native of Shao huan hsien, Che Chiang province. He is sagacious in temperament, and noble in character, being full of patience. When young, he was very much interested in the study of law. He came to Japan in 1904, and was graduated from the police school attached to the metropolitan office, Tokyo. On returning for his country, he was interested in the education of police in different capacities, having established even a school of his own for the purpose. In 1909, he was invited by the Chilin province to supervise the police work. In the first year of the Republic, he was elected a member of the medical assembly, and in the second year of the Redublic, a member of the Senate when the Parliament was properly opened. He was on the committee for drafting the Constitution, president of the Senate, and the president of the Constitutional Assembly etc. After the dissolution of the Parliament, he adopted the conservation policy, and was opposed the Imperial Movement. When the new president was elected, he worked for the restoration of the Paliament in which he was appointed a member of Senate, the position of honour which he now enjoys.

湯化龍　字濟武　歲四十二

選舉地　湖北省　衆議院議長
籍貫　湖北省蘄水縣
住址　北京石板坊頭條胡同

君秉性誠厚。天資聰穎。爲人精明強幹。自幼好學。鄉里有神童之稱。及梢長。喜爲詩歌。尤究心經史之學。嗣以甲辰科進士。咨送日本。留學法政大學專科畢業。歸國後。旋於宣統元年被選爲湖北諮議局議長。時鄂省方以鐵路國有問題。民論沸騰。君與同志。以此屢與政府力爭。是年武昌起義。君被舉爲民政總長。民國元年。被任爲法制院副總裁。旋又爲臨時參議院副議長。二年被選爲衆議院議長。三年任爲教育總長。兼學術委員長。適帝制問題發生。君慎慨不安。遂毅然棄職南歸。五年六月黎大總統繼任。君由上海入京。商恢復約法國會各問題。嗣以夫人於日本病故。君倉卒回里。國會開會後。群促君北上。時君既抱客旅斷絃之痛。復懷指揮大計之思。卒以急公後私之精神。不及摒擋家事。遽來京。復就衆議院議長之職。

君秉性誠厚にして天資聰穎なり。人と爲り精明強幹にして、幼より學を好み、鄉里神童の稱あり。稍や長じて詩歌を喜び、尤も經史の學に通曉す。甲辰科の進士を以て日本に留學し、法政大學專科を卒業す。宣統元年選ばれて湖北諮議局議長と爲る。鐵道國有問題起りて民論沸騰するや、君同志と偕に外資拒絕鐵道民營の議を主張して政府に迫りたり。未だ幾くならずして武昌革命の事あり君舉げられて湖北民政總長となる。南北統一後、法制院副總裁に任ず。旋て又た臨時參議院副議長と爲る。民國二年正式國會成立するや、衆議院議長に舉げらる。國會停止後、熊希齡內閣の教育總長に任じ、學術委員長を兼ぬ。四年帝制問題起るや、慨然其の職を棄てゝ南下す。五年黎元洪大總統となるや、上海より入京して約法及び國會恢復等の各問題を商籌したり。適ま夫人の死に會し國會開院後十數日、復た入京して衆議院議長の職に就きたり。

Mr. Tang Hua-lung, present speaker of the House of Representatives, forty two years old, a native of Chisuihsien, Hupeh. He was well known as clever when a youth. At that time he was fond of writing poems and devoted himself much to chinese history and classics. After obtainting the scholorship of "Chinshih" in 1904 he was sent to Japan by Government to study political sciences and graduated there some years afterwards. In 1909, he was elected as the president of the provincial assembly of Hupeh. When the question of railway nationalization arose, the people of Hupeh showed much dissatisfaction to it, and Mr. Tang and his comrades acted acording to the wish of their fellow provincials made strong protest against the goverument. But as the government declined to listen to his suggestion Mr. Tang immediatly reluctantly returned home. In 1911. the Wuchang outbreak took place, and Mr. Tang was elected as the civil governos. In the next year, he was appointed as the vice-president of the law compelation bureau in which post he remained not very long. Then he was elected as the vice-speaker of the national aseembly. In 1913. he was elected as the speaker of the House of Representatives. He was appointed the minister of education and concurrently the president for the scholars examination commission in 1914. At that time he enjoyed very high reputation, espeeed among moderates. But as failed to secure confidence from the late president Yuan Shih-kai he could do nearly nothing. When the Monarchical Movement came, he was even more anxious than ever, and adroitly resigned and started for South. His wife has died in Japan, while his children remain there. After the death of Yuan Shih-kai, both Houses were called to session by a presidental mandate. Although he was in a state of great sorrow for the death of his wife, he came to Peking resumed his duty as the immediately and speaker of the House of Rep resentatives. It is seen that he has given the countrv welfare the first consideration, and put the private matter last.

王正廷 字儒堂 歲三十五

選舉地　浙江省　參議院副議長

籍貫　浙江省奉化縣

住址　北京西城林清宮二十二號

君光緒二十四年卒業于北洋大學預科。隨即昇入大學法科。後以庚子事變。大學停辦。故未克畢業。三十年。被聘爲湖南高等學校教員。三十二年。赴日本留學。翌年。復渡美。入耶爾大學。卒業後。得文學士學位。宣統三年歸國。時值光復之初。君遂入武昌。爲軍政府外交部次長。南北和議既興。被舉爲湖北省代表。旋又被選爲南京臨時參議院副議長。民國元年。任命爲工商次長。旋署理工商總長。二年正式國會成立。復爲參議院副議長。旋棄職南歸。痛詆袁氏之暴虐。與同志等力倡反對。及至此次共和復活。君盡力尤多。民黨活動。多恃君之調遣指揮。五年六月。黎大總統繼任。君以南方代表之名義入都。遂遍說當局。示以大義。動以利害。並爲疏通意志。調融感情。使無復隔閡。卒使與國所企望之種種問題。皆克爲圓滿之解決。及國會恢復。遂仍就參議院副議長。

民國之精華　（傳記）　王正廷先生

君は明治三十一年北洋大學預科を卒業し進みて大學法科に入れり。偶々北清事變の爲め大學停止となりたるを以つて未だ卒業するに至らず。明治三十七年湖南高等學校教員となり、三十九年日本に留學す。翌年米國に赴き「ェール」大學に入り、四十三年成績良好を以つて文學士の學位を得、翌年歸國す。恰も武昌革命の時に遇ひ、直に湖北軍政府外交次長となる。南北和を議するや、湖北省代表となり、次いで南京臨時參議院副議長に當選す。

大正元年工商次長に任ぜられ、又た總長心得となる。二年正式國會成立するや選ばれて參議院副議長となりしが、袁氏の横暴を怒りて南方に歸り、極力之れに反對して共和復活に多大の貢獻をなせり。五年六月袁氏死して黎氏大總統に就任するや、南方代表として北京に來り、穩健なる政見を主持して常局を説き、遂に圓滿なる解決を見るに至りたるは君の力與つて大なり。國會の復活するに及び再び參議院副議長の職に就きたり。

Mr. C. T. Wang, the vice-speaker for the Senate, thirty five years old, a native of Funhuabien, Chekiang. He pursued the study of laws in Peiyang University after having graduated from its preparatory department in 1898, owing to the outbeak of the boxer trouble. Peiyang University exsted no longer, Mr. Wang was compelled to suspend his study. In 1904 he was a teacher in the Hunan High Sohool. Having studied in Japan for some time in 1906, Mr. Wang, started for America in the year following, and entered the Yale University where he received the M. A. degree. The Revolution took place in 1911, when Mr. Wang returned to the country from America. He was appointed by the Wuchang Military Government, as the vice-minister of foreign affairs. Later he participated in negotiating the terms for settlement between North and South in the capacity as a representative from the province of Hupéh. when the National Assembly held their meeting at Nanking he was elected the Vice-Speaker. In 1912 he was appointed to the vice-minister of agriculture and Commerce, and then the acting Minister of the same. Again he entered the legislative circle in the next year when was elected the vice-speaker of the Senate. As at variance with the policy of the Government, Mr. Wang resigned and went to South where he strongly voiced against the despotism of the late president Yuan Shih-kai. He was an important factor in the movement for over throwing the monarchical campaign and restoring the republicanism. After General Li Yuan-hung ascended to the presidentiaI chair, Mr. Wang came to Peking as representative for the South. He had a close contest with all the influencial men in the capital, and gave them proper advises as to how to act righteously in order to avoid all sorts of danger. By doing this, he succeeded in compromising the different views and opinions held by the so called Northern and Southern parties, hense many questions have been solved satisfactorily. Now Mr. Wang has resumed his duty as the vice-speaker of the Senate.

陳國祥　字敬民

選舉地　貴州省　衆議院副議長
籍貫　貴州省修文縣
住址　北京火道口

君賦性溫和。其父陳厚魄本以文學顯名。初在翰林。意氣盛。及改官縣令湖南。意忽忽不樂。飲酒賦詩自遣。即卒于官。遺孤數人。君其長也。時年弱冠。既知自刻厲爲文詞。由監生中貴州鄉試。逾年成進士。遂入翰林。時清廷方興新學。設進士館于北京。新及第者。法當入肄業。君乃呈請赴日留學。入法政大學畢業。還朝授編修。加侍講銜。豫撫林紹年。奏以君充法政學堂監督。在職三年。養成子弟千餘人。民國元年被選爲臨時參議院議員。遂應召入京。把持正論。贊勸建設。與褒念益陳敬第等。設立共和協進會。未幾。與共和民主統一各黨合併爲進步黨。君又爲進步黨員。二年正式國會成立。被選爲衆議院議員。被舉爲衆議院副議長。國會解散後。被任參政院參政。頗抱消極主義。不願贊勤帝政。及國會復活。仍復就衆議院副議長之職。

君賦性溫和なり。弱冠既に剃苦勉勵して文詞を作る。監生より貴州鄉試に及第し、年を逾へて進士と爲り、遂に翰林に入る。時方に清廷は進士館を北京に創設す。君乃ち進士館に入らずして日本に留學し、法政大學に入りて卒業す。歸國後翰林院編修を授けられ侍講銜を加へらる。河南巡撫林紹年より聘せられて河南法政學堂監督となり、在職三年、子弟千餘人を養生したり。民國元年選ば れて臨時参議院議員となる。褒念益、陳敬第等と共和協進會を設立し、其の後、共和民主統一各黨と合併して進步黨を組織さるゝや、同黨員と爲る。二年貴州より選ばれて正式國會衆議院議員と爲る。衆議院副議長に舉げらる。國會解散後、參政院參政に任せらる。五年國會復活して重ねて召集を行ふや、仍は復た衆議院副議長の職に就き たり。

Mr. Chen Kuo hsieng, otherwise known of Ching Min, is a native of Hsin wen hsien, Kuei Chuan province. He is a gentleman of quiet and severe temperament, while young he was a great student of books. He passed successfully the civil service examination, which made him a member of Han lin. He went to Japan to complete his education, and he entered the Hosei University. An returning to his country, he was appointed a member of the Hau lin. He went to Japan to complete his education, and he entered the Hosei University, an returning to his country, he was appointed a member of the Han lin yin, and later a director of the Hu nan law school, which post he occupied for three years, and meantime he educated over thousand young men. In the first year of the Republic, he was elected a member of the local assembly, and later, he enjoyed the honour of being the organizer of the progressive party. In the second year of the Republic, he was returned for the House of Commons of which he became to vice-president. When the Parliament was dissolved, has was appointed a member of the Senate. When the Parliament was restored, he was appointed the vice-paesident of the House of Commons

丁濟生　字梅嚴　歲六十九

選舉地　福建省
籍　貫　福建省建甯縣
住　址　北京東草廠二條胡同邵武會館

君爲人誠實篤厚。生平不爲僞言。雖疾惡如仇。不以疾言厲色。人以非禮相加。但以理責之。不出惡聲。自幼聰穎好學。弱冠以詩文知于鄉里。及長。尤銳志實學。造詣漸深。前清以拔貢生。用直隸州州判。畢業後。分發江西。補學堂學監。建甯縣瀾川書院學院。高等小學校校長。邵武中學校校長。君本洪都循吏。更以提獎後進。改良社會爲已任。惜在前清。限於階級。莫能展其所爲。惟對於官省學務。因其主政有年。頗有成效。現迄今。南昌學生。尤多出其門下云。民國成立。二年正式國會議員選舉。君被選衆議院議員。國會解散後。南旋歸鄉。誘導後進。從事教育。不問政治。國會恢復。君復應召入京。仍爲衆議院議員。

民國之精華　（傳記）　丁濟生先生

君人と爲り誠實にして篤厚、生平僞言を爲さず。惡を疾むこと仇の如しと雖、疾言厲色を以てせず。人の非禮を以て相加れば但だ理を以て之を責め惡聲を出さず。幼より聰穎にして學を好み、弱冠詩文を以て鄉里に知られ、長ずるに及び尤も實學に志して造詣漸く深し。前清時代拔貢を以て法政學堂に肄業し、卒業後江西に分ちて直隸州州判に補用せらる。客籍學堂學監、高等小學校校長、邵武中學校々長等に歷充す。君本

と洪都の循吏にして、更に後進を誘掖し、社會改良を以て已が任と爲したり。地方の學務を管掌すること久しく頗る成效し、現に今に至る迄南昌の學生尤も其の門下に出づと云ふ。民國樹立して正式國會議員選舉に際し衆議院議員に當選す。國會解散後南旋して鄉に歸り、依然育英に從事す。國會恢復するや、又身を政界に投じ出でゝ衆議院議員となる。

五

Mr. Ting Chi Sheng, another name Meng Yen, Native of Chien ning hsien, Fu chien hsing, sixty nine years old. He is a man of truth, never spoke a word which he does not believe. He disdains injustice as his enemy, yet he never reproaches him too hastely. If one does him wrong he asks him kindly to think it over and uses no hursh word. He was known as one of brightest boys in his town and had been looked for a future poet as he composed poems remarkably well. But growing older his expiration changed to be a lawyer. During the Imperial Regime he was an appointed fellow at the law school, Fa Cheng Hsiao tang, where he graduated with honour and made a prefectural justice of Chi li Later, he was appointed registrar of Ko Chieh Hsiao tang, then he accepted the professorship of Fu ning Hsiang Chuan Shu Yuan, from which position he was tranferred to superintend Higher Grammer School, and lastly he was promoted to the Shao Wu Middle School Principal. As an official of Hung tu he educated a thousand young men, improved the social condition and superintended successfully the local education for a prolonged period. It is told that the much of students of Nan Chuang go through his instruction before undertaking any advance study. On the establishment of Republican Government he was one of first elected members of the House of Representative. After the dissolution of the House he returned home in the South and devoted all his power for the education of youth. Having the Parliament reconvened in 1916 he has entered again into politics and was elected a member of the House of Representatives.

丁儼宣 字雨生 歲四十八

選舉地 浙江省

籍貫 浙江省新昌縣

住址 北京石燈庵浙江議員第二公寓

君爲人篤實無欺。而性聰敏善謀。膽識並富。維新後。極意考求新學。能得其精義。喜開通愚蒙。引證解釋。淳々不倦。早歲入學。科舉未廢時。即立志不後從舉業。自庚子至庚戌。歷充本邑沃西高等小學校長。縣學校董。辛亥。被選爲縣會議員。旋被舉爲澄潭鄉鄉董。光復時。匪徒竊發。聚集二千餘人。白日搶刼。地方糜爛。君集民團擊破之。由浙江都督朱。委任爲新昌縣知事兼任新昌民團局團長。旋被選爲衆議院議員。及國會解散。君即南旋創辦實業。經營安徽新昌縣榮昌公司煤鑛。絕口不談政事。及國會復活。始欣然入都。仍爲衆議院議員。

君人と爲り篤實にして欺かず、性聰敏にして膽識並び富む。維新後勉めて新學を攻究し、能く其の精を得て引證解釋淳々として倦まず。庚子より庚戌に至る諸年、本邑沃西高等小學校長、縣學校董等に歷任し。辛亥の歲、選ばれて縣會議員となる。旋て復た舉げられて澄潭鄉鄉董と爲る。革命光復の時、匪徒竊に衆を聚ること二千余人、白日搶刼を擅にして地方糜爛す。君乃ち民團を集めて之を擊破す。其の後朱浙江都督は君に委任するに新昌縣知事の職を以てし、新昌民團局長を兼充したり。旋て選ばれて衆議院議員と爲る。國會解散さるゝに及びて、君ち南旋して實業に從事し、安徽繁昌縣榮昌公司の炭鑛を經營して、暫らく政事を談せず。本年國會復活するに及び、欣然として再び北京に抵り、衆議院議員として政界に活躍の人となれり。

Mr. Ting Hsu-Hsun, another name Yu Sheng, is a native of Che chian hsing, Hsin chang chien. He is a man of sincerity, and people well know that he would never tell a lie through in all his life. He is also so sagacious, that he had become an accomplished savant of the modern sciences, after a few year's learning since the new era. During many years, he became the master of the Higher Common School at Wu hsi and the principal of the district high school. In the year of 19 Hsin kai he was elected to a member of district legislative, and also appointed the magistrate of Cheng Tan Ching. In the period of the Revolution, the bandits took the advantage of local disorder, and hands of more than two thousands plandered the villages rnd towns, causing a great fear of the people. It was through his exploit that the bandits were expelled and local disorder was recovered, because the people were wholly depended upon him, and obeyed to his order. The viceroy of the province of Cheh-king heard of this, and appointed him the sheriff of Hsin Chang district, and gave also the position of the group of the body of self-government. When the new Parliament was opened, he was returned a member of the Lower House. After the Coup d'Etat, he came back to the South, and engaged in business. The coal mines owned by the Jung Chang & Co., and situated in the district, Fan Chang of the province of Chung hui, was under his management. For a while, he paid no attention to the political affairs, but after the reopening of Parliament, he gladly hurried up to Peking, and as a member of the House of Commons, is enjoying the political life.

丁象謙　字六皆　歲四十

選舉地　安徽省

籍貫　安徽省　阜陽縣

住址　北京西城西斜街五十一號

君自幼好讀。弱冠即負文名。於前清光緒二十一年入郡庠。二十五年。肄業江南高等學堂。二十六年。入統領五省授軍程壯勤公幕府。二十七年。肄業江南格致書院。二十八年入第二次江南高等學堂。三十一年東渡留學日本。三十三年。畢業於東洋大學高等師範科。宣統二年。畢業於早稻田大學政治經濟科。旋入中央大學研究科。卒亥武漢起義。歸國。由皖軍都督府。聘為高等政治顧問。民國成立。被舉為臨時省議會議員。幷充安徽官立法政學校教員。與同志創辦江淮大學。任教授。二年。正式國會成立。被選為參議院議員。以守正不阿。為袁政府所深忌。追帝制發生。滇黔舉義。遂赴滬。與客居其一。幾瀕於死。三年出獄。杜門謝客。遂赴滬。與黎繼起。兩院同志。協謀恢復國會。及袁死黎繼。國會復活。遂來京供職。

君幼より讀書を好み、弱冠にして文名を負ふ。前清光緒二十一年、郡庠に入る。二十五年江南高等學堂に學ぶ。二十六年統領五省授軍程壯勤の幕府に入る。二十七年江南格致書院に學ぶ、二十八年再び江南高等學堂に入る。三十一年日本に留學し、三十三年東洋大學高等師範科を卒業す。宣統二年早稻田大學政治經濟料を畢へ、又た中央大學研究科に入る。辛亥武漢を起す。乃ち國に歸り、皖軍都督府の聘に應じ、高等政治顧問と爲る。民國成立し、選ばれて臨時省議會議員と爲り、幷に安徽官立法政學校教員に充てられ、同志と江淮大學を創辦して教授に任せらる。二年正式國會成立す、選ばれて參議院議員と爲る。正を守りて阿らざるを以て深く袁政府の忌む所と爲る。京畿軍政執法處違法に違ひて八議員を逮捕す、君其一に居り、幾んど死に瀕す、三年獄を出で、門を杜ぢ客を謝す、帝制發生して滇黔義を舉ぐるに追び、遂に上海に赴き、兩院同志と協謀して國會を恢復せんとす。袁死し黎繼ぎ、國會復活するに及び、遂に京に來りて就職す。

民國之精華　（傳記）　丁象謙先生

七

Mr. Ting Hsang Chien, another name Liu Chieh age forty, is a native of Fou Hsien, Ang Hui hsing. Since the boyfood, he has been a book-lover, and famous of his literary talent. In the year of 21 of the reign of Kwang hsü of the Manchu dynasty, he entered the district school, and in 25, the Chiang Nan Kiang nan High School, and the next year he became a member of the headquarters of the general Cheng Chiang chin. But after the resumption of the learning in the Kiang nan Ko Pei phu yuan, he came to Japan in 31, and studied the modern sciences. In 33 he was a graduate of a faculty of education in the Toyo-College. In the second year of Hsüan t'ung, he got a diploma of the faculty of the political and economical sciences of Waseda University, and was studying the special coarses in Chuo University, when the revolution broke out in Wu chang and Hun chiang. He soon went home, and became the Special Political Adviser, accepting the offer of revolutional military government. After the formation of Republic, he was returned a member of Provincial Legistrative in Extraordinal Session, and also appointed a professor of the Public Law School. After this, he became a professor of Chiang-huai University, of which he was a promoter. When the Parliament was regularly established in the second year of the Republic, he was elected the Senator of the people's acclamation, the responsibility of which position he faithfully observed. He is a sort of man who pursues only the course of righteousness, and naturally got a disfavor of the dictator Yuan, who ordered his arrest and sent him to prison, where he had nearly suffered the death. After he came out of the prison, he returned home and lived in a seclusive life. But when the new revolution broke out in Yun-nan, he went to Shanghai, and was planning a new movement to expel Yuanshih-kai. He is now fulfilling the duty of his former position as the Senator.

王玉琦 字慕韓 歲六十三

選舉地　吉林省

籍　貫　吉林省長春縣

住　址　北京西單、北芐于胡同四

君秉性誠實篤厚。爲人溫良恭謙而至
孝。質朴自持。不事浮華。有士大夫之
風。家世居長春縣城東北距城一百里。
村名冰泉觀。自幼好讀書。爲文崇唐卑
宋。不習時尚迄今。好古之心。不減於
當日。文采風貌。可掬可敬。年二十三
歲。諸生師友以功名勉之。方降格應
試。二十四歲。一擊而雋。二十七歲。即
得廩餼。三十二歲即以前淸恩貢生。候
選敎論。五十五歲。被選爲吉林諮議局
議員。民國成立。被選爲臨時省議會議
員。前後多年。盡力於地方公益事業。
不尠所貢献。民國二年。正式國會成
立。荷衆望。當選衆議院議員。國會解
散後。歸田閒臥。悠々自適。讀書自娛。
及國會重開。不厭老軀。應召抵京。復
就衆議院議員之職。

君秉性誠實にして篤厚、人と爲り溫良恭謙にして至孝。
質朴自ら持して浮華を事とせず。家世々長春縣城の東北
百支里冰泉觀村に在り。幼より讀書を好み、文を作りて
唐を崇び宋を卑みて時尚に習はず、今に至る迄好古の心
當日に減せず、文采風貌敬すべきものあり。二十七歲即ち
廩餼を得て三十二歲即ち恩貢生を以て敎諭候選と爲る。
五十五歲選ばれて吉林諮議局議員と爲る。民國成立して
共和の冀を肇ぶるや臨時省議會議員に選ばれ、前後多年
地方の公益事業に盡力して貢献する所尠からず。民國二
年正式國會成立するや、衆望を荷つて衆議院議員に當選
す。國會解散さるゝや田園に歸臥して悠々自適し、國會
重ねて開かるゝに及び老軀を厭はず山を出でゝ關を入
り、召集に應じて北京に抵り、仍ほ復た衆議院議員の職
に就く。

Mr. Wang Yu-chi, another name Jung-han, is a native of Chang chun hsien, Chi-lin province, sixty three years old. He was born honest and gentle and growing older, he is modest and kind to the parents and others. His home is in the town of Shui-chuan han, where his ancestors lived every generation, a hundred Chinese miles off north east of Chang chun. He has been a lover of books from his boyhood and now is a well own essaist, holding always a reverence to Tang and a contempt to Sung: study of ancient literature is his utmost pleasure. His refined manner and benevolent looks command all the people who meet him admiration. At his 27th age, he completed the highest education which could accomplish in China; at 32 he made an assistant professor, while he was a fellow, and at 55 he was appointed a member of Chi lin Advisory Board. When the Republic was organized, and the republican government was in full sway, he was elected a member of Prefectural Congress. During many years he served for his district in promoting public welfare. In the second year of the Republic he was elected a member of the Parliament and at the dissolution of it, he returned to his country home to enjoy the pural life. When the Parliament convened again this year, 1916, he was sent out again to the House by the voters.

王鳳義　字景檀　歳五十七

選舉地　山東省

籍貫　山東省諸城縣

住址　北京頭髪胡同四十一號

君幼好讀。及長。殫心經世之書。性任俠好義。喜周濟窮苦。中年喜談時務。於譯本及時人名著。無所不窺。清末。倡辦學校甚夥。校內職教各員。多採用醉心共和之士。辛亥革命。與各校率士子。組織學生團百餘人。聯合民軍。宣布獨立。被推掌民政事宜。共和宣布後。諸城爲官軍所襲。氏幾及於難。南北統一氏充省縣議會各議員。復被選爲正式國會參議員。袁世凱以暴力解散國會。氏匿迹燕都。期乘機光復。帝制亂生。魯省舉義。氏急回省。運籌一切。並膺山東護國軍代表之名義。張魯泉等奔走滬魯青島間。卒達再造共和之目的。克以恢復國會。仍來京。就參議院議員。

君幼にして書を好み、長じて治國經世の學を講す。性任俠にして義を好み、喜んで窮苦を周濟す。前清末年に於て學校を倡辦すること多く。校內の職員には共和主義の士を採用したり。辛亥革命の事起るや、各校の子弟を牽ひて學生團百餘人を組織し、民軍と聯合して獨立を宣布し、推されて民政事宜を管掌す。共和宣布後、諸城官軍の襲ふ所となるや、君幾んど難に及ぶ。南北統一後、君乃ち選ばれて省縣議會各議員となる。復た舉げられて正式國會參議院議員と爲る。旋て國會解散さるゝに及び、君迹を燕都に匿し、機に乗じて光復を期す。帝制問題に對し山東省義を舉げて反抗するや、君急ぎ歸省して一切を籌畫し、並に山東護國軍代表となり、張魯泉等と共に上海青島各地間を奔走し、卒に民國共和再造の目的を遂し、其の國會を恢復するや、仍ほ重ねて入京し、現に參議院議員の職に在り。

民國之精華　（傳記）　王鳳義先生

九

Mr. Wang Feng-chu, otherwise called Ching-tan, aged fifty seven, is a native of Chu-cheng hsing, Shan tung province. He received the literary education since the boyhood, but devoted his life to the study of politics. Chivalrous by nature, he would gladly give his things to the poor. During the last years of the Manchu dynasty, he became to manage many schools, and appointed the men of republicanism to the members of the schools. When the Revolution had happened, he became the leader of student troops and having had the support of the people's army, declared independence against the Manchus. He became an actual governor by the choice of people. When the Republic was proclaimed, the troops despatched by the central government attacked the people, and came very near to take him. After the compromise of the North and South, he became a member of district, and after that, provincial legislative body. He fulfilled the duty so well, that the people sent him to the Senate which was regularly opened very soon. In time of Coup d'Etat, he escaped himself from the arrest, and lived in secret metropols, planning the recovering of the parliamentary régime. When Shang tang province made a revolt against the imperial plan, he hurried back home, planned a successful demonstration, and became a delegate of the Shang-tung National Guard to Shan-ghai, Ching-tao and many other places, the cooperation with which was absolutely necessary to the cause of revolution. He accomplished this with great leaders of Chang Lu chuan, and with reopening of the Parliament, has again occupied the chair of the Senate.

王沚清　字石泉　歲五十六

選舉地　甘肅省
籍貫　甘肅省武威縣
住址　北京羅家大院

君秉性清高。言論風采。皆迥異庸俗。然謙和厚重。以禮自持。絕無虛驕習氣。稚齡即能爲詩文。吐芳新俊。鄉人皆以神童目之。及長。尤博及羣書。經史而外。諸子百家。皆取備讀。均能發微抉伏。得其眞精。中年。尤專攻于理義之書。屏棄考據詞章之學。常慨世道人心之是非。頗有廉頑立儒之志。而不以科舉縈怀。故雖淵博精深。乃僅以一衿自足。不復求進。及海內維新。遂慨然以提倡敎育爲已任。民國二年正式國會成立。被選爲參議院議員。國會解散後。歸里讀書。誘掖後進。不談時政。及國會重行召集。遂入京。仍爲參議院議員。

君秉性清高にして言論風采皆な迥に庸俗に異る。然かも謙和にして禮を以て自を持し、絕て虛驕な習氣なし。少年能く詩文を作り、吐芳新俊にして、鄉人皆な神童を以て之を目す。長ずるに及び、尤も博く羣書を涉獵し、經史以外諸子百家の書皆な通覽して、均しく其の徵を開きたり。中年尤も理義の書を修めて詞章の學を屏ぞけ、常に世道人心の是非を慨して、頗る高儒を以て立つの志あり。海內維新に及び、遂に慨然として敎育を普及し民智を開發するを以て己が任と爲す。民國二年正式國會成立さるや、選ばれて參議院議員となり。國會解散後、鄉里に歸省して讀書自ら娛み、時に出でゝ後進を誘掖して時事を談せず國會重ねて召集を行ふに及び、遂に復た入京して仍ほ參議院議員と爲る。

Mr. Wang Chi-ching, otherwise known as Shih Chuan, age fifty six, a native of Wu Wei Hsien, the Kan Hsing, is a born genius. His personal presence distinguishes himself from the common people. He is cautious to the extreme, and is free from arrangance and pride. He was a poet and essaist, and as he grew up, his information became comprehensive, himself being fond of a copious reading. Later in his life, he read books of phylosophical nature, and shunned the study of mere bombastic phraseology. Under the new world's is current, he has convinced himself that his duty was to make efforts towards the dessimination of education, thus developing the intellectual side of the people. In 1913 when the "Republic was established, he became a member of the Senate, upon the dissolu tion of the Parliament, he returned to his native district when his only friends were his books because he very little talked about politics. With the re-organization of the legislature body, he became a member of the House of Commons.

王人文　字朵丞　歲五十四

選舉地　雲南省

籍　貫　雲南省大理縣

住　址　北京長巷二條天順群

君爲人深沈多謀。喜怒不形辭色。然工
於交際。喜爲友朋助力。故鄉里皆以長
厚君子目之。以前清癸未進士。歷官貴
州湄潭貴筑鎮開泰縣知事。廣西南寧
平樂府奉天錦州府知府。廣西桂平梧
道。廣東按察使提學使。陝西布政使。川
滇邊務大臣。民國二年。由雲南省議
會。選舉爲參議院議員。曾於民國元年
加入國民黨。被舉爲理事。卒以國民黨
員。被選爲參議員。國會開會後。忽然
脫黨。爲無所屬議員。蓋君考于仕途。
與新進少年。自難於融洽。故入國民
黨。未久。終以氣味不相投之故。脫黨
獨立。國會解散後。隨遇而安。無所趨
向。及國會重開。遂入京。仍就參議院
議員之職。

君人と爲り深沈にして多謀、喜怒色に顯さず、交際に工
に、喜んで友朋の爲に力を致す。故に鄉黨皆な長厚君子
を以て之を目す。前清癸未進士を以て貴州湄潭貴筑渭鎮
開泰縣知事、廣西南寧平樂府奉天錦州府知府、廣西桂平
梧道、廣東按察使、提學使、陝西布政使、四川布政使、護
理四川總督侍郎銜、川滇邊務大臣等の官に歷任す。民國
二年雲南省議會より選ばれて參議院議員となる。曾て民
國元年國民黨に入り理事に舉げられたる事あるも、國會
開院後同黨を脫して無所屬議員と爲る。蓋し君の仕途に
考へ新進少年と自ら融合し難く、氣味相投せざるの故を
以て脫黨して獨立したる所以なり。國會解散せらる〻や、
退いて靜かに心神を養ひ、以て時運の再變を觀望す。此
次國會重ねて開かる〻に及び、遂に復た京に入りて、仍
は參議院議員の職に就きたり。

民國之精華　（傳記）　王人文先生

Mr. Wang Jen-wen, another name Tsai Cheng, aged fifty four, is a native of Ta-li hsing, Yunnan province. As a man of resourcefulness and sang-froid, he is well known among his friends who loved him heartily. He is also social to everybody, and has done many good things to the home-forks who take him as a true gentleman. During the Manchu era, he successfully passed the official exermination, and got the diploma of graduatariatship. He passed through many positions of sheriffaltydom of Mei-tan, Kuei-chu, of the province of Kuei Chuan, and after this, he was appointed the higher positions of prefect in the Nan-ning fu and Pin lo fu, Kuanghsi, Chin chou fu and Feng-tien, Cheng king. He was as succesful in each office, that he went higher in each step, and later he became successively the superintendent, inspector for iducation, magistrate, secretary to the viceroy in the provinces of Kuangtung, Kuang-hsi, Hsia-hsi, Si chuan, and lastly minister for the affairs of chuan-tien. In the second year of the Republic, he was elected the Senator from the province of Yun-nan by the legistlative body. He belonged once to the National Party, and was made the whip of that party, which he resigned after the opening of the session of the Parliament, and became an independent member. The long official life may have made his mingling with the younger radicals impossible. After the Coup d'Etat, he retired home, and enjoyed private life. But with the reopening of the Parliament, he came to Peking, becoming the Senator again.

王兆離　字伯明　歲四十七

選舉地　陝西省

籍貫　陝西省扶風縣

住址　北京校場六條路北劉廣

君秉性醇孝。篤於友愛。居恆勤謹自持。不苟言笑。與人交。喜勸善規過。然辭氣和婉。曲詞誘導。雖惡惡如仇。而不爲疾言遽色。故雖剛直不阿。而未嘗以是受小人之嫉恨。自幼天資聰慧過人。敏於悟性。然又謙虛好問。故其進猛。弱冠即以能文見知於時。及長。淹通經史。於前清光緒癸卯科舉人。歷充邑高等小學校。鳳翔西安中學校教員。民國成立後。被選爲臨時省議會議員。二年一月。復被選爲衆議院候補議員。二月。任陝西省教育科科員。五月。補衆議院議員。國會解散後。歸里從事教育。不談政治。及國會重開。始入京。仍爲衆議院議員。

君性や醇孝にして友愛に篤く、居常謹嚴自ら持して言笑を苟もせず。人と變るや喜んで善を勸め過を規し、然かも辭氣和婉にして曲詞を以て誘導す。惡を惡む仇の如しと雖、疾言遽色せず。故に剛直にして阿らずと雖、未だ甞て是を以て小人の嫉恨を受けざる也。幼より天資聰慧にして弱冠即ち能文を以て時に知らる。長するに及び經史に淹通し、前清光緒癸卯の歲舉人と爲り、本邑の高等小學校、鳳翔西安中學校教員を歷充し。民國成立後、選ばれて臨時省議會議員と爲る。二年一月復た選ばれて衆議院補缺議員と爲る。二月陝西省教育科科員に任ず。五月衆議院議員の缺を補す。國會解散さるヽや、郷に歸りて教育に從事して政治を談ぜず。國會重ねて開かるヽに及び、再び北京入り、仍は衆議院議員と爲る。

Mr. Wang Chao-li, another name Pai ming, age forty seven, is a native of Fiu feng-hsing, Hsia-hsi hsing. Filial, dutiful, gentle, frankful, he acts to everybody with whom he loves, and from whom he is loved. He would never laugh at the things immaterial, because it is unworthy. As a friend, he is a most worthy one who leads others to the good, and keeps them off of the vices. Although he hates the wicked people more than enemy, and never tell the flattery to the men of higher position, he never receives the enmity of them, because they know his sincerity. It may be the virtue of his reserved character. Sagacious and intelligent as he was, since the boyhood, he showed the marked distinction in literary talent, and classical study was of his special line. In time of Kwang-hsü of the Manchu dynasty, he passed the exermination, and appointed the principal of the common school in his own home town, and a teacher of the Sha-hsi middle school in the district of Feng hsiang successively. When the Republic came to the existence, he was elected a member as the provincial legislative which was summoned for extraordinary purpose. Next year he was returned a member of the House of Commons, which position he occupied until the Coup d'Etat. Temporarily he was also a member of educational board of the provincial government of Hsia-hsi. After the dissolution of the Parliament, he came home, and resumed the profession of the education. But with he reopening of the Parliament, he came to Peking, and has taken the duty as a member of Parliment.

王吉言 字颺廷 歲四十七

選舉地　直隸省
籍　貫　直隸省三河縣
住　址　北京西單牌樓二條胡同門牌三號

君秉性篤實。自幼勤學。不事嬉遊。弱
冠即廣通經史。長於詩文。以清朝光緒
甲午科舉人乙未科取謄錄。旋於光緒
二十四年註冊。揀選縣知事簽分廣東
後告假回籍養親。在本籍創立學校。充
當教員。復於光緒三十年創辦戒煙所
二處。光緒三十三年各縣劃區籌辦自
治。充當區萬併帮同本縣知事籌措警
欵。創立警務傳習所。充常警董後。居
京師。入法政專門學校肄業。因事告退
未獲卒業。民國成立。在第一區被選為
衆議院議員。國會解散後。歸里獨居。
不談政事。及國會重開。始來京。仍為
衆議院議員之舊職。

民國之精華　（傳記）王吉言先生

君秉性篤實にして幼より學に勤め嬉戲を事とせず、弱冠
即ち廣く經史に通じ詩文に長ず。前清光緒甲午科舉人を
以て光緒二十四年縣知事に選ばれ廣東省に分たる。後ち
請眼して鄉里に歸り、學校を創立して敎員に任ず。光緒三
十年戒煙所二箇處を創設して阿片吸煙の弊を矯めんと努
む。復た光緒三十三年各縣に於て地區を劃して地方自治
を準備するや、君其の區董に任ず。三河縣知事を助けて
財源を籌り、警務傳習所を創立して其の董事に任す。後
ち北京に抵りて法政專門學校に學びたるが、事を以て中
途退學す。斯くて民國成立後、正式國會議員選舉に會し、
君出で、衆議院議員に常選す。國會解散後は再び鄉里に
歸臥して獨居悠々政事を談せず、閑を普め淡を食つて靜
に身神を養ふ。國會恢復するに及び、復た召集されて京
師に入り、仍ほ衆議院議員の職に就きたり。

Mr. Wang Chi-yen, otherwise known as Yang-ting, aged forty seven, is a native of Sa-ho hsien. He in youth proved himself to be an admirer of books, and found very little enjoyment in the mere childish play. He is a student of classics and well posted up in poetry. Under the previous Chinese regime, he passed the civil service examination successfully, and was appointed the governor of Kuangtung hsien in 1891. On being permitted to leave the government service, he returned to his native district where he founded a school of which he became an instructor. In 1897, he established two smoking offices with a view to correct the habit of opium smoking while in 1900, preparation for the introduction of the civic body system was going on in every province, he was appointed the head of the section. While assisting the governor, he succeeded in establishing the police training institute of which he was appointed the director. He went up to Peking to study law in the law school there, but owing to some cause not repeated here, he had to leave the school. When the Parliament was opened, he ran as the candidate and was elected a member thereof. When the legislative body was shut down, he returned to his native country, and would not talk of any politics, but he beguiled his hours in a quiet study. With the restoration of the Parliament, he returned to Peking where he was returned for the House of Commons, the position he occupies in the present moment.

王茂材　字幼山　歲四十五

選舉地　江蘇省

籍貫　江蘇省沛縣

住址　北京米市胡同徐州會館

君為人長厚篤實。自幼攻苦讀書。喜為詩文。及海內維新遂盡棄舊學。殫心考求西化。旋入甯屬師範學校。畢業後。由兩江總督咨送日本。入法政大學第五班政治部。畢業。繼入本校法律專門部第二年級旋以光復歸國。任江北都督府秘書。兼江北民政司總務科科長。充江北財政公所蕩灘科科長。民國二年。被選為眾議院議員。國會解散後。返里閉門讀書。不談時事。及帝制發生。始赴滬上。與同志共圖倒袁。運動閩省及江北獨立。業已成熟。適袁氏逝世。約法恢復。遂應國會召集來京。復為眾議院議員。

君人と為り長厚篤實、幼より刻苦勉勵して書を讀み、喜んで詩文を作る。海內維新に及び遂に舊學を棄てゝ、西學の研究に志したり。曾て南京に抵り師範學校に學びて卒業す。繼で兩江總督より選派されて日本に留學し、法政大學政治科を卒業し、法律專門部に入る。旋て第一革命起りて歸國し、江北都督府秘書に任じ江北民政司總務科科長を兼ぬ。嗣で江北財政公所蕩灘科の長に充つ。民國二年選ばれて眾議院議員と為る。國會解散後、鄉里に歸りて杜門閉居讀書自ら娛み、また時事を語らず。帝制問題發生するに及びて、上海に赴き、同志と共に倒袁の事を圖り、閩省及び江北の獨立を運動す。事飯に熟して適ま袁氏逝き、約法恢復されて國會再び召集を行ふ。君遂に復た北上入京して、仍は眾議院議員の舊職に就く。

十四

Mr. Wang Mao-tsai sometimes known as Yu Shan, age forty five, is a native of Rei Chiong Su province. He is a gentleman of high virtue and sincere character. Even while young, he was a hard student, and fond of reading books and composing books and composing poem. At the time. of the Restoration, he abandoned the old learning, and took up the new. He went to Nanking when he entered the normal school whence he was graduated. He was sent to Japan by the government, and was graduated from the Hose Law University. In the first year of the Revolution, he was appointed the secretary of the governor general of Cheng pei. In the second year of the Republic, he has returned for the House of Commons. After the disolution of the Parliament, be returned to his native province where he devoted himself to reading, caring very little about the current topics. When the Imperial Movement took place, he planned for the downfall of Yuanshi-kai. With the death of Yuanshi-kai, however, the situation was changed so that he went up to Peking, and was returned for the House of Commons.

王蔭棠 字澤南 歲四十四

選舉地　奉天省
籍　貫　奉天省海龍縣
住　址　北京油房胡同

君性爽直任俠。詩文有奇氣。天資聰穎
敏捷。自幼好學。及長。新舊皆有素養。
夙抱經國濟民之志。長于幹濟之才。前
清廩生。保用直隸州知州。曾在里。辦
理山城子小學。籌欵甚裕。嗣充海龍府
勸學總董。剔除舊有積弊。學務蔚起。
旋充東平縣統計長兼收捐總董。清理
積欠。樽節浮濫。宣統元年舉充奉天諮
議局議員。提議積穀備荒。建修奉海鐵
路。編練堡防。民國二年被選爲衆議院
議員。國會解散後。歸里讀書。四年袁
世凱謀爲皇帝。君在籍極倡反對之說。
五年袁氏死。黎氏繼任。及共和克復。
國會重開。應召入京。仍爲衆議院議
員。

君性爽直任俠にして詩文奇氣あり。天資穎顯敏捷にして
幼より學を好み、長ずるに及び新舊共に素養あり。夙に
經國濟民の志を抱きて、幹濟の才に長ず。前清の廩生に
して直隸州知事保用たり。曾て鄉里に在りて山城子小學
校を經營し、嗣で海龍府勸學總董となり、多年の積弊を
剔除して學務蔚として起るを得たり。旋て東平縣統計長
兼收捐總董となり。缺損を整理して冗費を樽節したり。

宣統元年奉天諮議局議員に任じ、地方公益に關し、獻議
する所多し。民國二年選ばれて衆議院議員と爲る。國會
解散の後ち鄉里に歸りて頭書自ら娛み、四年袁世凱帝
制を謀るや、君鄉里に在りて極めて之に反對す。五年袁氏
死して黎氏繼任し、共和克復して國會重ねて開かるゝや。
遂に又た召集に應じて入京し、仍ほ衆議院議員となる。

民國之精華　（傳記）　王蔭棠先生

Mr. Wang Yin-tang, otherwise known as Tse-hsi, age forty four, is a native of Hai-lung, Feng-tien province. He is a man of gallant character and his literary productions are full of independent spirit. While Young he was greatly interested in learning. As he grew older he showed his practical ability being full of public spirit and sentiment. While in his province he was interested in the management of a primary school. In 1909 he was appointed a member of Hu-tien local assembly and public works to which he contributed great deal. In the 2nd year of the Republic he was elected a member for the House of Commons and when the Parliament was dissolved, he returned to his home where he devoted himself to reading. He was deadly opposed to the Imperial Movement of Yuanshi-kai but when this veteran statesman died and the Parliament was opened he was invited to Peking and was elected a member of the House of Commons.

十五

王侃　字補宣

選舉地　江西省
籍貫　江西省
住址　北京順治門外江西會館

君天資絕高。悟性敏捷。而頭腦周密。其言論思想。皆秩序井然絕無顛倒紊亂之弊。自幼讀書。即喜探索精義。不以文字自拘。以其能精思深入。抉其蘊要。故其見解思想。皆極明瞭切實。且洞悉事情。明察物理。長於幹濟之才。居常以誠厚待人。然於社會裏面鬼域情形。莫不深悉無遺。於前清時。留學東隣。入日本最高學府帝國大學法科。畢業歸國後。歷充江西省司法司司長。民國二年正式國會成立。被選爲衆議院議員。此次國會重開。遂又應召。仍就議員之職。

君天資高邁にして悟性敏活なり。頭腦明晰にして思慮周密。其の言を建つるや理路井然として、一糸亂れず。幼より書を好み、喜んで義に退ち精を究め、また文字章句の末に拘泥せず、書を讀む每に深く思索し、義理透徹、眼光紙背に徹するものあり。居常誠實篤厚を以て人を待ち。然かも社會の裏面を洞觀して、其の機微を知悉せり。前清時代笈を負ふて東渡し、拮据勉勵、遂に日本最高學府たる帝國大學に入りて法科に學び、業を畢へて新進法學士として歸國す。後ち江西省司法司長として令名あり。民國二年正式國會議員選舉に際し、民望を荷ふて衆議院議員に當選し。蘊蓄を傾倒して議政壇上大に參畫する所あり。國會解散後、野に在りて尚ほ智を磨き德を養ひ、國會恢復するに及び再び召集されて、仍ち衆議院議員の職に復す。

Mr. Wang Kan, known as Fu Hsuan is a native of Chiang hsi. He is a gentleman of noble character and of quick understanding, coupled with clear brain and deep thoughts. He is logical in his argument. In reading books, he is not slave to mere words but dive into the very depth of the significance of the text. He is a deep thinker who is able to comprehend the authors' meaning through and through. In dealing with others, he makes sincerity and honesty his highest virtue; moreover, he is conversant with the inner working of social ramifications. In the previous Chinese regime, he went to Japan where he entered the Imperial University of Tokyo and he took the regular course in law. On returning to his home, his reputation as the head of the Justice Bureau of Chiang-hsi stood very high. In the second year of the Republic, he was elected a member of the House of Commons with a large majority. The rich stock of knowledge he had in possession enabled him to steer his course in the Parliament. With the dissolution of the Parliament, he has been quietly studying, and improving himself in every respect. When the Parliament was summoned, he entered Peking, and has resumed his function as the member of the Parliament.

王多輔 字憲溥 歲四十

選舉地 安徽省

籍貫 安徽省太平縣

住址 北京西四大醫房胡同

君性聰慧。善悟能思。弱冠隨父歷遊各省。閱十有八年。足跡幾遍國境。二十三歲。以縣試第一入庠。二十四歲。以省試第一入安徽大學堂。二十七歲。以校試第一入京師大學堂優級師範科第三類。學習物理化學數學。三十一歲。畢業。得優等。三十二歲。任寧國府中學監督。旋兼充皖江中學監督。三十四歲。改任皖江師範學堂監督。中央教育會會員。民國元年充寧廣八屬教育特派員。二年一月。當選爲中華民國第一次國會衆議院議員。隸進步黨。國會解散。就安徽省立第一師範學校教務主任。兼物理化學教員。三年六月叛辦安徽省立第四師範學校。充任校長。先後造就學生甚衆。及國會恢復。遂入京。仍衆議院議員。

民國之精華 （傳記） 王多輔先生

君性や聰慧にして能く悟り能く思ふ。弱冠父に隨つて各省を歷遊すること十有八年、足跡幾んど國境に遍ねし。二十三歲縣試第一を以て庠に入り。二十四歲省試第一を以て安徽大學堂に入り。二十七歲校試第一を以て京師大學堂優級師範科第三類に入り、物理化學數學を學習し、三十一歲或國府中學監督に任ひ、皖江中學監督を兼充す。三十四歲改めて皖江師範學堂監督に任ひ、中央敎育會會員たり。民國元年寧廣八屬敎育特派員に充てられ、二年一月選ばれて衆議院議員と爲り、進步黨に隸す。國會解散さるヽや、安徽省立第一師範學校敎務主任として物理化學敎員と兼ぬ。三年六月安徽省立第四師範學校を創辦して校長と爲り、前後學生を敎養すること甚だ衆し。國會恢復するに及び遂に北京に入り、現に衆議院議員たり。

Mr. Wang To-fu, another name Chen-pu, age forty one, native of Ta-ping-hsing, An-hui hsien. He is one of the wisemen whom the country has rarely produced. He was accompanied by his father for the eighteen years since the boyhood from place to place of the country, the latter having been the official of the governmnt. So he is well acquainted with every corner of the country. When he was twenty three years old, he entered to the district school, passing the entrance excrmination with the mark of senicrity, which he monopolized during his student life. Next year he entered to the Provincial University of An-hui, and after he graduated there, he was sent to the great University of Peking, where he studied the physics and chemistry, and graduated at the age of thirty one. Next year he was appointed to the Superintendent of the middle school in the Ning-kou fu, as well as that of Pai-wan-chiang middle school. After two yeas he became the Superintendent of the teachers school in the latter place, and a member of the central Educational Society. In the first year of the Republic, he was despatched as a delegate to inspect the educational in some another provinces. In the second year, he was elected a member of the House of Commons, and belonged to the Progressive party. After the dissolution of the Parliament, he again took the educational profession as the head teacher of the Provincial First Teachers' School, teaching the physics, and chemistry. In the third year he endeavourel in establishing the Tourth Teachers' School of the same Province and became its President. Many students had been sent out of his school. After the reopening of the Parliament, he again became a member of the lower House.

王鑫潤 字廣山 歲四十

選舉地　甘肅省
籍　貫　甘肅皋蘭
住　址　北京三府胡同

君自幼好讀。喜博覽羣籍。任意所之爲快。而不屑規規然從事於科舉之業。故其讀書。純以主觀判斷是非。而不局於習俗之成見。及海內維新。愈立志求有用之學。於新書無所不覽。而尤醉心於法律之書。清末年。負笈入都。肄業於北京高等法律學堂。畢業後。適武昌革命起。君南下與諸同志共襄大計。多所擘畫。南京臨時政府成立。君被任爲司法部簽事。旋被選爲臨時參議院議員。政府北移。遂於司法部註冊爲律師。並爲參議院議員。居無何。被舉爲憲法起草委員。國會解散。君歸甘肅。爲公立法政專門學校敎授。旋復至上海。爲中華新報。任東文編輯。國會復活。遂來京。復爲參議院議員。

君幼より書を好み博く群籍を覽て意に任せて快を呼び殼々として科舉の業に從ふを屑しとせず。故に其の讀書は是非の判斷を主觀して習俗の成見に局せられざる也。海內維新に及ぶや、愈々志を立て〜有用の學を求め、新刊の書籍悉く之を讀破し、尤も法律の書に心醉せり。清末に於て笈を負ふて都に抵り、北京高等法律學堂に入り て業を畢ゆ。適ま武昌革命の事起り、君乃ち南下して同志と共に大計を勸助し、其の蠶畫する所多し。南京臨時政府成立するや、君は司法部簽事に任じ、旋て選ばれて臨時參議院議員と爲る。南京統一政府樹立後、君出で〜辯護士となり、後ち選ばれて參議院議員と爲り、旋て憲法起草委員に舉げらる。國會解散されて、君甘肅に歸り、公立法政學校敎授と爲る、嗣で復た上海に至り中華新報日文編輯に從事す。國會復活後、再び北上して重ねて參議院議員と爲る。

Mr. Wang Chin-jun, another name Keng-Shan. He was born in the prefecture of Kao-lan, Kan-hsi, in the year 1876. He showed a striking fondness for reading when very joung and amused himself, while searching for numerous books, with reading them as much as he pleased. However submitting himself tenaciously into the dry business of the scientific research was contrary to his nature, so it had the effect of causing him to pursue his upright course through reading. He had no regard for popular view but held to his purpose. But the intensive restoration which now broke in upon the country determined him to devote his entire energies to acquire of knowledge the most needful of the time. No new publication ever escaped from his attention and the books of law fascinated him especially. At the closing period of Ching he then decided to study law in the capital. He went to Peking and finished his courses satisfactory in the higher law college. No sooner the revolution at Wu-chang broke out than he went down into the south. He took active part in the revolution with his fellow-enthusiasts and effects of his responce to the cause exercised no slight weight in the struggle. When the temporal government of Nan-king was organized, he was appointed councilor of the department of justice and then he was elected member of temporal Parliament. However, on the organization of the union government of south and north, he resigned his office and was engaged in law practice. Later he was elected member of Parliament besides being one of committees entrusted with duty of drafting a constitution. When the Parliament was dissolved, he went to his native land Kan-hsi and accepted Chair of Professor in the public institution of Law and politics, afterward he went to Shanghai and was engaged in editing of the Japanese section of the Chung-hua news paper. The Parliament was reorganized. He went up to the north and has gained the former chair.

王觀銘 字箴 三 歲三十八

選舉地　直隸省
籍貫　直隸省寧晉縣
住址　北京西單牌樓二條胡同愛廬

君秉性剛健。操己極嚴。其處世接物。大都以約自持。言行皆取消極主義。雖有大利當前。苟非審慎周詳。決不輕於動作。迨及得失既明。方針已定。則又勇猛精進。決不人言動搖其意志。而當進退未決之前。則極為虛己從人。不恥下問。蓋心力極強。而又不執我見不拘偏私者也。自幼好讀書。喜探求義理。及長。尤富於研求之精神。具有科學的頭腦。前清時。以邑庠生。考入直隸省優級師範學堂。肄業二年餘。旋經本校選拔。以官費送往日本。早稻田大學。畢業回國。曾赴新疆漫遊。民國元年。被舉為直隸省議會副議長。民國二年。被舉為參議院議員。國會解散。絕口不談時事。亦無心仕進。及國會重開。始應召仍就參議院議員之職。

民國之精華 (傳記) 王觀銘先生

君資性剛健にして己を持する頗る嚴なり。言行多くは消極主義を取りて、大利ありと雖愼重周密の思索を盡して輕々しく動かず。得失既に明にして方針既に定まれば勇猛精進して決して其の意志を動搖せざる也。而して進退未だ決せざるに當りては、則ち己を虛ふして人に從ひ下問を恥とせず。蓋し心力極めて強固なる〻、我見に執せず私黨に偏倚せざる也。幼より書を讀て義理を求め、長じて尤も研究の精神に富み、科學的頭腦あり。前清時代邑庠生を以て直隸省優級師範學堂に入學し、修業二年餘にして本校選拔生として官費を以て日本に留學し、早稻田大學に入る。卒業後歸國して新疆に赴きて遊歷す。民國元年擧げられて直隸省議會副議長と爲り、二年選ばれて參議院議員と爲る。國會解散さるゝや、稻咽して時事を談せず、身を養つて德を修む。國會重ねて開くるに及び、再び召集に應じて、現に參議院議員の職に在り。

Mr. Wang Kuan-ming, another name Chen-sa. He was born in the prefecture of Ning-chin, Chi-li hsing in the year 1878. He is a man of energetic character inspired by a noble spirit, whose actions are governed by rectitude and the law of whose life is duty. He is just, upright, and honest in his words and in his work. Whatsoever being tempted, he never inclines to do anything until motive and delicate consideration shall determine him to take a final step and which once takes hold on him he shall never retreat from the cause. However, if needed, he never hesitates to call upon others even upon inferiors—for help in forming a decision. And a man of strong confidence as he is, he never persists his even view nor inclines to his own side. He showed a remarkable fondness for reading when very young. As he grew up, he had a fine scholarship and showed a marked ability for systematic investigations. At the closing period of Ching he entered with the senior normal school in Chi-li hsing. And for the next two years he remained there but the school finding in him remarkable element ordered him to go abroad to study in Japan. On his return to home after graduation of Waseda University he found himself in travelling and visiting at Hsin-chiang the first year of Republic, he was made vice-chairman of Chi-li hsing Provincial Assembly and the next year he was elected member of Parliament. When the parliament was dissolved, he retired himself from active life of politics but lived in quiet in taking care for his health and cultivating his virtue. No sooner the Parliament was reorganized than he was called out to take former chair there.

王錫泉 字卓甫 歲三十七

選舉地 直隸省

籍 貫 直隸省蠡縣

住 址 北京虎坊橋槩魁店

君爲人誠厚篤實。痛惡浮華。與人交。常硬直不阿。絕無世故之念。人告以過。亦欣然謝之。然居心仁厚。喜救人之難。絕不思報。自幼好讀。喜研究眞理。而不屑尋常摘句。以爲博取功名計。故其所讀多有用之書。及海內維新。決志求西學。醉心新書。尤喜政究教育學。及長。入直隸優級師範學堂肄業。後又負笈東渡。留學日本。入經緯學校師範科。畢業歸國。歷充直隸承德視學官。直隸學務處會計員直隸提學司科員。北洋法政專門學校庶務長。於直隸之文獻。勞苦顯著。旋被舉爲順直諮議局議員。民國二年正式國會成立。當選第一次衆議院議員。國會解散後。讀書靜養。不問時事。及國會重開。君復應召集。仍爲衆議院議員。

君人と爲り誠厚篤實にして浮華を痛惡し、人と交るに常に硬直阿らず、絕へて世故の念なし。人の告ぐるに過を以てすれば亦た欣然之を謝す。然り居心仁厚にして、喜んで人の難を救ひ、絕て報を思はず。幼より讀を好み、喜んで眞理を研究し、尋常章句を摘みて功名を博取するを屑しとせず、故に其の讀む所多くは有用の書なり。海內維新に及び志を決して西學を求め新書に心醉す。長ずるに及び直隸優級師範學校に入りて修養し、後ち又た笈を負ふて東海を渡り日本に留學す。經緯學校師範科に入り卒業して歸國す。直隸承德視學官、直隸學務處會計員、直隸提學司科員、北洋法政專門學校庶務長等の職に歷任し、旋て舉げられて順直諮議局議員と爲る。民國二年正式國會成立するや、衆議院議員に常選す。國會解散後、讀書靜養して時事を問はず。國會重ねて開かるゝに及び復た召集に應じて仍は衆議院議員と爲る。

Mr. Wang Hsi-chuan, another name Cho fu, thirty seven years old. Chi-li hsing. He is a man of candid and integrity, never likes flaunting and always open hearted to his friends. He does not act for the personal interest. If one tells him of his mistake he committed he thanks him and correct it immediately; he gives ready hand to the poor and misery, yet never seeks any sort of reward from anywhere. He surveyed various kinds of books, particularity phylosophical works drew more his attention. He did not think of making himself prominent by publication of his works. Decline of the old regime in China and introduction of western civilization gave him an inspiration that he must acquire fresh knowledge through the western publications. Later he entered the Chi-li Higher normal school where he graduated duly and went to Japan to pursue a further study. He completed courses on pedagogy in a Nornal school there. On his return home he was appointed to the positions of the Education Inspector, Treasuror of the Education Department, then the Director of Education, Secretary, the Pei-yang Law and Politics school, and finally appointed the member of Shun-chih Advisory Board. In the second year of the Republic he was sent out to Parliament from his district. When it was dissolved he returned home to rest and study but not to talk politics. In 1916 he was again elected the member of Parliament.

王汝圻　字甸伯　歲三十七

選舉地　江蘇省

籍　貫　江蘇省阜寧縣

住　址　北京棉花上四條二十三

君自幼聰穎絕倫。好讀深思。博而能約。及長。尤喜涉獵群籍。任意所之以為快。不屑規規然從事於科舉之業。故其讀書純以主觀判斷是非。而不為習俗之成見所局。然為人精明強幹、頭腦明晰。氣宇寬宏。夙求天下有用之學。尤喜讀治國濟民之書。專究其精。深明其義。遂貫笈東渡。留學日本八載。在早稻田大學大學部政治經濟科。畢業歸國。民國正式國會成立。君被選為眾議院議員。國會停止後。南下歸里。後于育英事業。歷充江蘇省立法政專門學校分校校長。江蘇省立第一商業學校校長。五年國會重行召集。君復應召北上入京。仍就眾議院議員職。

君幼より聰穎絕倫にして讀書を好み思索を喜ぶ。長ずるに及びて群籍を涉獵して意の往く所に任せて快を呼び、規矩に拘束されて科舉の業に從事するを屑しとせざるなり。故に其の讀書は主觀を以て是非を判斷して習俗の成見に局する所なし。然かも人と爲り精明強幹にして頭腦明晰、氣宇また寬宏なり。夙に天下有用の學を求め、尤も治國濟民の書を喜び、專ら其の精を究め深く其の義を明にす。遂に笈を負ふて日本に留學すこと八箇年、早稻田大學校政治經濟科を卒業して歸國したり。民國二年正式國會成立するや、君選ばれて眾議院議員と爲る。國會停止後南下して鄕里に歸り、育英事業に從つて江蘇省立法政專門學校分校長、江蘇省立第一商業學校長に歷任し、後進子弟の誘掖開導に力を盡したり。五年國會重ねて召集を行ふや、君復た之に應じて北上し、仍ほ再び眾議院議員の職に就きたり。

民國之精華　（傳記）　王汝圻先生

二十一

Mr. Wang Ju-tse, another name Tsao pai, a native of Fon-ning hsien, Chiang-su hsing, thirty seven years old. In his early age he was known with his brightness and sagacity; read well and found a pleasure in silent study. Growing older he read very widely and was hostile to formality which fetters his free will and action; for this reason he never sought to be an official. The sole aim of his study was in collecting new knowledge by which, he thought, he can only give right judgement, free from petty rules and conventions. His robust body, clear head, and magnanimity command his surroundings whether the friend or foe, yet, his ever increasing appetite for learning found him impossible to keep him home and consequently led him out of the country to Japan in hunt of the fresh knowledge. He studied economics in Waseda University for several years and graduated with honour. Returning China he found the Republican Government was established and the Parliament was formally installed. He was elected a member of the House which was dissolved soon. He returned home and devoted all his time in education of young men. He was made later the Director of the Branch school of the Chiang-su hsing Law and Politics school and then transferred to the President, the first commercial school of the district. Thus he devoted several years in education of young men. In the fifth year of the Republic Parliament again convened and he was called to Peking as a member of the Legislature.

王永錫 字眞存 歲三十六

選舉地 廣西省
籍貫 廣西省平樂縣
住址 北京延壽寺街平樂會館

君爲人頭腦明晰。意志堅強。能忍辱耐
勞。富于幹濟之才。然秉性仁厚。篤實
無欺。與人交。喜勸善規過。相其人必
能納諫者。始規正之。否則惟漸與疎
遠以示意。及其改悔。則愈以善律之。
人告以過。則直認不諱。自幼聰穎好
讀。弱冠即下筆千言。鄉里以神童目
之。然以不喜追隨俗尚。故學問雖極深
厚。而困于場屋。海內維新。君益研求
濟世之學。頗以天下興亡爲己任。第一
革命事竣。五大民族共和創奠民國二
年被選爲正式國會衆議院議員。把持
正論。提倡公議。翼贊建設之業。國會
解散後。南旋歸里。讀書自娛。及國會
重開。遂又入京。仍爲衆議院議員。

君人と爲り頭腦明晰にして意志堅強なり。能く辱を忍び
勞に耐へ、幹濟の才に富む。然り秉性仁厚にして篤實欺
かず、人と交るや善を勸め過を規すも、其の人必ず能く
諫を納るゝ者を相して之を正し、否らざれば唯だ漸く疎
遠となりて意を示し、其の悔改するに及びて善を以て
之を律す。幼より聰穎にして讀を好み、弱冠即ち筆を下
して千言立どころに成り、鄉里神童を以て之を目す。然
かも俗尚に追隨するを喜ばざるを以て、學問極めて深し
と雖、發用試驗に困したり。海內維新に及び濟世の學を
研究して天下の興亡を以て己が任と爲す。第一革命の事
竣つて五大民族共和の奠を剏むるや、民國二年選ばれて
正式國會の衆議院議員となり、正論を把持して公議を提
倡し、建設の大業を翼贊す。國會停止後、南旋して鄉里
に起臥し、讀書自ら娛む。國會重ねて開くるに及び、遂に
又た入京して衆議院議員たり。

Mr. Wang Yung-hsi, another name Chen-tsun, Ping-lo hsien, Kuanghsi province, thirty six years old. Clear head and strong will power are found remarkably in Mr. Wang Yung-hsi, whose patience and whose talent are very rarely seen any where. Yet, his kindness and honesty make one who meets him unable to forget him. He applauds good and corrects error of his friends, but doing so he always choses one, who is broad enough to accept his advice; as to one who seems impatient to listern to his wise words, he defers them to future occasion. When he was a boy the villagers admired him as a precocious child, who read well and wide and composed with ease a thousand word article. But he was not successful of civil service examination, because he was too independent to follow the custom and rule which had been observed in such a case. On the introduction of western knowledge, he resolved to study political science in view of serving the country in changed status. At the end of the first Revolution the five great races came to an agreement of establishing the Republic; consequently, in the second year of the Republic he was elected a member of the Lower House and has done a good deal in unifying the public opinions and solidifying the country. After the dissolution of the House returned South to enjoy himself with his books and quiet life, until he was re-elected in 1916.

王鴻龐　字亮齊　歲三十六

選舉地　廣東省
籍　貫　廣東省連山縣人
住　址　北京大外郎營連州會館

君天資聰穎にして悟性敏捷、尤も理想に富む。然かも人と爲り誠實にして欺がず。人と變るや善を勸め過を規すを喜ぶ。幼より讀書を好み、弱冠にして文采風韻己に儕輩に超出す。海内維新の後に及び、君慨然として舊を棄て新に從ひ、心を實學に傾注して新書を攻究す。夙に治國安民の志を抱き、長するに及び、廣東高等警察專門學校を卒業して後、地方の安寧を保全し人民の權利を保護するを以て自ら其の任と爲す。廣東の地素と革命首唱の地にして變亂相繼ぎ瘡痍屢々至る、君熱心地方の秩序を保つに努めたり。民國二年正式國會成立するや、選ばれて參議院議員と爲る。國會解散して後ち、南旋して鄉に歸り、地方公安の維持に盡瘁したり。五年共和克復して國會重ねて開かるゝに及び、遂に復た入京して仍ほ參議院議員と爲る。

君天資聰穎。悟性敏捷。尤富理想。然爲人誠實不欺。與人交。喜勸善規過。相其人必能納諫者。始規正之。否則惟漸與疏遠。以示意。及其改悔。則愈以善律之。人告以過。則直認不諱。自幼好讀。弱冠文采風貌。已超出儕輩。及海內維新後。君慨然棄舊從新。銳意西學。專心實學。夙抱治國安民之志。及長。入于廣東高等警察專門學校。畢業後。以保全地方之安寧。與保護人民之權利。爲其任。粵境素革命首倡之區。變亂數次。瘡痍屢至。君熱心力保地方秩序。勞苦顯著。民國二年正式國會成立。當選參議院議員。國會解散後。南旋歸里。盡力維持地方公安。及國會重開。遂復入京。仍爲參議院議員為。

民國之精華　（傳記）　王鴻龐先生

Mr. Wang Hung-pang, another name Liang chih, Chiung shan hsien, Kuangtung hsing, thirty six years old. He is quick to understand, keen-sighted and a man of idea; yet, he never betrays his friends and himself. He seems to find best pleasure to do good to others and to give a kind advice to his friends. He was distinguished in intelligence and task even he was a boy. On the introduction of western civilization he was one of few, who threw off the old and accepted the new instead; he took up the study of science and made up his mind to devote all his time for the people and the country. Graduating the Kwantung Police school he served to maintain peace of the locality and defend the right of people. Kwantung was sometimes a hot-bed of revolution and the successive revolt up-rooted order and place of the place. He was always insistent in keeping of the order among the populace. In the second year of the Republic. Parliament was formally organized and he was elected a member of the Upper House. On the dessolution of the House he returned South and devoted all his energy for the well-fase of the community. The restoration of the Republic called him to the Upper House of Parliament which was also restored in 1916.

二十三

王秉謙　字治安　歲三十六

選舉地　奉天省
籍　貫　奉天省錦西縣
住　址　北京西交民巷

君爲人倜爽有奇氣。於前清光緒三十二年。充本縣警務總局書記官。三十四年。經本縣咨送奉天全省地方自治研究所肄業。宣統元年。充奉天諮議局選舉調查員。得最優等獎牌。二年充本縣地方自治研究所所長。復被選爲城廂自治議事會議長。仍兼所長。及自治事務所辦事員。辛亥。武昌起義。即在本縣聯絡同志。就境內所有預警秘編義勇軍。以爲遼西義軍根據地。併奔走於大連烟臺等處。民國元年。充奉天臨時省議會書記員。二年。改任省議會秘書。併被選爲參議院奉天候補議員第一名。三年三月。省議會被解散。即停職。五年八月。國會恢復。參議院開幕。遂被補爲參議院議員。

君人と爲り倜爽にして奇氣あり。前清光緒三十二年錦西縣警務總局書記官となり、三十四年同縣より選ばれて奉天全省地方自治研究所に入りて修業す。宣統元年奉天諮議局選舉調查員となり、最優等獎牌を得たり。二年同縣地方自治研究所々長となり。復た選ばれて城廂自治議事會議長と爲り、所長及び自治事務所辦事員を兼ねたり。辛亥の歲、武昌に於て革命の事起るや、君は鄕里に在りて同志と聯絡し、縣內にある預備の巡警を集めて義勇軍を編成し、以て遼西義軍の根據地と爲したり。而して又た大連芝罘等の各地を奔走す。民國元年奉天臨時省議會書記となり、二年改めて省議會秘書に任じ、併せて參議院奉天補缺議員第一名に選ばれたり。三年三月省議會の解散と共に即ち停職す。五年八月國會恢復して、參議院開會す。君遂に補缺として召集され、現に督京して參議院議員の職に就きたり。

Mr. Wang Ping-chien, another name Chih-an. He was born in the prefecture of Chin-hsi, Feng-tien hsing. In the year of thirty two, in the Manchu Dynasty he was appointed secretary of the Metro-politan Police Board and thirtyfour, Chung chu, he was ordered to go to study the training institutions of provincial self-administrations at Fengtien. In the first year of I-tung he was made election-commissioner of Tzu-i-chu and was rewarded with the medal of the highest honour. In the following year he succeeded to the post of president of the training institutions of provincial self-administrations in this prefecture besides being appointed chairman Cheng-hsiang self-administration assembly and staff of office of the assembly. On the outbreak of the revolutions at Wu chang in the year of Tsu-shih, he hurried back to his native place and acting in concert with those fellow enthusiasts, collected the reserved soldiers in the prefecture in forming volunteer army. Thus he made it the basis of operation for Liao-hsi revolutionary army, while in the mean time he buried himself in running about all directions between Tai lien and Chie fu. In the first year of Republic he was made secretary of Fengtien temporal assembly and in the following he was appointed private secretary of it besides being elected the first Fengtien member of parliament. In the third year, march, the parliament was dissolved and he also resigned the office. However, in the fifth year, august, on the reorganization of parliament he has been called out to fill the vacancy of a chair.

王雙岐　字子邠　歲三十六

選舉地　直隸省
籍　貫　直隸北冀縣
住　址　北京六部口東雙栅欄五號

君秉性溫厚。然爲人顚直不阿。疾惡如仇。遇不平。輙當面痛斥其人。人以過相詰。恆自陳不稍隱諱。以前清癸卯科舉人屢試均落。時方海內維新。遂棄舊業。新考求西學。卒以自費留學日本。畢業于早稻田大學法政經濟科。歸國後。受學部試。授七品小京官。歷充直隸自治研究所長警務公所科員。直隸私立法政學堂教員。直隸諮議局籌備處司選員。民國成立後。曾充山東膠濟鐵路游擊隊長。內國公債局諮議員。中國銀行招股處經理員。直隸省議會議員。國會成立。被選爲衆議院議員。國會解散後。遇事持消極主義。絕無表見。及國會復活。遂復爲衆議院議員。

君秉性溫厚。然れども人と爲り頗る直阿らず。惡を疾む仇の如し。不平に遇へば輙ち面の當り其の人を痛斥す。人の過を以て相詰れば、恆に自ら陳して少しくも隱諱せず。前清癸卯科の累人を屢々試みて均しく落つ。時方に海內維新、遂に舊政を棄てて、新に西學を考求す。卒に自費を以て日本に留學し、學部の試を受け、七品小京官の業を授けらる。

直隸自治研究所長、警務公所科員、直隸私立法政學敎員、直隸諮議局籌備處司選員に歷充す。民國成立後、曾て山東膠濟鐵路游擊隊長、內國公債諮議員、中國銀行招股處經理員、直隸省議會議員に充てらる。國會成立後、選ばれて衆議院議員と爲る。國會解散後、事に遇ひて消極主義を持し、絕えて表見すること無し。國會復活するに及び。遂に復た衆議院議員たり。

民國之精華　（傳記）　王雙岐先生

Mr. Wang Shuans-chi, another name Tsu-Fen. He was born in the Prefecture of Poe-i Chi-li hsing in the year 1881. A man of amiable disposition as he is, he flattes no one. He is a man of upright and integrity, inspired by a sense of abhorrence of crime. So if he insulted, he never forget to reprove him to the face. However he is in turn, rebuked, he always ready to apologize for it. But the restoration which now broke in upon the country, effected him complete revolution in his mind. He turned his attention seriously to the study of western learning. He felt that if it was to be thorough, should be saught for in Japan. He entered Waseda University in Tokyo with his own expence and and completed the course of economics and politics. On his return to home, he passed the examination of Hsiaopu and was conferen the seventh grade of Shan-king kuan rank. He was appointed one after another to those offices of President of Chi-li traiming instituton of Proniacial self administration, staff of Metoropolitau Police Bureau, Professor of Chi-li private institution of Law and Politics, and commissioner of Chi-li Tsan chu. When Republic was estiblished he was appointed, successionaly to the post of those offices commander of Shangtung Miao chai flying column, commissioner of home loan, staff of Che chu ching of China Bank and member Chi li Provincial Assembly. Later on the organization of National Assembly he was elected member of Parliamen'. However its dissolvement caused him to take negative attitude to politics. He has been called out again to fill his chair in parsliament.

王烈　字少南　歲三十五

選舉地　浙江省

籍　貫　浙江省蘭谿縣人

住　址　北京前門外東大市蘇家坡金華會館

君秉性剛直。不隨俗浮沈。然居心仁
厚。雖仇敵。亦不忍窘迫之。與人交。喜
相責以善。人告以過。輒大喜。蓋謂其
能直言不欺。不以流俗相待也。以前清
拔貢。朝考列一等。旋留學日本。卒業
于法政大學。得法學士。歸國後。嘗上
書清政府。力言實行立憲及其他各項
新政。以救危亡之道。著有法家叢編。
世界大勢。中國現勢。政治革命論。軍
事淮覽。兵家輯要等書。民國元年。曾
充參謀部軍事秘書。二年當選爲衆議
院議員。國會解散。復歸里從事著述。
國會復活。仍爲衆議院議員。

君や賦性剛直、俗に隨つて浮沈せず。然り居心仁厚にし
て仇敵と雖亦窘迫に忍びず。然り人と交るや相責ひるに
善を以てし、人の告ぐるに過を以てすれば輒ち大に喜ぶ。
蓋し其の能く直言して欺かず、流俗を以て相待たざる所
以なり。前清時代、貢生を以て朝考一等に列し、旋て日本
に留學して法政大學校を卒業したり。歸國後嘗て清政府
に上書して立憲宣布並に其の他の新政を條陳す。法家叢
編、世界大勢、中國現勢、政治革命論、軍事淮覽、兵家
輯要等の書を著して時務を開導し時難を痛弁す。民國元
年參謀部軍事秘書に充任し、二年選ばれて衆議院議員と
爲る。國會解散さるゝに追び、復た鄉里に歸省し、筆硯
の塵を播つて悠々著述に從事す。既にして國會重ねて復
活さるゝや、再び召集に應じて北京に抵り、現に衆議院
議員として重ねて議政壇上の人となれり。

Mr. Wang-lieh, another name Hsiao-nah. He was born in the prefecture of Lan-chi, Che-chiang hsing in the year eighteen. He is the man of strong character governed by the principle. He puts his conscience into his work, into his words, into his every action and never makes his way compromisely through the world. He is generous and merciful to his opponent. He never condemns others but esteem, all such things as friends that desire to file off his betters and help him out of prejudice. During the period of Chin he was appointed a fellow and promoted to the rank of Chao lao. Then he went abroad to study in Japan and graduated the University of Law and Police. On his return to home, he memorialized Chin government, begging that a constitions should be promulgated and that new administration should be adapted. He published several works such as "The general meaning of law," "The general trend of the world," "The present condition of China," "Political revolution," "Review of military affairs," and "Military digestions" etc. The effect of these works exercised no slight weight in developing sentiment and enlightening knowledge of his age. In the first year of Republic, he was made private secretary of the military staff office and in the following year he was elected member of parliament. On the dissolvement of parliament, he found himself in his native place spending mostly his time in writing. However the parliament was reorganized, he has been called out and hold his former chair.

二十六

王靖方　字伊文　歲三十五

選舉地　河南省
籍貫　河南省沁陽縣清化鎮
住址　北京東城無量大人胡同

君賦性仁厚，自幼以孝行見知于鄉里。為人精明強幹。洞察事理。少年讀書。慕古任俠之所為。其為詩文。多激昂悲狀之詞。能使人感發興奮。稍長。喜為義舉。見人不平。常奮不顧身。欲捨身為之報復。唯一念及身體髮膚之訓。則又自儆其不孝。遂專從事於周濟貧乏。不復為從井救人之舉。人有困於貧者。常典鬻所有助之。不自為緩急之計以是鄉里皆奉若神仙。里中偶有爭報。常求取決於君。君出一言。無不立即解釋。戊戌政變後。君慨然以挽救危亡為志。遂以自費東渡。入東京明治大學。畢業後。歷充上海民呼民吁報駐東京通信員。上海北京民立報記者。正式國會成立。被選為參議院議員。國會解散時。歸里獨居。無所表見。及國會復活。始入京。仍為參議院議員。

君賦性仁厚にして幼より孝行を以て鄉里に知らる。人と為り精明強幹にして事理を洞察す。少年書を讀みて古へ任俠の所為を慕ひ、其の詩文は慷慨激越の詞多し。稍や長じて義舉を喜び、人の不平を見れば常に身を棄てゝ之が為に報復を欲す。唯だ一たび身體髮膚の訓を念ふに至り、則ち自ら其の不孝を咎め、遂に專ら貧家を周濟するの事に從ふ。人の貧に困する者あれば所有を典賣して之を助く。鄉黨省な君に信服して偶ま紛爭あれば決を君に求め、君一言を出せば直ちに解決す。戊戌政變後慨然として危亡を挽救するを志とし、遂に自費を以て東渡し、東京明治大學に學び、畢業後、上海民呼民吁報東京通信員、北京民立報記者に歷充す。正式國會成立の際補缺して參議院議員と為る。國會解散されて歸省蟄居す。國會復活に及び再び北京に入りて參議院議員と為る。

民國之精華　（傳記）　王靖方先生

二七七

Mr. Wang Ching-fang, another name I-wen. He was born in the prefecture of Hsin-yang, Ho nan hsing in the year 1882. He is a man inspired by a manly spirit. He exhibited his character in his youth, in its most dutiful aspects to his parents. He had such a clear head strong insight as to penetrate the point. In his youth, as he was charmed by reading ancient chivalry his poem and writing were always pitched up with phrases of grievance and indignant. All heroic deeds fascinated him. It had effect of causeing him to desire to plunge at the risk of his life wreak vengence upon for others. But the new light, which once broke in upon him, determined him to devote his entire energies to the completion of filial duties in keeping his body received from his parent uninjured and to the releef work for the poor, he would even help with his own money those who pressed for. Thus he commanded the affection and service of others by his uniform heartiness and sympathy. The Political disorder of Mou hsu had taken place, he realiyed himself, it was his duty to act in an emergency of the country and to deliver from its danger. So it determined him to devote his time to study in Japan. He entered Meiji University with his own expense. On his completion of course in the university he was appointed Tokyo reportor of the Shanghai nichiao besides being staff of Peking democratic news. The Parliament was organized and he was elected. However on its dissolvement he retired into private life in his native place. Happily for him, he has found himself again in a chair of Parliament as it was reorganized.

王文璞　字晦膻　歲三十五

選舉地　黑龍江省

籍貫　黑龍江省海倫縣

住址　北京順治門內兵部窪中街門牌卅一號

君為人頭腦明晰，意志堅強，能忍辱耐勞。於前清光緒三十二年，在北洋法政學堂肄業。為黑龍江第一次官費生，追畢業後，充諮議局選舉司選員，兼自治研究所所長。選舉事竣，又歷充巡防陸軍執法處書記等官。辛亥武昌起義，曾糾合同盟會同人，謀響應。未幾，和議告成，遂組織共和進行會，被舉為幹事部部長，又以同盟會改組國民黨，被舉為綏化分部部長，旋被舉為眾議院議員。緣愛護民權，深惡於本省長官。或迫而出止，或陷於貔狃，至丙辰反對帝制，為滬上議員團之一，及國會復活，遂來京，復為眾議院議員。

君頭腦明晰、意思堅固、能く辱勞を忍ぶ。前清光緒三十二年北洋法政學堂に修業し、黑龍江第一回の官費生と為る。畢業後乃ち諮議局選舉司選員に充てられ、自治研究所々長を兼ね。選舉事竣りて後、又た巡防陸軍執法處書記等の官に歷充す。辛亥の歲、武昌義を起すや、同盟會同人を糾合して響應を謀る。未だ幾くならずして和議其の成を告ぐ、共和進行會を組織し、幹事部々長に舉げらる。又た同盟會が國民黨に改組さるゝや、舉げられて綏化分部々長と為る。旋て選ばれて眾議院議員と為る。深く本省長官の憎惡する所となり、或は迫つて出で或は貔狃に陷る。丙辰の歲、帝制反對の風潮勃發するや、上海議員團の一員と為りて共和の恢復に運動盡瘁す。而して其の國會復活さるゝや、遂に北京に抵り、復た眾議院議員と為りたり。

Mr. Wang Wen-po, another name Hui-hsuan. He was born in the prefecture of Hei-lung chien in the year eighteen. He is a man of strong will and of clear head even of great fortitude. In the thirty-second year of Kuang chu he entered the Pe chin law and political college. As a result he was made, at their first trial, paid student by the Hei-lung chiang provincial government. On his graduation he was appointed election-commissioner in Jzu-i chu besides being president of training institution of provincial self-administration. Then he accepted the office of secretary of the standing military penal court. No sooner the outbreak of Revolution took place at Wu chang in the year Jsu shih than he called together those of the same mind among partizan society and responded to the cause. In the meantime the peace was concluded and subsequently an associations for carrying out a democratic government was organized to which he was made general secretary. And the amalgamations between his partizan society and the national party was anounced and he was made its leader. Then he was elected member of parliament and with impellent zeal he urged his view of democracy. However he was so opposed perhaps even hated and detested by the president of the government. On the growth of Anti-Imperialistic tendency in the year of Ping chen, he jointed member's society at Shanghai and devoted all his energies to the re-establishment of the democratic government. Subsequently the parliament was re-organized and he has been made member of it.

王文芹　字采章　歲三十五

選舉地　直隸省
籍　貫　直隸省清苑縣
住　址　北京絨線胡同成公府夾道三號

君天性沈靜謹默、富有實業思想。居恒以爲中國歷史流傳、自三代以還、素以農立國。迄今海禁大開列國莫不以謀農工商業之發達、爲富强之要素。倘中國能舉國一心、從事於重農主義、以求發展工商事業。潛滋暗長、則百年之後。何難與美洲合衆國亞駕齊驅、以故研究農商諸學。不遺餘力。生平熱心致育。聆君之議論風采。發聲振瞶。能發人深省。青年即潛心學理。汎濫古今。與君交游者。莫不深相稱許。以爲今世之有心人也。君以幾輔大學生出身。歷充直隸總商會協理。總農會協理。及湖北陝西等省敎育科長。於民國二年正式國會成立。被選爲參議院議員

民國之精華　（傳記）王文芹先生

君天性沈靜謹默にして實業の思想に富み空言空論の人にあらず。少より農商諸學を研究して餘力を遺さず。造詣頗る深きものあり。生平銳意地方敎育の振興を圖り、夙に世界の大勢に鑑み、開國以來の重農主義に併行して商工業の發展を期待す。議論着實にして豊富、能く豐を發し肯を開き、時人をして省察せしむるに足るものあり。幾輔大學校出身の秀才を以て、直隸總商會協理又は總理、同總農會協理等に推され、湖北陝西等各省の敎育科長に歷任したる事あり。民國二年正式國會議員選擧に際し參議院議員に當選したり。國會解散さるいや、君依然として農事の改良、商工の振興に靈瘁して國利民福の增進を念とす。飢にして國會重ねて開かるいに及び、再乃ち召集に應じて院に到り、仍は參議院議員の職に復す。

Mr. Wang Wen-chin, aged thirty five, is a native of Chin-yuan hsien, Chi-li hsing. He is a gentleman of taciturn temperament, being full of practical ability. He is far from being a dreamer. He grudges no efforts to complete his education: He put his entire energy to the building up of the education of the people. Perceiving the trend of the time, he encouraged the development of commerce and industry along with the agricultural efforts, which had been the policy of the country. His argument being solid and sound, it went far in arousing the people to the necessity of the time. He was elected the chief of the agricultural association as well as the director of the Chilin Chamber of Commerce. He was also appointed the educational head of Hu-pei and Shan-hsi. In the second year of the Republic, he was elected as a member of the Senate. With the collapse of the Parliament, he interested himself as before in the improvement of agriculture, the furtherance of commerce and industry as well as that of the national wellbeing. When the Parliament was opened for the second time, he resumed his senatorial function.

王試功　字嘯雲　歲三十四

選舉地　直隸省

籍　貫　直隸省恒來縣

住　址　北京象坊橋衆議院西寄

君爲人忠厚朴實。生平無僞言。弱冠
讀書。即抱大志。於前清光緒三十三年
卒業於直隸高等學校。隨升入北洋大
學。畢業後。被聘爲朝陽中學敎員。鐵
道國有問題起。即辭職。奔走南北運動
革命。民國元年。被舉爲直隸臨時省議
會議員。二年復被舉爲參議院議員。窺
袁氏有帝制自爲意。與同志力倡反對。
政變後。被聘爲宣化中學校敎授。滇省
護國軍起。即棄職赴滬。組織議員團。
通電全國力阻衰逆借欵。時兩院議員
在滬者僅卅餘人。復設立議員通訊處。
充當幹事。通告同人在滬集會。袁氏旣
死。國會重開。遂來京。仍就參議院議
員之職。

君人と爲り忠厚にして朴實、生平僞言無し。弱冠にして
書を讀み、即ち大志を抱く。前清光緒三十三年直隸高等學
校を卒業して北洋大學に入る、畢業後、聘せられて朝陽中
學校敎員と爲る。鐵道國有問題の風潮起るや、即ち職を
辭して南北に奔走して革命の事に從ふ。民國元年舉げら
れて直隸臨時省議會議員と爲り、二年復た選ばれて參議
院議員と爲る。袁世凱が帝制を志すや、君即ち同志と力
を併せて反對す。政變後、聘せられて宣化中學校敎授と
爲る。雲南護國軍起るや即ち職を棄てゝ上海に赴きて議
員團を組織し、全國に通電して帝制を力阻す。袁世凱借
欵の時、兩院議員の上海に在る者僅に三十餘人なりし。
復た議員通訊處を設け、其の幹事の職に當り、同人に通
告して上海に集會す。袁世凱旣に死して國會重ねて召集
さるゝや、遂に北京に入り、爾來重ねて參議院議員の職
に就きたり。

Mr. Wang Shih-kung, another name Hsiao yun. He was born in the prefecture of Heng-lai Chi-li hsing in the year 1883. He is of character inspired by patriotic spirit. He is just, upright and integrity in his words and in his work. A great fondness for reading when very young fostered in him an ambition. In the thirtythird year of Kuang chu, he graduated Chi-li higher school and entered Pe chin university. After the completion of the course he was engaged as teacher at the Chan yang Middle school. The rise of the question of nationalising the railways had the effect of causing him to turn his attentions seriously to politics to the cause of revolutions. As a result, he resigned his post and buried himself in running about in all directions in the country. In the first year of Republic, he was made member of Chi li temporary provincial assembly and in the following year he gained a chair in parliament. Co-operating with those of the same mind he strongly opposed Yuan-shih-kai who now turned his attentions toward the organizations of Imperialistic government. However the political disorder had taken place, he was again engaged as teacher of Middle school. No sooner the rise of "Yuu-nan guardian-army" was reported than he resigned his post and went to Shanghai. He organized member's society and thus communicated to away the people in all directions of the country as to fostering absolute opposition to the organization of Imperialistic government. However when the contraction of debt was proposed by Yuanshi-kai, members of both parliament at Shanghai were number but little more than thirty. So he took active part in organizing member's communications bureau to which he was made secretary. Thus he called together at Shanghai those of devoting themselves to the same cause. By the death of Yuanshi-hai the Parliament was re-organized and he has been duly elected member of it.

王鴻賓 字寅谷 歳三十三

選擧地　陝西省
籍　貫　陝西省臨潼縣
住　址　北京順治門外錢老鸛廟

君賦性慷慨尚義。見人患難。常不惜身命救之。然爲人精明强幹。雖剛直而未嘗以暴躁債事。於前清光緒末年。留學京師。辛亥各省起義。歸陝襄助民軍。民國元年。被選爲衆議院議員。國會解散後。從事社會教育。日與志士豪俠相往來。帝制發生。陝西民黨郭沈等首倡義擧。與君往復運籌。部置乃定。君始隻身赴滬上。與東南起義諸君子。互相聯絡。籍通聲氣。以期南北一致之進行。及共和重立國會復活。遂由滬來京。仍就參議員之職。

民國之精華　（傳記）　王鴻賓先生

君慷慨義を尚ぶ。人の患難を見るや、常に身を捨つるを惜まずして之を救ふ。然れども人と爲り精明强幹にして、剛直と雖も。未た嘗て暴躁を以て事を債らず。前清光緒末年、北京に留學す。辛亥の歳各省義を起す、君陝西に歸りて民軍を襄助す。民國元年、選ばれて衆議院議員と爲る。國會解散後、社會教育に從事し。日に同志の豪俠と相往復す。帝制發生するや、陝西民黨郭沈等を首として義擧を唱へ、君と往復運籌し、部累乃ち定る。君始めて隻身上海に赴きて東西起義諸君子と互に聯絡して氣脈を通し、以て南北一致の進行を期す。共和復活して國會再開するに及び、遂に上海より上京し、仍は衆議院議員の職に就く。

Mr. Wang Hung-pin, another name Yin-ku. He was born in the prefecture of Lin tung, Shan hsing in the year 1884. He is a man inspired by the most heroic spirit and values fidelity more than anything. He exhibits his character in enemy example of his heroic conduct with uniform heartiness and sympathy for others. He was of clear head of strong insight and of strict profity as he was, his conduct always anticipated the sound principle. At the closing year of Kuang chu, he went to study in Peking. No sooner the revolutions broke out among states than he returned to Hsia-hsi and responded to the cause. In the first year of Republic, he was elected member of Parliament. However on its dissolvement it caused him to engage in social educations work, while communicated with those eminent men in the same mind. On the outgrowth of tendency toward Imperialistic government, he opposed to in organizing anti-Imperialistic party, with Kuo-po and others of Hsia-hsi democratic as the sole wielders of influence. Having then firmly filed up their plan of operation he went alone to Shanghai and communicated and connected with those fellow enthusiasts from the all parts of the county and expected to advance keeping south and north in close touch all the while. When democracy was firmly guarded and the Parliament was reorganized, he comming up from Shanghai succeeded to hold his former chair in parliament.

選舉地　廣西省
籍貫　廣西省桂林縣
住址　北京西城闢才胡同二條三號

王乃昌　字季文　歲三十二

君自幼過異凡流。年十六便下筆萬言。
但矢志不應童子試。家雖足自給。而以
仰給父兄為恥。入工藝廠。學習織布。而
以圖自食其力。不貽父兄累。旋以迫於
父命。一應童試。為汪貽書文字所賞識
拔之前茅。送高等學堂肄業。改旋學師
範。卒業後。為師範中學各教師。旋以
提倡革命。為偵者報告當局。幾陷非
命。辛亥武昌起義。君倡捐義餉。為義
師援旋當選為臨時省議會議員。國會
選舉。當選為衆議院議員。迨及袁氏非
法解散國會。倡辦中華雜誌。攻擊袁氏
之不法行動嗣見袁氏有意恢復帝制。
遂與同志等。分途運動反對。乙卯冬。
在香港為選者所獲。因此入獄。興訟
二月始出。廣西獨立。始終與聞其事。
旋赴海上。爭約法與國會之恢復。及
國會召集。遂入京。仍為衆議院議員。

君幼より非凡、年僅に十六、筆下萬言を草す。但だ志を
失つて童子の試に應せず。自ら給するに足らずと雖、給を
父兄に仰ぐを恥とし、工藝廠に入りて織布を學習し、獨
立して父兄の累を免るゝとす。旋て父命に迫られて童試に應
じ、高等學堂に送られて修業す。旋て改めて師範學校に
學び、卒業後出でゝ師範中學各校教師と爲る。次で革命
提倡の故を以て探偵の爲に殆んど非命に陷る。辛亥武昌
義を起すや、君乃ち義餉を主張して義師の援を爲す。旋

て臨時省議會議員に當選し、復た衆議院議員に當選す。
袁世凱が國會を解散するや、去つて中華雜誌を創辦して
其の不法行動を攻擊す。乙卯の冬、香港に於て選者の爲に獲
らて入獄し、訴訟二ヶ月始めて出づ。廣西獨立の擧に
干預し、旋て上海に赴きて、約法と國會恢復の事を爭ひ、
途に北京に入りて再び衆議院議員と爲る。

Mr. Wang Nai-chang, another name Chi wen. He was born in the prefecture of Kuei-lin, Kuang-hsi hsing in the year 1885. He was an extraordinary genious even in his boyhood. He showed such a remarkable talent for writing when only sixteen years old as he composed a long prose at once as much natural as it was in his element. He had been designed by his parents for preparing child's examinations, but ambitions new fostered upon him, determined him to devote his energics while supporting himself, in learning the arts of fablic in the industrial building. Thus he struggled along by himself as he thought it shame to live in parents. However could not but obey his father. He passd the examinations and was accepted to study in the Higher school and later in the Normal school. After his graduation, he was engaged as teacher of both Normal and Middle school. In the course of the life there he was entrapted by a detective on suspicion of being respound to the cause of revolution. However, happily for him, he barely escaped with his life. On the outbreak of Revolution at Wuchang in the year of Tsu-shih he associated with them in proceeding of those equipment to their needs. In the meanwhile he was made member of provincial assembly and later elected member of parliament. When the parliament was dissolved by Yuanshi-kai, he attacked him his illegal act through the Chung hua magazine which he established on the occasion. The growth of tendency toward the organization of Imperialistic government arosed among them strong opposition. However, in winter Chi year, he was arrested by and put into prison. Happily for him he was released after two months, appeal to court. He took active part to undertaking of independence in Kuang-hsi and then he went to Shanghai. He urged his view on promulgations of constitution and re-establishment of parliament. He has been elected member of parliament.

王 槙　字曉秋　歲三十二

選舉地　雲南省

籍　貫　雲南省昆明縣

住　址　北京珠巢街雲南會館

君爲人精明強幹。富於忍耐。然情性圓
活。不固執己私。識力均極高。而又虛
心好問。能受盡言。于前淸。在雲南法
政學校。以最優等畢業。授內閣中書。
歷充雲南自治研究所。法政學校各教
員。民國成立。曾被委任辦理全省複選
選舉。暨地方自治等事。旋復代理雲南
警備隊總司令部執法處處長。並先後
署理雲南江川永北宣威大關等縣知
事。正式國會成立。被選爲衆議院議
員。國會解散後。歸里。歷充將軍行署
及巡按使公署秘書。及國會復活。遂來
京。仍爲衆議院議員。

民國之精華　（傳記）　王槙先生

君人と爲り精明強幹にして忍耐に富む。然り情性圓滿に
して我意を固執せず、識力均しく高きも又た虛心以て問
を好み能く盡言を聞く、前淸時代雲南法政學校に學びて
最優等を以て卒業し、內閣中書を授けられ、雲南自治研
究所、法政學校等の各教員に歷充したり。第一革命の事
就つて民國の樹立を見るや、全省複選選舉辦理及び地方
自治等の事宜を委任され、旋で復た雲南警備隊總司令部
執法處々長代理となり、並びに前後して雲南江川永北宣
威大關等の各縣知事に任せられたり。民國二年正式國會
の成立に際し君も亦た選ばれて衆議院議員と爲る。其の
後國會解散さるゝに迫び、君乃ち故山に歸りて雲南將軍
行署及び巡按使公署の秘書に歷充したり。本年重ねて國
會復活するに及び、召集に應じて再び晋京し、現に復た
衆議院議員として國政を議しつゝあり。

三十三

Mr. Wang Chen, another name Hsiao Chin, aged thirty two, is a native of YunNan.　He
is a man of magnanimous spirit and has extraordinary perseveranc'.　He is sociable and ready to listen
one's advice although he has his own opinion upon everything.　During the reign of Chin Dynasty, he
was appointed to Secretary after his graduation with honour from Yun Nan Law College, and subsequently to the headmaster of several schools.　After the establishment of the Republic, he was appointed to
the Committees of General Election and the Governers of Yun Nan, Chian Chuan, Yenpe, Hsen Wei,
and Tai Ruan.　In the 2nd year of the Republic, he was elected to a member of House of Commons.
After the dissolution of the Parliament, he returned to his province where he was appointed to the
Secretaries of Governor-General as well as the Chief of the Administration Office.　He is now a member
efthe House of Commons again.

王有蘭 字孟廸 歳三十一

選舉地　江西省
籍　貫　江西省興國縣
住　址　北京燈市口億昌飯店

君自幼好學深思。稚年讀書。即喜推求精義。不厭數問。塾師常爲所窘。益契重之。弱冠即有文名。詩文策論。皆有名家風味。及長。尤廣覽羣書。並喜涉獵周秦諸子。然不屑從事舉業。及海內維新。尤奮志新學。不以舊見自拘。遂東渡留學日本中央大學法律本科。辛亥革命時。充江西都督府參議官。旋派赴南京。充組織臨時政府江西代表兼臨時參議院議員。民國元年。充江西內務司長。兼交通司長。民國二年。當選衆議員。民國三年。赴歐洲各國考察政治。民國四年。返國。運動第三次革命。民國五年。革命軍政府成立。充軍務院軍事參議。雲南護國第二軍參議兼嶺南道尹。迄衆議院恢復。仍充議員。

日本中央大學法律本科出身の秀才なり。辛亥革命の時、江西都督府參議に任じ、旋て臨時政府組織江西代表として南京に赴き、後ち臨時參議院議員となる民國元年江西內務司長に任じ、江西交通司長を兼ね、本省の政治を刷新して功あり。民國二年正式國會議員選擧に際しては衆議院議員に當選して北上し議政壇上の闘士として名あり。國會解散さるゝや、君は蹶然國を去つて泰西に航し、歐洲列國各地を歷游して政治を視察して大に得る所あり。民國四年歸國して、力を第三革命に致す。五年革命軍政府成立するや、軍務院軍務參議となり。雲南護國第二軍參議となり、嶺南道道尹を兼ね。既にして共和政復活の目的を達し、國會重ねて召集せらるゝに及び、君踴躍して北京に抵り、現に仍は衆議院議員たり。

Mr. Wang Yu-lan, otherwise known as Weng-ti, age thirty one, is a native of Hsing-kuo hsien, Chiang-hsi-hsing. He is one of the foremost graduates of the Chuo university of Japan. In 1911 when the revolution broke out, he was appointed an adviser to the governor general of Chiang-hsin province. In the formation of the emergeny cabinet, he went to Nan-king representing his own province, and was elected a member of the Senate. In the first year of the Republic, he was appointed the head of the Home Bureau, that of the Communication Bureau, and succeeded in improving the provincial administration. In the second year of the Republic when the Parliament was opened, he was returned for the House of Commons with an overwhelming majority, and went up to Peking when his ability as the member of the legislative body became well known. However with the dissolution of the Parliament, he travelled through European countries when through his keen observation, he was greatly benefitted. On returning to his home, he was interested in the third revolution. When the military force of the revolutionists proved to be a success, he was the efficient member of the military staff. At the final restoration of the Republic, the Parliament was summoned when he hastened to Peking, and was returned for the House of Commons, the position he holds in the present moment.

選舉地　河南省

籍　貫　河南省武陟縣

住　址　北京達智橋嵩雲草堂

君自幼有大志。刻苦求學。尤喜王陽明
致良知知行合一之旨。在蒙養中學校
肄業。由河南學憲拔升。本省高等學校
預科畢業。考入直隷法律專門學校肄
業。宣統三年畢業。考取最優等第一
名適武昌起義。地方多事。閭閻不靖。
回籍由縣知事照會。辦理籌防總局事
宜。民國元年。被舉爲臨時省議會議
員。期滿閉會。河南都督。委辦全省籌
備選舉事宜。民國二年被舉爲衆議院
議員。國會解散後。回籍。從事實業。與
豫北道尹。本邑知事。籌資創辦工藝
廠。頗著成効。甲寅夏。丁內艱。乙卯冬
葬母後。復從事太行開探煤礦事業。丙
辰帝制將成。西南起義後。赴滬反對
帝制。維持共和。黎氏繼任後。約法國
會恢復。問題尚未解決。滬議員籍以督
促兩大問題之易于解決。嗣兩問題繼
續解決。復任衆議院議員。

君幼より大志あり、刻苦して學を求め尤も王陽明の知行
合一の主旨を喜ぶ。蒙養中學校に在りて修業し、河南當
局より抜擢されて同省高等學校預科に入りて卒業し、直
隷法律專門學校に入りて宣統三年優等を以て卒業す。適
ま武昌義を起して地方靖からず。歸省して籌防總局事務
を處理す。民國元年臨時省議會議員に舉げらる。閉會後、
河南都督より全省選舉準備事務を委託さる。民國二年正
式事會成立に際し、衆議院議員に當選す。國會解散後歸
郷して實業に從事し、河南北方道尹及び郷里の縣知事と
資を籌りて工藝廠を創立經營して頗る成功あり。甲寅の
夏喪に遭ひて其の冬母を葬りて後ち、復た太行炭鑛開堀
事業に從事す。帝制問題發生して西南地方義を起して後
ち、上海に赴きて同志と共に帝制に反對し、黎氏の大總
統繼後、約法と國會の復活を絶叫し、目的既に達するや、
遂に北上して衆議院議員と爲る。

民國之精華　（傳記）王廷弼先生

Mr. Wang Ting-pi, otherwise called Chang Chen, a native of Wu Chih, Ho Nan, 30 years old.
He was a very ambitions young man supported himself through his study, and one of adminers of
Wan yang-ming. He pursued the middle school courses at the Meng Yang, from which he was chosen
to be a stndent of the Preparatory course, the Higher School of the same prefecture. Graduating the
course he entered the Chi Li Law school and completed his study there with the honor in the third
year of Hsuantung, at that time an uprising occurred in Wu Chang, causing much disquietude. Returning home he directed the business of the General vigilance office. In the first year of the Republic he
was appointed a member of the Prefectural Congress, an which adjoinment he was invited by Governor-
General of Ho Nan to over-see the preparation of the prefectural election. In the second year Parliament was formally proclaimed to which he was sent out from his district. When it was dissolved he
went home to pursue industrial business. He with the assistance of Governor-General of Ho Nan ang and
Governor of his prefecture established successfully an industrial factory which turned out a great profit.
After a short interval he began the mining of coal at Tai Han. The problem of restoration of Imperial
Regime disturbed the country widely and deeply and the South western provinces revolted against the intended design. He went to Shanghai together the Anti-Imperial party in view of opposing execution of
the scheme. Since the inauguration of the present president he insisted to revive the Parliament formally created according to the provisional constitution. His desire was duly satisfied and now is a
member of the Lower House.

王恩博 字君雅

選舉地 湖南省

籍貫 湖南省慈利縣

住址 北京北柳巷北極庵五

君賦性慷慨好義。見人不平。常忿忿不自禁。過於自受。然天資豪放氣宇潤大。自幼有大志。少年好爲文。尤喜舊武。及長。出而游歷四方。行旅中。恆書豪傑之士。惟其處世接物。過於夾直。誠一時祇求有益於時事者。莫不咄張爲之初交君者。常怏敬憚之。壯年貟笈東渡。入日本大學法科畢業。歸國後。曾任前清郵傳部小京官。辛亥武昌起義。血鐘一鳴。烽火連天。君蹶然奮起赴難。歷充戰時總司令部秘書。北方招撫使秘書。大局已定。正式國會成立。被選爲衆議院議員。國會解散後。南旋歸里。橫劍說經。及共和克復。國會再開。遂蹻躍應名集。重入北京。仍復衆議院議員職。

君賦性慷慨義を好み人の不平を見て常に己が事の如く忿々として自ら禁せず。然かも天資豪放にして氣宇潤大なり。幼より大志あり、少年好んで文を作り尤も喜んで武を奮ふ。長じて四方に游歷し、行旅常に書劍之に隨ひ、悲歌慷慨實に一時豪傑の士に隨ひ。其の世に處し物に接するや夾直に過ぎ、君と初めて交はる者常に之を憚る。壯年笈を負ふて東海を渡り、新銳の強隣に游びて日本大學校法科を卒業して歸國す。曾て前清郵傳部小京官に任ず。辛亥の歲武昌義を唱へ、血鐘一鳴して烽火天に連るや、君蹶然奮起して難に赴き、戰時總司令部秘書、北方招撫使秘書に歷充す。大局旣に定りて正式國會成立するや選ばれて衆議院議員と爲る。國會解散後南旋して鄉里に歸り劍を橫へて經を說く。共和克復して國會再び開かるゝに及び、遂に踴躍して召集に應じ、重ねて北京に入りて仍ち衆議院議員の職に復す。

Mr. Wang En-po, another name Chun-ya a native of Hun Nan hsing, a patriot and a lovre of justice was whose nature inclined to be unreserved and broad-minded. He was ambitious in his boyhood, fond of writing and found a great joy in practice of military art. Growing a man he travelled extensively collecting knowledge and studying facts. First interviews felt mostly diffident against him, for he was too straight forward. He studied once at the Nihon University, Tokyo, Japan and completed the required courses in due time. Returning to home he was made Secretary in the Communication Department of the late Imperial Government. Subsequently Wu Chang revolted against the Government resounding the battle cry. Turning his heel he left for the disturbed province and served as the secretary of the Te Shih Wu and the same to the every sent to the North to solicit it as it may take the same course as the South. At the closing of the turmoil Parliament was formally instituted and he became a member of the Lower House. When it was dissolved he returned South to study quietly politics. Soon, the Republic was restored and Parliament re-convored; he was called to House to but fill his duty as a representative.

王 湘 字芷塘 歳四十二

選舉地 四川省
籍　貫 四川省軍慶
住　址 北京順治門外醒華報社

君賦性惇篤。天資英邁。居恆尚質惡文。不事無益之繁華。然富於學識。新舊皆有素養。故其見解氣慨。皆逈異凡流。夙抱濟民治國之志。專攻實學。最注重於生理衛生兩科。長于醫術造詣既深。嘗自負曰。不為良相便為良醫。足知其素志也。醫業之餘暇。喜讀政治法律之書。謂人生無政治智識。欲圖改良國家。莫之適從。其抱負之既可慨見。曾任四川軍醫院局局長。兼辦軍醫學校。雲南陸軍醫院院長。四川成武將軍署顧問。民國二年正式國會成立。被選為參議院議員。君於中國醫界學界政界。多有所貢獻。國會解散後。為國手有成名。及國會重開。遂復入京。仍為參議院議員。

君賦性惇篤にして天資英邁なり。居常質を尚び文を惡みて無益の繁華を事とせず。然かも學識に富み新舊皆な素養ありて、其の見解氣慨皆な逈に凡流に異なるものあり。夙に濟民治國の志を抱き、專ら實學を攻め、最も生理術生兩科を重んじ、醫術に長ずる造詣飫に深し。嘗て自負して曰く良相たらずんば良醫たるべしと、其の素志を知るに足る也。醫業の餘暇、喜んで政治法律の書を讀みて曰く、人生政治智識無くんば、國家の改良進展を圖らんと欲するも適從する所なかるべしと。曾て四川軍醫局局長に任じ、兼て軍醫學校を經營し、又た雲南陸軍醫院々長、四川成武將軍署顧問となる。民國二年正式國會成立するや、選ばれて參議院議員と爲る。君中國醫學界に於て貢献する所あり、國會解散後依然國手として成名あり、國會重ねて開かるゝに及び、遂に復た入京して仍ち參議院議員と爲る。

民國之精華　（傳記）　王湘先生

Mr. Wang-hsiang, otherwise called Chiu-tang, is native of Chung Ching, Ssu-chuan, 42 years old. He is a man of kindness and honest. He lives a plain life and dislikes a pomp and shaw. He is a learned scholar of old and new; he sees things which ordinary man can not and he thinks what others never dream. In his early life, he determined to be a friend of the people and enter into politics. He studied mostly science, particurarlly physiology and hygiene, which made him very prominent later in his medical knowledge, as it was told that he boasted himself one day to say, "If I could not be a good minister of state, I shall be a good doctor." His leisure time has been utilized for the study of law and politics. He is used to say that if one has no knowledge of politics, he could not sure for the country in promoting the national wellfare. He was once the Director, the Ssu-chuan army medical corps and at the same time, superintendent the army medical school. Then he was made the Superintendent, Yun-nan Army Hospital and was the Adviser to the Cheng-wu army Head-quarters. In the Second year of the Republic, when the Parliament was organized, he was a member of the Upper House, and has done a good deal for the political and medical worlds. After the dissolution of the House, he devoted all his time in practice of medicine and is now again in the Upper House since the re-opening in 1916.

王傑　字從周

選舉地　河南省

籍　貫　河南省西華縣

住址　北京北鬧市口溝頭路南三十一

君爲人剛正不阿。而秉性聰慧。思想活潑。頭腦明晰。讀書不執成見。不拘字句。故皆能得其眞義。弱冠即負文名。及長。尤廣覽羣書。自以遠大相期許。及海內維新。遂改志彈精西學。遍閱新書。慨然以挽弱爲强自任。曾畢業于河南法政學堂。民國元年。當選爲本省議會議長。二年。當選爲衆議院議員。二年十一月。袁氏以暴力解散議會。君遂去國留學日本。入法政學堂。孜孜不倦。五年八月一日。共和再造。仍就衆議院議員職。

君人となり剛正謹直にして阿らず、秉性聰慧敏捷にして、頭腦明晰、思想活潑なり。書を讀みて字句に拘泥せず成見に執着せず、以て其の眞義を究むるを得たり。弱冠にして文名を負ひ、長ずるに及びて博く百家の書を涉獵す。海內維新に及めて志を改めて西學を攻究し遍ねく新書を閱して、時艱匡救を以て其の念と爲す。曾て河南法政學堂を卒業す。民國成立して後ち、擧げられて同省議會議長と爲る。二年選ばれて衆議院議員となる。袁政府が威力を以て、橫まゝに民黨を壓迫し憲政を蹂躙して、國會を解散するや。蹶然國を去つて東渡し、日本法政學堂に入りて學び、孜々として倦まず、造詣盆々深し。既に再び共和克復し、國會重ねて召集さるゝや、君歸國して再び衆議院議員の職に復したり。

Mr. Wang Chieh otherwise known as Tsung Chou is a native of Hsi-hua hsien, the Ho-nan-hsing. He is a gentleman of straightforward character, not subject to the vice of flattery. Being sagacious and clear headed, he is full of active thoughts. In reading books, he is neither subject to mere words or forms nor to any of prejudices, but try to get into the real meaning of what he reads pure and simple. Early in life, he secured more or less literary reputation, and when grown up, he became conversant of celebrated authors. When China was working for the new state of affairs, he turned his attention to the perusal of new books, and was deeply impressed of his own duty of saving his country from its inevitable doom. He was graduated from the law college of Ho-nan. With the establishment of the Republic, he was elected a member of the local assembly. In the second year of the Republic, he was returned for the House of Commons. When the Yuanshi-Kai government dominated over the people's party trampling down upon the Constitution, and when the Parliament was shut down, he entered in the Japanese law school where he devoted himself to the acquiring of the thorough knowledge of law and politics. When the Republic was restored followed by the summoning of the Parliament, he returned to his native country where he was again returned for the House of Commons.

王洪身　字曦秋　歳三十五

選舉地　吉林省
籍　貫　吉林省
住　址　北京西單牌樓英子胡同四號

君爲松水望族也。年弱冠。負笈遠方。
潛心經世之學。迄畢業出校。君年已三
十矣。辛亥之役。秘謀改革。幾罹奇禍。
時新會陳公。治軍吉林。奇其才。延之
幕前。時賓倚任焉。維時政黨崛起。君
歷遊吉圉三十餘邑。所至政黨觀成。君
之力有足多也。越明年被選爲正式國
會參議院議員。以民黨精神。卓然不撓
之故。國會未經解散。君之證書徽章既
先入袁氏手矣。今者共和復活。君仍就
參議院議員舊職。後此之碩謀偉畫。更
不知凡幾僂就。

民國之精華　（傳記）　王洪身先生

君は松水の望族たるなり。年弱冠にして笈を負ふて鄉關
を出で、四方に遊學して經世の學を求め、業を畢り校を
出づ、君年既に三十なり。辛亥革命の事勃發するや、君
亦た遠く之に響應の策を講じて幾んど奇禍に罹る。時に
吉林都督陳照常、君の才を奇とし延いて幕客とし、時に
倚任に資したり。當時政黨崛起の大勢に乘じ、君乃ち吉
林省內各地三十餘邑を歷遊して遊說これ努めたり。民國
二年正式國會議員選舉に際し君は參議院議員に當選す。
君乃ち晉京して中央政界民黨の鬭士として活躍す。爲に
袁政府の忌む所となりて國會解散前に先ち、君が議員證
書並に徽章共に剝奪に遭ふ、君慾々として袁政府の專橫
を慷し、回天の謀を念ふ。既にして袁氏死して民國復活
し、國會重ねて開かるゝに及び、君亦た召集せられて、
參議院議員の舊職に復したり。

Mr. Wang Hung-shen, known as Hsi Chin is a native of Chilin. He left his home early in life and travelled throughout China devoting himself to the study of classics. When he finished his school course he was thirty years of age. In 1911 when the revolution broke out, he responded to the same at the peril of his life. His ability became known to the governor general of Chilin who treated him as his honoured adviser. Taking the advantage of the political situation, he travelled through more than thirty villages of the province urging his own cause. In the second year of the Republic when the Parliament was formed, he was elected a member of the Senate. Whereupon, he proceeded to Peking where he had a fine chance of showing his ability as an able combatant on the side of the people. Being suspected by the Yuanshi-kai government, previous to the suppression of the Parliament, he was deprived of his certificate and badge of the membership. He naturally cherished a great animosity to the Yuanshi-kai government and waited for the opportunity. With the death of Yuanshi-kai the Parliament was restored. On being summoned to Peking, he resumed the former senatorial function.

王篤成　字仲潛

選舉地　湖北省
籍　貫　湖北省
住　址　北京白廟胡同大同公寓

君天資聰慧。悟性敏捷。言論舉止。皆
極活潑。然其處世接物。又極尚氣節。
重信義。少年讀書。專求有用之學。不
從事於考据詞章。及長。尤精思深入。
洞悉事理。故工於詞令。長於幹才。君
性至孝。稚齡。即守遠惡崇善之庭訓。
故既入社會後。猶服膺不忘。故雖交遊
遍天下。而未嘗接近姦邪。所識稍有失
德。即與絕交。不復存世故之念。海內
維新。辛亥武昌倡義。天下饗應。民國
肇造。及正式國會成立。君荷衆望。被
選爲衆議院議員。國會解散後。南旋歸
里。觀望世變。懍然思念恢復大業。既
而袁氏死黎氏出。國會再開。君遂應召
入京。仍爲衆議院議員。

王篤成先生

君天資聰慧にして悟性敏捷なり。言論舉止皆な極めて活
潑にして。然も其の世に處し物に接し、又た極めて氣節
を尚び信義を重んず。少年嘗を讀みて專ら有用の學を求
め、長ずるに及び其の義を思索して事理を洞察し、詞令
に工なるも幹才に長ず。君性至孝にして即ち惡を遠ざけ
善を崇ぶの庭訓を奉じ、社會に入るの後も猶は服膺忘れ
す。故に交遊天下に遍しと雖も、未だ嘗て姦邪に接近せ
ざるなり。辛亥の歳、武昌義を唱へて天下響應し、民國
樹立して正式國會成立するや、選ばれて衆議院議員と爲
る。國會解散さるに及び、南旋して鄕里に歸臥し、世變を
觀望して大業の恢復を思ふ。既にして袁氏死し、黎氏出
で、國會再び開くや、君遂に召集に應じて北京に入り、
仍は衆議院議員たり。

Mr. Wang Tu-cheng is of the Ho-pe hsing. Both in words and behavior he is activity itself, to which may be added his fidelity to any cause he advocates. He is a copious reader of books, and sought what may be termed an efficient learning. He is also noted for his filial obedience, which virtue he never forgot even as he grew older, and had much chance of mixing with others in society. He is not known for any vice, although as a politican, he had numerous temptations. When the Revolutionary movement has taken place and attained its object, he was elected a member of the House of Commons. On the suppression of this legislative assemoly, he returned home keenly watching the course of the movement. With the death of Yuanshi-kai and the appearance of Leao on the scene, he entered Peking, and was returned for the House of Commons.

文篤周　字塞翁　歲四十三

選舉地　新疆省

籍貫　湖南省衡山縣

住址　北京虎坊橋聚魁店

君自幼聰穎絕倫。而賦性高潔。其文采風度。皆超出凡流。讀書博而能約。雖所造已深。然仍攻苦不倦。為人謙虛好問。喜聞蓋言。人告以過。雖未盡當。必欣然謝之。及長。以邑庠生。歷任新疆昌吉綏來等縣知縣。曾充發審局提調。平反疑獄多件。記大功五次。民國二年正月。當選為眾議院議員。十一月。被袁世凱迫去證書徽章。遂回籍辦理學務。五年八月。國會重開。始入京。仍為眾議院議員。所著有所新疆古蹟志。天山金石述則諸書。

君や幼より聰穎絕倫なり、賦性また高潔にして其の文采風度實に凡流に超出す。讀書該博にして所造既に深きも然り仍は刻苦玫究倦まざる也。其の人と爲り謙虛にして問を好み喜んで蓋言を聞く、人の告ぐるに過を以てすれば未だ盡く當らずと雖必ず欣然として之を謝す。長ずるに及び邑庠生を以て新疆昌吉綏來等の各縣知事に歷任し曾つて發審局提調に充てられ、疑獄多件を處理して大功を記せらるゝこと五回なり。民國二年正月衆議院議員に當選し、十一月袁世凱の爲めに議員證書徽章を奪はれて京を追はる遂に鄉里に歸省して學務を辦理す。民國五年八月國會重ねて開かるるや君も亦た再び晉京して衆議院議員と爲る。君常に政界に馳騁して忙中尙ほ且つ簾硯に親み、新疆古蹟志、天山金石述開等の著作ありて世に行はる。

Mr. Wen Tu-chou, another name Chai-Weng, was born in the prefecture of Heng-shan, Hu Nan hsing in the year 1874. He showed genuine excellence and cleverness when very young. His lofty character exhibited in its highest aspects which surpassed most people in his literary ability and talent. Though he gained the profundity and erudition of knowledge through his mids reading, he never tried to give himself up but worked very hard. As grew up, he became more and more modest and zealous for a new light. His keen attention would turn quick to one's view and if any fault willingly pointed out though not partinent to him, he thanked for. Later he was made fellow and appointed to those post of goveror of Hsim-chiang, Chang-chi Huan-lai and etc. He was made manager of communication Bureau and the merits were given him five times by the dint of having the most intricated cases skilfully settled. In January, 2nd year of Republic, he was elected to a member of the Parliment. However, in november Yuanshi-kai deprived him a bodge of member of Parliament and excelled him from Peking. Then returning to his homestead, he engaged in educational works. August 5th year of Republic the Parliament was norganized. He came up to the capital again, and gained a chair in Parliament. Busied himself as he was in running about all directions, in political field, he also engaged in writing and published those books entitled "archœological history of Hsin-chiang," "orcheological introduction of Ku-tien-shan" and etc.

文登瀛　字仙舟　歲三十五

選舉地　甘肅省
籍　貫　甘肅省武威縣
住　址　北京大佛寺街羅家大院

君賦性溫良。與人交。和藹可親。雖素
所嫌惡之人。亦必謙和相接。不以疾言
厲色加人。然言忠行篤。操守既甚嚴。
又極尚氣節重信義。少年讀書蒐求有
用之學。不從事於考据詞章。及長。尤
精思深入。洞悉事理。故工於詞令。長
於幹才。銳意盡力地方公益事業。鄉黨
頗以推重。辛亥武昌起義。天下響應。
傾覆前清之專制。釀造五族共和之新
政。民國二年正式國會成立。君被選爲
參議院議員。參畫議政。抱持公正。未
幾。國會解散。君乃歸省讀書。不聞時
事。共和克復。及國會重開。君復應召
集。入京師仍復就參議院議員之職。

君賦性溫良にして人と交はる私竊親びべし。素と憎惡す
る所の人と雖、亦た必す謙讓溫和の態度を以て相接し、
疾言厲色を以て人に加へざる也。然かも言は忠實にして
行は篤厚、操守既に甚だ嚴しく、又た極めて氣節を尚び
信義に重んじ、少年書を讀みて專ら有用の學を求め詞章
の末に拘泥せず。長ずるに及び尤も深く思索して事理を
洞察す。故に幹才に長じ、銳意地方の公益事業に盡瘁し
鄉黨頗つて以て之を推重す。辛亥の歲武昌義を倡へて天

下響應し、滿清政府の專制を覆滅して、五大民族共和の
新政を創め、民國二年正式國會を召集して萬機公論に決
せんとす。君乃ち選ばれて參議院議員となり正論を把持
して大政を翼贊す。未だ幾くならずして國會停止され、
君乃ち歸省して讀書自ら娛み遽に時事を問はず。既にして共
和克復し國會重ねて開かる、君復たを集に應じて仍ち參
議院議員の職の職に就きたり。

Mr. Wen Teng-ying, another name Shan Chou, a native of Wu wei hsien Kan-hsi hsing, 35 years old. He is a well-born, kind hearted man and never uses any hasty words even he talks to one with whom he is not in good terms. His words are always true and his conduct is sincere, which are the manifestation of his strong will-power. He was a book lover when he was a boy and found an unusual interest in valuable publications. When he reached a manhood he was a learned, clear sighted gentleman, whose endowment was a previous gift to the town and its vicinities. The promotion of public welfare was considered as his duty and the disinterestedness of this public man was acknowledged by all the people of the province. The revolt of Wuchang against the Imperial Government was followed by almost all Districts, which sueceded in vanquishing the Imperial Regime and establishing a new government of the "Five Great Races." In the second year of the Republic organized a National Congress, a fundamental element of the representative government. He entered the Congress as a Senator and gave invaluable assistance in unifying the country. Unfortunately the Congress was suspended in a short time, consequently he returned to his district to study but not to talk politics. In 1916 the Republic is restored and the Congress is again prorogued; he was called again to sit in the Upper House.

方聖徵　字紀周　歲四十一

選舉地　福建省
籍　貫　福建省雲霄縣
住　址　北京琉璃廠東南園八十三

君為人剛正不阿。然秉性仁厚。喜濟人急難。人有所求。必為暗中設法助之。不肯輕為承諾。而所承諾。則未有不成者。自幼好讀能文。喜為詩歌。及長。遂改志攻求新學。以前清優增生。巳西科副拔。入全閩第一師範學校肄業。于光緒三十二年畢業。三十三年被任為雲霄縣視學官。兼高等小學校長。三十四年。福建提學使姚。以君辦學為各屬冠。特獎教育先聲匾額。嗣復歷任各校視學校長。民國元年十二月。當選為福建省議會議員。民國二年二月。由省議會議員當選為參議院議員。國會解散。歸里不出。直至共和再造。始應召入京仍為參議院議員。

君人と為り剛正にして阿ねらず、然かも秉性仁厚にして喜んで人を済ひ難に赴く、人求むる所あれば必す暗中に法を設けて之を助く。輕々に承諾せざるも、承諾すれば則ち未だ成さゞるはなし。幼より書を好み文を能くし、喜んで詩歌を作る。長ずるに及び遂に志を改め求めて新學を攻究し、前清優増生巳酉科の副拔を以て全閩第一師範學校に入りて肄業し、光緒三十二年卒業したり。三十三年雲霄縣視學官に任せられ、高等小學校長を兼ね。三十四年福建姚提學使は君が學事を辨理すること部内の冠なりとなし特に「教育先聲」の匾額を獎したり、嗣後各校視學校長に歷任す。民國元年十二月福建省議會議員に當選す。二年二月省議會議員より選ばれて參議院議員と為る。國會解散後、鄉里に歸臥して暫らく出でず、其の國會重ねて恢復するや、召集に應じて晉京し、現に參議院議員と為る。

民國之精華　（傳記）　方聲徵先生

Fang Sheng-cheng, another name Chi-chou. He was born in the prefecture of Ynn-hsiao, Fu-chenhsing 1872. He is a man of just and strong will and never flatters. However he had such a sympathetic as it revealed itself in every example of his chivalrous conducts for others. Even he would respond to every condition of man if he asked. He is not a sort of man who easily be moved, but man who carries out what he consents. He showed a fondness for reading when very young, and also he had a talent for writing and lived in composing poems. As he grew up, he revolutionized himself in obtaining a new learning. The government of Chin let him to enter to Chuan-min first normal school In the 32nd year of Kuang Chu he graduated the school and the next year he made school-inspector of Yun-hsiao prefecture, besides being master of a senior school. In the 34th year, the commissioner of Chen tiao, Fu Chen, found in him ability of managing educational administration and gave him as its merit a frame tablet of "glorious voice of Education." Later he accepted successively the positions of master and inspector of numerous schools. December, the First year of Republic, he was elected member of Fu Chen provincial assembly and in the following year he gained a chair in Parliament. After its dissolvement he retired to his home. On the re-organization of Parliament he was called out to Peking and has been accepted to his former chair.

方鎭東　字德九　歲三十五

選舉地　河南省

籍貫　河南省沁源縣

住址　北京琉璃廠中間太平巷北口

君賦性耿介不阿。疾惡如仇。然其處世接物。不露鋒鋩。明友有過。雖至契非豫斷。其能納諫改過。決不輕於規勸。居恆以厚道待人。雖仇敵亦不忍無端虐待之。與人交。尙信義。重然諾。人有所託。既諾無不成者。自幼好讀書。弱冠即工於詩文。及長。遂專求有用之書。不復固執章句。不喜漢魏之學。西化既盛倡于海內。君復改志研究西學。遂至北京。肄業于京師法政學校。畢業後。于民國元年。被選爲河南臨時省議會議員。旋被選爲衆議院議員。及國會解散。至二年。張家口組織律師公會。被選爲該會々長。三四年至京津各法庭執行律師職務。及國會重開。始應召。仍爲衆議院議員。

君賦性耿介にして阿らず、惡を疾むこと仇の如し、然かも鋒鋩を露はさずして、朋友過あれば至契と雖豫斷を非とす。其の能く諫を納れ過を改め決して至則を輕んぜず、居常厚道を以て人を待ち仇敵と雖亦た之を虐待するに忍びず、人と交るに信義を重んず、人の託す所あれば、既諾して成さざる者無し。幼より讀書を好み弱冠即ち詩文工みなり。長ずるに及び遂に專ら有用の書を求め、復た章句に固執せず、故に讀む所多くは義理の書にして漢魏の學を喜ばず。西化既に盛なるや、君亦た學びて業を畢め。民國元年選ばれて河南臨時省議會議員となり、旋て衆議院議員に舉げらる。國會解散後、張家口に於て辯護士公會を組織して該會々長に選ばる。其の後京津に至り各法庭に於て辯護事務に當り、國會恢復するや、再び召集に應じて仍は衆議院議員と爲る。

Mr. Fang Chen-tung, another name Chiu-Chin, was born in the province of Tzu-Yuan, Ho-nan in 1885. He was a man of just and upright inspired by sense of abhorrence of crime. He never flattered but he had a nature incapable to endure anger or any sentiment of worth. However he was ready to listen to one's advices and followed it. He was generous and merciful even to his opponent. In intercourse with others, he set store by faith and never broke his promise. He responded to every condition of man if he asked. He showed a remarkable fondness for reading and excellent talent for poem when very young and he chosed many of useful books without paying any attention to the delicacy of literary style. So the books written about sentiment of justice and duty fascinated him, in turn he cared for no book of trades. The wave of western civilization which beated upon the country turned his on attention a new learning. He went to study in Peking and graduated King-Shih college of law and politics. In the first year of Republic, he was elected to member of Ho-nan temporary provincial assembly and then was made member of Parliament. After its dissolution he organized Lawyer Society at Chan-cha kon and consequently he accepted chair o president of the society. Later he went to King-tsin and engaged in law practice. And on the reorganization of Parliament he was called out to be a member of it.

尹宏慶　字蕊椁　歲四十五

選舉地　山東省
籍　貫　山東省高唐縣
住　址　北京鮑街家雅集公廟

君爲人老成持重。篤實不華。然天資聰慧絕倫。精明強幹。且有事務之才。其處世接物。大都崇尚堅實。尤卑輕舉妄動。自幼好學。弱冠有文名。及海內維新。薬舊從新。喜讀天下有用之書。專攻實學。夙抱治國安民之志。前清以舉人。揀選知縣。君乃不安小成。貢笈東渡。留學日本。肄業法政大學校本科。畢業歸國。歷任安徽鳳陽銅陵。山東鄆城。直隸易縣等知事。及武定府知事。治績大舉。百性感激。民國二年正式國會成立。被舉爲參議院議員。入京師到院。議政公正。時人推重。國會解散後。端里不出。及國會重開。遂復應召集抵京師。仍爲參議院議員。

民國之精華　（傳記）尹宏慶先生

君人と爲り老成持重、篤實を旨として華美を事とせす。然かも天資聰慧絕倫にして事務の才あり。幼より學を好みて弱冠早くも文名あり。海內維新の風潮に乘じて舊を棄て新に從ひ、喜んで天下有用の書を讀み、專ら實學を攻究し、夙に治國安民の志を抱きたり。前清時代舉人を以て知縣に選ばる。君乃ち小成に安んぜして笈を負ふて東海を渡り、日本に留學して法政大學校本科に入り卒業して歸國す。安徽省鳳陽銅陵各縣、山東省鄆城、直隸省易縣等の知事及び武定府知事等に歷任して治績大に舉り百性感激す。民國二年正式議會成立するや選ばれて參議院議員と爲る。院に到りて政を議すること公正にして時人推重す。旋て國會解散され、君乃ち、鄉里に歸りて杜門蟄居す。此次國會重ねて開かるゝに及び、遂に復た召集に應じて北京に抵り、仍ち參議院議員と爲る。

Mr. Ja Hung-Ching, a native Kao tang hsien, Shangtung hsing, is 45 years old. We can find a man of the most president and cautious in Mr. Chun Hung ching who is also sincere and keeps off display, yet he surposses any one within his sagacity and great business talent. From his boyhood he was observed in learning and was quite a scholar while young. At the time the western civization prevailed throughout the country, he was quick to catch books particularly scientific publications. His resolution at the time was to serve the country as as a public man. During the Imperial Regime he was appointed to a Governor, but he did not satisfy with such a little success; crossing the Eastern Sea and went to Japan where he enrolled as a student at the Hosci University and completed the required courses for graduation. On returned home he was appointed to governors of Teng-yang Tung Liu prefectures, An-hui District, Hhun-cheng Shan-tungi Chili and the city of Wuting his administrative ability was recognized and the people of the prefectures and city were very grateful to him. In the second year of the Republic he was a senator of the Parliament then organized formally. His views and speeches in the House of Commons were always impartial and just, undoubtedly persuaded listeners. But he did not have much chance to espound his political belief as the Parliament was dissolved. He returned home and spent very quiet life until he was called again in 1916 to resume the legislative duty in the upper House.

司徒頴　字仲實　歲三十八

選舉地　廣東省

籍　貫　廣東省開平縣人

住　址　北京李鉄拐斜街肇慶西館

君爲人精明强幹。好質惡文。與人交。
極重然諾。自幼即知好學不輟。喜捲卷
深思。有所得。如獲至寶。終身不忘。以
前清擧人。歷充禮部農商工部小京官。
旋入北京大學採礦冶金科畢業後。于
民國元年。由省議會選充臨時　參議院
議員。民國二年。再選充爲衆議院議
員。十月國會被袁氏非法解散。遂忿々
歸粤。不談政治。專從事於實業。民國
三年。往山陝一帶查砒石油礦。民國四
年。赴小呂宋。調査糖業。及今年國會
復活。遂來京。仍充衆議院議員。

君人と爲り精明强幹にして實を好み華を惡む。人と變る
や極めて然諾を重んず。幼より學を好んで輟まず。卷を
捲で思索し、得る所あれば至寶を獲るが如く身を終る
まで忘れず。前清時代擧人を以て禮部農商工部小京官と
なる。旋て北京大學採礦冶金科に入りて卒業す。民國元
年省議會よりばれて臨時參議院議員と爲る。二年再び選
ばれて衆議院議員と爲る。十月國會は袁氏の非法により

て解散さるゝや、遂に忿々として粤に歸り、竊かに時事の
非を嘆じて口暫らく政治を談せず、專ら實業に從事し三
年山陝一帶に往きて石油礦を調査し、四年小呂宋に赴き
て糖業を調査して富國の計を圖らんとす。今年國會の復
活するに及び、又た召集されて遂に來京し、仍は衆議院
議員の職に就き再び政界馳驅の人となりたり。

Mr. Ssu Tu-in, another name Chu-shih, was born in the prefecture of Kai-eing, Kuang-ting in the year 1876. He was a man of clear head and strong insight. He set value upon substance but never adhered too much to the forms and rules. In intercourse with others, he set stone by faith and promise. In his youth he loved to read books and used to put much consideration on every page. If he gained anything benefit out of it he vallved it as a treasure in his hand and kept it a life-long. During the period of Chin he was appointed to Hsiso King-kung of the Agricultural and Commercial Bureau in Lei-pu. Then he entered Peking University and finished the courses of mining and metelorology. In the First year of the Republic, he was elected to the provincial assembly member of temporal national assembly. And in the second year of Republic he gained a Chair, in Parliament. On August in the same year the Parliament was dissolved by illegal hand of Yuanshi-kai. He went back to his home with no least indigaation. However he took no active part to political discussion since, but engaged in business. In the third year with the purpose of enriching the country he went to the lands of Shan hsi and investigated a petroleum mine and in the following years he went to Hsiao-lu-sung to inquire into sugar business. And on the re-ganization of Parliament he has been elected to a member.

白常潔　字西垣

君天資聰慧にして悟性敏捷なり。言論舉止皆な活潑にして、然かも又た極めて義節を尙び信義を重んず。少年書を讀みて專ら有用の學を求め詞章の末に拘泥せず、長じて尤も思索を喜びて事理を洞察す、故に詞令に巧みなるも幹才に長じたり。夙に風土を以て自ら任じ、勉めて經國濟民の書を讀む。遂に笈を負ふて東海を渡り、新進の日本に留學して法政大學法律科專門部に學び、研磋捲まず其業を畢へて歸國したり。民國樹立して共和の莫を倡め約法によりて第一次正式國會成立するや、君選ばれて衆議院議員となり、多年修養せる新智識を傾倒して大政に贊勤する所ありたり。國會解散さるゝや郷里に歸省して讀書自ら娛み、時に出でゝ地方公益事業に從ひ、又た後進を誘導す。國會重ねて開かるゝに及び、遂に又た入京して仍ち衆議院議員と爲る。

選事地　陝西省

籍　貫　陝西省長安縣

住　址　北京西城邸祖胡同十二號

君天資聰慧。悟性敏捷。言論舉止。皆極活潑。然其處世接物。又極尚義節重信義。少年讀書。專求有用之學。不從事於考据詞章。及長。尤精思深入。洞悉事理。故工於詞令。長於幹才。君性至孝。稚齡即守遠惡崇善之庭訓。故既入社會後。猶服膺不忘。故雖交遊遍天下。而未嘗接近姦邪。所識稍有失德。即與絕交。不復世故之念。夙以國士自任。尤喜讀經國濟民之書。遂負笈東渡。留學日本東京。入法政大學法律科專門部。畢業歸國。民國二年正式國會成立。被選爲衆議院議員。傾注溢蓄贊勤大政。國會解散後。歸里省家。讀書自娛。時出從于地方公益事業。又誘導後進。及國重開。遂又入京。仍爲衆議院議員。

Mr. Pai Chang-chieh, another name Hsi-yüan, a native of Chang-an-hsien, Hsie-hsi hsing
Erudite and brilliant are the character of Mr. Pai Chang-chieh whose manner and habit are full of life, yet he never fails in fulfilling his duty, and does things with a good faith. From his youth the books were his best friends, growing old r he found his pleasure in investigation of problems and solving questions. He is quiet a diplomat in etiquette but his talent is distinguishable. Early in his age he resolved to be a pu'lic man and studied science serving for welfare of the state. He crossed s a to Japan to pursue his study in the progressive Japan. Reaching Tokyo he matriculated at the Hose University where he studied very hard, which r sult was honoured by the graduation. When he return d home the Republic was established and the first Parliament was formally organized according to the provisional constitution. He was successfully elected to a member of the Lower House and has done a good deal for the working of representative government, whi h knowledge he had acquired which he was in Japan. An the dissolution of the Parliament he returned to his district and enjoyed himself in quiet reading, sometimes engaged in the promotion of public welfare of the district and in the education of young people. Having the Parliament prorogued again he returned to the Lower House.

四十七

田應璜 字子琮 歲五十二

選舉地　山西省
籍貫　山西省渾源縣
住址　北京兵部窪十二

君氣度從容。性情和緩。與人交。溫良恭謙。不爲意氣之爭。雖有所忍恨。亦未嘗以疾言遽色加人。然意志極強。富於獨立之性。且喜聞忠告之言。勇於改過。人告以過。雖所言失實。絕不與辯。常語人曰。聞過而改。旣得無過之實。又居從喜如流之名。年少讀書。即以遠大自期。稍長。愈益從事於學養。故夫資雖非絕高。而明察事情。洞委眞理。初入仕途。即老成練達。措置行動輒得宜。曾以前清舉人。歷充湖北來鳳縣知縣。調署思施縣知縣。民國元年。充施鶴司令部參謀長。山西都督府高等顧問官。署歸綏觀察使。二年。被選爲參議院議員。現充參議院議員。

君氣度從容として性情圓滿なり。人と交りて溫良恭謙意氣の爭を爲さず、憤る所ありと雖も未だ嘗て疾言遽色を以て人に加へざる也。然かも意志極めて強くして獨立の性に富み、且つ忠言を聞くを喜びて過を改むるに勇なり。年少書を讀みて遠大を以て自ら期し、稍や長ずるや愈々學養に勵みたり。故に天資必ずしも絕高なりと雖ふべからざるも、事理を明察して眞義を洞察す。初め仕途に入るや、即ち老成練達にして措置行動共に宜しきを得たり。嘗て前清の擧人を以て、湖北來鳳縣知縣、思施縣知縣を歷任したり。民國元年施鶴司令部參謀長、山西都督府高等顧問官、歸綏觀察使署理等の職に歷充したり。民國二年正式國會參議院議員に選ばれ、五年國會復活するや、再び召集に應じて現に仍ほ參議院議員たり。

Mr. Tien Ying-huang, aged fifty two, is a native of Hun Yuan, Shan-hsi province. He is a quiet serious and magnanimous in character. He shows never any anger in his countenance. However he is a man of strong will full of independent spirit. He listens carefully to the advice given by others. While Young he was fond of reading books. and as he grew older he was interested in learning. When engaged once in the government service he was very successful. Therefore as the governor of a province he distinguished himself from others. In the first year of the Republic, he was appointed to an adviser to the governor-general of Shan-hsi. In the 2nd year when the Republic was established he was elected to a member of the Senate, and even in the 2nd year of the Republic when the Parliament was restored, he resumed the senatorial function.

田美峰 歲四十二

選舉地　黑龍江省
籍　貫　黑龍江省海倫縣
住　址　北京兵部窪中街胡同三十一

君氣度從容。性情和緩。與人交。溫良恭謙。不爲意氣之爭。雖有忿恨。亦未嘗以疾言遽色加人。然意志極强。富於獨立之性。且喜聞忠告之言。勇於改過。人告以過。聞過而改。雖所言失實。絕不與辯。常語人曰。讀書。以遠大自期。稍長。愈益從事於學養。故天資雖非絕高。而明察事情。又居恭善如流之名。利劫大焉。年少讀書。以遠大自期。稍長。愈益從事於學養。故天資雖非絕高。而明察事情。洞委眞理。初入仕途。即老成練達。措置行動輒得宜。於前清光緒年。在黑龍江通肯副都統衙門。歷充筆帖式之差。於宣統元年。當選爲諮議局議員。民國元年。改爲臨時省議會議員。二年。被選爲衆議院議員。

君氣度雍雅にして性情和平なり。人と交るや溫良恭謙にして爭を好まず。忿恨あるも亦た嘗て疾言厲色を以て人に加へず。然かも意志極めて强くして獨立の性に富み、且つ喜んで人の忠言に聞きて過を改るに勇なり。年少書を讀みて即ち自ら大成を期す。稍や長ずるに及びて益々研究修養に努め、天資必ずしも絕高ならざるも事理を明察して眞義を洞觀するに至れり。初め仕途に就くや、老成練達にして措置行動共に輙ち宜しきを得たり。前清光緒年間黑龍江通肯副都統衙門に在りて筆帖式の職に任す。宣統二年選ばれて諮議局議員と爲る。元年正式國會の成立に際し衆議院議員に當選す。國會解散後、田園に歸臥して讀書自ら娛み、國會重ねて開くるに及び、復た出でて仍は衆議院議員たり。

民國之精華　（傳記）　田美峰先生

Mr. Tien Mei-feng Hailin hsien, Hei-lung-chiang hsing, fortytwo years old. He is a man of taste and well-ballanced; and he is also gentle and modest to all, even his foes can not heat a hursh word from him, still he is determined and independent; in spite of that, he is ready to cortrect his fault whenever he finds it. In his yourth he was one of book-lovers as the rest of members of the Parliament and was enthusiastic in his study when grew older. He was not brilliant but he is apt to see the truth back of a fact. As an officer he managed the business with a great skill and wisdom. During Kuo ksu period he was secretary to the Hai-lung chiang, Tung ken futu tung yih men. In the second year of Hsuan-tung he was appointed a membar of the advisory Bureau. In the first year of the Republic was a member of the Provisional District Congress. In the second year of the Republic the national congress was formally organized and he was, this time, elected a member of Lower Houses. After the dissolution of the congress he went back to his district to enjoy himself in reading. Restoration of the Republican government has sent him back to the Lower House.

田　稔　字多稼　歲三十

選舉地　浙江省

籍　貫　浙江省紹興縣

住　址　北京象坊橋浙江議員公寓

君爲人頭腦明晰。意思堅強。能忍辱耐勞。富于幹濟之才。然秉性仁厚。篤實無欺。與人交。喜勸善規過。相其人必能納諫者。始規正之。否則惟漸與疏遠。以示意。及其改悔。則愈善律之。人告以過。則直認不諱。自幼聰穎好讀書。尤喜讀法律之書。以治國平天下自任。曾以前清附生。負笈東渡。留學日本。入法政大學專門部政治科。畢業歸國。歷充浙江行政公署科員。江西行政公署秘書。民國二年正式國會成立。被選爲衆議院議員。國會解散後。南旋歸里。費力于地方公益事業。及國會重開。遂又入京。現仍爲衆議院議員。

君人と爲り頭腦明晰にして意思堅強、能く辱を忍びて勞に耐へ、幹濟の才に富む。然かも秉性仁厚にして篤實欺くなし。人と交るや善を勸め過を規するを喜ぶ。幼より聰穎にして讀書を好み、弱冠早くも文を能くし、鄕里神童を以て之を目す。海內維新に及びて君專ら新學を攻究し尤も法律の書を喜び、治國平天下を以て已が任とせり。曾て前清時代附生を以て笈を負ふて東海に渡り日本に留學し、法政大學校專門部政法科に入り卒業して歸國す。而して浙江行政公署科員、江西行政公署秘書に歷任す。民國二年正式國會成立するや選ばれて衆議院議員と爲る。國會解散後南旋して鄕里に歸來し、地方の公益事業に盡瘁したり。國會重ねて開くるに及び遂に又た入京して、現に仍は衆議院議員と爲る。

Mr. Tien Jen, another name To-chia, nature of Shao hsing hsien, Che chiang, thirty years old. One can rarely find so clear headed man like Mr. Tien Jen who is also a man of strong will-power, patience and ability. A man of such an inclination is, often founds to be cold and indifferent but we find him quite contrary as he is true and kind to every one, always encourages good cause and excuses other people's error. He was an absorved reader in his child days and composed articles very remarkably, as the villagers looked him up as a prodigious child. Introduction of the western civilization had much influence upon him particulorly on his study; he begun to learn the western science specialy laws. The late Imperial government sent him to Japan for study of law and politics. He entered the Hosei University and took up courses on palitical science. On graduation he returued home to accept a position at Che chiang administrative office, then he was promoted to the position of secretary of the Chiang hsi admnistrative office. In the second year of the Republic the national Parliament was inaugulated formaly and he made a member of the Lower Hou·e, dissolution of which drove him back to his distriet in the South where he endeavored to promote the public welfare. The Republic is restored and so the Parliament where he has returned again from the original distsiet.

田桐 字梓琴 歳三十五

選舉地　湖北省
籍貫　湖北省
住址　北京西里頭條胡同

君秉性聰慧敏捷にして人と為り、慷慨義を好み尤も喜んで
不平の鳴と為す。然かも意思堅強にして居常正義を固持
して、權勢富貴た君の志を
換ゆべからざる也。幼より讀書を好みて弱冠既に文名あ
り。長ずるに及びて博く群籍を涉獵し國家の危亡を挽回
するを以て自ら任じ、舊同盟會中有名の鬪士と為る。第
一革命に際し君は漢陽に走せて民軍總司令部の高級副官
となる。旋て上海南京間を奔走して臨時政府組織の事に

君秉性聰慧敏捷為人懷慨好義。尤喜
為不平之鳴。然意思堅強。居常把持正
義。倘儻不羈。權勢富貴亦不可奪君之
志。壓迫誘惑亦不可換君之志。自幼好
讀。弱冠有文名。及長。博賢群籍。深思
明辨。以挽救危亡自任。舊同盟會中為
有名之鬪士也。辛亥武昌首義。君走赴
漢陽。任民國軍總司令部高級副官。旋
奔走滬寧間。干預於臨時政府組織事
宜。南北統一後。被選為臨時參議院議
員。在北京創辦國光新聞自任總理。民
國二年被選為眾議院議員。正論讜議。
袁氏尤忌。旋蒙非法壓迫。第二革命事
敗。亡命日本。與孫文等。重謀恢復。帝
制發生。冒險回國。潛洲長江中游。力
圖第三革命。旋滇黔起義。各地響應。
君鼓吹之力居多。目的既達。及共和再
造。國會重行召集。遂來京。仍為眾議
院議員。

民國之精華　（傳記）　田桐先生

預り、南北統一後、臨時參議院議員と為る。北京に於て國
光新聞社を創立して社長となる。民國二年眾議院議員に
常選す。其の正論讜議は袁氏の尤も忌む所にして旋て非
法の壓迫を蒙り、第二革命の事敗れて日本に亡命す。孫
文等と恢復を謀り、帝制問題發生するや、險を冒して歸
國し、上海より漢口方面に出沒して第三革命を圖る。目
的既に達して共和克復するや、再び出てゝ眾議院議員と
なる。

Mr. Tien-tung, otherwise known as Tzu-chin, aged thirty five, is a native of. Hu-pe hsing. He is a gentleman of heroic temperament and strong minded character. Any amount of temptation and pressure would win his strong determination. While young he was fond of reading books and took the duty of saving his country from the precarious condition. In the first revolution, he was appointed, the adjutant to the military staff. He was also chiefly interested in the formation of the democratic government. When the Republic was formed, he was elected a member of the Senate. He established a news paper, advocating the cause of the people. In the second year of the Republic, he was elected for the House of Commons. In the attempt toward the second revolution, he repaired to Japan. However with the outbreak of the Impereal movement, he returned to Shanghai where he planed for the thrid revolution. With the restoration of the Repubric, he became a member of the House of Commons.

石璜　字子佩　歲四十

選舉地　山西省

籍貫　山西平順縣

住址　北京西城報子街

君秉性剛正。不隨俗好。然居心仁厚。常喜周急貧困。與人交。和婉可親。見人有過。恆于無人處規勸之。示以利害。故人多爲所感動。早歲篤志舊學。海內維新後。盡棄所學。以專力西書。於前清光緒二十八年。入山西大學校中齋肄業。三十一年畢業。曾充潞安府中學校學監兼敎員。宣統三年。復肄業北京法律專問大學。民國元年三月。充山西臨時省議會議員。五月。潞安巡防隊譁變。山西都督委充潞澤遼沁鎮守使隨營參贊。協辦勦撫事宜。二年一月。被選爲衆議院議員。國會解散後。不復以政治介懷。日惟以詩酒自娛。絶口不談時事。及國會復活。始應召入都。仍爲衆議院議員。

君や秉性剛直にして俗好に隨はず。然かも居心仁厚にして常に人の窮困を濟ふを喜ぶ。人と交りて和婉親むべく、人若し過あれば恒に人無き處にて之を規勸して示すに利害を以てす。故に人多くは感動す。早歳舊學に志し海內維新後盡く學ぶ所を乘て專ら西學に勉む。前清光緒二十八年山西大學校中齋に入りて修業し、三十一年卒業す。曾て潞安府中學校學監兼敎員となり、宣統三年復た北京法律專門大學に入りて學ぶ。民國元年三月山西臨時省議會議員となり。五月潞安巡防隊譁變して亂を作すや山西都督は君をして潞澤遼沁鎮守使隨營參贊に任じ、剿撫事宜を協辦せしむ。二年一月選ばれて衆議院議員と爲る。國會解散後、復た政治を以て心に介せず、日に惟だ詩酒を以て自ら娛み、絶へて時事を談せず。國會復活するに及び、始めて召集に應じて晉京し、再び衆議院議員の職に就く。

Mr. Shih-kuang, another name Jzu Pei. He was born in the prefecture of Ping-Shun, Shan-hsi hsing in the year 1877. He is a man of strong character governed by the upright principle. So his way went straight through the world. He is generous and merciful and responded to every condition of man. In his intercourse he commanded the esteem and respect and secured the confidence of others. He would kindly remonstrate the fault of others in private stating minutely its intrests. The growth of spirit of restoration in the country had the effect of causing him turn his attention seriously from old sentiment to which he had been educated, to the study of new learning. As a result, in the 28th of Kuang-chu he entered middle department of Shan-hsi University and in the 31st of Kuang-chu he completed the courses. He was once engaged as secretary of the middle school in Lu-an fu besides being teacher. In the 3rd year of Hsuantung he found himself busy in studing in the College of Law at Peking. In the first year of Republic, he was elected member of Shan-hsi temporal provincial assembly. However, on may, on the outbreak of a rebellion of Lu-an guards corporal, the governer general of Shan-hsi appointed him staff of Lu-tse Lian-chin, Che-shon ship to assist in consulting of suppression of the rebellion. On january second year, he was elected member of Parliament. On its dissolvement he retired himself entirely from political circle and enjoyed the life of composing poem and drinking wine. However on the reestablishment of national assembly he has been elected member of parliament.

史澤咸　字剛峯　歲三十二

選舉地　山東省
籍　貫　山東省樂陵縣
住　址　北京順治門內頭髮胡同山東議員
　　　　通訳處

君于前清光緒二十八年。卒業於山東高等學堂。以山東官費生。派赴日本留學。三十一年。考入鹿島第七高等學校。在學三年正式卒業。遂升入東京帝國大學法科。逾二年。值武昌起義。君遂廢學歸國。投入民軍。組織山東軍政府。充外交司長。旋被舉爲南京參議院議員。洎南北統一。參議院北移。乃辭職回里。聯合各界。力圖民生發展。元年春。創立山東墾植協會。專以移民殖邊利國福民爲宗旨。是年。第一次國會開幕。被選爲山東省議會議員。旋被舉爲衆議院議員。充憲法起草委員。國會停止後。赴口北多倫赤峯。經枏開魯林西等地。調查墾荒狀況。藉以避袁氏暴橫之鋒。本年二月到上海。隨同人組織國會。未幾。大局解決。遂來京復就衆議院議員。

君は前清光緒二十八年山東高等小學堂を卒業し、同省官費留學生として日本に抵り、在學三年正式に卒業す。三十一年鹿兒島第七高等校造士館に入り、在學三年正式に卒業す。遂に東京帝國大學法科に入りて學ぶこと二年、時適ま武昌義を起すや君遂に學を廢して歸國し、民軍に投じて山東軍政府を組織し、其の外交司長となり、南北統一して參議院北京に移るや、職を辭して歸省し、各界を聯合して民生の發展を圖り、元年春山東墾植協會を創立し專ら移民殖邊を以て國を利し民を富すを主義とせり、同時に選ばれて山東省議會議員となり旋で衆議院議員に舉げられ、憲法起草委員となる。國會停止後、乃ち蒙古の多倫赤峯に赴き枏開魯林西等の蒙古各地を經て、墾荒の狀況を調査し、藉りて袁氏橫暴の鋒を避けたり。本年二月上海に到りて同人と國會を組織し、大局解決後、晉京して復た衆議院議員と爲る。

民國之精華　（傳記）史澤咸先生

Mr. Shih Tse-hsien, another name Kang-feng. He was born in the prefecture of Yo-ling, Shan-tung. In the twenty eight of Kuo-hsu, he graduated the Shang-tung Senior Grammer School. As a result, he was ordered by Shang-tung government to study in Japan. In the year of the thirty first of Kuo-hsu, he entered the "Zoshikan," the Seventh High College at Kagoshima, and completed the three year regular courses successfully. For next two years, he remained in the Tokyo Imperial University studying law, but revolution occurred in Wu-chang, which recalled him to his country. He at once plunged in dust and blood of the struggle and took an active part to the organization of Shang-tung republic. Subsequently he succeeded to take the post of the minister of foreign affairs in that provisional government. In the removal of the assembly to Peking after the union of the South and North, he resigned the office. He went back to his native place with an intention of enrichment of national welfair by establishing strong connections of people in all occupations. In the spring time of the fourth year of Republic, he organized the Shang-tung Colonization Company intending the betterment of national wealth by the expansion of industry and colonization. At about the same time, he was returned a member of Shan-tung provincial assembly, and afterwards gained a chair in the Republican Parliament. He was made a member of the committee, and entrusted with the duty of drofting a constitution. On the dissolution of parliament, he went to To-lin-chih-feng of Kou-pe. He passed through those places of Tau-kai-chin-lin-hsi in Mongolia, investigating both conditions of caltivating and waste lands. Thus he could escape the treacherous hands of the dictater Yuan. On february of 1916, he went to Shang-hai and established national assembly with those of same mind. On the settlement of general situation, he came to the capital, and was elected a member of the Parliament again.

朱溥恩 字稺竹 歲四十三

選舉地 江蘇省

籍貫 江蘇省武進縣

住址 北京前門內前紅井九號

君秉性聰頴。少時即有志農商。實習數載。後以父命迫令。專心讀書。旋即遊庠。並補優廩生。其爲人精明強幹。熱心公益。素爲鄉里所推重。自科舉停罷。講求法政。提倡學務。不遺餘力獨資創辦喬陰學校。任校長兼敎員。成績優良。地方風氣。賴以開通。歷任武陽敎育會長。武陽農會常任宣講員。武陽籌備縣自治駐所幹事。武進鄉董董。公所總董。常州府中學校庶務長。各省設立諮議局。被選爲江蘇諮議局議員及諮議局常駐議員。辛亥滬蘇獨立。在常與同志謀響應。組織軍政府及民政署君任民政總務長。將及一年。諸事就緒。即辭職。改組國民黨。任正部長。辦理國會省會選舉。大獲優勝。君亦被選爲衆議院議員。國會解散。歸里不問政治。因平日研究農商。確有心得。遂盡力於樹桑育蠶兼營商業。及推翻帝制。國會重開。將所辦農商各事。委人經理。仍出席於議院。

君秉性聰頴なり。少時農商に志して實習數年、遂に父の命によりて專心皆を讀み、優廩生に補せらる。人と爲り精明強幹にして、科舉の制能むや、法政の學を攻究し、熱心興學を提唱す。自ら資を投じて喬陰學校を創立して校長兼敎員に任す。武陽敎育會長、武陽農會常任宣講員、武陽縣自治準備所幹事、武進鄉董董公所總董、常州府中學校庶務長等の職に歷任したり。各省諮議局成立するや、江蘇諮議局議員に常選し、又た諮議局常駐議員と爲る。

辛亥の歲滬蘇獨立するや、同志と響應を謀り、軍政府及び民政署を組織し、君民政總務長に任ずること一年、後ち辭職して國民黨正部長に任じ、省議會及び國會議員の選舉を處理して大に勝を得、君亦た衆議院議員に常選す。國會解散後、歸鄉して政治を問はず、平日農商業上の素養あるを以て、蠶桑並に商業を營む。國會恢復するに及び、其の農商各事業を人に託して召集に應じ、仍は衆議院議員たり。

Mr. Chu Pu-en, known as Chi chu, age forty three, a native of Wu-chin-chien, Chang su, was brought up as a business man in young days, but never neglected his study since such was his father's wishes. He studied law, and at his own expense, he established a school called the Chiao yin of which he became the president and instructor. He was appointed a director of Wu Yan agricultural association, that of the preparatory committee for the Wu-yan civic body and several other similar institutions. He was also a member of the Chang Su advisory board. When the Chang Su became independent at the time of the Revolution, he was appointed the chief of the civil administration which function he most successfully discharged. He was then returned for the House of Commons. On the suppression of this assembly, he returned home, but never bothered himself with politics. For a while, he was interested in sericultural industry, and general lines of business, but when the Parliament was reopened, he became a member of the House of Commons.

朱觀玄　字碧齊　歲三十九

選舉地　福建省

籍　貫　福建省建陽縣

住　址　北京西長安街雙柵欄健盧

君為人正直耿介。不隨流俗浮沈。性喜
質樸。富於堅忍之力。自幼好為義舉。
然不肯輕于允諾。人有所託。必量其力
所至者。事成。應允之。既允後。雖赴湯燉。亦
所不辭。事成。絕無矜意。生平疾惡如
仇。見人不平。雖陷路。必奮身助之。常
以此自瀕于危。而不以告其人。故受恩
者。事後聞之。感戴愈摯。自幼聰頴絕
倫。稚齡讀書。即能領悟義理。年方弱
冠。即已下筆數千言。皆斐然成章。詞
達義明。脫盡彫刻之陋習。及長。尤博
覽羣書。頗以名儒自相期許。其為文喜
獨樹一幟。不矯襲古人之陳規。而學派
則不拘漢宋。考据義理。兼重不偏。民
國五年共和克復。及國會重開。君補缺
應召集。仍就眾議院議員。

民國之精華　（傳記）　朱觀玄先生

君人と爲り正直にして耿介、流俗と共に浮沈せず。性質
朴を喜びて堅忍の力に富む。幼より義を好み、輕々しく
允諾せず。人託する所あれば先づ自らの力を量って後之
を應諾し、既に諾したる後は湯燉に赴くと雖も亦た辭せず、
事成つて絕て矜意あるなし。生平惡を疾むこと仇の如く、
人の不平を見るや必ず身を奮つて之を助く。幼より聰頴
絕倫にして少年書を讀み即ち能く義理を悟了し、弱冠に

して下筆數千言、皆な斐然として章を成し、詞達し義明
に彫刻の陋習を脱す。長するに及び尤も群書を涉獵して
頗る名儒を以て自ら相許す。世に處し物に接して偏私な
く、正論を把持して公議を主張し、兼て地方の公益事業
に盡瘁して、鄉黨の推重する所となる。民國五年共和克
復して國會重ねて開かるゝに及び、君補缺として召集に
應じ、仍ほ衆議院議員の職に就きたり。

朱觀玄先生

Mr. Chu Kuan-hsuan, another name Pi-chi, Chien-yang, prefecture, Fukian district, thirty nine years old. He is honest, plain, and patient; never cares to follow the world, does not give any promise before he thoroughly measured the question, but gave once an assurance he is responsible to the end. Since he accomplished one thing he never thinks of any kind of reward materially and spiritually. He hates evils like enemy and always ready to rescue the unfortunate. He was very bright boy as he read through 2 cores of books and understood the meanings of all of them. He composeed many thousand words proses, all of which were elegant literally works, skillful are of words, abundant vocabulary, and the clear-cut style, entirely free from any kind of rules or customs, may be found scarcely anywhere. Growing older, he surveyed almost all books and was considered as an eminent scholar. Equity and justice to all men and things are motto of Mr. Chu Kuan-hsuan He was always insistent on having a popular assembly to discuss and decide the public affaires. He was an enthusiastic public man in his locality and has done a great deal in promoting the public welfare; for these reasons he is loved by all the people who know or hear of him. In the fifth year of the Republic the national congress has been restored and was sent to the Lower House as the favorable result of the by-election.

朱兆莘　字鼎青　歲三十八

選舉地　華僑

籍貫　廣東省花縣

住址　北京順治門外東椿樹胡同十八號

君爲人忠厚朴實。生平無僞言。弱冠讀書。即抱大志。於前淸時以優廩生。肄業于廣雅書院內學齋。旣畢業。獎給舉人。光緒三十三年。奉學部派往美國留學。兼辦華橋學務。先入紐約大學校商務財政科。畢業。得學士學位。繼入哥侖比亞大學法政科。畢業。得碩士學位。又入通儒院博士研究科。民國元年冬。充美洲華僑選舉代表回國。民國二年二月。當選爲參議院華僑議員。兼任北京大學校商科主任敎員。總統府秘書。總統府諮議。國會停止後。歸任廈門鼓浪嶼會審公堂堂長。旋復至京師充律師。因國會復活。遂應召。仍就參議員議員之職。

君人と爲り忠厚にして朴實、生平僞言なし。弱冠書を讀みて卽ち大志を抱き、前淸時代優廩生を以て廣雅書院西學齋に肄業し、旋て復た北上して京師大學優級師範科に入りて業を畢へ、獎して擧人を給せらる。光緒三十三年學部の命を奉じて米國に留學し、兼ねて華僑の學務を辦す。先づ紐育大學校商務財政に入りて卒業し、學士の學位を得たり。繼いで哥侖比亞大學法政科に入りて卒業し、碩士の學位を得たり。又た通儒院博士研究科に入り、碩士の學位を得たり。民國元年に米華僑選舉代表として歸國し、二年二月選ばれて參議院華僑議員となり、兼ねて北京大學校商科主任敎員、總統府秘書、總統府諮議に任す。國會停止後、南下して廈門鼓浪嶼會審公堂々長に任じ、旋て復た北京に抵りて辯護士の業を爲す。國會復活と共に召集されて再び參議院議員と爲る。

Mr. Chu Chao-hsin, another name Ting-ching. He was born in the prefecture of Hua, Kuang-tung province. He is a man of character inspired by patriotic spirit. He is just and upright in his words as well as in his deeds. Fondness for reading, when very young has fostered in him a great ambition. During the period of the Chin he proved himself an excellent pupil in the western learning department of Kuang-ya-shu-yuan Seminary. Then he entered King-shih University and completed higher normal department. He passed succesfully the exermination of the civil service for the second stage. In the thirtythird year of Kuang-hsu, he was ordered by the government to go abroad to study the modern science in the United States of America. He matriculated at first to the commercial department of New York University, and was confered the degree for B. A. Then he entered Columbia University, and remained there in the political department, until he was confered M. A.'s degree. He was also admitted to study in the Doctor's Institute. In the first year of the Republic, he returned to his beloved country as a representative of Chinese electors in America. And in the course of the following year, he was elected a member of the Parliament and at the sametime he succeeded to those parts of headprofessor of the commercial department of Peking University, and secretary to councelor of the government. After the Parliament was dissolved, he went down into the South and was made President of Ku-lang-hsing-hui-hsiao-kung-tang. In the meantime, however, he found himself in Peking, engaging in law practice. On the reestablishment of National Assembly, he was again elected a member of Parliament.

朱家訓　字述齊　歲三十七

選舉地　陝西省
籍貫　陝西省隴縣
住址　北京校場六條

君秉性剛直。不隨俗浮沈。然謙虛好問。喜聞蓋言。人告以過。雖未盡富。必欣然謝之。然使譽過其實。則反盛怒形于顏色。自幼慷慨好義。見人不平。常忿忿不自禁。過於身受。弱冠時。嘗以是與人爭。不顧已身之利害。及長。修養漸積。始稍趨和平。以前清廩貢生。於宣統元年。被任為本省諮議局議員。二年。保送孝廉方正。朝考一等。籤分甘肅知縣。民國元年任西安府佐治員。兼長安縣郡審員。二年被選為眾議院議員。國會解散任四川胖鎮鹽務權稅官。四年。任甘肅第三區於酒公賣局局長。及至國會復行召集。仍來京。就眾議院議員之職。

民國之精華　（傳記）　朱家訓先生

君資性剛直にして俗流に隨はす、然かも謙虛以て問を好み蓋言を聞くを喜ぶ。人若し告ぐるに過を以てすれば未だ盡く常らすと雖、必ず欣然として之を謝す。若し譽にして其の實に過ぐれば則ち反つて怒色あり。幼よりして慷慨義を好み、人の不平を見れば常に自ら忿々として禁せず。弱冠の時、嘗て是を以て人と爭ひ、己が身の利害を顧す。其の長するに及びて修養漸く積みや、始めて稍や和平に趨きたり。前清の廩貢生を以て、宣統元年選は

れて陝西省諮議局議員と爲る。二年孝廉方正を保送され、朝考一等にして、籤を甘肅知縣に分たれたり。民國元年西安府佐治員に任じ、長安縣審計員を兼ねたり。二年選ばれて眾議院議員と爲る。國會解散後、去つて四川胖鎮鹽務權稅官に任す。四年甘肅第三區於酒公賣局々長に任す。本年國會恢復して再び召集を行ふや、仍は普京して眾議院議員の職に就きたり。

五十七

Mr. Chu Chia-hsun, another name Shu chī. He was born in the prefecture of Lim, Hsia-hsihsing in the year 1880. He was the man of strong character governed by the principle of integrity. So he never made his way compromisingly through the world. Humbled himself, he liked to ask and enjoyed to hear advice. He willingly thanked for those who pointed out of his faults though not partinent to him, while displeased with those who praised him too much. From his boyhood he rejoiced to live in a heroic deed. Suffered and indignated at with those insulted, he risked his life in quarrelling with when he was a mere boy. However as he grew up, the gradual development of his culture brought along in him a gentle disposition. During the period of Chin Dynasty he was made fellow and was appointed member of legislative assembly of Hsia-hsi, in the first year of Hsuan hsu. In the first year of Republic he was appointed secretary of Hsi-an-fu besides being commissioner of Changan prefecture. For the next year he gained a chair in Parliament, and after its dissolvement he was appointed inspector of Salt Monopoly Bureau at Sze-shuen. In the fourth year he accepted the office of superintendent of the third district Wine Monopoly Bureau at Kan-suh. On the reorganization of national assembly he was called out to Peking and has been elected again member of Parliament.

朱騰芬 字馨梓 歲三十五

選舉地　福建省
籍貫　福建省屬鼎縣
住址　北京安福胡同双柳欄健廬

君賦性溫厚和平。工於交際。然又篤實不欺。動止以禮自持。為人精明強幹。富於忍耐。與人交。覷直不阿。人有過。輒直斥不諱。人告以過。雖未盡當。必欣然謝之。少好義。喜為人鳴不平。里人有以金錢受窘者。輒解囊助之。不復望報。遠近爭稱其名。中年。慨然有志以挽回危亡自任。遂決志以私費游學東京。肄業於日本法政大學。畢業歸國。充福建公立法政學校校長。民國二年國會成立被選為衆議院議員。兼院內典股常任委員。國會解散後。歸里獨居。絕口不談政事。人叩以政見。輒以提倡道德為言。不為具體之答覆。及國會重開。遂入都為衆議院議員。

君秉性溫厚にして和平なり。交際に工に、然かも篤實にして欺かず、動止禮を以て自ら持す。人と為り精明強幹にして忍耐に富む。其の少時義を好み喜んで人の為に不平を鳴らす、里人金錢を以て窘を受くる者あれば輒ち自ら囊を解いて之を助け、復た其の報を望まず。故に遠近争つて其の名を稱す。中年に及び慨然として國家の危亡を挽回する事を以て任じ、遂に志を決して私費を以て東京に游學し、日本法政大學に學び、畢業後歸國して福建公立法政學校々長となる。民國二年正式國會の成立に際し、選ばれて衆議院議員と為り、院内典股常任委員となる。國會解散後、南旋歸省以て郷關に韜晦し、絕へて政事を談せず、人若し政見を叩くあれば、輒ち道德を提唱するを以て言と為し、具體的答覆を為さず。以て嫌忌を避けたり。國會の復活と共に再び北上して政界に入り現に衆議院議員の職に在り。

Mr. Chu Teng-fen, another name Hsing-tzu. He was born in the prefecture of Fu-ting, Fu-chien in the year 1882. He was a man of amiable character and gentle disposition, whose actions are governed by politeness and the law of whose life is humble. In his skilful intercourse, he commands esteem and respect and secured the confidence of others. He was a man of clear headed and strong insight and even a man of fortitude. Quite as chivalrous was the conduct of him when very young. He would give help with his own money those villagers pressed for and expected nothing. Thus he commaned esteem and repect of them. As he grew up, he realized himself that it was his duty to act in an emergency of the country and to deliver from its danger. So it caused him to determine to denate his energies to study in Japan. With his own expense he entered the college of law and politics in Japan. He returned to his home after completion of courses and was appointed president of Fu-chien institution of law and politics. In the second year of Republic, when the national assembly was legally established, he gained a chair in Parliament and subsequently he was made acting committee of Tien shu in Parliament. After the dissolvement of Parliament he retired into his native place and hiddened himself. As a result, he took no active part of politics nor gave any concrete political view however he was asked, but simply stating his present participation of morality. Thus he concealed himself from being suspected. On the reorganization of national assembly, he plunged himself into the political world again and has been elected member of Parliament.

朱念祖 字伯箴 歲三十五

選舉地　江西省
籍　貫　江西省
住　址　北京棉花五條西頭

君賦性溫和。好靜能思。然志向既定。能奮迅直前不畏艱苦。自幼好讀。及長。博覽群書。尤注意經世之學。以前清優附生。入中學堂。旋考取官費。旋送日本留學。先畢業於宏文書院。復入明治大學政治科。既畢業得政治學士學位。歸國後。於民國元年調任吉安府知事。民國二年調任撫州知事。兼第四區衆議員覆選監督。旋被選爲參議院議員。在院內歷充議事細則起草及院治審查等委員。是年八月與褚補成趙世鈺等八人。以革命嫌疑同時被捕。留於皖垣之軍政執法處。直至民國五年七月始被釋出獄。時方國會復活。遂應召入京。仍充參議院議員。九月被舉爲參議院外交委員長。

君賦性温和にして静思を好み、然かる志既に定まれば勇往邁進して艱苦を畏れず。幼より讀を好み、長ずるに及び群籍を渉獵して尤も經世の學に注意す。前清優附生を以て中學堂に入り、旋て官費を以て日本に留學し、宏文學院を卒業して明治大學に入り政治科を卒業す。歸國後民國元年吉安府知事に任じ、二年撫州知事と爲り、第四區衆議院議員覆選監督を兼ぬ。旋て選ばれて參議院議員と爲る。院内に在りて議事細則起草及び院治審査等の委員に歷充す。是年八月、褚補成趙世鈺等と八人、革命嫌疑を以て同時に捕はれ、安徽の軍政執法處に抑留せられ時方に國會復活す、遂に召集に應じて入京し、仍ほ參議院議員と爲る。九月舉げられて參議院外交委員長と爲る。

民國之精華　（傳記）　朱念祖先生

Mr. Chu Nien-tsu, otherwise known as Pai-chien, age thirty five is a native of Chiang-hsi province. He is quiet and pensive, but when once his mind is made up, he pushes on without the fear of any suffering. As he grew older, he was sent to Japan where he was graduated from the Meiji University. In the first year of the Republic, he was appointed the governor of one of the provinces. Later, he was appointed a member of the Senate, and was on the committee of drawing up rules and regulations. It was in the same year that he was suspected of the implication with revolutionary movement, and was arrested but when the Parliament was restored, he was released from the prison, and elected a member of the Senate in the Parliament newly opened. He is appointed the chief of the diplomatic committee of the Senate.

朱甲昌　字仲夔　歲三十

選舉地　江蘇省

籍　貫　江蘇省泰縣

住　址　北京爛慢胡同七十三

君天資聰穎絕倫。富於理想。然爲人誠實不欺。雖年少氣盛。而無虛驕氣習。少時讀書。專求有用之學。不從事於考据詞章。及長。尤精思深入。洞悉事理。故工於詞令。長於幹才。君性至孝。稚齡,即守遠惡崇善之庭訓。故既入社會後。猶服膺不忘。故雖交游遍天下。而未嘗接近姦邪。所識稍有失德。即與絕交。不復存世故之念。以故里人皆極愛敬之。光復後。民國二年。正式國會成立。被選爲參議院議員。國會解散後。南旋歸里。五年及國會重行召集。遂又北上抵京。現仍復參議院議員職。

君天資聰穎頴偏にして理想に富む。然かも人と爲り誠實にして欺かず、年少氣盛なりと雖虛驕の氣風無く、少年書を讀み專ら有用の學を求めて詞章の末に從事せず。長するに及びて尤も思索して義理を洞悉す。故に詞令に工なるも幹才に長す。君性至孝にして幼より即ち惡を遠ざけ善を崇ぶの庭訓を守り、既に社會に出づる後も猶は服膺して忘れず。交游の士は天下に遍しと雖、未だ曾て姦邪を近けず、知人にして稍も德を失するものあれば即ち交を絕ちて復た世故の念を存せず。故に鄉人之を敬重す。漢土光復して後、民國二年正式國會成立するや、君選ばれて衆議院議員と爲る。國會解散後、南旋して鄉國に歸臥す。五年國會重ねて召集を行ふに及び、遂に又た北上して北京に抵り、現に仍は參議院議員の職に復した。

Mr. Chu Chia-chang, another name Chung Kuei, Tai prefecture, Chiang su district, thirty years old. We can find one of the most brilliant idealists in Mr. Chu chia chang, yet he is honest and true to every one. He was a dashing young man but these could not be seen even a least tint of vanity. He was fond of reading and study of literary works. Growing older a most thoughtful man we can find him; his fine etiquette and good manner can rarely be found outside of a diplomatic circle. It is said that his home training has built up his magnanimous quality and the instruction, received from his parents are considered as his guide even after he went into the world. He is very popular but never seeks an intimate friendship with a wicked man. If he finds that one of his friends does not maintain his virtue he never would see him again; this shows how he is strict and sincere, which was cause of reverence toward him on the past of the town people. In the second year of the Republic the National Parliament was formally inaugurated; he was then elected a member of the Upper House. On the dissolution of Parliament he went back to the South and lived easy life until the fifth year when Parliament convened again. He was called to resume the old seat in the House.

江贅桑布　歳四十三

選舉地　西藏
籍　貫　西藏
住　址　北京雍和宮北大門

君賦性誠實朴質。不喜浮華。生平不爲
妄言。雖有所秘密。亦但以不便詳告爲
言。決不飾詞搪塞。然天資絕高。悟性
敏捷。表觀雖極平凡。而當於內容。思
想活潑。好讀書。而不喜尋摘章句。唯
以推求義理爲懷。自幼慷慨好義。喜救
人急難。及長。尤有任俠之風。遠近部
落。爭稱其名。曾在西藏充當忠譯堪
布。於光緒三十四年。由達賴喇嘛奏
留駐京當差。充唐古忒學教習。民國
二年五月。被選爲參議院議員。是年
十二月。被任爲政治會議議員。民國三
年六月。得四等嘉禾章。國會解散後。
閉戶讀書。絕意政治。及國會復⋯。始
入京。仍爲參議院議員。

君や賦性誠實朴直にして浮華を喜ばず。生平妄言を爲さ
すして、秘密ありと雖亦た但だ詳言に便ならすと云ひて
決して詞を飾つて搪塞せざる也。然り天資高邁にして悟
性敏捷なるも、表面顏る平々凡々を極め、而して內に活潑
の思想を藏す。讀書を好みて、章句を摘むを喜ばず、唯だ
義理を推求するを以て念と爲す。幼よりして慷慨義を好
み、喜んで人の難を救ひ、長するに及びて尤も任俠の風あ
り、皇近の部落爭つて其の名を稱す。曾て西藏にありて
忠譯堪布に充つ。光緒三十四年達賴喇嘛より上奏して北
京駐在の職に當らしめ、唐古忒學教習となる。民國二年
五月選ばれて參議院議員となり。國會停止後、政治會議
議員となり、民國三年六月四等嘉禾章を得たり。本年重
ねて國會復活するや、再び出でゝ參議院議員と爲りたり。

民國之精華　（傳記）　江贅桑布先生

Mr. Chiang-tsan-Sang-pu. He was born in the prefecture of La-sa. He is a man of integrity
and upright which revealed both in his words and deeds. He is widely reputed to possess high intelligence and the keenest understanding, though never paraded it himself. He showed a striking fondness
for reading and pursued to take in the meaning of those books without keeping to the words or
phrases. In his boyhood, all the heroic deeds charmed him and as its results, it effected him, as he
grew, in his conducts with uniform heartiness and sympathy for others. Thus he secured esteem and
respect of all neighbouring villages. In may of the second year of the Republic, he gained a chair in
the Parliament, and on its desolation, he was appointed a member of Political Council. In the third
year of the Republic, he was confered a decoration of the "Fourth Rank" Chiaho-chang. On the
reorganization of the Parliament, he has been elected again a member of the Parliament.

江天鐸　字巚盫　歲三十七

選舉地　西藏

籍　貫　廣東省花縣

住　址　北京宣武門外大街萬家花園

君天資聰慧敏活。頗富進取之氣象。才華煥發。談論風生。蓋日本早稻大學校政治科畢業一秀才。而中國法律界一偉才也。少貧苦。未冠豪筆游四方。居滬較久。營出版業。編譯天下有用之書。又新聞雜誌記者。正論公議。爲一世之重。夙抱大志。前清壬寅。貢笈東渡。中外志士爭結契。在日本專心攻究政法之學。丁未歸國。充民政部則例局纂修。未幾。以政治革命嫌疑。被政府下命逮捕。潛避得免。復赴日本。專攻法律之學。造詣既深。宣統庚戌歸國。在京師高等警察學堂。執務鞭。民國成立以後。業律師。被舉律師公會會長。民國二年正式國會成立。被選爲衆議院議員。旋又爲徐國務卿顧問。共和克復。及國會重開。君仍充衆議院議員。

君天資聰慧にして敏活、頗る進取の氣象に富む。才華煥發にして談論風生す、蓋し日ト早稻大學政治科出身の一秀才にして、中國法學社會の一異才たるなり。少にして貧、弱冠筆を載せて四方に游び、上海に在りて出版業を營みて天下有用の書を編纂譯述し、又た新聞雜誌記者として正論公議一世の重を爲す。夙に大志を抱いて東海を渡り、日本に留學して政法の學を攻究し、丁未の歲歸國して民政部則例局纂修に任ず。未だ幾もなく革命の嫌疑を以て逮捕されんとす。潛に遁れて日本に赴き更ら法律學を修ひ。宣統庚戌の歲歸國して京師高等警察堂に敎鞭を執りたり。民國成立以後、辯護士を業とし、辯護士公會々長に舉げらる。民國二年正式國會成立に際し衆議院議員に當選す。國會停止後、徐國務卿の顧問に聘せらる。國會再び開くるに及び、仍は復た衆議院議員と爲る。

Mr. Chiang Tien-to, another name Chin-o, Hua prefecture, Kwantung district, thirty seven years old. He is one of the most sagacious and brilliant men and we can hardly find a parallel with his progressive and ambitious nature, and his eloquence. He was one of the most promising graduates of the Waseda University where he pursued courses on political science. He is really a prominent man among the jurists of China. Poverty in his youth completed him to earn his living by his writing which he was distinguished while very young. He established a publishing co. of himself in Shanghai, and edited or translated valuable books of the East and West. As an editor of certain newspaper or magazine made himself very popular throughout the country. During the late Emperial reign he went to Japan crossing the Eastern Sea with the ambition of studying political science. In due time he accomplished what he disired to complete. Returning to the Middle Kingdom he was appointed to counsellor at the Legal Buleau, administrative department. While he was in the office he was in danger of imprisonment on the assumption that he was a revolutionist. He escaped the country very quietly to Japan where he studied further laws. In the reign of Hsuan-tung he returned to China to take up a professorship at the Higher Police School of Peking. Since the Republic was established he was admitted to the Chinese Bar, later he was president of the Bar Association. In the second year of the Republic he was elected to member of the Lower House and after the dissolution he became the adviser to the secretary of state Hsu. On the reconvening of Parliament he has returned to the House to occupy the old seat.

江　浩　字注源　歲三十七

選舉地　直隸省

籍　貫　直隸省玉田縣

住　址　北京西單牌樓後牛肉灣二十二

君少好義。喜爲人鳴不平。里人有以困
于資者。輒解囊助之。不復望報。遠近
爭稱其名。然居心仁厚。雖仇敵亦不虐
待之。與人交。喜相責以善。人告以過。
輒大喜。自幼好讀。喜博覽羣書。純以
主觀判斷是非。而不局于習俗之成見。
故其文采風流。亦超出儕輩。弱冠時。
即以名儒自期。旋復立志棄舊從新。編
購譯本讀之。尤注意於政法之學。遂留
學日本。入警監學校。畢業歸國後。歷
充諮議局選舉調查員。罪犯習藝所所
長。自治預備會會員。中學校監。民國
元年被選爲省議會議員。現充參議院
議員。

君少にして義を好み、喜んで人の爲に不平を鳴らす。里
人資に窮する者あれば輙ち囊を解いて之を助け、復た報
を望まず、遠近つつて其の名を稱す。然かも居心仁厚に
して仇敵と雖亦た之を虐待せず。人と交るや喜んで善を
以て相責め、人の告ぐるに過を以てすれば輙ち大に喜ぶ。
幼より讀書を好み博き群書を覽る。是非の判斷を主觀し
て習俗の成見に局せず、故に其の文采風貌亦た儕輩に超
出す。弱冠の時、即ち名儒を以て自ら期したり。旋て復

た志を立て、舊を棄て新に從ひ、譯本を購求して之を讀
み、尤も政法の學に注意する所あり。遂に意を決して日
本に留學し、警察監獄學校に入り、業を畢へて歸國する
や、直隸省諮議局選舉調查員となり、罪犯習藝所長、自
治預備會々員、中學校學監に歷任したり。民國元年選は
れて省議會議員となり、復た舉げられて参議院議員と爲
りて、現に其の職に在り。

Mr. Chiang-hao, another name Chu-yuan. He was born in the prefecture of Yu-tien Chi-li hsing in the year 1880. All chivalrous deads fascinated him when very young. He would gladly help with his own many those who pressed-for and expected nothing. Thus he secured esteem and respect of all neighborning villlagers. He was generous and merciful to his opponent. He never condemned others but esteemed all such things as friends that desire to fite off his fetters and help him out of prejudice. He showed a striking fondness for reading when very young and chosed many of best books. Thus he passed his upright course through reading. He had no regard for popular vew but held to his purpose. So he surpassed most people in his literary ability and talent. He had designed himself in his youth for confucian scholar but the new light which now broke in upon him to denote his energies to the abolition of the electing educationed systms and to the establishment of a new. Happily for him, he was able to acquire a kowledge of law and politics as he succeded in obtaining books in traslation. These works effected complete revolution in his mind. He went to Japan and found himself, busy in study in the training istitution of police and judge. On his return to home after his graduation, he was appointed election-commissioner of legislative assembly of Chili. Later he succeded to these posts of police training institution, member of society for provinial administration and acting principal of middle-school. In the first year of Republic he was made member of provincial assembly and then gained a chair in Parliament.

江 琠 字玉泉 歲三十四

選舉地　廣東省
籍貫　廣東省廉江縣
住址　北京潘家河沿高州會館

君爲人慷慨尚義。海內維新後。銳意新學。以廣東高等學堂預科最優等畢業生。日本大學法科畢業生。歷任廣東各學校教員。辛亥光復。被選爲廣東臨時省議會議員。兼財政股委員。當國會爲議員。兼法律股審查員。當國會爲袁政府非法蹂躪。強索徽章證書時。遄返廣東。旋爲廣東當局所偵知。突派軍警數十人荷槍實彈。圍宅大索。倉皇逃避難於香港澳門廣州灣等地。幾爲所獲。繼復亡命上海。任進步書局及各館編纂事宜。足跡不涉鄉閭者三年。帝制禍興。更兼任報館筆政。盡筆誅口伐之責。及國會復活。遂入都仍任衆議院議員。君生平著述。除箸而未成者外。其已成者。有諸子通論。史學史。子學史。詩學史。說文古籀訂訛。毛詩釋例。經學講義。低文初步及筆記。詩文集等。

君人と爲り慷慨にして義を尚び、海內維新後銳意新學を攻究す。廣東高等學堂預科を最優等にて卒業し、又た日本大學法科を卒業す。斯くて廣東各學校教員に歷任し、辛亥光復後廣東臨時省議會議員に選ばれ、法律股審査員を兼ぬ。旋て衆議院議員に舉げられ、財政股委員を兼ぬ。既にして國會が袁政府の非法蹂躪する所となりて徽章證書を強索せられ、急ぎ廣東に歸るや廣東當局の爲に偵知され、軍警數十人武裝して其の宅を包圍す。君倉皇逃走して難を香港澳門廣州灣等の各地に避く。繼で復た上海に亡命し、進步書局及び各館の編纂事務に任ず、帝制の禍あるや、更に新聞記者として筆誅口伐の責を盡したり。國會復活するに及び、遂にまた都に入りて衆議院議員に任す。君生平の著述にして現に完成せる者、諸子通論、史學史、子學史、詩學史、說文古籀訂訛、毛詩釋例、經學講義、作文初步及び筆記、詩文集等あり。

Mr. Chiang Shien another name Yu-chuan. He was born in the prefecture of Lienchiang, Kuang-tung hsing in the year 1883. He was a man of patriotic spirit and valued heroic deeds highly. The intestine restration of the country had effect of causing him to turn his attention to the study of new learning. On his completion with honours of the preparatory department of Kuang-tung Higher School, he entered college of law and politics in Japan, and finished the law department. Then he was engaged successively as teacher in many schoo's at Kuang-tung. The revolution of Hrin shih had taken place, he was also elected member of Kuang-tung temporal provincial assembly besides being appointed committee of inquiring law affairs. Then in a meanwhile he gained a chair in Parliament and was made committee of financial affairs. No sooner the Parliament was dissolved by the legal hand of Yuanshi-Kai government and the members were striped off their badge and certificate than he returned to Kuangtung. However his presence had been ferreted out by the Kuang tung authorities. He scarcely escaped from seize which, while in his house, laid by a company of soldiers, into those places at Hsiang-chiang, Kuang Chon wan. Later he refuzd himself in Shanghai and was engaged in editing at the offices and progressive party bureau. On the growth of tendency toward Imperialistic government he opposed and attacked through his paper. The national assembly was re-opened and he was elected member of Parliament. He published those works on "Chu-Tzu-tung-lin" "History of historology," "Wen-hsiao shih, histiory of poetry," "Mas-shih-ticls-li," "Lecture on economic," "Introduction to composition and penmanship" and "a collection of poems," Etc.

仇玉珽　字黻忱　歲四十二

選舉地　奉天省
籍貫　山東省
住址　北京西鐵匠胡同

君自弱冠讀書。即抱大志。少時嘗從事
於詩古文詞諸文藝。嗣覽世界之趨勢
知非有用學。遂決然棄舊從新。前清
末季。以官費留學日本。入宏文學校師
範科。畢業歸國後。委充岫巖初級師
學堂校長。後充縣議會議長。兼充地方
自治事務所所長。於地方利弊。多所建
白。民國元年。充臨時省議會議員。二
年。被選爲衆議院議員。以剛正故。頗
爲袁政府所忌。後因錦洮四路綫問題
發生。上書質問。未及答覆。而取銷之
命令下矣。遂隱身學界。絕口不談政局
者二年。及帝制亂成。乃隻
身赴滬。呼號奔走。函電鼓吹。及至國
會恢復。遂入京。仍爲議員。

君幼より書を讀みて大志を抱き、少時詩古文詞の文藝に
沒頭したるも、世界の趨勢に鑑みて決然舊を棄て新に就
きて有用の學を求む。前清末官費留學生として日本に
遊び、宏文學校師範科に入り卒業して歸國す。後ち、縣議會議長となり、地方自治事
務所々長を兼ね、地方の利弊に於て建白する所多し。民國
元年臨時省議會員に舉げらる。二年選ばれて衆議院議員
となり、正式國會議員中、剛正の故を以て顏を袁政府の忌
む所となる。後ち錦洮四鐵道問題發生さる、や。政府に上
書して質問し、未だ其の答辯に接せざるに早くも取消の
命下る。遂に身を學界に隱して口また政事を談ぜざるも
の二年。帝制の事ありて雲南軍義を起すや、君乃ち身を珽
して上海に赴き呼號奔走これ努む。國會恢復するに及び、
欣然躍躍して召集に應じ、現に衆議院議員の職に在り。

民國之精華　　（傳記）　仇玉珽先生

Mr. Chou Yu-pan, age forty two, is a native of the Chan-tung province. Early in life, he was an ardent admirer of books, and was full of ambition. He indulged himself in the study of classics and poems. However, having become aware of the change of the time, he abandoned the old for the study of the new, seeking at the same time the study of useful learning. Under the previous Chinese regime, he went to Japan at the government's expense, and returned home after having graduated from the normal school course. He was appointed the head of the normal school, and later the president of the local assembly. Being the chief of the civic body, he pointed the evils connected with local districts. In the first year of the Republic, he was chosen a member of the special local assembly, while in the second year of the Republic, he was returned for the House of Commons. He became an object of odium to the Yuanshi-Kai government because of his strong argument. When the Parliament was suppressed, he took refuge in the world of scholarship, and never talked of politics for the space of two years. When the Imperial movement was started, he went to Shang-hai vehemently attacking the unworthy movement. When the Parliament was restored, he went up to Peking and was returned for the House of Commons.

牟　琳　字貢三　歲四十

選舉地　貴州省

籍　貫　貴州省遵義縣

住　址　北京宣武門內象來街八號。

君爲人老成持重。氣慨深厚。生平無
妄動妄言。萬事皆以約爲訓。不輕於作
爲。然秉性慷慨好義。故唯好爲俠舉。
人有困厄。常暗中助之。永不令知。匪
獨不圖報也。常語人曰。吾素愛簡約。
唯以性喜濟人之急。故常舍己芸人。然
必一施即了。始可無累。若因此惹出酬
報譽揚等事。相擾不已。則爲吾所深
惡。其純粹爲己之處。即此可見一斑
矣。前清時。以舉人留學日本。入宏文
師範科。畢業歸國。歷充遵義中學校師
範學校校長敎員。及勸學所總董。前清
宣統元年。舉充貴州諮議局副議長。繼
舉充資政院議員。因即請詣赴日本考
察政治。事畢。仍回京供職。民國成立
被舉爲衆議院議員。兼充進步黨交際
科主任。及帝政發生。回黔運動起義。
偕戴戡熊其勳出師纂江。及帝制取消。
國會恢復遂入京仍充衆議院議員。

君人と爲し老成にして持重し、生平妄動妄言なく、萬事皆
な約を以て訓と爲す。秉性慷慨にして義を好み、人の困
厄するあれば常に暗中に之を助けて永く知らしめず、獨
り報を圖らざるのみにあらざる也。常に曰く、吾素と簡
約を愛す、人の急を濟ふを喜ぶが故に己を舍てゝ人を助
くるもの、然り一たび施せば即ち了る。若し此に因て酬報
及び名譽等を惹出すは累しと。前清時代舉人を以て日本
に留學し、宏文學院師範科を卒業して歸國し、遵義中學
校、師範學校々長敎員及び勸學所總董に歷充す。宣統元
年貴州諮議局副議長に舉げられ、繼いで資政院議員に舉
げらる。即ち否を請て日本に赴き政治を視察し、事畢つ
て歸京其の職に就く。民國成立後、衆議院議員に選ばれ、
進步黨交際科主任たり。帝政問題發生後、貴州に歸りて
起義の事に干與し、戴戡、熊其勳と偕に師を纂江に出す。
帝制は取消され、國會は恢復するや、復た京に入りて衆
議院議員と爲る。

Mr. Mau-lin, another name Kung-sa. He was born in the prefecture Tsun-i, Kuei-Chou-hsing in the year 1866. He was a man of mature experience. He was just, upright and honest in all things in his words and in his work. He was a man inspired by patriotic spirit and fascinated by chivalrous deeds. He would often help in secret those who pressed for and expected nothing. His motto is, "Love simplicity. Be rejoice in sacrificing for those who suffered and expect nothing, for honour and reward participate troubles." During the period of the Chin, he was sent to go abroad to study in Japan. He entered the Normal Department of Hung-wen School and completed all the required courses. On his return to home, he was made successively teacher of Tsun-i Middle School, Master of Normal School, and Superintendent of Kuan-hsiao-pai-hsia. Then he was appointed a member of Tzu-cheng-yuan. Later he was sent at his own request to Japan to investigate politics. After the organization of Republic, he was elected a member of Parliament, and was made a secretary of external affair in the Progressive Party. On the growth of tendency toward Imperialistic government, he took active part to raise an army of righteousness with Tsai-kan, Nan-chi-tung as sole wielders of influence, and despatched troops. The Parliament was reorganized and he has gained the former chair in the Parliament.

札希土噶 字巫懷

選舉地　西藏

籍貫　西藏拉薩

住址　北京報恩寺胡同二十四號

君爲人誠實篤厚言動舉止皆確守古
訓。不稍縱肆。居常以厚道待人。秉性
聰敏異人。自幼即明察事理。思考敏捷
而意志堅強。弱冠讀書。即能發徹起
伏。別關新奇。尤深思明辦。勵行身心
之修養。亦是西藏人中新進之秀才也。
前清光緒三十一年。由西藏揀派來京。
曾歷任御前繙譯。滿蒙高等學堂藏文
敎習。辛亥革命。民國肇造。五大民族
共和告成。民國二年被選爲參議院議
員。代表西藏。翼贊建設。特授三等嘉
禾勳章。國會解散後。在京閑居。讀書
自娛。及國會再行召應。仍復就參議院
議員職。

君人と爲り誠實篤厚にして、言動舉止皆な寵として古訓
を守り、毫も放縱ならず。平生厚道を以て人を待ち、秉
性聰敏人に異る。幼より事理を明察して、思考敏捷、意
思堅强なり。弱冠書を讀みて徹を發し伏を起し、別に新
奇を關き、尤も身心の修養を屬み、亦た是れ西藏人中の
新進秀才なり。前清光緒三十一年、西藏より派遣され
て入京し、曾て御前繙譯に任じ、滿蒙高等學堂藏文敎習
に任す。辛亥の歲、命を革めて民國成立するや、二年選
ばれて參議院議員と爲る、西藏を代表して建設の業を翼
贊したり。功を以て特に三等嘉禾勳章を授けらる。國會
解散後、北京に在りて閑居し、讀書自ら娛む。五年國會
再び召集を行ふや仍ほ復た參議院議員の職に就きたり。

民國之精華　（傳記）札希土噶先生

Mr. Cha Hsi Tu Ko, otherwise known as Wu-i, a native of La Su Thibet, is a politician greatly
different from others. He clings to old traditional teaching. but being naturally quick in understanding
and strong in will power, he was full of original ideas, and is one of the most progressive young men of the
time. In 1905, he came to Peking from Thibet, and was translator and instructor in the high school
in Chind. With the outbreak of the Revolution and the formation of the Republic, he was elected a
member of the Senate, and on behalf of Thibet, he participated in the new movement. On the dissolution
of the Parliament, he stayed in Peking, and indulged himself in reading book. When the Parliament
was again summoned, he resumed his senatorial functin as the member of the body.

向乃祺 字北翔 歲三四

選舉地 湖南省
籍　貫 湖南省永順縣
住　址 北京宣武門外上斜街二十三號

君英資豪爽。才學傑出。亦近世卓異人才也。光緒二十七年。入郡庠。旋考入長沙高等學堂。三年畢業。湖南巡撫端方以官費咨送日本留學。入早稻田大學本科政治經濟科。民國元年卒業受政學士學位。歸國後。充湖南財政司職入科科長。嗣被選爲參議院議員。復由本院互選。爲憲法起草委員會委員。國會停止後。任中國公學大學部經濟科教授。年餘。由四川省巡按使陳廷傑。保免知事。署南部縣缺一年。及國會重開遂入都仍就議員之職。

君天資豪爽にして才學傑出し近世卓異の人才なり。光緒二十七年郡庠に入り、旋て長沙高等學堂に入りて卒業す。湖南巡撫端方より選拔されて官費を以て日本に送り留學せしひ、早稲田大學校本科に入りて政治經濟の學を修めて民國元年卒業歸國す。湖南財政司職入科々長に任ず。嗣民國正式國會成立に際し選ばれて參議院議員となる。開て憲法起草委員會委員に舉げらる。多年依養せる蘊蓄を傾注して國家建設の大業に翼贊せんとしたるも、未だ幾くならずして國會は停止さる。後ち中國公學大學部經濟科教授に任ずること一年餘、四川省巡按使陳廷傑より知事に保薦せられて南部縣知事の缺を署理すること一年。適ま國會再び召集を行ふ。君復た北京に入りて仍は參議院議員と爲る。

Mr. Hsiang nai-chi, another name, Pe yang, Yung shun prefecture, Hu-nan district, thirty-four years old. He is a most disinterested and gifted man China ever produced. In the twenty seven year of Kuang hsu he entered into a county school, then he transferred to the Chang sha Higher School and graduated with honour. The governor-general Tuan fang, of Hu-nan, finding in him an unusual talent sent him with the government expense to Japan where he enrolled in the department of politics and economics, Waseda University. In the first year of the Republic he returned home as soon as he graduated the University and made the head of revenue section, treasury department, Hu-nan government. When the Republican government was organized he was elected a member of the Senate; succeedingly he was appointed a committee man for drafting of the national constitution and his services on this were greatly looked forward. Unfortunately, however, Parliament was suspended; consequently he left the House to accept a professorship on economics in the college department of the Chun kuo kung hsiao, and kept that position for more than one year. Then, came another appointment to the governorship of Nan wu prefecture by the governor-general Chen-ting chieh, of Saichuan district. He held the office for an year, he was called to Peking to resume the seat he held in the Senate.

李保邦　字少文　歳六十二

選擧地　直隷省

籍　貫　直隷省樂亭縣

住　址　北京東四牌樓錢糧胡同東口路南三十四號門牌

君曾て山西隰州直隷縣知事に任じ、嗣で豐鎭廳撫民同知に任じ、至る所治績大に擧りて功勞あり。又た奉天の賑捐を辦理して知府在任候補を奬せらる。宣統元年解州直隷州知事に任じ、二年山西丁巡撫は、君を保薦して曰く才長く守り潔くして、惠政民に及ぶと、以て君の人と爲るを知り且つ其の牧民官としての才幹操守をも知るに足るなり。三年病を以て任を卸し、民國元年に至り、山西隰州並に所屬蒲縣の有力者より民政長に請ふて、君をして隰州知事の本任に返ることとを求め、即ち赴任したるも未だ幾くならずして辭職して鄉里に歸る。二年正式國會成立するに際し、選ばれて衆議院議員と爲る。國會解散後、敢て表見する所無く、閑臥悠々以て身心を養ふ。五年國會再び召集さるに及び、遂に入京して、仍ほ衆議院議員たり。

君爲前淸山西隰州直隷州知州。光緒三十一年到任。因徵稅溢額記功一次。又因挐獲隣境盜首記大功一次。光緒三十二年。調署豐鎭廳撫民同知。因挐獲著名盜犯加大功二次。恩詔加一級。又因辦理奉天賑捐。獎以知府在任候補。宣統元年。調任解州直隷州知州。因辦理警察列表最優等。記大功一次。又因徵兵案內記功一次。宣統二年十二月。山西撫院丁以才長守潔惠政及民註考保薦卓異。宣統三年。因病交卸。民國元年。經山西隰州幷所屬蒲縣紳學各界。在民政長公署呈准回隰州本任。是年四月。遂復返本任。旋因病告假。於五月交卸回籍。二年被選爲衆議院議員。國會解散後。無所表見。及國會重行召集。遂來京仍爲議員。

民國之精華　（傳記）李保邦先生

Mr. Li Pao-pang, otherwise called Shao-wen, age sixty two is a native of Lo-ting, Chi-li province. In his capacity of the governor, his services were extensively recognized. In 1909, he was the governor of the Chi-li province, where he spent over two years enjoying high reputation with the people as the successful governor. On account of illness, he had to resign his post; In the first year of the Republic, the people in Shanhsi district wanted him as the governor. He went to his post, but owing to illness, he returned to his home. In the second year of the Republic, when the Parliament was brought into existence, he was returned for the House of Commons. However, with the dissolution of the Parliament, he returned to his country, taking very little interest in public affairs. However, when the Parliament was restored, he was returned for the House of Commons, the position of honour which he now occupies.

李伯荊 字議軒 歲五十

選舉地　黑龍江省

籍　貫　黑龍江省呼蘭縣

住　址　北京堂子胡同東口外寬街九

君秉性篤實。不喜浮華。自幼聰慧善讀。弱冠即長於詩文。及長。尤奮志求博。經史之外。諸子百家。皆已窺堂奧。然志在淹博。不以舉業自拘。故其爲文常自立一派。以追隨俗尙爲深恥。然爲人慷慨好義。喜爲不平之鳴。見人爲強暴所窘。忿忿不自禁。過於身受。弱冠時常以是與人爭。不顧已身之利害。及修養既充。始稍趨平和。海內維新之際。君極意提倡西學。頗以開通民智自任。曾辦本省敎育二年。宣統元年。被選爲諮議局議員。二年被選爲諮議局副議長。民國元年。被選爲臨時省議會副議長。二年被選爲參議院議員。國會解散。歸里從事於地方公益事業。及國會重開。遂入都。仍就參議院議員職。

君秉性篤實にして浮華を喜ばず。幼より聰慧にして善く讀む。弱冠にして詩文に長じ、長じて群籍を博覽して堂奧を窺ふ。然かも志は淹博に在りて舉子の業を以て自ら拘らず、其の文を作る常に自ら一派を立て、俗尙に投ずるを以て深く恥と爲す。人と爲り慷慨にして義を好み、喜んで不平の鳴を爲し、人若し強暴の爲に窘む所となるを見れば、忿々自ら禁せざること自ら受くるものあり。是を以て常に人と爭つて己が利害を顧みざりし。

修養既に進むに及び始めて稍や平和に趨きたり。海內維新の際、君極めて西學を提倡し、民智を開通する事を以て自任したり。曾て本省の敎育を辦ずること二年、宣統元年選ばれて諮議局議員となり、二年諮議局副議長に舉げらる。又た參議院議員に選ばる。國會解散後、鄕里に歸省して地方の公益事業に從事す。國會重ねて召集さるや遂に都に入りて仍ほ參議院議員の職に就きたり。

Mr. Li-pai-ching, another name Shih-hsien. He was born in the prefecture of Tsie huli chou hsing in the year 1876. He was honest and integrity. He scorned insincerity. Quite as excellent and clever was he when he showed such remarkable talent for taking and composing poem. As he grew up, he chosed many of best books and took in the profoundest meaning of them. He pursued his own course through writing and he had no regard for popularity but held to his principle. He was a man inspired by a high-sense of patriotism and he exhibited character in its most heroic aspects. He suffered and indignated with those who violently appressed by high hand. Thus he would risk himself in quarreling with others. However the gradual development of his culture brought in him a gentle disposition. The intestive restoration which now broke in upon the country determined him to devote all his energies to the establishment of new learning for enlightening nation. For two years he engaged on educational work in his own province. In the first year of Hsuantung, he was appointed member of legislative assembly and in the course of the following year he was made chairman of the same assembly. At about the same time he was elected member of Parliament. On the dissolvement of Parliament he returned to his native place and engaged in enterprising of provincial public benefit. The Parliament was reestablished and he has been called out to be a member in it.

李景濂　字君周　歲四十八

選舉地

籍　貫　直隸省

住　址　北京東門騎河樓福祿館

籍　貫　直隸省邢郿縣

君天資聰穎。性敏捷。然為人老成厚
重。脫盡浮華之氣。少時從吳汝綸學為
古文。為甲午科舉人。甲
辰科進士。官內閣中書。學部總務司案
牘科主事。歷充直隸省城蓮池書院齋
長。直隸大學堂漢文教習。直隸學校司
編譯處編纂。進士館學員。學部專門普
通實業三司行走。北京法政專門學堂
國文教員。北洋五省優級師範學堂專
科國文教員。北洋大學堂霑辦兼預科
國文教員。直隸高等學堂漢文教務長。
直隸文學館副館長。民國以來。歷充北
京大學校預科國文教員。文科左傳門
教員。北京女子師範學校國文教員。被
選為眾議院議員。國會解散後。曾旋任
內務部地方行政講習所國文中央教
員。旋充清史館協修。北京大學校文科
中國哲學門宋學教員。著有學部條議
存稿。左傳講義。中史講義。詩文各集
均未經付梓。以國會復活。遂應召復為
眾議院議員。

民國之精華　（傳記）　李景濂先生

君天資聰穎にして、然かも人と為り老成厚
重にして浮華の氣を脫す。悟性敏捷なり、然かも人と為り老成厚
重にして浮華の氣を脫す。少時吳汝綸に從つて古文を學
び、甲午科舉人、甲辰科進士となり、內閣
中書、學部總務司案牘科主事となり。直隸省蓮池書院齋
長、直隸大學堂漢文教習、直隸學校司編譯處編纂、進士
館學員、學部專門普通實業三司行走、北京法政專門學堂
國文教員、北洋五省優級師範學堂專科國文教員、北洋大
學堂霑辦兼預科國文教員、直隸高等學堂漢文教務長、直
隸文學館副館長に歷充したり。民國成立後は北京大學校
預科國文教員、同文科左傳門教員、北京女子師範學校國
文教員、旋て眾議院議員に選ばる。國會解散後、曾て內
務省地方行政講習所國文中學教員に任じ、旋て清史館協
修、北京大學校文科中國哲學門宋學教員となる。學部條
議存稿、左傳講義、中史講義、詩文各集の著あるも未だ
梓に付せず。國會復活するや召集に應じて再び眾議院議
員と為る。

Mr. Li Ching-lien, another name Yu-chou, age forty, native of Chi-li hsing. He is a man of integrity and wide experiences, and is known of his matured judgment and lack of foisterous manner. Early is his life, he had a rare opportunity to study the classics under the far us scholar and states man E gu lin, and passed all the governmental examination Jen Chin shih with remarkable success. Most important posts is his province, chiefly in educational matters. Even after the formation of the Republic, he was professing the classics in the Peking University, when he was elected a member of the Parliament. After the coup d'etat, he resumed this profession, and became teacher in the schools of the interior department. He wrote many books on the question of eduction, the lecture on a classical history, and many other topics, which are waiting publication. With the reconvening of the Parliament, he became the member of the Parliament again.

七十一

李漢丞 字吟秋 歲四十九

選舉地　湖南省
籍貫　湖南衡山縣
住址　北京象坊橋泰議院西來道

君秉性鯁直好義。喜挫強扶弱。以前清
優附生。於光緒三十年留學日本。先後
畢業于法政大學第四班。及明治大學
警察分科。曾充留日湖南南路懇親會
會長。三十一年。與黃興劉揆一等組織
同盟會。君擔任幹事。三十四年回國。
捐貲創辦衡山開知實業女學校。由縣
詳請容部立案又充衡山勸業所所長。
宣統元年。由本省提學使委充湖南高
等學堂齋務長。兼湖南公立法政學校
教員。辛亥九月湖南光復。君籌辦軍
務。公擧爲湖南南路保安會會長。民國
元年九月。任命爲工商部僉事。二年二
月被選爲參議院議員。三年二月。取得
司法部律師證書。國會解散後。遂專營
律師業。不復與聞時政。及國會重會。
始來京。復供舊職。

君秉性鯁直にして義を好み、強を組き弱を扶くるを喜ぶ。
前清優附生を以て光緒三十年日本に留學し、法政大學第
四班及び明治大學警察科を卒業す。曾て留日湖南南路
懇親會々長に充てらる。三十一年黃與劉揆一等と同盟會
を組織し、君幹事を擔任す。三十四年團に歸り、資を投
じて衡山開知實業女學校を剏辦す。縣より郡に咨して案
を立つ。又た衡山勸業所所長と爲る。宣統貳年本省提學

使より委任せられ、湖南高等學堂齋務長兼湖南公立法政
學校教員と爲る。辛亥九月湖南光復す。君軍務を襄助し
公擧せられて湖南南路保安會々長となる民國元年九月任
命せられて工商部僉事と爲る。二年二月參議院議員に選
ばる。三年二月司法律師證書を領取す。國會解散後遂に專
ら律師業を營み、復た時政に與らず。國會重ねて開かる
、に及び、始めて京に來り復た實職に從ふ。

Mr. Li Han-ching, another name Yin-chin. He was born in the prefecture of Ho-nau-hsing in the year 1878. He was a man of just and upright inspired by chineleous spirit whose character revealed itself in its most heroic aspects. He was ordered by the Chin government to go abroad to study. In the year of 30th Kuang-chu, he went abroad to Japan. There he graduated Law and Political University and then he finished the Police-training department of Meiji University. He was once appointed president of the Union social gathering of Hu-nan and Nan Lu students in Japan. In the thirty one year, acting in concert with Huang-hsing, Liu-kueii and others, he organized a Union Society to which he held the post of secretary. On his return to home in the thirty four years, he established Kai chih practical girl's school in Heng-shan at the cost of his own expense, and he was appointed president of Bureau of encouragement of industry. In the first year of Hsuan-tung he was entrusted, by the educational commissioner of the province, with the duty of administeration of Hu-nan hihher institution, and at the same time he was engaged as teacher in the Public institution of Law and Politics. On aujust Hsin-shih, the revolution broke out in Hu-nan and he responded to the cause in helping military affair. And then he was publicly elected President of Hai-nan Safty-society. Now in the first year of Republic he was made councilor of commercial and industrial department and in the following year he was elected member of Parliament. January, the third year he was confered a certificate of lawyer. The Parliament was dissolved. Now he was engaged in law practice and took no active part to politics. On the reorganization of Parliament he gained the former chairs in it.

李兆年 字濬卿 歲三十九

選舉地　福建省
籍貫　福建省建甌縣
住址　北京棉花胡同五條

君為人頭腦明晰。意思堅強。能忍辱耐勞。富于幹濟之才。然秉性仁厚。篤實無欺。自幼聰穎好讀。弱冠下筆千言。文采大著。及長。專求天下有用之學。尤喜政法律之書。前清以優貢生。錄用知縣。君不甘小成。貢笈入都。肄業京師法政學堂。研磋不倦。造詣既深。以優等畢業。歷任廣東翁源縣。浙江新登縣知縣。又歸充京師初級審判廳推事。地方審判廳推事。治蹟大舉。遠近有令名。辛亥武昌起義。民國造肇。被選為臨時參議院議員。贊襄建設之業。民國二年正式國會成立。當選參議院議員。國會解散後。讀書自娛。及國會恢復。仍為參議院議員。

民國之精華　（傳記）　李兆年先生

君人と為り頭腦明晰にして意思堅強、能く辱を忍び勞に耐へ、幹濟の才に富む。然り秉性仁厚にして篤實欺く無し。幼より聰穎にして讀書を好み弱冠筆を下し千言立るところに成り文采大に著る。長ずるに及び專ら天下有用の學を求め尤も法律の書を究むるを喜ぶ。前清時代優貢生を以て知縣に登用せらる。君小成に甘んぜすして笈を負ふて都に抵り、京師法政學堂に入りて研磋倦まず、造詣既に深く、優等を以て卒業したり。廣東翁源縣、浙江新登縣の知事に歷任し、又た京師初級審判廳推事、地方審判廳推事に歷充し、治蹟大に舉り遠近令命あり。辛亥の歲武昌義を起して民國始めて樹立するや、選ばれて臨時參議院議員と為る。民國二年正式國會成立に際し參議院議員に常選す。國會解散後讀書自ら娛み、國會恢復するに及び、仍は復た參議院議員となる。

Mr. Li Chao-nien, Chien-ou prefecture, Fukiang district, thirty nine years old. Firmness of his will and clearness of his head can be hardly found their equals, above all of them he is indifatigable as well as full of ingenuity; yet, he is kind and true to all. He was very precaucious child, read widely and wrote often clever articles, which was wonder of neighbourhood. Growing older his intellectual taste turned to the study of law books. During the Imperial reign he, as the honorary fellow was appointed a governor. But he looked a still bigger thing and proceeded to Peking to enter the Metropolitan Law and Politics School where he assiduously pursued his study in law. After he graduated with honour he made governor of Heng-yuan, Kwantung district, and of Hsin teng, Che chiang district. Later, he made public procurator, at the Metropolitan court for the first instance, and at the district court successively. As the administrator and justice his fame was wide and far. Wu-chang seceded from the Empire in 1910, which gave impetuous to the whole country to rise against the Imperial authority that was duly upturned and the Republic was established instead. Then, he was a member of the Provisional State Council. In the second year of the Republic the National Parliament was constitutionally organized, and he was chosen as a member of the Upper House. There came a short suspension of the Republican Government after the dissolution of Parliament, during which period he was a book-lover at his home. Now, the order of things has been restored to that of the Republic; and he is a member of the Senate.

李揖榮 字笏辰 歲四十五

選舉地　直隸省
籍　貫　直隸省武清縣
住　址　北京糧食店同校橓

君幼承庭訓。長讀文書。世代揖紳。里稱榮幸。生平於教育事業。最能誦求。而爲人和藹可親。溫文爾雅。不以毀譽爲懷。不以權利爲動。同輩中推爲有器量之特色。前清。科舉廢。學校與。於是勵志興學。充武清縣勸學員。縣立高等小學校長。順天學務總滙處董理。兼調查員。順直諮議局議員。資政院議員。京兆教育會副會長。全國教育會聯合會。第一次。第二次會員。現充梅廠郵高等小學校。國民學校。志成女學校。又蒙善圍經理。衆議院議員。在議院持論和平。然又不同於唯唯否否隨聲附和者。故議員稱其垂紳揖笏之氣象。

君幼より庭訓を承け、長じて經史に親む。世々地方の揖紳として、君生平教育事業に從事す。人と爲り和藹親むべく、毀譽を以て懷と爲さず、權利を以て動かされず。前清時代科舉廢され同輩中推して以て君が特色と爲す。武清縣勸學員、縣立高等小學校長、順天學務總滙處董理、兼調查員、順直諮議局議員、資政院議員、京兆教育會副會長、全國教育會聯合會第一次第二次會員に歷充したり。民國正式國會成立するや、選ばれて衆議院議員と爲る。議院に在るや、持論和平にして然かも又た唯々諾々聲に隨つて附和する者と同じからず。國會解散後、依然育英の業に從事して、現に梅廠郵高等小學校、國民學校、志成女學校等に敎鞭を執り、又た蒙善圍經理となる。國會重ねて召集を行ふや、再び出でし現に仍は衆議院議員たり。

Mr. Li Chin Jung, otherwise called Au Chen, age forty five, a native of Wu Ching Hsien, the Chi Lin Hsing was thoroughly educated in classics. He was looked up to as a teacher by his fellow then. He is gentle in character, but not swayed by any criticism or by any power and influence. He started his career as the head master of the district primary school, and then the educational committee of the province. When the federated educational meeting was held, he was appointed a member representing his district. When the Parliament was brought into existence, he was elected as a member of the House of Commons. His argument in the assembly was always rational and to the point : He was very much unlike the blind follower of others. After the dissolution of the Parliament, he was an instructor in various schools. When the Parliament was reopened, he was returned for the House of Commons.

李振鈞

字澥荃 歳三十九

籍貫　安徽省合肥縣人

原籍地　安徽省

住址　北京賈家胡同五十九號

君秉性慷慨にして義を好み、平生人の爲に難を排し紛を解き、郷里不平の事あれば、君輙ち喜んで之が爲に報復す。然かも見解明晰にして、其の世に處し物に接す、皆な機敏人に過ぐ、動作する所あれば。必ず豫め未來を計り て措置す。生平尤も喜んで善行を獎勵す、里人一德の長ある者あれば之を扶持せざる莫し。幼より聰穎にして善く讀み、記憶に強し、少年時代日に數千言を誦し、詞句

歳君秉性慷慨好義。居常好爲人排難解紛。鄉里有不平之事。君輒喜爲之報復。然以見解明晰。其處世接物。皆機敏過人。有所動作。必豫計未來之如何措置。生平尤喜獎勵善行。里人有一德之長者。莫不扶持之。自幼聰穎善讀強於記憶。稚齡時。日誦數千言。詞句義理。能一一背誦。講解無稍遺忘。及長。尤能精通古義。時復發抒已見。爲理想上之新發明。前清時。曾留學日本。畢業回國。歷充交通部鐵路高級職務。前清知府。民國山東縣知事等。嘉禾勳章。現充衆議院議員。

義理、一々背誦して毫も遺忘するなし。長ずるに及びて尤も古義に精通し、時に復た私見を發抒して、理想上の新發明を爲す。前清時代曾て日本に留學し、業を擧へて歸國す。交通部鐵道高級職務、前清知府、民國山東縣知事等に歷任して、五等嘉禾勳章を授けらる。現に兼議院議員たり。

民國之精華　（傳記）李振鈞先生

Mr. Li Chen-chun, otherwise called Hsieh Chuan, age thirty nine, a native of An Hui Hsing is distinguished for his heroic and gallant temperament. When troubles or discontents arise in his native district he is always an the scene being actively engaged in the settlement of the affairs. He is clear headed and shrewed and takes great pleasure in accomplishing good deeds. He has always been a copious reader so that he has became a aquainted with the classical teaching : He is also quite a genuine original thinker. He went to Japan whence he retuned have loaded with stocks of new knowledge. He filled an important post in the communication department. When the Republic was formed, he was appointed the governor of Shan tung in which capacity he accomplished a great dead of work. With the reopening of the Parliament, he resigned his post, and entered Peking when he was returned as a member of the House of Commons.

春榮　三十七

君賦性仁厚。待人以誠。然為人剛直不
阿。慷慨好義。居恆疾惡如仇。人有過
失。輒當面痛斥。人以過相詰。恆自陳
不稍隱諱。見人為強暴所厄。常忿忿不
自禁。過于身受。弱冠時。嘗以與人爭。
不計己身之利害。故其接物。雖鋒鋩過
露。然以其出至誠。故人亦罕忌恨之
者。自幼好讀深思不倦。喜推求真義不
拘拘于文詞。及海內維新。力求有用之
學。專攻法律之書。前清宣統元年。在
北洋法政學堂畢業。曾充直隸自治總
局自治委員。翼贊地方自治事宜。民國
元年被選為直隸省議會議員。旋正式
國會成立。當選為眾議院議員。國會解
散後。歸田讀書。惟盡力于地方公益事
業。不問政事。及國會再開。仍復為眾
議院議員。

身地　直隷省
籍貫　直隷省平泉縣
住址　北京西單二條胡同二

君賦性仁厚にして人を待つに誠を以てし、然かも、人と
為り剛直にして阿らず、慷慨義を好みて居常惡を疾むこ
と仇の如し、人過ちあれば輒も面のあたり痛斥し、人の
過を以て相詰れば常に自ら稍も隱諱せず。人若し強暴の
為に押壓さるゝあらんか、忿忿として自ら禁せず。弱冠
の時甞て人と爭ひて己が身の利害を計らざりし。幼より
讀書を好みて思索倦まず、喜んで眞義を攻究して文詞に
拘らず。海内維新に及び、力めて有用の學を求め專ら法
律の書を學ぶ。前清宣統元年、北洋法政學堂に在りて卒
業す。曾て直隷自治總局自治委員として地方自治の事宜
を翼贊したり。民國元年選ばれて直隷省議會議員と為
る。旋て正式國會成立して衆議院議員と爲る。開會解散
後、田園に歸臥して書を讀み、時に唯だ地方公益事業に
盡瘁し、また政事を問はず。國會再び開かるゝに及び、
仍も復た衆議院議員と爲る。

七十六

Mr. Li-chun-jung, Ping chuan prefecture, Chi-li district, thirty seven years old. He is born kind and true, yet upright and straight-forward; never flatters anyone. He is a typical patriot, who hates the wicked as his enemy, and defends the weak even sacrificing his fortune. He never afraid to rebuke his friend's fault in his face, at the same time, he is willing to correct his own mistake if one pointed it out to him. As a boy he was fond of reading and never tired of study; he always sought truth assiduously. On the introduction of the western civilization he took his interest in search of legal theories. In the first year of Huan tung he entered the Pe-yang law and politics school which he duly graduated. Sometime, as a member of the Self Government Committee of Self-Government Bureau, Chi li district he devoted a good deal of his energy in promoting local self governments. In the first year of the Republic he was elected a member of the Chi li district Congress and chosen as a member of the Lower House when the National Parliament was constituted in the second year of the Republic. The suspension of Parliament sent him back to the native town to read, rest, and sometimes to give helping hand for the local welfare. The Republican government was restored and he was sent back to the Lower House as a representative.

李英銓 字鏡衡 歲四十

選舉地　廣東省
籍　貫　廣東省英德縣
住　址　北京東草廠二條韶州館

君爲人誠篤無欺。言動皆確守古訓不稍縱肆。居常以厚道待人。雖疾惡崇善而薄己厚人。不苟求人過。秉性聰慧異人。自幼即明察事理。思考敏捷。意志堅強。弱冠讀書。即能發微起伏。別開新奇。不爲流俗之成見所局。及長。尤深思明辨。勵行身心之修養。專攻有用之實學。前清以副貢。入廣東法政學堂政治科畢業。傾注蘊蓄。盡瘁地方公益事業。民國成立。被選爲廣東省議會議員。正式國會成立。常選參議院議員。北上到院。翼贊建設之業。國會解散後。南旋歸里。靜養英志。及國會重開。再應召集。現仍爲參議院議員。

民國之精華　（傳記）　李英銓先生

君人と爲り誠篤にして欺かず、言動皆な古訓を守りて稍も放縱ならず、居常厚道を以て人を待つ、惡を疾みて善を學ぶと雖、己を薄くして人に厚くし、人の過を苛求せす。秉性聰慧にして幼より事理を明察し、思考敏捷にして意思堅強なり。弱冠書を讀み即ち微を發して伏を起して別に新奇を開き流俗の成見に局せらるゝ所とならず。長ずるに及び尤も身心の修養に勵みて專ら有用の實學を攻究す。前清時代副貢生を以て廣東法政學堂政治科を卒し、蘊蓄を傾注して地方の公益事業に盡瘁したり。民國成立後選ばれて廣東省議會議員となり。正式國會成立するや參議院議員に常選し、北上して院に到り、國家建設の大業を翼贊したり。國會解散後南旋して鄉里に歸り靜に英志を養ふ、國再重ねて開かるゝに及び、再び召集に應じて現に仍ほ參議院議員と爲る。

Mr. Li Ying-chuan, another name Ching-heng, Ying te prefecture, Kwantung district, fourty years old. His horesty never disappointed others; wise ethics guides him in talk and conduct. He meets people with justice and kindness: He is always more considerates of others than to himself: He rebukes no fault of others with a hursh word. He is one of the most ingenious men, remarkably adroit in finding reason and truth. Strong is his will-power. In his boyhood he was fond of reading by which he gathered his knowledge and formed his opinion. Growing older, he took much pain in culture of himself and in study of science. During the late Imperial reign he studied in the political science department of the Kwantung Law and Politics School as an associate fellow. Since the graduation he devoted a good deal of his time for the local welfare. When the Republic was established he was elected and sent to the district Assembly and the National Congress was formally convened he was a member of the Upper House to which member he was duly elected, and assisted a great deal in unifying the country On the dissolution of the Congress he returned to the native town to nurture his ambition. The Congress was called again to convene and he was also called to set in the Upper House.

李夢彪　字嘯風　歲三十八

選舉地　陝西省
籍　貫　陝西洵陽縣
住　址　北京三眼井二號

君于光緒三十一年。肄業陝西高等學校。三十四年。從軍伊犁。九月伊犁將軍長庚。委充參謀處編纂略科員。兼兩等學校教員。武備學校編纂伊犁開辦日報。擔任編輯。辛亥九月。與湖北蘄春縣人郝可權。於伊犁組織革命軍。以應內地。民國元年。一月七日舉義。與郝可權率民軍。將軍志銳殺之。推前將軍廣福爲都督。君充軍政司次長。南北統一。辭職歸里。任三秦公學教員。兼第一師範教員。民國二年。南京討袁軍起。君馳往赴之。比至。則事已敗。遂往日本。三年返國。至上海。五年三月。由申返秦。與陝北鎮守使陳樹藩密謀獨立。以應義師。五月七日。陝西宣告獨立。君爲第一游擊隊參謀長。八月。國會重開。以候補當選。辭職入都。充衆議院議員。

君は光緒三十一年陝西高等學校に學び、三十四年伊犁に從軍す、九月伊犁將軍長庚は君を參謀處略科員に委充し、兩等學校教員、武備學校編纂を兼ぬ。伊犁に於ては報を創刊するや其の編輯を擔任す。辛亥の秋湖北蘄春縣人郝可權と伊犁に於て革命軍を組織して響應せんと圖り、民國元年一月七日郝可權と偕に民軍を率ゐて將軍志銳を擒とし之を殺す。前將軍廣福を推して都督と爲し君は軍政司次長となる。南北統一後辭職して歸省し、三秦

公學堂教員に任じ、第一師範學校教員を兼ぬ。二年南京討袁軍起るや、君馳せてこれに赴く。至る頃則ち事既に敗る。君遂に日本に往き、三年國に返りて上海に潛む。五年三月秦に返りて陝北鎮守使陳樹藩と密に獨立を謀り、五月陝西の獨立を宣言す、君第一游擊隊參謀長たり。八月國會恢復と共に君候補議員を以て缺を補ひ職を辭して入京し、始めて衆議院議員と爲る。

Mr. Li meng-piao, another name Hsia-min. He was born in the prefecture of Hsuan-yaug, Hsia-hsi-hsing in the year 1878. In the thirty one year of Kuang-hu, he entered Hsia-hii Higher School. However later he was attached to the army in I-che and on september, general Chang king of I-che appointed him member of staff-office. At about the same time he was made teacher of Shau kai School and secretary of Military School. Then he was engaged in editing newspaper which newly established at I-che. On the revolution of Hsin-shih he and Ho-ko-chuan from Chun prefecture Hu-pei, in acting concert, organized revolutional army to respond to the cause. He and Ho-ko-chuan, on january, 7th, the first year of Republic, accompanied by the revolutional army, caught general Shih-ju and put him to death. The ex-general Kuang-fu was appointed in his place and he succeeded to the post of Vice-president of military department. After the unification of South and North had been completed he resigned his office and engaged as teacher of San-chin Public School besides teaching in the first Normal School in his native place. No sooner Nan-king expedition army against Yuan-shi-kai government was raised than he ran and joined his side. However their course have gone completely wrong he refuged in Japan. In the third year he returned to the country and concealed himself in Shanghai. In the fifth year he went back to his native place and planed independence in concert with the inspector Hu-pei. Thus he responded to the revolutionary army. On may they declared the independence of Hsia-hsi. Subsequently he was made staff in chief of the first flying column. On the reorganization of Parliament, he resigned the office and to the vacancy of member of Parliament he has been elected.

李夢麟　字佛塵　歲三十七

選舉地　河南省
籍貫　河南省武安縣
住址　北京順治門內翠花街三十四

君秉性聰穎絕倫。而心力極強。不喜受人拘束。年七歲入私塾。以督責至嚴。稍一曠課。即遭呵斥。屢欲輟學改爲他業。未獲也。十九歲時。入邑庠。奉親命遊學大梁。入明道書院。越年。考入河南高等學堂。旋轉入師範學堂。乙巳年。由河南派遣留學日本。初入宏文學院。畢業後入正則英語學校。翌年。考入明治大學預科。由預科升入法科大學本科。至二年級。適革命軍起。遂罷學歸國。民國元年。歷充河南省議會議員。地方自治籌備處參議諸職。旋被選爲衆議院候補議員。二年。投身新聞界。四年冬。帝制發生。君歸里隱居。不問時事。及至此次約法恢復國會重開。遂以衆議院議員缺額故。依次遞補爲衆議院議員。

民國之精華　（傳記）　李夢麟先生

君や秉性聰穎絕倫にして心力極めて強く、人の拘束を受くるを喜ばず、年七歲私塾に入る、督責嚴重にして屢々呵斥に遭ひ、學を輟めて他業に轉せんと欲するも未だ獲ざる也。十九歲の時邑庠に入り、親の命を奉じて大梁に學び明道書院に入る。年を越て河南高等學堂に入り、旋て師範學堂に轉ず。乙巳河南派遣の日本留學生として宏文學院に入り、卒業後正則英語學校に學ぶ、翌年明治大學預科に入り、預科より本科に入りて二年級に至る。適ま革命軍起るを以て遂に學を罷めて歸國す。民國二年河南省議會議員、地方自治準備處參議諸職に歷充し、旋て衆議院候補議員に選ばる。二年身を新聞社會に投ず。四年の冬帝制問題發生するや鄉里に歸りて韜晦す。此次約法恢復して國會重ねて開かるに及び、遂に議員の補缺を以て召集せられ、現に衆議院議員と爲る。

Mr. Li meng-lin, another name Yo-yu. He was born in the prefecture of Wu-au, Ho nan hsing in the year 1879. He was a man of excellent intelligence and of strong insight and his nature ran counter to any restriction. He entered a Private School when seven years old. However under strict restriction and severe punishment which often inflicted on him, he would have deserted there and plunged into another life. At the age of nineteen, he entered the village school. Then, obeying his parents command he went to Tai-liang and studied in Ming-tao shu Yuan institution. For the next year he matriculated in Ho-nan Higher School but later changed it to the normal school. In the year of Chi, he was ordered by Ho-nan provincial government to go abroad to study in Japan. After his completion of his course at Hung-weu-hsiao-yuan school, he studied in Seisoku English School and in the following year he was allowed to enter in the preparatory department of Meiji University. For the two years he remained in the university department of Meiji, but then the revolution occured which recalled him to his beloved country. In the second year of Republic he was made member of Ho-nan provincial assembly besides being councilar of provincial self administration office. Later he was elected member of Parliament and in the third year he found himself a jurnalist. But the growth of tendency toward Imperialistic government had effect of causing him to retire into his home. However on the reorganization of Parliament he has been elected member to fill the vacancy of it.

李垚年 字淑庭 歲三十六

選舉地　福建省

籍貫　福建省建甌縣

住址　北京棉花胡同五條

君賦性仁厚。待人以誠。然爲人剛直不阿。慷慨好義。居恒疾惡如仇。自幼聰慧好讀。深思不倦。喜推求眞義。不拘拘于文詞。及海內維新。喜讀新書。專攻法政之學。浩詣漸深。浙江法政學堂。畢業。前清時代曾充山西知縣。五大民族共和光復。民國元年。被選爲臨時省議會議員。贊襄辦地方自治事宜。民國二年。正式國會成立。當選爲衆議院議員。把持正論。翼贊大政。國會解散後。南旋歸里讀書自娛。時出從事地方公益事業。此次及國會重開。遂又應召集。北上抵京。仍爲衆議院議員。

君賦性仁厚にして人を待つに誠を以てす。然かも人と爲り剛直にして阿ねらず、慷慨義を好み居常惡を疾むこと仇の如く、幼より聰慧にして讀書を好み、深く思索して倦まず、喜んで眞義を求め文詞に拘泥せず。海內維新に及び新書を涉獵して專ら法政の學を攻究して造詣漸く深く、浙江法政學堂に入りて卒業す。前清時代曾て山西知縣に任じ、漢土光復後民國元年選ばれて臨時省議會議員と爲り、地方自治の事宜を襄助す。民國二年正式國會議員選舉に際して衆議院議員と爲り、正論を把持して大成を翼贊す。國會解散後南旋して鄉里に閉居して讀書自ら娛み、時に地方公益事業に從事す。此次國會重ねて開かるヽに及び、遂に又た召集に應じ北上して京師に抵り、仍ほ衆議院議員と爲る。

八十

Mr. Li Tu-nien, another name Chien ou prefecture, Fukian district, thirty six years old. He is naturally kind and true to every one, yet up-right and straight-forward; never flatters anyone. He is a typical patriot, who disdains the wrong as his enemy and defend the weak against the strong even sacrificing himself. He never afraid of reproaching his friend's fault in his face, at the same time, he is willing to correct his own mistake if one tells him of it. He was a sagacious child, fond of reading, never tired of study and saught truth among facts and theories. On the introduction of the western civilization he surveyed the western books and absorbd in study of politics and laws. He entered, some-time, the Che-chiang Law and Politics School and graduated after the hard years study. Under the Imperial Government he was appointed the governor of Shan-hsi prefecture. After the fall of the Empire he became a member of the provisional district assembly in the first year of the Republic. He served invaluably to help the local self government. In the second year he was chosen as a member of the Lower House when Parliament was formally constituted and took a prominent part in solidifyng the country. During the suspension of Parliament he returned South to turn his activity on the local government. On the restoration of the Republic he has came back to the capital to sit in the Lower House.

李積芳　字筱溪　歳三十六

選舉地　湖南省

籍貫　湖南省平江

住址　北京都城隍廟街湖南李寓

君秉性誠厚篤實。痛惡浮華。居常以儉約自持。能耐勞苦。與人交。直而不諛。喜聞藎言。人告以過。不論當否。必婉詞謝之。若加以過度之譽。則反漠然待之。甚至示以怒容。視同欺侮。生平以文飾爲恥辱。常語人曰。有過而能直陳不諱。反足以增其令譽。有善而能不求人知。反足以減少謗言。其見解詢可云超出尋常數位矣。前清時以湖北仕學館學員。由張文襄選送日本留學。畢業于經緯學校及早稻田大學政治經濟科。歸國應學部試授法政科舉人。辛亥武昌起義。回湘充法制局參事。籌辦地方自治。旋組織湖湘法學校。兼充公立法政各校教員。二年。被選爲衆議院議員。國會解散後。專力經營商鑛。不問政事。及國會重開。始入京仍爲衆議院議員。

君秉性篤實にして浮華を憎悪し、倹約自ら持しで勞苦に耐ゆ。人と交りて正直、喜んで藎言を開く。生平其の過を飾るを以て恥辱とす。常に人に談つて曰く、過あれば直言して諱まずんば、反つて其の譽を増すに足る、善あれば人の知るを求めずんば、反つて其の謗を減ずるに足るなり云々。前清時代湖北仕學館學員を以て、張之洞より選拔されて日本に留學し、經緯學校及び早稻田大學政治經濟科に入りて業を畢へたり。歸國の後ち學部の試に應じて法政科舉人を授けらる。辛亥の歳武昌義を起すや、湖南に歸りて法政局參事に任じ、地方の自治を籌辦し、湖南法政學校を組織して公立法政各學校教員に兼充したり。民國二年選ばれて衆議院議員となり、國會解散後重ら商鑛事業を經營して暫らく政事を問はず。本年國會重ねて開かるゝに及び召集されて晉京し、仍ほ衆議院議員たり。

民國之精華　（傳記）　李積芳先生

Mr. Li Chi-fang, another name Yu-chi, was born in Pen-chiang hsien, Hu-nan hsing. He was a man of uprightness and simplicity. He was always ready to give his ear to any advice and felt it shame to disguise himself. During Chin Dynasty, being himself a fellow of Hu-Pei Shih Hsiao-Kwan Institution, he was adviced by Chang chih-tung to go to Japan for study. He graduated, at first, institution of economic and later completed satisfactory the department of economics and politics of Waseda University. On his return to home, he passed the examination of the government and was given a certificate of high official. After the revolution at Wu-chang, he went back to his native province and was appointed to councilar of the bureau of legistation, besides takeing charge in the work of provincial self-administration. He organized Hu-nan Institution of law and politics and at about the same time he was appointed to professor in the Public Institution of Law and Politics. In the second year of Republic he was elected as a member of the Parliament. However after its dissolvement, he took no active part to politics, but was engaged in business of mining as well as trading. But, now, the Parliament was reorganized and he has been called out to be its member.

李燮陽　字彌青　歲三十六

選舉地　雲南省

籍貫　雲南省昭通縣

住址　北京前門外長巷上二條十一號

君爲人精敏堅實。能耐勞苦。前清庚子。補縣學附生。旋隨軍勘桂匪。以功奏保知縣分發四川候補。抵蜀後。見國事日非。政途汚濁。遂舍官東渡留學。入東京宏文學院普通科畢業。考入大阪高等工業學校電氣科。旋赴美國。入卜技利大學豫備科畢業。考入阿海約大學電氣工程科。三年。再入鐵路工程科。適民國肇造。奉雲南軍政府電調回籍。贊勤一切。歷任雲南實業司副長。兼任雲南全省模範工廠監督。及鐵路局局長。民國二年。被選爲衆議院議員。國會解散後。曾任美國巴拿馬賽會雲南出品協會代表。民國四年。雲南起義。君招募精兵六營爲蔡鍔討袁後備軍。復任護國第四軍籌餉總辦。民國五年八月。以國會重行召集。遂辭差入都仍爲衆議院議員。

君人と爲り精敏にして堅實、能く勞苦に耐ゆ。前清庚子の歲、縣學附生に補し、旋て軍に從つて桂匪を勦し、功を以て知縣に奏保し四川候補に分發せらる。四川に抵りて後、國事日に非にして政途汚濁せるを見て、遂に官を令て東渡し、東京宏文學院普通科に入りて卒業し、又た大阪高等工業學校電氣科に學ぶ。旋て米國に赴きと卜技利大學豫備科に入りて卒業し、阿海約大學電氣工程科に學ぶこと三年、再び鐵道工事科に入る。適ま民國肇めて樹立するや、雲南軍政府より招かれて歸國し、雲南實業司副長、雲南全省模範工廠監督兼任及び鐵路局々長に歷任す。民國二年選ばれて衆議院議員と爲る。國會解散後、曾て米國巴拿馬博覽會雲南出品協會代表に任ず、四年雲南義を起すや、君は精兵六營を招募して蔡鍔の討袁後營軍と爲し、復た護國第四軍籌餉總辦に任ず五年八月國會の再召集に應じ遂に職を辭して晉京し衆議院議員となる。

Mr. Li Hsieh-yang, another name Yeh Chin, was born in Chao-tung, Yun-nan. He was a man of shrewdness and uprightness. He could endure difficulties, during the period of Chin Dynasty. He was made fellow of the prefecture. Once he, accompanied by army; sent to suppress the rebellion and he was made official despatch to Ssi Chuan for his good services. But the political disorder in the country had the effect of causing him to think that it was his duty to act in emergency of the country and to deliver its crisis. He resigned his office. He went to Japan, where he was matriculated in the Department of electricity in higher technical college, Osaka. Then he went to America where he learned several years the engineering in University. No sooner the government was established than he returned to home having engaged by Yun-nan Government. He was appointed successively to those offices of vice-chairman of Yun-nan Bureau of Commerce, inspector of factories and chief director of the Bureau of Railways. In the second year of Republic he was elected to a member of Parliament. After the Paliament was dissolved he was once appointed to representative of Yun-nan Chinese Department in Panama International Exhibition in America. On the outbreak of revolution in Yun-nan in the 4th year of Republic he, at once, raising six divisions of men and drafting them into second reserve of Tsai-e's Army Corps.

李茂之　字茂之　歲三十五

選舉地　廣東省

籍貫　廣東省新會縣

住址　北京順治門大街守真照相舊址

君秉性岐嶷。熟中同學。憑藉厚偕
改革を失ふ。紀堂家資幾百萬や、君力めて之を成す。
辛亥の歲武昌義を起すや、君は廣東軍政府樞密部參議と
なり、南京臨時政府組織さるゝや、君海を航して竊に入
り建議する所多し。嗣いで廣東に歸りて圖書館長を兼ぬ
時に廣東省の財政稍や紊亂す。君乃ち錢局を綜べて之を
整理したり。國會の開かるゝや、君擧げられて參議院議
員となり、大政大法に於て建白する所あり。袁政府が國會

君秉性岐嶷。熟中同學。冠同學。憑藉厚偕
從兄紀堂長香江。比長。共矢改革。紀
堂毀家幾百萬。君力成之。辛亥起義。
入粵政府樞密部參議。南京政府建同
容君開航海入寧。多所建議。嗣歸粵。
仍兼圖書館長。時粵財政稍紊。君綜官
錢局爲整理之國啓。被擧參議院議
員。大政大法。日有建白。袁府解散國
會。模被南返申江。同谷九峯諸子創正
誼雜誌社泰東書局等。更偕唐少川先
生擧辦實業。首組金星保險公司。以其
餘暇。築別業於杭州西湖。爲息塵勞之
居。岑。待士。笠屐清遊。蕭然有物外之
意。會時事趨下。政變日潯。君默運廣
濟泊。共和再造。國會恢復。由是離容
北來。其青年俠義之氣。出而爲公爲
黨。並不異昔時焉。

を解散するや、上海に南下し、谷鍾秀等と共に正誼雜誌
社、泰東書局等を創設經營し、更に唐照儀と實業に從事
して金星保險公司を組織す。其の餘暇を以て別業を杭州
西湖に築きて塵勞を息ゐの居と爲し、羣僚を備へて士
を待ち、笠屐を具りして清遊し蕭然として物外の意あり會
ま時事趨下して政變日に潯す、君默して廣濟を思ひ、共
和の再造を望む。國會恢復後北上して再び參議院議員と
なる。

民國之精華　（傳記）李茂之先生

八十三

Mr. Li Mao-chih, another name Mao-chih, was born in Hsiw-hui, Kuang-tunghsing. He was a man of lofty character, and surpassed all his fellow students in his talent. He acted in concert with his causion Chi-Tang-chang, Hsiang-chiang to the cause of revolution. On the outbreak of Revolution at Wu-chang he was appointed to the staff of privy council of the government of Kuang-tung Army and his exertion had no least exercise in the organization of Nan-king temporal government when he entered there secretly by sea. Afterward he returned to Kuang-tung and accepted the port of president of library. However at that time, the finances of the kuang-tung government appeared to be in some difficulties. So he took charge of finance bureau and readjusted it. On the organization of National Assembly he was elected member of Parliament and memorialized his views to the government on the day of promulgation of the constitution. When the National Assembly was dissolved by the government he went down into south at Shang-hai and published a magazine and organized a Buraru of Ching-tung, Shu-chu, acting in concert with Ku Chung-hsiu and others. He and Tang Chao-i while engaging in business, organized Insurance Company. He also managed another business at Hsi-hu Hong-chou and made it his lesting place. There he invited his friends and spent his quiet life. However Political disorder raised him up again to the active life in Politics. On the reorganization of National Assembly he has been called out and made member of Parliament.

李自芳　字仲翔　歲三十五

選舉地　廣東省

籍貫　廣東省廣州府台山縣

住址　北京東草廠二條胡同韶州館

君秉性嚴正不阿。然居心仁厚。雖素所厭惡。亦不慮待之。生平無以私隙仇人之事。爲人精明強幹。長于事務才。居恆以儉朴自勵。屏絕贅澤。然爲人助力。則又不吝于貲。常爲鄉人排難解紛。誘說勸導。兩造皆感其誠。雖有大爭。得君居中一言。無不立決。少年時。攻苦讀書。淹通經史。然喜求實學。不爲舉業所局限。海內維新後。彈精西學以副貢分部主事。入京師高等巡警學堂畢業。後又入京師法律學堂本科畢業。曾充京師地方審判廳民二庭推事。廣州地方審判廳刑一庭推事。廣東高等審判廳聯合庭推事。及廣東法政學校民法教員。民國二年。被選爲參議院議員。國會解散後。歸里從事公益事業。絕意政治。因此次共和復活。始來京。仍爲參議院議員。

新後西學を攻究し、副貢分部主事を以て京師高等巡警學堂に入り、卒業後又た京師法律學本科に入りて業を畢へたり。曾て京師地方審判廳民事部推事、廣東高等審判廳聯合法廷推事及び廣州地方審判廳刑事部推事、廣東高等審判廳聯合法廷推事及び廣東法政學校民法教員に歷任す。民國二年選ばれて參議院議員と爲り、國會解散後歸鄉して地方の公益事業に從事す。國會復活して再び晉京し、仍は參議院議員たり。

君秉性嚴正にして阿らず、然かも居心仁厚にして、其の厭忌する所の者も亦た之を虐待するに忍びず、生平私隙を以て人に仇する事無し。人と爲り精明強幹にして事務の才あり。居常儉朴自ら勵みて贅澤を排するも、人の爲に助力するには貲を吝まずして、常に鄉人の爲に難を排し紛を解き誘說勸導し、爭事結ぶで解けざるものも君が居中の一言を得て立どころに決す。少時剋苦精勵して經史に淹通し、喜んで實學を求め、舉子の業を爲さず。海內維

Mr. Li Tsu-fang, another name Chung-hsiang, was born in Tai Shanhsien, Kuang-tung. He is man of gravity and of strictures and flatters no one while he is generous and merciful even to his hatred person. He has a clear head, strong insight and fine talent for business. He showed striking fondness for reading history when very young. It had the effect of causing him to turn his attention from dry business of scholarship to the practical preparation. The restoration broke in upon the country determined him to study new learning and as a fellow he was accepted to Peking Higher Training Institution of Police. Then he graduated Peking Institution of Law. He was appointed to the post of public procurators in civil department of Peking Local Court, besides being procurator in Criminal Department of Kuang-chou Local Court. In the course of the following year he was made public proculators in the Union Court of Kuang-tung Higher Courts, besides being professor of Civil Law in the Kuang-tung Institution of Law and politics. In the second year of Republic he was elected to a member of Parliament, but its dissolvement caused him to return to home and engaged in the work of public benefit. On the re-organiation of Parliament he succeed to gain his former chair in Parliament.

李有忱 字蘭坡 歲三十五

選舉地　奉天省
籍　貫　奉天省新民縣
住　址　北京關才胡同

少聰穎。賦性整飭。孩提時如成人。稍
長即不喜理帖括業。留心時事。並好讀
史。每抵掌而談。授古證今。聽者動容。
暫入奉天兩級師範學校。適值徐世昌
督東。種種交涉失敗。憤不顧身。與同
志李紹白。連電政府。請罷徐以挽國
權。徐大震怒。將置重典。以提學張筱
闔與監督吳蓮伯營救得免。嗣歷充新
民師範中學教習監學。庶務長代理校
長。被選爲新民教育會長。自治開辦。
被選爲縣議會議長。是年秋武昌起義。
暗與同志企圖獨立。及謀稍就緒。而共
和宣布矣。民國元年。被選爲臨時省議
會議長。二年被選爲衆議院議員。國會
解散後。而專心實業經營。及帝制發
生。痛袁之殘暴。思所以推翻之。乃與
吳蓮伯合成一氣。密秘進行。奔走於奉
天大連上海之間。袁死。黎氏繼任。國
會復活。由滬來京。就衆議院議員之
職。復被選爲同院實業委員長。

民國之精華　（傳記）　李有忱先生

君や少にして聰穎、賦性整飭にして幼年の時歲人の如し。
稍や長じて帖括の業を理するを喜ばや、心を時事に留め
並に好んで史を讀む。曾て奉天兩級師範學校に入りて學
ぶ、時適徐世昌總督として種々外交上の失敗あり、君憤
然として李紹白と共に政府に打電して徐を罷めん事を請
ひ、徐の怒に觸れたるも、提學張筱闔と監督吳景濂の爲に
救はれて事無きを得たり。嗣で新民師範學堂、中學教習
監庶務長校長代理等に歷充し、新民郡教育會會長に選ば
る。後ち縣議會議長に選ばれ、武昌義を起すや暗に同志
と獨立を企圖す。民國元年臨時省議會議長に選ばれ、二
年兼議院議員に舉げらる。國會解散後即ち專ら實業に從
事す。帝制問題發生するに及び、之が推翻を思ひ、吳景
濂と志と併せて奉天大連上海間を奔走す。袁氏死して黎
氏繼任し、國會復活するや上海より晉京し衆議院議員の
職に就き、同院實業委員長に選ばる。

八十五

Mr. Li Yu-shen, another name Lan-po, was born in Asiu-ui, Feng-tien. He was sagacious and clearheaded even in his youth, whose character exhibited itself in its most intrinsic aspects. So shat they would often take him an adult when he was a mre by. As he grew up, he loved reading history and paid a special attention to the current events. However the diplomatic failure of governor general Hsu Shih-shan, which had been reported among them, raised him up to take a final step to memorialize through telegraph his view on immediate dismissal of Hsu Shih-chan from the post of the government. He should have aroused Hsu-shi-chan's wrath but for help of a educational inspector Chang Yu-tuan and superintendant Wu Ching-tun. Thus he scarcely escaped from the impending peril. Later he was appointed to a secretary of teacher's institutions of both middle and normal school and then he succeeded to the post of acting president of the same institution, besides being president of educational society at Hsiu-ni-fu. Then he was elected to the chair-man of provincial assembly. In the second year of Republic he was elected to a member of Parliament and after its dissolvement he was engaged in business. On the outgrowth of tendency toward imperialistic government, he acting in concert with Wu-ching-lin, ran about all directions between Teng-tien and Ja-lien. When the Yuanshi-kai was succeeded by Mr. To, the Parliament was re-opened. Subsequently he gained his former chair in Parliament and has been appointed to the committees in chief commercial affair in it.

李述膺　字龍門　歲三十四

議舉地　陝西省

籍貫　陝西省耀縣

住址　北京西城油房胡同關中李寓

君性豪爽。能文章。十五冠童試。陝學使。奇其才。薦赴日本留學。歷入經緯學校。第一第七高等學校。肆業。時適辛亥事起。奮然歸國。與同志潛約入魯。圖恢復山東。謀泄走津。當道索之急。復歸滬。充上海民立報編輯。旋被舉爲南京參議院議員。南北統一。議院北遷。復被選。正式國會成立。被選爲參議院議員。君主持正義。不爲強禦。十餘年如一日。國會解散。君隻身走東瀛。以時宜有待。潛心著述。有德意志主戰論。中立法規等譯。並撰正誼中華等雜誌。與黃克強李印泉等。組織歐事研究會。與滬上谷鍾秀徐傳霖等。互相呼應。民國四年歸滬。與諸同志。倡辦中華新報。痛關帝制。皷吹民權。及國會恢復。仍就參議院議員之職。

君性豪爽にして文章を能くす。十五歳童試に冠たり。陝西學使其才を奇とし、日本に留學せしむ。經緯學校、第一第七高等學校に修業したり。時適ま一革命の事起る、君奮然として國に歸り、同志と潛に山東に入り恢復を圖る、謀泄れて天津に走り、當局の搜索嚴重なるを以て復た上海に歸り、民立報編輯に任す。旋て南京參議院議員に舉げられる。南北統一するや北京參議院議員となる。正式國會成立して參議院議員となる。君正義を主持して

十年一日の如し。國會解散するや、隻身東瀛に走り、時運の再變を待ち、心を著述に潛め、獨逸主戰論及び中立法規等を譯述し、並に正誼、中華の二雜誌の編輯に任し黃克強李印泉等と歐事研究會を組織し、谷鍾秀、徐傳霖等と互に相呼應す。四年上海に歸り、諸同志と中華新報を主倡して帝制を痛斥す。國會恢復するに及び、仍は參議院議員となる。

八十六

Mr. Li Chiu-ying, otherwise called Pai-men, age thirty four, a native of Yao-hsien, the Shan-ssi hsien. When young, he was a good writer, and at the age of fifteen, he distinguished himself from his fellow students. He was sent to Japan, where he studied in the 7th High School. When the revolutionary movement broke out, he with his fellowmen, entered Shan-tung, and planned for the accomplishment of his ideas. He was sought mercilessly by the authorities so that he went back to Shanghai where he was interested in the newspaper work. He was elected member of the Nanking Local Assembly, and after peace between the north and south was concluded, he entered Peking, and was returned for the House of Commons. On the dissolution of the Parliament, he went to Japan, and bid the opportune time. He wrote during this time several books, one of which "Germany and the War" is most noted. Later he returned to Shanghai, and started a strong opposition against the movement favouring adoption of the Imperial Government. When the Parliament was restored, he was appointed a member of the Senate.

還舉地　湖南省
籍貫　湖南省岳陽縣
住址　北京都城隍廟街

君魁梧奇偉。賦性豪爽。有俠士風。不
屑屑舉子業。蓋天邁絕群也。前肄業湘
省時務學校。求實書院。以清政日非。
乃開辦小學校。旋以前湘督焦達峯擬密
秘連合各同志。共圖改革。焦任湘中
路。彭邦棟任南路。君任東路。焦任湘中
危。辛亥武昌起義。君隻身赴鄂。屢瀕于
日夕。急偕督繼悟唐蟒等籌設岳州鎮
守府。民國元年。任稽勳局湘調查員。
二年。被選衆議院議員。適袁世凱蹂躪
新政。潛與陳嘉會返湘。勸都督譚延
闓獨立。再謀改革。事敗。走日本。居數
月。更名返國。企圖再舉。迫滇黔起義。
往返滬湘。與各舊同志聯合響應及國
會復活。始入京。仍爲衆議院議員。

君魁梧にして奇偉、賦性豪爽にして俠士の風あり。前に
湖南の時務學校、求實書院に學び、乃ち小學校を創立經營
す。旋て前湖南都督焦達峯竊に各同志を糾合して共に改
革を圖るや、焦は湘の中路に任じ、彭邦棟は南路に任じ、
君は東路に任じ屢々危險を犯す。辛亥武昌義を起すや譚
人鳳等と籌畫して、響應の計を爲す。九月一日湖南獨立
し、十日焦達峯害に遇ひて秩序大に亂る。また清軍武昌
に迫りて漢陽守を失し、岳州危ふし。君急ぎ曾繼唐蛟

等と岳州鎮守府を設く。民國元年稽勳局湖南調査員に任
じ、二年衆議院議員に選ばる。適ま袁世凱は新政を蹂躙
す、潛に陳嘉會と湖南に返り、都督譚延闓の獨立を勸め
再び改革を謀る。事敗れて日本に走り、居る事數月更に
歸國を名として再舉を圖り、雲貴の義を起すに追び、上
海湖南を往返し舊同志と響應す。國會復活する
に及び、再び晋京して衆議院議員と爲る。

民國之精華　（傳記）李錡先生

Mr. Li-i, another name Yun-lan, was born in Yo-yang, Hu Nanhsing. He is grand and dignified in his appearence. No sooner the ex-governer Chiasta-feng called together those of the same mind secretly and intended reforms with Chiao as the sole wielder of powers and with Peng Ho-lien as his right hand than he was appointed his left hand. They advanced at their own risk. Acting in concert with Teng-ko, a man from Tan He responded to the cause of reformation which broke out in the year of Hsin-Wan. The first day of september, independence of Hu-nan was declared and on the tenth, the ex-governor Chiao was assassinated. It had the effect of causing the state out of order: At the same time Chin army advancing toward Wu chang stormed the fortification of Han-Yang and consequently it effected Ping-chon much fear of danger. So he and Tseng Chi-wu, Tang Fong hrstened to set up an army station at Yo-chu. In the first year of Republic he was appointed, Hu-nan commissioner of the bureau of decorations. In the second year he was elected member of Parliament. After its dissolvement he with Yuan-shi-kai secretly returned to Hu-nan and intended reform in assisting governor-general Tan Yen-kai. However, the scheme went all wrong and consequently he ran to Japan and remained there few months. He returned to home and planed a reform again. On the out-break of revolution at Yun Kui he responded to the cause, running about all directions between Shanghai and Yun-nan communicating with those old fellow-enthusiasts. The Parliament was re-opened and he has been made a member of it.

選舉地　陝西省
籍貫　陝西省臨潼縣
住址　北京潘家河沿五十四

李含芳　字可亭　歲三十三

君天資聰慧。悟性敏捷。然爲人誠篤無華。待人以直。喜規勸人過失。人告以過。亦直陳不諱。且謙詞謝其直言。幼時肄業私塾。稍長。入本省武備學校。改入西安府中學校。後升選省立高等學校。入預科五年。畢業後。遷入京師法律專問學校。辛亥革命軍起于武昌。君棄學歸陝。任陝督軍府秘書。未幾。復與陝西革命巨子井勿幕君。倡辦同盟會陝支部。及合併爲國民黨後。君任總務主任幹事。第一次國會選舉被舉爲衆議院議員。國會解散。君歸陝任本縣兩全鎮立高等小學校長。帝制發生。陝將軍陸建章。殘殺民黨。派兵抄沒家資。東行被阻。西逃甘肅平凉。潛匿商號。友人助資。使絰營布商業。現在平凉之吉祥合號。即君避難時之紀念也。及此次西南舉義。陝民黨應之。君在平凉。末幾。共和再造。國會復活。君遂北上。仍爲衆議院議員。

君天資聰慧にして悟性敏捷なり。然かも人と爲り誠篤にして華無く、人を待つに直を以てす。幼時業を私塾に受け、稍や長じて本省武備學校に入り、改めて西安府中學校に學び、後ち省立高等學校に遷りて預科五年に入學して業を畢へ、京師法律專門學校に入る。辛亥の歳革命軍武昌に起るや、學を棄てゝ陝西に歸り、陝西督軍府秘書に任ず。未だ幾くもなく同志と共に陝西革命の巨子井勿幕君と共に同盟會陝西支部を主倡して創立し、其の國民黨に合併するや君總務主任幹事に任ず。第一次國會選舉に當り衆議院議員に舉げられ。國會解散後歸省して同縣兩全鎮立高等小學校長となる。帝制發生するや陝西將軍陸建章は民黨員を私殺し家資を抄沒し君の東行阻まる、西の方甘肅平凉に逃れ潛に商店に匿れ、友人資を助けて布商を經營す。此次西南義を舉りて陝西の民黨之に應ず、君平凉に在りて耗を聞きて歸省す。共和既に復活し國會再蘇す。君遂に北上して衆議院議員と爲る。

Mr. Li Mao, another name Ko-tung, was born in Lin-tung, Hsic-hsi hsing. He is a man of clear head and good understanding. He is Ju and upright whose action is governed a private by the priciple of simylicity and the law of his life is honesty. In his youth he had been educated in school. But he grew up his entered H ia-hsi military school and then Hsi-antu middle school. Later he was matriculated as fifth year class student in the preparatony department in Hsia-hsi high s hool and finished the course. Then he remained in studying in King-shih Law college until the revolution was broke out which recall d him back to his home. He was appointed priqate secretary to Hsia-hsi military head quarter and at the same time he, in consulting with those of the syme mind, organized H ia-hsi Branch of the Union Society. After its amalgamation with the National party he was appointed to the general Secrelary. Later he was elected to a member of Parliament on its first trial of election. When Parliament was dissolved he reterned to his home and was master of Liao-chuan-chen-li Senior School. On the outgrouth of tendency toward Imperialistic Goverment, the government-general Liu-chien-chang, Hesia hesi issued an edict ordering the distriction of democratic party f llowing by imp isoning and subjecting into torture all members and those of the same mind. He ran to west ward and concealed in a store at Kan-hsi-pin with pecunial help from his friends he enjoyed there in trading. Just about this time the revolution of Hsi-nan broke out and the democratic party of Hsia-hsi responded to the cause. The Republic was firmly guarded and the Parliament was reorganiz d. He has been called out and was appointed to a member of Parliament.

李載賡 字竹亭 歲三十三

選舉地　河南省
籍　貫　河南杞縣
住　址　北京西草廠敷家胡同路東

君于前清光緒三十年。以首卷入庠。學使王序提送河南高等學堂肄業。三十一年。應出洋考試。取列前茅。是年八月。赴日本留學。初入宏文學院。習師範。旋改入東斌學堂。研究警察監獄諸學科。三十四年夏。畢業。復入早稻田大學專門部法律科。於宣統三年畢業歸國。經學部覆試合格。獎法政舉人。未幾。武昌起義。君見有機可乘。即號召同志。回河南運動革命。嗣因力薄不敢輕舉。由同志被舉為代表赴滬。與陳其美程德全聯絡。旋隨威武軍北征剛抵黃州。適清帝退位之詔既下。遂返旆南旋入南京臨時政府。從事建設。充交通部秘書官。復由河南諮議局被選為臨時參議院議員。迨政府北遷。君乃解職投身報界。主持正論。民國二年。復被選為眾議院議員。兼充律師。國會解散。君遂專業律師。不問政事。及國會重開。始到院。仍為眾議院議員。

に隨ひ、北征して黃州に抵るや、適ま淸帝退位す、遂に南京臨時政府に入りて建設に從事し、交通部秘書となる。復た河南諮議局より選ばれて臨時參議院議員となり、南北統一後君乃ち職を解いて新聞記者となり正論讜議を主持す。民國二年眾議院議員に舉げられ、傍ら辯護士の業務に從事す。國會解散後眾議院議員の業を專ら辯護士の業に擧げられ、國會恢復後再び院に到り仍は眾議院議員たり。

君は前淸光緒三十年首席を以て庠に入り、河南高等學堂に入學す。三十一年日本に留學して宏文學院師範科に學び、旋て改めて東斌學堂に入り警察監獄諸學科を修め、三十四年日本に留學して宏文學院師範科に學業す。復た早稻田大學專門部法律科に學び宣統三年卒業して歸國し、學部の試を經て法政舉人たらる。未だ幾くもなく武昌義を起すや、君則ち同志を起し河南に歸りて革命を志すも敢て輕舉せす。同志の代表として上海に赴き陳其美程德全等と聯絡し、旋て威武軍

民國之精華　（傳記）　李載賡先生

Mr. Li Tsai-keng, another name Chu-ting was born in Chi, Ho-nan hsing. He visited Japan and finished the law course of Waseda University. He was conferred a certificate of high official as the result of his passing the government examination. When the revolution broke out at Wu-chang, he responded to the cause with those of the same mind and went to Ho-nan. However his action was always anticipated delicate consideration. Then he went to Shang-hai as reprentative of those fellow enthusiast, and communicated with Chen Chi-mii Chang-Te-chuan to and others. Later he went to the bront as a general of Wei-wu army attacking the North. Just about this time the abdication of Chin emperor was reported. So he took active part in organizing of Nanking temporal government, as a result he was made private secrecary of the Commication Bureau besides being appointed by Ho-nan legislative assembly member of temporal Parliament. After the Unification of South and North he resigned his office and became a journalist. However in the second year of republic he was elected to a member of the Parliament besides having engaged in law practice. After its dessoliement, he denoted all his energies to his law and took no part to politics. The Parliament was reorganized and he has been re-elected to a member in it.

李肇甫 字伯申 歲三十二

選舉地　四川省
籍　貫　四川省巴縣
住　址　北京西長安街與隆大院孫宅

君賦性篤厚。以純孝見稱於時。然爲人剛直嚴正。不隨俗浮沈。其在議會。素爲袁政府所憚。與人交。喜於責以善。人告以過。輒大喜。居常勤謹儉約。既達後。尤力尚儉朴。不事虛華。自幼好讀。喜博覽羣籍。任意所之以爲快。而不屑規規然從事於科舉之業。及海內維新。愈立志求新學。於新書無所不觀。而尤醉心於法律之書。前清宣統三年。遂以官費東渡留學。入日本明治大學法科大學部。畢業歸國。民國年被任爲總統府秘書。同年三月。被選爲臨時參議院議員。並全院委員長。民國二年一月。被選爲衆議院議員。國會解散後。仍留意時事。極望共和之復活。然以屈於專制淫威。不能有所表見。及國會復活。遂應召。仍爲衆議院議員。

君賦性篤厚にして純孝を以て稱せらる。人と爲り剛直嚴正にして流俗と同じからず、其の議會に在るや議論公正嚴明、內外之を推重し、袁政府の憚る所となる。人と交るに善を以て責め、過を告ぐれば、輒ち大に喜び、信義を以て中外人と親睦す。居常勤儉己を持し、朴實以て人に對し、虛華を事とせず。幼より讀書を好み、群籍を博覽し意に任せて快を呼び、科舉の業に從ふを屑とせず。海內維新に及び、志を立て〻新學を攻究し、尤も法律の書に傾倒せり。宣統三年官費を以て日本に留學し、明治大學校に學び、業を畢へて歸國す。民國元年總統府秘書に任じ同年三月選ばれて參議院議員となり。並に全院委員長たり。曾て南京參議院に於ける臨時約法審議會議長に擧げらる。二年一月衆議院議員に選ばる。議會解散後袁政府の注目甚だしきを以て韜晦して孝養に勤む。今や國會恢復して再び衆議院議員として議政壇上の闘將たり。

Mr. Li Chao-fu, another name Pai-shen, was born in Pa hsien, Ssi Chuan hsing, was a man of lofty character and magnanimous spirit. His arguments with clearness and impartiality in Parliament commanded esteem and are respected from surroundings and in his intercourse with others, he was merciful and generous and was always ready to give his ear to remonstrations. He showed a striking fondness for reading when very young. The intestine resteration which now broke in upon the country determined him to devote his entire energies to the new learning and books of law especially absorbed attention. During Chin Dynasty, he was ordered to go to Japan for study. He remained there until the courses of Meiji University was completed. In the first year of Republic, he was made private secretary of the government and on may in the same year, he was appointed to a member of legislative assembly, besides being chief-committee of the assembly. He was also made chairman of temporal meeting of drafting a constitution in the legislative assembly of Nan-king. On january, second year, he was elected to a member of Parliament, after its dissolution, he retired in his home and devoted his energies to filial duty. Thus he abuided watch of Yuanshi-kai government. On re-organization of the Parliament he was been re-elected to a member and is an eminent figure in it.

李膺恩　字榮　九　歲三十二

選舉地　吉林省
籍貫　吉林省舒蘭縣
住址　北京中鐵匠胡同五號

君賦性溫厚。與人交。和藹可親。雖所素惡。亦假以顏色。不出惡聲。然爲人耿直不阿。言行以禮自持。故雖以和婉待人。而無形中自有不可侵越之界限。曾未嘗曲己狥人。扮尺直尋之事較之尋常無意識之同流合汚者。自屬大相庭逕。自幼聰慧好讀。深思明辨。故於古義多所領悟。然喜求有用之學。不爲舉業所拘。及海內維新。愈肆力于西學。于新書無所不觀。尤喜研究教育之學。曾肄業于吉林師範學校。畢業後。歷充高等小學校長。吉林教育總會評議員。模範區學務委員。民國二年。國會成立。被選爲衆議院議員。國會解散後。歸里閉戶讀書。不問時政。及國會復活始入京。爲衆議院議員。

君賦性溫厚にして和藹親しむべし。然かも人と爲り耿直にして阿らず、言行共に禮を以て自ら持す、故に和婉を以て人を待つも無形の中自から侵すべからざるものあり。幼より聰慧にして好んで書を讀み、深く思索して明に辨じ、古義に於て領悟する所多し。喜んで有用の學を求め、舉業の拘する所とならず。海內維新に及びて愈力めて西學を攻究し、新書は觀ざる所無く、尤も喜んで教育の學を研究す。曾て吉林師範學校に學び、卒業の後ち高等小學校長、吉林教育總會評議員、模範區學務委員に歷充したり。民國二年正式國會の成立に際し、選ばれて衆議院議員と爲る。國會解散後は鄕里に歸臥して杜門閉戶以て書冊に親しみ又た政事を問はず。既にして時運再び來して國會重ねて召集さるゝに及び晉京して仍は衆議院員たり。

之精華　（傳記）　李膺恩先生

Mr. Li Ying-en, known as Jung Chin, age thirty two, is a native of Chin-han hsien, Chi Lin hsing. He is a man of generous mind and a typical gentleman. After his graduation of Chi Lin Normal School, he was appointed to the head of a normal school, the Committee of Educational Conference in Chi Lin and the Committee of Educational Affairs. In 1913 he was elected to a member of the House of Commons. He is now a member of the House of Commons again.

李爲綸　字伯玉　歲三十一

選舉地　四川省

籍　貫　四川簡陽縣

住　址　北京四單牌樓興隆大院二十四號

君爲人耿介不阿。生平以緘默自持。不
苟言笑。不輕於擧動。然持己以嚴。待
人以和。與人交。極重然諾。人有所託。
雖充之。必待事成而後告。居恆以消極
自持。能堅忍耐勞。不爲意氣所動。迨
宗旨旣定。則又猛勇直前。不復觀望。
自幼聰敏異人。讀書深思明辨。探求
眞義。及長。尤奮勉求博。即以大器自
期。貢笈東渡留學日本。入明治大學政
治科。研磋不倦。畢業歸國。民國二年。
正式國會成立。君被選爲衆議院議員。
北上到院。傾注蘊蓄。翼贊大政。多有
所議。國會解散後。歸里韜晦。讀書自
娛。及國會重開。遂又抵京。仍爲衆議
院議員。

君人と爲り耿介にして阿らず、生平緘默自ら持して苟も
言笑せず、輕々に擧止せず、已を持するに嚴なれども人を
待つに和を以てす。人と交るや然諾を重んじ、人若し人を
託すことあれば、之を允すと雖、必ずや事成りて後ち告ぐ。
生平消極主義を持して、堅忍能く勞に耐へ意氣の動かす
所とならず、方針旣に定るに迨び猛然として奮進す。
幼より聰慧人に異り、深く思索して書を讀み、日本に留
學して明治大學校政治科に入りて研磋倦まず、能く新進
の學問を咀嚼して其の業を畢へ、歸國後正式國會議員の
選舉に會す、民國二年選ばれて衆議院議員と爲る。北上
して院に到り多年の蘊蓄を傾注して大政を翼贊したり。
國會解散後、蜀山に歸臥して讀書自ら娛む。國會重ねて
開かるゝに及び復た其の召集應じて京師に抵り、仍ほ衆
議院議員たり。

Mr. Li Wei-lun, known as Pai-yu, age thirty one, is a native of Chien Yang hsen, Hsu Chuan hsing. He is man of frankness and very few words. He is severe for himself, but so benevolent for others that he renders his service at any cost to any body, from whom he was entrusted with something. Having been fond of reading books from his boyhood, he later went to Japan where he finished the political course of the Meiji University after industrious study of a new learning. On return to his home he met the Revolution, and was elected to a member of the Parliament, in which he contributed much towards the course of the state's affairs. On the dissolution of the Parliament he returned home and has been spending much of his time for reading books; but when the Parliament reopened, he went to Peking, responding its summon, in the capacity of a member of the Parliament, which post he now holds.

選舉地 直隷省
籍　貫 直隷省
住　址 北京西單東二條胡同二

君賦性朴質篤實不欺。與人交。常鯁直
不阿。人有過失。無不逕情詰責。不稍
存世故之念。然爲人慷慨尚義。喜爲貧
困者助力。而不輕於允諾。既承諾。無
不成者,以是人愈信用之。自幼聰穎好
讀。然非有益於身心及足以爲經世濟
爲之資者。輒不終篇即棄擲之。故雖曾
殫精舉業。然經史之外。大都擇其富於
義理讀之。不喜拘章句。效彫蟲刻縷者
之所爲。辛亥武昌倡義。天下響應。漢
土光復。民國肇造。宣布共和。及正式
國會成立。君荷衆望。被選爲衆議院
議員。國會解散後。韜晦里園。讀書自
娛。及國會重開。又出應召集。仍爲衆
議院議員。

民國之精華　（傳記）李永聲先生

君賦性朴直にして篤實。人と交りて常に硬直自ら持し致
て阿らざるなり。人君し過失あらむか、逕情を以て詰責
せざる無く、少しも世故の念を存せず。然かも人と爲り
慷慨にして義を尚び、喜んで貧困者を助く、輕々に時人
せざるも、既に一諾すれば成さ〻事無く、爲に時人
の信用を得たり。幼より聰穎にして學を好み、喜んで身心
の修養及び經世濟物の資とするに足る者を讀み、曾て科
舉の業を指彈し、經史以外の群籍大約其の義理に富める
ものを擇びて讀破し、章句に拘泥せざること、到底彼れ彫
蟲刻鏤者の學び能ふ所にあらざるなり。辛亥の歳武昌義
を唱へて天下響應し、漢土を光復して民國を樹立し、以
て共和の新政を宣布して正式國會成立するに及び、君衆
望を負ふて衆議院議員に常選したり。國會解散後、里園
に韜晦して讀書自ら娛み。國會再び開くるに及び、又た
出で〻召集に應じ、仍は衆議院議員と爲る。

Mr. Li Yung-sheng, known as Li-shan, is a native of Chi-li hsing. He is frank and

righteous by nature, never flactuating his will with the worldly interests. He is respected by his

friends as a reliable person who does his best, once entrusted, for others. He read many books which

are benefitable for the promotion of his character. When the Rovolution took place and the Parlia-

ment was established, he was elected to a member of the Parliament. After the dissolution of the

Parliament, he has been enjoying a peaceful life in his home, but as soon as the Parliament was

reopened he went to Peking to occupy his seat, which he now holds with honour.

李景泉　心源

選舉地　山西省

籍貫　山西省歸化縣

住址　北京兵部窪十二號

君秉性清高。言動舉止。皆迥異凡流。

然爲人恪謹耐勞。自幼天資聰慧。悟性

敏捷。讀書能深思探究精義。不爲成見

所局。故思想豐富。見解新穎。人但見

其居常規規自守。不知其精神。固異常

活潑也。海內維新後。銳意求新學。造

詣日深。歷充山西省城中學教員。學務

公所議紳。又籌辦全省諮議局。並自治

事宜。被選爲諮議局議員。曾歷充撫藩

道各慕。佐理新政。又歷充薩拉齊五原

縣知事。將軍署書記。幹才大著。數年

來專研究佛理。理想高遠。現被選爲衆

議院議員。及國會重開。遂應召集。抵

北京仍任衆議院議員職。

君秉性清高にして言動舉止皆な迥な凡流に異るあり。然
かも人と爲り恪謹にして勞に耐へ、幼より天資聰慧にし
て悟性敏捷なり。書を讀みて深く其の義を探究して思索
これ勉む。故ゆ思想豐富にして見解新穎なり。山西省城
中學教員、學務公所議紳となり。育英の業に從事し、教
育の振興に努む。又た全省諮議局並に自治の事宜を處理
して、地方の公益增進を圖る。曾て巡撫布政使道臺等の
慕賓として新政を勤助したる事あり。又た薩拉齊五原縣
知事、將軍衙門書記等の職に任じて吏務幹才大に著る。
數年來專ら佛典を研究して理想高遠なり。現に衆議院議
員に選ばれ、民國五年正式國會第二次の開院式を舉ぐる
や君また召集に應じ、山を出でゝ北京に抵り、仍ち衆議
院議員の職に就きたり。

Mr. Li-chang-chuan, otherwise called Hsi yuan, is a native of Kuei-hua hsien, Shan-Hsihsing. His sustained and noble character are discernible in his daily conduct and common talk, while are subject of admiration for one who meets him. As a boy he was remarkably sagacious to find a truth among compled daily problems. Also he took an observing interest in reading and study, by which he has acquired the profound knowledge in facilitating him to solve difficult questions at ease. While he was a professor of the Shauhsi-hsing middle school and councillor of the Educational Board, he took unusual interest in instructing and training young people and rendered the supreme effort in improving the educational system. Also as a member of the district congress and of the self-government Board he has done a good deal for the local welfare. Once of the counsellor to the governor-general Kuo-shi, his helping hand was counted highly in the establishment of the new government. Later, he was made the governor of Sa-la-chi-uu yuan, then the secretary of the War Depertment, proved his ability as an able administrator. Recent year, he has became an ardent follower of Budda, and it is said that he devotes much time in study of buddhism. In the fifth year of the Republic he was elected and sent to the Lower House, as one of most accomplished statesmen.

李慶芳 字楓圃

選舉地　山西省

籍貫　山西省

住址　北京東四牌樓燈草胡同

君秉性溫厚。待人以和。與人交。直而
婉。談而能久。不爲疾言遽色。居常以
謹約自持。言動舉止。皆有本末。且重
信義。嚴取與。然天資聰穎。思想活潑。
非尋常拘拘自守之鄉愿可比。自幼即
負文名。好談宋儒義理之學。尤精詞
賦。童試輒冠其曹。弱冠。肄業山西晉
陽書院。旋調令德堂。年二十六。以官
費留學日本。初入經緯學校。旋復入日
本大學法科畢業得法學士學位。歸國
後。應留學生試。授法政科舉人。在籍
襄辦學務自治。卓著勤勞。民國元年。
當選爲衆議院議員。二年。復被舉爲憲
法起草委員。創辦民憲日報及憲法新
聞。國會解散後。以記名道尹。服職稅
務處。及國會復活。終應召。仍爲衆議
院議員。

民國之精華　(傳‧記)　李慶芳先生

君や秉性溫厚にして人を待つに和を以
てす。居常謹約を
以て自ら持し、言動舉止皆な本末あり、且つ信義を重ん
す。天資聰穎にして思想活潑、尋常拘々たる鄉愿と比すべ
くもあらず。幼より即ち文名あり、好んで宋儒義理の學
を談じ、尤も詞賦に精しく、童試其の曹に冠たり。業を
山西晉陽書院に受け、旋で令德堂に調せらる。年二十六、旋て日
官費を以て日本に留學し、初め經緯學校に入り、旋て
本大學法科に學びて業を畢り。歸國の後ち留學生の試に
應じて法政科舉人を授けらる。鄉里に在りて勞務と自治
を處理して勤勞卓著なり。民國元年衆議院議員に當選し
二年復た憲法起草委員に選ばれ、民憲日報及び憲法新聞
を創立經營したり。國會解散後、記名道尹を以て職を稅
務處に服す。國會復活するに及びて召集に應じ、仍ほ衆
議院議員たり。

Mr. Li Ching-fang, known as Feng Pu, is a native of Shan Hsi-hsing. He is a man of generous mind and benevolent for others. Early in his life he already gained a literary fame. After graduation of Pu Jang Institute he visited Japan where he finished a course of the Nihon University, and subsequently he passed successfully the Government's Civil Official Examination in his own country. In 1912 he was elected to a member of the House of Commons and appointed to a committee of the draft of constitution. He is now a member of the House of Commons again.

李紹白　字堅白　歲

選舉地　奉天省

籍貫　奉天省遼陽縣

住址　北京象來街八

君秉性溫厚。五歲讀書。中經亂雜。屬輟業。初習八股。嗣棄之。學爲古文辭。並及子史。詞筆翔實。爲儕輩冠。二十二歲。入邑學爲庠生。明年。入襄平公學。習科學。嗣入奉天師範學校。習物理化學諸科。迨徐東海總督三省。交涉失敗。乃與同學李有忱李及蘭等鳩集省垣各校學生二千人開議。電達中央。東海知之。立飭嚴除名籍。並擬以革命闌涉。交法司削辦。經學使知君力爭得免。君乃欲東渡。未果。乃遊理春哈爾濱齊々哈爾等處。以恣考查。行經五千里。歷時五閱月始歸。終專心敎育。歷辦中學師範各校。成績斐然。校務之暇。留心政治。民國二年。當選參議院議員入都。國會消滅後。仍回本省辦學。及帝制發生。乃潛赴滬上。與同志等共謀反對。國會重開。遂入都。仍爲參議院議員。

君や秉性溫厚、五歲にして書を讀む。初め八股を習ひ嗣之を棄て、舉んで古文辭を作り詞筆翔實にして儕輩に冠たり。二十二歲邑學に入りて庠生となる、翌年襄平公學堂に科學を習ふ、嗣で奉天優級師範學校に入り物理化學諸科を修め、徐世昌が總督となりて外交に失敗するや、仍ち同學李有忱、李行蘭等と省城各學校生徒二千人を糾合して會議し、中央政府に上陳する所あり。徐總督之を知りて直に學籍を削除し、法司に交附して嚴罰に處せしむ。

張學使力爭して漸く免かるゝを得たり。吾乃ち東渡を欲して○さず。乃ち哩春哈爾賓齊々哈爾等の各地を漫遊す。歸來專ら敎育に從事して中學師範各學校を創立し、校務の餘暇心を政治に留む。民國二年參議院議員に當選す、國會消滅後、歸省して學事を處理す。帝制問題起るや潛に上海に赴きて同志と共に反對を謀る。國會重ねて開かれ君また晉んして參議院議員たり。

Mr. Li Shao-pai, known as Chien Pai, is a native of Liao Yan hsien, Feng Tien hng. He of generous mind and fond of a learning early in his life. He learned the phisic and chemistry Higher Normal School. He was interested on education, so that he established several ure of his business he paid the attention on affairs of state. In 1913 he was elected uate. He is now a member of the Senate again.

李慶芳 字楓圃

選舉地　山西省
籍　貫　山西省
住　址　北京東四牌樓燈草胡同

君秉性溫厚。待人以和。與人交。直而婉。談而能久。不爲疾言遽色。居常以謹約自持。言動舉止。皆有本末。且重信義。嚴取與。然天資聰穎。心想活潑。非尋常拘拘自守之鄉愿可比。自幼即貢文名。好談宋儒義理之學。尤精詞賦。童試輒冠其曹。弱冠。肄業山西晉陽書院。旋調令德堂。年二十六。以官費留學日本。初入經緯學校。旋復入日本大學法科畢業。得法學士學位。歸國後。應留學生試。授法政科舉人。在籍襄辦學務自治。卓著勤勞。民國元年。當選爲衆議院議員。二年。復被舉爲憲法起草委員。創辦民憲日報及憲法新聞。國會解散後。以記名道尹。服職稅務處。及國會復活。紆應召。仍爲衆議院議員。

本大學法科に學びて業を畢ゆ。歸國の後ち留學生の試に應じて法政科舉人を授けらる。鄉里に在りて勞務と自治を處理して勤勞卓著なり。民國元年衆議院議員に當選し二年復た憲法起草委員に選ばれ、民憲日報及び憲法新聞を創立經營したり。國會解散後、記名道尹を以て職を稅務處に服す。國會復活するに及びて召集に應じ、仍ほ衆議院議員たり。

君や秉性溫厚にして人を待つに和を以にす。居常謹約を以て自ら持し、言動舉止皆な本末あり、且つ信義を重んず。天資聰穎にして思想活潑、尋常拘々たる鄉愿と比すべくもあらず。幼より即ち文名あり、好んで宋儒義理の學を談じ、尤も詞賦に精しく、童試其の曹に冠たり。業を山西晉陽書院に受け、旋で令德堂に調せらる。年二十六、官費を以て日本に留學し、初め經緯學校に入り、旋て日

Mr. Li Ch.ing-fang, known as Feng Pu, is a native of Shan Hsi-hsing. He is a man of generous mind and benevolent for others. Early in his life he already gained a literary fame. After graduation of Pu Jang Institute he visited Japan where he finished a course of the Nihon University, and subsequently he passed successfully the Government's Civil Official Examination in his own country. In 1912 he was elected to a member of the House of Commons and appointed to a committee of the draft of constitution. He is now a member of the House of Commons again.

民國之精華　（傳記）李慶芳先生

李紹白　字堅白

選舉地　奉天省
籍貫　奉天省遼陽縣
住址　北京象來街八

君秉性溫厚。五歲讀書。中經亂雜。屬
輟業。初習八股。嗣棄之。學爲古文辭。
並及子史。詞筆翔實。爲儕輩冠。二十
二歲。入邑學爲庠生。明年。入襄平公
學。習科學。嗣入奉天優級師範學校。
習物理化學諸科。迨徐東海總督三省。
交涉失敗。乃與同學李有忱李友蘭等。
鳩集省垣各校學生二千人開議。電達
中央。東海知之。立飾嚴除名籍。並擬
以革命關涉交法司削辦。經學使張君
力爭得免。君乃欲東渡。未果。乃漫遊
珥春哈爾濱齊々哈爾等處。以恣考查。
行經五千里。歷時五閱月始歸。終專
心教育。歷辦中學師範各校。成績斐
然。校務之暇。留心政治。民國二年。當
選參議院議員入都。國會消滅後。仍回
本省辦學。及帝制發生。乃潛赴滬上。
與同志等共謀反對。國會重開。遂入
都。仍爲參議院議員。

君や秉性溫厚、五歲にして書を讀む。初め八股を習ひ嗣で
之を棄て、學んで古文辭を作り詞筆翔實にして儕輩に冠
たり。二十二歲邑學に入りて庠生となる、翌年襄平公學
堂に科學を習ふ、嗣で奉天優級師範學校に入り物理化學
諸科を修め、徐世昌が總督となりて外交に失敗するや、
仍ち同學李有忱、李有蘭等と省城各學校生徒二千人を糾
合して會議し、中央政府に上陳する所あり。徐總督之を知
りて直に學籍を削除し、法司に交附して嚴罰に處せしむ。

張學使力を爭して漸く免かるゝを得たり。吾乃ち東渡を欲
して果さず、乃ち琿春哈爾濱齊々哈爾等の各地を漫遊す。
歸來專ら敎育に從事して中學師範各學校を創立し、校務
の餘暇心を政治に留む。民國二年參議院議員に當選し、
國會消滅後、歸省して學事を處理す。帝制問題起るや潛
に上海に赴きて同志と共に反對を謀る。國會重ねて開か
れ君復た晉京して參議院議員たり。

Mr. Li Shao-pai, known as Chien Pai, is a native of Liao Yan hsien, Feng Tien hsing. He

is a man of generous mind and fond of a learning early in his life. He learned the phisic and chemistry

in the Feng Tien Higher Normal School. He was interested on education, so that he established several

schools. At a leisure of his business he paid the attention on affairs of state. In 1913 he was elected

to a member of the Senate. He is now a member of the Senate again.

李永聲 字立三

選舉地　直隸省

籍　貫　直隸省

住　址　北京西單東二條胡同二

君賦性朴質篤實不欺。與人交常鯁直
不阿。人有過失。無不逕情詰責。不稍
存世故之念。然為人慷慨尚義。喜為貧
困者助力。而不輕於允諾。既承諾。無
不成者。以是人愈信用之。自幼聰穎好
讀。然非有益於身心及足以為經世濟
為之資者。輒不終篇即棄擲之。故雖曾
殫精舉業。然經史之外。大都擇其富於
義理讀之。不喜拘章句。效彫蟲刻縷者
之所為。辛亥武昌倡義。天下響應。漢
土光復。民國肇造。宣布共和。及正式
國會成立。君荷衆望。被選為衆議院
議員。國會解散後。韜晦里園。讀書自
娛。及國會重開。又出應召集。仍為衆
議院議員。

君賦性朴直にして、篤實。人と交りて常に硬直自ら持し敢
て阿らざるなり。人若し過失あらむか、逕情を以て詰責
せざる無く、少しも世故の念を存せず。然かも人と爲り
慷慨にして義を尚び、喜んで貧困者を助く、輕々に允諾
せざるも、既に一諾すれば成さざる事無く、爲に時人
の信用を得たり。幼より聰穎にして學を好み、喜んで身心
の修養及び經世濟物の資とするに足る者を讀み、曾て科
舉の業を措びし、經史以外の群籍大約其の義理に富める
ものを擇びて讀破し、章句に拘泥せざること、到底彼れ彫
蟲刻鏤の學び能ム所にあらざるなり。辛亥の歳武昌義
を唱へて天下響應し、漢土を光復して民國を樹立し、以
て共和の新政を宣布して正式國會成立するに及び、君衆
望を負ふて衆議院議員に常選したり。國會解散後、里園
に韜晦して讀書自ら娛み。國會再び開くるに及び、又た
出で〻召集に應じ、仍は衆議院議員と爲る。

Mr. Li Yung-sheng, known as Li-shan, is a native of Chi-li hsing. He is frank and righteous by nature, never fluctuating his will with the worldly interests. He is respected by his friends as a reliable person who does his best, once entrusted, for others. He read many books which are benefitable for the promotion of his character. When the Revolution took place and the Parliament was established, he was elected to a member of the Parliament. After the dissolution of the Parliament, he has been enjoying a peaceful life in his home, but as soon as the Parliament was reopened he went to Peking to occupy his seat, which he now holds with honour.

民國之精華　（傳記）李永聲先生

李景泉　心源

選舉地　山西省

籍　貫　山西省歸化縣

住　址　北京兵部窪十二號

君秉性清高。言動舉止。皆迥異凡流。然爲人恪謹耐勞。自幼天資聰慧。悟性敏捷。讀書能深思探究精義。不爲成見所局。故思想豐富。見解新頴。人但見其居常規規自守。不知其精神。固異常活潑也。海內維新後。銳意求新學。造詣日深歷充山西省城中學教員。學務公所議紳。又籌辦全省諮議局。並自治事宜。被選爲諮議局議員。曾歷充撫藩道各慕佐理新政。又歷充薩拉齊五原縣知事。將軍署書記。幹才大著。數年來專研究佛理。理想高遠。現被選爲衆議院議員。及國會重開。遂應召集。抵北京仍任衆議院議員職。

君秉性清高にして言動舉止皆な迥に凡流に異るあり。然かも人と為り恪謹にして勞に耐へ、幼より天資聰慧にして悟性敏捷なり。書を讀みて深く其の義を探究して思索之れ勉む。故ゝ思想豐富にして見解新頴なり。山西省城中學教員、學務公所議紳となり。育英の業に從事し、敎育の振興に努む。又た全省諮議局並に自治の事宜を處理して、地方の公益增進を圖る。曾て巡撫布政使道臺等の幕賓として新政を勸助したる事あり。又た薩拉齊五原縣知事、將軍衙門書記等の職に任じて吏務幹才大に著る。數年來專ら佛典を研究して理想高遠なり。現に衆議院議員に選ばれ、民國五年正式國會第二次の開院式を擧ぐるや君また召集に應じ、山を出でゝ北京に抵り、仍ち衆議院議員の職に就きたり。

九十四

Mr. Li-chang-chuan, otherwise called Hsi yuan, is a native of Kuei-hua hsien, Shan-Hsihsing. His sustained and noble character are discernible in his daily conduct and common talk, while are subject of admiration for one who meets him. As a boy he was remarkably sagacious to find a truth among compled daily problems. Also he took an observing interest in reading and study, by which he has acquired the profound knowledge in facilitating him to solve difficult questions at ease. While he was a professor of the Shaubsi-hsing middle school and councillor of the Educational Board, he took unusual interest in instructing and training young people and rendered the supreme effort in improving the educational system. Also as a member of the district congress and of the self-government Board he has done a good deal for the local welfare. Once of the counsellor to the governor-general Kuo-shi, his helping hand was counted highly in the establishment of the new government. Later, he was made the governor of Sa-la-chi-uu yuan, then the secretary of the War Depertment, proved his ability as an able administrator. Recent year, he has became an ardent follower of Budda, and it is said that he devotes much time in study of buddhism. In the fifth year of the Republic he was elected and sent to the Lower House, as one of most accomplished statesmen.

李國珍　字碩遠　歲三十五

選舉地　江西省

籍貫　江西省武寧縣人

住址　北京順治門大街路東李宅

前長江水師湖口總鎮雨亭公第三子。由日本東京早稻田大學政治經濟科畢業。前清授法科舉人。廷試優等。授度支部七品小京官之職。民國成立。充江西省議會議員。旋被選爲臨時參議院議員。正式國會告成。又被選爲衆議院議員。國會停職後。赴德國留學。未幾歐戰甚劇。輟學返國。歷充政事堂參議。國務院參議。教育次長。農商次長等官。歷兼編審處處長。全國專門以上學校成績審查會會長。林務處督辦等差。國會恢復。仍就議員。蓋世以雄辯稱之。而已以議會發言爲樂事也。然自充議員以來。小事不言。大事則登壇言之。滔滔不絕。理罄而止。其自重又如此云。

民國之精華　（傳記）　李國珍先生

君は前長江水師湖口總鎮雨亭公の第三子にして、早稻田大學政治經濟科出身の秀才なり、曾て法政科舉人を授けられ。廷試優等を以て度支部七品京官に敍せらる。民國成立するや、江西省議會議員となり、旋て選ばれて臨時參議院議員と爲る。二年正式國會衆議院議員に當選す袁政府より國會議員の職を停止されて後は、獨逸に赴きて留學す。未だ幾くもなく歐洲戰爭甚だ劇し、即ち學を輟めて歸國し、政事堂參議、國務院參議、敎育次長、農商次長等の要職に歷任し、兼ねて編審處々長、全國各專門學校成績審査會々長、林務處督辦等の職に歷充したり。其の議政檀上常に滔々たる雄辯家を以て名あり。其の議政檀上常に滔々たる雄辯滿場を壓す、蓋し言論界一方の關將たるなり。五年約法復活して國會重ねて召集を行ふに及び、再び出で、仍ほ衆議院議員と爲る。

Mr. Li Kuo-chen, otherwise known as She-yuan, thirty five years of age, is a native of Wu ning, Chiang-ssi. He is of a very good family in China, his father being the high official of the province. He studied in the Waseda university, and on returning to his home, he passed the civil service examination with honours. When the Republic was established, he was a member of Chian-hsi Assembly. In the second year of the Republic, when the Parliament was opened, he was returned for the House of Commons. Under the Yuanshi-kai, government, when he was deprived of his function as a member of the Parliament, he went to Germany to complete his education. When the European war broke out, he returned to his country where he occupied in turn such important posts as a member of the Senate, vice-president of the educational department and that of agricultun and commerce. He was also appointed the chief of committee investigating the technical schools. He was known for his eloquence, and the power of debate. When the Parliament was restored, he was elected a member for the House of Commons.

九十七

汪震東 字子陽 歲三十

選舉地　內蒙古

籍　貫　內蒙古之喀喇沁即河熱之平泉縣

住　址　北京東皇城根八顯槐西口外滄北

君秉性剛毅朴直。慷慨好義。居恆尚質惡文。不事無益之繁華。然文武兼資其學新舊有素養。劍膽琴心。橫劍說經。夙抱經世之志。專攻天下有用之實學。尤富於軍事學問。初入師範學校畢業。曾籌辦漢蒙小學堂歷充高等小學教員。前蒙藏局蒙文白活報編輯。以啓發民智。開化風氣。爲己任。並充口北騎兵團第一營副官。嚴守北門鎖鑰。多有所畫策。民國五年。五大民族共和之事。建置尤重。君鑑于中外之趨勢。庶稗挽回自疆。適及國會再開。君補缺當選衆議院議員。慨然應召抵京師。仍爲衆議院議員。

汪震東先生

君乘性剛毅朴直、慷慨義を好み。居常質を尚び文を惡む。然かも文武兼資して、其の學新舊共に素養あり。劍膽に して琴心、劍を橫へて經を說くの士なり。初め師範學校に入りて業を畢へ、曾て漢蒙小學堂を創立經營し、高等小學校教員、前蒙藏局蒙文白話報編輯等の職に任じ、民智を啓發し、風氣を開導するを以て己が任と爲す。並に口北騎兵團第一營副官に任じ、長城外に出で、鑰を橫へ、北門の鎖鑰を嚴守して貴憚する所多し。民國五年五大民族共和の新政再び克復さる。蒙古西藏の事、時下建設すべき要務尠なからず。君中外の大勢に鑑みて庶くは頹勢を挽回して邊務を振作せん事を思ふ。適ま國會重ねて開かるゝに及び、君補缺議員として召集せらる。君慨然としして立ち、踊躍して京師に抵り、仍は新に衆議院議員の職に就きたり。

Mr. Wang Chen-tung, another name Tzu-yang, Je Ho-ping-chuan, mongolier prefecture, thirty years old. Sturdy character and simple nature we find in him remarkably: his patriotic spirit defends the weak, loves justice, disdains the wicked and maintains plainness; yet he is distinguished both in letters and military art. He is a good scholar of classics and modern. He studied first at a normal school after completed his requirements there he established the Han meng grammar school. Later, he taught a higher grammar school for sometime, then he took charge of editing the Meng-Wen Pai Hou Pao published by the late Mongoria and Tibet Bureau and tried to educate and lead the people to culture and taste. As the aid of the commander of the Kou-pe Country regiment he lived a camplife outside of the Great Wall for sometime and had done his duty of guarding the northern frontier. In the fifth year of the Republic the new regime established by the five great races has been restored and the National Parliament has been called to existence. He was elected to the Lower House and stays in Peking. Recently, Mongolia and Tibet begun to draw much attention at home and abroad, man who has complete knowledge of present and past, like mr. Wang Chen-tung is expected much in unifying the frontier regions and improve the condition of the same territory.

汪喙鸞 字輸忱

選舉地 湖北省
籍　貫 湖北省武昌
住　址 北京打牌廠板井胡同三號

君秉性質朴惇篤。崇實惡華。言論思想。皆安于平易着實。不喜以怪奇。然天資聰慧。氣宇不凡。少時讀書。即抱大志。終年奮勉於學。不以嗜好縈懷。弱冠。即工於文詞。所作多富於理想。文格則近漢魏。稍長。改崇歐蘇。語調氣勢。愈益雄奇俊偉。超絕儕輩。讀書博而能約。淵博之上。加以精深。學派則不拘漢宋。皆深有所得。海內維新後。嘗入兩湖書院肄業。畢業後。又於庚子辛丑併科中試爲舉人。歷任山西大學堂教習。廣東優級師範管理員兼教員。高等工業學堂地理教習。及廣州工藝學堂監督。及廣東學務公所專門科長。辛亥改革。民國元年。被選爲衆議院議員，國會解散後。君歸里從事學問。不談政治。及國會重開。始入京就職。

君秉性質朴惇厚にして實を崇び華を惡む。其の思想言論皆な平易着實なり。然かも天資聰慧にして氣質凡ならざるものあり。少時書を讀みて大志を抱き、弱冠にして詞文に工に、作る所多く理想に富み、文格また漢魏に近し。稍や長して改めて歐蘇を崇び、搭調氣勢愈々益々雄奇俊偉にして僑儕を超絕す。讀書博くして能く約し、即ち淵博にして精深を加へたるもの、其の學派は漢宋に拘はらす、皆な深く造詣する所あり。海內維新に及び、曾て兩湖書院に入りて修め、卒業の後ち庚子辛丑の試に及第して舉人と爲る。山西大學堂教習、廣東優級師範學校管理員兼敎員、高等工業學校地理敎員、廣州工藝學堂監督及び廣東學務公所專門科長等の職に歷任したり。辛亥革命の事起るや、武昌に於て武昌群報を發刊す。民國元年衆議院議員に當選す。國會解散後君歸鄉して書齋に韜晦し、國會恢復に及びて召集に應じて再び出で〻衆議院議員の職に就きたり。

民國之精華　（傳記）　汪喙鸞先生

Mr. Wang Sei-luan, otherwise called Shu Chin, is a native of Wu-chang, Hu-pei hsing. He is a man of sound principle being honest and simple in character. His ideas as well as words are plain and yet sound. He had the natural gift and high aspiration. He was a copious reader of books and writer of rich and profound ideas. His strength of pen is rivalled only by few. His information is thorough and comprehensive. When the new current of thought was running in China, he studied in Lian-hu school and having passed the civil service examination he was appointed an instructor of the Kuangtung higher normal school, the higher technical school and several other important institutions of learning. When the revolution broke out he started news-paper in Wu-chuang. In the 1st year of the Republic he was elected a member for the House of Commons. With the dissolution of the Parliament he returned to his home where he spent most of his time in study. When the Parliament was restored he resumed the function of the member of the legislative assembly.

克希克圖　字仲養　歲三十

選舉地　外蒙古。

籍　貫　原籍蒙古。寄籍江蘇鎮江駐防鑲紅
　　　　旗。

住　址　北京隆福街。

君名克希克圖。漢名恩浩。賦性惇篤。
天資英邁。然富於學識。新舊皆有素
養。其見解氣慨。皆迥異凡流。夙抱大
志。專攻實學。造詣既深。傑出儕輩。年
十四。即前清光緒二十六年。入江南常
備右軍隨營學堂肄業。二十八年畢業。
入江南將備學堂。二十九年。由南洋考
送。日本留學。入振武學校。三十二年
卒業。入明治大學。肆習法科。同年並
入東京高等警察學校。因革命嫌疑官
費被停。三十三年警察學校畢業歸國。
宣統三年。充黑龍江交涉局飜譯科員。
科員。民國二年正式國會成立。當選為
由外蒙古札薩克圖汗部被衆議院議
員。國會解散後。曾充蒙藏院科員。五
年薦任為編纂。及國會重開。君復應召
集。現充衆議院議員。

君名は克希克圖、漢名恩浩と云ふ、其の先蒙古に出で江
蘇鎮江駐防鑲紅旗人となる。賦性惇篤にして天資英邁な
り。前清光緒二十六年、年十四にして江南常備軍右軍隨
營學校に入り、二十八年卒業す。又た江南將備學堂に入
り、二十九年南洋大臣より選拔されて日本に留學し、振
武學校に入りて三十二年卒業す。又た明治大學に入りて
修業し、次で東京高等警察學校に入る。革命嫌疑を以て

官費留學を停止されたるも、依然在學して三十三年卒業
歸國す。三十四年黑龍江交涉局飜譯科員となり、宣統三
年清華學校敎師となり、兼て印鑄局科員に任す。民國二
年正式國會成立するや、外蒙古札薩克圖汗部より選ばれ
て衆議院議員と為る。國會解散後。曾で蒙藏院科員に充
り、五年編纂に薦任さる。本年國會再び國會召集さるゝ
や、仍は復た衆議院議員と為る。

Mr. Ko Hsi-ko-tu, Cha Su-ko-tu Chien Chi, Wai Mongolia, thirty years old, his
ancestors were mongolians. He is most truthful and sincere man; but very brave gentleman
he is. In the 26th year of Kuang-hsu at his forteenth year he entered the military school
organized under the Chiang-nan standing army and graduated in the 28th year. Then he advanced to
the Chiang-nan officers school; next year he was picked out by the minister for the eathern district
and sent to Japan where he entered as a student of the Shinbu school which he graduated in the 32nd year.
As soon as he completed the study at the Shinbu school, he enrolled as a student at the Meiji University, finally he matriculated at the Tokyo higher police school, then he was suspected of revolutionary
design and suspented the government allowance; still them, he continued his study at the school and
accomplished his cherished object without any hindrance whatever. In the 33rd year he graduated the
Meiji and returned home: next year he was appointed the translator of the foreign bureau, Heilung
Chihsing district. The third year of Hsuan tung he taught the Chin-hua school and held an office at
the printing bureau. In the second year of the Republic the national Legislature formally inaugulated
and he was elected a member of the Lower House. When the regislature dissolved he was appointed
to an office at the Mongolia and Tibet Board. In the fifth-year he was promoted to the position of
chief compiler. In the same year the central Legislature was restored; consequently he was again
sent back to Lower House.

吳景濂 字蓮伯 歲四十三

選舉地　奉天省
籍　貫　奉天省錦州
住　址　北京新簾子胡同

君容貌魁偉。天資精明强幹。思想堅實。頗有氣慨。自幼好讀。弱冠有文名。夙抱經世之志。專攻實學。前清庚子後。以高才貢進。入京師大學堂。畢業後。肄業奉天自治研究所。以進士資格。佐理新政。歷充奉天教育會會長。師範學堂監督。及諮議局開。君遂被選爲議長。辛亥武昌起義。黨人入奉者甚衆。君糾合同志官紳。謀獨立。保全地方免糜爛。以奉天代表赴上海。旋充南京臨時參議院議員。勸助建設之業。臨時參議院移於北京。君被推爲議長。遂携統一共和黨與同盟會合併。爲國民黨。被公推爲代理理事長。正式國會成立被選爲衆議院議員。與湯化龍爭議長敗。時人惜之。國會解散後。爲大總統府顧問。不就而韜晦。帝制發生。滇顯起義。君赴滬。與同志計大局。目的既達。國會再開。君仍應召集。直抵北京。復就衆議院議員職。

君秉性聰穎にして天資英邁なり。容貌魁偉頗る氣慨に富み、凤に經世の大志を抱きて、學識亦た新舊共に造詣深し。前清庚子高才貢生を以て京師大學校に入り、卒業後奉天自治研究所に修業し、出でゝ進士の資格を以て新政を勸助したり、奉天教育會長、師範學校監督等の職に充り名望大に著る。奉天諮議局開くるや議長と爲る。第一革命當時多數の黨人滿洲に入りて變を企つ、君同志の官紳を糾合して獨立を謀り以て地方の平和を保全す。旋て奉天代表として上海に赴き嗣で南京臨時參議院議員と爲る。臨時參議院が北京に移るや、舉げられて議長と爲る。遂に統一共和黨を牽ねて同盟會と合併し國民黨を組織し其の理事長代理と爲る。民國二年衆議院議員に當選す。國會解散後大總統府顧問に聘せられしも就かず、帝制問題發生して雲南義を起すや、上海に抵りて同志と偕に大局を圖り。國會恢復するや再び北上して衆議院議員と爲る。

民國之精華　（傳記）　吳景濂先生

一百

Mr. Wu Ching-lien, another name, Lien-pai Chin prefecture, Feng-tien district, forty three years old. He is bright and brilliant gentleman who can hardly find a parallel; his massive figure in commanding, spiritous nature of him led him to give up old and new he acquired profoundly. During the late emperial reign he was admitted to the Mepoliton University as honorary fellow. On the graduation he took up further study at the Feng-tien self Government institute. Later, in the capacity of counsellor he assisted in establishing the new order of things. His popularity did not find any competitor when he accepted the positions as the president, Fengtien educational association, and later the supe intendent of normal school. When the Fengtien Legislative assembly was organized he made the speaker. At the time of the first Revolution various political party men gathered themselves in Manchuria to reflect another up-rising; he persuaded almost all officers to declare independence against the central government in view of maintaining peace of the locality. Succeedingly he represented Pao-tin at the Shanghai Conference; then, he was a member of the Provisional Nankin Assembly which transparted to Peking and he was elected the president of the assembly. Amalgamating the Union Republican party with the Union party organized the national party of which he was the charge of director-genernal. In the second year of the Republic he was chosen as member of the Lower House. At the dissolution of Parliament he was asked to be an adviser at the presidents' office but he declined it. Question of the Restorations of Emperial Regime gave high tention to throughout the country. As soon as Yun-nan rose up against the scheme he went down to Shanhai to prevent the retrogression. Fortunately the Parliament came to existense again and he is now a member of the Lower House.

吳榮萃　字拔其　歲三十八

選舉地　江蘇省

籍　貫　江蘇省六合縣

住　址　北京香爐營頭條三十四

君爲人耿直不阿。疾惡崇善。朋友有
過。常直辭規勸。不復存世故之念。人
或矯詞辯護。則不復與言。人告以過。
輒欣然謝之。絕不文飾。常語人曰認錯
二字。是文過之不二法門。日本法政大
學速成科。明治大學法律專門部卒業
生。兩江師範學堂教員。江南高等商業
學校教務長兼教員。並歷充江南法政
學堂。浙江法政學堂。高等巡警學堂。
法官養成所等處教員。前淸諮議局議
員。民國二年正式國會成立。被選爲衆
議院議員。國會解散後。歸里從事教
育。及國會復活。始入京。仍爲衆議院
議員。

君人と爲り耿直にして阿らず、惡を疾んで善を崇ぶ、朋
友過あれば直言以て之を規勸し、復た世故の念を存せず
人或は詞を矯めて辯護すれば、則ち復た與に言はず、人
の告ぐるに過を以てすれば、輙ち欣然として之を謝し、
絕えて文飾する事なし。夙に日本に游學して法政大學速
成科に學び、明治大學法律專門部に入りて卒業す。歸國
して後ち兩江師範學堂敎員、江南高等商業學校敎務長敎

員に歷充し、並に江南法政學堂、浙江法政學堂、高等巡
警學堂、法官養成所等各學校の敎員を歷す。復た選ば
れて前淸時代江蘇省諮議局議員と爲る。後ち民國樹立し
て民國二年正式國會成立するや、衆議院議員に舉げられ
中央議政檀上の人となれり。國會解散後歸鄉して再び敎
育に從事したり。其の國會が再蘇するに及びて重ねて晋
京し、仍は衆議院議員と爲る。

Mr. Wu Jung-hua, another name Pachi, age thirty eight, native of Liu-ho hsien, Chiang su hsing. He is a sincerely straight forward man, who hates the vices, and loves the good. He would suggest to his friends without hesitation, whenever he has found their fault. When he met one who says some excuse, he would never talk again to him, but if one apologizes him sincerely, he would gladly welcome him, and becomes his true friend. Early in the youth, he studied in a japanese law school, and is a graduater of special course of Meiji Law-University. After he returned home, he passed through several positions of teacher of Lin Chiang Teachers' school, head teacher of Chinag-nan Commercial High School, as well as teacher of Chiang nan Law School, Tai san Law School, Higher Police School, and Judge Training School. During the period of the Manchu dynasty, he was a member of Legislative of the province of Chiang-su. In the second year of the Republic, the Parliament opened its session regularly, and he was returned a member of it, and became one of its prominent figure. After the Coup d'Etat, he resumed the profession of teacher. With the recover of the Republic, he went to Peking to take his duty of the representative of the people.

吳宗慈 字靄林 歲三十七

選舉地 江西省

籍 貫 江西省南豐縣

住 址 北京順治門外醒華報社

君天資聰慧。自幼好學。以前清優貢生。自光緒甲辰年。均從事教育。歷充廣東潮州府中學堂監督。韓山師範學堂監督。廣東兩廣隨官學堂教員。廣東學務公所會計課長。江西建昌府中學堂監督。江西學務公所視學官。實赴日本考察學務。又曾歷充上海警鐘報。名譽撰著員。廣東汕頭曉鍾報。上海民呼報撰述員。又在江西接辦自治日報。今尚開辦在京主辦醒華報館。始終皷吹革命。民國二年當選為衆議院議員。嗣被選為憲法起草委員。國會解散後。被任為四川政務廳廳長。旋代行四川巡按使職務。兼充四川全省警備隊總司令官及四川陸軍軍法處長。五年在滬發起議員通訊處。反對帝制。袁政府屢次密屯通緝。均未遭其毒。共和克復。及國會重開。遂入京應召集。復為衆議院議員。

民國之精華 （傳記） 吳宗慈先生

君天資聰慧にして強幹。前清の優貢生を以て光緒甲辰以來均しく教育に從事し、廣東潮州府中學堂監督、韓山師範學堂監督、廣東兩廣隨官學堂教師、廣東學務公所會計課長、江西建昌府中學堂監督、江西學務公所視學官、等の職に歷充し、曾て日本に赴きて學政を視察調査したる事あり。又た曾て上海警鐘報名譽主筆、廣東汕頭曉鍾報、上海民呼報等各新聞記者となり、又た江西に於て自治日報を經營し、今ま尚は北京に在りて醒華報社を經營主宰

しつゝありて、終始革命を皷吹す。民國二年衆議院議員に當選し、憲法起草委員に舉げらる。國會解散後、四川廳政務々長に任せられ、旋て四川巡按使の職務を代理し、四川全省警備隊總司令官及び四川陸軍々法處長を兼任す。五年上海に在りて議員通訊處を發起して帝制に反對す。袁政府屢々捕縛の密電を發したるも幸に免る。共和克復して國會重ねて開かるゝに及び仍て復た衆議院議員と為る。

Mr. Wu Tsung Tzu, otherwise called Ai Lin, thirty seven years old, amative of Nan Feng Hsien, the Chiang Hsi. He as a fellow engaged during the Emperial Reign for the education of young people. Later, he was appointed the superintendent of the Chao Chon Fu middle school, Kwantung, then of Han Shan normal school, professor at the Kwantung Liang Kuang private school, the head of the treasury department, the Kwantung education office, the superntntendent of the Chen Chang Fu middle school of Chiang Hsi, from which position he was transferred to the capacity of the educational imspector at the Thiang Hsi Educational office. Since he went to Japan to investigate the educational system. Sometime he was honorary chief editor of a news of Shang hai, then the editor of a news of Shan Toa of Kwantung and the other news of Shanghai, also in Chiang Hsi he edited the Self Government Daily News at present, he is the director as well as manager of a news in Peking. He was earnest revolutionist against the Empire and expounded this veiws through his papers. In the second year of Republic he was chosen as the member of the Lower House and appointed a committee man for drafting the constitution. After the dissolution of the Congress he made director of the Ssu Chuan administrative office, subsequently, he took charge of the office of governer-general of Ssu Chuan and at the same time he was commander-in-chief of the Ssu Chuan defence army and the head of the Ssu Chuan war department. In the fifth year of the Republic he made himself a leader of anti-emperial party, for while he was many times at the danger of imprisonment by order of Yan-ahi kai. On the restoration of the republican order, he returned to the Lower House.

吳日法　字審度　歲三十五

選舉地　安徽省

籍貫　安徽省歙縣

住址　北京西四南大醬坊胡同莊宅

君爲人個儻不羣。言論風采。皆超出儕輩。自幼家于黃山三十六峰之下。崇之靈秀所鍾。故其稟賦尤較一般爲深厚。少年時。頗篤志舊學。常以淵博自期。及海內維新。始改途專攻新學。清時歷任本縣水南公立兩等小學。安徽省立第四師範。安徽省立第三中學等處教員。爲本縣縣議會議員。並創設本縣南一鎭地方自治及水南公學。民國成立。當選爲衆議院議員。國會開議時。君曾主張。先定總統選舉法之一部。後定憲法之全部。提案逾二月。卒以時勢所趨得以通過。旋又組織政學社於龍泉寺。以調和黨爭。國會停止後。君歸里讀書。時復發表意見。唯多言他方面之進行。不直接干與政治。及國會重開。遂入京。仍就議員之職。

君人と爲り倜儻にして不羈、言論風采、皆な儕輩を超出す。約より黃山三十六峰の下、山水の靈秀鍾る所に家して、其の稟賦に是れ天然の感化を享くるものあるか。少年時代頗る舊學に志し、海內維新に及び改めて新學を專攻す。前淸末季に於て、本縣水南公立兩等小學、安徽省立第四師範學校、安徽省立第三中學校の各敎員に歷任し、並に本縣南一鎭地方自治及び水南公學校を創設辨理す。民國成立して後ち衆議院議員に南々議會議員となり、民國成立して後ち衆議院議員に當選す。國會開議の時、君曾て先づ大總統選舉法の一部を定め、後ち憲法の全部を定むる事を主張して提案二ケ月を與へ、卒に時勢の趨く所、通過するを得たり。旋て又た政學社を龍泉寺に組織し、以て黨爭を調和す、國會停止後君歸省して書を讀み、時に意見を發表するも、直接政治に干與せず。國會重ねて開くるに及び、遂に入京して衆議院議員と爲る。

Mr. Wujih-fa, another name Shen-to, age thirty five. Native of Hsi An-hui hsing. Though excentric, and lonely, he is a man, for whose ability of debeting and fine complexion one can rarely find the equal. He lived since the childhood in the section of the finest scenery under the beautiful mountains San shih lin, Huang-shan. At first he studied the classic, but after the Revolution, he began to study the modern sciences. In the last years of the Manchu dynasty, he became the teacher of the common school in the district Hsi, the Provincial Fourth Normal School, and Third Middle School successively, and became a member of local legislative. He established also Shui kung nan school and succeeded in the promoting of the local self government. After the formation of the Republic, he was returned a member of the Parliament, where he moved a plan which intended to regulate one part of the election of the president of the Republic, and then to go forward to discuss each articles of the new constitution. He fought for this plan for two months, and got a remarkable triumph. Nextly, he established a society for the study of the poliotical affair in Lung Chuan Ssu, and wanted to harmonize the partisan struggle. After the Coup d'Etat, he came home, and spent the hour in the reading of the book, from which he caltivated himself immensely. Sometime he made a statement of his own opinion, but refrained from the politics, and with the reopening of the Parliament, he became a member of the Parliament again.

吳 湘 字楚碧 歲三十五

選舉地　華僑
籍貫　廣東省潮州府潮安
住址　北京延壽寺街潮州七邑館

君聰慧剛直。待人以誠。於陽明先生之學。深有心得。先世經商新嘉坡。爲吾國到南洋之先導者。戊戌政變後。即信學校實勝於科舉。乃將家塾改爲尚志學堂。捐資甚鉅。前清政府嘗獎勵之。壬寅遊學日本東京同文書院。甲辰春畢業。考入千葉醫校。適丁憂回國。及服闋。而取締風潮起。因胞兄崇在度支部服務。赴京相視。並以道員歸直隸候補。丙午考入北京譯學館肄業。辛亥夏優等畢業獎舉人。仍以原官歸直隸補用。秋武昌起義。潮州官吏均逃走。匪孔多。地方大亂。公正紳士憂之。乃設立維安社。舉君正社長。君以仁慈之心。起救濟之念。排難解紛。抑強扶弱。地方大定。宗羲稱義。民國元年。潮安縣議會成立。被舉爲正議長。二年國會成立被舉爲參議院華僑議員。蓋君在新嘉坡營商。自祖若父。以至於今。已近百年。商務發達。產業亦多。以之當選代表華僑。名實相符云。

君や聰慧剛直にして人を待つに誠を以てす。陽明先生の學を以て深く造詣する所あり。君が先世新嘉坡に通商して圖南の先導者たり。戊戌政變後乃ち家藝を改めて尚志學堂とし。資を捐する甚だ鉅し。前清政府嘗して之を獎勵す。壬寅の歲日本東京同文書院に入學して甲辰の春卒業す。千葉醫學專門學校に入り、適ま喪に遇ふて歸り服終るに及び、胞兄崇が度支部に在り、京に入りて相視る、而して道員を以て直隸候補に歸す。丙午の歲譯學館に入りて學び。辛亥の夏優等等にて卒業し、舉人を授けらる。仍ほ原官を以て直隸補用に歸す。武昌義を超ゆや、潮州の官吏を以て直隸補用に歸す。武昌義を超ゆや、潮州の官吏均しく逃亡して盜匪出でゝ地方大に亂る、乃ち維安社を設立して君を正社長に舉ぐ。民國元年潮安縣議會成立し君を正議長に舉ぐ。二年選ばれて參議院華僑議員と爲る。蓋し君が家新嘉坡に在りて商を營むこと旣に百年に近し、之れ華僑を代表する所以なり。國會恢復後今ま現に參議院議員たり。

民國之精華　（傳記）　吳湘先生

Mr. Wu Hsing, otherwise called Chu-Pi, age thirty five, is a native of Chao-chuan Fu Kuang-tung hsing. In dealing with others he is sincere and true although he personally is a man of strong will. While he is deeply in love of classical teachings, he is interested in commerce as his father traded with Singapore. After the political change of 1898, he contributed his service towards the country by offering his own private school to the educational cause. In 1902 he came to Japan and entered the Dobun shoin where he was graduated in 1904. He studied medicine the Chita medical school. On account of the mourning he had to return to his country. In 1906 he studied in one of the schools in his province whence he was graduated in 1911. He was appointed again the official of the Chi-lin province. When the trouble of Wu-chuan broke out, the officials of his province took flight plunging the district in commotion. Hereupon a society was formed at once to bring about the order, of which he became the president. In the 1st year of the Republic when Chao-chun local assembly was brought into existence he was appointed the president thereof. In the 2nd year of the Republic he was a member of the Senate, representing the Chinese residence abroad. His business connection in Singapore has no doubt placed him in his position. When the Parliament was restored he resumed at once the senatorial function.

一百五

吳作棻　宇南屏　歲三十三

選舉地　貴州省
籍　貫　貴州省遵義縣
住　址　北京象來街八號

君自幼好學深思。稚年讀書。即喜推求精義。不厭數問。熟師常爲所窘。益契重之。弱冠即有文名。詩文策論。皆有名家風味。及長。尤廣覽羣書。並喜涉獵周秦諸子。以前清文生本省師範畢業生。法官養成所畢業員。歷充遵義勸學員。兩等小學校長。暨貴陽商業養成所。時敏樂羣廣益各學校教員。貴州公報鐸報總編輯。省議會議員。洪江軍事會議代表。關嶺縣知事。滇黔首義。任貴州護國軍。東路司令部秘書長。兼諮議官。民國再復活。召集議會。仍充參議院議員。

君幼より學を好みて深く思索す。少年書を讀むや義理を推求し、精を究めて問ひ、藝師常に窘む所と爲る。弱冠にして文名あり、詩文策論皆な名家の風味あり。長ずるに及び、尤も群書を閲し、喜んで周秦諸子を渉獵す。前清の文生、本省師範學校卒業生、法官養成所卒業員を以て、遵義勸學員、兩等小學校長及び貴陽商業養成所、時敏樂群廣益の各學校教員、貴州公報鐸報等の新聞編輯、省議會議員、洪江軍事會議代表、關嶺縣知事等に歷充したり。帝制問題の風潮發生して雲南貴州天下に先ちて義を唱ふるや、君出で、貴州護國軍東路司令部秘書長に任じ、諮議官を兼ねたり。天下響應して民國再び復活し、國會重ねて召集せらる、や、君乃ち北上して院に到り、仍ほ參議院議員と爲る。

Mr. Wu Tse-fun, otherwise called Nan Ping, age thirty three, is a native of Tsu hsien, Kuei-chuan hsing. While young he was a lover of learning himself being a deep thinker. His study went so deep that his questions were great puzzles to his instructors. When he was still young he won a literary fame. His poetry and writing show marks of great scholarship. As he grew older he became throughly conversant with classical writings. Under the previous Chinese regime he was graduated from the normal school, the judge training institute and was appointed the principle of a primary school as well as an instructor of the commercial school in the province. After successfully occupying various posts of importance he was finally appointed the governor of one of the provinces. When the Imperial movement of Yuanshi-Kai was started, his province became the leader of opposition; he at once was appointed the chief secretary of the military headquarter of the province, at the same time acting as an adviser to the government. The Republic was again restored and the Parliament was opened when he went up to Peking and was appointed a member of the Senate.

吳 淵　字仲遙　歲三十

選擧地　蒙古伊克昭盟
籍貫　四川省達縣
住址　北京前門外延壽寺街羊肉胡同華賓旅館

君少慧能文。於經史學皆已窺堂奧。並喜研究新學。年十六。赴日本留學。初入弘文學院。繼入早稻田大學。與同志等組織政文社。嗣以患腦病歸國。歷任吉林巡撫公署秘書。吉林都督府秘書。綏遠將軍府總務廳廳長。及吉林巡按使公署外交顧問。吉林伊通稅捐總局局長等職。旋交政事堂以簡任職存記任用。又歷任各新聞雜誌記者。並創辦共和建設討論會。及民主黨。君爲領袖。旋被選爲衆議院議員。國會解散。君專心從事著述。所著有擺倫傳。湘夢痕館韻文集、湘夢痕館筆記。社會主義論。湘夢痕館公牘存草。陰山歸客談。德皇威廉二世傳等書 及小說數種 國會復活。遂來京復爲議員。

吳少にして慧、文を能くし、經史の學に於て皆な既に堂奥を窺ひ、並に喜んで新學を研究す。年十六、南京高等學校に入り、十九日本に留學して、初め宏文學院に入り、繼で早稻田大學に入り、同志等と政文社と組織す、嗣で腦病を以て歸國す。吉林巡撫公署秘書、吉林都督府秘書、綏遠將軍府總務廳々長、吉林巡按使公署外交顧問、吉林伊通稅捐總局々長等の職に歷任し、旋て政事堂に交して簡任を以て存記任用す。又た各新聞雜誌記者となり、並に共和建設討論會及び民主黨を創立經營して君其の領袖と爲る。旋て衆議院議員に選ばる。國會解散後、專心著述に從事し、擺倫傳、湘夢痕館韻文集、湘夢痕館公牘存草、陰山歸客談、德皇威廉二世傳等の書及び小說數種等の著作あり。國會復活するや、遂に北京に抵り、復た衆議院議員と爲る。

民國之精華　（傳記）　吳 淵 先生

一百七

Mr. Wu Yu-an, otherwise called Chung Yao, age thirty, is a native of Ta hsien, Hsi-chun hsing. He was a precocious child and when quite young he was already a master of the classics and historical works. He took delight in the study of new learning. At the age of sixteen he entered the Nanking high school while at the age of nineteen he came to Japan and entered the Waseda University where he organized a party with his fellow thinkers. On account of the brain trouble he returned to his home, when he was appointed the secretary of the Chi-lin governor general, the Chi-lin foreign adviser and several other important positions were offered to him. He also used to write for journals and magazines and became the leader of various societies established for the purpose of discussing preparations for the Republic. When the Parliament was opened he was elected a member of the House of Commons. On the dissolution of the Parliament he devoted himself to the literary work. Among his writings there are quite a number of new books worthy of our special attention. He was indeed a prolific writer. When the Parliament was restored he was elected a member of the House of Commons.

余紹琴　字朋期　歲三十

選舉地　四川省
籍　貫　四川省平武縣
住　址　北京前青廠大院四號

君少好義。喜爲人鳴不平。里人有以因
于貧者。輒解囊助之。不復望報。遠近
爭稱其名。然居心仁厚。雖仇敵亦不虐
待之。與人交。喜相責以善。人告以過。
輒大喜。自幼好讀。喜博覽羣籍。純以
主觀判斷是非。而不同于習俗之成見。
故其文采風貌。亦超出儕輩。弱冠時。
即以名儒自期。旋復立志棄舊從新徧
購譯本讀之。尤注意於政法之學。曾肄
業于四川法政學校法律專科。畢業後
曾充北京法院律師。旋又留學日本畢
業于中央大學高等研究科。得法學士
學位。旋充中華民國駐日四川留學生
經理員。歸國時。適正式國會成立。被
選爲衆議院議員。國會解散後。歸里閉
戶讀書。不談時事。及國會重開。始入
京。仍充議員。

を畢ゆるや、北京法院辯護師となれり。旋て又た日本に
留學して中央大學高等研究科に入りて卒業す。嗣で日本
駐在の四川留學生經理員に任ず。後ち歸國するや、時適
ま正式國會議員選舉に會す、君選ばれて衆議院議員とな
る。國會解散するや、田園に歸臥し書齋に蟄居して、亦
た時事を問はず。國會電ねて開かるに及び、君また召集
に應じて入京し、仍は衆議院議員と爲る。

君少より義を好み、喜んで人の爲に不平を鳴らす。里人
貧に困する者あれば、喜んで囊を解きて之を助け、復た報を
望まず、遠近其の名を稱す。然かも居心仁厚にして仇敵
と雖ぬ之を虐待せず、人と交るに相責むるに善を以て
することを喜ぶ。幼より書を讀み博く羣籍に親みて文采
風流儕業に傑出す。弱冠の時即ち名儒を以て自ら期し、旋
て復た志を立て舊を棄て新に從ひ尤も意を法政の學に注
ぐ。曾て四川法政學校法律專門科に入りて學び、其の業

Mr. Yu Shao-chin, otherwise known as Min Chi, age thirty, is a native of Ping-wan hsien,
Hsi-chuan province. While young he was noted for his gallant and heroic conduct. He was ready to
help his country men in need without any idea of compensation. In dealing with others, even with his
enemy he was guided by the principle of love. He was an ardent reader of books which made him a
gentleman of culture and refinement. Leaving aside the old he took up the new learning especially the
study of law. He was graduated from the law college of Hsi-chuan and became a lawyer in the
Peking court. He came to Japan and was graduated from the Chuo university and was appointed an
inspector of the Chinese students in Japan from his province. On his return home he was elected a
member of the House of Commons. However with the dissolution of that assembly he returned to his
home and kept aloof from politics. When the Parliament was reopened he entered Peking to resume
his former function as the member of the House of Commons.

呂復　字健秋　歲三十八

選舉地　直隸省
籍貫　直隸省涿鹿縣
住址　北京半壁街

君爲人慷慨好義，富於感情，然居恒以謹約自持，絕少囂張氣習，且秉性篤實，不事浮華，生平極尚信義，重然諾，雖好義舉，而人有所託，不輕于承諾，聰慧善讀，弱冠即有文名，曾肄業于直隸高等學校，光緒甲辰，遊學日本，先入經緯學校，改入明治大學預科，畢業，升入本大學法科，並爲民報記者，歸國後，曾於某鐵路局辦理華洋文牘事宜，民國元年被選爲順直省議會議員，二年，被選爲衆議院議員，國會解散復遊學日本，五年三月，返國，在滬上，充新中華雜誌及新中國報記者，及國會重開，始入京，仍爲議員。

君人と爲り慷慨義を好みて所謂感情家なるも、秉性篤實にして浮華を事とせず。生平極めて信義を尙び然諾を重んず。曾つて直隸高等學校に入りて學び、光緒甲辰の歲、海外に出でゝ新學を求め、初め日本經緯學校に入り、後ち改めて明治大學預科に入り、卒業して本科生となる。學業の餘暇艇を操つて民報記者となる。歸國の後も曾て某鐵道局に於て華洋文牘事宜を處理したり。民國元年選ばれて順直省議會議員となる。二年正式國會議員選舉に際して衆議院議員に當選したり。國會解散さるゝや、再び東渡して日本に游學し、五年三月歸國し、上海に在りて新中華雜誌及び新中國報の記者として樣大の筆を振ひ、約法恢復して國會重ねて召集さるゝに及び、君復た北上し、仍は衆議院議員となる。

民國之精華　（傳記）　呂復先生

Mr. Lu Fu, age thirty eight, is a native of Chi lin province. He is what may be called is a man of sensitive temperament. Therefore he always is faithful to his promise. He studied in the high school of his province. In 1904 he came to Japan where he entered the Meiji university. While he was in school he spent his leisure in writing for the paper. On returning to his home he was connected with a certain railway bureau as a secretary. In the 2nd year of the Republic he was elected a member of the Parliament. However when the assembly was broken up he went to Japan to continue his study. On returning to China he was in Shanghai as a journalist when he used to write a great deal for periodicals. When the parliament was reopened he came up to Peking and was returned for the House of Commons.

呂志伊 字天民 歲三十六

選舉地 雲南省
籍貫 雲南省思茅縣
住址 北京西單牌樓橫二條十二號

君性慧。弱冠即舉孝廉。旋留學日本。入速成師範。復入早稻田大學政治經濟科。中國同盟會成立。任雲南支部長。戊申夏。雲南河口事起。君與同志等倡設雲南獨立會。爲義軍後援。冬十一月。赴南洋謀起義。未成。辛亥春。與趙聲黃興等舉義於廣州。事敗。赴滬。任民立報記者。旋赴香港。復入滇謀響應。雲南光復。任都督府秘書。兼參議院參議。後充赴寧會議全權代表。被任爲司法部次長。壬子夏。政府北移。辭職。任上海同盟會機關部副部長。民國新聞總編輯。秋赴南洋。設立國民黨支部。癸丑春。被選爲參議院議員。並充憲法起草委員。國會解散後。寄迹上海。乙卯春。回滇。及帝制議起。遂與滇軍同志。共定大計。任護國第一軍參議。充南洋籌餉代表。事竣回至肇慶。任軍務院法制顧問。及國會重開。遂來京。仍爲參議院議員。

君や、性慧敏にして弱冠即ち孝廉に舉げらる。旋て日本に留學して速成師範學校に入り、復た早稻田大學政治經濟科に學ぶ。中國同盟會成立して雲南支部長に任す。戊申の夏雲南河口の事起るや、君は同志と偕に雲南獨立會を創立す。後ち、南洋に赴き起義を謀りて成らず。辛亥の春黃興と趙聲等と義を廣州に舉げ、事敗れて上海に赴き民立報記者となる。旋て香港に赴き復た雲南に入りて響應を謀る。雲南獨立して都督府秘書兼參議院參議に任じ、後ち雲南代表として南京に赴き、南京臨時政府司法部次長となる。南北統一後辭職して上海同盟會機關部副部長となり、民國新聞總編輯を兼ぬ。また南洋に赴きて國民黨支部を設立す。民國二年參議院議員となり、憲法起草委員たり。國會解散後上海に寄居し、五年春雲南に歸る。第三革命に際し護國第一軍參議に任じ南洋籌餉代表となる。後ち肇慶に抵り、軍務院法制顧問に任す。國會恢復後、北上して仍ほ參議院議員と爲る。

Mr. Lu Shih-i otherwise called Tien Min, age thirty six, is a native of Ssu-mao-hsien, Yun-nan province. While quite young he was chosen as the candidate among young men to be educated in Japan. He entered the University of Waseda. When the Chinese alliance society was formed he was appointed the chief of the Yun-nan section of the society. When the trouble arose in Yun-nan he advocated with his fellow thinkers the necessity of declaring independence. In 1911 when his movement was defeated he went to Shanghai and remained there as the journalist. However when Yun-nan finally became independent he was appointed a private secretary to the governor general and a member of the Senate. Later he went to the south sea islands and established the branch of the national party. In the 2nd year of the Republic, he became a member of the Senate and was appointed a committee for drafting the constitution. When the Parliament was broken up, he went to Shanghai and was waiting for another chance in the Republican movement. As soon as his cause was won and the Parliament was reopened he went to Peking and was elected a member of the Senate.

選舉地　湖北省
籍　貫　湖北省竹山縣
住　址　北京永光寺西街

君賦性仁厚。喜周濟貧困。常傾囊無各
色。然平時自奉甚薄。不知者見其計及
錙銖。莫能辦其為慷慨好義之人也。以
前清光緒乙酉科拔貢。大考得知縣。旋
入京師法律大學堂畢業後。復研究醫
算學。皆能力求精微。各有心得。猶復
以餘力研究政治。著有醫義又醇。算數
簡括。政治新編等書。歷任豫陝蜀等省
知縣。光復後。回籍。民國二年。國會肇
開。被選為衆議院議員。國會解散。仍
從事學問。不以政治介懷。及國會復
活。遂應召入都。仍供舊職。

民國之精華　（傳記）　杜樹勳先生

君賦性仁厚。貧困を周濟するを喜び。常に囊を傾けて客
色無し。然れども平時自ら奉ずるこを甚だ薄し。知らざ
る者、其の計錙銖に及ぶを見て、能く其の慷慨義を好むの人
たるを辨ずる莫し。前清光緒乙酉科拔貢を以て、考せら
れて知縣を得たり。旋た京師法律大學堂に入る。業を畢
ふるの後、復た醫學算學を研究す。皆力を極めて精微を
求む、各々心得あり。猶ほ復た餘力を以て政治を研究し。

「醫義又醇」「算數簡括」「政治新編」等の書を著す。河南
陝西四川各省の知縣を歷任す。光復の後籍に回り。民國
二年國會肇せらるゝや、選ばれて衆議員と為る。國會解
散の後、仍ほ學問に從事し、政治を以て懷に介せず。國
會復活するに及び、遂に召集に應じて都に入り、仍ほ舊
職に供す。

Mr. Tu Shu-tung, age sixty, is a native of Chu-shan hsien, Ho-pe province. He is a gentle-man of charitable turn of mind and finds pleasure in helping the poor. Those who are not acquainted with this part of his life are liable to misjudge him, because he is frugal in the mode of living. In the previous Chinese régime, he passed the civil examination and was appointed the governor. He studied law in the Peking law college. He was also interested in medicine and mathematics. Any time left at his disposal he employed for the study of politics. He wrote books on medicine, mathematics as well as on politics. In the 2nd year of the Republic he was returned for the House of Commons. However when the Parliament was dissolved he became an ardent scholar of books and no more troubled himself about politics. He went up to Peking and resumed his function as the member of the Parliament as soon as it was reopened.

辛際唐　字逑祖　歲

選舉地　江西省

籍　貫　江西省萬載縣

住　址　北京板章胡同宜分萬館

君秉性剛直。重廉恥。尚信義。勇於任
事。自幼聰頴好讀。頗有文名。以舉人
授內閣中書。轉授郵傳部主事。民國紀
元。回籍辦地方自治事宜。維持桑梓。
不避勞怨。二年。當選爲衆議院議員。
主張正大。不受誘脅。袁氏當國。久蓄
異謀。因贛寧事起。欲藉以解散國會。
先除國民黨員。既被羅織罪狀。布告
全國。旋復被勒繳證書徽章。放歸田
里。偵探布密。絕少自由。幸託跡商界。
謝絕交游。得免于禍。及帝政發生。雲
貴起義。天相中國。國會重開。鄉人父
老。敦促就道。遂欣然整裝北上。應召
爲衆議院議員。

君秉性剛直にして廉恥を重んじ信義を尙び事に任する勇
あり。幼より聰頴にして讀書を好み顏る文名あり。舉人
を以て內閣中書を授けらる。轉じて郵傳部主事を授けら
る。民國元年鄕里に歸りて地方自治事宜を處理し勞怨を
避けず斡旋盡力す。二年正式國會衆議院議員に當選し、
正論を主張して壓迫又は誘惑に動かされず。袁氏政柄を
執つて久しく異謀を蓄へ、江西南京等所謂第二革命の事
起るや、之に藉りて國會を解散すべく、先づ國民黨議員
を除かんとし、罪狀を羅織して全國に布告し、旋て議員
證書並に徽章を脅迫して剝奪したり。君亦國民黨員と
して此非法に遭ひ慨然として田園に歸臥す、探偵嚴重に
して自由を拘束さる。君幸に跡を商業に託して交涉を絕
ち漸く禍を免かるを得たり。帝政問題發生して雲貴義
を起し、國會重ねて開かるゝに及び、鄕人に促されて立
ち、欣然北上して仍ほ衆議院議員の職に就きたり。

Mr. Hsin Chi-tang, otherwise called Shu-tsu is a native of Wan-tsai, Chiang-hsi. He is a gentleman of strong mind and faithful to his cause while he has courage to take upon himself a heavy responsibility. While young he attained literary fame and was appointed the secretary of the Cabinet and also a secretary of the Communication Bureau. In the 1st year of the Republic he returned to his home and worked for the development of local interests. In the 2nd year of the Republic he was elected a member of the House of Commons. Neither threats nor temptation could disturb his strong determination. He strongly opposed Yuanshi-Kai for his audacious conduct of depriving the members of the national party the certificate and the badge of the parliamentary membership. Being a member of the national party he was subjected to this unlawful treatment. Although he went back to his home he was subject to strict espionage. He only escaped the fatal doom by engaging in business. When the Imperial movement of Yuanshi-Kai took place, he came to the front and fought his way. As soon as the Parliament was reopened, he was returned for the House of Commons, which post he gladly accepted.

辛漢　字濯之　之歲三十九

選舉地　江蘇省

籍貫　江蘇省江寧縣

住址　北京變輿衛夾道

君為日本東京帝國大學畢業之秀才也。恆曰新進之士。不患無學識。患無品行。君天資總穎敏捷。學識優良。為人誠實悼篤。品行端正。其卒業歸國後。凡所行事。莫不持重出之誠。非輕躁浮薄之士所能望其項背。氣度雍容。性清和美。文采風品。可掬可敬。前清以法科舉人。任民政部主事。充浙江高等撿察長。漢土光復。民國樹立。共和肇造。君任南京府知事。愛民慰撫。治政大舉。百性感激。推稱良二千石。民國二年正式國會成立。被選為參議院議員。把持正論。主張公議。翼贊建設之大業。未幾。國會停止。帝制發生。君快快不娛。共和恢復。及國會重開。欣然應召集。遂又北上入京。仍為參議院議員。

民國之精華　（傳記）辛漢先生

君は日本東京帝國大學卒業の一秀才なり。然かも常に曰く新進の士學識なきを患へず、品行無きを患ふと。君天資聰穎にして學識優良、人と為り誠實にして品行端正、蓋し品學兼資の士なり。氣度また雍容にして性情和美、文采風品共に掬すべく敬すべし。前清法科舉人を以て民政部主事に任ひ、浙江高等撿察長に任ず。漢土光復して民國樹立するや、南京府知事に任ひ、民の父母として治蹟大に舉り百性感戴す、眞に良二千石の名に愧ぢず。民國二年正式國會成立するや、選ばれて參議院議員と為り、正論を把持して公議を主張し、建設の大業を翼贊する所あり。未だ幾くならずして國會停止し、次で帝制問題發生す、君快々として娛まず。共和克復して國會重ねて開かるゝに及び、君復た欣然眉を開きて召集に應じ、仍は參議院議員の職に就く。

Mr. Hsin-han, otherwise called Cho-chih, is a native of Chiang-ning prefecture, Chiang-su district. He was bont thirty nine years old. He is a graduate of the Tokyo Emperial University, Japan and is always reluctant of the bad morals of scholars, but not of the poor knowledge of them. He is the most bright man and the man of profound knowledge. His up-right conduct and honesty are combined with the deep learning, which is rarely found among scholars now-a-days. His mild appearance, noble look and loving nature demand the respect of all who meet him. During the late Emperial Regime he was once chief of the administrative bureau, then he was appointed to the chief of the Cho-chiang higher police court. At the time of establishment of the Republic he was appointed to the governor of the city of Nankin; he was estimated by the people as their father, which tells us how good administrator he was. He is really a model of good governor. In the second year of Republic the National Parliament was formally constituted and he was elected as the Upper House member. In solidifying the new state he can be estimated as one of the most prominent figures. The Enapenton of Parliment and progress of the Emperial design gave him such a disgust as he determinded that he would not talk politics ever in his life. Fortunately the Republic was restored and so the Parliament. He went gladly to Pekin to resume his old seat in the Upper House.

何士果　歲五十

選舉地　廣東省

貫籍　廣東省大埔縣

住址　北京丞相胡同潮州館

君賦性誠篤。尚質惡華。然天資聰頴。思想活潑。與人交。常喜爲規勸。辭直而婉。懇切而不數。以故人多爲所感動。爲人精明幹練。明察事理。言動舉止。皆有定則。自幼好讀書不事嬉戲。能深思精進。弱冠卽能悟古人精義及長。尤肆力求博。謙虛好問。不以小成自肅。以前清戊戌進士歷任吉林提學司僉事。吉林府知府。吉林調查局總辦清理財政局駐局會辦。吉林法政學堂總理並曾充日本公使署商務委員。北京憲政編查館諮議員。著有日本國民敎育二十八卷。吉林調查局文牘初二編。吉林調查報告。日本市町村制理由書。日俄戰時紀要。支那法制史等書。民國二年。正式國會成立。被選爲參議院議員。國會解散。歸里從事學問著述。及國會重開。始來京。仍爲議員。

君賦性誠實篤厚にして質を尙び華を卑む。人と交る常に規勤を喜び、辭直にして婉、人多く感動す。人と爲り精明幹練にして事理を明察し、言動舉止井然として紊れず。幼より讀書を好みて嬉戲を事とせず、力を盡くして博を求め、巳に虛ふして問を好む。前清戊戌の進士を以て、吉林提學司僉事、吉林府知府、吉林調查局總辦、財政整理局駐局會辦、吉林法政學堂經理等の重職に歷任し、並に曾て日本公使署商務委員、北京憲政編查館諮議員たりしことあり。公務の餘暇筆硯に親みて、日本國民敎育二十八卷、吉林調查局文牘初二編、吉林調查報告、日本市町村制理由書、日露戰時紀要、支那法制史等の著作あり。民國二年正式國會參議院議員に常選す。國會解散して鄕里に歸り學事に親み著作を試む。國會復活するや復た召集されて仍ほは參議院議員たり。

Mr. Ho Shih-kuo, age fifty, is a native of Tai-po, Kuang-tung province. He is a gentleman of solid virtue despising pomp and vanity. In talking to others his language is always inspiring. He is logical to the extreme and all his conduct is regulated thereby. He was a great lover of books which afforded him a very wide scope of information. In the previous Chinese regime, he successively filled many important government posts. At one time he was an commercial attache to the Chinese legation in Shanghai and a committee on drafting the history of the constitutional government in China. He wrote several books of which the "Japanese national education" consists of twenty eight volumes. Besides, he wrote the history of the Chinese law, the outlines of the Japan Russian war and the account of the municipal organization of Japan. In the 2nd year of the Republic, he was elected a member of the Senate. When the Parliament was closed he went to his native province where he devoted himself to book writing. With the restoration of the Parliament, however, he was reinstated to the former senatorial position.

何海濤 字伯龍 歳四十四

選舉地　新疆省

籍　貫　甘肅省皋蘭縣

住　址　北京太僕寺街三府胡同

君秉性聰穎。爲人恪謹耐勞。然富於學識。新舊皆有素養。故其見解氣慨。迥異凡流。壯歲幀遊天山南北。歷辦教育事宜。以勞績補庫車。直隸知州。辛亥起義。在廸苦心擘畫。遙爲武昌聲援。事洩。卒爲袁撫破壞。莫能成功。民國成立時。新撫袁大化唆使旅新甘人滋擾。藉圖不軌。君責以正義。袁撫愧恼。乘夜遯去。彼黨以所謀不成。賄買土匪暗殺。身受重創。積欠乃瘥。民國二年被選爲參議院議員。國會中挫後。遯身待時。民國五年及約法恢復。國會重開。仍爲參議院議員。

君秉性聰慧にして人と爲り恪謹勤勞に耐ゆ、然かも學識に富み、新舊皆な素養ありて其の見解氣慨な迥に凡流に異る。壯年にじて天山南北を跋渉して敎育に從事し。勞績を以て庫車に補し直隸知州に分たる。辛亥義を起すや事洩れて袁巡撫の爲めに破壞さる。民國成立の時、巡撫袁大化新疆に在る甘肅人を使嗾して反對せんとするや、君責ひるに正義を以てす。袁乃ち夜に乘じて遁れ去る。袁大化の黨與は爲に君を恨み、土匪を買收して暗殺を試み、君重傷を受け、久ふして漸く愈ゆるを得たり。民國二年正式國會の成立に際し選ばれて參議院議員と爲る。國會中止後、身を逃れて時運の再變を待ち、五年約法恢復して國會重ねて開かる〻や、其の召集に應じて仍ほ參議院議員たり。

民國之精華　（傳記）　何海濤先生

一百十五

Mr. Ho Hai-tao, otherwise named Pai Lung, age forty four, a native of Kao-lan hsien, the Kan-su hsing is a shrewd strong-minded and well informed gentleman whose opinion differs from that of the common people: He was deeply interested in education, and after passing through various government post he was appointed to the governor of a province. When the Revolution took place, he rendered some help to Wu chang which plan was destroyed by Yuanshi-kai. Once he most vehemently opposed to the instigatory act of Yuanshi-kai which caused the latter to fly from the district under the cover of night. The Yuan party held grudge against him, and bribing the bondits, tried to assasinate him. He was seriously minded from which he recovered but slowly. In 1917, he was appointed to a member of the Senate. After the suppression of the Parliament, he fled from Peking bidding a fair opportunity for the future activity. When the Parliament was opened, he was elected to a member of the Senate.

何雯　字宇塵　歲三十三

選舉地　安徽省

籍貫　安徽省懷寧縣

住址　北京南柳巷

君資質聰穎。總角時。即以文學有名。雖耆宿不能難也。東渡後。留學日本法政大學。畢業。前清舉人。歷充湖南岑撫院。揚撫院。余撫院。憲政文案會議廳參事。湖南調查局。法制科長。元年被選爲衆議院議員。憲法起草委員會委員。清末。在上海。曾任神州日報總編輯。民國元年。任民聲日報總理。繼在京。與王君揖唐。創立中華大學。又曾主任醒華報。新中國報。因反對帝制。與宋遯鵠。同被繫於軍政執法處。新中國報。亦被封閉。國會復活。仍復衆議院議員兼充新中國報主任。著有湖南風土記十二卷。論符二卷。澄園文稿四卷。龍潭室詩鈔二卷。累辭二卷。（獄中作）居易錄一卷。（獄中作）

君資質聰穎にして少年の時即ち文字を以て名あり。長ずる及び笈を負ふて東海を渡り、日本に留學して法政大學を卒業す。歸國後、即ち前清の舉人を以て湖南岑巡撫、相介巡撫、余巡撫等の文案並に憲政文案會議廳參事、湖南調査局法制科長に歷任したり。民國二年憲法起草委員に舉げらる。之より先、前清末、上海に於て神州日報の編輯に任じ、民國成立後は民聲日報社總理に任じ、旋て北京に抵りて王楫唐と共に中華大學を創立經營す。曾て醒華報、新中國報の主筆として帝制に反對し、遂に筆禍を買ふて軍政執法處の獄に繫がれ。斯くて共和克復する及び、仍は衆議院議員の職に復し、新中國報社主任を兼ぬ。其の著湖南風土記十二卷、論符二卷、澄園文稿四卷、龍潭室詩鈔二卷、及び獄中の著作として、累辭二卷、居易錄一卷あり。

Mr. Ho-wen, otherwise named Yu-chen, age thirty three, is a native of Huai-ning An-hui. He is one of the most sagacious men ever gathered in Peking; as a youth he was known as a writer. Growing older he went to the new progressive country an East and entered in the Hosei University and graduated there in due time. Since returned home he held offices of counsellorship to the constitution drafting committees anthorized by the governor-generals, of Tsen-yany-yu of Hu-nan and made the chief of the legal department of the Hu-nan Inquiry Board. He was chosen by the people of his district as the member of the Lower House, later, he was appointed to the member of the Constitution drafting committee. Prior to this time toward the end of the Empire, he published a daily paper, the Shen-chuan Daily news at Shanghai. After the establishment of the Republic he organized a news, of which he was president. Then he founded in Peking, the Chun-hua University with Mr. Wang-i-tang. At times, he expounded anti-Emperial doctrine as the Chief-editor of the Hsing-hua news, and also the new centre-nation. Almost every time he demanded the Emperial Government, he was sent to the military prison by the government of that time. On the restoration of the Republic Regime he was released from the Prison and returned to the Lower House to resume his old seat. He is still the Head of new Centre-nation, Hsin-chun-kuo-pao she among the various publications of himself the Hu-nan geography, 12 volumes, essays, 2 volumes, the Cheng-yuan-wan-kao 4 volumes, the Lung-tan-shih-chao 2 volumes, and the Lei-tzu 2 volumes and Chu-i-lu are value as written during he was in prison.

宋 揙 字維周 歲四十五

選舉地　直隷省
籍　貫　直隷省永平縣
住　址　北京西城二龍坑北貴人關路南十五號

君爲人誠厚篤實。不喜浮華。生平以險約自持。痛惡奢侈。然唯自待歉薄。而厚於待人。且喜爲善舉。鄉里之困於貧者。無不曾受君惠。少年時。好爲詩詞。而不汲汲於科第。及長。遂改志求有用之學。嘗謂。章誤人之事功。而舉業。則錮人之情性。清時。以優廩生。爲江蘇試用典史。旋辭職歸里。入天津自治研究所肄業。畢業後。又入天津法政講習所。亦畢業。歷充本縣自治研究所所長。本縣自治預備會會長。順直諮議局議員。天津廣仁堂董事。民國第一次國會成立。被選爲參議院議員。國會解散。君萬事取消極主義。於時事無所可否。日惟以研究學問自娛。絕口不言政治。及共和復活。國會重開。始應召復爲議員。

君人と爲り誠厚篤實にして浮華を喜ばず、勤儉自ら持して痛く奢侈を惡む。然り自ら待つこと甚だ薄く、人を待つに頗る厚し。年少の時、好んで詩詞を作り、長じて志を改めて有用の學を求め、曾て詞章の人が事功を誤るを論じたる事あり。前清時代優廩生を以て江蘇典史試用となり、旋りて職を辭して歸鄉し、天津自治研究所に入りて學び、卒業後又た天津法政講習所に入りて卒業したり。夫れより鄉里に歸りて本縣自治研究所々長、本縣自治預備會々長、順直諮議局議員、天津廣仁堂董事等の公職に歷充し、地方の自治に貢獻する所あり。民國第一次國會參議院議員に當選す。國會解散するや、君暫らく消極主義を標榜して時事の可否を論ぜず、日に誰ぞ學問を研究して自ら娛みたり。共和復活して國會再び開かるゝに及び復た出でゝ召集に應じ、仍ほ參議院議員と爲る。

民國之精華　（傳記）　宋揙先生

Mr. Sung Chen, otherwise known as Wei Chou, age forty five, is a native of Chen-ping, Chi Li province. The hatred of pomp and vanity and the love of sincerity and frugal living was his motto. He was sociable in his nature which manifested itself in his dealing with others. When young he composed poems and wrote essays. As he grew older he became the seeker of new learning and attacked the old method of the civil examination in China which was the fettering of the dividualism of man. However in previous Chinese period he passed the examination with honors and had a service in the government. Later he studied in the law school of Tientsing from which he was graduated. His contribution towards the development of the civic body in China was not to be underlated. In the 1st year of the Republic he was elected a member of the Senate. However with the shutting down of the Parliament he held his peace not discussing politics any longer. He found pleasure in the perusal of books. When the Republic was restored he went up to Peking to resume his senatorial function.

宋梓　字子材　歲三十六

選舉地　甘肅省
籍貫　甘肅省伏羌縣
住址　北京棉花下六條二號

君恬慷慨性成。多材多藝。自幼讀書
潁悟殊絕。心得甚超。著書累千百萬
言。其于實業。尤多所發明。平生好讀
柳子厚梓人傳。故自名曰梓。在前清
以優廩生。肄業蘭州大學堂。宣統巳西
科考取優貢。庚戌科朝考一等。以七品
小京官用籤分郵傳部。歷委川粵漢鐵
路籌備處。編案校對路政司額外科員
等差。民國元年八月。交通部派赴甘
肅。調查電報線路。二年三月。省議會
選充第一次國會參議院議員。十一月。
前大總統命令停止職務。三年十一月。
教育部函記。在甘調查教育。五年七
月。今大總統電集。續開國會。仍充參
議院議員。論事持正。無偏無黨。每出
抗議。必占優勝。

君性懷慨にして多藝多能なり。幼より書を讀みで聰慧頴
悟、造詣飫に深くして著書千百萬言を累ぬ。其の實業に
於て尤も發明する所あり。平生好んで柳子厚梓人傳を讀
ひ、故に自ら名けて梓と云ふ。前清時代優廩生を以て蘭
州大學堂に修養し、宣統巳酉優貢生となり、庚戌の試驗
に一等を以て及第し、七品小京官を以て郵傳部に分たる。
川粵漢鐵道籌備處編案校對、路政司額外科員等の職に歷

任したり。民國元年八月交通部より甘肅に派遣され電信
線路を調査す。二年三月第一次國會參議院議員となり、
不偏不黨にして事を論ずる公正なり。十一月前大總統の
命令によりて議員の職務を停止さる。三年十一月教育部
よりの命により、甘肅に在りて。教育を調査報告す。此
次國會重ねて開くるに及び、復た其の召集に應じて北京
に抵り、仍は參議院議員の職に就く。

Mr. Sung Tzu, otherwise called Tzu-tsai, age thirty six, is a native of Fu-cha prefecture, Kan-su district. We find in him a full of patriotic spirit; he is a man of accomplishment and talents. He had a striking fondness of reading, which made him bright and wise. He wrote and published books of no less than ten million words. He discovered a great truth industriously; he read assiduously biography of Liu-tzu-hou-tzu and named himself Tzu which shows how much he took interest in the book. During the Shin Dynasty he studied at the Lan-chuan university as a scholar later a fellow and graduated there with the first honor. As an officer of seventh grade he served in the department of communication. Later he made a designer at the head office of the Chuan-Yueh-han Railway, then a member of the Rood Commission. In August of the first year of the Republic he was sent by the Communication Department to investigate telegraph in Kan-su. In March of the second year he was chosen as a member of the Upper House. As the member he spoke what he thought just and benefit for the country, which occassionary wounded the feeling of Yuanshi-kai; consequently the latter suspended the right of representative of Mr. Sung-Tsu. In November, the third year, of the Republic he investigated by the request of the Educational Department the educational condition of Kan-su. Having Parliament again convened in the fifth year, he was called to Pekin to take up the seat in the Upper House.

選舉地　福建省

籍　貫　福建省永春縣

住　址　北京西長安街東頭健廬

君天資聰慧敏捷。頗富熱烈之氣象。爲福建下江之勢力家。熱心政治。又長于言論。然秉政和易。與人交。藹然可親。自幼好學。夙抱經世之志。攻究新學。自任以天下有用之材。負笈東渡。入日本明治大學校政治科畢業。歸來歸走國事。無寧日。癸丑失敗後。曾來往海外于閩事多有所計畫。亦民黨中之一重鎭也。辛亥武昌起義。天下響應。君兼閩南安撫使。福建臨時省議會正議長。國民黨閩支部長。民國二年正式國會成立。君被選爲參議院議員。正論公議。爲政府所懼。國會非法解散後。南旋與同志密圖挽回大局。目的旣達。共和克復。及國會重開。欣然踴躍。應召北上。仍爲參議院議員。

君天資聰慧敏捷にして頗る熱烈の氣象に富み、福建下江地方の勢力家なり。政治に熱心にして又た言論に長す。然かも秉性和易にして人と交る藹然親ひべし、幼より學を好みて夙に經世の志を抱き新學を攻究して自ら天下有用の材を以て任す。笈を負ふて日本に留學し、明治大學校政治科に入りて卒業す。歸來國事に奔走して寧日無く、癸丑の事敗れて後ち海外に來往し、福建の事亦た多く計畫する所ありて、蓋し民黨中の一重鎭たるなり。辛亥武昌義を唱へて天下響應するや、君福建に在りて大計を圖り、福建都督府參事員、閩南安撫使、福建臨時省議會正議長、國民黨福建支部長等に歷充す。民國二年正式國會成立するや君選ばれて參議院議員となり、其の正論公議頗る袁政府の懼かるゝ所と爲る。國會が非法に解散さるや、南旋して同志と偕に密に大局の挽回を圖る。目的の旣に達して國會重ねて開くるに及び、欣然踴躍して召集に應じ、仍ほ參議院議員と爲る。

Mr. Sung Yuan-yuan, atherwise named Tzu-ching, is a native of Yung Chun prefecture, Fukian district. He is one of the most bright and sagacious men and is a full of spirit. He is very influencial in Hsia chiang province, Fukian, as he is an enthusiastic politician, of great eloquence, kind and considerate to all. Even he was a young man, he read widely and nurtured an ambition of serving the country with his new knowledge obtained by the study of new science. He once studied at the political science department, the Meiji University, Japan. After the graduation of the institutions returning home, he had hardly time of rest as he was fully occupied on the national politics. Failing an up-rising he fled to foreign countries. He was leader in Fukian in fact, he was one of magnate of the people's party. In 1910 Wu-chang rose against the later Emperial government, calling the whole country to fallow its example; then he was in Fukian working hard for the revolutional course. Counsellor of the Fukian government-general, governor-general of Men-nan, president, the Fukian provisional Legislature and director of the Fukian Brande of the people's party were all rewards he accepted as his disinterested activities. In the second year the national Legislature was formally organized, to which he was an elected member from his district. As the senator his views and speaches offended the Yuan government a good deal. When the Legislature was dissolved un-contitutionally he returned South to plan to set things right, which was accomplished on the recovering of the Legislative organ. He is now a member of the Upper House.

沈河清 字曙秋 歲三十

選舉地　雲南省
籍　貫　雲南省建水縣
住　址　北京西栓馬椿

君秉性溫恭謙讓。待人以誠。生平以虛己。下問自喜。人告以過。卑詞謝其忠告之厚意。然後細辦其是否合理。人言當。固不吝卽改。卽有不當。亦絕不辨釋。居常以退讓自持。人有與爭者。常以柔制勝。不逞意氣而自甘於兩敗俱傷。自幼卽知苦讀求進。及長。愈益奮勵。故天資雖非絕倫。而其所造。則甚遠大着實。前清時法政畢業生。歷充辦理地方自治學務實業。雲南光復後。充富滇銀行經理。民國二年被選爲衆議院議員。國會解散後。歸里從事實業。及至共和再造。國會重開。始應召入京。仍爲衆議院議員。

君秉性溫良恭謙、人を待つに誠を以てす。己を虛ふして人に問ふを喜び、人若し告ぐるに過を以てすれば詞を卑ふして其の忠言の厚意を謝し、然る後ち其の是非を仔細に省察して改むるに吝ならず。居常退讓を以て自ら持し、人と爭へば常に柔を以て勝を制す。幼より刻苦精勵して學を求め、長ずるに及び益々奮勵努力す。故に天資必ずしも絕倫ならざるも、其の造詣甚だ深し。　前清時代法政學校卒業生を以て地方自治の進步、學務の振興、實業の發展に盡力する所あり。第一革命當時、雲南獨立して後ち、富滇銀行經理に任じたり。民國二年選ばれて正式國會衆議院議員に當選す。國會解散後、歸鄉して再び實業に從事す。共和復活して國會重ねて開かるヽに及び、其の召集に應じて入京し、仍ほ衆議院議員と爲る。

Mr. Chen Ho ching, sometimes called Shu Chin, age thirty, is a native of Chien shui, Yunnan. He is humble in his character and open minded enough to receive any advice of others with thanks. He was ready to rectify any fault of his. In quiet and humbleness, there is strength. He was an ardent scholar in youth, which practice has been continued even when grown up. In the previous Chinese regime, he as a graduate of law college was deeply interested in the development of the civic body, the expansion of learning and the development of industry. At the time of the 1st revolution, with the independence of Yun-nan, he was interested in the management of a bank. In 1913, he was elected to a member of the Parliament, but on the disolution of the same, he became interested in business. With the reopening of the Parliament, he has resumed the function as the member of the Parliament.

谷嘉蔭 字芷航 歲五十六

選舉地 吉林省
籍貫 吉林省扶餘縣
住址 北京順治門裏中鐵匠胡同路北

君爲人精明強幹。當於忍耐。居心仁
厚。痛惡陰險。然惟喜規人過失。輒直
斥不諱。甚至聲色俱厲。人告以過。亦
直認不諱。故其於人雖有過詰之嫌。人
亦無疾恨之者。自幼聰慧好讀能文。及
長。尤活潑自喜。富于好奇之性。然其
立身行已。多厚重自持。不效時髦青年
之浮薄踐躁。蓋君之思想極放膽。而行
爲則極規則也。清時。以恩貢生得候選
通判。旋充黑龍江善後局委員。承辦呼
蘭田房稅契。兼征收稅務委員。及諮議
局議員。民國二年。被選爲參議院議
員。國會解散後。歸里隱居。不問時事。
及共和恢復。國會重開。始入京。仍爲
參議院議員。

君人と爲り精明強幹にして忍耐に富み、居心仁厚にして
陰險を憎惡す。幼にして聰慧、讀を好み文を能くす。長
じて尤も活潑自ら喜び、好奇の性に富む。然かも其の身
を立て己を行ふや、厚重自ら持して時髦青年の浮薄踐躁
なるに效はず。蓋し君の思想極めて放膽にして君の行爲
は則ち極めて規則的なり。前淸時代に於て恩貢生を以て
候選通判の官を待たり。旋て黑龍江善後局委員に任せら
れ、呼蘭の田房稅契を處理し、稅務征收委員及び黑龍江
省諮議局議員を兼たり。民國二年正式國會議員の選擧に
際して參議院議員に常選す。其の國會が解散さるゝに及
び、君乃ち田園に歸臥して韜晦自ら心を養ひ、敢て時事の
擾々を問はざる也。共和政治恢復して民國議會重ねて開
かるゝや、君復た召集に應じて晋京し、仍ほ參議院議員
の職に就きたり。

民國之精華 （傳記）
谷嘉蔭 先生

Mr. Ku Ko-in otherwise known as Jui-hang, age fifty six, is a native of Fu-yu, Chilin. He is frank and open minded and entertain dead animosity against any nafarious conduct. He was an admirer of books when young and as he grew older he was very much fond of taking active steps in anything he undertook and yet he was far from being rush and careless. He was comprehensive and bold in thought but strictly regular in his conduct. In the previous Chinese regime, he obtained government services of various kinds. He was on the committee of taxation system and also on advisory board. In the 2nd year of the Republic he was appointed a member of the Senate, when the Parliament was dissolved he went back to his home and spent his time in selfculture. With the Restoration of the Republic, the Parliament was reopened and he was once more appointed a member of the Senate.

谷思愼　字仲言　歲三十六

選舉地　山西省

籍　貫　山西省神池縣

住　址　北京西單石橋異馥館

君爲人慷慨好義。自幼即自負不凡。年方十九。值庚子拳匪變亂。在本地倡辦團練。捕首要。散脅從。地方賴以安謐。二十一歲。就學於本省大學堂。二十三歲。留學日本。與革黨首領訂交。同盟會之組織。君身與其謀。同盟會成立後。同人以北方事委君。乃定三方並進之策。遂歸國着實進行。銳意聯絡有力人物。凡秦晉魯豫志士。無不傾心結納。其最知名者。爲秦督張。晉督閻。他如井勿幕。趙戴文。丁惟汾等。咸爲君所動。以故武昌起義。秦繼之。晉又繼之。清軍攻入娘子關。君同閻督退守北方。轉戰歸綏。共和成立。君解甲赴南京。會商一切。旋歸晉襄助閻督。整理山西善後事宜。國會成立。君被選爲衆議院議員。國會解散後。君退隱鄉里。無所表見。及至國會重開。始應召入京。仍爲議員。

君人と爲り慷慨義を好み幼よりして非凡を以て自負す。年十九庚子義和團事變に際會す、君乃ち郷關に在りて團練を組織して匪首を捕へ雷同者を解散し、地方賴つて以て安謐を得たり。二十一歲本省の大學堂に入り、二十三歲日本に留學し、革命黨の首領と交を訂し、同盟會組織の議に預る、君乃ち歸國してより銳意其の實行を計り有力の人物と聯絡に努め、張陝西都督、閻山西都督君くは趙戴文、丁惟汾等の如き咸な君が爲に動かさるゝ所となりし者なり。故に武昌義を起すや、陝西之に繼ぎ、山西又之に繼ぐ、清軍攻めて娘子關に入るや、君は閻都督と退いて北方を守り歸化綏遠に轉戰す。民國成立後君乃ち甲を解き南京に赴きて一切を會商し、旋て山西に歸り閻都督を助けて山西善後事宜を整理す。國會成立の際乘議院議員に選ばれ、國會解散後田園に歸臥す。今ま國會第二次の召集に應じて入京し仍は衆議院議員たり。

Mr. Ku Ssu-chen otherwise called Ching-yen, age thirty six is a native of Shen-chih, Shanhsi province. Naturally being a man of heroic temperament he associated himself with something beyond a ordinary level. At the age of nineteen he encountered the Boxer trouble when he arrested the leader and brought back order in his province. At the age of twenty three he went to Japan where he came into contact with leaders of revolution in forming the society for the accomplishment of their object. When the revolution was started in Wu-chung which was rapidly followed by other promises he was a leader of a section defending the cause of the revolutionists. When the Republic was established he went to Nanking and arranged everything. As soon as the Parliament was brought into existence he was elected a member of the House of Commons. As soon as the legislative assembly was suppressed he returned to his native province. He once more took up the legislative function when the Parliament was reopened.

岳秀夫 字宋生 歳三十五

選舉地 河南省

籍貫 河南省蘭封縣

住址 北京達智橋嵩雲草堂

君秉性聰慧。而沈默寡言。喜讀書兼善拳術。年十五。應府縣院童試。三冠全軍。遂入庠。次考補廩膳生。旋考入本省高等學校預科卒業。又考入優級師範學校理化專科。以最優等卒業。得獎理科舉人。簽分學部爲小京官。以不甘小就。遂不到部。仍在本省任高等學校教員。並歷任開封工業中學校。許州陝州各中學校理科教員。共和告成。開封鄭州十八屬。舉爲同鄉聯合會會長。又舉爲臨時省議會議員。閉會後。任實業司工科長。國會選舉。當選爲衆議院議員。學會解散後。蟄伏里門。不求榮達。民國五年春。應滬上同志約。赴滬電請政府恢復舊約法。及國會續開。遂入京。就議員之職。

民國之精華 (傳記) 岳秀夫先生

君秉性聰慧にして沈默寡言、讀書を喜び學術を喜ぶ。歳十五重試に應じ三たびとも首席を占む、遂に庠に入りて學び廩膳生に補す、旋りて本省高等學校預科に入りて卒業し、優級師範學校理化專門に入り最優等を以て卒業す。理科舉人として學部小京官となりしも就かす。仍ほ本省に在りて敎育事業に從事し、高等學校敎員、開封工業中學校及び許州陝州各中學校理科敎員に歷任したり。民國成立するや開封鄭州等十八管區より舉げられて同鄉聯合會々長となる。又た選ばれて臨時省議會議員となる。閉會後同省實業司工科長に任す。正式國會議員選舉に際し衆議院議員に當選す。國會解散後は里門に蟄伏して榮達を求めす、悠々自適す。民國五年の春上海の同志と約して同地に赴き、政府に電致して舊約法の恢復を請ふ。國會再び召集さるべきに及び、北上して衆議院議員の職に復したり。

Mr. Chin Hsin-fu otherwise called Sung Sheng, age thirty five, is a native of Lan-fing, Honan hsing. He is a gentleman of taciturn temperament but well read and fond of boxing. He entered the high school of the province and the higher normal school from which he was graduated with honors. He was engaged in educational works being an instructor of various middle schools. With the establishment of the Republic he was appointed a member of the special local assembly. When the Parliament was opened he was returned for the House of Commons. With the suppression of the Parliament by Yuanshi-Kai he went back to his home where he was quietly devoting himself to study. With the death of Yuanshi-Kai, order was established in China and he was elected a member of the House of Commons.

尚鎮圭 字連池 歲四十二

選舉地　陝西省
籍　貫　陝西省大荔縣
住　址　北京爛熳胡同漢中館

君為人慷慨好義。喜為不平之鳴。前清時。曾肄業陝西宏道高等學校。嗣充渭南高等小學校教習。旋辭職東渡留學。先入早稻田大學預科。復轉學于東京實科學校理化專修科。並與同志等組織同盟會陝西分會。被選為分會書記兼會計。兼總會評議員。畢業後。回國充陝西同州府中學校監督。所聘教習管理等均係革命鉅子。專以鼓吹改革輸播新知織為宗旨。辛亥陝西獨立後。君赴省視軍械乏情形。遂隻身赴滬。聯合旅滬同鄉于君右任等。籌辦大宗軍械運陝。以濟陝危。適戰事初息。方組織臨時省議會。遂被選為陝西臨時省議會議員。旋復被選為眾議院議員。國會解散後。君歸里。無所表見。直至共和再造。始入京應召。仍為議員。

君人と為り慷慨義を好み喜んで不平の鳴を為す。前清時代曾て陝西宏道高等學校を修業し、嗣で渭南高等小學校教習に任じ、旋て辭職して東渡留學す。先づ早稻田大學預科に入り、復た東京實科學校理化專修科に轉ず。並に同志等と同盟會陝西分會を組織し、分會書記兼會計及び總會評議員に選ばる。卒業後歸國して、陝西同州府中學校監督となり、聘用せる敎員事務員等均しく革命の鉅子に係り專ら改革を鼓吹し、新知識の輸入播布を以て主義と為す。卒亥の歲、陝西獨立するや、君乃ち省城に赴きて、陝西民軍が東西敵を受け軍器糧食缺乏の實狀を觀て、遂に上海に赴きて同地に在る鄉人于右任等と籌りて軍器を購入して陝西に運ぶ。戰事息みて後ち陝西臨時省議會議員に選ばれ。旋で正式國會の眾議院議員となる。國會解散後、鄉鄉閑臥し、共和復活するに及び、再び國會の召集に應じ、仍は眾議院議員たり。

Mr. Shang Chin-kuei, otherwise called Lien Chi, age forty two, is a native of Tai-li, Hsia-hsi hsing. Being naturally of impulsive temperament he was prove to get malcontented. After receiving primary education in China he entered the Waseda University and later took the special course in the Tokyo Jikka School. With his fellow thinkers he formed a society preparing for the revolution of which he became the secretary and accountant. On return to his home he was appointed a director of the Hsia-hsi middle school. He made it point to introduce and propagate new knowledge inspiring the people with revolutionary ideas. As soon as the revolutionai movement was ripe and Hsi-hsi declared its independence he went to Shanghai and bought arms for his people. When peace was restored he was elected a member of the local assembly and later the member of the House of Commons. When the Parliament was broken up he went back to his home and waited for the opportunity. With the restoration of the Republic he went to Peking and was returned for the House of Commons.

周廷弼　字右卿　歲四十六

選舉地　山東省

籍貫　山東省壽光縣

住址　北京中京畿道西口下崗古剎周高

君自幼功舉業有年。及光緒二十九年。始考入山東初級師範學堂完全班肄業。二年。以自費留學日本。入東京私立法政大學政治科速成班。畢業回國。充本縣視學員長。歷任四年。武漢起義時。至濟南提倡獨立。被推爲臨時省議會議員。旋又被選爲衆議院議員。民國二年冬。袁氏以非法解散國會。乃由都返里。杜門不出。日惟以詩文自娛。絕口不談政治。雖至契者強使述其政見。亦以消極的語調對付之。及雲南起義。欲由濟南赴滬。共襄大業。以中途被阻。直至六月中旬。始達上海。適值黎大總統恢復國會之命令。已於其時頒布。乃由滬入都。仍充衆議院議員。

民國之精華　（傳記）　周廷弼先生

君や幼より舊學の功を積み、光緒二十九年始めて山東師範學堂完全班に入りて修養するこど二年、自費を以て日本に留學し、東京私立法政大學校政治科速成班に入りて卒業す。歸國後壽光縣視學員長に任ずる事四年なり。武漢義を起すの時、君や濟南に至りて獨立を主張し、推されて臨時省議會議員と爲る。民國成立後・選ばれて衆議院議員となる。民國二年の冬國會解散さるゝや、君乃ち鄉里に歸去業を賦して杜門閉居悠々自適し、日に詩文を以て自ら娛み、敢て政治を談せず。恥近者強いて其の政見を叩けば、亦た唯い消極的語調を以て之に對するのみ。雲南に於て義を起すに及び、君馳せて濟南より上海に赴き、同志と共に大業を襄助せんとして中途に阻まれ、六月中旬始めて上海に至るを得たり。適ゝ黎大總統でゝ國會を恢復し、君亦た召集されて北京に入り、仍は衆議院議員となる。

Mr. Chou Ting-pis, otherwise called Yu-chiang, age forty six, is a native of Shou-kuang, Shantung hsing. He is a scholar of classics. In 1903 he was graduated from the normal school of the Shantung province and at his own expense he came to Japan where he was graduated from the Hosei University of Tokyo. On return to his conntry he was appointed the chief of the school inspector. When the revolutionary movement took place he was also interested and claimed independence for his own province. When the Republic was established he was returned for the House of Commons. In the 2nd year of the Republic when the Parliament was broken up he went back to his home where he beguiled his time in writing poems. When he was pressed by others to give an opinion on politics he always replied in conservative tone. When the movement for the Restoration of the Republic took place he went to Shanghai to help the work. When the new president summoned the Parliament he went to Peking and was elected a member of the House of Commons, the position he holds in the present moment.

周震麟　字道腴　歲四十二

周震麟先生

選舉地　湖南省

籍　貫　湖南省寧鄉縣

住　址　北京西草廠裏共和報館

君於十九舉秀才。旋入兩湖書院研究科學。尤長於地理。卒業後。極力提倡教育。創立湖南私立官立各學校。握湖南教育界之中心。其講學以喚起學生進取奮鬥精神及政治革命思想為宗旨。故湖南青年出其門者。多其一種特別學風。革命巨子黃興張繼吳祿貞諸人。皆由君延入湖南任教授。甲辰。湖南革命之役。黃興張繼逃命日本。君亦以充同盟會支會長。為前清官吏所偵知。遁入日本。與黨人共謀大計。旋又歸國。在安徽任教授一年。在北京任教授三年。並營新聞事業。辛亥起義。被充湖南籌餉局長。幫辦軍務。事定。被選為參議院議員。旋回湖南。共舉第二次革命。失敗後亡命日本。滇黔起義之先。君奔走南洋香港。以共成大計。袁死遂仍就今職。兼營新聞事業云。

君や十九歳にして秀才となり、旋て兩湖書院に入りて科學を研究す。卒業後乃ち教育の普及を提唱し、湖南官私立各學校を創立して湖南教育界の中心を把握せり。其の學を講ずるや、奮闘進取的の精神及び政治革命的の思想を鼓吹し、爲に湖南の青年にして其の門を出る者は多くは一種特別の學風を具ふ。黃興、張繼、吳祿貞等の諸名士の如き、皆な君が延ひて湖南各學校の敎授に任じたるものなり。甲辰の歳湖南革命の役、黃興張繼等日本に亡命し、君も亦た日本に遁る。其後歸國して安徽北京等にて敎育に從事し並に新聞事業を經營す。第一革命には湖南籌餉局長として軍務を幫辦し。後ち參議院議員に選ばる。第二革命には其の擧を圖りしも事敗れて日本に亡命す。雲貴義を起すの初、君は南洋香港に走せて大計を圖る。國會恢復するや、仍ほ參議院議員となり兼て新聞事業を經營せり。

Mr. Chou Chen-lin otherwise called Taolehn, age forty two, is a native of Ning-hsing hsien, Ho-nan hsing. At the age of nineteen he already became famous and studied science in Lian-hu school. As soon as he was graduated he became the founder of the private school and became the central figure of the Hu-nan educational circle. In giving lectures he inspired students with progressive and revolutionary ideas. Consequently from his school, there appeared many men of importance who took active steps in revolutionary movements: He came to Japan as a political fugitive but on his return to China he was interested in education and journalistic works. In the 1st revolution he did a great service as the chief of the commissarit department. He was chosen a member of the Senate. In the 2nd revolution his plans were frustrated and he again escaped to Japan. As soon as the Parliament was restored he was appointed a member of the Senate, at the same time having management of a newspaper.

周慶恩　字次瑾　歳四十一

選舉地　山東省
籍貫　山東省歷城縣
住址　北京順治門外大街醒華報館南鄰

君自幼好學。弱冠即有文名。及長。尤彈心新學。旋以官費咨送日本。入法政大學畢業。歸國後。由司法部調部。參訂各級審判廳試辦章程。試署京師內城東廳初級檢察官。旋充天津北洋高等警察廳法律教員。及北洋譯學館教員。居無何。歸山東。任法政專門學堂教習。辛亥起義。與同志設機關分部於濟南。謀洩被捕。民國元年出獄。公推至烟臺組織臨時省議會。被舉爲烟臺臨時議會議長。迨正式省議會成立。復被舉爲山東省議會副議長。民國二年。被選爲衆議院議員。是年十月被袁政府違法取消。遂在北京濟南以律師營業。旋被聘爲大理院特約律師。及國會復活。仍爲衆議院議員。

民國之精華　（傳記）　周慶恩先生

君や幼より學を好み、弱冠にして文名あり。長ずるに及び尤も心を新學に留む。旋て官費留學生として日本に抵り、法政大學に入り卒業して歸國す。司法部より調せられて京師内城東廳初級檢察官試補となり、次で天津北洋高等警察廳法律教員及び北洋譯學館教員となる。居ること幾くもなく、山東に歸りて法政專門學堂教官に任じたり。辛亥革命の事起るや同志と共に機關を設け、濟南支部を置きしが、謀洩れて捕はれ、民國元年獄を出づ。即ち烟臺に於て臨時省議會組織さるゝや、君擧げられて臨時議會議長と爲る。正式省議會成立するや、また擧げられて山東省議會副議長と爲る。民國二年選ばれて衆議院議員と爲り、同年十月袁政府が違法を以て議員資格を剝奪するや、君北京と濟南とに在りて辯護士を營み、旋て聘せられて大理院特約辯護士と爲る。國會復活するに及び、復た出でゝ衆議院議員と爲る。

Mr. Chou Ching-en otherwise called Tzu Chin, age forty one, is a native of Li-cheng, Shantung hsing. When quite young he secured his literary fame. As he grew older his attention was called to new learning so that he went to Japan at the government expence where he was graduated from the Hosei University. He was appointed the assistant public procurator in Peking as well as the instructor of law in Tientsin and Pe-yang high police office. On returning to Shan-tung he was appointed an instructor of the law college. When the revolution broke out he worked with his fellow thinkers for the cause of revolutionists but was arrested by the government official. In the 1st year of the Republic he was released from his prison and when the special local assembly was held in Yen-tai he was elected the president thereof. In the 2nd year of the Republic he was elected a member of the House of Commons. When Yuanshi-Kai government deprived some members of the membership certificates, he stayed in Peking and practiced law. When the Parliament was opened again, he became the member thereof.

周擇 字無擇 歲三十七

選舉地 四川省
籍貫 四川省成都縣
住址 北京宣武門內東城根剛家大院

君以成都名諸生見知于時。年二十一
歲時。歷充四川夔州府立中學校及師
範學校歷史國文主任教習。旋遊學日
本法政大學。畢業歸國後。送任四川官
立法政學校教習。成都縣立中學校教
習。公立法政學校教務長。四川商報主
筆。先後六年。被選爲四川全省敎育總
會會長。反正後。充四川都督府秘書。
民政省顧問。被選爲臨時省議會議員。
復被舉爲預算審查委員會委員長。民國二
年被選爲參議院議員。國會解散後。仍
充四川巡按使公署顧問。復充幣制局
鈔券處委員。四年至吉林。署理五常縣
知事。前任內務總長王揖唐氏。以循良
特保。由今大總統發交國務院存記。及
國會復活。遂立辭五常縣知事職。即赴
京。仍充參議院議員。

君や成都著名の學生として時に知らる。年二十一歲の時、
四川夔州府立中學校及び師範學校歷史國文主任教習に歷
充し、旋て日本に遊學し法政大學に入り卒業して歸國す。
迭次四川官立法政學校教習、成都縣立中學校教習、公立
法政學校教務長、四川商報主筆に歷充し、後ち選ばれて
四川敎育總會々長となる。第一革命後四川都督府秘書、
民政署顧問となり、臨時省議會議員に選ばれ、復た豫算
審査委員會會長となる。民國二年選ばれて參議院議員と爲
る。國會解散後、歸鄉して仍ち四川巡按使公署顧問とな
り、復た幣制局鈔券處委員たり。四年吉林に抵りて五常
縣知事署理となり、前任內務總長王揖唐は特に君の材幹
を保薦して現大總統より命じて國務院に記錄せしむ。此
の次國會復活するに及び、君乃ち地方官の職を辭して召
集に應じ、仍は參議院議員たり。

Mr. Chou Chai otherwise called Wu Chai, thirty seven years of age, is a native of Cheng-tu hsin, Hsi-chuan province. As a student, he was already famous, and at the age of twenty, he was an instructor of history and national literature in middle and normal schools of the province. He studied in the Hosei University of Japan. On returning to Japan, he was an instructor of the Hsi-shuan law college, the Cheng-tu middle school and other important concerns. Finally, he was elected the President of the Hsi-chuan educational society. After the first revolution, he was appointed the private secretary of the governor general of Hsi-chuan and adviser to the civil administration of the province. In the special local assembly he was elected a member, and was on the committee of Budget investigation. In the second year of the Republic, he became a member of the Parliament. When the Parliament was closed he returned to his home and was on the committee of the mint in his province. As soon as the restoration of the Republic became a fact he responded to the call and was appointed a member of the Senate.

民國之精華　（傳記）　周克昌先生

周克昌　字峻青　歲四十三

選舉地　山西省

籍貫　山西省平定縣城內

住址　北京前門外西河沿大耳胡同十六

君賦性戇直。不隨流俗浮沈。然居心仁厚。以寬恕待人。雖仇敵亦不忍窘迫之。與人交。喜相責以喜。人告以過。輒大喜。蓋謂其能直言不欺。不以流俗相待也。自幼好讀。喜博覽羣書。任意所之業。故其讀書純以主觀判斷是非。而不局于習俗之成見。及海內維新。愈立志求有用之學。於新書無所不覽。而尤醉心于西學之書。遂肄業於山西大學堂西學專齋。優等畢業後。爲陝西補用知縣。民國二年。被選爲衆議院議員。國會解散後。無所表見。及共和復活。國會重開。仍復爲衆議院議員。

君賦性剛直流俗に隨つて浮沈せず。然かも居心仁厚にして寛恕を以て人を待ち。仇敵と雖ぁ亦た之を窘窮するに忍びず。人と交つて相責むるに善々を以てし、人若し過を以て告ぐれば輒ち大に喜ぶ。幼より讀書を好み、群籍を涉獵して意ぐ往く所に任せて快とし。矩々然として科擧の業に從事するを屑しとせず。故に其の讀書は專ら主觀を以て是非を判斷し、習俗の成見に局限されざる也。海內維新に及び志を立て～有用の學を求め、新書殆んど觀ざる所無く尤も西學の書に心醉す。山西大學校西學專科に入りて修業し、優等を以て卒業し。陝西省の補用知縣と爲る。民國二年正式國會成立に際し衆議院議員に當選す。國會解散後、歸里に韜晦して時事を談せず。共和復活して國會再ねて開かる～に及び、仍は復た衆議院議員の舊職に就きたり。

Mr. Chou-ko-chang, otherwise called Hsuan ching, Ping-ting prefecture, Shan-hsi district, forty three years old. He is a man of resolute, never follows the tendencies of time; but he is always kind and warm hearted, as he overlooks even his enemies. He encourages good of others and corrects gladly his own fault if one tells him of the fact. He was inclined to have had a striking fondness reading and went through a thousand volumes. He did not study so hard for the civil service examination but for his own pleasure. On the introduction of the western civilization he turned his attention toward new science and new books, particularly foreign publications. He entered in the Shan-hsi University as a special student in the western science. On graduating there with honour he made the acting governor of Hsia-hsi district. In the second year of the Republic he was elected by his district to serve a time in the House of Representative, which was formally organized both with the Upper House. Service of the Parliament was dissolved by Yuán he was spending his time unpleasantly. But, fortunately the Republic was restored and so the Parliament of which he is now a member of the Lower House.

周澤　字潤生　歲四十二

選舉地　四川省

四川　四川省雙流縣

住　址　北京前門內小四眼井黎宅

君秉性誠實悃篤。居恒尚質惡文。天資
聰慧敏活。自幼好讀。弱冠有文名。及
海內維新。決志涉獵新書。遂頁戻東
渡。留學日本。博覽群籍。研磋不倦。專
究其精。深明其義。造詣既深。學識傑
出儕輩。歸國後。以開導後進。啓發民
智自任。銳意從事育英之業。熱心盡力
教育之普及。曾歷任本省中小學堂。師
範學堂教員。管理員。及省視學諸職。
宣統庚戌。受地方長官委託。赴日本
考查教育。歸國仍傾注蘊蓄。改良教
育。民國肇造。正式國會成立。被選為
眾議院議員。嗣國會停止。囘籍任四川
師範學校校長。管理校務。養成子弟。
不談政事。本年及國會重開。遂又入
京。仍為眾議院議員。

君秉性誠實悃篤にして居常質を尚び文を惡む。天資聰慧
敏活にして幼より讀書を好み、弱冠早くも文名あり。海
內維新に及び志を決して新書を涉獵し、遂に笈を負ふて
東海を渡り、新進の文明懷爛たる日本に留學して研磋倦
まず、新智識を咀嚼して造詣僭饕に傑出す
るものありたり。國に歸つて後も後進を誘掖して民智を
開發するを以て自任し、銳意育英の業に從つて熱心教育
の普及に盡瘁したり。曾つて本省各中小學校、師範學校

教員乃至は管理員又は省視學等の諸職に歷任す。宣統庚
戌の歲、地方長官の委託を受けて日本に赴き教育を視察
し、歸國乃ち蘊蓄を傾住して教育の改良に從事したり。
民國二年正式國書成立に際し選ばれて眾議院議員と為
る。國會停止後歸鄉して四川高等師範學校々長に任じて
校務を管理し、子弟を養成して政事を談せず。國會重ね
て召集さるゝに及び、遂に又た入京して仍ほ眾議院議員
たり。

Mr. Chou-tse, another name Jun-sheng, Chien-i prefecture, Ssi-chuan district, fourty two years old. He is a man of truth and kindness, loves plainness and dislikes pomp. At the same time he is very bright and keen; from boyhood he has found best pleasure in reading and he had a reputation of a good writer which he was very young. On the introduction of the western civilization he begun to look into the western books, finally deciding to complete his study in a foreign country he chosed young progressive country in the East and went to Japan where he studied untiringly and gathered new knowledge. Returning home, he made it his duty to educate young men and advance the average knowledge of the people, accordingly he engaged assiduously to educate entire young people of the distrist. He was once teacher of, grammer school, middle school, and normal school, then the principal of the district educational inspector. During Hsuan-tung era he was sent by a local governor to Japan to investigate the educational condition there. Having returned home he reformed the educational system. In the second year of the Republic the national congress was formally organized and he having been chosen held a seat in the Lower House until it was suspended by Yuan. During the interval returned to his native town and made president of the Ssichuan, Higher Normal School. Parliament has convened again in the 5th year and he was called to resume his duty in the Lower House.

周之翰　字文山　歲三十六

選舉地　甘肅省

籍貫　甘肅武威縣

住址　北京背陰胡同羅家大院

君秉性剛正。待人以誠。自幼篤實不欺。尚質惡文。不事無益之繁華。然天資聰穎。悟性極高。讀書能精思深入。探求眞義。雖博及經史。而不喜摘華飾藻尋摘章句。與人交。重然諾。尚信義。人有所託。雖擬爲盡力。常於事前陽爲拒絕。然後暗中援助之。事成絕不望報。夙抱經世之志。從事地方公益。多有功勞。民國肇造。共和創莫。民國二年正式國會成立。被選爲衆議院議員。把持正論。主張公議。翼贊建設之偉業。未幾。國會停止。君歸里快快不娛。五年及約法恢復。國會重開。君欣然應召入京。仍復就爲衆議院議員。

民國之精華　　（傳記）周之翰先生

君秉性剛直にして人を待つに誠を以てす。幼より篤實にして欺かず。質を尚び文を惡みて無益の繁華を事とせず然かも天資聰穎にして悟性極めて高く、書を讀みて能く義理に通曉し、博く經史を涉獵すると雖も章句の末を摘ひを喜ばず。人と交りて然諾を重んじ、信義を尚ぶ。人の託する所あれば陽に拒絕して暗中に援助し、事成つて絕へて報を望まず。夙に經世の志を抱きて地方の公益に從

事し、功勞尠なからず。民國樹立して共和の新政を創むるや、君選ばれて正式國會衆議院議員と爲る。遂に京師に入りて院に到り、正論を把持して公議を主張し、以て建設の偉業を翼贊す。未だ幾くもなく國會停止す、君鄉里に歸臥して快々樂まず。五年約法復活して國會重ねて開かるゝに及び、君復た召集に應じて入京し、仍は衆議院議員たり。

Mr. Chou Chi-han, otherwise called Wen Shan, age thirty six, a native of Wu Wei Hsien, the Kan-su Hsing, is straight forward in dealing with others. He hated vain pompasity and highly valued the real and substantial of any thing. He is a well read man free from any prejudice. He is not slave to mere words but enters into the spirit of the letter. He helps others in secret and late publicity of good works. His service in the opening-up of local district is indeed very great. When the Republic was established, he was returned for the House of Commons. He entered Peking, and was known for his distinguished services in attending the mighty work of government with the suppression of the Parliament, he returned home when he waited for an oppotunity. When it was decided to reopen the Parliament, he was elected as a member thereof.

周澤南 字達之 象三十四

選舉地 江西省
籍 貫 江西省萍鄉縣
住 址 北京北半截胡同

君爲人倜儻不羈。處事精敏活潑。勇於
決斷。居常持己以嚴。不隨同流俗。與
人交。直而不黨。有所規勸。聽者無不
爲所動。自幼好讀。然喜探求眞義。不
以博聞強記尋摘句章爲懷。少時。好爲
詩歌。及長因得宋儒學說之訓。斥爲
玩物喪志。遂棄不復爲。專肆力於有用
之學。及海內風氣開通復改志殫精西
學。遍讀新書。於西人邸治保邦之要。
均確有把握旋又東渡留學。入早稻田
大學政治經濟科。畢業歸國後。應學部
留學生試驗。考取法政科舉人。民國二
年。被選爲參議院議員。國會解散後。
歸里獨居。不談政事。五年八月。及國
會重開。始來京復爲參議院議員。

り、日本に留學して早稻田大學政治經濟科に入りて研磋
倦まず、遂に北の業を畢へて歸國す。即ち前淸學部の留
學生試驗に應じて法政科舉人と爲る。漢土光復して民國
成立して共和の新政を創むるや、民國二年選ばれて參議
院議員と爲る。國會解散後、鄉里に歸り獨居して出でず
五年八月國會重ね開かるゝ及び、復た其の召集に應じて
仍は參議院議員と爲る。

君人と爲り倜儻にして不羈、事に處するや精敏にして活
潑顏る決斷に勇む。居常己を持する嚴にして流俗に同せ
ざる也。人と交りて直にして硬、幼より讀書を好みて眞
義を探求することを喜ぶ。少時好んで詩歌を作りしも長
するに及び之を斥け、專ら天下有用の實學を攻究するに
勉め、海內の風氣開通するに及びて進んで心を西學に傾
注して遍ねく新書を涉獵し、西人邸治保邦の要を究めて
均しく確かに造詣する所あり。曾て笈を負ふて東海を渡

Mr. Chou Tse-nan, another name Te-yuan, Ping-ching prefecture, Chiang-hsi district, thirty four years old. We find him most prudent and independent, and quick to handle things and ready to give a decision. He is rather vigolous to himself and never follows the daily tendency. He is also just and aquire to all, From youth he has been great reader of books and silent researcher of truth. As a boy he camposed well verses but as a man he would not look for them. The study of valuable science became his choise. At the time of introduction of the mixture civilization he was absorved in study of the westren science by that he gaind immense quantity of the fresh knowledge. Once he went to Japan clossing the Eastern Sea and entered into the Waseda University to study economics and political science. The hard study rewarded him with the honorable graduation. He pass d the examination of the education department of the late Emperial Government for the student returned from foreign countries and admitted as the scholor on politics and laws. On the establishment of the Republican Government he was elected a member of the Upper House in the second year of the Republic, when the national Parliament was suspended he returned to his native country and lived very quietly until he was again sent to the Upper House in the fifth year as the Parliament has reconvened and the Republic order of things is restored.

周嘉坦　字履安　歲三十

選舉地　山東省
籍　貫　山東省長山縣
址　住　北京西城安福胡同○嶽廬

君賦性篤實不欺。而氣宇深厚。不苟言
笑與人交。談而能久。以雖疾惡崇善。
而不露鋒鋩。相其人必能納諫者。始懷
慨規正之。否則惟婉詞示意。不聽。然
後漸與疎遠。喜求有有用之學。新學既盛倡
于海內。君遂盡棄舊學。篤志研究西
學。遂於光緒末年。入山東優級師範學
堂。畢業後。自宣統三年至民國四年。
任山東農業專門學校數學教員。旋被
選爲衆議院議員。國會解散後。仍返里
任原校教員。著有幾何學解題類編四
年六月。以縣知事分發浙江任用。五年
及國會重開。遂辭職應召入京。仍充衆
議院議員。

民國之精華　（傳記）　周嘉坦先生

君賦性篤實にして欺かず、而かも氣宇深厚にして言笑を
苟もせず。人と交るや淡として能く久し。惡を惡み善を
崇ぶと雖も、鋒鋩を露はさず。幼より刻苦精勵以て學を
求め、長するに及び有用の學に志して西學を研究し切磋
倦まず。光緒末年山東優級師範學校に學びて業を畢ゆ。
即ち志を育英の業に立てゝ、前清宣統三年より民國四年
に至るの間、山東省農業專門學校に教鞭を取りて後進を
誘掖するに努む。之より先、民國二年正式國會乘議院議
員に當選し、出でゝ議政檀上の人となること半年有餘、
國會解散さるゝや、即ち郷里に歸りて舊の如く教育に從
事し、幾何學解題類編の著あり。民國四年六月、縣知事
に任じて浙江省に分たる。五年國會復活す、仍ほ職を辭
して召集に應じ乘議院議員と爲る。

Mr. Chou Chia-tan, otherwise called Lian, age thirty, is a native of Changshan, Shan-tung hsing. He is broad minded and sociable but he never betrayes either in anger or joy. He is a hard working student who has devoted his attention to the acquisition of new learning. At the end of the previous Chinese regime he entered the higher normal school of his province, when he made up his mind to enter into educational work. From 1911 to 1912 he was an instructor in the agricultural school of his province. In the 2nd year of the Republic he was elected a member of the House of Commons which post he occupied a little over half a year. With the breaking up of the Parliament he returned to his native country where he was interested in education. He wrote book called a Key to Geometry. In the 4th year of theRepublic he was appointed the governor of the Shang Chiang hsing. With the Restoration of the Parliament he resigned the post and was elected for the House of Commons as its member.

邵長鎔　字冶田　歲五十三

選舉地　江蘇省

籍　貫　江蘇省灌雲縣

住　址　北京騾馬市虎坊橋聚魁店

君賦性仁厚誠實。為人嚴重。饒歷練。
每以寬恕應物。自幼好學。及長。博覽
群籍。探究精義。海內維新後。銳志西
學。新書無所不視。思想豐富。見解新
頴。具有幹濟之巨手。鄉黨皆推重之。
前清補歲貢生。旋被選江蘇諮議局議
員。光復後。民國元年歷任江蘇都督府
審計科員。實業科長。交通科長。復被
選充江蘇臨時省議會議員。二年正式
國會成立。當選衆議院議員。被舉進步
黨交際幹事。嗣以國會解散旋里。由江
蘇民政長聘任。為江蘇籌辦巴拿馬賽
會出品協會名譽經理。五年國會恢復。
遂應召入京。仍為衆議院議員。

君賦性仁厚誠實、人と為り嚴重にして經驗に富む。常に
寬恕を以て物に應じ、幼より學を好み、長ずるに及び、
群籍を涉獵して精義を探究す。海內維新後、西學に志し
て薪書觀ざる所なし。思想豐富にして見解新頴にして、
幹濟の巨手を具ふ。前清歲貢生に補し、旋て江蘇諮議局
議員と為る。第一革命後、民國元年、江蘇都督府審計科
員、實業科長、交通科長に歷任したり。復た選れて江蘇
臨時省議會議員となり。二年正式國會衆議院議員に當選
す。舉げられて進步黨交際幹事と為る。國會解散後、鄉
里に歸り、江蘇民政長より聘せられて江蘇準備巴拿馬博
覽會出品協會名譽經理となる。五年國會恢復するに及
び、遂に召集に應じて入京し、仍ほ衆議院議員と為りた
り。

Mr. Shao Chang Jung, otherwise called Yeh Tien, fifty three years of age, a native of Kuan Yun Hsien, the Chiang Su Hsing, is a gentleman distinguished for his honesty, sincerity, magnanimity and rich experience. He was a well read and ardent reader of books, but he is far from being a casual reader. He made it point to dive into the deep significance of what he read. He is greatly interested in new learning, and as a matters of fact, there are few books which he has not read. Rich thoughts coupled with practical ability makes the leader of the people in his district. He was appointed a member of the Chiang Su Advisory Assembly, while after the Revolution, he occupied numerous positions of importance. In 1913, he was elected a member of the House of Commons, in which capacity he assisted the work of the government. He was also appointed the ship of the progressive party. On the dissolution of the Parliament, he returned to his home where he was at the request of the Chiang Su Civil Adminstraton was appointed the honorary director of the Chiang Su Exhibition Association of the Panama Exposition. When the reopening of the Parliament was actualized, he entered Peking, and was returned for the House of Commons.

邵仲康　歲三十四

選舉地　黑龍江省

籍　貫　黑龍江巴彥縣

住　址　北京順治門內抄手胡同

君天資聰穎敏捷。然爲人誠篤無華。好
質惡文。不事無益之繁華。與人交。直
而婉。淡而能久。不爲疾言遽色。居常
謹約自持。言動舉止。皆確有本末。自
幼好學深思。稚年讀書。即喜推求精
義。不厭數問。進境嶄然。超出儕輩。及
長。博覽群籍。造詣旣深。遂專求有用
之學。不復固執章句。夙抱興學之志。
以開通文化自任。嘗入師範學校畢業。
歷充視學勸業等差。銳意力圖地方敎
育之普及。於北境之文化開發。貢獻不
尟少。聲望日大著。民國二年正式國會
成立。被選爲衆議院議員。國會解散。
歸里讀書。尤喜誘掖後進。不問時政。
五年及國會重行召集。遂出閭門。抵京
師。仍爲衆議院議員。

君天資聰穎敏捷にして人と爲り誠篤華なし、質を好み文
を惡みて無益の繁華を事とせず。人と交りて直にして婉、
淡として能く久しく、疾言遽色を爲さず。居常謹約自ら
持し、言動舉止皆な確として本末あり。幼より學を好み
深く思索す。少年書を讀みて即ち其の精義を推求する事
を喜び、進境嶄然として濟輩を超出す。長するに及び博
く群籍を覽びて造詣旣に深く、遂に專ら有用の學を求め復
た章句を固執せず。夙に興學の志を抱き、文化を開通す
るを以て自ら任す。曾て師範學校を卒業し、視學及び勸
業等の職に歷充し、銳意地方敎育の普及を圖り、北境の
文化開發上貢獻尟なからず、聲望日に著る。民國二年正
式國會衆議院議員に當選す。國會解散するや、鄕里に歸
りて後進を誘掖するに力めて時事を問はず、五年國會重
ねて召集を行ふに及び、遂に閭門を出で、京師に抵り、
仍ほ衆議院議員と爲る。

民　國　之　精　華　（傳　記）　邵仲康先生

邵　仲　康

衆議院議員

Mr. Shao Chung-Kang, thirty four years of age, is a native of Pa zen, Hei lung province.
He is quick witted and sincere, and is a lover of substance and hater of vain pomp. He is sociable
in nature, and does not show his anoyance, since his selfcontrol is so strong. While young, he was
a lover of learning, and a deep thinker. As he grew older he distinguishad himself from others. He
devoted his attention to the study of useful learning. He considered himself to be the pioneer of introducing civilization to his own country. After he was graduated from the normal school, he was interested the promotion of local education and in the dissimination of knowledge among his countrymen. In
the course of time his popularity grew to such an extent that in the second year of the Republic, he
was returned for the House of Commons. When the Parliament was dissolved, he returned to his
native province when he devoted himself to the instruction of the rising generation. When the Parliament was summoned, again, he went up to Peking where he was returned for the House of Commons,
the position of honour he now enjoys.

林玉麒 字式言 歲四十五

選舉地　浙江省
籍　貫　浙江省永嘉縣
住　址　北京絞場六條

君為人誠厚篤實。痛惡浮華。與人交。常硬直不阿。絕無世故之念。人告以過。亦欣然謝之。然居心仁厚。喜救人急難。故其接物。雖稍露鋒芒。而人亦罕忌恨之者。自幼好讀深思。喜研求眞理。而不屑尋章摘句。以為博取功名計。故其所讀多有用書之書。及海內維新。志西學遂肆于新書無所不觀。而尤醉心于教育之書。曾充福建蒲田永福等縣知縣。浙江優級師範學校庶務長。廣東官銀號經理。民國二年正式國會成立。被舉為衆議院議員。國會解散後歸里不問政事。及國會復活。始入京復為衆議院議員。

君人と為り誠厚篤實にして浮華を痛惡す。人と交りて常に硬直阿らず、絶へて世故の念無し。人の告ぐるに過を以てすれば欣然之を謝し、然かも居心仁厚にして喜んで人の急を救ひ、其の事に接して稍や鋒鋩を驚すと雖、人亦之を恨む者少なし。幼より書を讀みて深く思索し、真理を研究するに勤めて、章句の末を摘むことを屑しとせず。海內維新に及びて遂に博く新書を涉獵して、尤も教育學に心醉したり。曾て福建省の蒲田永福等各縣知事に任じ、又た浙江省優級師範學校庶務長、廣東官銀號經理等の職に歷任し、幹濟の才大に著る。民國二年正式國會成立するや、舉げられて衆議院議員と為る。國會解散されてより鄉里に歸省して讀書自ら娛み、また時事を談せず。國會復活するに及び、遂に又た其の召集に應じて入京し、仍は衆議院議員と為る。

Mr. Lin Yu-chi, otherwise named as Shih Yen, age forty five, a native of Che chiang Hsing, is straight forward in character, but wide enough to accept the advice of otheres. He is sympathetic with the misfortune of others. Even if he may treat the subjects rathers roughly on that account he never incurs the hatred of others. He was from youth a great admirer of books, but he was rather a thinker not caught up by the empty philascology. With the new current of thought, he was interested in reading most copiously books on various subject, but he is greatly interested in reading educational books. He was the governor of Fukien-chou and other provinces while his service as the instractor in normal schools was by no means to be ignored. Under the Republic, he was a parliamentary member, but that assembly was suspended, he was returned to his native province when he spent his time mostly in reading books. When the Parliament met once more, he was returned for the House of Commons.

林長民 字宗孟 歲四十一

選舉地　蒙古
籍　貫　福建閩侯縣
住　址　北京南府口御澔河邊謙女橋西

君自幼聰穎絕倫。讀書遇目成誦。鄉黨宗族。目爲神童。而其彬彬儒雅。從無自滿自矜之態。故同輩皆以兄事之。及至成年。以爲世界交通。斷非拘守經史所能濟世。於是立志。究心科學。遂留學于日本。入早稻田大學。政治經濟科。宣統元年。畢業歸國。任福建諮議局書記長。民國元年。任臨時參議院秘書長。二年當選爲衆議院議員。兼同院秘書長。三年任政事堂參議。五年任法制局局長。辭職。現復爲衆議院議員。舊爲民主黨派。合併進步黨爲政務部長。今任憲法研究會編輯事務。該會即進步黨之結合而成者。當袁世凱僭稱帝制時代。君長法制局。乃憤然而欲曰。違法行爲。眞至此爲甚。於法制何有焉。辭職出京。與同志謀復共和。甚力云。

君幼より聰穎絕倫にして目に觸るゝの書誦を成す、鄉黨宗族即ち目して神童と爲す。而して其の彬々たる儒雅の風また自矜自滿、態無くして同輩皆な之に師事したり。成年に至りて世勢の大勢に稽へ、志を決して科學を攻究し、遂に新進の日本に留學して早稻田大學校政治經濟科に學び、明治四十二年卒業歸國して福建諮議局書記長に任す。民國元年臨時參議院秘書長となり、二年衆議院議員に常選し同院秘書長を兼ぬ。當時民主黨が共和黨及び統一黨と合併して進步黨を組織するや、君は其の政務部長と爲り、後ち同黨員にて組織せる憲法研究會編輯事務に任じたり、國會停止後、三年政事堂參議に任じ。五年法制局々長に任す。會ゝ袁世凱が帝制を僭稱せる時代なりしを以て憤然として其の違法行爲を歎じ、職を辭して北京を去り、同志と偕に共和の恢復を圖り、國會復活するに及びて再び出でゝ兼議院議員と爲る。

民國之精華 (傳記) 林長民先生

M. Lin-chang-ming, otherwise called Tsung-meng, Min-hou prefecture, Fukian district, forty one years old. When he was a boy brightness surpassed every friend; if once he read a book he memorized it well; the villagers thought him an infant prodigy. His scholarly manner and knowledge made others to follow him as the master. Growing a man he understood throughly the tendency of world and determind to study siencce. Finally he went to the new and progress country, Japan, to take up the cherished study. He entered the Waseda University where he pursued courses on economics and politics, and completed his work there in the 42nd year of Meiji. Returning home he was appointed the secretary general of the Fukians Legislature. In the first year of the Republic he made the chief secretary of the Provisional State Council. Next year, he was sent to the Lower House from his district to occupy a seat there and the position of chief secretary of the same. At the time Democratic, Republican and unionist parties fused one political party, and organized progressive party; He was nominated the chief of the Political Department, later the compilr of the constitution committee formed by the party. Since the suspension of Parliament he was a counsellor of the administrative Council and in the fifhh he made director of the Legal Bureau. When Yuan-shi kai basely designed to restore the Emperial regime making himself the Emperor he pointed cut Yuan's inegulality and illegality and resigned his position. Soon, he left Peking to make the plan of restoring the Republican order. Without waiting very long Yuan fell and the Republic cames to existence again. He is now a member of the Lower House.

林輅存 字景商 歲三十七

選舉地　福建省

籍貫　福建省安溪縣嵩住里臚傳鄉

住址　北京板章胡同同安會館

君少居臺灣。臺灣之茶葉樟腦金鑛等。皆由君祖遠芳所開創。君少負詩名。乙未自臺渡閩。入籍安溪。由清秀才疊薦經濟特科戊戌上書言變法。光緒帝甚寵之。以郎中用。充總理衙門英國股章京。後以政變故。日本兒玉源太郎伯爵攜之避居東京。旋歸國。改道員分發江蘇。調廣東。歷保記名公使。掌敎安溪同安馬巷龍溪各書院。倡辦泉漳廈門南洋各學校。爪哇中華商會。多半出其組織。以唐才常案嫌疑。流寓歐美各地。旋復歸國。爲前清福建諮議局議員。資政院補缺議員。民國成立。海外及本省皆選爲議員。君辭華僑議員。充福建臨時省議會議員。又爲臨時參議院議員。後又爲衆議院議員。國會解散後。華僑擧爲福建暨南局總理。嗣當選國民會議議員。立法院議員。皆託故不就。及今國會恢復。始來京充今職。五年九月授三等嘉禾章。

林輅存先生

君少にして臺灣に居る。臺灣の茶業樟腦金鑛等は皆な君の祖遠芳の創めたるもの。君少小詩名を負り、乙未の歲福建に歸りて籍ゝ安溪に移す。前清の秀才を以て經濟特科に應め、戊戌上書して變法を言ひ、光緒帝之ゝ愛して郎中を以て用ひ、總理衙門英國部章京に任す。兒ゝ源太郎伯に携られて政變を東京に避け、後ち歸國するや道員に分ち廣東に調し、記名公使に保せらる、安溪同安馬巷龍溪各書院教師となり。泉漳廈門南洋各學校同中華商會等、牛は其の組織する所なり。唐戈常案の嫌疑を受け、出で、歐米各地に流寓し、歸國後福建諮議局議員、資政院補缺議員となる。第一革命後福建臨時省議會議員、臨時參議院議員となり。又た正式國會衆議院議員に常選す。國會解散後、福建暨南局總理に舉げられ、國民會議議員、立法院議員に常選したるも皆な故に託して就かす。國會恢復後出で、衆議院議員の職に就き、五年九月三等嘉禾章を授けらる。

Mr. Lin Lu-tsun, otherwise called Ching-Ti, age thirty seven, is a native of An-chi, Fu-chien hsing. While young he lived in Formosa. His grandfather started business in Formosa tea, conphor, and gold mining. In 1895 he came to Fu-chien and made his home in An-chi hsien. He was known to the late Chinese Emperor and served in the court. He was with Count Kodama and stayed in Tokyo during the political trouble. On returning to his home many important posts were offered to him. Being suspected by the government, he went to Europe and America and when he returned again to his country the situation was rapidly changing and he was appointed a member of various committees in his province. When the Parliament was opened he was elected a member of the House of Commons. With the dissolution of the Parliament a provincial assembly invited him to take part in the business but he declined. As soon as the Parliament was opened he was elected a member of the House of Commons.

選舉地　廣東省

籍　貫　廣東省雲浮縣

住　址　北京潘家河沿二十號

君秉性溫厚篤實。待人以和。雖盛怒。無疾言遽色。然持己甚嚴。言動不苟。自幼好讀遇目成誦。並能深入精微。洞悉義理。及長。博覽群籍。涉獵新書。立志尤求實用之學。造詣漸深。乃達觀強鄰列強之大勢。即以從事育英。開發民智為己任。曾歷充廣州嶺南學校教員。澳門明新中學校校長。民國二年正式國會成立。被選為眾議院議員。把持正義。翼贊建設。國會解散後。南旋歸里提倡道德。誘掖後進。不談時政。五年及約法恢復。國會重開。遂又應召北上。到院。仍復就眾議院議員舊職。

君秉性溫厚にして篤實、人を待つに和を以てす。然かも已を持すること甚だ嚴正にして言動苟もせざる也。幼より讀書を好みて目を過ぐれば誦を爲し、且つ能く其の精徽を究めて義理を洞察す。長するに及びて博く群籍を讀み新書を涉獵し、尤も實用の學を喜びて研磨倦まず、造詣漸く深し。乃ち強隣列強の現勢に觀て、民智の開發を以て己が任と爲す。曾て廣州嶺南學校敎員に任じ、又た

澳門明新中學校校長と爲り、銳意育英の業に從事す。民國二年正式國會の成立に當り選ばれて眾議院議員と爲り、正義を把持して建設の業を翼贊す。國會解散されて後ち南旋歸鄉し、道德を提唱して後進を誘掖し、又た時政を論せず。五年約法復活して國會重ねて開かるゝに及び、途に又た其の召集に應じて北上し、仍ほ眾議院議員たり。

mr. Lin Pai-ho, native of Yun Fon Hsien, the Kuntung Hsing, is gentle in dealing with others but very strict with himself. He never utters even one word for which he claims his responsibility. From childhood, he read books copiously; but at the same time he was a great thinker, and took pleasure in the practical application of his learning. Perceiving the present force of other powers of the world, he felt most keenly the necessity of disminating knowledge among his own country, with that object in view he most realously applied himself to the education of the people himself becoming the insluctor and maker of various schools. Under the Republic, he was returned for the House of Commons, as a member of which he contributed a great deal to the interest of his own country by advancing strong argument on the cause of justice. On the dissolution of the Parliament, he went to the South when he preached high morality, guiding the young generation at the reopening of the Parliament, he was elected as a member of the House of Commons.

阿旺根敦　字雲亭　歲五十八

選舉地　西藏
籍　貫　西藏
住　址　北京雍州宮北大門

君爲人嚴正耿介。接物以約。自治以
勤。居常極守儉樸。飽煖而外。決不稍
行耗費。然居心仁厚。自處極薄。而不
以啬啬加人。且對於地方公益之事。亦
勇於出資。常語子弟曰。儉之爲德。在
於約束其身心。使毋放縱。非僅爲節用
計世。自幼以孝友見稱于人。及長。尤
善措置家政。待下以寬。而不爲姑息
之愛。少時。曾學漢文漢語。皆純熟無
訛。中年。遂克充西藏商務繙譯員。光
緒三十四年。由駐藏大臣奏派駐京充
官唐古忒學繙譯員。民國二年。正式國
會成立。被舉爲衆議院議員。國會解
散。仍旅居內地。絕不發表政見。及國
會復活。遂復就職爲衆議院議員。

阿旺根敦先生

君人と爲り嚴正耿介にして居常極めて儉朴を守り、然も
居心仁厚にして自ら處する事極めて薄きも敢て客嗇を以
て人に加へず、地方公益の事業に對しては亦た出資を惜
まず。幼より孝友を以て鄕人に稱せられ、長ずるに及び
て最も善く家政を措置し、下を待つに寬を以てし姑息の
愛を爲さざるなり。少年の時曾つて漢文漢語を擧び皆な
通曉して訛なきに至る。中年時代に及び遂に西藏商務局

繙譯員となる、前清光緒三十四年駐藏大臣の奏派により
て北京駐在の唐古忒學或繙譯員となる。第一革命後民國成
立して五大民族共和の新政を創め、民國二年正式國會成
立するや君選ばれて衆議院議員となる。國會解散して後
支那本土に客寓して讀書自ら樂しみ絕へて政見を發表す
る事なし。國會復活するに及び君再び召集に應じて遂に
仍は衆議院議員の職に就きたり。

Mr. A-Wang-kentun, another name Yun-ting, Tibet, fifty eight years old. He is most vigorous man we can find very rarely; his daily life is very simple and plain, yet he is very kind. He is never afraid to spend a thousand tails for the public work, though he is rather too close to himself. From youth he was commented by the villagers as the most faithful son. Growing older he managed skillfully his family finance and treated the household very tenderly. During the boyhood he learned thoroughly chinese language and letters and his middle age he made the translater at the Tibet Commerce Bureau. In the 34th year of Kuang-hsu he was appointed on the recommendation of the Chinese Minister at Tibet the translator at the office of Tang-ku te-hsiao, then stationed in Peking the first Revolution broke out and the Republic was organized by the five great races. In the second year of the Republic the National Parliament was inaugurated formally and he was, then, elected by people a member of the Lower House. Since the dissolution of Parliament he staid in the China praper and amused himself in reading and never spoke politics. On the restoration of the Republic and Representation Government he has been called to Peking to take up the old duty in the Lower House.

邱冠棻 字贊宣 歲三十一

選舉地　江西省

籍貫　江西省吉安縣

住址　北京官菜園上街五號

君秉性仁厚。富於感情。自幼好爲義舉。喜爲不平之鳴。鄉人有處困厄者。輒竭力救援之。事成不望報。不成則引爲絕大恥辱。蓋君素尙信義。重然諾。故人有所託。恆佯拒不允。復暗中爲之盡力。以免貪不成之責。居常以勤儉自持。衣食居住。皆極簡約。與人交。務以勸善爲訓。然嚴已。而薄責於人。朋友有過。唯避人。直言諫止之。而對他人則力爲之隱飾。有善行。則揄揚之。不遺餘力。前清時。以附生。留學日本東京。入早稻田大學專門部政治經濟科。畢業。授得業士。歸國後。于宣統二年由學部考試。獎給法政科擧人宣統三年。殿試。以知縣分發陝西。民國元年。任江西埋財局長二年。任財政司主計科長。同年。被選爲衆議院議員。國會解散。歸里任江西法政學校講述員。兼充律師及此次國會復活。遂入京充衆院議員。

早稻田大學專門部政治經濟科に入りて卒業す、宣統二年學部の試驗に及第して法政科擧人に擧げらる。宣統三年知縣として陝西に分たる。民國元年江西埋財局長、二年財政司主計長の職に歷任す。同年選れて衆議院議員とな る、國會解散するや都に歸り西江法政學校講述員となり兼て辯護士を營み、國會復活するや、入京して再び衆議院議員となる。

君は性仁厚にして感情に富む。幼より義擧を好み、喜んで不平を鳴らし、都人の窮する者あれば全力を擧げて之を救濟し、事成るも決して報を受けず。成らされば絕大の恥辱と爲す。蓋し君素ら信義を受けて然諾を重んず。常に勤儉を以て自ら持し衣食住共に質素を崇びて然諾を旨とす。人と交りて已に嚴にして人を責むる事薄く。朋友過あれば人を避けて諫止し、他人に對して力て之を隱くし、善行われば則ち之れを稱揚す。前淸の時附生を以て日本に留學し

民國之精華　（傳記）邱冠棻先生

Mr. Chin Kuan-fen, another name Tsau-hsuan, Chi-an prefecture, Chianghsi district, thirty one years old. He is a man of kind heart and sympathetic; from his boyhood he found utmost pleasure in charity; whenever he heart or see misery of the townsman he saved him sacrificing even his entire fortune and received the reward for the deed; If he fails in rescue he was ashamed of himself; these due to his truthful nature and up-right mind. He minds himself to be economical, and plain and simple in food, clothing, and habitation. To meet others he is generous though vigorous to himself. If he finds that his friend made mistake he worns him kindly and never uses hasty words to him. He k eps other man's fault to himself and tells about it to third man and applauds a good conduct of others. During the Emperial Government he was sent as the scholar to Japan and entered into the Waseda University, pursued courses on politics and economics. After the graduation he returned home to take the examination of the education department in the second year of Hsuan-tung and passing it successfully he was admitted to the scholar on plitics and law. In the third of Hsun-tung he was named as the governor of Hsia-hsi, director of the Chang-hsi Finance Bureau, in the first year of the Republic, and the head of the accounting department in the third year were the offices he occupied. During the latter year he was sent to the Lower House on the dissolution of which he returned to his district and taught at the Chang-hsi Politics and Law School. Sometimes, he was attorney-at-law: On the restoration of the Republican order he has returned to the Lower House.

孟昭漢 字羨亭 歲四十八

選舉地　黑龍江省

籍貫　山東省兗州府鄒縣

住址　北京順治門內中街胡同三十一

君秉性醇厚。篤於友愛。居恆勤謹自持。不苟言笑。與人交。喜勸善規過。然不爲疾言遽色。故雖剛直不阿。而未嘗辭氣和婉。曲詞誘導。雖惡惡如仇。而不爲小人之嫉恨。自幼天資聰慧過人。敏於悟性。然又謙虛好問。故其進愈猛。弱冠即以能文見知於時。及長。淹通經史。由邑庠生考補增生。嗣於辦理地方保甲。由地方官紳舉充孝廉方正。朝考列二等。二年。因辦理地方防務。肅淸後。防務案內。保爲異常勞績。免補本班。以知縣分省試用。部議核准後。時値武昌起義。民國告成。及至國會告成。被選爲衆議院議員。國會解散後。歸里獨居。無所表見。又至國會重開。始入京仍爲議員。

君秉性醇厚にして友愛に篤く、居常恪謹自ら持して輕々しく言笑せす。善を勸めて過を規するを喜ぶと雖も辭色共に和平婉曲なり。故に硬直阿らざるも未だ甞て小人の恨を受けざるなり。幼より天資聰慧人に過ぎ悟性に敏なるも謙讓以て問を好び。弱冠即ち能文を以て知らる。長するに及び經史に通曉し、邑庠生を以て增生に補せられ嗣で地方の保甲事務を處理して功あり、爲に府經歷に擢用せらる。宣統元年地方官紳により考廉方正に舉げられ朝試の二舉に列す。二年地方の防務事宜を處理して肅清の後ち知縣を以て試用さる事となれり。時適ま第一革命の事起りて民國成立す。正式國會の成立に際し遂に選ばれて衆議院議員と爲る。國會解散して後ち田園に歸臥して政見を發表する爲く悠々自適す。國會重ねて開くるに及び復た出でゝ仍は衆院議員と爲る。

Mr. Meng Chae-han, another name Shen Ting, Tsou prefecture, Yeu Chou-fu Chonfu Shantung district, forty eight years old. Warm hearted he is and kinds to his friends; he is vigorous to himself and does not talk or laugh carelessly; he encourages good and corrects mistake, yet he appears weak and peaceful. He never made enemy though he is sturdy. From youth he is very bright and quick to understand, still loves to ask others opinion with utmort modesty. As a young man he was known as a good writer; growing older he had a thorough knowledge of the chinese ethics. He was once appointed the village scholar. Later superintendng the local guard he did a great deed, on that account he was promo ed to the position of the city guardian. Iu the first year of Hsun tung he advanced to the positon of Kan-lienfang cheng from the local high official, then he was admitted to the second degree of Chang hsih. In the second year he looked after the local defence and was to be appointed a governor. At the time the first Revolution broke out, the Republic was established. On the organization of the national Parliament he was elected a member of the Lower House. In short time, Parliament was dissolved by Yuan, and he returned to his home to rest himself, but not to talk his political view. Fortunately, the representative government has been restored and so the Parliament to which he was called to take the old seat he held in the Lower House.

易宗夔　字蔚儒　歳四十二

選舉地　外蒙古札薩克圖汗部

籍　貫　湖南省湘潭縣

住　址　北京潘家河沿四十五號

君幼孤貧稍長。知勤學。年十八。遂籍學官爲諸生。年少才美。喜爲詩歌。及駢體文。丁酉戊戌間。梁啓超在湖南總敎時務學堂。並與譚嗣同熊希齡唐才常等。設立南學會湘報館。著文講學。開通風氣。君於其時。著以弱爲強論登之湘報。羣士大譁。甲辰。遊學日本。以學費不繼。返國。主長沙各學校講席。已酉冬。由湖南諮議局被選爲資政院議員。庚戌九月。開會。以彈劾軍機大臣慶親王。見稱於時。武昌事起。君乃棄職經海上返湘。民國元年入都。由陸徵祥薦爲法典編纂會纂修。是時同會與統一共和黨合併國民黨。君爲本黨政事部主任幹事。二年。國會成。由外蒙古札薩克圖汗被選爲衆議院議員。旋被舉爲憲法起草委員。國會解散後。挈眷回湘。與諸鑛商營實業。絕口不談時政。及今年三月。始走上海會合舊時議員。倡議規復二年國會。七月。始來京供職云。

君幼より孤にして貧、稍や長じて學に勤め年十八諸生と爲る。年少にして才美、詩歌及び駢體文を作る。丁酉戊戌間、梁啓超が湖南務學堂總敎として譚嗣同熊希齡唐才常等と南學湘報館を設立して文を著し學を講ずるや、君即ち弱を以て強と爲する論を著して世論を喚起したり。甲辰の歳日本に游學し、歸國後長沙各學校訓師となり、已酉の多資政院議員となり、庚戌九月開會するや慶親王を彈劾す。第一革命の事義を起すや職を棄で湖南に歸る民國元年北京に入り法典編纂會纂修に任ず。當時同盟會と統一和黨と合併して國民黨を組織す、君其の政事部主任幹事と爲る。二年外蒙古札薩克圖汗より推されて衆議院議員と爲り、旋て憲法起草委員に擧げらる。國會解散後、家族を挈げて歸省し、鑛山業者と共同して實業を經營して時事を談らず。本年三月上海に赴きて舊議員と合して國民黨、倡議規復二年國會の復活を主張し、目的旣に達して今全現に衆議院議員と爲る。

Mr. I-tsung-ku i, another name Wei-ju Hsiang-tan prefecture, Hu-nan district. Fourty two years old. He was a poor orphan and began study after grown up: At his 18th year he became a student: He was a bright boy, then, composed verses remarkably well. Sometime, Mr. Liang-chi-chao as the dean of the Hu-nan political school, established the N u h iao Hsiang pao huan with Jan-Ssu tung, Hsiang hsi ling and, Tang Tsai Chang in view of publishing books as well as to use it as lecture hall. Then he wrote a book entitled "Subjugation of strong by weak" which gave much stimurant to the intellectual world. Once, he studied in Japan from where he returned to take up positions of teacher at the C ang sha schools. Soon after he was nominated to be a member of the advisory council while convened in september, next year he was appointed. He impeached Ching hsin wang at the meeting which undoubtedly offended the Royality. When the first Revolution broke out he returned to Hu nan throwing off his position. He engaged in drafting the code of laws, at Peking in the first year of the Republic, At the time, union party, and unionest Republican Party united and organized National party. He was nominated to be the Director of the political department of the new party. In the second year he was requested by Su-ko tu-han outer Mohgolia, to represent his province in the Lower House and accepted the request. Subsequently he was appointed the committee man to draft the constitution. An the dissolution of Parliament he returned home with his family and engaged in the mining business. In march, 1916, he went to Shanghai with intention of restoration of the republican order. Soon his hope has been realized and now he is a member of the Lower House.

易次乾　字次乾　歲三十六

君天資明敏透徹にして敢為の氣象に富み時勢の才幹なり。前清の偽廩生を以て若埔水陸師學堂及び水雷學堂を卒業す。前清政治の壞敗を慨して學を棄て、竟に革命を謀り、清吏之を捕ふること急なり、乃ち香江に走せて商に隱れ、日に書報を以て民族民權民生主義を鼓吹す。尋で同盟會南部幹事となる。辛亥の歲廣東獨立するや香軍の參謀に任じ並に北伐の事を經營したり。南北統一後宋敦仁が農部幹事及び公報處々長林部總長となるや、君は同部の編纂僉事及び公報處々長

選舉地　廣東

籍貫　廣東肇慶府鶴山縣

住址　北京驛馬市街金星保險公司

君為剛直堅強。而頭腦明晰。不執偏私自誤。於前清時以優廩生。黃浦水陸師學堂及水雷學堂畢業。清政失綱。乃棄所學。潛謀革命。清吏捕之急。乃走香江。隱於商。日以書報。鼓吹民族民權民生主義。所辦新報數種。皆輪灌革命思想。發揚民主精神。一時革命風潮風起水湧。尋被舉為同盟會南部幹事。益端力實行革命事業。辛亥粵省光復。任香軍參謀。並經營比伐事。冀共和告成。宋君敦仁。長農林部。邀君共襄部務。任該部編纂僉事。旋被舉為衆議院議員。時袁氏違法。君反對袁氏。崢崢有聲。暨袁氏非法解散國會。君遂南下。逃亡海上。改圖實業。與唐少川君等組織金星保險公司。被舉為該公司總理。經營三年。成效大著。袁氏稱帝。海宇騷然。四方志士咸集滬上。以為西南義帥應。君奔走其測。多所盡力。袁氏死。黎氏繼。國會復活。君復充衆議院議員職。

の職に任じたり。民國二年舉げられて衆議院議員と為る。既にして袁政府が非法を以て國會を解散するや君南下して上海に逃れ、實業に從事して、曾照儀等と金星保險公司を組織して其の總理となりたり。帝制問題發生して海內騷然として四方の志士上海に集るや、君其の間に奔走して盡力する所移し。袁氏死し黎氏繼ぎて國會復活するに及び、君復た北上して衆議院議員の職に就く

Mr. I Tzu-huan, Hao shan, Kugng-tung Chao-ching fu, thirty six years old. He is sagacious as well as very resolute and full of business talent. During the late imperial reign he graduated the Hsiang navy school and Topedo school with honour. Finding the corruption of the Emperial Government he gave his study and planed secretly the revolution. The secret service man tried to arrest him, he quietly escaped to Hsiang Chiang and hid among merchants. He wrote many letters daily expounding the rights of people, race, and man. Subsquently he was nominated to be the manager of the southern branch of union party. In 1910 Kwantung declared independence, and he made the staff-officer of the army and planed the invasion of North. After North and South united to form one Republic he made compiler and director of the official gazette Bureau under the direction of the minister of agriculture. Sang-jen. In the second year of the Republic he was chozen by the people of his district to hold a seat in the Lower House. When Yuan Government disouted Parliament unconstitutionary he went to South, Shanghai and engaged in business. He organized the Hsing insurance company with Tung chao and he made president of it. When the question of restoration of Emperial government came up the country boiled over and the patriots gathered to Shanghai from all directions. He was one of pirots around which the anti-emperial plans were laid down. Mr. Li succeeding Yuan reconvened Parliament and called the old member of both House. He is now in Peking holding a seat in the Lower House.

杭辛齋　字辛齋　歳四十七

選舉地　浙江省
籍　貫　浙江省海寧縣
住　址　北京琉璃廠西南園

君は前清の中書科中書にして光緒二十三年、天津に於て國聞報を發刊す、北支那に於ける新聞の嚆矢なり。庚子以後北洋官報商報等の要務に任じ、嗣で北京に於て中華報、京華日報を創立す。後ち筆禍を買ひて一年の禁錮に處せられたるも有力者の庇護によりて漸く免かれ、浙江省に歸りて實業の振興に努む。旋て農工研究會々長、浙江農會總理に舉げらる。農工雜誌及び愛國白話報を發刊す。第一革命の軍起るや、同省の匪徒及び旗兵皆な機に乘じて亂を唱ふ、均しく君の盡力によりて治安を維持するを得たり。民國成立後、君乃ち社會事業に盡力して迭に國民協濟會幹事長、浙江工會總理、國民公所主任、團體聯合會副會長等の職に舉げらる。又た漢民日報を創立して民生主義を主張す。國會成立に際し衆議院議員に當選し、後ち帝制反對を以て捕はれ獄中に在る者七箇月、共和恢復して後ち獄を出で仍は衆議院議員の職に就く。

君爲前清中書科中書。光緒廿三年。剏辦國聞報於天津。北方之有新聞事業。自此始。庚子後。尤多盡力於新聞事業。歷充北洋官報商報要任。嗣來京創辦中華報。京華日報。北方風氣之開通。多出自兩報提倡之力。後因叛議國民捐爲常軸所忌。以妄議朝政爲詞。處以遞藉禁錮。在獄年。經紳耆力保。留辦浙江省實業。由浙撫奏。請報可。旋被舉爲農工研究會會長。浙江農會總理。叛辦農工襍誌。及愛國白話報。皆風行一時。辛亥革命起。浙省匪黨及旗兵皆欲乘機倡亂。均賴君竭力維持。得免糜爛。光復後。君仍盡力於社會事業。迭被舉爲國民協濟會幹事長。浙江工會總理。國民公所主任。團體聯合會副會長等之職。又叛辦漢民日報。提倡民生主義。遂于第一屆國會常選爲衆議院議員。帝制發生。以反對故被捕。陷獄中者七閱月。共和恢復。始得出獄。復充衆議院議員。

民國之精華　（傳記）　杭辛齊先生

一百四十五

Mr. Hang-hsin-Chi, another name Hsin-chi, Hai-ning prefecture, Che-chiang district, forty seven years old. He was doctor of letters under the Empire and published the Kuo Wen-pao at Tien-sin in the 23rd year of Kuoh su, which was first newspaper ever published in northern China. He held the important position at the Pe yang Official Report and the commercial news. Then, he established the Chung-hui News, and the King-hui Daily Papers offending the authority of the time he had been sentenced to one year's imprisonment, but he was saved from the penalty by the good offices of dignitories. Returning to Chi-chiang district he did much in promotion of industry. He made president of the industrial investigation association, and the Che-chiang agricultural association. At this time he published the agricultural and industrial magazin and the Ai-kuo pa huo News. At the time of the first Revolution brigand of the district and the soldiers tried to break order, but his effort prevailed and was able to maintain peace and order. After the Republic was organized, he devoted himself improve the social condition. President of the National Aid Society, the Che-chiang industrial association, chief of the National Public Office, and Vice-President of the union of associations were the offices he held, different time. Also he established the Han-ming Daily Paper and empounded the popular rights. On the organization of Parliament he was elected a member of the House of Commons and having opposed bigorously the Emperial scheme, he was imprisoned for 7 months. The Republic has been restored and he is released and returned to the Lower House to held the old seat.

金溶熙　字溶仲　歲五十一

選舉地　浙江省

籍貫　浙江省杭縣

住址　北京施家胡同二十二

君賦性堅實。長於經營工商。遂以是見知於世。而浙中人則稱爲織物專家。以其曾繼金源泰號之後。製造絹織物。並曾創辦金源昶絹織物商號。振新絹織物廠。日新絹織物公司等。織物之專門營業也。宣統三年。浙商總會推舉君赴東考察實業。因武昌起義。未果行。是年。辦保衛團。君自任團長。復歷充全浙國貨維持會會長。綢業公所總董。絲綢觀成機業三學校校董。商務總會董。兼評議員。改良織物公會會長。民國二年。公舉君爲赴東大正博覽會觀光團團員。同年被選爲衆議院議員。議會解散後。仍南旋經營實業。並指揮後進。示以趨避棄取之機。及國會復活。適被舉爲商會聯合會代表。遂以此名義入都。復入衆議院爲議員。

君賦性堅實にして商工業の經營に長す。曾て金源泰號の後を繼ぎて絹織物を製造し、また曾て金源昶絹織物商會、振新絹織物廠、日新絹織物公司等織物專門の工場商店を創設經營し、浙江省中有名の商店なり。宣統三年浙江商務總會は君を推して日本に赴き實業を視察調査せしめたるも、適ま第一革命の事起りて未だ行くを果さず。保衛團を組織して君自ら其團長に任ず。復ヵ浙江全省國貨維持會々長、綢業公所總董、絲綢觀成機業の三學校々董、

商務總會々董兼評議員、改良織物公會々長等の職に歷充したり。民國二年衆議院議員に當選す。同年大正博覽會觀光團員として日本に赴く實業を視察して歸國す。國會解散後は仍ほ南旋して專ら實業の振興を圖り、後進を指導す。此次共和復活するや適ま商務總會聯合會代表とし て北上す。旋て再び國會の召集に遭ひ君復た衆議院議員の職に就く。

Mr. Chin Jung-hsi, otherwise called Jung-chung, is a thoroughgoing businessman being the founder of various textile fabric companies in China. In 1911 he was to be sent over to Japan with a view to investigate the business condition of the country, but owing to the outbreak of the 1st revolution he was not able to accomplish his object. During the revolution, the order preservation society was established of which he was appointed the president. Besides, his connection as a business man is very extensive, he himself being the president of various commercial and industrial associations. In the 2nd year of the Republic, he was elected a member of the Parliament and went over to Japan to investigate the business condition of the country. With the breaking up of the Parliament he devoted himself to his own business. However with the Restoration of the Republic he went to Peking representing the commercial union. He has also taken up the membership of the House of Commons.

金詒厚　字篤生　歳三十二

選舉地　直隸省

籍貫　直隸省大興縣

住址　北京西單牌樓一條胡同

君少穎悟。而專勵學問。識見豐富。有新舊素養。光緒二十八年。入北京順天中學堂肄業。課餘輒縱談時事。畢業後。升入順天高等學堂唯時政局漸益索亂。黨禁日嚴。有志之士亦輩出。君居校中。時形憤慨。審知事變。當前以無所表見爲憾。宣統二年試。畢業列優等。三年就聘爲山東高等學堂英文教員。武昌首義。君約同志二三。共旋里。謀建設。比民國成立。遂被選爲直隸省議會議員。二年。被選爲衆議院議員。海內粗平。當局之暴橫漸肆。國勢亦日微。君則抱憤獨深。杜門謝客。四年。籌安會議起。爰藉細事赴蒙古。以避地絕人之行。作韜光養晦之計。洎滇黔義起。始再入京師。及國會復活。仍就衆議院議員之職。

君少より穎悟にして專ら學を賜み、識見豊富なり。光緒二十八年北京順天中學校に入り、卒業後順天高等學校に入る。時適ま政局漸く紊亂して黨禁日に嚴しく、有志の士亦た多く君が同窓中より輩出す。君隠忍して時を待ち、宣統二年優等を以て卒業し、三年聘せられて山東高等學校英文教師と爲る。武昌義起るや、君は二三の同志と約して郷里に歸りて呼應の策を計り、民國成立する頃、途に選ばれて直隸省議會議員と爲る。民國二年衆議院議員に當選す。時や將に海內略ば平ぎて常局の橫暴漸く肆に、國勢亦た日に傾く。君則ち時事を慷慨して憂憤の極途に門を杜して客を謝す。四年籌安會發起されて帝制問題起るや、君乃ち遠く蒙古に赴きイ韜光養晦の計を爲したり。雲南貴州義を舉ぐるに及び始めて再び北京に入り、國會復活するに及びて仍ほ復た衆議院議員の職に就きたり。

民國之精華　（傳記）　金詒厚先生

Mr. Chin-i-hou, another name Tu-sheng, Tai hsing prefecture, Chi-li district, thirty three years old. From childhood to manhood he has been a brilliant scholar of profound knowledge of the old and new. In the 28th year of Kuank hsu he entered in the Pekin Shun-tien Middle School, after the completion of study there proceeded to the Shun-tien Higher School. The political confusion was brewing everywhere and political parties recieved undue restraint. Many of the political leaders came out of his alma mater but he waited proper time for him to rise up. In the second year of Hsuan-tung he graduated the school with honour and next year he secured a chair of english professor at the Shan-treng Higher School. Soon Wu-chang province rose up against the Emperial Government: he returned to his native town after made understanding with his friends in view of effecting the revoluional caurse. About the time the new Republic nearly established he was chosen as a member of the Chi li District Legislature. In the second year of the Republic he was elected the member of the Lower House. As soon as the new organization completed persons in power abused their rights and suspended the national Parliament, it secured certain that at the time, another trouble was brewing. His patriotic indignation drove him to give up all his social intercourse and closed his door against callers. In the fourth for the Chou an hui was organized with the aim of supporting Yuan's views and of restoration of the emperial order, he travelled for to Mongolia to find the means of checking the emperial progress. On the up-rising of Wun-nan Kuli-chuan, he went again to Peking and re-occupies the seat he held in the Lower House a year ago.

金承新　字子銘　歲四十三

選舉地　山東省

籍　貫　山東省寧陽縣

住　址　北京宣武門外永光寺內

君天資明敏。富於學識。即奉山東巡撫
李委。充河防局文案。兼中游稽查。清
光緒二十五年。爲山東巡撫袁保用知
縣指分浙江候補。歷充紹興府屬酒稅
委員。法審局委員等差。二十六年。山
東拳匪肇亂。袁撫調委辦理兗沂府屬
團練事宜。二十八年。游歷日本。考查
政治實業。二十九年。回國。魯撫楊委
充河防局文案。三十三年。因病回籍。
督。農桑會會長。巡警教練所董事。宣
辦理地方公益。歷充寗陽高等小學監
統三年。奉兗州府知縣陶委辦兗屬團
防清鄉事宜。民國元年。被選爲衆議院
議員。二年。國會遭政府非法蹂躪解
散。君慨然歸里閉門謝客。大有披髮入
山之志。帝制澎漲。君更憤憤。迨共和
復活。國會重開。君躍起曰。今而後可
盡吾職矣。乃復到院。

り、又た寗陽高等小學校監督、農桑會々長、巡警教練所
董事等に歷充し、宣統三年兗州府陶知縣の委託により其
の管下の治安保警事務を處理す。民國元年選ばれて衆議
院議員と爲る。二年國會が政府の非法蹂躪に遭ふや、君
慨然として鄉里に蟄居し、杜門客を謝し、帝制問題發生
するや抑欝甚だし。國會重ねて開くるに及び跼躍して召
集に應じ仍は復た衆議院議員たり。

君天資明敏にして學識に富む。青春早くも山東李巡撫の
命を奉じて河防局書記に任じ、中流の稽査を兼ねたり。
光緒二十五年山東巡撫より知縣に保薦されて浙江省に
分たる。紹興府管下の酒稅委員、法審局委員等の職に當
り、二十六年拳匪亂を起すや、袁巡撫の命を受けて兗沂
府管下の團練事務を處理す。二十八日本に游歷して政
治及び實業を調查す、翌年歸國して再び河防局書記とな
る。三十三年病を以て田園に歸臥しつゝ地方の公益・計

Mr. Chin-cheng-hsin, anothername Jzu ming, Ning yang prefecture, Shan-tung, forty three
years old. This brilliant gentleman of profound knowledge was, for the first time appointed by the
governor general of Shan tung, the clerk of the River Defence Bureau, then he was very young. In
the 20th year of Kuang-hsu he was appointed a governor Che chiang district by the governor general,
Yuan of Shan tung. At the sametime, he made the liquor tax collector in the city of Shao-hsing, and
a commissioner of the legal investigation commission. In the 26th year, at the time of the boxer uprising
he was directed by the governor-general Yuan to look after the affairs of the city of Chung chim. In
the 28th year he crossed Japan Sea to study the condition of industry and politics of that country and
next year, he took office of secretary in the River Defence Bureau. In the 33rd year he returned to,
his home on account of his health; yet he could not refrain from doing public good; he made himself a
counsellor to the local welfare, superintended the Ning-yang higher grammor school, made the president
of the farm association, and lastly the director of the police school. In the third year of Hsuan tung
he was commissioned by the governor of Chang chon fu to took after the pense and welfare within the
limits. In the first year of the Republic the people of his district sent him to the Lower House which
was dissolved, next year. He returned home indignantly and kept his door closed, for he could not bear
to see any politician at the time. When the question of establishment for retrogression to the
Emperial order came up his disappointment was very great. Fortunately the Republican government
was restored and so the National Parliament. He accepting gladly the call to the House he went to
Peking to resume the old seat in the Lower House.

金尙詵 字苑秋 歲四十九

選舉地　浙江省
籍　貫　浙江省台州溫嶺縣
住　址　北京南關市口二十七號

君爲人精明强幹。洞悉事理。思想活潑。而行動謹嚴。生平不苟言笑。不輕然諾。居常以緘默自持。然一有發揮。則又娓娓動人。聽者無不爲之感化。常訓其晚輩曰。求工辯。須自少說話起。求幹練。須自少做事起。與人交。淡而能久。以其能以恕道待人。雖疾惡崇善。而未嘗稍露鋒芒也。前淸時。歷充本邑民團水利工藝禁烟各局總理。並創辦中學校及自治研究所。前後從事公益者共十六年。旋被選爲本省諮議局議員。民國二年。國會成立。被選爲衆議院議員。國會解散後。歸里欝欝獨居。不談時政。直至共和再造。國會重開。始入京仍爲議員。兼浙江顧問官。

民國之精華　（傳記）金尙詵先生

君人と爲り精明强幹にして事理を洞悉す。思想活潑にして行動謹嚴、生平苟も言笑せず、居常緘默自ら持するも、一たび口を開けば娓々として人を動かす。前淸時代曾て本邑民國水利工藝禁烟各局の總理に歷充し、並に中學校及び自治研究所を創立經營し、前後して地方の公益事業に盡力すること計十六年、旋て選ばれて本省諮議局議員と爲る。民國二年正式國會議員選舉に會して衆議院議員に當選す。國會解散さる〻や、快々として鄕里に歸り、獨居抑欝また時事を談せず。旣にして共和政治復興して約法は恢復され國會亦た重ねて開院さる。君始めて愁眉を開き、出で〻召集に應じ　現に衆議院議員の職に就き、浙江都督府顧問を兼ぬ。

一百四十九

Mr. Jung Shang-shen, otherwise called Yuan-chin, age forty nine, is a native of Tai-chuan, Wen-ling, Che-chiang. He is a gentleman of sound understanding and active ideas. He is a man of few words but once start on his argument he would not stop until he convinces others. In the previous Chinese regime he was connected with various offices such as riparian works, fine arts and prohibition of opium smoking etc. He established a middle school and the civic body institution of which he became the director. For the space of sixteen years he was interested in pushing local public works. In the 2nd year of the Republic he was returned for the House of Commons but when that legislative assembly was closed, he went back to his home where he never allowed himself to talk about current topics. With the Restoration of the Republic and the reopening of the Parliament he responded to the call and resumed his Parliamentary function. Besides, he is an adviser to the governor general of Che-chung.

金兆棪　字仲蓀　歲三十八

選舉地　浙江省
籍　貫　浙江省金華縣
住　址　北京石燈庵

君爲人惇篤。朴直不欺。然性聰慧。好
讀書。多所領悟。故其文采風流。亦超
出儕輩。弱冠時。即以博通羣書自期。
旋復立志棄舊從新。以前淸鄉人入北
京大學堂。畢業後。授官中書。歷任浙
江金華地方自治籌備處坐辦。浙江金
華府中學堂監督。浙江第七中學校校
長。浙江全省農業敎育講習所所長。浙
江臨時省議會議員。浙江永嘉縣知事。
福建福淸縣知事。民國旣興。曾充浙江
都督府機要秘書。旋當選爲參議院議
員。兼充憲法起草委員。國會解散。歸
里不復與聞政事。惟時時從事於公益
事宜之提倡。及國會復活。遂來京。復
爲參議院議員。

君人と爲り惇篤にして朴直欺かず。然かも性聰慧にして
讀書を好み造詣深く、其の文采風流亦た儕輩に超出す。弱
冠の時群書に博通するを以て自ら期す。旋で復た志を立
て、舊を棄て新に從ひ、前淸の擧人を以て北京大學堂に
入り、卒業後中書を授けらる。浙江金華地方自治籌備處
坐辦、浙江金華府中學校監督、浙江第七中學校々長、浙江
全省農業敎育講習所々長、浙江臨時省議會議員、浙江永
嘉縣知事、福建福淸縣知事等の官職に歷任したり。民國

樹立後、浙江都督府機要秘書に任じ、正式國會の成立に
際し、選ばれて參議院議員と爲りて大政を議し、兼ねて
憲法起草委員に舉げらる。國會解散さる、に及び、南旋
して鄉關に韜晦し、暫らく政事を聞かずして、唯い地方
公益事業の振興を主張す。共和政治復活して國會重ねて
開かるゝに及び、君復た召集に應じ、家門を出でゝ北京
に抵り、仍ほは參議院議員の職に就く。

Mr. Chin Chao-o, otherwise called Ching-un, age thirty eight, is a native of Chin-hu hsien, Che-chiang hsing. He is simple and straightforward being very well read man. His personal refinement distinguishes him from others. Casting away the old he took to the study of the new. He studied in the Peking university and later he became the president and inspector of middle schools in his province and a member of the local assembly as well as the governor of the province. With the establishment of the Republic he was appointed the private secretary of the governor general of Che-chiang. When the Parliament was brought into existence he was elected a member of the Senate and was on the committee for the drafting of the constitution. With the dissolution of the Parliament he returned to his home and turned a deaf ear to politics. He only devoted himself to the upbuilding of local interest. When the reopening of the Parliament was announced he responded to the call and went up to Peking where he resumed the senatorial function.

胡壽昌 字擎懷 歲四十八

選舉地　湖南省

籍　貫　湖南省寶慶

住　址　北京西城屯絹胡同棗林街

君賦性高曠。自幼從伯兄曙軒修陽明學。不屑從事科舉。海內維新後。同邑英俊。多赴日本求學。君以親老不獲遠遊。亟遣子晃往學海軍。而獨留國內籌辦一邑學務。時新學阻障甚鉅。君不避艱險。與留東同邑諸君。內外提挈。卒成風氣。縣屬各校女塾暨駐省師範中校。皆嘗持教鐸。戊申劉君人熙招君充優級師範總務。旋由蔡君鍔雷君颷先後招赴桂林。充陸軍學堂教職。庚戌遊京師。任陸軍部錄事官。辛亥改革。南歸襄助湖南招撫事宜。民國元年。選充臨時省議會爲員。二年。被選爲衆議院議員。國會解散。歸蟄園。清理全縣反正以後財用及公產。帝制亂起。滇黔倡義。君赴滬與同志協謀倒袁。及國會重開。遂來京。仍爲議員。

民國之精華　（傳記）　胡壽昌先生

君人と爲り高曠。幼より從伯兄曙軒に從ひ、陽明學を修め、科舉に從事するを屑しとせず。海內維新の後、同邑の英俊多く日本に留學す。君親老いたるを以て遠遊するを獲ず。子息晃をH本に遣はして海軍を學ばしめ。獨り國內に留まりて一邑の學務を創辦す。時に新學阻礙甚だ大なり。君艱險を避けず、留東同邑諸君と、內外提挈し、卒に風氣を成す。縣下各校女塾、及び駐省師範中學、省に嘗て敎鐸を執れり。戊申劉照君招かれて優級師範學務に省長たり。尋いで蔡鍔君需鑾君より前後招かれて桂林に赴き、陸軍學堂に敎官たり。庚戌、北京に遊び、陸軍部錄事官に任せらる。辛亥改革の時。南歸して湖南招撫事宜に充てらる。民國元年選ばれて臨時省議會議員と爲る。二年選ばれて衆議院議員と爲る。國會解散後歸りて故國に蟄居し、全縣反正以後の財用及び公產を清理す。帝制の亂起り、滇黔義を倡ふるや、君上海に赴きて同志と議し、袁を倒さんことを謀る。國會重ねて開かるゝに及び、上京して仍は議員と爲る。

Mr. Hu Shou-ping otherwise known as Chih Huai, age forty eight, is a native of Pao-ching, Ho-nan hsing. While young he studied classics with his uncle but seeing the change of the current thought in China he was desirous of going to Japan like others but owing to the fact that he had aged parents he sent his son to Japan to study naval affairs. He stayed at home and was a village teacher, teaching in various girl, normal and middle schools. In 1910 he went to Peking and was appointed the secretary of the military department. In the 1st year of the Republic he was a member of the local assembly and in the 2nd year a member of the House of Commons. With the dissolution of the Parliament he returned to his home. As soon as the Republic was established he became again a member of the Parliament.

胡祖舜　字玉齊　歲三十二

選舉地　湖北省

籍　貫　湖北省嘉魚縣

住　址　北京宣武門外南橫街大川淀七號

君自幼慷慨好義。戊戌政變後。即立志
從事革命。辛亥之役。當其運動時代。
君爲革命機關本部參議。奔走部置歷
有年所。八月十九夕之役。躬與其事。
歷充都督府參謀秘書。及管理交通事
務。迨清兵南下。調充鄂軍輜重管帶。
擔任全軍後方勤務。南北統一充副總
統府參議。兼任漢口警察幫辦。及漢口
警察上局局長。同時又兼任中央稽勳
局名譽審議員。及湖北稽勳局調查會
審議兼審調查員。旋授陸軍少將銜並四
等嘉禾章。國會成立。被選爲衆議院
議員。癸丑之役君以嫌疑被遣。退處江
漢。專精從事著述。帝制問題起。君糾
集同志。謀舉義師。因事前洩漏。功敗
乖成。又創辦武漢新報。大肆鼓吹。未
幾。共和再造。遂應召入京。仍復就議
員職。

君幼より慷慨義を好み、戊戌政變後即ち志を立てゝ革命
の事に從ふ。辛亥の舉義に先ち君は革命機關本部參議と
して奔走盡力す。既にして武昌義を起すや、君は鄂軍都
督府參謀秘書及び交通事務管理の任に當り、清軍南下す
るに追び君乃ち民軍の輜重管帶となる。南北統一後、副
總統府參議に任じ、漢口警察部幫辦及び漢口警察上局々
長を兼ぬ。同時に又た中央稽勳局名譽審議員及び湖北稽
勳局調查會審議兼調查員に任じたり。旋て功によりて陸
軍少將銜を授けられ、並に四等嘉禾章を獎せらる。正式國
會議員選舉に際し衆議院議員に當選す。第二革命の變に
處して嫌疑を受け、君暫らく退いて江漢の間に韜晦し、
專ら筆硯に親みて著作に從事す。帝制問題起るや、君早
くも同志を糾合して義を計り、事洩れて敗る。又た武漢
新報を創辦して大に共和擁護を鼓吹す。未だ幾ならず國
會復活し、君亦た召集に應じて衆議院議員たり。

Mr. Hu Tsu-shun, known as Yu-chi, age thirty three, is a native of Chao-yu, Hu-pei
province. He is heroic in temper, and was deeply interested in public affairs which fact naturally
brought him into contact with revolutionists. When the revolution took place, he was an adviser to the
headquarters of the revolutionay party. When Wu-chung was in trouble, he occupied the post of secretary-
ship to the governor general and also had charge of communications. He was also interested in
commissariat department. When the south and the north were united, he was an adviser to the vice president,
and had interest with the Hankow police at the same time, he was an honorary judge of the Central
Merit and Decoration Bureau, as well as that of the Hu-pei province. When the Parliament was formed,
he was elected as a member of the House of Commons. In the second revolution, he was suspected
by the government so that he in private he devoted himself to writing. On the occasion of the outbreak
of the Imperial movement, he with his fellow men attempted to take a strong attitude, but was frustrated
in his attempt. When the Republic was restored, he was elected for the House of Commons.

胡鄂公　字新三　歲三十二

選舉地　湖北省
籍貫　湖北省江陵縣
住址　北京鮑家街

君性豪邁不羈。剛毅果決。幼時。即嶄然露頭角。於鄉里。喜結納。好爲維新之論。嘗於鄉塾中。創立日新輔仁諸社。同學咸推戴焉。稍長。游學京保懃諸校。目擊清政暴虐。乃倡立共和會。聯合同志數萬人。奔走呼號。幾遍禹域。辛亥武昌義起。君任鄂寅水陸指揮。首挫清軍之銳。湘鸒諸省。始因之響應。嗣鄂都督黎元洪。以清政府根基未能搖動。乃使君之燕趙。甫至。即成立北方革命協會。衆舉君爲北方總司令。明攻暗襲。退遏震動。清廷始宣布共和。民國元年。任荆州旗民善後督辦。一年。被選爲衆議院議員。至國會解散後。復歷任法政專門校長。公府政治諮議。四川將軍署秘書。四川宣慰使等諸職。當帝制發生。滇黔首義。陳四川將軍。主持於內。君奔走於外。四川遂以獨立。君嗜力古文。農林諸學。手選五十家論文書牘一卷。古文詞粹八卷。著有原農。原林各一卷云。

民國之精華　（傳記）　胡鄂公先生

君性豪邁不羈にして剛毅果決なり。幼時即ち嶄然頭角を露し、曾て鄉塾中に於て日新輔仁諸社を創立して同學咸な推戴したり。稍々長じて各地に游學し、清政の暴虐を慨し共和會を組織して同志數萬人を聯合し、南船北馬殆んど全國を周游す。第一革命當時君鄂軍の水陸指揮に任じて清軍の銳に當る。嗣で黎元洪の命を受けて燕趙各地に赴き即ち北方革命協會を成立して北方總司令と爲る。二年選清廷退位後、民國元年荆州旗民善後督辦に任す。

ばれて衆議院議員となる。國會解散後、復た法政專門學校々長、總統府政治諮議、四川將軍衙門秘書、四川宣慰使等の諸職に歷任し、帝制問題發生して雲貴兩省義を倡ふるや、陳四川將軍は內に主持して君は外に奔走し、四川遂に獨立するに至れり。君古文並に農林諸學の造詣深く、手選五十家論文書牘一卷、古文詞粹八卷、原農、原林各一卷の著作あり。國會恢復後再び入京して、仍ほ衆議院議員たり。

Mr. Hu-i-kung, another name Hsin san, Chiang-ling Prefecture, Hu pe District, thirty three years old. He is the most undanuted and independent, sturdy and resolute. He was distinguished as boy from others, and once organized several associations in a town school and commanded the respect of all. Growing a little older went round to study, and disgusting of the despotic administration of the Chin Dynasty he organized the Republican association which members were counted as many as ten thousands. He made campaign trip all over the country for the advancement of the republican course. At the time of the First Revolution, commanding army and navy held off the army of the Empire. Later, by order of Yuan-hung he went to North and organized the Northern Revolutional Society and he made Commander-in-Chief of the Northern army. On the retirement of Chin Dynasty he was appointed to the Governor of the Ching chan in the first year of the Republic. Next year, he was elected a member of the Lower House. Then, he made President of the Law and Politics school, as the National Legislature was dissolved. The Counsellor of the President's political Council, Secretary at the Ssi chuan military Department, and the envoy to Ssi chuan here the offices held by him during a short periods. The question of the imperial restoration drove the two Districts of Yun kuei to declare independence against the Yuan's Government. Governor-General, Chen-huan, of Ssi-chuan maintained the order within and Mr. Hu ex hanged views and plans with other Districts, and finally the District declared independence. He is a man learned, particularly classics and agricultural science and wrote many books. He is now a member of the Lower House.

胡璧城 字蘗文 歲四十六

選舉地 安徽省
籍　貫 安徽省涇縣
住　址 北京ノ庫胡同

君秉性清高。言論風采。皆過異庸俗。然謙和厚重。以禮自持。絕無虛驕習氣。稚齡即能爲詩文。吐芳新俊。鄉人珍重之。及長尤博及群書。經史而外。諸子百家。皆取備讀。均能發微抉伏。得其眞精。中年尤專攻于理義之書。屏棄考据詞章之學。及海內維新。醉心西學。於新書無所不視。以前淸丁酉科舉人。北京大學校師範專科畢業。在本省。從事育英之業。辦理安慶府中學。後諮議局成立。充秘書長。光復時。被舉爲安徽臨時省議會議長。聲望益著。民國元年被選爲臨時參議院議員。二年正式國會成立。常選爲參議院議員。國會停止後。曾充審計院審計官。本年及國會重開。君辭審計官職。仍應召集現復爲參議院議員職。

胡璧城 先生

君秉性清高にして言論風采皆な遇に庸俗に異るものあり。然かも謙讓にして溫和、自ら持するに禮を以てし、絕へて虛驕の風なし。少年即ち詩文を能くして吐芳新俊、鄉人之を珍重す。長じて益々群籍を涉獵し、諸子百家の書均しく徹を開ら伏を抉って其の眞義に精通す。中年專ら理義の書を攻究して考据詞章の學を屏ぞく。前淸丁酉科の舉人を以て北京大學校師範科に入りて學び、卒業後本省に在りて育英の業に從事し、安慶府中學校を經營す。

後ち諮議局成立するや秘書長に任じ、第一革命後舉げられて安徽臨時省議會議長となり、聲望日に著る。民國元年臨時參議院議員に選ばれ、民國建設の大業を勸助す。二年正式國會成立に際し衆望を荷つて參議院議員に當選す。國會停止後、曾て審計院審計官に任じたり。本年國會重ねて開かるゝに及び、審計官の職を辭し、仍ほ召集に應じて參議院議員の職に就きたり。

Mr. Hu-pi-cheng, another name Kuei-wen, Ching prefecture, Au-hui district, fourty six years old. He is a man of pure nature, his views and his appearance widely deffer from ordinary people; but he is very modest and mild, courteous to all and never assuming. As a youth he versed well as the towns man wondered of his ability. Growing older he read through a hundred boocks and understood their truth. An his middle age he took his interest in phylosophical works and did not care to look mere literary publications. During the imperial government he entered as a fellow into the normal department of the Pekin University and worked for the educational advancement at the education department after the graduation. Later, he founded the An-ching-fu Middle School and made the chief secretary of the district legislature which was organized at the time. After the first Revolution he was nominated to preside over the An-hui Provisional Congress, then his name was known wide and far. In the first year of the Republic he was chosen as the member of the provisional national council and had done a good deal in establishing of the new order. In the second year, on the formal installation of Parliament he was elected a member of the Upper House. When it was suspended he made an accountant of the accounting Board. The House reconvened this year, 1916, and he came back to the original seat resiging the position of accountant.

胡源滙　字海門　歲三十五

選舉地　直隸省
籍貫　直隸省
住　址　北京南太常寺街十一

君賦性清高。言動舉止。皆過異凡流。為人勤謹耐勞。人有所託。輒喜為盡力。不以功自居。以故里人皆極愛敬之。偶有糾紛。得君出一言。無不立即解釋。自幼天資極高。悟性敏捷。讀書能深思探究精義。不為成見所局。故思想豐富。見解新頴。人但見其居常規規自守。不知其精神固異常活潑也。海內維新後。銳意西學。旋以前清廣緒生留學日本。入早稻田大學政治經濟科畢業歸國後。歷充北洋法政學校校長。北京法政專門學校教員。直隸臨時省議會議長。全國平民生計籌備委員。民國二年。正式國會成立。被選為衆議院議員。國會解散後。從事教育事業。及共和復活。國會重開。仍為衆議院議員。

民國之精華　（傳記）胡源滙先生

君賦性清高にして言動舉止亦た過な遉に凡流と異るものあり。然かも人を為す恪勤にして勞に耐へ、人若し託する所あれば輒ち喜んで力を盡し功を以て自ら居らず。故に鄉黨極めて君を敬重し、偶ま紛糾あれば、君の一言によりて立どころに解決す。幼より天資聰慧にして悟性敏捷。故に書を讀みて深く義理を探究し成見の局する所とならず、故に思想豐富にして見解新頴なり。海內維新後、進んで西學に志し、前清廣緒生を以て日本に留學し、早稻田大學校政治經濟科に入り、新進の學問を修めて卒業歸國後北洋法政學校々長、北京法政專門教員に歷充して後進を誘掖啓發し、又た直隸臨時省議會議長に舉げられ、全民平民生計籌備委員と為り、聲望益々著る。民國二年正式國會成立に際し、衆望を荷つて衆院議員に當選す。國會解散後、再び育英事業に從事す。共和克復して國會重ねて開かる〻に及び、再び出で〻召集に應じ仍ほ衆議院議員と為る。

Mr. Hu-yuan-hui, otherwise called Hai-men, Chi-li, thirty five years old. His nature is pure, his conduct is just; yet he is enduring and industrious. Asked by one he accept the appeal gladly and does the best for him. For the reason the entire villagers respect him: His one word is enough to settle a serious difference among the villagers. From youth he has been very bright and quick to understand: he took much interest in reading and studied truth deeply. It was told that his thoughts are rich and views are always new. Since the introduction of the modern civilization he studied the western science and had been sent to Japan for the further study. In Japan, he entered into the Waseda University to politics and economics. On the completion of the study he returned home and accepted the positions of President, the Pe-yang Laws and Politics School, and professor of the Peking Law and Politic School. Later he was nominated to the speaker of the Chi-li Provisional Legislature, and as the committeeman for the investigations of living condition of whole people his name grew very popular. In the second year, he was chosen by the people, on the formal organization of the National Congress, to sent in the Lower House. Having the Congress been dissolved he again engaged in education of young people. The Republican order has been restored and the Congress came to convene again. So, he is sent by the people to hold the former seat in the Lower House.

姚桐豫 字吾剛 歲四十八

選舉地　浙江省
籍　貫　浙江省臨海縣
住　址　北京敎場三條十一號

君秉性仁厚。喜周濟貧乏。雖自處窘
中。亦不以已事而綏人之急。自幼即好
讀書。不事嬉戲。及長愈益攻苦。於資
質雖非絕倫。然所學輒能深入。扙其精
微。年二十即以博學名。然其讀書喜求
實學。注重義理。以祿位縈懷。旋中鄉
試。時方海內維新。乃盡棄舊學。篤志
研究西化。遂以自費東渡留學日本。入
法政大學。　畢業後。　歷任廣西撫署秘
書。桂林地方審判廳廳長。廣東審判籌
備處處長。民國元年。調充浙江都督府
秘書長兼法制局局長。旋改充江蘇都
督府秘書。正式國會成立。被選爲衆議
院議員。國會解散後。任京師高等檢察
廳檢察官。及國會復活。遂應召。仍復
爲議員。

君秉性仁厚、喜んで貧窮を周濟し、自ら窘中に處すと雖、
亦た人の急を赴き助く。幼より讀書を好み嬉戲を事とせ
ず、長ずるに及び刻苦精勵これ努め、資質絕倫と云ふに
非るも、然り其の學ぶ所報ち造詣あり、年二十即ち博學
の名あり、旋て鄉試に及第す。時方に海內維新、乃ち盡
く舊學を棄て專ら西學を研究す。遂に自費を以て東渡留
學し、日本法政大學校に入りて卒業す。歸國後、廣西巡
撫署秘書、桂林地方審判廳々長、廣東審判準備處々長等に
歷任したり。民國元年聘せられて浙江都督府秘書長兼法
制局々長に任じ、旋て改めて江蘇都督府秘書と爲す。正
式國會議員選舉に際して衆議院議員に常選し、中央に抵
りて議政壇上の人となる。國會解散後、京師高等檢察廳
檢察官に任じたり。此次國會復活するに及び、遂に召集
に應じて復た衆議院議員の職に就く。

Mr. Tiao Tung-yu, age forty eight, is a native of Lin-mei, Che-chiang hsing. Although he is satisfied with his poor condition he is never slow to help others in need. He was when young an ardent book reader. As he grew older he became known for the rich stock of his knowledge. At the age of twenty one he was already known for his comprehensive information. He passed successfully the local examination. Perceiving the change of the time he turned his attention to the study of the new learning. At his own expense he studied in Japan graduating from the Hosei University. On returning to his country he was successively appointed various important posts in his province. In the 1st year of the Republic he was a private secretary of the Che-chiang governor general. When the Parliament was opened he was elected a member of the House of Commons and was interested in the Parliamentary work. With the breaking up of the Parliament the was appointed a higher public procurator. When the Parliament was opened again he was returned for the House of Commons.

選舉地　江蘇省

籍貫　江蘇省上海

住址　北京東太平街路南天仙巷

君賦性清高。然爲人勤謹耐勞。人有所託。輒喜爲盡力。不以功自居。自幼天資聰慧。讀書深思。探究精義。不爲成見所局。故思想豐富。見解新穎。前清以優貢生。授舉人。補知縣。曾被選爲議上海全縣學務公會會長。旋充勸學所總董。被選爲江蘇諮議局議員。被舉爲財政審查長。又歷經被選第一屆常駐議員候補。資政院議員。民國江蘇臨時省議會議員。上海市議會議長。第一屆正式國會衆議院議員。由院被舉預算股委員。國會解散後。南旋歸里。依舊熱心于地方公益事業。又經上海縣議事會。被舉爲續修上海志主纂員。及國會再行召集。遂又入京。仍爲衆議院議員。

君賦性清高にして然も人と爲り勤勞に耐ゆ。人若し託する所あれば輒ち喜んで力を盡し功を以て自ら居らず。幼より天資聰慧にして書を讀み、深く其の義を究め成見の局する所と爲らず、故に思想豐富にして見解新穎なり。前清優貢生を以て舉人を授け知縣に補せらる。曾て選ばれて上海全縣學務公會長と爲り、旋て勸學所總董に任じ、又た江蘇諮議局議員に選ばれて財政審査長に舉げらる。

次で資政院第一期常駐議員補缺員に選ばる。民國成立して江蘇臨時省議會議員に當選す。舉げられて上海市議會議長と爲り、第一期正式國會衆議院議員に當選して預算委員に舉げらる。國會解散後、南旋して上海に歸り、熱心に地方公益事業に從ひ、又た上海議事會より舉げられて上海志續修主纂員と爲る、國會再び召集を行ふに及び遂に又た入京して、仍ほ衆議院議員と爲る。

民國之精華　（傳記）　姚文枏先生

Mr. Tiao Wen-sen, otherwise named Tzu-jang, is a native of Shanghai, the Chiang-su hsing. Nobleness of the character is particularly noteworthy in him. He takes great pleasure in doing service for the interest of others at his own sacrifice. He is therefore far from egoistic, and would not have his merit advertised. He is a copious and appreciative reader of books which supplies the rich ideas. He was appointed the governor, and the president of the educational society of Shanghai. He was also appointed a member of the Chung su advisory Board, and was the head of the financial investigation committee. He was also the president of the municipal assembly of Shanghai, and in the 1st session of the Parliament, he was on the budget committee. After the suspension of the Parliament, he returned to Shanghai, and was most keenly interested in public works. Besides, he filled many important posts in Shanghai. When the Parliament was decided to be sermoned, he entered Peking and was returned for the House of Commons.

姚守先 字警甤 歲四十六

選舉地 陝西省
籍貫 陝西省西鄉縣
住址 北京敄子胡同內沙欄胡同

君秉性清高。言論風采。皆過異庸俗。
然謙和厚重。以禮自持。絕無虛驕之
氣。稚齡即能為詩文。吐芳新俊。鄉人
皆以神童目之。及長。尤博及羣書。經
史而外。諸子百家。皆取備讀。均能發
微抉伏。得其眞精。中年。尤專攻于理
義之書。屏棄考据詞章之學。常慨世道
人心之是非。頗有廉頑立儒之志。而不
以科舉榮懷。故雖淵博精深。乃僅以一
衿自足。不復求進。及海內維新。遂慨
然以提倡教育為己任。前清時。曾任本
邑勸學總董辦理白話勸學報。創立初
等小學七十餘所。歷充縣立高等小學
國文經學敎員。及中學校學監兼國文
敎員。民國成立。當選為衆議院議員。
國會解散後。君遂歸里仍從事于敎育
之提倡。五年及國會復活。始應召。入
京就職。

君秉性清高にして言論風采皆な逈に庸俗に異る。然かも
謙讓溫和、禮を以て自ら持し、絕えて虛驕の風無し。少
年即ち詩文を能くし鄉人皆神童を以て之を目す。長じて
博覽强記、經史以外諸子百家の書皆な讀破して均しく其
の微を啓さて其の精を究む。常に世道人心の壞破を慨し
て廉頑立儒の志を抱く。海內維新に及び、遂に慨然とし
て敎育を提倡して後進を誘掖し、民智を啓發するを以て
己が任と爲す。前清時代曾て鄉里の勸學總董に任じ、白

話勸學報を發刊す。而して初等小學校を創設すること七
十餘箇所に及ぶ。又た縣立高等小學校國文經學敎師及び
中學校學監兼國文敎員に歷充す。民國成立するや地方の
民望を荷つて衆議院議員と爲る。國會解散するや、君遂
に再び鄉里に歸りて地方敎育發展の爲に奔走盡力する所
あり。國會復活するに及び、其の召集に應じて入京し、
仍は復た衆議院議員の職に就きたり。

Mr. Yao-shou-hsien, otherwise called Ching-chih, Hsi-ching prefecture, Shan-hsi district, fourty six years old. He is man of pure nature, and his manner and language are entirely different from others. Yet he is modest and mild; never lacks courtesy to anyone and would not assume in any case. When he was very young he composed verses so well that the villagers considered him as an infant prodigy. Growing a man his profound memory could find no equal, he read a thousand volumes and understood all of them. On the introduction of the western civilization he determined to devote all his time and energy for the education of young people. During the Imperial Regime he served as the principal of a village school, then he published the Pai-hus Educational News. It is estimated that he founded 70 grammar schools and he held resiponsible positions at the following schools: the prefectural higher grammar school, and the middle school. He also held offices of the examinar of the chinese language. When the Republic was organized he was sent to the Lower House. On the dissolution of Parliament he returned home to educate young folks. The Republican order has been restored and so the national Parliament. He is now a member of the Lower House as before.

姚華 字重光 歲四十一

選舉地　貴州省
籍　貫　貴州省貴筑縣
住　址　北京爛熳胡同遞花寺

君為人深沈厚重。不苟言笑。與人交。常守緘默。然氣慨溫和舒綏。靄然可親。故人皆樂與交游。自幼聰慧異人。讀書能領會其意義。弱冠即工於文詞。氣慨語調。皆極雄奇俊偉。超出儕輩。及長。頗以遠大自期。好求有用之學。而於舉業。則唯以其一部分之時力為之。於前清光緒二十一年補縣學生。明年試列優等。補廩膳生。二十三年。丁酉科。中式為舉人。三十年甲辰科。中式貢士。賜同進士出身。以主事用籤分工部。任虞衡司主事。調補郵傳部船政司主事。旋派往日本留學。入法政大學。畢業歸國。于民國元年被選為臨時參議院議員。二年復被選為正式國會參議院議員。兼任北京女子師範學校校長。國會解散。仍居都門。從事教育。不復為關於時政之表見。及國會重行召集。遂復為參議院議員。

民國之精華　（傳記）　姚華先生

君人と為り深沈にして厚重、苟くも言笑せず。人と交りて常に緘默を守る。然かも氣質溫和にして靄然親むべく、故に人皆な樂んで交游す。幼より聰慧人に異り、弱冠早くも文詞に工に其の調格極めて雄奇俊偉なり。長ずるに及び大成を以て自ら期し、好んで有用の學を求め研磋倦まず、其の舉業に於ては則ち唯だ一部分の力を割くのみ。前清光緒二十一年縣學生に補せられ、翌年優等を以て廩膳生に補せらる。丁酉の科に及第して舉人と為り、三十年甲辰の科に及第して貢士出身を賜ひ、主事を以て工部に分たれ虞衡司主事に任じ、郵傳部船政司主事に補せらる。旋て派せられて日本に留學し法政大學に入り業を畢へて歸國す。民國元年臨時參議院議員となり、二年正式國會參議院議員に當選し、北京女子師範學校々長を兼ぬ。國會解散後　依然都門に在りて教育に從事す。國會復活に及び復た出でて仍は衆議院議員たり。

Mr. Yao-hua, otherwise-called Chung-kuang, Kuei-chu prefecture, Kuei-chou district, fourty one years old. He is a deep and quiet man; does not talk or laugh easily. He is really a man of silence, yet his nature is gentle, and loveable. From child-hood he is brilliant, wrote several articles remarkablly well when he was a mere boy. His verses were forcible and revelent. Growing older he felt causcious of his future success and read widely and studied hard. In the 21st year of Kuang-hsu he was appointed to the prefectural student and next year the fellow. In the 23rd year passing examinaton he made the scholar, in the 30th he was graduated the highest scholary degree on passing very rigid examination. Then he was appointed to the position of the chief of the weights and measures section, industrial department. Later he made the chief of the marine section, communication department. Finally he was sent to Japan to study, and he entered into the Hosei University. After completion of the work there returned home. In the first year of the Republic he was a member of the probisional national council. Next year, parliament was formally organized, he was elected the member of the Upper House and at the same time, he was appointed to superintend the Peking Girl's Normal School. Even after the dissolutions he staid in Peking occupying himself in education of young persons. Having Parliament been reconvened he has returned this time to the Lower House.

姚翰鄉　字介忱　歲三十九

選舉地　黑龍江省
籍　貫　黑龍江省齊岡縣
住　址　北京宣武門內糖坊胡同六

君人爲精明強幹。富於忍耐。然鯁直好
義。人有過。輒直斥不諱。甚至聲色俱
屬。人告以過。亦直認不諱。故其於人
雖有過詰之嫌。人亦無疾恨之者。自幼
好讀能文。壯年入仕途。歷官各處。頗
有令名。及海內維新後。尤銳意實業。
曾在黑龍江辦理荒務。創設學校。並組
識吉林雙城縣輕便鐵路。及電燈電話
各項公司。民國二年春。被選爲參議
院議員。國會解散。即行歸里。專注意
發展實業。絕口不談政事。及國會恢
復。始來京。仍爲參議院議員。

君人と爲り精明強幹にして忍耐に富む。然かも硬直にし
て義を好み、人過われば輒ち直斥して諱まず、甚だしき
は聲色俱に屬しきに至る。人若し過を以て告ぐれば亦た
直ちに認めて諱まず、故に人と爲り嚴峻に過ぐるの嫌あ
るも人之を恨まず。幼より讀書を好みて文を能くし、壯
年仕途に入りて歷任せる各地均しく介名あり。海內維新
後は尤も意を實業の振興に注ぎ、曾て黑龍江に住りて開
墾事業を處理し、又た學校を創立して敎育の普及を計り、
並に吉林雙城縣輕便鐵道を布設し、電燈電話等の事業をも
創設經營して、地方の開發に盡瘁する所あり。民國二年
の春、選ばれて參議院議員と爲る。國會解散さるや、即
ち鄕里に歸省して專ら實業の發展を介圖して絕へて政事
を談せず。國會恢復して再び召集を行ふに及び、復た出
でゝ北京に抵り、現に仍は參議院議員たり。

Mr. Yao-han-hing, otherwise called Chieh-shen, Ching-kang prefecture, Hei-lun-chiang district, thirty nine years old. He is a man of a great talent and ability. If he finds one's mistaken he never afraid to reproach him in his face, sametimes even using harsh language. It was thought that he is a little too severe but no one resents him. From his boyhood he read much and composed articles and verses. Grown up a man he held several offices in local government and maintains a good reputation wherever he went. When the western civilization introduced into the country he turned his attention toward the development of industry, once, in Hei-lung-chian, he superintended cultivation of land and established schools for the advancement of education. He built at a time, the Chi-lin Chih-cheng Light Railways and established the electric high and telephon companies, which served a good deal to open up the remote regions of the country. In the second year of the Republic he was elected a member of the Upper House. On the dissolution of parliament he went back to his native district, and devoted all his time for improvement of industries. The Republican Regime was restored and so the parliament. He came back to the Upper House to resume his duty as a legislator.

恒　鈞　字詩峯　歲三十歳

選舉地　直隸省
籍貫　直隸省
住址　北京係公園夾道

君少好義。喜為人鳴不平。里人有以困
于資者。輒解囊助之。不復望報。遠近
爭稱其名。然居心仁厚。雖仇敵。亦不
虐待之。與人交。喜相責以善。人告以
過。輒大喜。自幼好讀。喜博覽羣書。純
以主觀判斷是非。而不局于習俗之成
見。故其文采風貌。亦超出儕輩。弱冠
時。即以名儒自期。旋復立志棄舊從
新。遍購譯本讀之。尤注意於政法之
學。遂遊學日本。入早稻田大學。畢業
歸國後。充大同報總經理。民國成立
後。被選為眾議院議員。

君少より義を好み、喜んで人の為に不平を鳴らし、里人
資に困する者あれば、輒ち囊を解きて之を助け、復た報
を望まず、遠近爭つて其名を稱す。然かも居心仁厚にし
て仇敵と雖も亦た之を虐待せす。人と交りて喜んで相責
ひるに善を以てし、人告ぐるに過を以てすれば輒ら大に
喜ぶ。幼より讀を好み、群籍を涉獵して主觀を以て是非
を判斷し、習俗の成見に囚れざる也。故に其の文采風貌
亦た儕輩に超出す。弱冠の時、即ち名儒を以て自ら期し、
旋て復た志を立て、舊を棄てて新に從ひ、遍ねく譯本を購
讀し、尤も意を政法の學に注ぎたり。遂に日本に留學し
て早稻田大學校に入りて卒業す。歸國後、大同報總理に
任す。民國二年正式國會眾議院議員に常選して、此次國
會重ねて開くや、再び召集に應じて、現に仍は眾議院議
員たり。

民國之精華　（傳記）　恒鈞先生

Mr. Heng Chun, sometimes known as Shih Feng, age thirty five, is a native of Chi-lin province. He is a man of heroic temperament and ready to help his friends in need which made him a very popular among the people in his province. Even towards his enemy he was quite open minded and did not hasitate to make him correct his faults. While young he was fond of reading books and very seldom bound up with traditional influence. His personality distinguished him from his friends. While young his ambition was to become a learned Chinese scholar, but as he grew older he devoted himself to the study of new learning particularly in matters relating to the law. He entered the Waseda University. In the 2nd year of the Republic he was elected a member of the Parliament. Under the new president when it was decided to open the Parliament, he was summoned to Peking and has returned for the House of Commons.

邴克莊　字敬如　歲三十五

選舉地　奉天省
籍貫　奉天省盤山縣
住址　北京前細瓦廠八號

君為人精明強幹。懷慨好義。自葉畢業後。在海城縣。創辦鄉團。聚黨里之健者數千人。辛丑壬寅伏莽叢生。其時盤山尚未設治。地屬海城。舉辦鄉團。所以謀自衛也。嗣因地方漸安。鄉團解散。舉辦初等高等各小學校。多方勸導。咸使就學。然自問實於新學無所得也。乃棄辦學之業而就學。考入奉天高等警察學校。卒業後。創辦警察協會。冀促警政之進行。旋被選為省議會議員。當民國元年武昌開第一次國慶紀念會。曾經被舉為省議會代表。又被選為眾議院議員。國會停議後。歷充奉天民政公署顧問。兼辦保衛團講習所。嗣以帝制發生。乃北走龍門。西上太原。冀與當世同志萍水相遭。回奉。遊說當道。後旋旅滬。志之委託。回奉。遊說當道。後旋旅滬。兩院同人。有在滬開會之舉。乃潛行赴滬與議。現值國會重開。遂仍就職。

君人と為り精明強幹にして懷慨義を好む。曾て海城縣に於て鄉團を組織し、鄉里の健兒數千人を聚む。但し辛丑壬寅の頃、土匪橫行す。當時盤山の地海城縣の管轄に屬す。地方自衛、もたるなり。初等高等各小學校を創設して、教育の普及を圖る。嗣で地方漸く安く鄉團解散す。後ち自ら新學の智識なきに顧み、卒業後、警察協會を創設す。旋て選ばれて省議會議員に入り省議會議員と為る。武昌に於て第一國慶紀念會を開くや、省議會代表として臨席す。民國二年眾議院議員に當選す。國會解散後、奉天民政署顧問に任じ、兼て保衛團員講習所を經營す。帝制問題發生するや、北は龍門に走り、西は大原に赴き、同志と萍水相遭ふ事を冀ふ。旋て南方同志の委託を受け奉天に歸りて常局を遊說す。後ち同志の兩院議員上海に於て國會を開かんとす。君乃ち潛に上海に抵り加はる。現に國會重ねて開き、遂に上京して眾議院議員たり。

Mr. Ping Ko-chuang, otherwise known as Chiug ju, age thirty five, is a native of Pan shan, Fengtien province. He is a gentleman of heroic temperament and as such was respected by his countrymen who used to congregate under him by thousands. He established a primary school with a view to the dissmination of popular education. He was very much interested in new learning. He was graduated from the high police school in Fengtien and established the police association. When the first meeting comemorating the birth of new nation in Wu Chun he was elected a member of there. In the 2nd year of the Republic he was returned for the House of Commons. When Yuanshi-kái Imperial movement broke out he was travelling all over the country proposing to hold a special national assembly in Shanghai. With the death of Yuanshi-kai, the parliament was restored. Thereupon he came up to Peking and resumed his parliamentary function.

一百六十三

范 樵　字鶴侶　歲三十三

選舉地　陝西省
籍貫　陝西省郃陽縣人
住址　北京松樹胡同

君賦性耿介不阿。疾惡如仇。然其處世
接物。不露鋒鋩。朋友有過。雖至契非
豫斷。其能相納諫改過。決不輕於規
勸。居恒以厚道待人。雖仇敵。亦不忍
無端虐待之。與人交。尚信義。重然諾。
人有所託。既諾無不成者。自幼好讀
書。弱冠即工於詩文。及長。遂事求有
用之學。不復固執章句。故雖淵博。而
所讀多義理之書。西化既盛倡于海內。
君復改志研究西學。造詣既深。民國二
年正式國會成立。被選爲參議院議員。
國會解散後。歸里讀書。不問時政。五
年及國會復活。遂又應召入京。現仍爲
參議院議員。

民國之精華　（傳記）　范樵先生

君賦性耿介にして阿らず、惡を憎むこと仇の如く、然か
も其の世に處し物に接して鋒鋩を露さず、朋友過あれば
至契と雖も豫斷を非とし、其の能く諫を納れ過を改むる
ことと相して、決して輕々しく勸告せず。居常厚道を以
て人を待ち、仇敵と雖も亦た端なく之を虐待するに忍び
ず。人と交りて信義を尚び然諾を重んず。人若し託する
所あれば、既に諾して後ち之を成さゞる者無し。幼より
讀書を好み、弱冠即ち詩文に工なり。長ずるに及び遂に

専ら有用の學を求め、復た章句を固執せざる也。故に學
頗る淵博なりと雖も讀む所は多く義理の書なり。西洋の
文學旣に盛んに海內に唱へらるや、君復た志を改めて
西學を研究し、造詣旣に深し。民國二年正式國會成立に
際し、選ばれて參議院議員と爲る。國會解散後、鄉里に
歸りて時事を問はず、五年國會復活するに及び、遂に又
た召集に應じて入京し、仍ほ參議院議員と爲る。

Mr. Fan Chiho, otherwise called Haolu, age thirty three, is a native of Shan-hsi province. While gentle in character, he is not subject to the vice of flattery. Being a great hater of the evil, but he does not show his hatred on surface. He does not hesitate to warn his friend against their faults, while on his past, he is open to listen to any advice. In dealing with others, he makes frankness and gentleness his motto. Being faithful to his promise, he would accomplish anything that he promises. While young, he is greatly fond of the art of versification. As he grew older, he sought useful learning, and was far from being slave to mere words and expressions what he took great delight in reading was books on reasoning and phylosophy. With the introduction of the western civilization, he also devoted himself to the study of occidental learning. In the second year of the Republic, when the Parliament was formed he was elected a member of the Senate. However with the disolution of the Parliament, he kept himself aloof from politics, spending most of his time in his native province. When the Parliament was restored, he was appointed a member of the Senate.

范殿棟　字雲卿　歲五十一

選舉地　吉林省
籍　貫　吉林省楡樹縣
住　址　北京西城中鐵匠胡同

君賦性誠厚篤實。好賀惡文。不事無益
之繁華。與人交。直而婉談而能久。不
爲疾言遽色。居常謹約自持。言動舉
止。皆有本末。且重信義。嚴取與。故雖
和藹可親。而無形中自有不可侵越之
界限。曾未嘗曲己狥人枉尺直尋之事。
較之尋常無意識之同流合汚者。自屬
大相逕庭。自幼好學深思。稚年讀書。
即喜推求精義。不厭數問。及長。遂導
求有用之學。不復尚執章句。前淸以附
貢生。創辦本縣地方自治。充常縣議事
會議長。民國二年正式國會成立。君荷
衆望。當選爲衆議院議員。國會解散。
歸里讀書。不問時政。五年及約法恢
復。國會再行召集。遂乂入京。仍爲衆
議院議員。

范殿棟 先生

君賦性誠厚篤實にして質を好み文を惡み、無益の繁華を
事とせず。人と交りて直にして婉、談じて久しく敢て疾
言遽色を爲さず。居常謹約自ら持し、言動舉止皆も無
あり、且つ信義を重んず。故に和藹親むべしと雖も無形
の中自ら侵越すべからざる限界あり。未だ曾て己を曲げ
て人に從ふ事を爲さい也。幼より學を好みて深く思索し、
少年書を讀みて其の義理を推求する事を喜ぶ。長じて遂

に專ら有用の學を求め章句の末に囚はれず。前淸時代附
貢生を以て、鄉縣に於ける地方自治を處理し、縣議事會
議長に舉げらる。民國二年正式國會成立するに際し、衆
望を荷つて衆議院議員に當選したり。國會解散するや、
鄉里に歸省して書を讀み、また時政を問はず。五年約法
恢復して國會再び召集を行ふに及び、遂に又た入京して
衆議院議員たり。

Mr. Fan Tien-tung, sometimes known as Yun ching, age fifty one, is a native of Yu-shu, Chilin province. Being sincere and serious minded, he is fond of the substance, but hates vain pomp as he hates the evil. He is quiet and sociable, and master of conversation. Both in words and deeds he attaches great importance to the preservation of fidelity. While he is sociable enough, then is something that makes him quite inaccessible as to others. He would never bend himself to meet the whims of others. When young, he was a lover of learning and deep thinking. He attaches importance to the practical side of his learning, and does not trouble himself with mere external phrases. In the previous chinese regime, he was deeply interested in the study of local civic institution, and was appointed the president of the local assembly. In the second year of the Republic when the Parliament was opened, he was elected for the House of Commons with a great majority. Upon the shutting up the Parliament, he returned to his home where he devoted himself to the study of books, caring very little about politics. When the Parliament was re-opened under the new president, he was elected for the House of Commons, the position of honour he now holds.

選舉地　浙江省

籍　貫　浙江省紹興縣

住　址　北京象坊橋浙江議員公寓

君天資絕高。悟性敏捷。而頭腦周密。

其言論思想。皆秩序井然。絕無顛倒索

亂之弊。自幼讀書。即喜探索精義。不

以文字自拘。故其於學問。雖所歷未

深。然每有所讀。必大有進益。以其能

精思深入。抉其竅要。故其見解思想。

皆極明瞭切實。且洞悉事情。明察物

理。辛亥革命。宣布憲政共和。民國肇

造。正式國會成立。被選爲衆議院議

員。國會解散。南旋歸里。隨時從事地

方公益之提倡。本年及至約法恢復。國

會重行召集。遂又北上入京。仍就議員

之舊職。

民國之精華　（傳記）戚嘉謀先生

君天資絕高、悟性敏捷にして頭腦周密なり。其の言論思

想皆な秩序井然として絕へて顛倒索亂の弊なし。幼より

書を讀み、其の義理を探求して文字に拘泥せず。故に其

の學問に於て、經歷未だ深からざるも、讀む每に必ず大

に進境ありて、其の能く思索して竅要を抉くが故に、見

解思想皆な極めて明瞭切實なり。且つ事情を洞察して物

理を明察したり。辛亥命を革めて憲政共和を宣布し、民

國初めて樹立して正式國會を開くや、君選ばれて衆議院

議員と爲る。國會解散後、南旋して鄉里に歸臥し、時に

地方公益事業の提唱を爲したり。本年約法恢復して國會

重ねて召集を行ふに及び、遂に又た北上入京して仍ち衆

議院議員の舊職に就く。

一百六十五

Mr. Chi Chia-mou, age thirty seven, is a native of Shao hsing, Che-chiang province. He is a man quick understanding and through in the made of thinking. His words and thoughts are always logical. In reading books he makes it point to understand the real meaning of the books and are not slave to mere outward words and forms. Therefore his thoughts are very deep and clear and can appreciate the real feature of the subject he handles. When the Republic was established he became a member of the Parliament. When the Parliament was dissolved he went to his native country and was interested in the promotion of public works. When the Parliament was re-opened under the new order of things he was elected a member of the House of Commons.

席　綬　字克南　歲三十七

選舉地　湖南省
籍　貫　湖南省
住　址　北京李鐵拐斜街永豐寄廬

君秉性慷慨好義。居常好爲人排難解紛。鄉里有不平之事。君輒喜爲之報復。然以見解明晰。其處世接物。皆機敏過人。有所動作。必豫計未來之如何措置。生平尤喜獎勵善行。里人有一德之長者。莫不扶持之。自幼聰穎善讀。强於記憶。稚齡時。日誦數千言。詞句義理。能一一背誦。講解無稍遺忘。及長。尤能精通古義。時復發抒己見。爲理想上之新發明。以前清附生。法部郎中。資政院納稅多額議員。民國反正初湖南南路公舉。爲南路保安總會會長。並在湘。組織天民報館。及湯薌銘督湘時。被封。現充衆議院議員。

君は秉性慷慨義を好み、居常好んで人の爲に難を排し紛を解く、鄉重不平の事あれば君輒ち喜んで之が爲に報復す。然かも見解明晰にして其の世に處し物に接す、皆な機敏人に過ぐるものあり。其の起つて事を爲すや、必ず豫め未來の如何を計りて措置し、不遠の復は未だ爲さざるの先に於て審にす。幼より聰穎にして學を好み、長じて博觀强記なり。尤も能く古義に精通して、時に復たる己見を發抒して理想上の新發明を爲す。前清の附生を以て法部郎中を授けらる。前清末、納稅多額議員として資政院議員と爲る。辛亥革命に際し、舉げられて湖南南路保安總會に長と爲る。嗣で湖南に在りて天民報社を創設すだるも、湯薌銘が湖南都督時代に於て封鎖せられたり。君は民國二年常選の正式國會衆議院議員にして、國會解散後、南方に在りて種々奔走する所あり。國會復活するに及び、再び出でゝ衆議院議員たり。

Mr. Hsi Shou, otherwise called Ko-nan, age thirty seven, is a native of Hoo-nan province. Being heroic in temperament, he is keenly interested in working for the interest of others. He always gladly took the side of the people in his province, whenever there was any feeling of dissatisfaction among them. His judgement was always correct and quick. In any enterprise, he is far-reaching in ideas so that he takes into consideration the cases of emergency. While young, he distinguished himself for his wonderful retentive faculty. Being well posted up in classics, he is quite original in his ideas. At the last days of the Chinese regime, he was a member of the assembly as a highest taxpayer. When the revolution took place, he was elected the head of the Hoo-nan Peace Preservation Association. He was also interested in the starting of a newspaper, which was shut down. In the second year of the Republic, he was returned for the House of Commons. When Yuanshi-kai suppressed the Parliament, he went to the south and was keenly interested in the promotion of his own cause. With the restoration of the Parliament, he was returned for the House of Commons.

俞鳳韶　字寰澄　歳三十六

選擧地　浙江
籍貫　北江省奧興縣
住址　北京兵部窪牛壁街

君爲前清擧人。然自幼即不滿於前清政治。常慨然有革命之志。家族強使應試。非所願也。君曾受業於湯蟄僊。湯創辦浙江鐵路。招任會記局長。鐵路規程。君手定甚多。嗣去之上海。與陳其美張人傑計畫大事。往巴黎經理通運公司通義銀行。以營業所入。賞助革命。辛亥。武昌義起。適在上海聯絡軍警。兼財政總參議。嗣湯任浙江都督。以湖州匪亂蜂起。防營蠢動。調任湖州軍政分府。撫馭驕兵。三月中。捕誅巨盜百餘人。地方以寧。民國元年。陳其美任工商總長。調任工商部秘書。兼署秘書長。唐內閣倒。去職。二年。當選衆議院議員。國會解散後。伏處上海。經商爲生。潛爲倒袁之計畫。五年夏。浙江獨立。君被任爲財政參議。銀行監理兼機要秘書。及國會重開。遂來京供職。

君は前清の擧人だり、然れども幼よりして前清政府の政治に滿足せず、常に慨然として革命の志を抱く。君曾て業を湯蟄僊に受け、湯が浙江鐵道を創設するや會記局長に任す。嗣いで上海に往き陳其美張人傑等を創設するや會記局長す。巴里に往きて通運公司、通義銀行を經理して其の營業又た所得を以て革命の資を助く。辛亥の歳武昌義を起すや、上海の軍警を聯絡して陳其美を助け、事就つて即ち滬軍都督參議に任じ、財政總參議を兼ぬ。嗣いで湯が浙江都督となるや湖洲の匪徒蜂起して防營蠢動す。君乃ち湖州軍政分府長に任じて驕兵を制御し又た巨盜百餘人を法に正して地方の安寧を致せり。民國元年工商部秘書長に任す。二年衆議院議員に當選す。國會解散後上海に在りて商業を營み、潛に討袁の計畫を志す。五年の夏浙江獨立するや財政參議、銀行監理に任じて機要秘書を兼ぬ。後ち國會再召集に應じ、北上入京して仍は衆議院議員たり。

Mr. Yu Feng-shao, otherwise called Huan-cheng, age thirty six, is a native of Wu Che-chiang province. He belongs to the last Chinese regime but with the system of the government he was quite dissatisfied and entertained always ravolutionary ideas. He was connected with the railway enterprise and then went to Shanghai where he worked with revolutionists. In Paris he was interested in banking the receipts were applied to help the revolutionary movement. In 1910 when the movement took place in Wu-chuang he was deeply interested in it having occupied the position of the member of the staff of the Shanghai army and also was a financial advisor. He was also interested in the suppression of bandits thus restoring peace to the district. In the 1st year of the Republic he was the private secretary to the industrial and commercial department. In the 2nd year of the Republic he was elected for the House of Commons. When the Parliament was disolved he went to Shanghai and was engaged in business at the same time planning for the downfall of Yuanshi-kai. When the Parliament was summoned he went up to Peking and was returned for the House of Commons.

姜毓英　字孟斐　歲四十

選舉地　奉天省

籍貫　奉天省蓋平縣

住址　北京永寧胡同二

君天資聰慧。為人誠篤。尚質卑文。不事浮華。居心仁厚。喜周濟困窮。不望報復。幼受庭訓。長攻舉子業。才具明敏。為鄉黨所推重。停科後。研習師範。歷辦學務。嘗入奉天法政學校為得業士。前清時。歷充籌辦諮議局司選員。及奉天提學使署科員。後入統計講習所畢業。改元統計員。民國二年正式國會成立。被選為衆議院議員。國會解散後。即往黑龍江經營墾務。從事實業。不聞時政。惟隨時襄助地方公益之事。不遺餘力。適湯原縣大饑。君襄辦賑務暨接濟平糶事宜。功勞顯著。里人應激。五年及約法恢復。國會重開。遂又應召入京。仍為衆議院議員。

君天資聰慧にして人と為り誠篤、質を尚び文を卑み、浮華を事とせず。居心仁厚にして喜んで困窮を周濟し、報復を望まず、幼にして庭訓を受け、長じて科學の業を攻究し、才識明敏なり。科學廢止後、師範の學を研習して學務に從事したり。嘗て奉天法政學校を卒業す。前清時代、諮議局司選員及び奉天提學使署の科員となり、旋て統計講習所に入りて卒業し、統計員となる。民國二年正式國會衆議院議員に當選す。國會解散後、即ち黑龍江に往きて墾務を經營し、實業に從事し、時政を聞かず、唯だ時に隨つて地方公益の事を襄助して餘力を遺さず。適ま湯原縣大に饑へ、君賑務を辦理し、平糶事宜を接濟、功勞顯著にして里人感激す。五年約法恢復して國會重ねて開かるゝに及び、遂に又た召集に應じて入京し、仍は衆議院議員と為る。

Mr Chiang Yu-ying, otherwise known as Meny Fei, forty years of age, is a native of Kai-pin, Fengtien province. He was smart, and bright in nature, which virtue was strengthened by his sincerity. He was the lover of the substance rather than the mere form. He took a great delight in helping the poor. As he grew older, he was a student of chinese classics, but later, he directed his attention to the study of new learning, particulary that of teaching. He was graduated from the law school in Fientsin. He studied in the institute of statistics. In the 2nd year of the Republic he was returned for the House of Commons. With the disolution of the Parliament he was intrested in the work of exploitation of the land but kept aloof from current politics. When there was famine in the district he contributed his service to such an extent that he won respect from the people in the district. When the Parliament was re-opened he accepted the summon and entered to Peking where he was elected a member of the House of Commons.

選舉地　雲南省
籍　貫　雲南省思茅縣
住　址　北京未央胡同五號

君於淸季赴日本。肄業鐵道學校。時淸室親貴用事。國政敗壞。乃出與留東諸志士組織同盟會。謀推倒淸廷。發展民主主義。適英法有滇緬滇越種種交涉。君則之憤。遂與雲南同志。特開雲南獨立之大會。與淸廷斷絕關係。丁未。君偕諸同志赴河口起義。事敗回日。志愈堅決。辛亥武漢事起。乃回上海謀進行。會漢陽失守。民軍勢漸孤弱。君與同志密謀定計取上海。攻南京。以爲第二根據。上海軍政府成立。復組織先鋒隊。君任指揮長。南京既下。臨時政府成立。君任司法部僉事。南北統一。君以不願受勳賞故。乃託故回鄉。辦理滇省黨事。二年被選爲衆議院議員。癸丑十月。袁世凱以暴力解散國會。下通緝之令。君回鄕養晦兩年。帝制議起。君愼不可過。乃與滇省軍政各要人。分別聯絡。共謀獨立。時機既熟。滇省遂以首義聞於世界。及議會重開。君遂入京。就衆議院議員職。

民國之精華　（傳記）　段雄先生

君前淸末に於て日本に留學し鐵道學校に修業す。時に國政敗壞す。乃ち諸志士と同盟會を組織して、淸廷を傾覆して民主々義の振興を謀る。適ま英佛兩國が西南支那に於て種々の交渉あるを聞き、慨然として雲南に歸り同志と共に雲南獨立大會を開く。丁未の歲諸同志と河口に赴きて義を起し、事敗れて日本に亡命す。第一革命の事起るや、乃ち上海に赴く。會ま漢陽守を先す、君密に同志と計を定めて上海を取り南京を攻む。上海軍政府成立す

るや先鋒隊を組織して其の指揮長に任す。南京既に下るや先鋒隊を組織して其の指揮長に任す。南京既に歸りて黨務を省く、二年衆議院議員に常選して北上す。袁政府が國會解散するや、命を下して君を捕縛せんとす。君鄕里に韜晦して漸く免る。帝制問題發生するや、君復た蹶起して雲南省軍政當路と聯絡して共に獨立を謀る。目的既に達して、國命再び召集せられ、君復た入京して、衆議院議員となる。

Mr. Tuan Hsiang, otherwise called Yu-ju, is a native of Ssu-mas, Yun-nan province. At the latter days of the previous Chinese regime he came to Japan, where he studied in the railway school. Seeing the decline and corruption of the government he acting in conjunction with others planned for the downfall of the Chinese government. When apprised of the fact that England and France had some negotiation with China, he went to Yun-nan where with his fellow thinkers he secured the independence of the Yun-nan province. In 1907 he went to Ho-kow where he was interested in revolutionary movement but was defeated and made his escape to Japan. In the first revolutionary movement he attacked Shanghai bearing pressure upon Nan-king. With the surrender of Nan-king the union of south and north was arrived at. In the 2nd year of the Republic he was elected a member of the House of Commons. With the dissolution of the Parliament he was in the personal danger of arrest but goingover to his native home he saved his life. When the Imperial movement took place he secured the independence of the Yun-nan province and when the Parliament was reopened he entered Peking and became a member of the Parliament, the position of honour he now occupies.

徐承錦　字尚之　歲四十二

選舉地　貴州省
籍貫　貴州省銅仁縣
住址　北京西城新建胡同

君天資聰慧絕倫。爲人精明強幹。富於忍耐。長于幹濟之才。然情性圓活。不固執己私。自幼好讀。博而能約。識力均極高。而又虛心好問。能受盡言。及海內維新。再求天下有用之學。攻究新書。造詣既深。且洞察事理。其文來風貌。迥超出凡流。以前清光緒丁酉優貢。授戶部主事。入京師大學堂仕學館畢業。獎員外郎。歷任務民政部員外郎。民政部參事。民政部左參議。記名截取知府。記名御史。民國二年選任正式國會參議院議員。國會停止後。歷任司法部秘書。前肅政廳蕭政史。五年及國會再行召集。仍復任參議院議員。

君天資穎絕倫にして人と爲り精明強幹、忍耐に富み、幹濟の才に長ず。然も情性圓活して我見を固執せず。幼より讀書を好み、博くして能く約し、識力均しく高く、又た心を虛ふして問を好み、能く盡言を聞く。海內維新に及び、專ら天下有用の學を求め、新書を攻究して造詣深かに且つ事理を洞察し、其の文采風貌迥かに凡流に超出す。前清光緒丁酉の優貢生にして戶部主事を授けらる。京師大學堂仕學館を卒業して員外郎を獎せらる。民政部員外郎、民政部參事、民政部左參議、記名知府、記名御史等の官に歷任歷敍されたり。民國二年正式國會參議院議員に當選す。國會停止後、司法部秘書、肅政廳肅政史に任ず。五年國會再び召集を行ふに及び、仍は復た參議院議員に任じたり。

Mr. Hsu Cheng Chin, otherwise known as Shaug chih, forty two years of age, is a native of Tung Jen, Kuei chou province. He is a gentleman of energy and patience, possessing very necessary quality for the practical turn of business. While young, he was deeply interested in reading, the result being that he is a gentleman of wide information. He is ready to listen to suggestions from others. With the introduction of new trend of thought into the country he was interested in the acquisition of new learning, and accumulated a stock of knowledge in these respects. In 1897, he passed the civil service examination with great success. He occupied successfully the government positions of importance, being the adviser of various civil and diplomatic institutions. In the second year of the Republic, he was returned for the House of Commons, but when the Parliament was disolved by Yuanshi-kai, he was appointed the private secretary to the Department of Justice when the Parliament was restored under the new president, he was elected a member of the Senate.

徐傳霖　字夢巖　歲三十八

選舉地　廣東省
籍　貫　廣東和平縣
住　址　北京西城油房胡同十一號

君三歲失怙。性豪俠。重然諾。博覽羣
書。能文章。尤精刑名之學。優廩繕生。
副貢。少年慕游長江大河南北足跡遍
十餘行省。京師國立法政專門學堂優
等畢業。日本法政大學法學士。廣東省
議會議員臨時參議院議員。衆議院議
員。及袁世凱非法解散國會。知袁氏有
帝制自爲之決心。東渡日本。與同志多
所籌畫。民國四年四月回滬。充正誼雜
誌新中華雜誌編輯。常籌安會發生。君
與谷君鐘秀。楊君永泰。歐陽君振聲。
發起共和維持會。最先反對帝制。以號
召國人。復倡辦中華新報。任主筆之
職。當時稱爲擁護共和唯一之報。君爲
護國軍主動之一人。充雲南浙江都督
府顧問。美洲籌餉代表。國會恢復。仍
就衆議員職務。

君三歲にして怙を失ふ。性豪俠にして然諾を重んず。博
く羣書を閱して文章を能くし、尤も刑名の學に精しく・
優廩膳生、副貢と爲る。少年長江南北に慕游して足跡十
餘省に遍し。北京國立法政專門學校を優等にて卒業し、
日本法政大學法學士たり。選ばれて廣東省議會議員、臨
時參議院議員、衆議員議員に歷充す。袁世凱が非法を以
て國會を解散するや、日本に赴きて同志と籌畫する所多
し。民國四年四月上海に歸りて、正誼雜誌、新中華雜誌の
編輯に任ず。嘗安會發起さるゝに當りて、谷鐘秀楊永泰歐
陽振聲等と共和維持會を發起して帝制反對の先聲を舉げ
て天下に號召す。復た中華新報を創立して其の主筆と爲
る。當時共和擁護唯一の新聞なりし。又た君は護國軍主動
者中の一人にして雲南浙江都督府の顧問に充ち、米國華
僑の籌餉代表たり。國會恢復するに及び、仍ほ衆議院議
員の職に就く。

民國之精華　（傳記）徐傳霖先生

Mr. Hsu Fu Lin, age thirty eight, is a native of Hai ping hsien, Kuangtung province. At the age of three, he was left as orphan. Being heroic in temperament he makes it point to keep promise at any cost. He is a copious reader of books and excellent writer. He is very well versed with the penal science. While young he travelled a great deal in China covering more than ten provinces. He was graduated from the Peking Law School with honours and also the law college of the Hosei University of Japan. On returning to his country he was elected a member of the special assemblies held in his province. Finally he was returned for the House of Commons. When Yuanshi-kai disolved the parliament, he went Japan where with his fellow sympathizers he entered various consultation. In the 4th year of the Republic he was in Shanghai publishing magazines. He was a pioneer of the antimovement against Yuanshi-kai's Imperial project. He established a newspaper which was only organ of the Republican ideas of those days. He became a representative of the Chinese residents in America. When the parliament was restored he was returned for the House of Commons.

徐象先 字慕初 歲三十七

選舉地 浙江省

籍貫 浙江省永嘉縣

住址 北京校場六條

君為人精明强毅。頭腦明晰。氣量寬宏。然性喜質朴。不事浮華。自幼好為義舉。喜周濟貧乏。雖自處窘中。亦不惜解衣推食濟之。尤喜獎勵善行。里人有純孝而貧者。母死。無以為葬。君時亦困於貧。乃益盡所有給之。知其猶不足。則强求貸於友朋以充之。以是自陷於窘中者累月。君天資絶高。弱冠即以能文著。然其讀書。喜推求義理。不肯拘拘於章句。及海內維新。益求有用之學。乃入京肆業于北京大學堂仕學館。畢業後。歷充北京高等巡警學堂教員。順天學堂教務長。並任郵傳部主事。及江蘇縣知事。民國二年正式國會成立。被選為衆議院議員。國會解散。遂以律師營業。不問時事。及國會復活。始仍就議員職。

君人となり精明剛毅、頭腦明晰にして氣量寬弘なり。然も性喜質朴、浮華を事とせず、幼より義舉を好み人の困苦を周濟するを喜ふ。君天資絶高にして弱冠即ち能文を以て著はる。然も其の讀書は喜んで義理を究めて章句の末に拘泥するを屑ぎよしとせず。海內維新に及び有用の學を求め即ち北京に入り、北京大學校に入りて肄業す。業を畢へて後ち北京高等巡警學堂教員、順天學堂教務長等に歷任し、並びに郵傳部主事、江蘇縣知事等に任せられ、や選ばれて衆議院議員となる。民國二年正式國會成立さるゝや選ばれて衆議院議員となる。國會解散するに及び辯護士を業としてまた時事を問はず、帝制問題に對し國論沸騰して共和政治を復活するや、國會重ねて召集を行ひ、君亦曾でゝ衆議院議員の職に就き、兼て辯護士の業を執る。

Mr. Hsu Wsiang-hsien, otherwise known as Mu-chu, age thirty seven, is a native of Yung-chia. Che-chiang hsing. He is a gentleman of clear head, minute observation and comprehensive views. Being a man of simple life he hates vanity. He was very much interested in working for the interests of others at his own expence. While young he showed his ability as a writer. When the new ideas swept over the country, he went up to Peking where he studied in the Peking University and after graduation he was an instructor of the Peking high police school and later he was promoted to the governor of one of the prefectures. In the 2nd year of the Republic when the Parliament was brought into existence he was returned for the House of Commons. With the dissolution of the Parliament he practiced law and was not interested in politics. When the public opinion rose against the Imperial movement and the Republic was restored, he was elected a member of the Parliament and also practiced law.

徐蘭墅　字樹馨　歲三十二

選舉地　江蘇省
籍　貫　江蘇省崇明縣
住・址　北京棉花上四條二十三

君賦性溫厚和平。工於交際。然又篤實
不欺。動止以禮自持。為人精明強幹。
富於忍耐。與人交。鯁直不阿。人有過。
報直斥不諱。人告以過。雖未盡當。必
欣然謝之。於前光緒二十九年。以諸生
遊滬肄習師範。曾辦本縣教育會及其
他公益事務三十三年遊學日本。在早
稻田大學政治經濟科畢業。宣統三年
夏間歸國。被選為崇明縣會議員。民國
光復。被推為本縣學務科科長。元年八
月辭職。改任律師。在江蘇省內行使
職務。嗣被選為眾議院議員。國會停止
後。充任浙江省杭縣地方審判廳推事。
現遵約法。國會重行召集。仍就眾議院
議員之職。

君賦性溫厚にして和平、交際に巧なり。然も亦篤實にし
て欺かず動止共に禮を以て自ら持す。人と爲り精明にし
て強幹、忍耐に富む。人と交つて鯁眞阿らざるなり。前
清光緒二十九年に於て諸生を以て上海に遊學し師範學校
を修業す。曾て郷里の縣教育會及び其他の地方公益事務
を處理したり。三十三年笈を負ふて日本に遊學し早稻田
大學校政治經濟科に入りて其の業を畢ゆ。宣統三年の夏
間に歸り。後ち選ばれて崇川縣會議員となる。民國光復
するや推されて同縣學務科長となる。民國元年八月職を
辭し、改めて辯護士を營み、江蘇省內に於て其の職務に
從事したり。次いで選ばれて衆議院議員となる。國會停
止されて後、浙江省杭縣地方審判廳推事に任す。現に約
法に遵つて、國會重ねて召集を行ふや仍ほ衆議院議員の
職に就く。

民國之精華　(傳記)　徐蘭墅先生

Mr. Hsu San-shu, otherwise known as Shu-hsing, thirty two years of age, is a native of Chung-min, Chiang-su province. Se is gentle, peaceloving and sociable in character. He is sincere to his friends and conducts himself by the strict code of ettiquet. Besides he is strong minded and full of patience. Being straight forward in character he does not bend himself against his own will. In 1903 he went to Shanghai where he was graduated from the Normal School and was interested in the local prefectural education and was engaged in various public works. In 1907 he went to Japan where he was educated in the Waseda University. In 1911 he returned to his country and was elected a member of the local assembly. When the Republic was established he was a chief of the educational department of the province and in the 1st year of the Republic he practiced law. Later he was returned for the House of Commons. When the Parliament was stopped he was appointed the local judge of his native province. When the Parliament was reopened he was returned for the House of Commons.

唐寶鍔 字秀豐 歲三十九

選舉地　蒙古

籍貫　廣東香山縣

住址　北京順治門內前王公廠門牌七號

君秉性清高。言論風采。皆超出凡流。以前清翰林院檢討。游學日本。畢業于最高學府帝國大學。得法學士學位。光緒二十五年。充隨使日本繙譯。旋調歸山東北洋襄辦新政。兼充陸軍部民政部法律館。川粵漢鐵路督辦諮議官補陸軍省一等參事官。居無何。奏調憲政館外務部行走。歷官至存記使才記名交涉提法使。民國元年。充直隸都督府顧問。調綏襄辦邊務。充歸綏警察廳長兼領化縣知事。及阿爾泰駐綏委員。國會成立。由內蒙古被選爲衆議院議員。兼充律師。充陸軍部諮議。旋調充江蘇中立處主任。派駐京津。四年八月。奉交政事堂存記。十月浦口商埠督辦聘任爲顧問。五年以國會重行召集。遂來京仍爲議員。

君秉性清高にして明敏、其の言論風采時流に超出す。前清翰林院の檢討を以て日本に游學して最高學府たる帝國大學卒業の法學士なり。光緒二十五年駐日公使に隨つて繙譯となり、旋て山東及び北洋に調派されて新政を佐理し、兼ねて陸軍部、民政部、法律館、川粵漢鐵道督辦等の諮議官に任ひ、陸軍省一等參事官に補せらる。後ち憲政館外務部行走に調せられ、提法使に記名さる。民國元年直隸都督府顧問に任ひ、綏遠地方に調せられて邊務を佐理し、歸化綏遠警察廳長に任ひ、歸化縣知事及び阿爾泰駐綏委員を兼ねたり。國會成立するや内蒙古より選ばれて衆議院議員となり、兼ねて辯護士を業とす。國會停止後、陸軍部諮議に補し江蘇中立處主任に任じて京津に駐在す。四年八月政事堂に登録せらる。十月浦口商埠督辦より聘せられて顧問となる。五年八月國會重ねて召集を行ふに及び途に入京して仍ほ衆議院議員と爲る。

一百七十四

Mr. Tang Pao-e, otherwise called Hsiu-feng, age thirty nine, is a native of Hsiang-shan, Kuang-tung province. Both his personality and learning distinguish him from others. He studied in Japan, and graduated from the Imperial University. In 1892, he was an interpreter to the Chinese minister in Japan. He was an official in the new government in Shan tung and Pe yan. He was also an official in military and civil offices and adviser to the Railway office. In the first year of the Republic, he was an adviser to the Chilin governor general. When the Parliament was brought into existence, he was returned for the House of Commons, and practiced law. After the dissolution of the Parliament, he was appointed a member of the Board of advisers to the Military Department. When the Parliament was reopened, he was appointed a member of the Parliament.

高仲和　字重源　歲四十

選舉地　湖北省

籍貫　湖北省棗陽縣

住址　北京後閘三號

君賦性惇篤。天賦英邁。然富於學識。新舊皆有素養。其見解氣慨皆過異凡流。夙抱大志。專攻實學。前清時。由鄂方言學堂。經張文襄派赴日本。學於早稻田大學法科。畢業歸國。充黑龍江陸軍學堂正教習。從事育英之業。辛亥武昌起義。南旋赴鄂。任鄂民政部參事。旋從軍北征。歷收附宜城棗陽隨州等各地。大局既定。民國肇造。君功就歸省。任鄂民政府簽事。民國二年正式國會成立。當選爲參議院議員。國會解散後。南旋歸里。帝制議出。赴滬從事操觚。歷充民信民意各新聞主筆。首倡秩序的改革。正論公議。時人推重之。共和復活。及國會再開。君仍入京。復就參議院議員職。

君賦性惇篤にして天資英邁なり。然かも學識に富み、新舊な素養あり。其の見解氣慨皆な適に凡流に異る。夙に大榮を抱ゥ專ら實學を攻究す。前清時代湖北方言學堂に入り、張之洞より選拔派遣されて日本に留學し、早稻田大學校法科を卒業して歸國す。後ら黑龍江陸軍學堂正敎習に任じ、育英の業に從事す。辛亥の歲武昌義を舉ぐや、南旋して之に投じ、湖北民政部參事となる。旋て從軍して北征し、宜城、棗陽、隨州等各地を收めたり。大局既に定りて民國樹立さるゝや、凱旋して湖北民政部簽事に任ず。民國二年正式國會成立に際し選ばれて參議院議員となる。國會解散して帝制問題發生するや、上海に赴きて民信報、民意報等の新聞記者となり、秩序的改革を主張す。共和復活して國會再び開かるゝに及び、君仍は入京して復た參議院議員の職に就きたり。

民國之精華　（傳記）　高仲和先生

Mr. Kao Chung-ho, otherwise called Chung-yuan, age forty, is a native of Tsao-yang, Hu-pei province. He is a gentleman of sincere character and the best scholarly attainment. His views were greatly different from those of common people. He was ambitious and devoted himself to the study of practical learning. At the latter days of the previous Chinese government he went to Japan where he was graduated from the Waseda University. On return to his country he was appointed an educator of the military school in Hei-lun-chen. In 1910 when the trouble arose in Wu-chung he was interested in the movement and was engaged in the expedition against the northern force. When the Republic was established he was appointed the director of the Hu-pei civil administration. In the second year of the Republic when the Parliament was called he was elected a member of the Senate. With the desolution of the Parliament and the outbreak of the Imperial movement, he went to Shanghai where he was interested in journalism. With the restoration of the Republic he was again returned for the House of Commons and became a member of the Senate.

高家驥　字季喆　歲三十六

選舉地　黑龍江省
籍　貫　黑龍江省巴彥縣
住　址　北京西單牌樓二子胡同東口外寬街

君為人精明剛毅。尚質惡文。自幼讀書。便知讀書大體。尤郵藥尋章摘句之學。故其知識之成。就在大凡。不在一隅。且世界新進之人。恒多失於浮華。君獨接物以禮。處事不阿。此誠新進人物中之翹望也。夙抱治國平天下之志。專求有用之實學。負笈入都。學於國立北京法政專門學校法律科畢業。時適民國肇造。元年被選為臨時參議院議員。抱持正論。主張公議。翼贊建設之偉業。二年正式國會成立復被選為參議院議員。國會解散後。歸里省家。不聞時事。及國會復活。始來京。仍充參議院議員職。

君人となって精明剛毅、質を尚び文を惡む。幼より讀書を好んで便ち讀書の大慨を知り、尤ゝ章句の末を摘むを卑む。且つ世界新進の人にして常に浮華に失する者多き中、君獨り物に接するに禮を以てし事に處して阿ねらず、夙に治國平天下の志を抱き專ら有用の實學を求め、笈を負ふて郡に入り、國立北京法政專門學校法律科に學びて卒業したり。時適々第一革命の事起りて民國肇造せらるゝや、元年選ばれて臨時參議員となり、正論を持して公議を主張し國家建設の偉業を翼贊したり。二年正式國會の成立に際して復た選ばれて參議院議員となる。國會解散されて後ち鄉里に歸りて家を省みまた時事を開かず。國會復活する及び再び其の召集に應じて北京に入り、現に仍は參議院議員の職務に就く。

Mr. Kao Chia-chi, age thirty six, is a native of Pa-yen, Hei-lung-chiang province. He entertains greater love of substance than mere outward forms. While being a copious reader of books he was interested in arriving at intelligent understanding of what he reads. He conducted himself in accordance with the strict code of ettiquet. Indeed he is one of the rising man of the period. He was deeply interested in politics and became an ardent student of practical learning. He went to Peking and was graduated from the law college. When the Republic was formed he was elected a member of the special assembly. He was a stout advocate of the Republicanism and in the second year of the Republic he was again elected a member of the Senate. With the desolution of the Parliament he went back to his native country and for the time being kept aloof from politics. With the restoration of the Parliament he entered Peking and was elected a member of the Senate.

高増融　字仲昭　歳五十四

選舉地　陝西省
籍貫　陝西省米脂縣
住址　北京順治門外上斜街陝西文獻局

君秉性誠篤。不事虛華。自幼聰穎好
讀。弱冠即以詩文著於鄉里。及長。乃
肆力舉業。所造甚深。以縣學廩生中光
緒戊子科鄉試。己丑成進士。以主事用
籤分戶部。是年。充順天鄉試受卷官。
歷任江南四川兩司正主稿。則例館纂
修。緻定庫監理。三十二年。改組部務。
任田賦司司長統計處總辦。及造幣鄂廠會
辦。改充甘肅省清理財政監理官。著有
隴政私議一書。於甘省吏治財政各利
弊指陳詳盡。武昌起義。西安響應。陝
甘邊境官民各軍戰爭激烈。死傷枕籍。
同人組織紅十字分會。君被公推爲會
長。共和成立。被選爲衆議院議員。國
會解散。君因丁內艱先期旋里。怳於時
變讀禮。家居喪服既除。國會重開。復
就衆議院議員。

君秉性誠篤にして虛華を事とせず、幼より聰穎にして讀
書を好み、弱冠即ち詩文を以て鄉里に著る。縣學廩生を
以て光緒戊子科鄉試に中り、己丑の歳進士となり、主事を
以て戶部に分たる。順天鄉試受卷官に充てられ、次で江
南四川兩司正主稿、則例館纂修、緻定庫監理に歷充し、
三十二年部務を改組するや、田賦司々長統計處總辦に任
ず、嗣いで喪に服して職を罷め、後ち出で〻湖南銅元局
總辦及び造幣鄂廠會辦となり、改めて甘肅省清理財政監
理官に任ず、隴政私議の一書を著す、甘肅省吏治財政の
各利幣を指摘詳論せるもの也。武昌義を起すや、西安は
た響應し、甘肅陝西邊境の官民各軍の戰爭激烈にして死
傷多し、君は同人と紅十字會を組織して會長に推さる。
共和成立後選ばれて衆議院議員となる。國會解散さる〻
や君歸鄉して家居喪に服す。國會恢復して君復た召集に
應じて衆議院議員の職に就く。

Mr. Kao Tseng-jung, otherwise named Chung Chau, age fifty five, is a natwe of Hsia hsi
province. He is a stronge lover of simplicity and hater of vanity. When young, he was interested in
the art of versification and writing in which he won a certain fame in his province. In 1889, he passed
the examination, and entered the government employ in diverse capacity. He incurred the mourning,
and had to resign his numerous posts, but shortly after he was appointed an official of the mint. He
was also appointed the officer of the Han Chu province about whose misad ministration, he wrote a
book. When the trouble in Wuchung broke and, he organised the Red Cross society of which he
was appointed the president. When the Republic was established, he was elected for the House of
Commosn. As the suppression of the legislative body, he retired to his home when he was in mourning.
With the restoration of the Parliaments, he was returned for the House of Commons.

高蔭藻 字際唐 歲三十六

選舉地 安徽省

籍 貫 安徽省合肥縣

住 址 北京西單牌樓拾飯寺胡同

君秉性溫厚。與人交。靄然可親。然為
人誠實不欺。生平重然諾。嚴取與。鄉
里皆信仰之。每有爭執。得君一言。即
可雙方解釋。自幼好讀。及長。遂貢文
名。海內維新後。遂銳意西學。遍閱新
書。旋復東渡留學東京。習普通既畢。
得考入長崎高等商業學校。畢業歸國。
適民國成立。由安徽都督孫聘請為安
徽都督府參事官。旋又由安徽都督柏
聘請為安徽都督府高等顧問官。兼安
徽殖邊銀行籌備處副辦。並任安徽皖
報館總經理。民國二年。被選為參議院
議員。國會解散後。專心從事學問。不
聞時事。及國會重行召集。始來京。仍
為參議院議員。

君や秉性溫厚にして靄然親ひべし。然かも人と為り誠實
にして欺かず、生平然諾を重んず。幼にして讀書を好み、
長するに及びて遂に文名を為す。海內維新後、遂に意を
西學に注ぎて遍ねく新書を閱讀す。旋て東渡して日本に
留學し、東京にて普通學を修め、後ち長崎高等學校に入
りて學び、業を畢へて歸國す。適ま民國成立するや、安
徽都督孫號篤より聘せられて安徽都督府參事官と為る。
旋又た安徽都督柏文蔚に聘せられて安徽都督府高顧問
となり。安徽殖邊銀行創立事務所副辦を兼ね、並に安徽
船館總經理に任じたり。民國二年選ばれて參議院議員と
為り。國會解散後、專心學問に從事してまた時事を聞か
す。國會重ねて召集を行ふに及び、再び出でゝ京に抵り、
現に仍は參議院議員の職に任り。

Mr. Kao Yin-sao, otherwise known as Chi-tang, thirty six years of age, is a native of Ho-pe
hsien, An-hui province. He is sociable and gentle in nature. Being straightforward in his character,
he is not known as having ever gone back on his word. He is an ardent reader of books, and won
literary fame. He was deeply interested in the Eastern learning: He studied in Tokyo and entered
the Nagasaki commercial school, where he completed the required course. On returning to his home,
he was appointed an adviser to the governor general of An-hui province. He had charge of the An-hui
bank and the An-hui shipping yard etc. In the second year of the Republic, he was elected a member
of the Senate. On the dissolution of the Parliament, he devoted himself to study and not interested to
current topics. Under the new president, when the Parliament was summoned, he went up to Peking,
and is at present a member of the Senate

選舉地　山西省

籍　貫　山西省崞縣

住　址　北京西城察院胡同

君秉性誠篤。生平無戲言戲動。然爲人
藹然可親。與人交。不立岩岸。然眉目
間。具有一種聲嚴氣象。故人皆敬畏
之。以前淸優貢生朝考二等爲芮城縣
訓導。旋轉任爲山西大學堂敎習。癸
卯中試。次年蟬聯入翰林院。以官費
送往日本留學。入法政大學速成科畢
業歸國。歷任山西籌辦諮議局局長。諮
議局議長。民國成立。被選爲衆議院議
員。國會解散後。曾任敎育部次長。籌
安會發生。以反對故辭職。國會恢復。
仍充衆議院議員。

君秉性誠篤にして生平戲言なく妄動せず。人と交りて障
壁を設けざるも、眉月の間一種の威嚴を具ゆ。前淸時代
優貢生を以て朝考二等及弟、芮城縣訓導と爲る。旋で轉
じて山西大學堂敎習に任す。癸卯の試驗に及弟して次年
翰林院に入り、官費を以て日本に留學し、法政大學速成
科に學びて業を畢ゆ、歸國して後ち山西諮議局準備局長
となり。其の成立後諮議局議長に舉げらる。民國第一次
國會議員選舉に際して衆議院議員となり。國會解散して
後ち、敎育部次長に任す。籌安會發起されて帝制の實行
を唱導するや、君之に反對し、職を棄てゝ民間に歸臥す。
旣にして帝制運動蹉跌して、共和政治恢復し、其の國會
再び召集さるゝに及び、君復た出でゝ現に仍は衆議院議
員の職に任り。

民國之精華　（傳記）梁善濟先生

Mr. Liang Shang Sei sometimes known as Pei Ching, fifty five years old, a native of Shan-Hsi-Shang being a gentleman of high, noble and sincere character, has never, in his career, been known as being guilty of idle and vain words nor of rash and unprinciples conduct.　In associating with others, he is very broad minded and sets up no barrier ; there is something in his whole appearence which maked him the possessor of an over jowering dignity.　In the preceding regime in China, he passed the the civil examination with honours, and was appointed an instructor in the Jui Cheng Ken ; thence he was promoted to the professorship of the Shan-Hsi university.　Having successfully passed the required examination, he was admitted to the Han-Lin-Yuang.　At the government's expenses, he studied law in a special course of the Hosei university of Japan.　Having graduated from the university, he returned to his country where he was appointed as head of the Burean Preparing for the Local Assembly, of which he was leter elected as the president.　On the occasion of the formation of the first National Assembly, he was returned as the member of the House of Commons.　When the National Assembly was displayed, he enjoyed the honour of being appointed the Vice-minister of the Educational Department. When an association was formed with a view to the restoration of the Imperial regime, he proned himself to be a staunch opponent of the new movement, and resigned his post to cash his lot with the people.　When the movement for the restoration of the Imperial regime was checkmated, and the Republic was brought into existence followed by the summoning of the National Assembly, he was as returned for the Houce of Commons which port he most ably occupies at the present moment.

梁 培 字桂山 歲三十五

選舉地 廣西省

籍貫 廣西省扶南縣

住址 北京東南園三條北口三十四號
廣西議員俱樂部

君爲人慷慨好義。喜周濟貧困。自幼好讀書。喜求實學。於前清光緒丁未年。畢業于兩廣高等學堂預科。自後歷充各學校教習者兩年。已酉。選拔貢。轉入官途。辛亥九月。往雲南參與革命事。傷足。民國元年。回南寧辦理西江報。並爲國民黨總務主任。二年。被選爲廣西省議會議員。旋被選爲參議院議員。是年十一月。因不見容于袁世凱出京。自是奔走江湖。力謀倒袁之策者二年。護國軍起。在兩廣都司令部充秘書。八月國會復活。遂來京。復就參議院議員之職。

君人と爲り慷慨にして義を好み、喜んで貧困を周濟す。幼より讀書を好み、專ら有用の實學を求む。前清光緒丁未の年、兩廣高等學校豫科を卒業す。爾來各學校教員に歷任すること二年、巳酉の歲選拔貢生を以て轉じて官途に就く。卒亥九月雲南にありて第一革命の事に參與して足を傷ふ。民國元年南寧に歸りて西江報を經營し、並に國民黨同地支部の總務主任となる。二年選ばれて廣西省議會議員となり、旋てまた選ばれて正式國會參議院議員となる。袁政府が國會を停止するに及びて京を去り、爾來江湖に流寓し、南北に奔走して倒袁の策を圖るもの二年、斯くて護國軍起るや、乃ち兩廣都司令部に在りて秘書に任ず。飢にして袁死して約法復活し國會また再蘇するに及び、君復た召集に應じて北上し、仍は參議院議員の職に就きたり。

Mr. Liang Pei otherwise called Kuei Shan, thirty five years of age, is a native of the Fu-Nan-Ken, the Kan-hsi-province. Being heroic in temperament, he is noted a loner of justice and fond of assisting the poor and oppressed. In his childhood, he showed remarkable propensity for book study. Having been graduated from the Preparatory Department of the Lian-Kan high school under the previous Chinese regime, he spent about two years as a teacher in various schools. He was then a government official for the time being having been specially chosen for the post. When the first Revolution took place, he participated in it in Un-Nan where he was wunded in the leg. In the first year of the Republic, he returned to Nan-Ning where he had charge of the Sei-Kiang news paper while at the some time he discharged the function as director of the local department of the National party which post he occupied for one year; in the second year of the Republic he was chosen as member of the Kan-Hsi-sho Assembly. He then proceeded to Peking as a member of the Senate. When two Yuan Shih-Kai government suspended the parliament, he quitted the capital, and for the space of the years, persistently worked for the dounfall of Yuan Shih-Kai, and when the war broke out he was the private secretary to the military staff. With the death of Yuan Shih-Kai, the parliamentary work was resumed when he responded to the government's call, and was appointed the member of the senate, a position he now enjoys.

梁成久　字樫濤　歲五十七

選舉地　廣東省
籍　貫　廣東省海康縣
住　址　北京西草廠裘家街雷陽新館

君本為粵東之大家世族。自幼好讀詩書。不求聞世故。著述宏富。為世所稱。辛亥革命後。被選為眾議院議員。推避亦始認就職。然亦觀於國家危亡之勢。有不容不出者。每逢議事。出席最多。誠議院中之健將。前清拔貢生。廣雅書院齋長。海康官立兩等小學堂校長。現充眾議院議員。家有漱芳園。藏書五萬卷。所著有溫故知新齋書目六卷。漱芳園詩文稿十二卷。又史記漢書。地理。今釋史例纂要。郡縣志例纂要。讀史隨筆。詩文流派徵評論書。未成。當世之士。俱拭目以待。剞劂而供世覽。

民國之精華　（傳記）梁成久先生

君本と廣東の世族大家に生れ、幼より好んで詩書に親しみて世故を求めず。前清拔貢生を以て曾て廣雅書院齋長海康官立兩等小學堂校長に歷充して青英の事業に從ひ、銳意後進を誘掖したり。家に漱芳園あり、藏書萬卷。君該博の學識を傾注して著作豐富なり。即ち溫故知新齋書目六卷、漱芳園詩文稿十二卷の著世に稱せられ、史紀、漢書、地理、今釋史例纂要、群縣志例纂要、讀史隨筆、詩文流派徵評論等諸書の著未だ成らず、當世の士俱に拭目して剞劂に附せらるゝ事を待つ。辛亥革命の後ち選ばれて衆議院議員と爲る。議事ある每に出席最も多く穩健公正の議論を主張して院內に重きを爲す。國會解散後、南旋して鄉里に歸り、詩書を友として悠々自適す。國會復活するに及び再び召集に應じて北上入京し、現に仍ほ衆議院議員と爲る。

Mr. Liang Cheng-chiu sometimes called Sheng-tao, age fifty seven, is a native of Hai-kang, Kuang-tung province. He is of the noble family in China. Early in life, he is fond of poetical and classical books. He has as many as fifty thousand volumes in his library. There are besides, a large number of his own literary production on various subjects. He is one of the more promising men in China. After the revolution of 1911, he was returned for the House of Commons: His argument in the Parliament is rational and unbrassed so that naturally it commands great respect. After the dissolution of the Parliament, he returned to his vative province where he was interested in the study of poetry. When the Parliament was restored, he entered Peking and was elected a member of the House of Commons.

梁登瀛 字曉舲 歲三十九

選舉地 甘肅省

籍貫 甘肅省金縣

住址 北京順治門外閘書館

君天資聰慧。悟性敏捷。然爲人誠篤無華。待人以直。喜規勸人過失。人告以過。亦直陳不諱。且謙詞謝其直言。自幼好讀。研磋不倦。弱冠即有文名。及長。博覽群籍。能深思明辨。及海內維新。遂專求有用之書。不復固執章句。故雖淵博。而所讀多義理之書。不喜漢魏之學。貿入律學館。以優等畢業。前清丁酉解元。丁未會考一等。叙官司法部主事。歷充京師地方審判廳推事。京師第二初級檢察廳檢察官。民國二年正式國會成立。被選爲參議院議員。此次國會重開。再應召集。復就參議院議員之舊職。

君天資聰慧敏捷にして、人と爲り誠篤華なく、人を待つに直を以てす。喜んで人の過失を規勸し、人若し過を以て告ぐるあれば亦た直諫して諱まず、且つ謙辭を以て其の直言を感謝す。幼より讀書を好みて研磋倦まず、弱冠即ち文名あり。長ずるに及び、博く群籍を涉獵して深く其の義理を究め、海內維新後、專ら有用の書を求めて復た章句を固執せず。故に其の學淵博なりと雖も、讀む所は多く義理の書にして漢魏の學を喜ばざる也、嘗て律學館に入りて優等を以て卒業す。前清丁未の試驗に於て一等に列し、司法部主事に叙せらる。京師地方審判廳推事、京師第二初級檢察廳檢察官に歷任したり。民國二年正式國會參議院議員に當選し、此次議會重ねて開院するや再び其の召集に應じて仍は入京し、參議院議員の職に就きたり。

Mr. Liang Teng-ying sometimes called Hsiao-lei, age thirty nine is a native of Chin, Kan-su province. Being naturally guick-witted and bright he is also sincere in dealing with others. He listens carefully and gladly to the advice given by others. He appreciates and takes in good humor straight forwared suggestions made to him. While young he was fond of study and secured some literary fame. With the introduction of new trend of thought to China he turned his attention to the study of more useful learning. He was graduated from one of the Chinese schools with honors and appointed an official of the Justice Department and occupied a series of important positions in Peking. In the 2nd year of the Republic he was a member of the Senate. When the Parliament was re-opened he responded to the government call and became a membea of the Senate.

民國之精華 （傳記） 梁士模先生

梁士模 字範西 歳三十四

選舉地 廣西省
籍 貫 廣西省北流縣
住 址 北京東南園

君爲人天資穎悟。好學深思。軍興時。
即以救國自任。呼號奔走。曾前清光緒
三十一年。畢業於兩廣師範學堂。隨當
悟州府中學堂教習。歷四寒暑。至己酉
選拔被貢。於都授職知縣。民國元年被
選爲廣西省議會議員。二年復被選爲
參議院議員。憤袁氏暴虐。旋棄職南
歸。投身軍界。爲第三革命之準備。其
充桂軍軍法司時。用人立法。秩序井
然。賞罰既明。三軍莫不翕服。於是聲
譽颺起。人咸謂君軍事家兼法律家也。
五年六月袁氏死。及共和復活。國會重
開。遂應召來京。仍就參議院議員之舊
職。

君人となり天資穎悟、學を好みて思索す。曾て前清光緒
三十一年、兩廣師範學校を卒業し、悟州府中學校に教鞭
を執ること四ヶ年、已酉の歳に至りて貢生に選抜され、
知縣の官に授けらる。民國元年選ばれて廣西省議會議員
と爲り、二年正式國會參議院議員に當選す。袁氏の暴虐
を憤りて、旋て職を棄てゝ歸鄕し、身を軍人社會に投じ
て第三革命の準備を爲したり。其の桂軍の軍法司に任じ
たる時、人を用ゐる法を立つ、共に秩序井然として、賞罰
飭に明なるを以て、三軍共に翕服せるなく、聲譽大に
擧り、時人咸な君を稱して、軍事家にして法律家を兼ぬ
るものと曰ふ。五年六月袁氏死して共和復活し、國會重
ねて開かるゝや、君亦た召集に應じて遂に入京し、仍ほ
參議院議員の舊職に就きたり。

Mr. Liang Shih-mo otherwise called Fan-tien, age thirty four is a native of Pe-lin, Kuang-hsi province. While young he was an ardent scholar of Chinse classics and in the previous Chinese regime he studied in the normal school of his province. While in the course of a few years he was appointed the governor of the province. In the 1st year of the Republic he was elected a member of the local assembly and in the 2nd year a member of the Senate. Being indignant at the attitude of Yuanshi-kai he gave up his position and became one of the soldiers waiting for the revolution. While he was interested in the military character his fame stood very high. When Yuanshi-kai died and the Republic was re-opened he went to Peking responding to the summoned and became a member of the Senate.

孫世杰　字俊之　歲四十五

選舉地　貴州省
籍　貫　貴州省銅仁縣
住　址　北京新建胡同

君爲人誠厚篤實。痛惡浮華。與人交。常硬直不阿。絕無世故之念。人告以過。亦欣然謝之。然居心仁厚。喜救人之難。絕不思報。自幼好讀。喜研究眞理。而不屑尋常摘句。以爲博取功名計。故其所讀多有用之書。及海內維新。決志求西學。醉心新書。尤喜攻究教育學。以前清光緒癸卯科優貢留學日本師範畢業。歷充貴州通省公立中學堂教務長齊務長監學兼教員。優級師範學堂教員。開封官立法政學堂監師範學堂教員。北京女子師範學校教員。教育部主事。現充衆議院議員。

君人と爲り誠厚篤實にして浮華を痛惡す。人と交りて常に硬直阿らず、絕て世故の念なし。人告ぐるに過を以てすれば亦た欣然として之を謝す。然かも居心仁厚にして人の難を救ふを喜び、絕て報はざる也。幼より讀書を好みて理義を研究す。海內維新に及び、志を決して西學を求め、新書に心醉して尤も教育學を攻究する事を喜ぶ。前清光緒癸卯科の優貢生を以て日本に留學し、師範學を修めて卒業歸國す。貴州通省公立中學校教務長齋務長監學兼教員、優級師範學校教員、開封官立法政學堂監學兼教員。北京女子師範學校教員、教育部主事等に歷充したり。而して君は民國二年當選の正式國會衆議院議員にして、國會解散後は依然敎育に從事して、暫らく政治に干預せざりしも、此次國會の復活するに及び、再び召集に應じて、仍は衆議院議員たり。

Mr. Sun Shih-chieh otherwise called Chun chih, age forty five, is a native of Tung-jin, Kuei chuan province. He is a gentleman who is sincere in all his deeds and attacks any action vain and pompous. In dealing with others he is straight forward and never bends himself against his will he is ready to listen any suggestions made to him. He takes also a great delight in helping those in need. He is a great lover of books and deep thinker. While a student of classics he is also interested in reading new books and interested in education. He was graduated from a normal sehool in 1903. Since then he was a teacher of the higher normal school, the higher girl school and several other institutions of learning. In the 2nd year of the Republic, he was elected a member of the House of Commons and after the dissolution of the Parliament he was interested in education and kept himself away from politics. However when the Parliament was restored he was again elected a member of the House of Commons.

孫正字 字調元 歳四十五

選舉地　河南省
籍貫　河南省開封縣
住址　北京達智橋豫學校

君賦性硬直にして洗俗に随つて浮沈せず。居心仁厚にし
て寛恕を以て人を待ち、仇敵と雖も亦た之を窘窮するに
忍びざるなり。人と交つて相責むるに善を以てするを喜
び、人の告ぐるに過を以てすれば輒ち、大に喜ぶ。幼より
讀書を好み、群書を渉獵して意の往く所に任せて快とな
す。而して矩々然として科舉の業に從事するを屑とせず
故に其の讀書は主觀を以て是非を判斷し、習俗の成見に
局せられざるなり。海内維新に及び志を立て有用の學を

君賦性贛直。不隨流俗浮沈。然居心仁
厚。以寬恕待人。雖仇敵亦不忍窘迫
之。與人交。喜相責以善。人告以過。輒報
之以爲快。自幼好讀。喜博覽群書。任意所
待也。
大喜盖謂其能直言不欺。不以流俗相
而不屑規規然從事於科舉
之業。故其讀書。純以主觀。判斷是非。
而不局于習俗之成見。及海內維新。愈
立志求有用之學。於新書無所不觀。而
尤醉心于政法之書。遂肄業於河南高
等警察學校。畢業後目觀警界汚穢。不
屑就職。復入學界。充校長者十餘年。
豫督張委任臨潁縣知事。辭不就。民
國成立後。被選爲衆議院議員。國會解
散。君歸里門。閉戶讀書。不復留意政
治。及國會重開。始應召入都。仍爲衆
議院議員。

求め新書見ざるものなし。尤も政治法律の書に心醉して
遂に河南高等警察學校に修業す。卒業の後ち警察界の腐
敗を見て職に就くを屑しとせず、復た教育界に入りて校
長の職に當る事十餘年なり。河南張都督より臨潁縣知
事に任じたるも辭して就かず。民國成立後歸鄉して閉臥し、國會復活後再び出
當選し、國會解散後歸鄉して閑臥し、國會復活後再び出
て仍ほ衆議院議員となる。

民國之精華　（傳記）　孫正字先生

百八十五

Mr. Sun Cheng-yu otherwise known as Tiao-yuan, age forty five, is a native of Kai-feng hsien, Ho-nan province. Being a man of straight-forward character, he is not swayed by any external pomp and popular taste. He is friendly to all, and even with his enemy he deals with a great deal of indulgence. He is always kind, friendly and sympathetic towards others making either sorrow or joy of others those of theirs. While young he was greatly fond of books and particularly in the interpretation of these he was not trammelled by any traditional influence. When the new trend of thought was introduced into the country he became a seeker of useful knowledge for which purpose he studied new books. He is also interested in the study of books on politics. He was graduated from the Ho-nan high police school but seeing the corruption of the police he did not take any work in this capacity. He entered the educational circle again and spent some ten years as a head master of a school. He declined the offer for the governorship of the province, but declined. When the Republic was brought into existence he was elected a member of the House of Commons. He returned to his home when the Parliament was dissolved but when under the new president the Parliament was re-opened he was returned for the House of Commons.

孫潤宇　字子涵　歲三十八

選舉地　江蘇省
籍　貫　江蘇省吳縣
住　址　北京西單、東斜街昌堂門

君賦性誠實不欺。然自幼聰敏絕倫。讀書能深思。務求眞義所在。弱冠好爲詩歌。甲午後。時人尙務科舉。而君即立志改求有用之學。嗣入北洋大學堂。預科畢業。適逢庚子之變。遂爾歸里。辛丑赴南洋新加坡等處考察實業。翌年應奉天增將軍之聘籌辦盛京大學堂。兼任敎授。甲辰以江蘇省官費。往日本留學。畢業于法政大學。得法學士。歸國後。歷充前淸民政部憲政籌備員。陸軍部統計科長。並財政學堂。高等巡警學堂。法政學堂各敎習。民國元年。任內務部警務局局長。兼高等警務學校校長。嗣被選爲江蘇省律師總會會長。二年一月。當選爲衆議院議員。由衆議院爲憲法起草委員。國會解散後。外交部派充駐日本公使館頭等參贊。此次國會召集。仍充衆議院議員。嗣被選爲外交委員會理事。兼任律師。

君賦性誠實にして欺かず。幼より聰慧にして、其の書を讀むや深く思索して眞義の所在を求む。甲午以後、時人尙ほ科舉の業に務む、君即ち志を立てゝ有用の學を求め、嗣で北洋大學堂豫科を卒業す適きて庚子の變に逢ひて歸鄕し。辛丑の歲、南洋新嘉坡等に赴きて實業を視察し。翌年奉天增將軍の聘に應じて盛京大學校を經營して敎授に任す。甲辰の歲、江蘇省費を以て日本に留學し、法政大學校を卒業す。歸國後、民政部憲政籌備員、陸軍部統計科長、財政學堂、高等巡警學堂、法政學堂の各敎師に歷充す。民國元年、內務部警務局長に任じ、高等警察學校長を兼ぬ。嗣で江蘇省辯護士總會長に選ばる。二年衆議院議員に當選す。憲法起草委員に舉げらる。國會解散後、日本駐在支那公使館一等參贊に任す。五年國會再び召集さるゝや、復た衆議院議員と爲り、外交委員會理事を兼ね、辯護士を業とせり。

Mr. Sun Jun-yu otherwise known as Tzu-han, age thirty eight, is a native of Wu, Chiang-su province. He is faithful, bright and sincere. In reading books he is always very careful to arrive at the truth. He became an ardent seeker of the new and useful knowledge, and entered Peking university whence he was graduated. In 1901, he went to south seas and Singapore where observed the business condition of the district. In the following year hs was appointed a professor of the Sien-king. He was sent to Japan in 1904 at the government expense where he was graduated from the Hosei university. On return to his home he occupied various posts of importance among which we may mention the chief statistician of the military bureau and the instructor of the law college etc. In the 1st year of the Republic he was appointed the chief of the police bureau of the home department and the president of the high police school. Then he was the president of the lawyer's association of Chiang su province. In the 2nd year of the Republic he was returned for the House of Commons and was appionted on the committee of drafting the constitution. After the dissolution of the Parliament he was the first seeretary of the Chinese legation in Japan. When the Parliament was restored he was again elected a member of the House of Commons.

孫鏡清　字性廉　歲三十二

選舉地　四川省

籍　貫　四川省江津縣

性

址　北京西長安街與隆大院

君爲人誠篤。不事欺飾。然性慧。好讀
善思。所爲詩文。皆深厚幽遠。超出儕
輩。弱冠。即連抉科第。前清光緒三十
一年。以中書科中書。送往日本留學。
習普通學年餘。入早稻田法政預科肄
業。三十二年以反對取締規則退學。與
同志多人回上海。開辦中國公學。三十
四年入京師法律學堂正科。宣統二年。
畢業。奏獎副貢生。以直隸州知州分發
河南省候補。歷任中州法政學校及法
官養成所教員。三年委署光州直隸州。
民國元年。署商城縣知事。二年被選爲
衆議院議員。兼營律師業。國會解散。
專爲律師。不與聞政事。及國會二次召
集。遂來京。復爲衆議院議員。

民
國
之
精
華
（傳記）　孫鋭清先生

君人と爲り、誠篤欺飾を事とせず。幼より性慧、好んで
讀み善く思索す。爲くる所の詩文、皆深厚幽遠、儕輩に
超出し、弱冠にして科第に連抉す。前清光緒三十一年中
書科中書を以て日本に送りて留學せしめらる。普通學を
習ふこと年餘、早稻田法政預科に入りて學ぶ。三十二年
取締規則に反對するを以て退學せられ、同志多人と上海
に回り中國公學を創設す。三十四年京師法律學堂正科に
入り、宣統二年業を畢へ、副貢生に奏獎せられ、直隸州
知州を以て河南省候補に分發せらる。中州法政學校及び
法官養成所教員を歷任し、三年署光州直隸州署理に委せ
らる。民國元年商城縣知事を署理すること二年。選ばれ
て衆議院議員と爲る。兼ねて律師業を營む。國會解散後、
專ら律師と爲り、政事に與り聞かず。國會再び集せらる
に及び、遂に京に來り、復た衆議院議員と爲る。

Mr. Sun Ching Ch'ing otherwise called Hsing Lien is thirty two years of age, being a native of the Chiang Chin Ken, Ssū Chuan Sheng. He is sincere and honest in temperament, not being addicted to vanity and deceitfulness. Naturally, being sagacious, he is a great a mirer of books and is a deep thinker. Poems and literary productions of this eminent scholar is deep and far-reaching in thought which make him distinguished from his contemporaries. While young, he passed a series of civil examination with a great success. In the previous Chinese regime, he went to Japan where he pursued a course of liberal education over a year. He studies law in the Preparatory Department of the law College of Waseda. Not being able to meet the requirements of the regulations controlling Chinese students in Japan, he left the college, and started for Shanghai with many of his fellow thinkers. In Shanghai, he had a school of his own. He entered the regular course of the Ching Si Law college where he was graduated in the 2nd year of Hsiian Tung. His promotion since then was very rapid, going through a series of official career until he was appointed an official in Ho Nan Hsing. He was also an instructor of the Central Law College and the Judge training institute, and in the first year of the Republic, he was the governor of the Chancy Ch'eng. Two years later, he was returned for the House of Commons. At the same time, he practiced law. After the disolution of the Parliament, he devoted himself to his profession, paying little attention to politics. In the second session of the Parliament, he came up to the capital, and was elected as a member of the House of commons.

孫乃祥　字瑞丞　歲四十一

選舉地　奉天省

籍　貫　奉天省瀋陽縣

住　址　北京順治門內銅幌子胡同十四號

君爲人誠篤無欺。言動皆確守古訓。不
稍縱肆。居常以厚道待人。秉性聰慧異
人。自幼即明察事理。思考敏捷。而意
志堅強。弱冠讀書。卽能發微起伏。別
關新奇。不爲流俗之成見所局。及長。
尤深思明辨。勵行身心之修養。前清宣
統己酉科優貢。直隸補用知縣。自治研
究所畢業。歷充諸議局議事課員。省議
會秘書長。民國二年正式國會成立。被
選爲參議院議員。國會解散後。歸里獨
居。靜觀世變。五年六月袁氏死。黎氏
繼任。及國會重開。遂應召來京。復爲
參議院議員。

君人と爲り誠篤な古訓を確守す。居常厚
道を以て人を待つ。秉性聰慧人に異り、幼より即ち事理
を明察して思考敏捷、意志堅強なり。弱冠書を讀み即ち
其の徴を發し其の義を究めて別に新奇を開き、流俗の成
見に囚る、所と爲らず。長ずるに及び尤も深く思索して
身心の修養に勵みたり。前清宣統己酉科の優貢生にして、諸議局議
事課員、省議會秘書長に歷充す。民國二年正式國會成立
に際し選ばれて參議院議員と爲る。國會解散して後ち鄉
里に歸りて、閉臥し靜に世變を觀望す。五年六月袁氏死
して黎氏繼任し、約法復活して國會重ねて開かるゝに及
び、君復た其の召集に應じて北京に抵り、現に仍は參議
院議員たり。

直隸補用知縣となる。自治研究所を卒業して、諸議局議

Mr. Sun Nai-hsiang otherwise called Jui-cheng, age forty one, is a native of Pan yang. Honesty of character and strict observance of ancient ettiquet, the friendship to others all go to make up the character of our hero. He has quicker understanding and strong will. He entered most deeply so that he never became subject of popular ideas. As he grew older he became a deeper thinker than ever. In 1909 he was appointed a governor of the Chi-lin province and was graduated from the civic system investigating bureau. He was appointed the chief of the secretary of the provincial assembly. In the 2nd year of the Republic he was elected a member of the Senate. With the dessolution of the Parliament he returned to his native country where he quietly observed the change of the time. With the death of the Yuanshi-kai the position was changed. Under the new Emperor the Parliament was opened so that he went to Peking and was elected a member of the Senate.

侯汝信　字意樵　歲四十八

選舉地　河南省
籍　貫　河南省扥縣
住　址　北京西單牌樓二條胡同

君天資絕高。悟性敏捷。而頭腦細密。
其言論思想。省秩序井然。絕無顛倒紊
亂之弊。自幼讀書即喜探索精義不以
文字自拘。故其於學問。雖所歷未深。
然每有所讀。必大有進益。以其能精思
深入。抉其竅要。故其見解思想。皆極
明瞭切實。且洞悉事情。明察物理。長
於幹濟之才。居常以誠厚待人。然於社
會裏面鬼蜮情形。莫不深悉無遺。自學
成後。歷充農林分會會長。巡警局正警
董。城議會議員。國會選舉事務所所
長。省議會議員。正式國會成立。被選
爲候補參議院議員。後歷任山東兵工
廠火藥工監。鑄鐵所工監。管庫員。陝
西蜥蜴蛤百貨徵收局局長。及此次國
會復活。循例補充參議院議員。

民國之精華　（傳記）侯汝信先生

君天資絕高、悟性敏捷にして頭腦細密なり。其の言論思
想秩序井然として顛倒紊亂の弊なし。幼より書を讀み常
に其の精義を探索して文字の末に拘泥せず。故に學に於
て深からずと雖も讀む處あるに從つて大に進益あり。以
て能く其の竅要を抉り、其の見解思想極めて明瞭切實な
り。且つ事情を洞察して物理を明かにし幹濟の才に長す
然かも常に人に接して誠實なるも、社會の裏面即ち鬼蜮
の情形を洞察して遺す處なし。學成りてより後ち農林分
會會長、巡警局正警董、城議會議員、縣議會議員等に歷任
す。正式國會成立するや選ばれて參議院議員補缺員とな
る。次いで山東兵工廠火藥工監、鑄鐵所工監、管庫員、
陝西蜥蜴蛤百貨徵收局々長に歷任す。次いで國會復活す
るに及び缺員を補充して參議院議員と爲る。

Mr. Hau Ju-hsin, age forty eight, is a native of Pa hsien, Ho-nan hsing. He is a gentleman

of bright nature being well informed on books. While young he proved himself to be a great seeker

of truth from these books. Therefor all his reading was greatly beneficial to him. In dealing with

others he had penetrating force of character so that he could show sympathy to proper parties. He

was the president of agriculture and forrestry accociation, and the member of the local assembly.

When the Parliament was opened he was elected a member of the Senate and occupied various import-

ant government offices in different provinces of China. When the Parliament was re-opened he was

appointed a member of the Senate. Among others we may mention his work connected with the Shang-

tung arsenal and iron works etc.

恩華　字詠春

選舉地　西藏
籍　貫　西藏
住　址　北京錦什坊街東籤馬營

君賦性敦厚溫和。與人交。和藹可親。
雖仇敵。亦假以顏色。不出惡聲。然為
人篤實不欺。動止以禮自持。雖長於交
際。而無形中自有不可侵越之界限。曾
未嘗曲已從人。較之碌々追隨俗者。自
屬大相逕庭。自幼好讀。喜博覽羣書。
任意所之以為快。而不屑規規然從事
于科舉之業。故其讀書絕以至主觀判
斷是非。不局于習俗之成見。及海內
維新。慾立志求有用之學。遂留學日本
入法政大學畢業。歸國後。前清癸卯進
士。充江南三江師範學堂提調。學部總
務司長。憲政編查館法制局科員。弼
德院參議。資政院議員。民國成立。任
為國務院秘書。現充衆議院議員。

君賦性敦厚溫和にして人と交りて和靄親しむべし。仇敵と
雖も顏を和げ惡聲を出さず。然かも人と爲り篤實にして
欺かず。動止禮を以て自ら持す。交際に長ずと雖も無形
中自ら侵越すべからざる限界あり。幼より讀書を好みて
群籍を涉獵し、意の向ふ所に任せて快とす。故に其の讀
書は專ら主觀を以て是非を判斷し習俗の成見に囚るゝ所
とならず。海內維新に及び、志を立てゝ有用の學を求む。
遂に笈を負ふて日本に留學し、法政大學に入りて卒業す。
歸國の後ち前淸癸卯の試に及第して進士と爲る。江南師
範學校提調、學部總務司長に歷任す。又た憲政編查館法
制局科員となり、弼德院參議に列し、資政院議員に選ば
る。民國成立して後ち國務院秘書に任じたり。民國二年
常選の正式國會衆議院議員にして、五年國會恢復するや、
再び其の召集に應じて現に仍は衆議院議員たり。

Mr. En Hua otherwise called Yung-Chun is a native of Hsi-Tsang. In dealing with others, he is sociable and sincere. Even towards his enemy, he can maintain this attitude, and will not betrry his anger. Although sociable, he is far from being obsequious. While young he was an extensive reader of books. He formed his judgement in accordance with the information he thus obtained so that he is not bound up traditional inflnence as others are. When the new trend of thought was introduced to China, he sought a useful learning. Coming to Japan with this object in view, he was graduated from the law college. On returning to his own country, he successful passed the civic service examination. He was then appointed an in structor of the Cheng-nan normal school, and a member of the board of the legislature; Besides being a member of the local assembly, he was appointed a secretary of the state bureau after the formation of the Republic. In the second year of the Republic, he was returned for the House of Commons, Later when the new president was appointed he was again returned for the House of Commons the honor he at present eujoys.

翁恩裕　字問卿　歲四十一

選舉地　奉天省

籍貫　奉天省本溪縣

住址　北京闢才胡同西楡錢胡同

君秉性溫厚篤實。居恒恭謙自持。待人以和。雖所素惡。亦假以顏色。不出惡聲。雖所仇敵。不忍虐待之。然其言動舉止皆確有本末。而無形中自有不可侵越之界限。曾未嘗曲己狥人。拄尺直尋之事。自幼聰慧好讀。深思明辦。故於古義多所領悟。然喜求有用之學。長及。遍購新書讀之。造詣極深。前清任筆帖式。授官候補主事。辛亥革命。宣布憲政共和。民國肇造。正式國會成立。被選爲衆議院議員。國會解散後。歸里讀書。時時從事於地方公益之提倡。及國會重開。再應召集。遂又入京。仍爲衆議院議員。

民國之精華　（傳記）　翁恩裕先生

君秉性溫厚篤實にして居常恭謙自ら持し、人を待つに和を以てす。平生憎惡せる者に對しても惡聲を出さず、仇敵と雖も之を虐待するに忍びず。然かも其の言動舉止皆な本末ありて、無形の中自から侵越すべからざる限界あり。未だ嘗て己を曲げて人に狥ふこと無し。幼より聰慧にして學を好み、深く思索して明に辨す。故に古義に於て領得する所多し。長ずるに及びて遍ねく新書を購求して之を讀む。前清時代、筆帖式に任じ、候補主事となる。辛亥命を革め憲政共和を宣布して民國の基を開くや、選ばれて正式國會衆議院議員と爲る。國會解散後、歸鄕して讀書自ら娛み、時に地方公益の事に從ふ。太年約法恢復して國會重ねて開かるゝに及び、再び召集に應じて入京し、仍ほ復た衆議院議員となる。

Mr. Weng En-yn, age forty one, is a native of Pen chi, Fengtien province. He is a gentleman of quiet and humble disposition. In associating with others, he was guided by the prinaple of loves and kindness. Even towards the eveing, he cultivated this virtue. He had within himself the personal command worthy of the respect from others. He could not bend himself simply to win the good will of others. When young, he is fond of learning, and at the same time a deep thinker. As he grew older, he was an ardent reader of new books. When the Republic was formed, he was elected a member of the House of Commons. After the dissolution of the Parliament, he was fond of reading books, and interested himself with the work of public nature. When the Parliament was re-opened, he responded to the call from the new president, and has returned for the House of Commons.

凌發彬 字雅林

選舉地　廣西省
籍　貫　廣西省靖西縣
住　址　北京後青廠廣西三館

君秉性仁厚。富於感情。自幼好爲義舉。喜爲不平之鳴。鄉人有處困厄者。輒竭力救援之。事成不望報。不成則引爲絕大恥辱。蓋君素尚信義。重然諾。故人有所託。恒佯拒不允。復暗中爲之盡力。以免貪不成之責。居常以勤儉自持。衣食居住。皆極簡約。與人交。務勸善爲訓。然嚴己而薄責於人。朋友有過唯避人直言諫止之。而對他人則力爲之隱飾。有善行。則揄揚之。不遺餘力。前清時留學日本。入明治大學法科專門部。畢業後歸國。從事教育。民國成立後。投身軍界。現充衆議院議員。

君秉性仁厚にして感情に富む。幼より義舉を好みて、鄉人の困窮する者あれば力を竭して之を援ひ、事成りて報を望まず、成らざれば大恥辱と爲す。蓋し君素と信義を尚びて然諾を重んず。故に人若し託する所あれば、恒に佯びて允さず、而して暗中窃かに之が爲に盡力して、成らざる時の責を免かる。居常勤儉を以て自ら持し、衣食住皆共に極めて簡便なり。人と交りて努めて勸善懲惡を以て訓と爲し、然かも己に嚴にして人を責むるに薄し。會て前清時代笈を負ふて日本に留學し、明治大學校に學びて法科を卒業す。歸國して後ち育英の業に從事して後進を誘掖し、民國成立後、身を軍界に投じて我軒に從ひ、民國二年衆議院議員に選れて議政壇上の鬪士と爲る。此の次國會復活と共に再び出でゝ仍は衆議院議員たり。

Mr. Ling Fa-shan sometimes called Ya liu is a native of Ching-hsi, Kuang-hsi province. Naturally he is a gentleman full of sympathy so that being heroic in temperament he was always ready to those in need apart from any consideration of rewards. He was faithful to his promise and was ready good and kind turns to others without their knowledge. He is a strong advocate of frugality and simplicity in the mode of living. In the previous Chinese period he went to Japan where he studied law in the Meiji University. On his return home he was interested in the education of the younger generation. In the 2nd year of the Republic, he was elected a member of the Parliament when he proved himself to he a strong debator in the House of Commons. When the Parliament was restored he was returned for the House of Commons.

凌 鉞 字子黃 歲三十四

選舉地　河南省
籍貫　河南省固始縣
住址　北京買家胡同十三

君幼讀書。慷慨有志節。而天性疏放。不屑爲章句之學。曾肄業河南開封正誼中學。天津南開中學。北洋法政專門學校等處。辛亥八月。革命軍起。潛伏天津。與白雅雨張良珅諸君。組織北方共和會。身任軍務。十月被舉爲炸彈隊隊長。前往直隸灤州超義。民國元年五月。由津回豫。復經三十六團體公舉。爲全省國民捐代表。赴京師。因見惡於袁氏。被捕入京畿軍政總執法處。侃侃陳詞。卒不力屈。趙秉鈞乃代袁謝罪。釋放。其冬歸里。適第一次國會舉行選舉。遂當選爲衆議院議員。癸丑之役。討袁軍起。復微服出京。潛往上海。未幾。民軍失敗。出亡日本。至五年六月六日。袁氏暴亡。國會復活。始歸就衆議院議員。

君幼より書を讀み、慷慨にして氣節あり。天性粗豪にして章句の學を屑とせず、曾て河南開封府の正誼中學校、天津の南開中學校、北洋法政專門學校等に入りて修業す。辛亥八月革命軍起るや、潛に天津に於て白雅雨、張良珅等と北方共和會を組織して自ら軍務に服し、十月爆烈彈隊長に舉げられて直隸省灤州に往きて事を舉ぐ。民國元年五月天津より河南に歸り、三十六團體より國民捐代表に舉げられて北京に赴く、袁政府に忌れて京畿軍政總執法處に捕る、君侃々として屈せず、趙秉鈞乃ち謝罪して釋放す。其の冬、鄕里に歸臥するや、適ま第一次國會議員の選舉に會し、遂に選ばれて衆議院議員となる。癸丑の歲、討袁の軍起るや復た徽服して京を出で、窃に上海に赴き、事敗れて日本に亡命す。五年六月六日袁氏死し、旋て國會復活す、君蹶躍して歸國し、其の召集に應じて再び衆議院議員と爲る。

民國之精華　（傳記）　凌　鉞　先生

Mr. Ling Yueh otherwise called Tzu-huang, thirty-four years of age, is a native of Ku-shih, Ho-nan province. While young he was a great admirer of books and naturally a man of heroic temperament. Being imperious in nature, he did not care to be bound up mere forms and words of literary character. He studied in the Pe-yang law school and when in 1910 the revolutionary movement took place he went to Chi-lin province where he showed his keen interest in this movement. In the 1st year of the Republic he went back to Ho-nan and went to Peking representing thirty six associations. He was suspected by the Yuanshi-Kai government and was held in custody but since he held out his own he was released and went back his native province. When the 1st Parliament was opened he was appointed a member of the House of Commons. In 1913 he left Peking with a view to attack Yuanshi-Kai after consulting with his friends in Shanghai. His plans having been failed he escaped to Japan. With the death of Yuanshi-Kai he returned to his country and was elected a member of the House of Commons.

耿臻顯 字

歲三十一

選舉地　山西省
籍　貫　山西省渾源縣
住　址　北京兵部窪十二

君秉性誠篤朴實。脫盡浮華。生平極尚信義。言動舉止。確有本末。與人有約。雖遇意外危險。亦必拾身踐履。前言。若以實際上無可排除障碍。致未克如約以行。則引爲絕大恥辱。以故人有所託。常不肯輕於承諾。有時或先託詞拒絕。然後暗中爲之盡力。事不成。可不負責。事成亦不望報。蓋生性使然。非有意造作以博浮名也。前清末期遊學日本。入盛岡高等農林學校。民國元年畢業歸國。由山西高等農林學校被聘。爲該校農科主教。八月兼充勸學公所。礦農科副科長。二年一月。被選爲衆議院議員。三年一月。國會停止。乃應粤海關監督之招。充石岐稅關總辦。五年八月。國會重開。復就衆議院議員之舊職。

耿臻顯先生

君秉性誠實にして素朴。生平極めて信義を尚びて言動舉止確かに本末あり。人と約するや、萬一危險に遭遇するも亦た身を捨てゝ前言を履行す。故に人若し託する所あるも輕々しく承諾を與へず、時ありて或は先づ詞に託して拒絕し、然る後ち暗に之が爲に盡力し、事成るも亦た報を望まず。前清の末期に於て笈を負ふて日本に游學し、盛岡高等農林學校に入

りて修業し、民國元年其の業を畢へて歸國す。爾來山西高等農林學校に聘せられて同校農科主任教師と爲り、勸學公所礦農科副科長を兼任したり。二年一月國會停止さるゝや、乃ち粤海關監督より招聘されて石岐稅關總辦に任す。五年八月國會重ねて開かるゝに及び職を辭して其の召集に應ひ、復た仍ほ衆議院議員の職に就た

Mr. Keng Chen-hsien, otherwise called Yang-ting, age thirty one, is a native of Hun-yuan, Shan-hsi hsing. He is a strong man of fidelity to his couse, so that when he makes a promise he will keep it even at the risk of his life. He hates any ostensible conduct so that what he does for his friends he does it unknown to others. At the latter days of the Chinese regime he went to Japan and entered the Morioka High Agricultural College and returned to his country. In the first year of the Republic, he returned to his home completing the course of study. In the second year of the Republic, he was returned for the House of Commons. When the Parliament was reopened he went back to his country and was returned for the House of Commons, the position of honour he enjoys at present.

耿春宴 字杏珊

選舉地　河南省
籍　貫　河南省孟縣
住　址　北京象牙胡同四

君賦性至孝。一舉一動。必曲體親心。順其意志。非親所喜之事。必先時請命。察親辭色以定行止。親有所訓。雖有不當。必先確守不移。然後乘間婉陳利害得失。迨至親心已悟。始敢變其所為。親有過。先假他事比譬。以顯明得失。不改。然後婉詞曲陳。復不聽則哀泣減食。卒能感動親心。居常事親。以養志為宗。而不專為口體之奉。自少即以能文見稱。於癸卯科舉于鄉。旋遊學日本東京。入宏文學院速成師範博物班。嗣入實科學校速成理化班。卒業歸國後。歷充孟縣勸學所總董。許洲中學監督。衛輝府中學監督。河南優級師範齋務長。中央教育會會員。河朔法政學校校長。民國二年。被選為眾議院議員。國會既停。君歸里讀書。時復從事于地方公益之事。及國會復活。遂來京復為議員。

君賦性至孝にして一舉一投足必ず父母の命を戴して其の意見に順ふ。親の訓る所あれば當らすと雖必ず先づ之を守り、然る後ち間に乘じて利害得失を陳べて徐らに其の所為を改む。少より即ち能文を以て稱せらる。癸卯の歲鄉試に及第し、旋て日本に留學して宏文學院師範博物速成科に入り、嗣いで實科學校理化速成科に入りて卒業す。歸國して後ち育英の事業に從事して孟縣勸學所總董。

許州中學監督、衛輝府中學監督、河南優級師範齋庫務長、中央教育會々員、河朔法政學校々長等の職に歷任し、後進を誘掖して令名あり。民國二年正式國會の成立に際し衆望を荷つて衆議院議員に常選す。既にして國會停止さるゝや鄉里に歸省して讀書自ら娛み、時に復た地方公益の事業に盡力す。國會復活するに及び、復た出でゝ其の召集に應じて仍ほ衆議院議員と爲る。

民國之精華　（傳記）　耿春宴先生

一百九十五

Mr. Keng Chun-yen, sometimes called Hsing-shan, is a native of Meng hsien, Ho-nan province. He is well known for his filial obedience and obeys to parents order in every small particular. While young he was well known for his book learning. In 1903 he went to Japan where he was graduated from the normal school. On returning home he was interested in the educational work, so that he passed through a series of various important government posts. In the 2nd year of the Republic when the Parliament was brought into existence, he was returned for the House of Commons. When Yuanshi-kai stopped the Parliament he returned to his country, where he devoted himself to the upbuilding of local interests. With the reestablishment of the Parliament he responded to the summon and returned for the House of Commons, the position of honour he now holds. It may also be mentioned that for sometime in the past he was the president of the law school in his province.

馬維麟　字豫勤

選舉地　甘肅省

籍貫　甘肅省道河縣

住址　北京李鐵拐斜街三元店

君秉性敦篤朴實。不喜浮華。爲人嚴正剛毅。不阿權貴。疾惡崇善。鄉里有不平之事。輒喜爲弱者盡力。必辦其曲直而後已。自幼聰慧過人。讀書過目成誦深入精微。洞悉義理。然信念鞏固。意志堅强。回族中之雋傑也。曾入本省文高等大學堂畢業。民國肇造五大民族共和成立。元年被選爲本省臨時省議會議員。二年正式國會組織。當選爲參議院議員。綜計民國國會中。回族議員唯有二名。君其一人也。對于憲法草案。以孔教爲國教條文。君爲極端反對者。蓋囙教中之新進秀才也。國會解散後。歸里熱心提倡回族之振興。五年及國會重召集。遂又入京。仍爲參議院議員。

君秉性敦篤にして篤實、浮華を喜ばず。人と爲り嚴正剛毅にして權貴に阿らず。惡を惡み善を擧びて、鄉里若し不平の事あれば輒ち喜んで弱者の爲に盡力し、必ず其の曲直を辨きて後ち已む。幼より聰慧人に過ぎ、然かも信念鞏固にして意志堅强、回敎徒中の雋傑なり。曾て甘肅省立文高等大學校に入りて卒業す。五大民族共和の新政を初めて民國を樹立せんとするや、元年臨時省議會議員に選ばる。二年正式國會の組織に際し、參議院議員に當選す。民國議會參衆兩院議員八百餘名中、回敎徒の議員は君を加へて僅に二人のみ。憲法條項中孔子の敎を以て國敎とするの一條に對し極端に反對す。蓋し亦た回敎族中の新進秀才なり。國會解散後、鄉里に歸りて熱心に回敎徒の開發振興を提唱したり。五年國會重ねて開かるゝに及び、遂に又た入京して仍は參議院議員と爲る。

Mr. Ma Wei-lin, known as Yu Chin, a native of Tao-ho hsien, the Kan-su hsing, is a friend of the poor and oppressed. He is honest and sincere, gentle to others, out strict to himself, but will not Kowtow to the influence. He has strong will, and the most influential figure among the Mahomedans in the country. He was educated in the university of Kan-su hsing. When the five leading tribes in China combined their efforts to establish a Republic, he was elected a member of the Extraordinary meeting held for the purpose. In 1917, when the Parliament was opened, he was appointed a member of the Senate. Of eight hundred members which composed the Parliament, there were only two Mohamedans of whom he is one. He most vehemently opposed so a clause in the Constitution which would have Confucian teaching as the state religion. On the dissolution of the Parliament, he returned to his home where he was most ardently engaged in the propagation or Mohamedanion. When the Parliament was opened again, he was elected a member of the Senate.

馬蔭榮　字樾盦　歲四十五

選舉地　山東省

籍貫　山東省荏平縣

住址　北京茄子胡同十六

君賦性高潔消介。言動風采。皆絕異凡
流。然爲人篤實不欺。脫盡虛驕氣習。
自幼聰穎絕倫。悟性敏捷。年方弱冠。
即以詩文書法著于郷里。稍長。尤奮勉
求博。頗以遠自期。不專其心力於舉
業。然卒能連抉科第。直成進士爲翰林
院編修。曾於前清派充駐日山東留學
生監督。旋歸國歷充山東學務公所議
長。自治籌辦處會辦。山東優級師範學
堂監督。全省農會協理。都督府參議。
山東高等農業學校監督。省議會議員
民國正式國會成立。君被選爲參議院
議員。國會解散。歸里閉戶讀書不談時
政。直至國會恢復。始入京就職。

君賦性高潔にして消介、言動風采皆な凡流に異る。然り
人と爲り篤實にして欺かず、虛驕の氣習を脱す。幼より
聰穎絕倫にして年方に弱冠即ち詩文書法を以て郷里に著
る。稍や長して研學益々精を究め、進士に及第して翰林
院編修と爲る。旋て歸國して後ち山東學務公所議長とな
る。曾て前清時代日本駐山東留學生監督と爲り、山東自治籌
辦處會辦、山東優級師範學堂監督、全省農會協理、山東
高等農業學校監督、省議會議員等の職
に歷充したり。民國成立して正式國會議員選擧の事ある
や、君選ばれて參議院議員と爲る。國會解散さるゝや、田
園に歸去來を賦し、杜門閉居偏に書册に親しみて時事を
談せず。既にして國會恢復するに及び、君復た召集され
て北京に抵り、仍ほ參議院議員の職に就きたり。

都督府參議、山東高等農業學校監督、省議會議員等の職

民國之精華　（傳記）馬蔭榮先生

Mr. Ma Yin Yung aged forty five is a native of Jen P'ing Hsien, Shan Tung Sheng. He is
a gentleman whose integrity of character need hardly any comment. Both in deed and words as well
as in personal presence he is above the men of common calibre. Being honest in character, he is above
any deceitful acts, and is absolutely free from vain and arrangant temperament. While Young, his
sagacity knew no equal and his name became widely known in his native place as one superior to others
in the art of versification and writing. As he grew older, he progressed in study and successfully passed
the examination to become a Chin-Si and was appointed a compiler attached to the Han Lin Yuang.
In the previous Chinese regime, he was appointed the inspector of the Chinese students of Shan Tung
sheng studying in Japan. On return to China, he occupied many an important posts such as the president of the Shan Tung Educational Department, the director of the Shang Tung Normal school and
the Agricultural school. He was interested in the development of the Shang Tung Civie body besides
being the member of district assemblies. When the National Assembly was summoned under the
Republic he was appointed a member of the senate. When the National Assembly was disolved, he
returned to his home, where he spent his days in peace, indulging himself in composing poems and
producing literary works, but with the opening of the National Assembly for the second time, he
repaired to Peking, and was elected a member of the House of Commons.

馬小進　字退之　歲二十八

選舉地　廣東省

籍　貫　廣東省臺山縣

住　址　北京西城臨清宮馬宅

君。資質聰穎。自幼好學。喜爲詩文。及
長尤醉心新學。加以家本富豪。故能專
心於學。不憂乏資。曾肄業于廣東法政
學堂法律本科。畢業于香港聖士提反
高等學堂。旋復肄業于美國哥林比亞
大學文科。及紐約大學商業財政科。君
舊爲同盟會人。由國民黨選出爲衆議
院議員。發丑二次革命。遂脫國民黨。
民國三年。歷充總統府秘書。財政部秘
書。稅務處幫辦。叙官中士。國會復活。
遂復爲衆議院議員。兼任憲法起草委
員。外交股常任委員。

君資質聰順にして幼より學を好み、喜んで詩文を作る。
長ずるに及び尤も心を新學に傾注す。家本も富豪なるが
故に學に志して資の乏しきを憂へず。曾て廣東法政學堂
法律本科を修め、香港聖士提反高等學堂を卒業す。旋て
復た米國に游學して哥倫比亞大學文科及び紐約大學商業
財政科に學ぶ。君素と同盟會員にして、民國成立後、國
民黨より選ばれて衆議院議員となる。第二革命に際して、
君途に國民黨を脱會したり。國會解散後、民國三年大總統
府秘書、財政部秘書、税務處辦等の職に歷任す。國會復
活後、復た召集されて衆議院議員となる。

Mr. Ma Hsiao Chin who styled himself as Tui Chih is twenty eight years old, being a native of the Tai Shan Hsiang, the Kuang Tung Sheng. He exhibited his sagacity of nature on many occasions, and was deeply addicted to study and even in his youth, he found pleasure in poetical and literary works. As he grew older, he turned his attention to the study of the new learning. Being of a wealthy family, he had never to trouble himself about plenniary matters in accomplishing his study. After graduating from the Law department of the Kuang Tung Law school, he entered the St. Timothy's High school, Hongkong, whence he went over to America where he entered the university of Columbia where he took the literature course, and then attended the commercial and financial course of the New York University. At the time when the Republic was established, he was returned for the House of Commons, as a member of the National party, but in the second Revolution, he left the National party, In the third year of the Republic, he was appointed the private secretary of the President, that of the Financial Department, the chief of the Taxation Burean. When the Parliament was opened, he was elected the member of the House of Commons.

袁弼臣　字朝佐　歳四十五

選舉地　四川省
籍　貫　四川省長寧縣
住　址　北京潘家河沿

君爲人忠實無欺。性喜質朴。不事浮
華。而氣字深厚。不輕於表示意志。故
雖遇事出以至誠。而人究莫能窺其深
淺。與人交。淡而能久。然亦喜爲規勸。
惟辭氣和婉不使人因羞忿而强辯且
必相其人能納諫者。然後慨慨開導之。
否則惟漸與疏遠。不露絕交之痕迹。自
幼聰慧絕倫。弱冠卽著文名。及長尤
博及羣書。討求眞義。故其爲文工于說
理。不屑從事于推砌。壯年。頗以名儒
自期。及海內維新。乃盡棄舊學。肆力
新書。遂肄業于四川通省師範學堂。畢
業後復肄業于北京法律學堂正科班。
於前淸以拔貢朝考一等。南京臨時政
府成立之際。君任內務部禮敎局科長。
民國二年。被選爲衆議院議員。國會解
散後。歸里讀書。遇事取消極態度。及
國會復活。始來京。仍就議員之職。

民國之精華　（傳記）袁弼臣先生

君人と爲も忠實にして欺かず、性質朴を喜びて浮華を
事とせず、氣字深沈にして輕々に意見を表示せず。人と
交るや淡さして能く久しく、然かも亦た喜んで規勸を爲
すも辭氣和婉なり。幼より聰慧絕倫にして、弱冠尙ほ且
つ文名著はる。長するに及びて尤も群書を涉獵して眞義
を討究し、其の文を作るや說理に工みなり。壯年に至り
頗る名儒を以て自ら期す。海內維新に及び、乃ち舊學を
棄て〻勉めて新書を購讀し、遂に四川通省師範學校に入

りて學ぶ。卒業の後ち、復た笈を負ふて京師に抵り、北京
法律學堂正科に學ぶ。前淸拔貢生、朝考第一等の成績を
以て及第す。第一革命の事起りて南京臨時政府成立に際
するや、君其の內務部禮敎局科長に任ず。民國二年選ば
れて衆議院議員となり、國會解散後歸省して書冊に親み、
事に遇へば消極的態度を持して時事の變を待つ。國會復
活するに及び、召集されて再び衆議院議員となる。

Mr. Yuan Pi Chen, sometimes known as Chao Tso is a native of the Chang Ning Hsiang, Ssu Chuan Sheng. This year he has seen forty five summers. Honesty and faithfulness are the two words which describe his personality. He lones simplicity, but hetes any extravagance and vain glory. Being meditative turn of mind, he does not express his thonght without deep consideration. In associating with others; he is simple and straightforward: Even in giving warning to others, his language is full of charms. He showed his wisdom while quite young and his literary fame stood quite high. He was a copious reader of books. He dived into the deep significance of the works he read, and his literary works are full of sound reasonings. His ambition was to be a grand scholer. With the progress of the time, he turned his attention to the perusal of new books. He entered the Normal school in Ssu Chuan Tung Sheng. On finishing the course in the Normal school, he repaired to Peking when he entered the Peking Law college. In the Previous Chinese regime, he passed the civil competetive examination with honours. With the 1st Revolutionary movement, the extraordinary Nanking Government was formed, when he was appointed the head of the Religlous Burean of the Home Department. In the 2nd yeer of the Republic, he was returned for the House of Commons. On the disolution of the parliament, he returned to his home, and bid the fair time, while he beguiled his own by reading books. When the National Assembly met for the second time, he was returned for the House of Commons.

袁景熙　字光泗歳四十五

選擧地　山東省

籍　貫　山東省済寗縣

住　址　北京西城取燈胡同門牌壹號

君幼ら貧文名工科擧業。然ら運蹇屢試
不中。中年棄舊從新。以附貢生考補
濟南尚志堂學長。光緒廿四年。因條陳
新政。由山東巡撫以人才保薦並聘充
撫署文案。廿五年。充曹縣書院院長。
廿六年充山東右路防軍總文案。兼營
務處。廿七年。上善後十八策于北洋大
臣。以學諳中西。填備諮詢。調赴保定。
派充兵備處文案提調。嗣充北洋財政
局提調。三十四年。丁憂回籍。應上海
中外日報之聘任駐京新聞記者。民國
元年。六月。委署登州府知府。旋留省改
充高等顧問。又爲山東統一黨支部長。
及共和黨支部長。二年被選爲衆議院
議員。國會解散後。歷任塞北關監督。四
局局長。塞北關監督。四年敍官上大夫
稅釐徵收局々長。塞北關監督に歷任す
以不贊成帝制免職。及國會復活。始來
京就職。

君幼より文名を負ひ、然かも屢々試を受けて及第せす。
中年舊學を棄てゝ新學を求め、附貢生として以て濟南尚志學
堂校長に補す。光緒二十四年新政を條陳したるを以て山
東巡撫より保薦せられて巡撫衙門文案となる。二十五年
曹縣書院々長となり、二十六年山東右路防軍總文案兼管
務處出仕となる。二十七年善後十八策を北洋大臣に上陳
して其の學を賞せられ、調して保定に赴き兵備處文案提
調に補せらる。嗣で北洋財政局提調に任じ、三十四年喪
に服して鄕里に歸り、後ち上海中外日報北京通信員とな
る。民國元年山東都督府政治顧問兼秘書となり、次で登州
府知府署理に補せられしも、省城に留りて高等顧問とな
り、又た山東統一黨支部長及ひ共和黨支部長となる。二
年選はれて衆議院議員となり、國會解散して後ち、塞北
關監督に歷任す。帝制に贊成せざ
るを以て職を免せらる、國會復活するや、召集せられて
復た衆議院議員たり。

Mr. Yuan Ching I, otherwise called Kuang Ssu is forty five years old. While young, he enjoyed a fame for his literary production. He went up for the examination more than once, but failed. He began to acquire the new learning, and was appointed the assistant to the president of the Chi Nan Shang Chih School. His memorial concerning the new government has highly approned by the authority, and he was appointed the literary secretary of the Shan Tung Governor, and then appointed the president Tsao Hsien Shu Yuan, and obtained an appointment as a sort of literary secretary to the Shang Tun Yu Lu Fang Military headquarter. He addressed a memorial to the Pei Yang Minister which comprised the celebrated eighteen plans. Passing through various official career of high importance, he was finally appointed the governor of the Pei Yang Financial Burean. On account of mounning, he returned to his native country. Before long, he became the Peking correspondent of a Shanghai paper. In the 1st year of the Republic, he was appointed the political axviser and secretary to the governor of the Shang Tung. Under various other capacities, he was deeply interested in the promotion of political wellfare of the Shang Tung Sheng. In the 2nd year of the Republic, he was elected as a member of the House of Commons. As he was a supporter of the Yuan Shi-Kai's cause in adopting the Imperial system, he was relieved of some of the Government's services, but when the National Assembly was opened, he was again returned for the House of Commons.

袁炳煌 字經凡 歲三十六

選舉地 新疆省
籍　貫 湖南省湘陰縣
住　址 北京兵馬前街湘館

君秉性篤實堅強。富于忍耐之力。居常
以緘默自持。待人以和。而操已以嚴。
言動皆簡約平易。不以矜奇立異爲懷、
其處世接物。大都謙虛退讓。不執我
私。不持偏見。生平未嘗爲無意識之
爭。然當其志向既定。則又猛進力前。
堅忍不拔。雖迭遭挫折艱險層生。亦
百折不撓。必達目的而後已。君行爲雖
極拘謹。而其思想則頗放達不羈。且富
于好奇之性。唯不喜以此驚駭世俗而
已。年少讀書。即抱大志。不屑以文章
斷送其一生。甫及冠。即投筆出關。
於新疆天山南北之間。專力研究游牧
情況。數年之間。堅苦卓絕。艱險備嘗。
旋肄業於省城警察學校。卒業後。即於
該省以作幕僚爲生。民國二年。以被選爲
議員。始束就職。國會解散。遂歸故
鄉蟄居。不問時事。直至共和再造。國
會重開。始入京仍爲衆議院議員。

民國之精華　（傳記）　袁炳煌先生

君秉性篤實にして堅強、居常緘默自ら持し、人を待つに和
を以てし、已を操るに嚴を以てす。言動皆な簡約にして
平易、其の虛世謙讓にして偏見を持せず、生平未だ嘗て
無意識の爭を爲さず。然り其の志既に定まるや則ち邁進
して屢々挫折するも撓まず、必ずや最後の目的を達す。少
年書を讀みて即ち大志を抱き文章を以て一生を送るを屑
しとせず、後ち筆を投じて關を出で、新疆天山南北の間
を跋涉して專ら游牧の情況を視察し、數年の間困苦艱難
具さに嘗めたり。旋て省城の警察學校に學びて卒業後即
ち同省の幕僚として事に預る。民國二年正式國會議員
選舉に際し同省より選ばれて衆議院議員となる。國會解
散するや、鄉里に歸り蟄居し出でず、また時事を開ふな
し。國會重ねて開くるに及び、再び召集されて入京し、仍
ほ衆議院議員となる。

Mr. Yuang Ping Huang or Ching Fan is thirty six years old being a native of the Hsiang Yin Hsiang, the Hu Nan sheng. He is honest and solid is his character. Silence is his chief trait, being gentle towards others but strict to himself. Simple in language and humble in life, he is never prejudiced against others, but when he makes up his mind, nothing can prevent him from accomplishing his ends. He never slackens his efforts until he wins the last victory. He was ambitions, and did not rest contented with his literary attainment alone. He observed in person the condition of pasturage in the valleys of Hsin Chiang and Tien Chan for the space of several years during which time he encountered all manner of suffering and hardship. He studied in the Hsing-Chieng police school; after graduating from the school, he was a sort adviser to the province, and in the 2nd year of the Republic, he was returned for the House of Commons. Like many other leading men of the country, when the parliament was disolved, he returned to his home, and kept aloop from politic He entered Peking when the National Assembly was again opened, of which he now has become a member.

陳經鎔 字紹聞 歲四十九

選舉地　江蘇省

籍　貫　江蘇省泰興縣

住　址　北京後孫公園如泰會館

君秉性誠篤不欺。而資質聰穎絕倫弱
冠即有文名。喜爲詩歌。及長尤殫心漢
魏六朝之書。並廣覽諸子百家。時復涉
獵宋明理義之學。頗以調和漢宋自期。
及海內維新。見國事日非。慨然有澄清
天下之志。遂肆科舉業。奮志新學。旋
毀家獨創宗孟兩等小學校。并附設師
範講習所。振興教育。兼辦地方水利橋
梁慈善事業。復赴日本留學。入早稻田
大學畢業。嗣以江督端方奏獎知縣。簽
分山東。遂廢學歸國。民國元年。正式
國會成立。被選爲衆議院議員。國會
解散後。歸里讀書。時復贊襄地方公
益之事。五年及國會重開。始來京。復
爲衆議院議員。

Mr. Chen Ching-jung, otherwise called Shao-wen, age forty nine, is a native of Chin hsien, Chiang-su province. He is noted for the virtues of faithfulness and honesty. While young, he was fond of poetry, and attained more or less literary fame; he made himself the master of ancient classic. With the introduction of new trend of thought into this country, he perceived the fact that China was not quite up to standard. Then he at once proceeded to the study of new learning. He established a normal school with a view to the extention of learning, and at the same he was deeply interested in the work of charity. He went to Japan where he was educate in the Waseda University. At the first year of the Republic when the Parliament was brought into existence, he was elected for the House of Commons. With the desolution of the Parliament, he devoted himself to reading at his native country. At the same time he was interested in public works of those districts. When the Parliament was reopened he was returned for the House of Commons.

陳燮樞 字贊政 歲四十三

選舉地 浙江省

籍　貫 浙江省紹興縣

住　地 北京象坊橋浙江議員公寓

君賦性誠實篤厚。尚質惡文。不事無益之繁華。天資聰慧敏捷。自幼好學。弱冠有文名。及長。博覽群籍。專求眞義。不拘章句之末。及海內維新。喜求西學。凡譯迻之新書。無有所不覽。造詣漸深。新舊皆有素養。前清優廩生。賀笈東渡。留學日本。入早稻大學專門部政治經濟科。畢業歸國後。曾充紹興龍山法政學校校長。銳意從事育英。指導後進。開化民智。共和光復民國肇造。被選爲浙江臨時省議會議員。民國二年正式國會成立。君當選爲衆議院議員。把持正論。主張公議。翼贊大政勤助建設。國會解散後。南旋歸里。五年。及國會重開。君復應召。北上抵京。仍就衆議院議員舊職。

民國之精華　（傳記）　陳燮樞先生

君賦性篤實にして質を尚び文を惡む。天資聰慧敏捷にして幼より學を好み弱冠文名あり。長ずるに及びて群籍を涉獵して專ら眞義を求め章句の末に拘泥せず。海內維新に及び喜んで新學を求め、遂に笈を負ふて東渡し日本に留學す。早稻田大學校專門部政治經濟科に學びて卒業歸國す。曾て紹興龍山法政學校長に任じ、後進を誘掖して民智を開導するに努めたり。漢土光復して民國樹立するや、浙江臨時省議會議員に選ばる。民國二年正式國會議員選擧に際し、君乃ち民望を負ふて衆議院議員に當選す。正論を把持して公議を主張し、大政を翼贊して建設を襄助する所ありしも、未だ幾くならずして國會解散す。五年國會重ねて開かるゝに及び、君復た召集に應じて北京に入り、仍は衆議院議員の職に就きたり。

Mr. Chen Hsieh-hsu, otherwise called Hsan-cheng, age forty three, is a native of Shao-hsing, Che-chiang province. He is a gentleman of honor and high virtue. While young he was interested in the reading of books but as he grew older he sought more of the meaning of these books. When the new trend of thought became vogue in China, he made up his mind to acquire new learning and for this purpose he went to Japan. He entered the Waseda university and was graduated there from. He was appointed on return to his home the president of the law school in his province and devoted his energy to the guidance of the people. In the second year of the Republic he was elected for the House of Commons. He advocated a great cause and was to accomplish the mighty deed of the government but shortly the Parliament was dissolved. However with the Restoration of the Parliament he entered Peking and resumed his function as the Parliamentary member.

陳鴻疇 字錫九 歲三十九

選舉地 河南省

粋貫 河南省長葛縣

任址 北京達智橋嵩雲草堂

君爲人誠實不欺。喜爲貧困者助力。而
不輕於允諾。既承諾無不成者。以是人
愈信用之。自幼性慧頴。於舉業之術。
巳深有所造。然以傾心西學故。但以一
衿自足。不復從事科舉。遂河南高等學
校畢業後。自費留學日本。入早稻田大
學預科。旋改入岩倉鐵道學校建築科。
畢業歸國。任洛潼鐵路材料總廠廠長。
武昌起義時。赴漢口。有所謀未成。九
月。至上海。任都督府軍事科一等科
員。繼任威武軍駐漢兵站長。後因共和
告成。仍就洛潼鐵路材料總廠之職。第
二次革命時。遭政府疑忌。辭職歸家。
終日閉戶。談古人書。絶不與聞政事。
及國會復活。始應召來京。就職衆議院
議員云。

君人と爲りや誠實にして欺かず。貧困者の爲に助力する
ことを喜び、允諾を輕々しく爲さず、既に允諾すれば、成
さざること無し。是を以て人愈彼を信用す。幼より聰頴、
舉業の術に於て已に深く造詣する所あり。然れども心を
西學に傾くるの故を以て、復た科舉に從事せず。途に河南高等學校に入り業を
畢ふるの後、自費を以て日本に留學し、早稻田大學豫科
に入り、改めて岩倉鐵道學校建築科に入る。業を畢へて
國に歸り、洛潼鐵路材料總廠廠長に任す。武昌義を起す
時、漢口に赴き謀る所あり、未だ成らず。九月、上海に至
り、都督府軍事科一等科員に任せられ、繼いで威武軍駐
漢兵站長に任せらる。後共和成るを告ぐるに因り、仍は
洛潼鐵路材料總廠の職に就く。第二次革命の時、政府の
疑忌に遭ひ、職を辭して家に歸り、終日戶を閉ぢ、古人
の書を讀み、絶えて政事に興味せず。國會復活するや、
始めて召に應じて京に來り、職に衆議院議員に就く。

Mr. Chen Hung Chou sometimes known as Hsi Chiu, thirty nine years of age, is a native of the Cheng Ko Hsiang, the Ho Nan Sheng. He is sincere and honest in dealing with others. He takes a great delight in helping the poor. He is slow to give his consent, but once given he never wavers from his decision. He is deeply interested in the promotion of industry. He is quite satisfied with his learning, and never coveted any government position. He studied in the Ho Nan High School. At his own expense, he went to Japan where he studied in the preparatory course of the Waseda University and then entered the architectural department of the Iwakura Railway School. Having completed the regular course, he returned to his home where he was appointed the chief of the General Railway Material Department of the Lo Tung Railways. When General Wang started on his plan, he went to Hankow, but finding that the situation was premature, he returned to Shanghai. He had charge of military supply department in its various branches. When the Republic was brought into existence, he was again interested in the Lo Tung Railways, but on the occasion of the 2nd Revolution, he was suspected by the government which made him resign his post. He returned to his home where he spent the time in indulging himself in books, and never showed any interest in politics. However, when the National Assembly was opened, he went up to Peking, and was elected a member of the House of Commons.

陳光譜 字耀遠 歲三十七

選舉地　安徽省
籍貫　安徽省宣城縣
住江　北京前門內草帽胡同

君爲人剛毅不阿。然肯爲理屈。不喜爲意氣之爭。於前清光緒二十八年。以諸生入本省高等學校。三十二年。改入陸軍醫學校。次年因丁外難輟學。在籍從事教育。歷宣統二三年。所瓣辦學校。有法政講習所。自治研究所。師範講習所。公私立高初等小學數十所。該縣教育之發達。一時稱爲全省之冠。多出自君提唱之力。民國成立。在本省瓣辦民嵒日報。身任主幹。持論正大頗善聲譽。二年。當選爲衆議院議員。到京後。入民主黨。國會解散後。三四兩年充任本省視學。奔走各縣。多所提唱。及帝制之亂已兆。遂辭去視學職務。在本縣組織華興煤礦公司。一心從事實業。不談時事。國會重開。始於本年七月到京供職。國會開設之後。對於議員兼行政官之事。反對極力。

民國之精華　（傳記）　陳光譜先生

君人と爲り、剛毅阿らず。然れども肯て理の爲に屈し、意氣の爭を爲すを喜ばず。前清光緒二十八年、諸生を以て本省高等學校に入る。次年外難に丁るに因り學を罷め、郷に於いて教育に從事し、宣統二三年の間、學校法政講習所、自治研究所、師範講習所、公私立高初等小學校數十所を創設す。該縣教育の發達、一時稱して全省の冠と爲す、多く君が提唱の力より出づ。民國成立後、本省に在りて民嵒日報を創立し、自から其の主幹に任ず、持論正大、頗る聲譽を博す。

二年當選して衆議院議員と爲る。北京に到るの後、民主黨に入る。國會解散後、三四の兩年本省視學に充てられ、各縣を奔走し、提唱する所多し。帝制の亂已に兆するに及び、遂に視學を辭し、本縣に於て華興煤礦公司を組織し、一心實業に從事し、復た時事を談ぜず。國會重ねて開かるに至り、本年七月初めて北京に到り職に從ふ。國會開設後、議員にして行政官を兼ぬるの事に對して極力反對を唱へたり。

Mr. Chen Kuang Pu is thirty seven years old, being a native of the Hsuan Cheng, the An Hui Hsing. Being high spirited and imperious in nature, he never kotow to others, but he is amenable to reason, and will not fight others because of sentimental considerations. He received early education in the high school of his province, as well as in the Military Medical School. When the country was in trouble, he gave up his schooling, and at home, he was interested in the promotion of education. Under him, there are various institutes of learning some relating to the study of law and others to the investigation of the civic body system. It may not be amiss to say that a great deal of the success in the educational institutes of this province may be attributed to his efforts. After the Republic was brought into existence, he started the news paper in which his argument won the high confidence of the public. He was returned for the House of Commons. After the disolution of the Parliament, he was appointed the school inspector of the province in which capacity he contibuted a great deal to the interest of the country. On the ever of the outbreak of the trouble relating to the restoration of the Imperial regims, he organised a coal Mining Co. of which he became the director, and devoted all his energy to the promotion of its interest. In July, the present year, he went to Peking. He strongly opposed that a parliamentary member should retain an executive office.

陳承箕　字子裘　歲四十八

選舉地。福建省

籍　貫　福建省泰寧縣

住　址　北京敦場五條榕廬門牌十八號

君爲人老成持重。篤實不華。然天資聰慧絕倫。頭腦明晰。意志堅強。且富于忍耐之力。其處世接物。大都崇尚消極。不輕於舉動。唯其志向所在。則猛勇精進。不以艱重而餒其氣。自幼讀書。即能領悟眞義。得其精華。及長。尤博學愼思。洞悉事理。於前淸時。以廩貢生。任汀州府學敎授。兼中學監督。並籌辦泰寧選舉諮議局事務。歷充自治研究所所長。農林會會長。臨時省議會議員。正式國會成立。被選爲衆議院議員。國會解散。歸隱不出。迨及國會恢復。始應召入京。仍爲議員。

　君人となり老成持重、篤實にして華ならず。然も天資聰慧絕倫にして頭腦明晰、意志堅強なり。且つ忍耐力に富み、其の世に處し物に接するに當り舉動沈靜にして輕措なく、一度志せる所に向つては則ち勇猛精進し、常に艱難を以て其の氣を餒さず。幼より書を讀みて能く其の眞義を悟り、其の精華を得たり。長ずるに及びて尤も博く學び愼みて思ひ、悉く事理を究む。前淸の時に當り廩貢生を以て汀州府學敎授に命ぜられ、兼ねて中學監督の職に就く。亦た曾て泰寧諮議局選舉事務を處理す。次いで自治研究所所長、農林會會長、臨時省議會議員等の職に歷任す。正式國會成立するや、選ばれて衆議院議員となり。國會解散するに及びて、鄉里に隱退して出です。再び國會恢復するに際し、召集せられて之れに應じ、北京に入りて仍は衆議院議員の職に就く。

Mr. Chen Cheng-chi, otherwise called Tzu-sang, age forty eight, is a native of Tai-ning, Fuchien province. He was a gentleman of mature thought when young being clear brained and strong willed. Besides, he was noted for his patients and was not disturbed when he met any emergency. While young he was deeply interested in reading books the meaning of which he thoroughly comprehended. As he grew older he was a comprehensive as well as deep scholar. He was an educator in the middle school under the previous Chinese regime. He was also the chief of the agricultural association and the member of the special council. When the Parliament was brought into existence he became a member of the House of Commons. However with the dissolution of the Parliament he returned to his country where he kept to himself. When the Parliament was restored he went to Peking and was returned for the House of Commons.

陳 堃 字伯簡 歲四十四

選舉地　福建省第四區
籍貫　福建省建甌縣
住址　北京敎場五條十八號

君秉性樸實篤厚。不喜浮華。然天資顏高。思想活潑。居恒以禮自持。言笑不苟。與人交。溫恭謙下。不爲意氣之爭。人告以過。雖不當。亦謝其厚意決不自爲辯護。友朋有所託。無不勉強盡力。雖以此自陷於窘亦所不惜。自幼好學深思。不恥下問。弱冠時。酷好詩文。頗爲前輩所契重。及長遂改途求身心修養之學。不專心于舉業。既中鄉試。遂肄精有用之學。不復以仕進爲懷。旋入法政畢業後。以知縣分發浙江。宣統庚戌。考取法官。復以推檢分發浙江。歷任浙江寧波地方檢察廳檢察官。寧波地方審判廳刑庭推事。民事庭長。福建閩侯地方審判廳刑庭推事等職。民國二年。正式國會成立。被選爲衆議院議員。國會解散後。歸里閉戶讀書。不談時事。及國會重開。遂來京。復爲衆議院議員。

君性樸實にして篤厚、浮華を喜ばず。然も天資高潔、思想活潑なり。常に禮を以て自ら持す。人と交はず、己の過を人に警告せらるゝや喜んで之を受け、當らずと雖も其の厚志を感謝し、決して其の非を辯護せし事なし。朋友託する所あれば自己の利害を顧ずして盡力す。幼より學を好み詩文に巧なり、先輩の重んずる處となる。長ずるに及びて身心の修養に努め、擧業に意を傾注せず。既にして鄉試に及第するや、有用の學を攻究し、致仕を懷とせずして法政學校に入りて業を畢へり。知縣として浙江に分たれ、宣統康戌の歲司法官試驗に及第し、浙江寧波地方檢察廳檢察官に任じ、同じく地方審判廳刑事部推事、民事部長、福建閩侯地方審判廳刑事部推事等に歷任す。民國二年正式國會成立するや衆議院議員となる。國會解散後鄉里に歸りて閉戶讀書す。五年國會重ねて開かるゝに及び又來京して仍は衆議院議員となる。

民國之精華　（傳記）　陳堃先生

Mr. Chen Fany, otherwise known as Pai-chien, age forty four, is a native of Chien-ou, Fuchien province. Being a man of simple living, he was opposed any vain glory and pomp. He was man of active thought but was sociable to the extreme. He was ready to accept any warning with appreciation. In helping his friends he was never slow and hasitating. While young he was deeply fond of poetry. As he grew older both in mind and body, he was anxious to bring him to culture and advancement. As he grew older he was deeply interested in the useful learning and studied law and politics. He was the judge of the local courts and when the Republic was formed and the Parliament was brought into existence, he became a member of the House of Commons. When the Parliament was dissolved he went back to his home, and devoted himself to reading but as soon as the Parliament was opened, he went up to Peking and was elected a member of the Parliament.

陳鴻鈞　字容甫　歲三十六

選舉地　江西省

籍貫　江西省上猶縣營前鎮

住址　北京宣武門內油房胡同北頭陳寓

君為人篤實誠厚。生平無戲言戲動。然天資極高。悟性敏捷。讀書能以主觀判斷是非。不為成見所囿。故思想豐富。見解新穎。人但見其居常規規自守。不知其精神固異常活潑也。海內維新之後。君銳志西學。遂以前清優廩生。入江西高等學校。畢業後。留學日本。入巢鴨宏文學院習普通學。旋入日本中央大學豫科二年。升入法律本科畢業歸國。被選為江西省議會副議長。旋又為參議院議員。嗣轉眾議院議員。國會解散後。充北京法政專門學校教員。此次國會重開。遂克仍充眾議院議員。並財政委員長。

君人と為り篤實誠慇、生平戲言戲動無し。然れとも天資極めて高く。悟性敏捷、書を讀み、能く主觀を以て是非を判斷して成見に局せられず。故に思想豐富、見解新穎、人但だ其の居常規々自ら守るを見て、其の精神異常活潑なるを知らず。海內維新の後ち。君志を西學に銳くし。遂に前清優廩生を以て、江西高等學堂に入りて業を畢ふ。後日本に留學し、巢鴨宏文學院に入り、普通學を習ひ。旋て日本中央大學豫科二年に入り、升りて法律本科に入る。業を畢えて國に歸り、選ばれて江西省議會副議長と為り、又た參議院議員と為り、次いで轉じて眾議院議員と為る。國會解散の後、北京法政專門學校教員に充てらる。此次國會重ねて開くに及び、遂に仍は眾議院議員に充てられ、並に財政委員長に任せらる。

Mr. Chen Hung Chun otherwise known as Yüng Fu is aged thirty six, being a native of the Shang Yu, the Chiang Hsi Hsing. Honesty, sobriety and faithfulness are marked characteristics of this gentleman. He is never guilty of words or deeds short of seriousness. He is endowed with noble spirit. Quick of comprehension, he reads books, of which he can pars judgement almost intuitively. His views are never hampered with any prejudices. Rich in thought and fresh in views, he often prones himself beyond the scope of being understood by others. Perceiving the necessity of acquainting himself with the occidental learning, he entered the Chiang Hsi High School where he completed the course prescribed. In Japan, he received the liberal as well as legal education in the Central University. On return to his home, he was appointed the Vice-President of the Chiang Hsi Hsing Assembly, then a member of the Senate, and later a member of the House of Commons. After the disolution of the National Assembly, he was appointed the Law Technical college of Peking. When the Parliament was opened again, he was elected as the member of the House of Commons in which he was appointed the chief of the financial committee.

陳允中　字權均　歲四十二

選舉地　江蘇省

籍　貫、江蘇省金壇縣

住　址、北京丞相胡同二十三

君自少即勵行道義。以氣節著聞于世。
而天資聰敏。年弱冠。爲瞿鴻機所賞
識。入南菁書院。由是得與大江南北豪
儁交游。而學乃益進。戊戌政變後。慨
然以天下爲已任。頗銳意革新。於是漫
游日本。得遍察其風俗政教之進步之
籍後。曾任師範校長。兼爲本省籌辦蘇
屬地方自治。同時當選爲省議會議員。
及武昌起義。君爲都督府參謀。于軍
事多所擘畫。國會開幕。當選爲衆議院
議員。及爲袁政府非法停職。乃杜門謝
客。羈居京師者逾年。雖經當道送薦。
君夷然弗屑就之。及帝制發生。憤然南
下。先是項城授意某丞。欲以爵祿羈縻
君之。君遂匿居海上。並與同志等協力
共爭約法。及目的既達。國會重開。遂
來京就職。

君少より道義を重んじ氣節を以て世に聞こゆ。天資聰敏
にして弱冠其の才を瞿鴻機に愛せられて南菁書院に入
る。是より大江南北の豪儁と交游して學益々進む。戊戌
政變後慨然天下を以て己が任と爲す。政界の革新を志し
て日本に漫游して其の政教の進步を視察す。曾て師範學
校々長を任じ、兼ねて本省蘇屬地方自治を處理し、同時
に省議會議員に當選したり。武昌義を起すに及び、都督府
參謀として軍事に於て擘畫する所多し。正式國會成立す

るに際し衆議院議員に當選す。袁政府の非法によりて國
會議員の職を停止さるゝや、杜門閉居して客を謝し、京
師に羈居する者年餘、當局より屢々致仕を薦められたる
も君之を却けて就かず。帝制問題發生するに及び憤然と
して南下せんとす、袁世凱は爵祿を厚ふして之を留めた
るも君屑しとせずして上海に走り、同志等と協力して約
法の恢復を圖る。目的既に達して復た北上して遂に再び
來京し約法の恢復を圖る。目的既に達して復た北上して
衆議院議員と爲る。

民國之精華　（傳記）　陳允中先生

Mr. Chen Yuu-chung, otherwise called Chuan-chun, forty two years of age, is a native of Chin-
tan, Chiang-su province. While young he attached great importance to his moral virtue. Being a man
of bright temperament he was much beloved by his betters. In 1898 when there started in Wu-chun
he was one of the staff to the leader. When the Parliament was brought into existence he was elected
for the House of Commons. Owing to the illegal conduct of the Yuanshi-kai government, Parliament
was stopped. He stayed in Peking over a year but refused was trouble in the country he became greatly
interested in public works. With a view to the improvement of the political circle in China he came
to Japan and observed the progress that Japan was making. He was the head of the normal school
and the member of the local assembly. When the movement was to accept any offer to government
post when the Imperial movement broke out he went to Shanghai although Yuanshi-kai tried to stop it.
With the final restoration of the Parliament his object was accomplished he became a member of the
Parliament.

君幼より倜儻不羈、好んで詩歌を作り吟咏の快を遺る。稍や長じて大梁明道書院に修業して性理學を講じ程朱陸王門戸の見無く、而して西學を研究して餘力を遺さす。

光緒二十九年鄉薦により上京して私立東文學校に學び、旋て豫南師範學校に入りて飛優等を以て卒業す。又た北京中華大學法科に學びて卒業す。河南學務公所、省視學、教育總會評議、汝甯府師範學校、第二中學校及び汝州中學々長等の職に歷任したり。民國二年二月選ば

陳銘鑑 字子衡 歲四十

選舉地　河南省
籍　貫　河南省西平縣
住　址　北京右驍馬大街如意胡同

君幼時。倜儻不羈。好爲詩歌。以風流名士自命。弱冠後。肆業大梁明道書院。講性理學。無程朱陸王門戶之見。而於西學尤研究不遺餘力。光緒二十九年。癸卯科。領鄉薦入京師。私立東文學校肄業。旋入豫南師範學校。以最優等第一名卒業。又在北京中華大學法科。卒業。歷充河南學務公所。省視學。教育會評議。汝甯府師範學校。第二中學校暨汝州中學校校長。民國二年二月。被選爲參議院議員。復經院選爲憲法起草委員會委員。三年春。國會中沮。經營省長聘爲行政公署調查員。未幾。被任命爲總統府政治諮議。當即上書項城。力請恢復議會。大赦黨人。重州賢材。屬行共利。書上不報。四年四月。又上書復申前請當道卒弗省。迨帝制議起。遂以近江知事名義離京。南遊凡武漢滬、甯蘇浙名勝之地。踪跡殆遍。國會復活。仍就參議院議員。

れて參議院議員と爲り、復た憲法起草委員會委員に舉げらる。國會停止さるに及び山東省長より聘せられて行政公署調查員となり。嗣で總統府政治諮議に任せらる、即ち上書して議會の恢復、黨人の大赦、賢材の重用、共和の勵行を請ふて用ゐられす。帝制問題起るに及び遂に浙江知事の名義を以て北京を去りて南遊す。國會復活して再び召集に應じ北上して仍ほ參議院議員の職に就く。

Mr. Chen Ming-chien, sometimes known as Tzu-heng, age forty, is a native of Hsi-pin, Ho-nan province. While young he was known for his independent spirit and as he grew older he was deeply interested in the teaching of some of classical writers. In 1703 he went to Peking and was graduated both from the normal school and Peking University. He was also a member of the educational assembly and the head of the middle school. In the second year of the Republic he was elected a member of the Senate and on the committee of drafting the constitution. When the Parliament was suspended he was appointed the political adviser to the president. He appealed to the president pointing out the necessity of restoring the Parliament of giving amnesty to party men, of appointing geneous to better position and the practical enforcement of Republican ideas. But his appeal was not accepted. When the Imperial movement took place he left Peking and went to the South. However soon as the Parliament was reopened he was appointed a member of the Senate.

陳善 字敬夫 歲四十

選舉地　雲南省

籍貫　雲南鹽豐縣

住址　北京宣武門內西栓馬樁三號

君性誠厚。尚質惡文。然爲人精明強幹。頭腦縝密。其於社會備悉情敵。而仍以厚道待人雖仇敵亦不以苛待。生平喜爲友朋盡力。絕不受報。強之。亦力却不受。更強之則正顏曰。子欲沒我之善。以陷戒于不義乎以是鄉人皆敬畏之。視爲一方之表率。自幼聰慧異人。工于文詞。及長。喜求有用之學。時新學盛倡于海內。君遂盡棄舊學。潛心考求西化。而于政法之書。尤有研究之趣味。曾於清末肄業于法政專門學校。畢業後。被選爲諮議局議員。民國元年被選爲臨時省議會議員。二年被選爲參議院議員。並充憲法起草委員會委員。國會解散後。回里充富。滇銀行總理。及國會重開。遂入京仍就參議院議員之職。

君賦性誠厚、質を尚び文を惡む。然も人と爲り精明強幹頭腦綿密なり。社會の情敵を知悉して、人に接するや仇敵と雖も苛刻を以て過せず。常に喜んで朋友の爲めに盡力し、事成るも絕へて報を受けず、之れを強ゆるも亦た却ぞく、更に之れを強ゆれば則ち顏色を正して曰く、子我が善を沒して不善を爲さしむるか、爲に鄉人に畏敬さる。幼より聰慧人と異り、文詞に巧なり。長ずるに及び喜んで有用の學を求む。時に新學海內に盛んなり、君遂に舊學を棄て心を西洋文明の攻究に潛め、政治法律の書に於て尤も研究の趣味あり。曾て清末に於て法政專門學校を修業し、後ち選ばれて諮議局議員となり、民國元年臨時省議會議員となり、同二年には參議院議員となり、憲法起草委員會委員に舉げらる。國會解散の後ち鄉里に歸りて富滇銀行總理に任ず。國會重ねて開かるゝに及び遂に入京して仍ほ參議院議員の職に就く。

Mr. Chen-shan, age forty, is a native of Yen-fang, Yun-nan province. He is a gentleman of noble and sincere temperament and was noted for his minuteness and energy. In dealing with others he is gentle and sociable and on many occasions he sacrificed his own interests for to sake of his friends. He is highly respected by his countrymen. He is an excellent writer and versifier. As he grew older he studied new learning and took great delight in the study of law. At the last days of the Chinese regime he was graduated from a law college and was elected a member of the local assembly. In the 2nd year of the Republic he was a member of the Senate and on the committee of drafting the constitution. When the Parliament reopened he went to Peking and became a member of the Senate.

民國之精華　（傳記）陳善先生

陳蓉光 字蘊齊 歲三十八

選舉地　福建省

籍　貫　福建省惠安縣

住　址　北京南柳巷晉江會館

君爲人溫厚平和。與人交。靄然可親。然秉性鯁直不阿。疾惡如仇。遇不平。常忿忿不自禁。過於身受。弱冠時。輒以爲人鳴不平。故與人爭。不計已身之利害。自幼聰慧異人。悟性敏捷。及長尤活潑自喜。富於好奇之性。然其立身行已。多厚重自持。生平無戲言戲動。讀書能以主觀判斷是非。不爲成見所局。故思想豐富。見解新穎。人但見其爲長厚而好義之君子。而不知其精神固異常之活潑也。海內維新之後。以舉人入法政學校。未及畢業。被選爲福建諮議局議員。並充全國諮議局聯合會代表。旋復爲福建臨時省議會議員。被選爲全會委員長。國會成立。被選爲衆議院議員。兼充預算股委員。國會解散後。歷里讀書。絕口不談時政。及國會復活。始來仍爲衆議院議員。

君人となり溫厚人と交つて一見舊知の如し。天性人に阿らず、惡を疾むこと仇敵の如く、人の不平を見る每に忿々自ら禁せざるなり。正義の爲めに人と爭つて利害得失を顧みず。幼より聰明敏捷人と異る。長ずるに及び活潑自ら喜ぶ。而も厚重自ら持し平生戲言妄動せず。書を讀みて主觀を以て是非を判斷し、其の思想豐富にして見解頗る新穎なり。海內維新の後ち、舉人を以て法政學校に學び未だ業を畢ゆるに及ばず。選れて福建諮議局議員となるも、次いで全國諮議局聯合會代表となり。福建臨時省議會議員に舉げられ、全會委員長となる。國會成せらるゝに及び、衆議院議員に當選し。同院預算委員に舉げらる。國會解散の後ち鄕里に歸り閑居して書を讀み、また時事を談せす。國會復活する及び、其の召集に應じて上京し、復た仍ほ衆議院議員の職に就く。

Mr. Chen Jung-kuang, otherwise called Yun-chi, age thirty eight, is native of Hui-an, Fuchien province. He is gentle and sociable in character. He had a great aversion to any form of flattery. He hated the evil like a devil, fighting always for the cause of justice. As he grew older he was very active but will not he swayed by any frivorous ideas. He was a great reader of books and his judgement was always correct. With the entrance of the new trend of thought he entered the law school and was elected a member of the local advisory assembly before graduation. He occupied various important memberships of associations in China. When the Parliament was established he became a member of the House of Commons. With the dissolution of the Parliament he went back to his country but seldom spoke of current topics. When the Parliament was restored he was elected a member of the House of Commons, the position of honour which he now holds.

陳祖基　字獻湖　歲三十七

住　址　北央胡同五
籍　貫　雲南省宜威縣
選舉地　雲南省

君自幼聰穎絕倫。好讀深思。博而能約。及長。尤喜涉獵羣籍。任意所之以為快。而不屑規規然從事於科舉之業。故其讀書純以主觀判斷是非。而不為習俗之成見所局。為人卓犖不羈。夙抱大志。因憤深政之專制。抱定改革宗旨。然舉動極慎。無猾邊躁急之氣。並喜研究法學。洞悉西人到治保邦之原則。前清時。修業於雲南算學校及師範學堂。嗣以己酉科拔貢。授廣東知縣。到省未久。適辛亥革命。辭職回滇。研究實業。於本省銅礦。認為富國大原。悉心考察。著有雲南銅礦土法說略一書。民國二年。主任雲南民報及共和滇報總編輯。其於共和精神。多所發揮。雲南共和黨支部成立。被舉為理事。國會選舉。旋被選為衆議院議員。國會解散後。遇事持消極主義。無所表見。及國會復活。始入京。復為衆議院議員。

君幼より聰穎絕倫にして好んで讀書し深く思索す。長するに及びて尤も群籍を涉獵し、而して矩々然として科學の業に從事するを屑しとせず、故に其の讀書は主觀を以て是非を判斷して習俗の成見に局せらる〃所とならず。人と為り卓落不羈にして夙に大志を抱き、清廷政治の專制を憤りて革新主義を思ふも、舉動極めて謹慎にして急遽輕躁の氣なく、專ら法學を研究して西人到治保邦の原則を洞察するに努めたり。前清時代雲南算學校及び師範學校に修業し、嗣て己酉科の拔貢生として廣東省內の知縣を授けらる。適〻辛亥革命の事起り職を辭して雲南に歸り實業を研究し。省內の銅鑛を探查して雲南銅鑛土法說略一書の著あり。民國二年雲南民報及び共和滇報總編輯に任じ、雲南共和黨支部成立するや舉げられて理事と為る。正式國會議員の選舉に際し衆議院議員に當選す。國會解散後、韜晦して出です。國會復活するに及び復た

民國之精華　（傳記）陳祖基先生

Mr. Chen Tsu-chi sometimes known as Hsiao-hu, age thirty seven, is a native of Hsuan-hsien, Yun-nan province. He was a copious reader of books and a profound thinker. As he grew older he turned his attention to the study which was far advanced to any traditional influence. He was a man of independent and ambitious spirit. While he was cautious he was deeply intrested in the revolutionary movement and studied laws and constutions of other countries. When the revolution broke out he resigned all the important posts and returned Yun-nan where he was interested in copper mining and as a matter of fact he wrote a book on the mining industry of Yun-nan. In the second year of the Republic when the branch office of the Republican party was established in Yun-nan he was appointed a director, when the Parliament was established he was elected for the House of Commons. With the dissolution of the Parliament he lived in retirement. With the Restoration of the Parliament however he was returned for the House of Commons.

陳 策 字勤宣 歲三十二

選舉地　安徽省

籍貫　安徽省壽縣

住址　北京西城拾飯寺西頭二龍坑下
　　　崗二十一號

君天資聰慧。悟性敏捷。言論舉止。皆
極活潑。然其處世接物。又極尙氣節重
信義。少年讀書。專求有用之學。不從
事於考据詞章。及長。尤精思深入。洞
悉事理。故工於詞令。長於幹才。君性
至孝。雅齡。即守遠惡崇善之庭訓。故
旣入社會後。猶服膺不忘。所識稍有失
德。即與絕交。不復存世故之念。前淸
時。以官費留學日本。入岩倉鐵道學
校。旋改入明治大學政治科。畢業歸
國。卒亥改革時。曾任臨時參議院議
員。及總統府高等諮議。民國元年。任
安徽蕪湖安撫使。七月。任國民黨本部
幹事。二年被選爲衆議院議員。國會
解散。歸里隱居。無所表見。及共和再
造。始仍京入爲議員。

君天資聰慧にして悟性敏捷なり。言論舉止皆な活潑にし
て、然も世に處し物に接するや極めて氣節を尙び信義を
重んず。幼時書を讀み專ら有用の學を求め、考据詞章に
從事せず。長するに及び深く思索して事理を究め、詞令に
巧にして幹才に長す。然も其の性至孝にして惡を遠ざけ
善を崇ぶの庭訓を守る。故に交游天下に遍しと雖も、嘗て
姦邪に接せず、知人にして失德の者あれば交を絕ちて世
故の念心を存せず。嘗て前淸時代官費を以て日本に留學

し岩倉鐵道學校に入り、改めて明治大學政治科に學びて
卒業歸國す。辛亥革命の時臨時參議院議員に選ばれ總統
府高等諮議に任す。民國元年安徽撫湖安撫使に任じ、七
月國民黨本部幹事に擧げらる。二年中華民國衆議院議員
に當選す。國會解散せらるや郷里に韜晦してまた政見
を發表する無し。再び共和政體を布くに及び、入京して
仍ほ衆議院議員となる。

Mr. Chen Tse, otherwis called Chin-hsuan, age thirty two is a native of Shou, An-hui province.
While he is very active in his movement and very strong in his arguments, he is full of faithful and
noble ideas. While young he read books and sought usefull learning. As he grew older became a
thinker deeper than ever. He went to Japan at the government expence and studied in the Meiji
Undversity. In 1911 he was a member of the Senate and adviser to the president. In the 1st year of
the Republic he was appointed the director of the national party while in the 2nd year of the Republic
he was elected a member of the Parliament. With the shutting down of the Parliament he returned to
his country and gave no utterance to his political views. When the Parliament was reopened he went
to Peking where he resumed the Parliamentary function.

陳嘉會 字鳳光

選舉地　湖南省

籍貫　湖南省湘陰人

住址　北京都城隍廟街湖南李宅

君沈默寡言。工詩文。性果毅。有卓拔
不搖之慨。前畢業湖北兩湖書院及日
本法政大學。歸國創立湖南法政學堂。
辛亥武昌起義。參與南北議利。與黃興
共籌進行。民國元年。南京新政府成
立。任陸軍部軍法局長。旋任南京留守
府秘書長。是年秋。袁世凱任爲國務院
秘書長。辭之。二年。被舉爲衆議院議
員。卓卓有聲嗣以袁氏驕橫。共和將
覆。急返湘。與譚延闓謀改革。事敗遯
跡荒山。乃免。自此閉門一榻。潛心禪
悅。慕倪雲林斥張士信事因亞肆力於
畫。作詩數百首。曰白燕盦集。有白燕
詩云。故宅今朝是也非。當時侶伴認眞
稀。自隨湘水孤花到處
歸。欲定新巢樓是玉。好翻雙翦雪爲
衣。愁看豈獨昭陽殿。更莫江南巷口
飛。蓋感於袁景文陸柈亭之所遇有同
慨也。五年。帝制事起。與譚
延闓范源濂孫伊諸人。共謀國事。盖
共和復起。君力居獨多也。

君沈默荏言にして詩文に工みに、果斷剛毅にして卓拔不
動の慨あり。前に湖北兩湖書院及び日本法政大學校に學
びて卒業す。後ち湖南法政學堂を創立して後進を誘掖し
たり。第一革命當時南北の講和に參與して黃興と共に進
行を籌る。民國元年南京臨時政府成立するや陸軍部軍法
局長に任す。旋て南京留守府秘書長の任に任す。南北統一政
府樹立後、袁世凱より國務院秘書長の内命を受けたるも
之を辭す。民國二年衆議院議員に當選す。第二革命に際

して湖南に歸りて譚延闓と改革を謀り、事敗れて荒山に
遯れて禪に匿れ、飛を擧じ詩を作り、白燕畫集あり。白
燕詩あり曰く故宅今朝是也非、當時侶伴認眞稀、自隨湘
水孤花到處歸、不飛揚花到處歸、欲定新巢樓是玉、好翻雙翦
雪爲衣、愁看豈獨昭陽殿、更莫江南巷口飛と。五年密に
出でヽ上海に赴き、譚延闓、范源濂、孫洪伊等と共に帝
制に反對して共和恢復を謀る。國會復治するに及び、仍
ほ衆議院議員と爲る。

Mr. Chen Chia-hui, otherwise called Feng-kuang, is a native of Hsiang-yin, Hu Nan province.
Although a man of taciturn temperament he was well posted up in the study of poetry and classics. He
is bold and inmorable in his spirit. He was graduated from the law college in Japan and establishing
a law school in his province, he was interested in the education of rising generation. In the first revolution
he participated in the movement bringing about both the North and the South under unity. In the 1st
year of the Republic when the Nan-king special government was established he was appointed the head
of the military law office. When the Republic was formend he was urged by Yuanshi-kai to become
the private secretary of the statedepartment but he declined to accept the offer. In the 2nd year of
the Republic he was elected for the House of Commons. His poetical work are quite numerous. With
his fellow thinkers he was strongly opposed to the Imperial movement and when the Parliament was
restored he was elected a member of the House of Commons.

民國之精華　（傳記）　陳嘉會先生

二百十五

陳洪道 字演九 歲三十七

選舉地 浙江省

籍 貫 浙江省溫嶺縣

住 址 北京東順城街八十八號

君性喜朴實。爲人鯁直不阿。與人交。
尚信義。重然諾。喜規善而不數。雖疾
惡崇善。而不露鋒鋩。是以里人皆敬愛
之。不相仇視。自幼讀書。卽能領悟義
理。精思深入。不徒記誦其文辭。及長。
尤殫精宋明學者之書。而於漢學。亦時
喜研究之。以求古義之所在。戊戌變政
後。君適舉於鄉。然以國事日非。知非
革新無以圖存。遂銳志西學。不復求進
于科第。旋肄業于法律學校。卒業後。
歷任廣西永福縣知縣。梧州府桂林府
地方審判廳廳長。廣西高等審判廳廳
丞。民國成立。被任爲浙江省法院院
長。及都督府秘書長。旋被選爲參議院
議員。國會解散。歸里獨居。不談時事。
直至共和再造。始仍出爲議員。

君性朴實にして人と爲り硬直にして阿らず。人と交りて
信義を尚び然諾を重んず。幼より書を讀みて義理を究む
長するに及びて尤も宋明學者の書に通ず。戊戌政變後、
慨然として西學を攻究す。旋て法律學校に學びて其の業
を畢る。廣西永福縣知事に任じて、地方行政を處理して
生民を安撫す。後ち司法官に轉じて梧州府、桂林府の各
地方審判廳々長、廣西高等審判廳々丞に歷充したり。民
國成立して後ち浙江省法院院長及び都督府秘書長に任ず、
正式國會の組織に當り選ばれて參議院議員と爲る。國會
解散されて後ち、鄉里に歸臥して學に親み、また時事を
談せず。斯くて共和政治克復して約法恢復し、國會重ね
て召集を行ふに及び、君再び出で〻北京に抵り、現に仍
ほ復た參議院議員となりたり。

Mr. Chen Hung-tao, known as Yen chiu, age thirty seven, a native of Wen-lin-hsien, is a gentleman of high character. With him, yes means yes and nothing else. He knows how to keep his word. He made up his mind to pursue the course in the western learning, and studied law in one of the law colleges. He was the governor of Kuang Hsi in which a capacity, he contributed a great deal to the development of the local administration. Afterwards, he was a judge in various districts. When the Republic was established, he was appointed the chief of the Che Chiang Hsing High Court and the secretary to the governor general: When the Parliament was opened, he was elected a member of the Senate. On the disolution of the Parliament, he returned to his home when he kept to himself, keeping aloof from politics. When the Republic was securely established, and the Parliament was summoned, he repaired to Peking, and was returned for the House of Commons.

陳耀先　字紹蕃　歲三十五

選舉地　黑龍江省
籍　貫　黑龍江省綏化縣
住　址　北京宣武門內小市南口七

君賦性溫和。與人交。和藹可親。雅素
所厭惡之人。亦必謙和相接。不以疾言
厲色加人。然言忠行篤。操已甚嚴。與
曲已從人同流合汚者。自相懸絕。自幼
好讀。喜考求眞義。不屑沾沾于章句之
學。時清末方興新學。遂於光緒三十二
年肄業于師範學堂。卒業後。充本郡勸
學員三年。勸學員長兼視學員二年。自
治公所紳董一年。民國元年。當選爲臨
時省議會議員二年。當選爲衆議院議
員。國會解散後。諸事抱消極主義。及
國會復活。仍入京爲衆議院議員。

民國之精華　（傳記）　陳耀先先生

君賦性溫和にして人と交る和藹親むべし。素と厭惡する
所の人と雖も必ず謙讓を以て相接し、疾言厲色を以て
人に加へす。然かも言忠にして行篤く、操守甚だ嚴にして
己を曲げて人に從ひ流に同じて汚に合する者と自ら懸絕
するものあり。幼より讀書を好みて眞義を攻求し、章句の
學に拘泥するを屑しとせず。時に清末方に新學を興すや、
光緒三十二年師範學堂に修業し、卒業後鄕里の勸學員と
なり、嗣で勸學員長に昇り視學員を兼ね、地方教育の振興
を圖りて民智の開發に努力盡瘁する所ありたり。後ち自
治公所紳董に任じて地方自治の發達に從事したり。民國
元年臨時省議會に當選し、二年正式國會成立に際し選ば
れて衆議院議員と爲る。國會解散して後ち諸事消極主義
を抱き、時に地方公益事業に力を盡したり。國會復活す
るに及び、仍ほ入京して衆議院議員と爲る。

Mr. Chen Yao-hsien, sometimes called Shao-fan, age thirty five, is a native of An hua hsien, the Hei-lung-chiang hsing. Being quite gentleman in temperament, he makes every one his friend when once they meet. He is a man of high moral character, and who should be clearly distinguished from the man who is addicted to the superficial view of learning. He made up his mind to acquire new learning, and in 1906, he was graduated from the normal school in his district, and ever since he devoted himself to the promotion of learning in local districts. He also was intensted in the development of the idea of selfrule among the people. In 1913, when the 1st Parliament met, he was chosen as a member of the House of Commons. On the disolution of the Parliament, in all things, he acted moderatey devoting his time more to the advancement of public interest. When the Parliament was formed again, he became the member of the Parliament.

陳祖烈 字繼庭

選舉地　福建省
籍貫　福建省
住址　北京校場五條十八號榕廬

君自幼聰慧絕倫。好讀深思。博而能約。尤喜涉獵群籍。及海內維新。夙求天下有用之學。醉心新書。專究其精。深明其義。君為人至孝。昏定晨省。終年不輟。且廉謹自持。非分內所得。從未見其有所干請古之人歟。君前清癸卯科舉人。負笈東渡。留學日本。入法政大學校畢業。歸國後。仍充福建公立法政學校教授。從事育英。誘導後進。民國肇造。被選為福建省議會議員。劻助地方自治事宜。多有所貢獻。民國二年正式國會成立。被選為參議院議員。國會解散後。南旋歸里杜門讀書。悠悠自適。不問時事。及國會重開。君復應召集。北上抵京。仍為參議院議員。

君幼より聰慧絕倫にして讀書を好みて深く思索す。海內維新に及び夙に天下有用の學を求め、新書に心醉して專ら其の精を究め深く其の義を明にす。君人と為り至孝にして且つ廉潔自ら持す。前淸癸卯學人を科せられ、笈を負ひ東海を渡りて日本に留學し、法政大學校に入りて其の業を畢へたり。歸朝後、福建公立法政學校教授に任じ、育英の業に從事して後進を誘掖す。民國の創立に際し選ばれて福建省議會議員と為り、地方自治の為に盡力して貢獻する所多し。民國二年正式國會の成立に際し選ばれて參議院議員と為る。國會解散されて後も、南下して鄉里に歸臥し、門を閉ぢて書を讀み、悠々自適また時事を問はず。國會重ねて開かるゝに及び、君復た召集に應じて北京に抵り、仍は參議院議員と為る。

二百九十八

Mr. Chen Tso-lich, otherwise known as Chi ting, is a native of Fu chien. He was both the reader and the thinker. He indulged himself to the reading of new books. He is a man of great filial obedience. He came to Japan where he was educated in law in the Hosei University. On return to his home, he at once was appointed an instructor in the law college of the Fu chien and devoted himself to the instruction of the rising generation. When the Republic was established, he contributed a great deal to the ideas of civic body, and in the 2nd year of the Republic he was elected a member of the Senate. When the Parliament was dissolved, he returned to his home where he spent most of his time in the study of books, but when the reopening of the Parliament was decided upon, he entered Peking and resumed the senatorial function

陳家鼎 字汗圓 歳四十一

選舉地 湖南省
籍貫 湖南省
住址 北京中華飯店内

君秉性正直。天資高邁。為人豪爽氣宇潤達。居恆以公明正大自持。疾惡如仇。直斥陰險。稍不假借。與人交。磊磊落落。披握至誠。吐露肝膽。故中外正義之士。深敬重之。自幼聰穎好讀。冠有文名。工於詩賦及長。博覽群籍。深明精義。尤喜求有用之學。夙抱澄清天下之志。與黃克強。宋遯初等同志。皷吹革命。幾陷囹圄者數次。民國成立後。被選為臨時參議院議員。又被推為北京新聞團團長。民國二年被選為衆議院議員。及袁氏違法剝奪議員職。君東渡日本。與諸同志協謀大計。袁氏帝制發生。君與令夫人飛微。反對帝制。筆誅袁氏。於喚起人心。多有功勢。滇黔起義。袁氏死。君乃返滬。督勵同志。大謀響應。黎氏繼任。結束在滬議員團。力倡恢復舊約法。目的既達。遂來京。仍為議員。

民國之精華 （傳記） 陳家鼎先生

君秉性正直にして天資高邁なり。人と為り豪爽にして氣宇潤達なり。居常公明正大を以て自ら持し、人と交りて磊々落々、至誠を披握して肝膽を吐露するが故に内外正義の士顔ある君を敬重す。幼より聰穎にして讀を好み、弱冠既に文名ありて詩賦に工なり。長じて群籍を渉獵して其の義理に精通し、尤も有用の學を求めて夙に天下澄清の志を抱き、黃與宋敎仁等の郷友と共に多年革命を皷吹して屢々危險に瀕す。民國成立後、臨時參議院議員に選ばる。又た北京新聞團々長に推さる。民國二年衆議院議員に常選す。一部同志より議長候補に推されたるも辭したり。後ち袁氏の違法壓迫に遭ふて日本に逃れ、諸同志と共に大計を謀る。帝制問題發生するや、君の令夫人亦た微を飛ばして帝制に反對し天下中外の人心を喚起した り。雲貴起義後、上海に歸りて奔走盡力し、國會復活す るに及び遂に入京して仍は衆議院議員と爲る。

Mr. Chen Chia-ting, othewise called Han Yuan, aged forty one, is a native of Hu-nan hsing. He is a man of straight-foward character and of bright temperament. He is sencere in all his dealings and open minded in listening to the advice of others. These characteristics of him won him many friends. While young, he was fond of reading and acquainted literary fame. As he grew older, he became an ardent scholar of useful learning, and was interested in inspiring the people with revolutionay ideas. When the Republic was established, he was elected a member of the Senate. In the second year of the Republic, he was elected a member of the House of Commons, some of his friends proposed to elect him for the chair of the Speaker, but under the pressure of Yuanshi-kai, he escaped Japan as a fugitive, but as soon as the Imperial movement took place, he strongly opposed thereto, and went to Shanghai to plan for the restoration of the Republic. However, when Yuanshi-kei died, he entered Peking and was again returned for the House of Commons.

陳子斌　字南屏

選舉地　江西省

籍貫　江西省石城縣

住址　北京棉花五條

君氣度從容。性情和緩。與人交。溫良恭謙。不爲意氣之爭。雖有所忿恨。亦未嘗以疾言遽色加人。然意志極强。富於獨立之性。且喜聞忠告之言。勇於改過。人告以過。雖所言失實。絕不與辯。常語人曰。聞過而改。既得無過之實。又居從善如流之名。利孰大焉。年少讀書。即以遠大自期。稍長。愈益從事於磁日以其效之積み、天資必ずしも聰穎絕倫なりと云ふ

故天資雖非絕高。而明察事情。洞委直理。前清時北京法律學堂畢業。曾充大理院法官。現充衆議院議員。

君氣度從客、性情和藹なり。人と交りて溫良恭謙にして意氣の爭を爲さず。嚇怒する所あるも亦た未だ疾言遽色を以て人に加へず。然かも意志極めて鞏固にして獨立の氣象に富み、且つ忠言を聞くの度量あり、常に人に談つて曰く、過を聞きて改むるに勇ならば、既に過無きの實を得るものなりと。少年書を讀みて孜々倦まず、即ち大成を以て自ら期したり。稍や長じて益々研學に勉めて切にあらざるも、終に深く其精義を探究して明に事理を洞觀するに至れり。前清時代、北京法律學堂に入りて學び、其業を畢ゆるや、即ち出で〻大理院法官に任じ、理據至正、裁斷公平、頗る令名あり。曾て正式國會衆議院議員に當選して議政擅上正義を把持して國家立法の大業を勳助す。國會重ねて召集を行ひ、現に仍は衆議院議員たり。

Mr. Chen Tsu-pin, is a native of the Chiang-ssi hsing. He is typically an oriental hero, possessing every quality of such an ideal being. He never shows anger. He is strong willed and full of the spirit of independence, but has capacity to listen to the advise of others. He is represented to have declared that he who has capacity to listen to the advice of others has already given an assurance of the fact that he will not be guilty of the same fault He was a great reader of books, and has won whatever he has through the means of hard fight and struggle. In the previores chinese regime, he was graduated from the Peking Law College, and was appointed the judge of the court in which capacity his fair judgement and high sense of justice won for him great fame. He wer returned for the House of Commons in which capacity he participated in the administration of the country when it was deceded to open the Parliament, he resumed the funotion as the member of the House of Commons.

陳煥南　字山畝　年三十六

選舉地　湖南省
籍貫　湖南省東安縣
住址　北京象坊橋衆議院西夾道

君以前清附生。入湖北文普通中學堂。旋由政府諮送日本留學。畢業於宏文警務科。歸國後。歷辦教育及警務事宜有年。功勞顯著。武昌首義。在龍州謀響應。充都督府軍事參議官。民國元年。四月辭職。走南京。充陸軍第八師秘書官。九月改充陸軍第二師軍顧問官。赴湘襄助解散軍隊事。十一月。改充湖南都督府政治顧問官。二年二月。被選爲參議員。國會解散。回湘蟄居。三年五月。以二次革命嫌疑被兵團捕以計出險。四年秋。集資在新寗縣。創辦建興錦鑛公司。舉充經理。滇南首義。君多所贊助。旋被舉爲湘南代表。赴廣西。陸督幕籌商軍事。並代表湘南護國軍。赴肇慶。加入軍務院。居無何。以國會集會於上海。遂至滬。八月抵京。仍爲參議院議員。

民國之精華　（傳記）　陳煥南先生

君前清の附生を以て湖北文普通中學校に入り、旋て政府より選抜されて日本に留學し、宏文學院師範科を卒業し次で警務科を卒業す。歸國後、多年教育及び警務を處理功勞あり。第一革命當時、龍川に在りて武昌に響應し、都督府軍事參議官と爲る。翌年南京に赴きて陸軍第八師團秘書と爲る。旋て陸軍第三師副軍事顧問官と爲り、湖南に歸りて軍隊解散の事を襄助したり。後ち湖南都督府政治顧問と爲る。二年參議院議員に當選す。國會解散後、湖南に歸りて蟄居す。三年五月革命の嫌疑を以て捕はれ、たるも計を以て險を脱したり。四年秋、資を集めて新寗縣に於て建興錦鑛公司を創設し、其の經理に舉げらる。雲南義を首むるや君贊助する所多く、旋て湖南代表に舉げられて廣西に赴き陸榮廷の幕内に軍事を商り、並に湖南護國軍を代表して肇慶に赴き軍務院に入る。既にして國會上海議員に集るや上海に赴き、後ち又た北京に抵り、仍は衆議院議員と爲る。

陳煥南先生

Mr. Chen huan-nan, sometimes called Shan yú, aged thirty six, is a native of Tung an, Hunan province. In the previous Chinese regime he was sent to Japan by the government where he studied in the normal school. On return to his country he was interested in police and educational affairs. In the first Chinese revolution, he occupied in many military offices in ... character of secrectary and adviser. Latery he was the political adviser to the Ho nan governor general. In the second year of the Republic he was elected a member of the Senate. When the Parliament was dissolved, he returned to Ho nan and kept himself quiet, but he was arrested being suspect of being interested in the second revolutionary movement. He went to Shanghai with a view to fight for the reopening of the Parliament, and when was decided to open the Parliament again he was elected a member of the House of Commons..

陳九韶 字雯裳

選舉地　湖南省

籍　貫　湖南省郴縣

住　址　北京西城廣寗伯街二十號

君天資聰穎。悟性敏捷。尤富理想。然
爲人誠實不欺。與人交。喜勸善規過。
相其人必能納諫者。始規正之。否則惟
善律之。人告以過。則直認不諱。自幼
好讀。弱冠文采風流。已超出儕輩。及
海內維新之後。君慨然銳意攻究實學。
尤喜讀政治經濟之書。前清以廩貢生。
任度支部軍餉司主事。曾入財政學堂。
國立法政學校政治經濟科。畢業。造詣
既深。民國二年。正式國會成立。君被
選爲衆議院議員。傾注蘊蓄。把持正
論。翼贊建設之偉業。國會解散後。南
旋歸里。讀書自娛。竊念挽回大局及
共和恢復。國會重開。君復踴躍應召集
北上抵京。仍爲衆議院議員。

君天資聰穎にして悟性敏捷し、尤も理想に富む。然かも人
と爲り誠實欺かず、人と交りて善を勸め過を規し、其の
人必ず能く諫を納る〻者を相し始めて之を正す。幼より
讀を好み、弱冠にして文采風流既に儕輩に傑出する。海內
維新の後ち慨然意を決して實學を攻究し、尤も政治經濟
の書を喜ぶ。前清廩貢生を以て度支部軍伺司主事に任
ず。曾て財政學堂、國立法政學校政治經濟科に入りて其の
業を畢へ、造詣旣に深し。民國二年正式國會成立に際し、
衆議院議員に當選し、多年の蘊蓄を傾注して正論を把持
して民國建設の大業に翼賛す。國會解散されて後ち南旋
して鄕里に歸り讀書自ら娛み、竊に大局の挽回を念ふ。
共和恢復して國會重ねて開くるに及び、君復た踴躍して
召集に應じ、仍ほ衆議院議員と爲る。

Mr. Cheu Chin-shao, otherwise called Wen Shang, is a native of Ho-nan. He is bright, quick of understanding and full of high ideals. He was an ardent book reader, and distinguished himself from his collegers in valters of literary refinement. Later, he took up the new study and was particularly interested in the study of politic and economic science. He studied law and economic in the National Law College, and in 1913, when the Parliament was opened, he was elected as a member thereof, and participated in the building up of the grand fabric of the Republic. On the disolution of the Parliament, he went back to his native place, where he spent his time in study, and secretly bid for the time when it was announced that the Parliament was to be opened again, he went up to Peking where he has resumed the membership of the House of Commons.

郝濯 字仲青 歳三十八

選舉地　直隷省
籍　貫　直隷省蠡縣
住　址　北京西單、二條胡同

君秉性溫厚。待人以和。然喜朴質。不
事浮華。舉止皆以禮自持。不苟言笑。
故和藹之中。復寓有莊嚴可畏之氣象。
稚齡讀書。卽能深造有得。明于理義。
年方弱冠。卽已畢諸經。旁及子史。及
長。尤務求淵博。廣覽群書。造詣漸深。
夙抱興學之志。曾入直隷師範學校畢
業。歷任保定公立第一中學國史教習。
育德中學校長。從事育英。誘掖後進。
民國元年被舉爲順直臨時省議會議
員。二年正式國會成立。由順直省議會
選舉爲參議院議員。國會解散後。在郷
縣。讀書自適。惟隨時從事地方公益。
五年國會重開。遂又應召。仍爲參議院
議員。

民國之精華　（傳記）　郝濯先生

君は秉性溫厚にして人を待つに和を以てす。然かも朴實を喜びて浮華を事とせず。舉止皆な禮を以て自ら持し、言笑を苟もせず。故に和藹の中復た莊嚴畏るべきの氣象あり。少年書を讀みて即ち能く深く理義を明にす。年方に弱冠、即ち諸經を畢りて子史を修め、長ずるに及びて尤も淵博を求め、群籍を閱して造詣漸く深し。夙に興學の志を抱き、曾て直隷師範學校に入りて卒業す。保

定公立第一中學國史敎師、育德中學校長に、歷任して、育英の業に從事し後進を誘掖して功あり。民國元年選ばれて順直臨時省議會議員と爲る。二年舉げられて正式國會参議院議員と爲る。國會解散後、郷里に在りて讀書自ら娯み時に地方公益の事を助く。五年國會復活するや、遂に又た召集に應じ、仍は參議院議員と爲る。

Mr. Hocho, sometimes called Chung Ching, age thirty eight, is a native of Chilin province. He is gentle and quiet in temperament. Being simple and frank, he has opposed to anything pompous and vain. His every dead and words are conducter by the strict code of ettiquet; therfore while gentle, he has something one inspiring and inaccessible in him. While young, he is fond of reading books which he was able to digest. As he grew older, his knowledge of books covered a vast field. He was graduated from the Chilin Normal School, and was greatly interested in education, and in guiding the rising generation, as he was an instructor of several middle schools. In the second year of the Republic, he was a member of the special provinciable assembly while in the second year of the Republic, he was elected a member of the House of Commons. When the Parliament was dissolved, he went back to his native province when he interested himself in the promotion of local interests. When the Parliament was restorned, he was appointed a member of Senate, the position of honour he holds in the present moment.

陸宗輿　字潤生　歲四十一

選舉地　浙江省
籍貫　浙江省海寧縣
住址　北京東城樓鳳樓小土地廟

君幼より聰穎絕倫にして夙に日本に留學し、早稻田大學專門部を卒業す。光緒三十一年金邦平等と第一次留學生試驗に及第して舉人となり內閣中書を以て補用せらる。同年七月各國憲政視學大臣一行の二等參贊官に任じ、翌年迄醫部主事に補せられ、旋て員外郎に昇級し郎中候補と爲る。同年御史となり、徐世昌が東三省に總督たるや鹽務局總辦となる。八月民政部の奏薦により左右參議に登錄せらる。三十四年四品京堂を以て任を東三省鹽務督辦に改む。宣統元年憲政編查館員と爲り、交通銀行協理を兼ぬ。二年資政院議員に勅選され、三年內閣印鑄局々長に補せられ、十二月度支部右丞を兼署す。民國元年三月度支部副首領と爲る。九月總統府財政顧問を兼任す。二年浙江省議會より舉げられて參議院議員に當選す。同年十二月日本駐箚全權公使と爲りて任に赴き、五年歸國す。此次國會重ねて開かるゝや召集に應じて仍は參議院議員たり。

君自幼聰穎絕倫早遊日本。在早稻田大學專門部畢業。光緒三十一年。與金邦平等應第一次留學生考試。賞給舉人出身。以內閣中書補用。是年七月。考察各國憲政大臣派爲二等參贊官。明年補巡警部主事。旋升員外。以耶中候補。是年考送御史。徐世昌爲總督東三省。調爲鹽務局總辦。八月。民政部奏保。以左右參議記名。三十四年。遂爲四品京堂改東三省鹽務督辦。宣統元年。爲憲政編查館員。充交通銀行協理。二年。欽選資政院議員。三年。補內閣印鑄局局長。十二月。兼署度支部右丞。民國元年。三月。爲度支部副首領。九月。兼總統府財政顧問。二年。由浙江省議會選舉爲參議院議員。是年十二月。拜日本駐箚全權公使。五年。召還。此次國會重開。始應召。仍爲參議院議員。

Mr. Liu Tsung-yu, otherwise called Jun-sheng, age forty one, is a native of Hai-ning, Che-chiang province. He was distinguished for his intelligence when quite young. He came to Japan and was graduated form the Waseda University. In 1905 he passed the civil service examination and was appointed a secretary of the cabinet and also he was the second secretary to the special envoy of China despatched to foreign countries. Since then his promotion was very rapid. In 1909 he was a member of the committee appointed for drafting the particulars regarding the constitutional government. He was also the head of the several bureaus is the cabinet. In the 1st year of the Republic he was appointed a adiviser to the president, and in the 2nd year of the Pepublic he was appointed a member of the Senate and went to Japan as the Chinese minister plenipotentiary. When the Parliament was reopened he responded to the call and was appointed a member of the Senate.

選舉地　山東省

籍貫　山東省惠民縣

住址　北京石駙馬大街鮑家街雅集公寓

君性鯁不欺。然謙虛好問。喜聞盡言。人告以過。雖未盡當。必欣然謝之。然謂言者之欺我也。少好讀。及長。有文名以前清丁酉科拔貢。肄業北京師範傳習所。畢業。丁未會考及第。分發雲南補用知縣。歷充雲南兩級師範學校教員。中等農業學校教員。兼監學。陸軍督練處文案委員。光復時。辭歸。民國元年。被選爲衆議院議員。國會解散後以前清原有資格。署理河南睢縣知事。在官二年。頗著政績。然以拙於貪緣。不受請託。有力者忌之。無肯爲之表彰者。五年五月。辭職歸。及國會恢復。遂來京。充衆議院議員。

民國之精華　（傳記）　曹瀛先生

君性鯁直にして欺かず、然かも謙虛以て問を好み、蓋書を聞くを喜ぶ。少にして讀書を好み、長ずるに及びて文名あり。前清時代丁酉科拔貢生を以て北京師範傳習所に入りて卒業す。丁未の際歳試を受けて及第し、補用知縣として雲南省に分發せらる。雲南兩級師範學校教員、中等農業學校教員兼監學、陸軍督練處文案委員に歷充したるが、第一革命に際し職を辭して歸る。民國元年選ばれて衆議院議員となり、北京に抵りて國政を議す。國會解散後、前清時代に有せる資格を以て河南睢縣知事を署理し、在官二年政績顯る顯著なるものあり、然かも貪緣に拙にして請託を受けず、故に長上の爲に忌まる。五年五月職を辭して歸れば、旋て適ま國會の恢復に遇ひ、復た出でて北京に入り、仍は衆議院議員の職に就く。

Mr. Tsao Ying, otherwise called Tzu Teng is fifty two years old. He is honest and straight as an arrow. He is quite open to the information which he is anxious to obtain from others Early in life, he was an ardent reader of books, and when grown up, he won fave in his literary career. In the previous Chinese regime, he entered Peking Normal Institute as a chosen student from his district. Having graduated from the school, he passed the civil service examination, and was appointed the acting governor of the Yun Nan Sheng while at the same time he was the professor at the Normal School in Yun Nan as well as an instructor in the agricultural school. He was on the literary committee for the military training institute. On the outbreak of the revolutionary movement, he resigned his post, and returned to his home. In the 1st year of the Republic, he was returned as a member of the House of Commons. When the Parliament was broken up, he was appointed the governor of the Ho Nan in which capacity he accomplished a great deal of the interest of the province, although the tenure of the office extended only two years. He was deadly opposed to any nepotic advancement; consequently he incurred the displeasure of his sevior officials. In May, the 5th year, he resigned his post, and returned to his native country. With the reopening of the Parliament, he went up to Peking and again became the member of the House of Commons.

曹振懋　字勉盦歲四十四

選舉地　福建省

籍　貫　福建省沙縣

住　址　北京宣武門外校場五條十八號榕廬

君爲人篤實無華。少常從事舉業。頭腦極舊及長。游學省垣。遍覽新書。思想眼光。均爲之一變。嗣以清廷國政日非。仕途日益污濁。知非革命不足救亡。曾在粵西。與同志等鼓吹革命。幾陷囹圄者數次。未幾。武昌起義。君由桂入閩。被選爲省議會副議長。民國二年。被選爲衆議院議員。到院數月。而袁氏違法專制。推殘民意。蹂躪國會。君屢於院中。爲反抗强權。主持正義之提議。卒以少數。不能貫徹其目的。及袁氏解散國會。君遂轉從嶺外。爲各新聞執筆。以主特正論。喚起人心。滇黔起義後。兩粵聞風響應。汕頭軍。以一團之師。起義潮汕。君于軍中盡力甚多。居無何。滬上有國會議員通訊處之設。君時方往來南寗肇慶間就商軍事進行事宜。聞訊。走赴滬上。與諸同志協謀恢復國會。目的既達遂來京。仍爲議員。

君人と爲り篤實にして華なし。少時科擧の學に從ひ頭腦極めて舊なりしも、長じて省城に遊學し、新書を讀みて思想一變したり。清廷の國政日に非にして仕途益々混濁せるを慨して革命を思ひ、廣西にありて同志と共に革命を鼓吹し、囹圄に陷ること數次なり。武昌義を起すや、君廣西より福建に入りて省議會副議長と爲る。民國二年選ばれて衆議院議員となる。君袁政府の政策に反對して正論を讜議これ好む。國會解散さるゝに及び遂に轉じて嶺外に移り各新聞の爲に筆を執りて正論を鼓吹す。雲貴各軍義を起すや、兩廣風を聞いて盡力頗る多し。汕頭軍乃ち義を潮汕に起すや、君軍中に在りて盡力頗る多し。旋て上海に於て國會議員通訊處の設あり、南寗肇慶間を奔走して軍事進行事宜を商りつゝありし君は、走せて上海に赴き、諸同志と偕に國會の恢復を謀る。目的既に達して、遂に北京に入り、仍ほ復た衆議院議員から。

Mr. Tsao, Chenl-cou, aged forty four, is a native of Sha Hsieng, the Fukieng Hsing. Simplicity and honesty untainted with the least sign of vanity is the characteristic of this gentleman. While young, he was a Chinese scholar of note, especially distinguished for the clearness of his brain, but as he grew older, a change of thought came over him as he became a reader of new books. Perceiving that the maladministration of the Chinese Government has reached the breaking point he came to the conclusion that the Revolution was the only effective method of salvation, he stayed at Yueh Hsi, inspiring the people with the revolutionary ideas, as a consequence of which he was imprisoned more than once. When the 1st revolution took place, he was elected the Vice-president of the local assembly. In the 2nd year of the Republic he was appointed a member of the House of Commons. He was a strong opponent of the Yuanshi-Kai Government but when the parliament was dissolved, he took up his mighty pen attacking the Government's policy without mercy. When the war broken out, he as a civilian, made efforts in diverse ways, gathering wang men of influence around him with whom he consulted in Shanghai the vest wears of accomplishing their end. When the Parliament was re-opened he entered Peking, and was returned as a member of the House of Commons.

曹汝霖　字潤田　歳四十一

選舉地　蒙古
籍貫　江蘇省上海縣
住址　北京東安門外錫拉胡同

君爲人老成練達。明察事情。意志堅
強。而頭腦明晰　不以感情用事。其處
世接物。絕少事實上之失敗。光緒二十
四年。赴日本留學。卒業於法學院光
緒三十年回國。入農工商部爲主事。編
訂商律及商標法草案。嗣調外務部自
光緒三十一年迄宣統三年。前後八年
間。中日交涉。殆歸一人經理。在外部
自主事擢員外郎。以徐世昌之密保召
見。特以京堂候補。遂補外部參議。復
升右丞。拜右侍郎。民國成立。君遂辭
職。爲律師。由蒙古被選爲參議院議
員。並任大總統顧問。民國二年八月。
命爲外交次長。五年五月。段內閣成
立。任爲交通總長。復兼任外交總長。
袁氏既逝。君又辭職。今黎大總統復任
爲大總統顧問。仍爲參議院議員

民國成立と共に其の職を辭し、辯護士を業とす。民國二
年選ばれて參議院議員となり、並に大總統顧問に任す。
嗣で外交次長となり、五年五月段祺瑞內閣組織さるゝや、
交通總長に任じ、復た外交總長を兼ねたり。既にして袁
世凱死すや君また冠を桂けて野に下る、黎大總統復た君
を起して大總統顧問とす。國會復た召集せられて、君仍
ほ參議院議員の職に在り。

君人と爲り老成練達にして頭腦明晰、經驗亦た富む。光
緒二十四年夙に笈を負ふて東渡し、日本法學院に學びて
業を畢ゆ。光緒三十年歸國して農工商部に入りて主事と
爲り、商法及び商標法草案を起草したり。嗣で外務部に
調せられ、光緒二十一年より宣統三年に至る前後八年間、
日支兩國間の交涉に干預す。外部主事より員外郎に擢用
され、徐世昌の保薦により特に京堂候補を以て外部參議
に補せられる。遂に右丞に升り、右侍郎の官に到る。

Mr. Tsao Ju-cin, otherwise styled as June Tien, was born in Chiang Hsing Cheng and aged forty one. He is a gentleman of mature thought, clear brain and rich experience. He accomplished his study in Japan where he was educated in the Japanese Law College. On returning to his home, he entered the government service in the Department of Agriculture, Artisan and Commerce, where he was employed in drafting the commercial code and trade mark laws. Then his service was employed in the Foreign Department: For the period of eight years, he was interested in diplomatic relations between Japan and China. His promotion in diplomatic service was indeed rapid, and reached the position of the councellor comparatively young. When the Republic was brought into existence, he resigned his office, and practiced law. In the 2nd year of the Revolution, he was chosen a member of the senate and adviser to the President simultaneously holding the position the Minister of Foreign Affairs. With the death of Yuanshi-Kai he resigned his post, but the new President again offered to employ his service, and has appointed him as his adviser. With the opening of the Parliament, he as appointed a member of the Senate.

民國之精華　（傳記）　曹汝霖先生

曹玉德 字運生

選舉地　安徽省

籍貫　安徽省靈璧縣

住址　北京崇城根中和醫院西首安徽曹屬

君賦性溫厚。與人交。和藹可親。雖所素惡。亦假以顏色。不出忿激之詞。然又篤實不欺。動止以禮自持。故雖長於交際。而無形中自有不可侵越之界限。曾未嘗曲己從人。較之碌碌追隨流俗者。自屬大相逕庭。自幼好讀書。然喜推求真義。不拘拘于文詞。維新後。入安徽求是學堂。畢業後。復入安徽法政學堂別科。以最優等畢業。民國元年。以安徽臨時省議會議員。為北京臨時參議院議員。國會成立。當選為眾議院議員。國會解散後。復從事學問。不聞政事。與人言。恆守消極。不置可否。朋輩強詢之。則以抽象的學理相答。決不涉及。帝制之亂發生。始赴滬。與同志等奔走國事。旅滬議員通訊處成立。君為常駐幹事。及國會實行二次召集。遂來京仍為眾議院議員。

君賦性溫厚、人と交る和藹親む可し。平素惡む所のものと雖も、亦假すに顏色を以てし、忿怒の詞を出さず。又篤實にして欺かず、動止禮を以て自ら持す、故に交際に長ずと雖も、無形の中、自ら侵越すべからざる限界あり。未だ嘗つて已を曲げて人に從はず。之を碌碌として流俗に追隨する者に較べば、自ら大に逕庭あり。幼より讀書を好み、然れども真義を推求するを喜び、文詞に拘泥せず。維新の後、安徽の求是學堂に入り、最優等を以て業を畢ふ。民國元年、安徽臨時省議會議員となり、北京臨時參議院議員となる。國會成立後、當選して眾議院議員となる、北京臨時參議院議員と爲る。國會解散の後、復た學問に從事し、政事に與らず、人と談論するに、恆に消極を守り、可否を置かず。朋輩強ひて之を詢へば、抽象的學理を以て答へ、決して政見に涉及せず。帝制の亂發生するや、始めて上海に赴き、同志等と國事に奔走す。在上海議員通訊處成立するに及び、君常駐幹事と爲る。國會再び召集するに至り。遂に上京して仍は眾議院議員と爲る。

Mr. Tsao Yu-te, otherwise called Yun Sheng is a native of Ling Pi, An Hui Hsing. He is a broad and gentleminded and extremely sociable. Even toward his enemy, he never shows his indignation in wither countenance nor in words. He is sincere and guide himself according to the strict law of courtesy. Therefore although sociable, he is morally superior and his influence as such is very great. However gentle he may be, he never bends himself without rational grounds; he is far from being a syncophant who Kowtows to influence. He is a reader as well as a deep thinker. He is above the study of were expression or turn of sentences. Under the new regime, he studied law in the law college of An Hui, and in the 1st year of the Republic, he was a member of the An Hui Special Local Assembly in which capacity he took part in the Extraordinay Senatorial Assembly hold in his own province. After the formation of the Parliament, he was elected a member thereof, but with the dissolution of the Parliament, he held his peace, and never talked of politics except in abstract and theoretical reasoning; when the movement for the Imperial Government took place, he went to Shanghai and proned himself to be an ardent educate of the opposition cause. When the Parliament was called again, he became the member thereof.

張相文 字蔚西 歲五十一

選舉地　江蘇省
籍　貫　江蘇泗陽縣
住　址　北京西單達智營

君秉性堅實誠篤。不喜浮華。而資質聰敏。穎於悟性。少時家綦貧。能刻苦勵學。有聲庠序間。年既壯。感於世變之亟。乃棄科舉業。殫心新學。尤好治中外輿地之學。遂以是名家。以此授徒爲活者凡三十餘年。成就弟子甚衆。所著有地誌地文諸書。風行海內。清末創地學會於天津。被推爲會長。自是編輯雜誌。月刊一册。學界爭寶貴之。生平性好遊歷。名山大川。足迹幾遍。民國成立。被選爲衆議院議員。國會解散後。出關薄遊塞外。實證秦長城所在。又發見成吉思汗陵寢。且糾歷史地理家之失。因以考訂其地點旋歸里仍從事研究。絕不談及時政。及國會復活。始應召來京。仍衆議院議員職。

君秉性堅實誠篤にして浮華を喜ばず、而して資質聰敏なり。少時其の家貧にして刻苦勉勵經史を攻究し、年既に壯なるや時事に感ずる所ありて科學の業を棄て專ら新學を求め九ゝ中外輿地の學を好み遂に一家を成して子弟に教授すること二十餘年、地誌地文に關す諸書を著はして海內に行はる。前清末季天津に於て地學會を創設して會長に推さる。爾來月刊雜誌を發行して其の蘊蓄を講述す。民國成立生平遊歷を好みて名山大川足跡幾んど遍ねし。民國成立後、選ばれて衆議院議員となる。國會解散さるや、關を出でゝ遠く塞外を跋渉して秦長城の所在を實査し、又た吉思汗の陵墓を發見し、且つ歷史地理家の失を糾して其の地點を考訂したり。旋て鄉里に歸臥して政事を談ぜざるも依然研究に從事して學術界に貢献する所尠なからず。國會復活するに及び其の召集に應じ再び北上入京して仍ち衆議院議員の職に就く。

Mr. Chang Hsiang-wen, otherwise called Wei-hsi, age fifty one, is a native of Ssu-yang, Chiang-su province. He is a gentleman of simple mode of living who cherishes strong hatred against anything vain and pompous. He was brought upon the lap of penury. As he grew older he was greatly impressed with the condition of affairs and he made up his mind to seek new learning. He wrote a well known geography and devoted himself to the education of the young more than twenty years. At the latter days of the Chinese regime he founded the geographical institute of which he became the president. He travelled a great deal to enrich the stock of knowledge. With the establishment of the Republic he was elected a member of the House of Commons. With the dissolution of the Parliament he went back to the life of a scholar deeply interested in history and geography. While he was back in his country he contributed a great deal to the interest of his country by his study. With the restoration of the Parliament he entered Peking and became a member of the House of Commons.

張錦芳　字綱庵　歲四十三

選舉地　河南省

籍　貫　河南省項城縣

住　址　北京北池子中州張宅

君爲人誠篤無欺。言動皆確守古訓。不
稍縱肆。居常以厚道待人。秉性聰敏異
人。自幼明察事理。思考敏捷。而意思
新奇。不爲流俗之成見所局。及長。九
堅強。弱冠讀書。即能發微起伏。別闢
深思明辨。勵行身心之修養。前清由廩
生在順直賑捐報捐道員。宣統元年改
度支部郎中。歷充庫藏司。鹽務處。兩
淮司各科員。民國二年被選爲衆議院
議員。國會解散後。歸里閑臥。時出從
事地方公益。五年及約法恢復。國會重
行召集。遂又入京。仍爲衆議院議員。

君人と爲り誠篤にして欺かず、言動當な古訓を確守す。
居常厚道を以て人を待ち、秉性聰敏にして幼より事理を
明察し思考敏捷なり。弱冠書を讀みて徽を發し伏を起し
て別に新奇を開き、流俗の成見に局さる〻所と爲らず。
長ずるに及び 深く思ひ明に辨じて身心の修養に勵みた
り。前清の廩生を以て、順直賑捐報捐道員たり。宣統元
年改めて度支部郎中と爲る。庫藏司、鹽務處、兩淮司等
の各科員に歷任して事務の才幹あり。民國二年正式國會
成立に際し衆議院議員に當選す。國會解散さる〻や、河
南に歸りて家を省み、時に出で〻地方の公益に從事す。君
が郷里項城は昔時項羽の出でし所にして近くは袁世凱の
郷里なり。五年約法恢復して國會重ねて召集を行ふや遂
に又た入京して仍ち衆議院議員たり。

Mr. Chang Chin-fang, age forty three, is a native of Hsiang Cheng, the Ho-nan-hsing. Honesty is the best palicy is his motto. He is interested in the classic teaching. He was bright and keen as the thinker. He was a great reader of books in his youth, and his judgement stood very high compared with most of the people. He was very careful in both mental and physical culture. His official career was commenced in 1909 when in the financial department he exhibited his ability. In 1917, when the Republic was established, he became a member of the House of Commons, on the disolution of which, however, he returned to Ho-nan, his native place where he gave his service to the benefits of local districts. Hsiang Cheng is the home of Yuanshi-kai. When the Parliament was summoned again, he entered Peking where he resumed his former service as the member of the House of Commons.

二百三十一

張嘉謀　字中學　歲四十三

選舉地　河南省

籍貫　河南省南陽縣

住址　北京崇來街西邊草廠

君爲人剛正不阿。而秉性聰慧。思想活
潑。頭腦明晰。讀書不執成見。不拘字
句。故皆能得其眞義。弱冠即負文名。
及長。尤廣覽群籍。自以遠大相期許。
前清由拔貢舉人。歷充南陽中學敎習。
河南商業中學校長。學務公所議紳。銳
意從事育英。熱心企圖敎育普及。多有
所貢獻。旋選爲諮議局議員。被推爲副
議長。被舉充請願國會聯合會會員。民
國肇造。被選爲省議會副議長。民國二
年正式國會成立。當選衆議院議員。國
會解散後。又充中州文獻徵輯處調查
員。五年及國會重開。遂又應召入京。
仍爲衆議院議員。

民國之翰
（華僑記）

張嘉謀先生

君人と爲り剛正阿らず、秉性聰慧にして思想活潑頭腦明
晰なり。其の讀書は成見に執せず字句に囚れず、皆に能
く眞義を得たり。弱冠早くも文名を負ひ、長じて尤も廣
く群籍を閲して大成を期したり。前清時代、拔貢舉人と
して、南陽中學敎習、河南商業中學校長。學務公所議
紳等の職に歷任し、銳意育英に從事し、熱心に敎育の普
及を企圖して、貢獻する所多し。旋て選ばれて諮議局議
紳と爲り、副議長に推さる。又た國會請願聯合會會員に
舉げらる。民國の樹立に際し、省議會副議長に舉げらる。
民國二年正式國會成立に際し衆議院議員に當選した
り。國會解散されて後も、又た中州文獻徵輯處關査員と
爲る。五年約法恢復して國會重ねて開かるゝに及び、遂
に又た其の召集に應じて入京し、仍ち衆議院議員と爲
る。

Mr. Chang Chia-mou, age forty three, is a native of Nan-yang-hsien, He-nan-hsing. Frank-ness of character and the boldness of temperament are combined in this gentleman who is the possessor of active thoughts and clear brains. Not being bound up with traditional influence nor by the study of mere phrases he was able to comprehend the real meaning of the book. Under the previous Chinese regime he was the head of the Ho nan commercial school and in similar capacity he was interested in education and contributed a great deal to the defusion of liberal knowledge. He was a member and later the vice president of the local assembly. When the Republic was brought into existence he was returned for the House of Commons. While this legislative body was kept in abeyance, he was keenly watching for the chance of the restoration of the Republic. Under the new president he entered Peking and was returned for the House of Commons.

張塡　字伯衍　歲四十三

選舉地　安徽省
籍貫　安徽省懷德縣
住址　北京草帽胡同

君少好學不喜制藝。專精經術。尤致力於易。偶有所得。惟書之秘編。不以問世。爲人慷慨好義。見人不平。常忿怨過於身受。然其舉動極爲愼重。不逞一時之意氣以爲從井救人之行爲。故生平所爲義舉極多。然未曾以此陷於絕境。前清癸卯科舉人分發廣東知縣。法政專科畢業。民國元年充本縣縣議會副議長。二年正式國會成立被選爲衆議院議員。國會解散後。消極自持。無所表白。及國會重開。復爲衆議院議員。

張塡先生

君少にして學を好み制藝を喜ばず。專ら經史に精しく、力を易に致し、偶を得る所あれば之を秘編に書して世に問はす。人と爲り慷慨義を好むも其の舉動極めて愼重、敢て一時の意氣に乘じ、并に從つて人を救ふの舉を爲さず、故に生平爲せし所の義舉極めて多きも、未だ曾て絕境に陷ゐりし事無し。前清癸卯科の舉人にして知縣として廣東省に分たる。曾て法政大學校專門科を卒業す。民國樹立するや、懷德縣會の副議長に舉げられ地方自治の事に盡瘁す。民國二年正式國會議員の選舉に際し衆望を荷つて衆議院議員に當選す。國會解散されてより、南旋して鄉里に閑臥し。消極主義を持して政見を表示する事無く、讀書自ら娛む。五年國會復活するに及び、再び立ちて其の召集に應じ、北上入京して仍ち衆議院議員の職に就く。

Mr. Chang yin, age forty three, is a native of Huai wang, Au-hui-hsing. While young he was an ardent scholar and was well versed in the classical history. He compiled for his own interest in a book form the points of interest which he observed in the course of reading. He is cautious in his movement and measures every step he takes. He was graduated from the law college in his province. When the Republic was established he was appointed the vice president of the local assembly. In the 2nd year of the Revolution, he was elected a member of the House of Commons with a overwhelming majority. When the Parliament was put down he went to his native country he adopted a conservative principle and seemed to care very little about politics. When the Parliament was to be opened again he went to Peking where he was elected a member of the House of Commons.

張雅南 字龍軒 歲五十

選舉地　吉林省
籍貫　吉林省
住址　北京糧食店同興旅館

君少好學。性謹飭。彬彬然有儒士風。中年究心學子業。速不得志于有司於是棄而從政。歷官任職。十有餘年。經驗宏富。由前清主事。己酉科歲貢生。歸充吉林練軍馬隊頭二三起營務帖式。靖邊新軍營務差遣委員。靖邊後路營務辦事官。隨同辦事委員。水陸捕盜軍隨營辦事委員。由甲午至癸卯。共在軍營。十年癸卯冬。充五常廳清賦放荒委員。乙巳轉吉省荒務總局差遣委員。丙午冬出爲拉林城荒務委員。共在荒務。四年丁未入省城法政學堂附設之憲政研究所肄業。戊申畢業。又入官紳自治研究所肄業。己酉畢業。被選爲吉林府城議會議員。庚戌入法官養成所肄業。壬子再被選爲城議會議員。互選爲副議長。又被選爲衆議院議員。癸丑到京。是冬解散回籍。五年七月。由上海到京。就議員席。提議要政。時論趙之。

民國之精華　（傳記）　張雅南先生

君幼より學を好み性恪謹、彬々然として儒士の風あり。中年科舉の業に勉め、後ち業を棄て〻致仕し、在職十餘年經驗豐富なり。前清己酉科歲貢生を以て、吉林練軍馬隊頭二三起營務筆帖式、靖邊新軍營務差遣委員、靖邊後路營務辦事官隨同辦事委員、水陸捕盜隨營辦事委員に歷充す。甲午癸卯間、軍營に在ること十年、癸卯の冬、五常廳淸賦放荒委員に任じ、乙己の歲、吉省荒務總局差遣委員に轉ず。丙午の冬、拉林城荒務委員として開墾事務を處理すること四年。丁未の歲、省城法政學校附設憲政研究所に入りて修業し。戊申の歲、官紳自治研究所に入りて修業す。己酉の歲、其の業を畢へて吉林府城議會議員に選ばる。庚戌の歲、法官養成所に入りて修業す。壬子の歲、省議會議員に選ばれ副議長と爲る。又た衆議院議員に當選す。國會解散するや、歸鄕して地方公益事業に盡力し、民國五年七月上海より北京に抵り、衆議院議員の職に就く。

Mr. Chang Ya-nan, otherwise called Ching-hsien, age fifty, is a native of Chi-lin hsing. While young he had an air of a scholar. After graduating from the middle school he spent over ten years in the government post. He spent over ten years of his life in the military circle. During different years he was connected with various organizations in the chinese regime. In 1907 he studied law in the law school of the province. After graduating from the school he again entered official career and became a vice-president of the local assembly. He was elected for the House of Commons. With the dissolution of the Parliament however, he returned to his home where he was deeply interested in the public enterprise. When the Parliament was reopened he entered Peking and was elected to a member of the House of Commons.

張 樹 桐　字鳳廷　歲五十

選舉地　內蒙古

籍　貫　蒙古卓索圖盟喀喇沁中旗

住　址　北京東皇城根達敎胡同

君少慧。年甫九歲。通達蒙文。鄉里有
才子之稱。及稍長。精通漢文。詩詞歌
賦。工巧不輩。尤究心經史之學。嗣以
繙譯進士。法政學堂畢業。歷任蒙旗司
法行政長官。管旗章京等職。素抱民權
政治。辛亥改革有勞。於民國元年被舉
爲臨時參議院議員。著作蒙藏交通公
司蒙漢旬報。以開邊。知宣慰卓昭兩盟
各旗。傾心內向。勳勞卓著。任命副都
統。四等嘉禾章。二年被選爲衆議院議
員。初袁氏經營帝制時。誘君以爵祿。
而不動。惟主持民權。保障憲法。隨袁
氏破壞國會時。被逐於海外議員之一。
當改元洪憲。君奔走蒙邊。反對帝制。
呼號討賊。三過其門而不入。迨雲貴首
義。即附旅滬之諸大名流議復民國之
策。至袁斃。國會復活。仍未歸蒙。摒家
事。旣抱棄家抛業之痛。復懷指揮大計
之思。卒以急公後私之精神。迺來京。
復就衆議院議員之職。

二年衆議院議員に當選す。初め袁氏が帝制を志す時、君
を誘ふに爵祿を以てしたるも動かず。袁氏が國會を破壞
するや、君亦た海外に逃れ、其の元を改めて洪憲と爲す
に及び、帝制に反對し、蒙古各地を奔走して討袁を呼號
す。後ち即ち上海に赴き諸名士と民國恢復の策を議し、
袁氏斃れて國會復活するや、蒙古に歸りて家事を顧ふの
遑なく、遂に入京して復た衆議院議員の職に就く。

君少より慧敏、年九歲、蒙文に通じ、稍や長するに及び
て漢文に精通し、詩詞歌賦に巧に、尤も心を經史の學に
注ぐ。嗣で繙譯進士を以て法政學校を卒業し、蒙旗司法
行政長官、管旗章京等の職に歷任す。素と民權政治の志
を抱き、第一革命に際し功勞あり。民國元年臨時參議院
議員に當選す。
蒙藏交通公司發刊の蒙漢旬報の編輯に任
す。卓昭兩盟の蒙古旗人を宣慰して民國に心を寄せしむ
其の勳功により副都統に任命して四等嘉禾章を授けらる

Mr. Chang Shu-tung, otherwise called Feng-ting, age fifty, is a native of Mongolia. He was
very precocious, having been able to read heavy classics at the age of nine. He was very much interested in the classical study and then in law. In the first revolution he rendered a great service to
his cause. In the 1st year of the Republic he was elected to a member of the local assembly. In the
second year of the Republic when the Parliament was opened, he was elected to a member of the House
of Commons. It is a fact, that Yuanshi-kai employed every means to get him on his side, when he proposed to adopt Imperial system. When the Parliament was dissolved, he went abroad where he strongly
opposed to the plans of Yuanshi-kai. With the death of Yuanshi-kai and the restoration of the Parliament he went to Peking and returned to the House of Commons.

張敬之　字翰鄉　歲四十九

選舉地　直隷省
籍　貫　直隷曲周縣
住　址　北京西城二龍坑貴人關

君賦性嚴正剛直。不隨流俗沈浮。然能
以厚道待人。雖所痛惡。亦不虐待之。
生平疾惡如仇。然但嚴其交游之界限。
絕不疾言遽色待人。居恒以禮自持不
輕於動止。唯見人不平。則喜爲不平之
鳴。不惜犧牲其個人之利益。自幼聰慧
絕倫。弱冠爲文。常下筆數千言。頃刻
立就。及長。愈求淵博精深。明於是非
利害之辦。前淸時。曾以地方推舉。辦
理本地團練事務。旋入地方自治研究
所。畢業後。歷充本縣自治預備會會
員。縣議事會議員。縣參事會參事員。
道省戒烟總會稽查員。民國成立。被選
爲正式國會衆議院議員。國會解散後。
萬事取消極態度。不問時事。及至國
復活。始應召仍爲衆議院議員。

君賦性嚴正剛直にして俗流に棹して浮沈するを欲せず。
然も厚道を以て人を待ち、憎惡する所のものと雖亦た之
を虐待せず。而して其交游の限界を嚴にするも、絕へて
疾言遽色を以て人を待たず。居常禮を以て自ら持し輕々
しく進退せず。幼より聰慧絕倫にして弱冠文を作りて筆
を下せば數千言頃刻にして成る。長ずるに及びて意々該
博を求め是非利害の辦を明にす。前淸の時曾て地方推舉
を以て鄉里の團練事務を辦理し、旋て地方自治研究所に
入りて卒業す。本縣自治預備會々員、縣議事會議員、縣
參事會參事員、直隷省戒烟總會稽査員等の公職に歷充し
て地方自治の發展に畫策努力する所ありたり。民國成立
の後ち選ばれて正式國會衆議院議員と爲る。國會解散す
るに及び、萬事消極的態度を持して時事の狂瀾に投せ
す。其の國會再び召集を行ふに及び復た出で、仍は衆議
院議員と爲る。

民國之精華　（傳記）　張敬之先生

Mr. Chang Chin Chih, otherwise called Han hsing, age forty nine, is a native of Chin Chou, the Chi len hsing. He does not care to nien with men of common caribre, and yet he is hospitable to every one whom he meets. In all things, he observes courtesy and do not show any anger if annoyed. He is an able writer, being very quick in the art of composition. He received his education in the local institute of learning. It appears that he attaches great interest to the development of local civic bodies, and as such occupied many important government offices. When the Republic was established, he was elected to a member of the House of Commons in which capacity he contributed a great deal to the interest of his countrymen. Upon the dissolution of the Parliament, he quietly returned to home, and never plunged himself into the mad vortex of political agitation with the reopening of the Parliament, he was elected to a member of the House of Commons.

二百三十五

張坤 字子厚 歲四十三

選舉地　河南省

籍貫　河南省陝縣

住址　北京石駙馬關橋西大院門牌三十二號

君賦性清高。為人勤謹耐勞。自幼天資聰穎。讀書能深思。探究精義。不為成見所局。故思想豐富。見解新俊。海內維新後。銳志西學。專攻新書。造詣既深。前清癸卯料舉人。庚戌會考。授度支部主事。曾任河南陝州中學堂監督。旋被選為河南諮議局副議長。兼河南高等學堂監督。民國成立。被選為河南臨時省議會議員。辭職。被選為河南臨時教育會議副議長。又歷充秦軍第二師第二軍參謀。上海公學總務幹事兼代校長。民國二年正式國會成立。被選為眾議院議員。國會停止後。從事育英。誘掖後進。不問時政。五年及國會重開。遂又應召人京。仍為眾議院議員。

君賦性清高にして人と為り恪謹勞に耐ゆ。幼より天資聰穎を讀みて其の義を探究し、思想富見解新俊なり。海內維新後、西學に志して專ら新書を攻究し、造詣飽に深し。前清癸卯の舉人にして庚戌の試に會して度支部主事を授けらる。曾て河南陝州中學堂監督に任じ、旋て河南諮議局副議長に舉げられ、河南高等學堂監督を兼ぬ。民國成立に際し選ばれて河南臨時省議會議員と為る。後辭職して河南臨時教育會議副議長に舉げらる。又た秦軍第二師第二軍參謀に任じ、上海公學總務幹事となり代理校長を兼ぬ。民國二年正式國會眾議院議員に當選す。國會停止後、鄉里に歸りて育英の業に從事し、後進を誘掖して暫らく時事を問はず。五年約法恢復して國會重ねて召集を行ふに及び、遂に又た入京して院に臨み、仍ほ眾議院議員と為る。

Mr. Chang Kun, otherwise known as Tzu Hon, age forty three, is a native of Shan hsien, Honan hsing. He had rich natural gifts when young, and became a reader of books, which he digested and reduced to practice for the interests of the people. Later his attention was turned to the new learning, of which he became very proficient. In 1910 he passed successfully the civil service examination and was appointed to one of the secretaries of finances. Later he was the vice-president of the Ho-nan local assembly. With the establishment of the Republic he was elected to a member of the Ho-nan special local assembly. On resigning this post he became the vice president of the educational society in his province. He also acted for the president of the Shanghai public school. In the 2nd year of the Republic he was returned for the House of Commons. When the Parliament was closed up, he was interested in the education of the younger generation. When the Parliament was summoned, he entered Peking and was elected to a member of the House of Commons, the position which he holds at present.

張伯烈 字亞農 歲四十三

選舉地　湖北省

籍　貫　湖北省隨州

住　址　北京南橫街大川淀南口路北七號

君爲人放達不羈。天資聰敏。年十八。補博士弟子員。中年以廩生。光緒乙巳。以官費留學日本。習普通既畢。考入日本大學法科肄業。半途歸國。與諸同志。創辦湖北地方自治研究會。君爲會長。未幾。川粤漢鐵路借欵問題發生。由反對留學界。被選爲代表。旋由湖北推選劉公源密昌堰。爲入都交涉代表。並推君並行。事竣。仍返日本卒學。所著假定中國憲法草案一書旋至汴。幇辦學務。並創辦女子師範學堂。及湖北起義。潛行回鄂。遂奔海上。旋由鄂省議會。被選爲南京參議院議員嗣又被舉爲北京參議院議員。正式國會成立。被選爲衆議院議員。君由民社發起人。改爲共和黨。迄今獨樹一幟。及國會解散。爲大總統政治諮議。民國三年辭職。遯跡韜晦。袁氏死。黎公繼任。君廳電召入都。創辦張維學社。提倡道德。改良社會。及國會重開。仍爲衆議院議員。

君人と爲り瀾達豪俠、天資聰明俊敏なり。年十八、博士弟子員に補し、中年廩生となる。光緒乙卯官貴を以て日本に留學し、日本大學校法科に入り、中途歸國し、湖北地方自治研究會を創立して會長と爲る。川粤漢鐵路借欵問題反對留學生の代表となり。旋で湖北代表劉公源密昌堰と共に北京に赴き、事竣つて復た日本に抵りて學事を畢ゆ。假定中國憲法草案を著す。旋て汴に至りて學務を助け、並に女子師範學校を創立す。第一革命には湖北に歸り途に上海に奔る。選ばれて臨時參議院議員と爲り。二年正式國會衆議院議員に常選す。君民社を發起し、共和黨となるや、依然として別に一旗幟を樹てゝ今に迫ふ。國會解散後、大總統政治諮議と爲りしも、三年辭職して韜晦し。五年黎公繼任するや、君を電召す、張維學社を創設し、道德を提倡して社會改良を圖る。國會復活するに及び、仍ほ衆議院議員と爲る。

Mr. Chang Pai-lieh, otherwise called Ya Nung, age forty three, is a native of Sui hsien, Hu-Pe hsing. He was naturally a gentleman of active and heroic spirit. Under the previous chinese regime he visited Japan and entered the Nippon University. On returning home he was organized civic system institution in Hu-pe, of which he became the president. He went to Peking representing the student class against the famous railway problem. Again he returned to Japan where he was graduated from the Nippon University. He founded the Female Normal School. In the 1st Revolution he went back to his province and then to Shanghai, when he was elected to a member of the special senatorial assembly. In the 2nd year of the Republic he was elected to a member of the House of Commons. When the Parliament was dissolved, he was once an adviser to the president but on resigning the same, he led the life retirement. He was also interested in the social reform movement. As soon as the Parliament was reopened, he was elected to a member of the House of Commons, the position he now holds.

民國之精華　（傳記）張伯烈先生

張國淩 字濟川 歳三十九

選舉地　直隷省

籍　貫　直隷省保定府清苑縣

住　址　北京石駙馬大街路南王庽

君秉性聰明穎達。爲人富于進取之氣象。由來。幽薊人民渾樸。開化最遲惟此君獨得風氣之先。醉心歐美之學。且尤於提創教育一途。不遺餘力。識時務之萬傑。微君其誰與歸。壯年入直隷大學堂畢業。光緒癸卯科副榜。歷充本省趙州中學堂教員。保定府中學堂監督。中州公立中學堂監督。淸苑勸學所總董。官立公立高等小學堂校長。從事育英。誘拔後進。旋被舉爲淸苑縣議會副議長。民國二年被選爲衆議院議員。國會解散後。歸里讀書。惟籌畫地方教育之普及。企圖民智之開發。不問時政。五年及國會重開。遂應召。仍爲衆議院議員。

君秉性聰明穎達にして人と爲り進取の氣象に富む。由來幽薊の民渾撲にして開化最も遲く、獨り君其の風氣に先を爲して歐米の學に心醉し、尤も教育の振興に關して餘力を遺さず、蓋し時務を識るの儁傑なり。壯年の頃、直隷大學堂に入りて卒業す。癸卯科の副榜を以て、本省趙州中學校教員、保定府中學校監督、中州公立中學校監督、淸苑勸學所總董、官立公立各高等小學校長に歷任し、育英中學校監督、淸苑勸學所總董、官立公立各高等小學校長に歷任し、青英の業に從事して後進を誘掖する所ありたり。旋て淸苑縣議會副議長に舉げらる。民國二年正式國會議員選舉に際し衆議院議員に當選す。國會解散されて後ち鄕里に歸り書に親しみ、時に出でゝ地方教育の普及を飾り、民智の開發を圖り、また時事を問はず。五年國會復活するに及び、遂に又た召集に應じて北京に抵り、現に仍は衆議院議員たり。

Mr. Chang Kuo-chun, otherwise called Chi Chuan, age thirty nine, is a native of Pao-ting fu, the Chi-lin hsing. He is full of progressive spirit. The people of his district generally speaking are slow to move, and grew benighted in the adoption of civilization, but he proved himself to be the pioneer in acquiring foreign civilization, and employed to the best of his ability every possible means necessary for the dissimination of the modern education. In his younger days, he studied in the Chi-ling university, since then he was an instructor in a number of middle schools and institutes of learning of all sorts. He contributed all his efforts to the promotion of the younger generation. In the 2nd year of the Republic, he was returned for the House of Commons. When this assembly was suppressed, he made his way to the native district, where he devoted himself to the education of the people. However, with the re-opening of the Parliament, he was again elected as the member of the House of Commons.

選擧地　貴州省
縮貫　貴州省盤縣
住址　北京驛馬市大街蘇線胡同中間路東

君為剛直堅強。而頭腦明晰。不執偏私
自誤。以前清光緒庚子辛丑併科舉人。
授知縣分發四川。旋丁父憂回籍宣統
元年。被選為諮議局議員。資政院候補
議員二年。各省諮議局開聯合會於北
京。君被舉為赴京代表。三年。起服回
川。適諮議局長蒲殿俊等以爭鐵路事
被捕。當事者多承總督趙匱豐意旨。煅
煉成獄。君知其冤。力諫趙以為不可。
不聽。川省光復。被任為青神縣知事。
調充財政部科長。四年。應調赴滇。未
至。而籌安會發生。因留黔不進。五年
一月。閏滇起義。始兼程前往。充都督
府諮議官。四月一日。滇人以衰世凱取
消帝制。開大會徵求意見。君極力主
戰。謂非令衰氏退位。終非民國之禍。
并倡議派議員赴滬組織國會。未幾共
和再造。重行召集國會。遂復至京。為
參議院議員。

君剛直にして堅強、頭腦明晰にして偏見を固執せす。前
清光緒庚子辛丑併科の舉人を以て知縣を授けられ四川に
分たる。旋て父の喪に服して郷里に歸る。宣統元年選ば
れて諮議局議員となり、資政院候補議員に舉げらる。二
年各省諮議局聯合會を北京に開くや、貴州諮議局代表と
して北京に赴き、三年喪に服して歸郷す。時適ま鐵道國
有問題の風潮起りて四川諮議局議長蒲殿俊等逮捕されて獄
に下る。君其の冤を知りて總督趙匱豐を諫めしを聞かれ

ず。旋て四川獨立して後ち君即ち青神縣知事に任す。
國元年都督府秘書長に任す。二年參議院議員に當選す。民
國會解散後、財政部科長に任す。四年雲南派遣の途上、
籌安會發起の事を聞きて貴州に留りて進まず。五年雲南
義を起すと聞きて出發前進して都督府諮議官となる。袁
氏帝制を取消すや、其の退位を主張す。袁氏死して國會
復活するや、再び召集に應じて入京し、現に仍は參議院
議員たり。

民國之精華　（傳記）　張光煒先生

Mr. Chang Kuang-wei, otherwise called Lien-hsien, age forty two, is a native of Pan Kuei-Chou province. Being a man of strong will and clear brain, he is not bound up with any prejudices. In 1901, he passed the civil service examination, and was appointed to a local governor, but on the death of his father, he returned to home. In 1909, he was appointed to a member of the local assembly. When the federate meeting of different provinces took place in Peking, he attended the meeting representing his own province. When the railway nationalization problem took place, the president of the Shu-chuan local assembly was imprisoned, when he worked very hard to get the president out of the prison. In the first year of the Republic, he was appointed to a private secretary to the governor general, and in the second year, he was elected to a member of the Senate. After the dissolution of the Parliament, he remained the head of the financial bureau. When Yuanshi-kai with-drew his proposal for the Imperial movement, he pressed Yuanshi-kai to give up his presiding. With the Restoration of the Parliament, he entered Peking, and was elected to a member of the Senate.

張琴　字治如　歲四十一

選舉地　福建省

籍貫　福建省莆田縣

住址　北京永光寺中街亞東新聞

君天資聰慧。為人誠篤。自幼好學。以優貢生中副車。登癸卯賢書。甲辰。成進士。改庶吉士。授翰林院編修。前清之季。嘗與邑中名宿創辦崇實中學校。暗以革命宗旨輸入諸生。時滿州寶康為太守。偵知之。遂遭停閉。後創辦與化中學校。旋為京師閩學堂監督。辛亥革命。起著共和論數千言。陳說袁世凱贊同民軍。南苑姜軍及禁衛軍要人來索書者踵相接。知交皆為之危。民國元年。簡任福建教育司長。辭不就。被舉為眾議院議員。任亞東新聞主筆。攻擊袁氏。遏其帝制自為之心。湖口獨立。著論勸袁氏辭職。登之報瑞。遂被警廳逮捕。報舘亦被封。旋由友人在外保釋。國會解散後。仍歸里主持教育。不涉足政界。及國會重開。始來京供職。

君天資聰慧にして人と為り誠實。幼より學を好み、優貢生副車及第を以て發卯の賢書に登り、甲辰の歲進士となり、庶吉士に改めて翰林院編修を授けらる。前清末季、曾て鄉里の先輩と籌りて崇實中學校を創設經營し、暗に革命主義を子弟に注入す。地方官滿人寶康之を偵知して遂に學校を閉鎖す。後も興化中學校を創立經營し、旋て京師閩學堂監督となる。第一革命に際し共和論數千言を著す。民國元年福建省教育司長に任せられたるも辭して就かず、嗣で正式國會の成立に際し乗議院議員に當選す。兼て亞東新聞主筆に任じ袁氏の政策を攻擊し、第二革命の變に際して袁氏辭職勸告論を著して紙上に揭載したるを以て新聞社は營業を停止され君は逮捕さる、旋て漸く友人の盡力によりて保釋された。國會解散後、鄉里に歸りて教育の振興を計り、また政界に遠ざかりしも、國會復活するに及び、再び出てゝ衆議院議員の職に就く。

Mr. Chang Chin, otherwise called Chih-yu, age forty one, is a native of Pu-tien, Fu-chien province. He is bright in nature and sincere in his efforts. While young, he passed the government examination successfully, and became a member of the Han-lin-yin. At the latter days of the previous Chinese regime, he established a school in his province in conjunction with his friends, and inspired the pupils with revolutionary ideas. But being suspected by the Manchu Government, he had to close it. When the revolution was starting he wrote a book on the movement. In the first year of the Republic, the chief of the educational department of Fukien was offered to him, but he gove it up. When the Parliament was opened, he was elected a member of the House of Commons. He opposed most strongly the policy of Yuanshi-kai in his paper, and at one time even his personality was endaugered. With the dissolution of the Parliament, he returned to his home where he was interested in education. With the restoration of the Parliament, however, he was elected a member of the House of Commons.

張宏銓 字伯衡 歳三十七

選舉地　湖南省

籍貫　湖南省乾城縣

住址　北京新簾子胡同二十四

君以前清廩生。入長沙師範館肄業。畢業後。歷任西路師範。乾城鳳永師範。及中學各教員。光緒乙己以官費咨送日本。入宏文學院尚等師範預科畢業歸國。歷充奉天農業試驗場。清理財政局。造幣廠等處職任。君好研究農學財政學幣制學。各有心得。凡所調查各項。均選簀報告。裏然巨快。辛亥國體變更。君由奉赴滬。偕熊希齡張學濟等發起共和協會。既而改為共和黨。遂歸乾城組織黨事。旋被選為衆議院議員君秉性公平正直。尤不好為無意識之爭執。唯對于國家重大事。則持正不阿。及國會解散。遂返乾城。獨居不與政事。及西南起義。袁氏派兵入湘。人民塗炭。君與熊希齡等從事賑撫事宜。張學濟在乾城縣獨立。聯合黔軍以抵制袁兵。其中秘密計畫。君皆與有大力。及國會恢復。始入京仍為議員。

民國之精華　（傳記）張宏銓先生

君や前清の廩生を以て長沙師範學校出身の秀才なり。西路師範學校、乾城鳳永師範學校及び中學校等の各教授に歷充し、光緒乙己の歳官費留學生として日本に游び、宏文學院高等師範豫科を卒業す。歸國の後ち奉天に赴きて奉天農業試驗場、財政整理局、造幣廠等に職を奉す。君好んで農學財政學幣制學を研究して各々素養あり。辛亥の歳、國體變更するや、君上海に赴きて熊希齡張學濟等と共和協會を發起す。後ち改めて共和黨を組織するや、乾城に歸りて同黨地盤の開拓に從事す。民國二年選ばれて衆議院議員と為る。君秉性公平にして正直。主張穩健なり。國會解散するに及びて乾城に歸り政事に與らず、西南義を起して袁政府の派兵湖南に入り人民塗炭に苦しや、君熊希齡等と賑撫事宜に從事し、張學濟が乾城縣に在りて獨立し、以て貴州軍と聯絡して袁政府の兵を牽制するや、其の秘密計畫に豫りて大に力あり、國會恢復後、再び出で、衆議院議員たり。

Mr. Chang Hung Chuan, otherwise called Pai Jen, is a native of the Ho-nan Hsing, and is thirty seven years old this year. He is a graduate of the Cheng Sha Normal School, and taught in a number of normal schools in his province. In 1905, he came to Japan at the government expense, where he was graduated from the Higher Normal School. On way home, he stopped at Mukden where he found a position in the government mint and agricultural farm. He was greatly interested in agricultural economy and mint system. In the time of the revolution, he went to Shanghai where he joined with others to form the Republic Association which was advanced to the political party of the same name. In the 2nd year of the Republic, he was elected a member of the House of Commons. His views are quite rational, but in furthering the cause of the Republic against the userpation of Yuanshi-kai, he was indeed on important factor. He is at the present moment an important member of the House of Commons.

張華瀾 字鏡滄 歲三十七

選舉地　雲南省
籍貫　　雲南省石屏祥
住址　　北京校場二條三十六號

君為人倜儻不羈。然居心仁厚。喜為義舉。自幼讀書。即慨然有為天下第一人之志。及長。不從事舉業。唯肆力新學。前清時。曾肄業雲南經正書院旋留學日本宏文學院。入中國同盟會。與胡漢民呂志伊等為友。歸充臨安師範學堂及雲南農業學堂教習。辛亥革命。被舉為雲南保安會會長。民國元年。被選為臨時參議院議員二年。被選為衆議院議員。國會解散後。隱居石屏異龍湖。不問國事。及滇省起義。出任護國第一軍秘書。隨攻瀘州。及共和恢復。國會重開。遂入都。仍為議員。

君人と為り倜儻にして不羈。然かも居心仁厚にして喜んで義舉を為し、幼より審を讀みて慨然天下第一人たるの志を抱く。長ずるに及びて科舉の業に從事せず、專ら新進の實學を攻究す。前清時代曾て雲南經世書院に學び、旋て笈を負ひ、日本に留學して宏文學院に修業す。中國同盟會に加入して胡漢民呂志伊等と友とし善し。歸國して臨安師範學校及び雲南農業學校教員に任ず。辛亥革命に際し舉げられて雲南保安會會長と為る。民國元年選ばれて臨時參議院議員と為り、民國建設の大業を翼賛す。二年正式國會成立に際し衆議院議員に常選したり。國會解散後は石屏異龍湖に隱れ超然自適また國事を問はず。雲南義を起すに及び、蹶然從起して護國第一軍秘書に任じ、軍に從つて瀘州を攻む。共和恢復して國會重ねて開院すや、遂に都に入りて仍は衆議院議員と為る。

Mr. Chang Hua Lan, otherwise called Ching Tsng, age thirty seven, is a native of Shih Ping Yun Nan. He is a gentleman of independent views and are not to be trammelled by any party feelings. He was deeply interested in the new learning. After studying in one of the schools in Yun Nan, he came to Japan where he studied in the Kobun-gaku-in. He had among his friends many leading men of the Revolution party. On returning to his home, he was appointed an instructor of the Yun nan Agricultural School. During the revolutionary period, he was appointed the president of the Yun-nan peace preservation association. In the 1st year of the Republic, he was elected a member of tha Special Senatorial Assembly in which capacity he assisted the work of completing the Republican form of goverment. When the Republic was securely established, he was returned for the House of Commons. He returned to his home when the Parliament was suppressed. However, when the Parliament was opened again, he came up to the capital to resume his function as a member of the House of Commons.

張魯泉　字魯泉　歳三十七

選舉地　山東省
籍　貫　山東省桓臺縣
住　址　北京順治門内頭髮胡同四十一號

君自幼有志實業。稍長。遂入山東農業學校。畢業後。遍遊内地。並赴日本。攷查農政。旋歸國。與魯省革命巨子徐鏡心等。交遊密切。第一次革命。牽師光復。高諸等縣。南北統一後。君歷辦山東省實業財政各要務。並充省縣各議會議員。正式國會成立。復被選爲參議院議員及袁世凱以暴力推倒國會。君遂歸治農業。當道察其淡泊無異志。亦不嫉視之。民國五年。滇黔起義。君偕民黨同志。舉兵膠濟。聯合居正吳大洲。準備北伐。事迹昭著。及袁氏死。今大總統繼任。民軍推爲總代表。奔走蘇滬京肇間。主張要求中央。依據元年約法。招集國會。改組内閣。均得一一貫徹。及一切問題完全解決後。始來京復爲參議院議員。

幼よりて實業の振興に志し、稍や長じて山東農業學校に入り卒業後遍ねく内地を游歷し、並に日本に赴きて農政狀況を視察す。歸國の後ち山東省革命の志士徐銳心等と交を訂し、第一次革命に際しては軍を牽ゐて高諸等各縣の獨立を圖りたり。南北統一の後ち山東省實業財政等の各要務を處理し、並に省議會縣議會の各議員と爲り。正式國會成立に際し參議院議員に當選す。袁政府が國會を

停止するに及び、君遂に歸省して農業を治め、當局其の淡泊にして異志無きを察して亦た之を嫉視せず。民國五年雲南貴州獨立するや、君民黨の諸士と偕に兵を膠州濟南等に舉げて居正吳大洲等と北伐を準備す。袁死して及び黎大總統繼任するに及び山東民軍より推されて總代表となり各地の間を奔走す。約法復活して國會再び召集を行ふに及び、仍は復た參議院議員たり。

民國之精華　（傳記）　張魯泉先生

Mr. Chang Lu-chuan, age thirty seven, is a native of the Huan Tai Hsien, the Shan tung Hsieng. Even in his younger days, he was greatly interested in the development of the industry. He was graduated from the Shan tung Agricultural School, he most extensively travelled in various parts of his district. He went even to Japan to observe the agricultural condition of that country. On return to his home, he was greatly interested in the revolutionary movement. When both North and South were united, he was commissioned to settle all the financial and industrial affairs of the Shan tung Hsing. When the National Assembly was formerly declared he was appointed a member of the Senate. When the Yuanshi-kai government suppressed the Parliament, he was interested in the promotion of agricultural interest. With the death of Yuanshi-kai, the situation was completely changed, and the Parliament came to be formally declared ; he is now elected a member of the Senate.

張官雲　字紀五　歲三十六

選舉地　　直隷省
籍　貫　　直隷省束鹿縣人
住　址　　北京西單二條胡同東頭二號

君秉性溫恭謙讓。待人以誠。生平虛已
下問自喜。人告以過。卑詞謝其忠告之
厚意。然後細辨其是否合理。人言當。
固不吝即改。即有不當。亦絕不辯釋。
居常以退讓自持。人有與爭者。常以柔
制勝。不逞意氣而自甘於兩敗俱傷。自
幼即知苦讀求進。及長。愈益奮勵。故
天資雖非絕倫。而其所造。則甚遠大著
實。前清時。天津北洋大學校預科畢
業。曾充保定育德中學校校長及教習。
民國二年被選爲衆議院議員。國會解
散後。歸里閉居。不問時政。及約法恢
復。國會重開。君復應召入京。仍就衆
議院議員舊職。

君秉性溫良恭謙にして人を待つに誠を以てす。生平已を
虛ふして下問自ら喜び、人告ぐるに過を以てすれば詞を
卑ふして其の忠言を陳謝し、而して後ち其の當否を省察
し、人言若し當らば改むるに憚らず、若し當らざるも絕
へて辨解する無し。居常退讓を以て自ら持し、人と爭あ
れば常に柔を以て剛を制す。幼より即ち拮据勉勵して學
を求め、長ずるに及びて益、切磋琢磨の功を積み、天資

必ずしも絕倫なりと云ふにあらざるも、遂に造詣深し。
前清時代、天津北洋大學校預科を卒業し、曾て保定育德
中學校長及び教員に任じたることあり。民國二年正式國
會衆議院議員に當選す。國會解散後は歸里に閉居して時
事を問はず。五年約法復活して國會再開するに及び、君
復た其の召集に應じて入京し、仍は衆議院議員の舊職に
就きたり。

Mr. Chang Kan Yun, otherwise known as Chi Un, age thirty six, is a native of Sulu. In dealing with others he is humble and op minded. He is ready to listen to the advice of others for which he humbly offers his appreciation. He ponders carefully of these words and are benefited thereby. He always teaches others the value of humility. He was in youth a very hard student and as he grew older his views have grown very wide. Although naturally not very bright he through his steadiness obtained rich stock of knowledge useful for him. In the previous Chinese period he was graduated from the Peiyang University. In the 2nd year of the Republic he was elected a member of the House of Commons. However when under the pressure of Yuanshi-kai the Parliament was desolved he retired from the public life for the time being, but as soon as the Parliament was reopened he entered Peking and resumed his function as a member of the Legislative body.

張復元　字復元　歲三十七

選舉地　浙江省
籍　貫　浙江省天台縣
住　址　北京象坊橋石燈庵浙江議員二公寓

君賦性篤厚。不喜虛華。然爲人精明強
幹。富于忍耐。自幼好讀。弱冠即以能
文見知于世。及長。遂銳意新學。旋以
官費留學日本。畢業于中央大學。得法
學士學位。歸國後。任浙江法政專門學
校教授。辛亥武昌起義。與同志奔走杭
滬。謀響應。浙江光復。被推爲浙軍政
府民政科長。尋轉浙江省法院推事。兼
庭長。復署理省法院院長。民國二年。
被選爲參議院議員。國會解散。歸國卧
西湖。旋任浙江巡按使署機要秘書。兼
司法秘書。代理承審處處長。必警務
處處長。以勳受四等嘉禾章。西南起義
後。浙江獨立。君任都督府政務廳廳
長。國會復活。遂入都。仍任參議院議
員。

君賦性篤厚にして虛華を喜ばず、人と爲り精明絕幹にし
て忍耐に富む。幼より學を好み弱冠即ち能文を以て世に
知らる。長ずるに及びて遂に意を新學に注ぎ、官費を以
て日本に留學し、中央大學に入りて卒業す。歸國後、
浙江法政專門學校敎授に任ず。辛亥の歲武昌義を起すや
同志と偕に杭州上海に於て饗應を謀る。浙江省獨立する
に及び浙江軍政府民政科長に推さる。尋で浙江省法院推
事に轉じて部長となり。又た法院々長を署理す。民國二
年參議院議員に常選す。國會解散して鄉國に歸りて西湖
の畔に閑臥して風月を友とす。旋で浙江巡按使署機要秘
書に聘せられ、司法秘書を兼ね、承審處々長を代理し、
警務處々長をも兼ねたり。後ち勳功を以て四等嘉禾章を
受く。西南義を起して浙江獨立するや、君即ち都督府政
務廳々長に任す。國會復活して再び入京し、復た參議院
議員に任じたり。

Mr. Chang Fu Yuan. who is otherwise in styled as Chang Yuan, age thirty seven, and is a native of the Tien Tai Hsien. He is simple in life, and hates vain pomp. He is both energetic and and patient. While young, he already enjoyed the fame as being an able writer. As he grew older, he turned his attention to the new learning. At the expense of the government, he went to Japan when he studied in the Chuo University. On return to his country, he was appointed a professor in the Che Chiang Law College. In 1911 when the revolution broke out under Wu chung, he met with his fellow thinkers in Shanghai. When the Che chiang Hsing declared its independence he was appointed the head of the civil administration. He occupied several other important posts in all of which he manifested his ability. In the second year of the Republic, he was elected a member of the Senate. On the disolution of the Parliament, he returned to his native district where he beguiled his time in the persued of books. His talent could not be left unemployed, he soon found positions where his talent could be employed with advantage. He was appointed the private secretay of Justice and the chief of the police bureau With the announcement of the reopening of the Parliament he was appointed a member of the Senate.

張廷弼　字西崑　歲三十六

選舉地　甘肅省

籍　貫　甘肅寧夏道屬寧朔縣

住　址　北京梁家園後身八號

君性聰穎耐艱苦。夙抱與學之志。曾由師範畢業。歷充兩等小學校校長。兼任正教員。銳意從事育英。熱心企圖地方教育之振興。多有所貢獻。聲望大著。辛亥反正。力居多焉。從此窜固民權可望。民國元年被選充臨時縣議會副議長。二年被舉爲正式國會參議院議員。國會中挫。歸里後。勵務農桑。組織學會。力謀地方公益。不問時事。民國五年。及約法恢復。重召國會。遂應召入京仍充衆議院議員。

君性聰穎にして親苦に耐へ。曾て師範學校を卒業して兩等小學校長兼正敎員の職に任ず。銳意育英の業に從事して地方敎育の普及並に振興を企圖し、貢獻する所多く。聲望漸く高し。辛亥の歲。武昌義を唱へて天下響應し、民國を樹立して共和の莫を創めて、民權の進展を圖るや。君舉げられて甘肅省寧朔縣臨時縣議會副議長と爲る。民國二年正式國會成立に際し選ばれて參議院議員と爲る。國會挫折するや、鄉里に歸りて、專ら農桑の改良進步に勵み、又た學會を組織して地方敎育の普及を圖り、地方公益事業に盡瘁して時事を問はず。民國五年約法復活して國會重ねて開院さるゝに及び、再び其召集に應じて遂に入京し、仍は衆議院議員と爲る。

Mr. Chang Ting Pi, age thirty six is a native of Ning So, Ning Hsia Tao, Kan Su hsing. After graduating from the normal school he became a teacher of a primary school in his province and devoted himself to the education of the young and to the dissimination of education among the people. His fame rose very high and he became very popular. In 1911 when the Revolutionary movement was started by Wu Chun which was supported by the public at large, he was interested to assist the work and was appointed the vice-president of the local assembly. In the 2nd year of the Republic he was elected a member of the Senate. When the Parliamentary movement was crushed he returned to his native country and turned his attention to the improvement of agriculture and to the promotion of local education but scrupulously kept away from the discussion of any current topic. When the Parliament was reopened he entered Peking and returned for the House of Commons.

張聯魁 字星五 歲三十六

選舉地 山西省
籍貫 山西省代縣
住址 北京琉璃廠廠甸十三號

君爲人誠實不欺。而心思細緻。于前清
光緒二十八年。由附生考入山西農林
學堂肄業。三十一年。以山西省官費
遊學日本。是年秋考入日本東京帝國
大學農科大學。三十四年。畢業歸國。
應學部試。取列優等。以農科舉人出
身。宣統元年至三年。歷充山西直隸湖
南陝西各省高等農業學堂教員。敎務
長。旋任山西提學使署實業科長。宣統
三年。廷試一等。即候補學部主事。民
國元年。由山西省議會被舉爲臨時參
議院議員。二年。被舉爲山西省議會
議員。又由山西省議會被舉爲參議員。
國會解散後。復從事敎育。任北京農業
專門學校專任敎員。四年。兼任該校
學監主任。及此次召集國會。遂復爲參
議院議員。

君人と爲り誠實にして欺かず。而して思想周密なり。前
清光緒二十八年附生を以て、山西農林學に入りて修業し三
十一年山西省官費を以て日本に遊學し、東帝京國大學農
科大學に入り、三十四年卒業歸國す。清政府學部の試驗
に應じ、優等に列して農一舉人を授けらる。斯くて宣統
元年より三年に至る間、山西眞隸湖南陝西等各省の高等
農學校敎師乃至は敎務長に任じ、旋て山西提學使署實業
科長に任じ、農業敎育の普及開發に從事したり。宣統三
年延試一等に及第して學部主事候補を授けらる。民國
元年山西省議會より參議院議員に舉げ
立して共和の新政を創むるや、民國元年臨時參議院議員
と爲り。二年正式國會の組織に當り參議院議員に舉げら
る。國會解散されて後ち、再び敎育に從事して北京農業
專門學校專任敎員と爲る。四年同校學監主任を兼任した
り。此次國會重ねて召集を行ふに及ひ、遂に復た參議院
議員と爲りたり。

民國之精華 (傳記) 張聯魁先生

Mr. Chang Lien Kuei, otherwise called Hsing Uu, age thirty six, is a native of Tai Hsien, Shan Ssi. He is a gentleman of the closest thinker, and in 1902, he entered the Shan Ssi Agricultural School. Three years later, he came to Japan at the government's expense where he studied in the Agricultvral College of the Imperial University of Tokyo. In 1908, he returned to his home. He passed the chinese government's examination with great success, and for three years he was an instructor of the higher agricultural college. He was also the chief of the Industrial Bureau of the Shan Ssi. Thus he was interested in the development of agricultural knowledge throughout the country. In 1911, having successfully passed the civil examination his future was full of hopes, and when the Republic was established, he was appointed a member of the Senate. However when the Parliament was dissolved, he employed himself as the instructor of the Peking Agricultural College. He is at the present moment a member of the Senate.

張恩綬 字澤餘 歲三十六

選舉地　直隸省

籍　貫　直隸深縣

住　址　宣武門外海北寺街三十三號

君于光緒三十年。由前保定大學堂選送日本留學。初入經緯學堂普通科。卒業後。入早稻田大學政治經濟科。宣統二年六月。卒業歸國。應學部游學生考試。考取法政科選人。三年。朝考一等。授七品小京官。籤分郵傳部供職。辛亥革命事起。與同志組織保安會於津門。津埠秩序多賴以維扶。民國成立。歷充順直臨時省議會議員。衆議院議員。北洋法政專門學校教員。教務主任。校長。北洋法政學會會長。民國法政講習所教務主任。中華武士會會長。前共和黨幹事。進步黨地方科主任。京兆地方自治研究所教員等職。此次國會復活。遂復爲衆議院議員。

君は光緒三十年、前保定大學校より選拔して日本に派遣せる官費留學生にして、初め經緯學校普通科に入りて卒業し、早稻田大學政治經濟科に學びて宣統二年六月卒業歸國せる一秀才なり。學部に於ける留學生試驗に及第して法政科擧人と爲る。三年朝試一等に列して七品小京官を授け、郵傳部に分たる。辛亥の歲、第一革命の事起るや、同志と偕に天津に於て保安會を組織し、天津市街の秩序維持に努めたり。斯くて民國成立するや、選ばれて順直省議會議員となり。正式國會の組織に當り衆議院議員に擧げらる。曾て北洋法政專門學校教員、教務主任、校長に歷充し、又た北洋法政國會々長、民國法政講習所教務主任、中華武士會々長、前共和黨幹事、進步黨地方科主任、京兆地方自治研究所教員等の職に歷任したり。此次國會復活するや、遂に復た衆議院議員の職に就きたり。

Mr. Chang En Shou, otherwise known as Tse-yu-i; is a native of Chi-lin-Hshing, and thirty six years old the present year. In 1904, under the present Chinese regime, he was sent to Japan by the government. He studied at the law department of the Waseda University. In 1910, he returned to Japan, and after successfully passing the required examination, he was appointed an official of the communication department. When the revolutionary movement broke out, he formed a society with a view to keep order in Tientsin. When the Republic was established, he was returned for the House of Commons. He was the president of the Pei Yan Law College, the chief of the progressive party, and numerous other associations. When the Parliament was re-opened, he resumed the function as the member of the legislative body.

張善與 字天放 歲三十五

選舉地　河南省

籍　貫　河南省新鄉縣

住　址　北京宣武門內什家戶

君賦性惇篤。尚質惡文。不事無益之繁
華。然富於學識。新舊皆有素養。故其
見解氣慨。迥異凡流。二十歲入邑庠。
翌年入衛輝中學。其後三年。蒙河南巡
撫。選送游學日本。畢業於早稻田大
學。清國留學生部豫科。高等豫科。升
入大學部政治經濟科。武昌起義。歸國
抵滬。入威武軍。民國元年。本省諮議
局。委托為代表。列席南京臨時參議
院。二年被選為衆議院議員。國會停止
後。復往日本。補習繼續前學。畢業。適
籌安會發生。上書袁項城。諷其勿信讒
言。並同陳君祖虞等。因請願參政
解散籌安會。以遏亂萌。除梁任公汪伯
唐兩參政外。莫肯表示反對意見者。卒
以介紹人。不足法定人數。不果。現國
會重開。仍充議員。

民國之精華　（傳記）　張善與先生

て前學を繼續し、以て其の業を畢ゆ。適ま籌安會發起さ
る。袁世凱に上書して諷諫する所あり、又た陳祖虞等と
共に參議院に向つて籌安會の解散を請願せんとしたる
も、梁啓超、汪大燮の兩參政以外、敢て籌安會反對意見
を表示する者無く、為に紹介人法定數に足らずして果さ
いりし。現に國會重ねて開く、君復た其の召集に應じて
仍ち衆議院議員の職に充る。

君賦性惇篤にして質を尚び文を惡みて無益の繁華を事と
せず。然かも學識に富み新舊皆な素養あり故に其の見解
氣慨な迥に凡流と異る。二十歲邑庠に入り、翌年衛輝
中學に學ぶこと三年、河南巡撫より選拔されて日本に留
學し、早稻大學豫科を經て大學部政治經濟科に入る。適
ま第一革命の事起り歸國して上海に赴き威武軍に入る。
民國元年河南諮議局代表として南京臨時參議院に列席し
二年衆議院議員に當選す。國會停止後、復た日本に抵り

張　浩　字雨樵　歲三十六

選舉地　浙江省

籍　貫　浙江省東陽縣

住　址　北京右駙馬大街

君性豪邁。有大志。弱冠見清政不綱。即從事於革命事業。由浙江高等巡警學堂畢業。充省城警官。故浙江警界多革命種子。旋即棄去。至日本留學警監學校。卒業回國。益刻苦自勵。辛亥春。赴滇。圖謀根據地。滇督偵知君行。電越南總督捕禁。諸同志多方營救。得不死。浙江光復。任省城警察廳長。兼稽勳局浙調查會編纂。旋辭去。當選爲衆議院議員。帝制發生。君奔走呼號。糾集同志。謀浙江獨立。類出諸君。浙督聘君爲顧問。兼公府秘書。旋被選爲浙參議會副議長。以道制爲吾國神政。力主裁撤。故浙省今已無道缺。國會恢復。仍充衆議院議員。著有咳根堂詩存。

君性豪邁にして大志あり、弱冠滿朝政治の紊亂を見て即ち革命の事を圖る。浙江高才巡警學校を卒業してより省城の警察官に任じ、密に浙江警察官中に革命思想を宣傳し、旋て去つて日本に留學し、警察監獄學校を卒業して歸國す。辛亥の春、廣州に於ける革命計畫に際して香港に抵る。事旣に敗れて雲南に赴き根據地と爲さんとす。諸同志の盡力によりて死を免常局之を偵知して捕縛す。れたり。浙江省獨立するや警察廳々長に任じ、稽勳局浙江調査會編纂を兼ね、旋て辭職して衆議院議員に常選す。帝制問題發生するや、君四方に奔走して同志を糾合し、以て再び浙江の獨立を謀り、浙江都督府顧問兼秘書となり、旋て浙江參議會副議長に舉げらる。後ち國會恢復すに及び其の召集にに應じ仍ち復た衆議院議員と爲る。君政界活躍の餘眼吟嘯の快を遣り咳根堂詩存の著あり。

Mr. Chang Hao, otherwise known as Yu Chiao, age thirty six, is a native of Tung Yang, the Che Chiang Hsing. He is imperious and full of ambition. When even in youth, perceiving the maladministration of the Manchu dynasty, he took up revolutionary measures. Upon graduating from the police school of his province, he became an official in the police department. In this capacity, he inspired the police with revolutionary ideas. He came over to Japan where he studied in the police and prison school. He went to Hongkong relating in the revolntionary movement of 1911, but was failed in his attempt. Thereupon, he went to Yun-nan to make it his headquarter, but was arrested by the government authorities. Through the influence of his friends, he escaped death. When the independence of his province was secured, he was appointed the chief of the police, and a committee of investigation of police affairs. Shortly, he was elected a member of the House of Commons. At the outbreak of the Imperial movement, he worked with his friends planning for the independence of his own province. He was elected the vicepresident of the Che Chiang Hsing local assmbly. On the summoning of the Praliament for the second time, he was elected a member of the House of Commons

張瑾雯　字次瑜　歳三十五

選舉地　四川省
籍　貫　四川省南部縣
住　址　北京校塲五條十號

君人と為り誠厚にして篤實、質を尚んで華を惡む。賦性高潔にして言動舉止皆な凡流に傑出す。幼より恪謹自ら持し言動を苟もせす。書を讀みて審かに問ひ愼みて思索し、力めて精義を探求して字句に執せす。長ずるに及びて群籍を渉獵し造詣漸く深し。君本と事務の才に通じ及び經學の造詣亦た漸く精明に趨き能く繁劇に堪ゆ。海內維新後また舊を棄て、新に從ひ專ら西學を攻究し、遂に笈

君為人誠厚篤實。尚質惡華。賦性高潔。言動舉止。皆超出凡流。自幼勤謹自持。不苟言行。讀書能審問慎思。力探精義。而不執於字句。及長。尤博及羣書。然謙虛好問。不以淹博自畫。故所造日益深遠。君本跳於事務之才。及經學之濡涵。遂漸趨精明。能任繁劇。海內維新後。復棄舊從新。專精西學。遂柬渡日本。入中央大學。畢業歸國於宣統元年。由商科舉人。考得內閣中書。民國二年。被選為衆議院議員。國會解散後，歸里獨居，無所表見。及國會重開，始入京。仍供舊職。

を負ふて東海を渡り、先進日本に留學して中央大學に入り、其の業を畢へて歸國す。宣統元年商科舉人として内閣中書に及第す。民國元年四川財政實業兩司々長に歷任す。二年正式國會議員選舉に際し舉げられて衆議院議員と為る。國會解散さる、や郷里に歸臥して政見を發表する無し。國會重ねて召集を行ふに及び、君復た之に應じて入京し、仍は衆議院議員の舊職に就きたり

民國之精華　（傳記）　張瑾雯先生

Mr. Chang Chin Wen, otherwise named Yeh Yu, age thirty five, a native of the Ssi Chuan Hsing is a gentleman of high integritys. He read ands appreciates what he reads. He is straight forword in character, and as such he distinguishes himself from his collegers. Perceiving the utility of studying the western learning and new books, he came over to Japan where he entered the Chuo University. After- graduating from the University, he returned home in april 1909, and passed the civil examination in China, as a consequence of which he was appointed the secretary of the cabinet, and in 1912, he was appointed the chief of the financial and industrial bureau. In the following year, he was returned for the House of Commons. On the disolution of the Parliament, he returned to his home, and never cared much about politics. With the announcement of the re-opening of the Parliament, however, he resumed the membership of the legislature.

張大義 字直卿 歲三十四

選舉地　雲南省第二區

籍貫　雲南省大理府

住址　北京西單牌樓廣二條

君為人慷慨尚義。海內維新後。銳意新學。以雲南經世書院高才生。移入雲南高等學校肄業。以鼓吹革命故為當道所不容。亡命南洋。轉徙日本。先後畢業于岩倉鐵道學校及法政大學。歸國後。從事新聞。旋趲復至日本。愈益猛勇進行。多所擘畫。武漢起義。君與同志十餘人。籌畫光復上海事。親冒槍彈。往攻上海道署及製造局。迫上海光復。即組織滬軍先鋒隊。准備南征。曾隨聯軍之後攻克金陵。臨時政府成立。任內務部秘書長。政府北遷。辭職回滇。任雲南高等審判廳廳長。兼辦稽勳局事。民國二年被舉為衆議院議員。國會解散。隨時歸隱雲南之開化廣南間。創辦開廣三七公司。以提倡實業為職志。不復出問世事。迨至雲南倡義。義旗重開。遂赴京仍就議員之職。

君人と為り慷慨にして義を尚ぶ。雲南經世書院の高才生を以て雲南高等學校に入りて修業す。革命を皷吹するの故を以て當局に忌まれ遂に南洋に亡命し轉じて日本に抵る。岩倉鐵道學校及び法政大學を卒業す。歸國して後ち新聞事業に從事し、旋て復た日本に抵りて革命計畫の進行を圖る。武漢義を起すや、君即ち同志十餘人と上海に赴き、親しく彈雨を犯すや上海道臺衙門及び製造局を攻む。上海獨立後即ち滬軍先鋒隊を組織し、諸軍と聯合して南京を攻略す。臨時政府成立して內務部秘書長に任じ、南北統一後雲南に歸り、雲南高等審判廳々長に任じ、兼て稽勳局の事を處理す。民國二年衆議院議員に當選す。國會解散されて雲南省開化廣南地方に歸來して開廣三七公司を創立經營して專ら實業の振興を企圖す。五年雲南再び義を唱ふるに及びて再び出で、護國軍秘書に任す。國會再び召集を行ふや遂に又た上京して仍ほ衆議院議員の職に就く。

Mr. Cang Tai i, known as Chi Hsing, age thirty four, is a native of Taili fu, th Yun nan hsing. He was graduated from the Unan high School, but being suspected as working for the interest of the Revolutionists, he had to flee to South Sea island whence he went to Japan. He is a graduate of the Iwakura Railway School and the Hosei University. On returning home, he was interested in the newspaper publication; He visited Japan for the second time to plan for the revolutionary movement. He joined Wu-han movement by which Shanghai declared the independence. He was at the head of the movement attacking Nanking. When the government was formed to meet the emergency, he was appointed the secretary of the Home Department. Later he went back to Unnan, where he was interested in police affairs. In 1913, he was returned for the House of Commons, but when the legislative assembly was shut up, he became interested in industrial development at home. When Yuanshikai died, which put a stop to the Imperial movement, he went to Peking, and resumed the function of the member of the House of Commons.

張 治 祥　字輯五　歲三十三

選舉地　四川省
籍　貫　四川省彭山縣
住　址　北京西單牌樓與隆大院孫宅

君賦性慷慨好義・見人不平・常忿忿不
自禁・過於自受・弱冠時・骨以是與人
爭・不顧己身之利害・及長・夙抱天下
國家之志・遇事敢爲・歷驗其生平・均
艱虞險阻之事・雖困於縲絏・曾未具有
戚容・亦豪傑之士也・壯年負笈東渡・
留學日本・前清光緒三十三年・畢業法
政大學・歸國後・君見清政不綱・謀革
命於成都・事泄・被捕入獄・宣統三年・
四川光復・君出獄・任軍政府參贊・兼
成渝聯合使・嗣充四川外交司司長・民
國二年・正式國會成立・被選爲衆議院
議員・國會解散後・慨然南旋・遍游各
地・與諸同志・圖恢復大業・及國會重
開・遂應召入京・仍爲衆議院議員・

民 國 之 精 華　（傳記）　張 治 祥 先 生

君賦性慷慨義を好み、人の不平を見て常に忿々自ら禁せ
ず。弱冠の時嘗て是を以て人と爭ひ、己が身の利害を顧
みず。長ずるに及び夙に天下國家の志を抱き、事に遇つ
て敢爲、生平の經歷均しく險阻艱難の事にして縲絏の厄
に困むと雖も、未だ曾て戚容あらず。壯年笈を負ふて日
本に留學し、前清光緒三十三年法政大學校を卒業す。歸
國後革命を成都に謀り、事洩れて捕はれ、宣統三年第一

四川獨立するに及びて獄を出づ。而して
四川軍政府參贊に任じ、成渝聯合使を兼ぬ。嗣で四川外
交司長に任ず。民國二年正式國會衆議院議員に當選す。
國會解散されてより、慨然として南旋し、各地を遊歷し
て諸同志と聯絡し、以て大業の恢復を圖る。既にして約
法復活し、國會重ねて開く、遂に其の召集に應じて入京
し、仍ち衆議院議員と爲る。

革命の事起りて四川獨立す

二百五十三

Mr. Chang Chih Hsing, otherwise called Chi Uu, age thirty three is a native of Peng Shan. Being of heroic temperament he often fought for the interests of others at the expence of his own. When he grew older he became ambitious and was keenly interested in public affairs. Open handed he was ready to meet any danger even at the risk of his own life. In 1907 he went to Japan and was graduated from the Hosei University. On returning to his home he worked with Revolutionists which being found out he was arrested. In 1911 the Revolution took place and Hsi heng declared its independence, when he was released from the prison. Then he was appointed the adviser to the military government as well as the chief of the Bureau of Foreign Affairs of his own province. He travelled various districts of China with a view to the Restoration of the grand work then proposed. When the Parliament was reestablished, he compiled with the summon and entering Peking was elected a member of the Parliament.

張蔚森 字蔭廷 歳三十三

選舉地　陝西省

籍　貫　陝西省渭南縣

住　址　北京外城藏家橋渭南會館

君自幼慷慨好義。慕古任俠之言行。及
長。尤喜赴人之急。千金不靳。弱冠時。
即喜談革命。然爲人精明愼重。不肯輕
於發難。以徒誤事機。故與海內志士奔
走聯絡。卒未陷于絶境。清末。以自費
遊學日本入。明治大學。畢業。得政學
士學位。歸國後。適武昌起義。君與諸
同志共籌大計。多所主持。南北議和之
際。曾充南京代表團陝西代表。復歸任
陝西都督府司法顧問。居無何。被選爲
調査日本實業委員。歸國時。適省議會
成立。被選爲陝西省議會議員。正式國
會成立。遂得當選爲參議院議員。國會
解散後。歸里蟄居。不復于與政治。迨
國會重開。始入京。仍任舊職。爲參議
院議員。

君幼より慷慨義を好み、古へ任俠の言行を慕ふ。長ずる
に及びて尤ゝ人の急に赴くを喜び、弱冠にして早くも革
命の志を抱く。然かも人と爲り精明愼重にして輕々に難
を發して徒に事機を誤るを肯せず。遍ねく海內志士との
聯絡に努めたり。前清末季、自費を以て日本に游學し、
明治大學校政治科に入りて卒業す。歸國の後、適ま第一
革命の事起るや、君乃ち諸同志と共に大計を籌りて主持
する所多し。南北和議進行に際して南京代表團陝西代表に
任じ、後ち復た歸省して陝西都督府司法顧問に任ず。居
ること幾くも無く日本實業調查委員に選ばれて日本に至
りて實業を視察調查す。歸國の時適ま省議會成立に際す
即ち選ばれて陝西省議會議員と爲る。正式國會成立する
や參議院議員に常選す。國會解散後、鄉里に歸臥し、國
會復活するに及び其の召集に應じて京に入り、仍ち復た
參議院議員と爲る。

Mr. Chang Wei sen, otherwise called Yin ting, age thirty three, is a native of Wei nan, Shan Ssi Hsing. Heroic in temperament, he risked his own interest to save the people from dangerous or trouble. Early in youth, he had the revolutionary ideas, but being very thorough, he would not attempt anything without careful consideration. He was in constant communication with those fellow thinkers staying abroad. At the latter days of the previous chinese regime, he visited Japan at his own expense. He was graduated from the Meiji University. At outbreak of the Revolution, he was in constant touch with other leaders. In the peace negotiation between the South and the North, he was a representative of the Shau Ssi Hsing. Before long, he visited Japan for the Empire of investigating commerce and industry. On returning to his home, he was elected a member of the Shau Ssi local assembly. With the formation of the Parliament, he was elected a member of the Senate. At the suppression of the Parliament, he returned home, and waited for the opportune time. When it was decided to reopen the Parliament, he was appointed a member of the Senate.

張于潯 字惠民 歲二十九

選舉地　江西省

籍貫　江西省南昌縣

住址　北京東城王府井大街長安飯店

君秉性慷慨好義。居常好爲人排難解紛。然以見解明晰。其處世接物。皆機敏过人。生平尤喜獎勵善行。里人有一德之長者。莫不扶持之。自幼聰穎善讀。强於記憶。稚齡時。日誦數千言。詞句義理。能一一背誦。講解無稍遺忘。及長。尤能精通古義。時復發抒己見。爲理想上之新發明。前清時。曾入江西陸軍學校。畢業後。以官費留學日本。入東京振武學校。旋復渡海留學法國。入巴黎國立法科大學。歸國後。歷充鄂皖贛軍政府參謀。及江西都督府副會長。兩廣都司令部參議。民國二年。國會成立。被舉爲衆議院候補議員。國會解散後。雲南護國軍第二軍司令部參議。曾授陸軍步兵中校。及此次國會復活。以候補資格。得補充議。

民國之精華　（傳記）張于潯先生

君秉性慷慨にして義を好み、屑常人の爲に難を排し紛を解く。然かも其の見解明晰にして世に處し事に應じて機敏人に過ぐ。生平尤も善行を獎勵する事を喜び、里人一德の長あれば必ず之を扶持す。幼より聰穎にして博覽强記なり。弱冠の時、日に數千言を誦して其の字句其の義理一々忘れず。長ずるに及びて尤も古義に精進、時に出意見を發表し、理想上の新發明あり。前清時代、曾て江西陸軍學校に入り、卒業後、官費を以て日本に留學して振武學校に學ぶ。旋て復た佛國に留學して巴里國立法科大學に入る。歸國の後ち湖北安徽江西等の軍政府參謀、江西都督府副官長、兩廣都司令部參議に歷充したり。民國二年正式國會衆議院補缺議員に當選す。國會解散後、鄉に歸り、雲南義を起すや、雲南護國軍第二軍司令部參議に任ず。曾て陸軍步兵中佐を授けらる。國會復活するに及び、補缺として召集され、仍ち衆議院議員の職に就く。

Mr. Chang Yu Hsuan, otherwise called Hui Min, age twenty nine, is a native of Nan Chang hsien, Chiang Hsi hsing. Being heroic in temper, he always works for the interests of his fellowmen. His farsighted and shrewed beyond the men in common life. He is fond of doing good and takes pain to support the least virtue found among his country men. Being a copious reader of books he is also a logical writer. As he grew older he became conversant with classical writings. After graduated from the military college of his province at the government expence, he went to Japan and spent several years in Paris where he studied in the law college. In the 2nd year of the Republic he was elected a member of the House of Commons and when the assembly was closed up, he returned to Yun nan where he became attached the staff of the army. He was appointed commander of infantry. When the Parliament was opened again he became the member thereof.

二百五十五

張　漢 字佩紳

選舉地　湖北省

籍　貫　湖北省

住　址　北京石駙馬大街東頭湖北董宅

君爲人精明強幹。當於忍耐。居心仁
厚。痛惡陰險。然惟喜規人過失。輒直
斥不諱。甚至聲色俱厲。人告以過。亦
直認不諱。故其於人雖有過詰之嫌人
亦無疾恨之者。自幼聰慧好讀能文。及
長。尤活潑自喜。富于好奇之性。然其
立身行己。多厚重自持。不效時髦青年
之浮薄踐躁。蓋君之思想極放膽。而行
爲則極規則也。及民國成立被選爲參
議院議員。授三等嘉禾章。

君人と爲り精明強幹にして忍耐に富む。居心仁厚にして
陰險を痛惡す。然かも喜んで人の過失を規し、輒ち直斥
して諱まず、甚だしきは聲色倶に屬しきに至る。幼より
聰慧にして讀書を好み文章を能くす。長ずるに及びて尤
も活潑自ら喜びて好奇の性に富む。然り而して其の身を
立て己を行ふや、厚重自ら持して時流青年の浮薄淺躁な
るものに效はず。蓋し君の思想極めて放膽なるも行爲極
めて規則あり。辛亥の歳武昌天下に先ちて義を舉げて以
來、國事に奔走して功勞顯著なり。三等嘉禾章を授けら
る。民國二年正式國會成立に際し、參議院議員に當選す。
此次國會復活するや、再び其の召集に應じて入京し、仍
は復た參議院議員たり。

Mr. Chang han, is a native of Hu Pei province. He is a gentleman full of patients and
sincerity. While Young he was fond of reading books but as he grew older he was very active in his
thoughts but always cautions as to his movements. In 1911 when trouble arose in Wu-chuong he was
also interested in the movement. When the Parliament was opened in the 2nd year of the Republic he
was appointed a member of the Senate. As soon as the Parliament was restored he went up to Peking
where he was elected a member of the Senate, the position which he holds at present. Although a man
of gentle character he is very strong when he makes up his mind to uphold any cause.

張樹森 字蛻覺 歲三十六

選舉地　陝西省

籍　貫　陝西安康縣

住　址　北京爛熳胡同濟中館

君早究心陽明之學。以良知良能知行
合一。爲人世法門。清季補增生。負笈
東游。留學日本。入法政大學畢業。歸
國後。中部試。授法政科舉人。時値淸
政不綱。國政日衰。君慨然以救國爲已
任。奔走呼號。凡瀕于危者屢。辛亥武
昌首義。天下響應。君往來于長江一
帶。進行尤力。南北統一。君實有以促
成之。曾與殷汝驪等。在南京組織統一
共和黨。旋統一共和黨與同盟會合倂。
改組國民黨。君復創超然社。先之。民
國二年正式國會成立。被選衆議院議
員。國會解散後。與諸同志交游。竊冀
恢復國勢。及國會再行召集。仍就衆議
院議員舊職。

君凡に陽明の學に心を潛め、良知良能
知行合一を以て世法に入るの門と爲す。
前淸末季增生に補せられ、笈を負ふて
東遊して日本に留學し、法政大學に入
りて卒業す。時に淸政振はず國政日に
衰ふ。君慨然として國家の頹勢を挽回
するを以て己が任と爲す。斯くて四方
に奔走呼號して危に瀕する事屢々なり。
辛亥の歲武昌義を首め天下響應す、君
長江一帶に往來して進行尤も力む。南
北の統一實に君之を促成す。曾て殷汝
驪等と南京に在りて統一共和黨を組織
するや、旋て統一共和黨が同盟と合倂
して國民黨を組織す。之より先、君復
た超然社を創む。之より先、民國二年
正式國會衆議院議員に當選す。國會解
散されて後ち諸同志と交渉し竊に國勢
の恢復を冀ふ。國會再び召集を行ふに
及び仍ち復た衆議院議員の舊職に就く。

國民之精華　（傳記）張樹森先生

Mr. Chang Shu-lin, otherwise known as To Chiao, age thirty six, is a native of the An kang-hsien, Shan Hsi province. He was trained in the school of Yang Min School, and was a strong advocate of the union of knowledge and ability in starting oneself in the world. He went to Japan where he graduated from the Hosei University. On his return to his country, he successfuly passed the civil service in the examination. Perceiving the decline of the Chinese government, he arrived at the conviction that it was duty to save the country from its inevitable doom. In 1911; with the trouble in Wu Chaung other provinces rapidly followed the example. In bringing about this state of affairs his efforts can by no means ignored. When the national party was organized, he established a society known as the Transcendental Association. In the 2nd year of the Republic, he was returnd for the House of Commons. However, with the shutting down of the Parliament by Yanshi-kai he worked with his fellowmen to bring about the Restoration of the Republic. When this was accomplished, he resumed the function as a member of the House of Commons.

張良弼 字佑卿

選舉地　直隷省

籍　貫　直顯省獲鹿縣人

君天資聰慧絕倫。富於理想。然爲人誠實不欺。自幼勤學。不事嬉遊。弱冠即廣通經史。工於詩文。及長博覽群籍。涉獵新書。深入其精。明察其義。前清以舉人。被用直隷州知州。曾醉心新學。專求有用之學。遂賚笈東渡。留學日本。入弘文學院師範科畢業。歷充直隷學務處查學員。直隷提學使司省視學。直隷補習學校校長。直隷提學使司省視學校校長。銳意於敎育之普及。熱心於民智之開發。多有所貢献。民國二年正式國會成立。被選爲衆議院議員。國會解散後。歸里讀書修養身心。又從事育英。誘掖後進。及國會再行召集。仍爲衆議院議員。

直隷提學使司省視學、直隷補習學校長、直隷甲種工業學校長等の職に歷任して敎育の普及を計りて民智の開發を計り貢献する所多し。民國二年正式國會衆議院議員に當り。國會解散されて後ち、鄉里に歸りて身心を修養し、又た育英に從事して後進を誘掖す。約法恢復して國會再び召集するに當り、復た出でゝ仍ち衆議院議員と爲る。

君天資聰慧絕倫にして理想に富む。然かも人と爲り誠實欺かす。幼より學に勤めて嬉遊を事とせす。弱冠即ち廣く經史に通じ詩文に工みなり。長するに及び群籍に涉り新書をも獵りて深く其の精に入り義を究む。前淸擧人を以て直隷州知州補用と爲る。曾て新學に心醉して專ら有用の學を求め、遂に笈を負ふて東海に渡り、日本に留學して宏文學院師範科に入りて卒業す。直隷學務處查學員

Mr. Chau Liang-pi, otherwise called Yu Hsing, a native of Hao Lu, the Chi Ling Hsing, is a gentleman full of thoughts and ideas, deeply interested in learning. He is a copious reader of books both ancient and modern. He became intensely interested in the new learning, and crossed the sea to Japan where he graduated from the Normal School Department of the Kobun Gakuin. He was interested in the educational matters of Chi lin province, being appointed the head of various local school. He contributed a great deal towards the diffusion of learning among the local people. In the 2nd year of the Republic, he was elected a member of the House of Commons. On the disolution of this legislative body, he returned to his province, where he was chiefly interested in the education of the young. When the Parliament was re-opened, he resumed the function of the member of the House of Commons.

選舉地　浙江省

籍　貫　浙江省鄞縣

住　址　北京象坊橋浙江議員公寓

君賦性剛毅不阿。而積極好進。不屑因循追隨人後。前清時。以壬寅舉人。歷充鄞縣勸學所總董統計調查總編纂。甯波府中學堂監督。浙江諮議局議員。兩次被舉為常駐議員。宣統三年諮議局議決浙江地方行政經費預算案。君充預算審查會長。光復後。充甯波軍政分府財政主任。二年。被舉為眾議院議員。國會停止後。充中國銀行嘉興分號溫州分號管理。國會重開復充眾議院議員。院內選舉常任委員。被舉為預算委員。兼充財政討論會會員。並聞君不日將在議會提出恢復縣議會及城鎮鄉自治會議案附議。通逃後。決意積極進行。務求從速完成。以遂各省之企望云。

君賦性剛毅にして阿らず、幼より向上心強くして人後に追隨するを屑しとせざる也。前清壬寅の舉人を以て鄞縣勸學所總董、統計調查局總編纂、甯波府中學校監督等の職に歷任し、後ち浙江諮議局議員に選ばる。宣統三年諮議局に於て浙江地方行政經費豫算案を議するや君其の豫算審查會々長となる。第一革命の事起りて浙江省獨立するや、君即ち甯波軍政分府財政主任に任ず。民國二年正式國會の成立に際し眾議院議員に當選す。國會停止後は中國銀行嘉興分店、同溫州分店の管理となりて銀行事務を處理し。共和克復して國會重ねて開かるゝや、君復た其の召集に應じて入京して現に仍ち眾議院議員と爲る。

Mr. Cheng Chuan-pao, otherwise called Shen-chih, age forty, is a native of Che-chiang province.

Being a man of strong will, full of ambition, he always took the position of the leader. He passed the civil service examination, and filled successsively important posts of the government, being the head-master of Ning pao middle school, and a member of the local assembly. In 1911, he was elected the chief of the Budge Committee of the province. In the first revolution, when Chen-ching province became independent, he was appointed to the financial chief of the Military Government. In the second year of the Republic, when the Parliament was brought into existence, he was returned for the House of Commons. When the Parliament was shut down, he was connected with banking bussiness. When the Parliament resumed its function, he was returned for the House of Commons.

黃汝瀛 字儼舫 歲四十三

選舉地 廣東省第二區
籍貫 廣東省龍川縣
住址 北京東草廠二條 韶州館

君秉性忠厚。生平不爲僞言。雖疾惡如仇。然富干忍耐。不以疾言厲色。引起少人之忌恨。人以非禮相加。但以理責之。不出惡聲。自幼聰穎好讀。弱冠以詩文知于鄉里。及長。尤銳志實學。不隨俗尙。其干舉業。雖淵博精深。然不屑執意於科第。故雖淵博精深。而僅一副貢生而自足。蓋非圖以高尙自詡。實以人爵之不若天爵也。及海內維新。愈立志求有用之學。於新書無所不視。而尤專心於法律之書。曾肄業於廣東法政學堂法律別科。畢業後充北京律師。民國二年。被選爲衆議院議員。第一期常會及第二期常會。均被選爲本院法律股委員。

君秉性忠實溫厚にして平生僞言を語らず。惡を疾む仇敵の如しと雖も然も善く忍耐力に富み、疾言厲色を以て小人の恨を惹起さず。人非禮を以て相加ふれば理を以て之れを責め、惡聲を出して罵詈を加ふる事なし。幼より聰慧にして讀書を好み弱冠早くも詩文を以て鄉里に知らる。長するに及び尤も志を實學に傾注して、俗尙に隨はざる也。其の科舉の業に於て造詣深しと雖も然も及第を念とせず。海內維新に及び愈々志を立て有用の學を求め、新書殆ど視ざる事なし。尤も心を法律の書に專にし、曾て廣東法政學校法律別科に修業す。卒業の後ち北京に於て辯護士を業とす。民國二年選ばれて衆議院議員となり。法律審查委員に舉げらる。國會停止後、依然野に在りて辯護士の業に從事し。國會重ねて開かるゝに及び再び衆議院議員と爲る。

Mr. Huang Ju-ying, sometimes known as Hsien-fang, age forty three, is a native of Lun-chuan, Kuang-tnng province. Being sincere and gentle in his nature, he is never guilty of lies. While he hates the evil, he is also forgiving. While young, he was fond of reading; as he grew older, he was greatly interested in solid learning, and was above the men of common level. With the introdunation of new ideas into the country, he sought more useful learning. He studied law, and graduated from the law school of Kuan-tung. After graduation, he prachiced law in Peking, In the second year of the Republic, he was returned for the House of Commons. When the Parliament was suspended, he practiced law, but with the re-opening of the Parlia   was returned for the House of Commons.

黃宏憲 字用溥 歲四十二

選舉地　廣西省

籍貫　廣西省容縣

住址　北京後青廠廣西三館

君爲人精明强幹。富於忍耐。長於幹濟
之才。然情性圓活。不固執己私。自幼
好讀。博而能約。識力均極高。而又虛
心好問。能受讜言。及海內維新。專求
天下有用之學。攻究新書。造詣既深。
即立志興學。開通民智。以挽救危亡自
任。歷辦上海中國公學。廣西桂平縣梧
灣各府中學。銳意力圖教育之普及。熱
心從事育英。誘掖後進。聲望大著。旋
被舉爲廣西諮議局副議長。辛亥革命。
民國肇造。被選爲南京臨時參議院議
員。把持正論。提倡民權。贊勳共和政
府建設之偉業。民國二年正式國會成
立。被選爲參議院議員。國會解散後。
南旋歸里。五年及約法恢復。國會重
開。遂又應召。北上入京。仍爲參議院
議員。

民國之精華　　（傳記）　黃宏憲先生

吾人と爲り精明强幹にして忍耐に富み幹濟の才に長す。
然かも情性圓活にして己私を固執せす。幼より讀書を好
み、博にして能く約し識力均しく高く、又た心を虛ふし
て問を好み、能く讜言を受く、新書を攻究して造詣既に深く、即ち天
下有用の學を求め、新書を攻究して造詣既に深し、即ち天
學の志を抱き、民智を開通して、危亡を挽救するを以
て自ら任す。上海中國公學、廣西桂平縣梧灣各府中學を
歷辦して銳意教育の普及を計り、育英の業に從事して聲
望大に著はる。旋て廣西諮議局副議長に舉げらる。辛
亥命を革めて民國肇造するや、南京臨時參議院議員と爲
り、正論を把持し民權を提倡して共和政府建設の偉業を
贊勳したり。民國二年正式國會參議院議員に當選す。國
會解散後、南旋して鄉里に歸り、依然興學に力を致して
後進を誘掖す。五年約法恢復して國會再び召集を行ふや、
更に北上入京して仍ち參議院議員と爲る。

Mr. Huang hung hsien, sometimes called Yung-su, age forty two, is a native of Jung, Kuang-hsi province. He is a man of impulsive nature, but full of patience. While young, he was interested in reading books. He was a man of high aspiration, but he is always ready to listen the advice given to him by others. When the new trend of thought was introduced to China, his attention was called to the study of new books and necessity of saving the situation by the development of local educational systems. He became very popular because of the interests shown to the Chinese residence in various parts of the world. Once he was a vice-president of the Kuang-hsi Board of Investigation. When the Revolution led up to the formation of society he became a member of the Senate. In the 2nd year of the Republic, when the Parliament was opened, he was elected to a member of the Senate. After the disolution of the Parliament, he went back to his conntry, where he devoted himself to the guidance of the rising generation. When the Parliament was re-opened, he went to Peking where he was selected to a member of the Parliament.

二百六十一

黃象熙　字星衡　歲四十一

選舉地　江西省

籍貫　江西省臨川縣

住址　北京達智橋東口七號

君賦性仁厚。自幼以孝行見知于鄉里。為人精明强幹。洞察事理。少年讀書。多激昂悲慕古任俠之所為。其為詩文狀之詞。見人不平。常奮不顧身。唯一念及身體髮膚之訓。則又自給其不孝。遂專從事於周濟貧乏。不復從井救人之舉。人有困於貧者。常典鬻所有助之。不自為緩急之計。以是鄉里皆奉若神仙。里中偶有爭報常求取決於君。君出一言。無不立即解決。前清孝廉。歷充本省諮議局議員。及資政院議員。民國二年正式國會成立。被選為衆議院議員。國會解散。南旋歸里。讀書自娛。唯隨時襄辦地方公益事業。不問時政。及國會重開。遂應召入京仍為衆議院議員。

君賦性仁厚にして幼より孝行を以て鄉里に知らる。人と為り精明强幹にして事理を洞察し、少年書を讀みて古仁俠の所為を慕ふ。人の不平を見て常に奮然として身を顧みざるも、一たび身體髮膚の訓を念ふては則ち自ら其の不孝を咎め、遂に專ら貧困を救濟する事に勤め、井に從つて人を救ふの事を為さず。前清の孝廉を以て、江西省諮議局議員に選ばれ、資政院議員に舉げらる。辛亥革命を革めて民國樹立するや、二年正式國會衆議院議員に當選す。國會解散後、南旋して鄉里に閒臥して讀書自ら娛ひ。唯だ時に隨つて地方公益事業を勸助し、また時事を論せず。五年約法復活して國會重ねて開かるゝに及び、君再び出でゝ其の召集に應じ、北上入京して仍ち衆議院議員と為る。

Mr. Hung hsiang hsi, forty one years of age, is a native of Lin Chuan, Chiang hsi province. While young, he was known among his people for his filial obedience. As he grew up, he had a gift of strong reasoning power and clear brain. While young, he was a copious reader of books. He was heroic in temperament, and would rush to the rescue of his friends in need, but he was always mindful of the code of filial obedience, so that he would not risk his life even on those occasions. He turned his attention towards helping the poor. When the Revolution was established in the second year of the Republic, he was returned for the House of Commons. When the Parliament was disolved he returned to his home and devoted his time in reading. He stimulated local interests, but kept away from politics. When the Parliament was restored, he responded to the summon, and was returned for the House of Commons.

黃序鵷　字季飛　歲三十九

還畀地　江西省清江縣
籍貫　江西省萍鄉縣
住址　北京宣武門外北半截胡同定盧

君為人鯁直不阿。不苟取與。然居心仁厚。肯急人之難。事成。絕不言報。前清以優附生。留學日本。初學普通。畢業後。入早稻田大學政治經濟科畢業歸國。受前清學部試。授法政科舉人。民國元年一月。任法制院法制調查委員。是年四月。由財政部調充財政部籌備處員。歷充江西財政視察員。賦稅司科長。財政討論會議員。編輯處編輯員。財政調查委員會委員等差。旋補任僉事。十二月。辭職。被選為衆議院候補議員。三年一月。充漢口民國日報館總理。九月。復由財政部調充稅法委員會委員。嗣復歷充整理賦稅所議員。清查官產處委員。清理大清銀行委員會委員等差。民國五年五月辭職。七月補充衆議院議員兼財政委員會委員。

民國之精華　（傳記）　黃序鵷先生

君人と為り硬直にして阿らず、然かも居心仁厚にして人の難に赴き、事成るも絕えて報を言はざるなり。前清優附生を以て日本に留學し、初め普通學を修め、後ち早稻田大學校政治經濟科に學びて業を畢り。歸國して前清政府學部の試驗に及第して法政科舉人を授けらる。民國元年一月法制院法制調查委員に任す。是年四月財政部より財政部籌備處員に調せられ、江西財政視察員、賦稅司科長、財政討論會議員、編輯處編輯員、財政調查委員會委員等の職に歷充し、旋て財部僉事に補せらる。十二月職を辭して衆議院補缺議員に選ばる、三年一月漢口民國日報社總理に任ず。九月復た財政部より調せられて稅法委員會委員に任じ、嗣で復た賦稅整理所議員、官產清查委員、大清銀行整理委員會委員等の職に歷任す。五年五月官職を辭し、七月國會再び召集の令下るや、其の補缺として仍ち衆議院議員の職に就きたり。

Mr. Huang Hsu Yuan, otherwise named Li Fei, age thirty nine, is a native of Ping Hsing. Straightforward in character, and not kotowing to others, he is ready to help his friends in need, but not expecting any reward thereof. He was sent to Japan by the government, and studied law and economics in the Waseda University. On returning to his country, he passed the examination, and was appointed on the committee of legal investigation. In the Chiang Ssi province, he was appointed various committees relating to finances and other branches of local administration. He was elected a member of the House of Commons after resigning his post. In the third year of the Rupublic, he was interested on the news paper. When the parliament was opened again, he was elected a member of the House of Commons for the second time, when he was interested in the diffusion of education among the people. When the re-opening of the Parliament was settled, he came up to Peking, and resumed his function as the member of the House of Commons.

黃寶銘 字叔箴 歲三十六

選舉地 廣西省第一區

籍貫 廣西省賓陽縣

住址 北京賈家胡同廣西南館

君幼有大志。稍長習章句之學。不屑棄去。專攻經史。意猶以爲未愜也。旋游庠。未幾。入兩廣師範學校。畢業後慨然以興學爲己任。首創家族兩等小學校。並充該校校長。宣統元年。往桂學習法政。嗣畢業於廣西法政學校。同時值旅桂同鄉組織同鄉會。被舉爲武鳴府同鄉會會長。光復時。曾與同志組織北伐隊。隨同北伐。而南北和議告成。民國統一。解甲旋里。而南北和策進會成立。被舉爲共和策進會會長。賓陽縣分會會長。旋又被舉爲同盟會賓陽縣分部部長。旋之邑。又充同盟會廣西北部聯絡員。夏間在邑。與同志創辦嶺南法政學校。於邑垣。民國二年。被選爲衆議院議員。國會解散後。歸里獨居。國會復活。遂入京。仍爲衆議院議員。

君幼より大志あり、稍や長じて章句の學を習ひ專ら經史を專攻して意猶ほ慊らず、遂に新學を求めて兩廣師範學校に入りて卒業す。爾來興學を以て自ら任じ、家族兩等小學校を創立して其の校長に任す。宣統元年桂に往きて廣西法政學校を卒業す。時適ま在桂の同鄉人が同鄉會を組織す、君を舉げて武鳴府同鄉會々長と爲す。第一革命に際し同志と偕に北伐隊を組織して北伐の軍に從ひ、南北媾和して民國統一するや甲を解いて歸鄉す。共和策進會賓陽縣分會會長に舉げられ、旋て又た同盟會賓陽縣分部々長に推さる。嗣で邃に往き又た同盟會廣西北部聯絡員となる。當時在邑の同志と籌りて嶺南法政學校を創立經營したり。民國二年正式國會成立に會し衆議院議員に當選す。國會解散後南旋歸鄉して地方教育の普及を計り、國會復活するに及びて其の召集に應じ仍ほ復た衆議院議員たり。

Mr. Huang Pao-ming, sometimes known of Shu Chen, age thirty six, is a native of Pin Yung, the Kung Ssi Hsing. He was quite ambitious from youth and studied history and classics very extensively. Seeking the new knowledge, he entered the Lian Kuang Normal School; even since, he was intersted in educational affairs. In 1909, he graduated from the Kung Ssi Law college. At the time of the first revolution, he started an expedition against the Northern Government, and when peace was concluded, he returned home where he was keenly interested in the promotion of the Republican Form of the Government. He is the founder of the Lien Nan Law School. In the 2nd year of the Republic, he was elected a member of the House of Commons. With the shutting down of the legislative assembly by Yuanshi-kai, he returned his home.

黃懋鑫　字頴亭　歲三十四

籍　貫　江西省武寧縣
住　址　北京宣武門外棉花下六條
選舉地　江西省

君賦性純孝。舉止必請命於親。親有疾。嘗十餘日衣不解帶。侍側奉湯藥不稍離命往息。陽作歸寢狀出。仍入伏親疾。不見處以待。及親愈。而君乃以勞成疾。因恐貽親憂。遂秘不示人。伴爲健康狀。力疾承歡親側。及病增劇不可復支。蓋以久出。亦同一貽親憂也。以前清優附生。先後卒業于本省初級師範學校。暨資政院速記學校。復修業于法政學校。歷充本省諮議局速記員。及各小學校教員。本省速記學校主任教員。兼教務長。民國元年。被選爲衆議院議員。國會停職後。任本縣小學校校長。五年八月。以共和再造。復應國會召來京就職。又君于地方公益事件。辦理甚多。聞仲先後。被選爲本縣教育會會長。農會會長。禁煙公所所長。等職云。

君賦性純孝にして進退共に必ず親の命に從ふ。親疾あれば曾て十余日衣を解かずして湯藥を奉じて看護之れ努ひ。前清の優附生を以て、前後して江西省初級師範學校及び資政院速記學校に學び其の業を畢へ、又た法政學校に修業したり。學就つて後ち出で〜江西省諮議局速記員及び各小學校教員、江西省速記學校主任教員兼教務長等の職に歷充す。民國正式國會成立に際し選ばれて衆議院議員と爲る。國會停止後、南下して鄕里の縣小學校々長に任じ、又た曾て同縣教育會長に舉げられ地方教育の普及に盡力すると共に、同縣農會々長、阿片禁止所々長等の職に當りて地方公益事業に貢献する所尠なからず。五年八月再び國會開業さる〜に及び君仍ち其の召集に應じて北京に抵り復た衆議院議員と爲る。

民國之精華　（傳記）　黃懋鑫先生

Mr. Huang Won-chin, otherwise known as Ying-ti, is a native of Wu-ning, the Chen Sei hsing. He is noted for his filial obedience, so that he conducts himself strictley in accordance with his arent's wishes. He completed the conrse in the normal school of his province, besides attending a mumber of other institutions of learning. He also taught in primary schools, which were left under his charge. When the Republic was established, and the Parliament was opened, he was returned from his province for the House of Commons. After the closing up of the assombor, he went back to his home, where he was appointed the president of the Government Primary School, that of the educational society, and the head of the Opium Prohibition Bureau; In these respects, he considerably contributed to the public interests of his own country. When the Parliament was re-opened in China, he went up to Peking, and became a member of the House of Commons.

黃雲鵬　字默咸　歲三十四

選舉地　四川省

籍　貫　四川省永川縣

住　址　北京順治門外上斜街二十三號

君自幼穎悟。而老成幹練。爲郷黨推重。以前清廩生。入四川東文學堂。優等畢業。咨送日本留學。宣統三年。在早稻田大學部政治經濟科。畢業。學部試驗。列最優等。奬給法政科進士。民國元年。被選爲四川臨時省議會議員。並審查長。閉會後爲財政部委員爲四川大清銀行清理處清理員。兼重慶瀘川源銀行總理。旋被選爲衆議院議員。二年制定憲法。被選爲憲法起草委員會委員。國會解散後。任中國公學大學部校長。三年。任四川瀘川源銀行總理。五年國會復活。仍任衆議院議員。

君幼より穎悟、而して老成幹練、郷黨以て之を推重す。前清の廩生を以て四川東文學校に入り優等を以て卒業し、官費を以て日本に留學し、宣統三年早稻田大學校政治經濟科の業を畢へて歸國す、清政府學部の試驗を受けて最優等を以て法政科進士を授けらる。未だ幾くもなく民國成立し、選ばれて四川臨時省議會議員と爲り、審査長に推さる。閉會後、財政部より命じて四川大清銀行整理委員を委托され、重慶瀘川源銀行總理を兼ぬ、四川財界に於て聲望あり。正式國會成立に際し衆議院議員に當選し、憲法起草委員會委員に擧げらる。國會解散されて後ち中國公學大學部校長に任じ後進を誘掖指導す。民國三年復た四川瀘川源銀行總理と爲る。五年共和克復して國會重ねて召集を行ふに及び遂に又た北上して仍ほ衆議院議員の職に就く。

Mr. Huang Yun Peng, age thirty four, a native of Ssi Chuan Hsieng, is highly respected by his countrymen for his personal weight. In the previous Chinese regime, he was educated in the primary school in his native province. He went over to Japan at the government's expense. In 1911, he entered Waseda University. On returning home, he passed with honours the public examination of the Government. As soon as the Republic was established, he became a member of the Ssi Chuan Local Assembly. He was entrusted with the settlement of the Tai-tsin Bank in Ssi Chuan and as the president of other financial institutions, his fame stood high among the people in his district. As soon as the Republic was formed, he was elected a member of the House of Commons, and appointed the committhe for drafting the constitution. After the disolution of the Parliament, he was appointed the president of the college. When peace was regained, and the Republic was established, he went up to Peking and was returned for the House of Commons.

黃霄九　歲三十二

選舉地　廣東省
籍　貫　廣東省新會縣
住　址　北京李鐵拐斜街門牌四十

君爲人頭腦明晰。意志堅強。能忍辱耐勞。富于幹濟之才。然秉性仁厚。篤實無欺。與人交。喜勸善規過。相其人必能納諫者。始規正之。否則惟漸與疏遠。以示意。及其改悔。則愈善律之。人告以過。則直認不諱。自幼聰穎好讀。弱冠即下筆千言鄉里以神童目之。然以不喜追隨俗尙。故學問雖極深厚。而困于場屋。海內維新。君益研求濟世之學。頗以天下興亡爲己任。曾于中華民國元年。充新會縣署民政科員。民國二年。被選爲衆議院議員。及國會停職。充內國公債局文牘員。今秋召集國會。遂復入京仍充衆議院議員。

民國之精華　（傳記）黃霄九先生

君人と爲り頭腦明晰にして意志堅強、能く辱を忍び勞に耐へ事務の才に富む。然かも氣性仁厚にして篤實欺く無く、人と交りて善を勸むるを喜び、人の告ぐるに過じてすれば、直に認めて諱まず、幼より聰穎にして學を好み弱冠已に文名あり、鄉里神童なりと雖も科舉の業に困しむ。海內維新に及び、盆々濟世治國の學を求め、天下の興亡を以て己が任と爲す。民國樹立して共和の新政を擧ぐるや、民國元年新會縣民政科員に任ず。民國二年正式國會議員の選擧に當り衆議院議員に當選す。未だ幾くもあらずして國會解散され、君乃ち聘せられて內國公債局文牘員となる。共和克復して約法に準據し、國會重ねて召集さるゝに及び、君遂に復た院に到りて現に仍ち衆議院議員を爲る。

Mr. Huang Hsiao Chin is a native of Hsin hui, the Kangtung hsing. He is a gentleman of clear head and strong will, yet he is ready to listen to the advice of others, and gladly tries to rectify his mistakes. He was a precocious child, but never cared to mix himself up with men of common heads. He is greatly interested in the acquisition of new learning, and considered it to be his mission to work for the interest of his people. In the 2nd year of the Republic, he was returned for the House of Commons. With the disolution of the Parliament, he is appointed an official of the Home Loan Bonds Bureau. With the restoration of the Republic, he was returned for the House of Commons.

黃汝鑑 字筱衡 歲三十一

籍　貫　四川省榮經縣

鄉擧地　四川省

住　址　北京潘家河沿十七號

君賦性朴實。不喜浮華。與人交。鯁直
不阿。疾惡如仇。人有過失。無不逕情
詰責。不稍存世故之念。爲人精明强
幹。少好義。喜爲人鳴不平。里人有以
金錢受窘者。輒解囊助之。自幼聰慧好
讀。多所領悟。弱冠時。其文来風貌。已
超出儕輩。讀書能以主觀判斷是非。不
爲成見所局。故思想豐富。見解新頴。
海內維新之後。君慨然棄舊從新。銳意
西學。旋以公費留學日本。入東京帝國
大學法科。於清末畢業。歸國。經學部
考試。授官內閣中書。嗣改調民部營繕
司行走。民國二年。被選爲衆議院議
員。國會解散。歸里獨居。不聞時事。及
國會復活。始來京仍充衆議院議員。

君賦性朴實にして浮華を喜ばず、人と交るや硬直にして
阿らず、惡を惡むこと仇の如く、人過失あれば直言以て
之を詰責し稍しも世故の念を存せず。人と爲り精明强幹
にして少より義を好み喜んで人の爲に不平を鳴らす。幼
にして聰慧、書を好みて領悟する所多く、弱冠早くも文
采風貌嶄然として傑出したり。思想豐富、見解新頴、後ち
新學に志して、官費を以て日本に留學し、東京帝國大學
法科に入り、先進强鄰の最高學府に學びて研磋倦まず、

其の業を畢へて造詣飯に深し。歸國して清政府學部の試
驗に及第し內閣中書を授けらる。嗣で改めて民政部營繕
司行走に調せらる。民國樹立して正式國會組織さるゝに
際し衆議院議員に當選す。議政檀上多年の蘊蓄を傾注し
て民意を代表し建國の大業を贊勤す。國會停止さるゝに
及び、韜晦して讀書自ら娛む。國會復活するや復た出で
て仍は衆議院議員たり。

Mr. Huang Ju-Chien, otherwise known as Su Hui, age thirty one, is a native of Jung Ching,

the Ssi Chuan-hsieng.　He is simple in the mode of living, and hates vain pomp.　Being straightward

in character, he does not hesitate to attack the evil, but is always ready to extend the aid to those in

need.　While young, he had mature throughts, and looked quite distinguished from his fellowmen.　He

went to Japan where he studied in the Law College of the Imperial University of Tokyo.　He passed

the civil examination successfully and was appointed the secretary of the Cabinet.　When the Republic

was formed, he was returned for the House of Commons, in which capacity, he contributed a great deal

to the service of the country.　With the re-opening of the Parliament, however, he was elected a

member of the House of Commons.

黃增耇　字元白　歲三十一

選舉地　廣東
籍貫　廣東省羅省縣
住址　北京宣武門內滌水河十一號

君生於光緒十一年。舊名元白。二十九年遊日。專攻政治學。曾畢業於慶應大學。其時改革論起。君遂與世界著名改革家。孫逸仙。胡漢民。汪兆銘諸氏。為中國同盟會之組織。主稿民聲天聲各報。排滿立憲論。遂風靡海內外。三十一年君偕同學同志多人返國。擬舉高、雷、羅、陽、欽、崖各州為革命之簧源地。適受萍鄉醴陵失敗之影響。事遂中嫌。乃力從事于教育實業水利各事業之進行。又任籌辦地方自治所長。蘊蓄革命之潛勢力。尤為磅礴。民國元年。被舉為眾議院議員。國會破壞。君復遊歷各邦。與民黨馮自由。葉夏聲。發刊民日雜誌實為此次討袁之先河。更實行其計畫。奔走南洋羣島。為革命之指導。現國會再集。復充議員。君性慷慨。情報讜學博思銳。而十餘年對于自信之主義。不撓其政見尤亟亟以保持東亞和平不為主。

君舊名元白。人と為り剛毅にし卓落不羈なり。幼より學を好み十九歲笈を負ふて日本に留學し、專ら政治學を攻究して慶應大學を卒業す。孫逸仙、胡漢民、汪兆銘諸氏と中國同盟會の組織に參與し、民聲天聲各新聞の主筆として革命を鼓吹す。光緒三十一年同學同志の多數と偕に國に歸り、高、雷、羅、陽、欽、崖の各州に於て革命の策源地と為さんと謀りしも、適ま萍鄉醴陵に於ける失敗の影響を受け中途にして挫折す。乃ち教育水利各事業の發展を計り地方自治所長に任じたり。民國元年廣東省議會議員に舉げられ、辭して就かず。二年衆議院議員に當選す。國會破壞するや、君復た各國に游歷し、民黨の志士と謀し、更に討袁の計畫を實行すべく南洋群島各地に奔走する所ありたり。現に國會再び召集さる、や、復た北上して仍は衆議院議員と為る。

Mr. Huang Tseng Kou, thirty one years old, is a native of Lao Tin, the Kuang-ting province. Early in youth, he was fond of study, and at the age of eighteen, he came to Japan, and was graduated from the Keiogijuku, taking lessons in the political science. With some of the leaders of the Revolution, he started a federated society, inspiring the people with revolutional ideas. In 1905, he went about throughout China trying to form headqnarters in pivotal points, but he was frustrated in the attempt, so that he planned for the development of local interest, helping educational and riparian works. In the first year of the Republic, he was elected a member of the Kuangtung Local Assembly, but would not accept the election. In the second year of the Republic, however, he was elected for the House of Commons, but when this Legislative Assembly was suppressed, he travelled through different parts of China, trying to form plans to attack Yuanshi-kai. To accomplish this object in view, he even went as far as the South Sea Islands. When the Parliament was re-opened, he was returned for the House of Commons.

黃錫銓　字鈞選

選舉地　廣東省

籍貫　廣東省梅縣

住址　北京冰窖胡同十八

君賦性仁厚。待人以誠。然爲人剛直不
阿。慷慨好義。居恆疾惡如仇。人有過
失。輒當面痛斥。人以過相詰恆自陳不
稍隱諱。見人爲強暴稿所厄。常忿忿不
自禁。過于身受。弱冠時。嘗以是與人
奮爭。不計已身之利害。故其接物雖鋒
鋩過露昧于社交之術。然以其萬事出
至誠。故人亦罕忌恨之者。自幼好讀能
深思不倦。喜推求眞義。不拘于文詞。
民國元年　被選爲廣東臨時省議會正
議長。正式省議會成立。被選爲省議
會議員。二年被選爲國會參議院議員。
國會解散後。歸里從事地方公益。及國
會重開。始來京復爲參議院議員。

黃錫銓先生

君賦性仁厚にして人を待つに誠を以てす。人と爲り剛直
阿らずして慷慨義を好む。居常惡を憎むこと仇の如く、
人若し過失あれば面の當り痛斥し、人の過を以て相詰る
あれば恆に自ら陳べて稍も隱諱せず。人若し強暴の爲に
窘むを見れば常に恣々として自ら禁せず。是を以て嘗て
相爭ひ已が身の利害を顧みざる也。幼より學を好みて研
磨倦まず。博く讀み深く思索して其の眞義を究むるを喜

びて章句の末に囚はれざる也。民國元年選ばれて廣東臨
時省議會正議長と爲る。後ち正式省議會成立するや、復
た選ばれて省議會議員と爲る。二年正式國會參議院議員
に當選す。國會解散されてより鄕里に歸りて地方公益の
事に從ひ貢献せし所尠からず。約法恢復して國會重ねて
開かるゝに及び、其の召集に應じて入京し、復た仍は參
議院議員たり。

Mr. Huang Hsi Chuan otherwise called Chun, Hsuan, is a native of Mei-hsien, Kuangtung hsing

He is full of spirit of justice and heroism. In dealing with others he is charitable. If he finds anything distasteful in others, he always rebukes them in their face, but never behind them. At the expense
of his own interests he helped many. He was always an industrious student, always trying to appreciate
what he reads. In the 1st year of the Republic, he was elected the president of the Kuangtung Local
Assembly, and, in the 2nd year of the Republic, he was elected a member of the Senate. When the
Parliament was shut down, he returned to his native country, where he contributed a great deal to the
building up of local interests. He contributed a great deal to the promotion of education among the
people. When the Parliament was restored he entered Peking, becoming the member of the House of
Commons, the position which he now holds.

黃贊元 字鏡人 歲三十七

選舉地 湖南省
籍　貫 湖南省長沙縣
住　址 北京宣武門大街善化館

君為人精明強幹。洞察事理。思想活潑。而行動謹嚴。生平不苟言笑。不輕然諾。居常以緘默自持。然一有發揮。則又娓娓動人。聽者無不感之應化。常訓其晚輩曰。求工辯。須自少說話起。求幹練。須自少做事起。與人交。淡而能久。以其能以恕道待人。前淸時曾在長沙。倡辦小學及師範傳習所。旋游日本。留學東京。法政大學畢業。後與同志回國。請願速開國會。旋充四川總督趙爾巽幕職。四川憲政籌備處主任。四川湖南各法政學堂教授。軍政府法制局參事。湖南外交司科長。北京幣制局調查員。浙江將軍署秘書員。浙江長與縣知事。現任衆議院議員。兼充憲法起草委員。

君人と為り精明強幹にして、事理を洞察して思想活潑なり。而して行動謹嚴にして、生平言笑を苟もせず然諾を輕々しくせず、又た娓々として人を動かし、聽者之に一たび口を開けば、又た娓々として人を動かし、聽者之に感動敬服せざるなし。常に其の晚生に訓して曰く、辯舌に工みならば、須らく少なく說くべし、事務に練達せむ事を求む、須らく少なく事を做すべしと。人と交りて淡とし能く久しく、其の能く寬恕の道を以て人を待つ。前淸時代會て長沙に在りて小學校及び師範傳習所を開設す。旋て日本に留學して法政大學校を卒業す。後ち同志と歸國して、國會の開設を請願す。旋て總督趙爾巽の幕僚となりて四川憲政籌備處主任となり四川湖南各法政學校教授、軍政府法制局參事、湖南外交司科長、北京幣制局調查員、浙江將軍署秘書員、浙江長與縣知事に歷任す。民國二年當選の衆議院議員にして憲法起草委員を兼任せり。

民國之精華　（傳記）　黃贊元先生

Mr. Huang Tsan-yuan, otherwise known as Ching-Jen, age thirty seven, is a native of Chang Chou, Hunan province. He is a gentleman of clear understanding and active thoughts. Being very strict in his character he is never guilty of careless conduct. He is naturally a man of taciturn temperament, but once when he starts in his argument he is able to inspire others. While young, he was well known for his eloquence and thoughtful consideration for others. He established a primary and teachers school in his province. He came to Japan where he graduated from the law college. On his return to his country, he was an instructor of the law school in his province, the committee on the Peking Financial Bureau, and many other important functions were assigned to him which he most ably discharged. In the 2nd year of the Republic, he was elected a member of the House of Commons and the Committee for drafting the constitution.

黃荃　字獻襟　歲三十三

選舉地　福建省

籍貫　福建省泉州南安縣

住址　北京後孫公園泉郡會館

君爲人精明強幹。洞察事理。思想活潑。而行動謹嚴。生平不苟言笑。不輕然諾。居常以緘默自持。然一有發揮。則又娓娓動人。聽者無不感之應化常訓其晚輩曰。求工辯。須自小說話起。求幹練。須自少做事起。以其能以恕道待人。與人交。淡而能久。雖疾惡崇善。而未嘗稍露鋒鋩也。前清法政畢業生。學識優良。兼長于幹濟之才。民國二年正式國會成立。被選爲衆議院議員。國會解散。南旋歸里。從事地方公益事業之提倡。五年及約法恢復。國會再行召集。遂又入京。仍爲衆議院議員。

君人と爲り精明強幹にして事理を洞察す。思想活潑にして行動緘嚴なり。生平言笑も苟もせず、然諾を輕んせす。居常緘默を以て自ら持し、然かも一たび發揮する所あれば則ち又娓々人を勤かし、聽く者之に感せざる者無し。常に其の晚靏に訓しにて曰く、能辯ならんひ事を求む、須らく少より演說せざるべからず、幹練あらひ事を求む須らく少より事を做さるべからずと。人と交りて淡として能く久しく、寬恕を以て人を待ち、惡を憎み善を舉ぶと雖も、未だ嘗て稍も鋒鋩を露さいる也。前清時代法政學校の出身にして、學識優良に加るに事務の才あり。民國二年正式國會成立するや選ばれて衆議院議員と爲る。國會解散後南旋して鄉里に歸り、地方公益事業に從事す。五年約法復活して國會再び召集を行ふに及び遂に又た入京して仍ほ衆議院議員たり。

Mr. Huang Chuan, age thirty three, is a native of Nan-an, Chuan Chuan, Foo Chien province. He was a gentleman of comprehensive views and quick understanding. He is known for the tenacity of his character naturally, he is a man of few words, but, once roused, he would not stop until he could convince others. He used to tell his friends about the importance of eloquence when young. He is sociable in temper, and generous to all. In the previous Chinese regime, he graduated from the law school with honours. In the second year of the Republic when the Parliament was brought into existence, he was returned for the House of Commons. After the disolution of the Parliament, he returned to his native home when he was interested in public enterprise. With the restoration of the Parliament, he entered Peking, and was returned for the House of Commons, the position of honour which he now holds.

陶保晉 字席三 歲四十一

選舉地　江蘇省

籍貫　江蘇省江寧縣

住址　北京香爐營頭條西頭路南

君天資聰穎絕倫。頭腦明晰。思考敏捷。少時讀書。即以大器自期。專其心於義理之學。周秦諸子。及宋明學者之學說。皆一一涉獵及之。均有所得。稍長。思想見解。皆極放達活潑。不拘守一隅。然其爲人耿介廉潔。言動舉止皆以禮節自持。嚴取與重信用。雖一介之微。一言之細。亦決不任意出入。苟且偸安蓋放縱於理想。而拘謹於行爲之人也。前淸時。以官費留學日本。入法政大學。卒業歸國。歷充江蘇諮議局議員。金陵法政專門學校長。江蘇銀行檢查員江寧律師公會會長。南京總商會法律顧問。民國二年。國會成立。被選爲衆議院議員。兼全國商會聯合會南京總商會代表。並充律師。國會解散。仍專以律師爲業。不于財政。及此次國會重開。始入京就議員職。

君天資聰穎絕倫にして頭腦明晰なり。少より書を讀みて大器を以て自ら期し、專ら義理の學を修め、周秦諸子及び宋明學者の學說、皆な一々涉獵して均しく所得あり。人と爲り耿介廉潔にして言動舉止皆な禮節を以て自ら持し、蓋し理想に放縱にして行爲に恪謹なる人なり。前淸時代官費を以て日本に留學し、法政大學校に入りて研磨怠まず、其の業を畢へて歸國す。江蘇諮議局議員、金陵法政專門學校々長、江蘇銀行檢查員、江寧辯護士公會々長、南京總商會法律顧問等の職に歷充し、多年蘊蓄せる新智識と明敏なる才幹とを以て地方の開發に任じて聲名日に著る。民國二年正式國會成立に際し衆望を荷つて衆議院議員と爲り、全國商業會議所聯合會南京總商會代表を兼ぬ。國會解散するや、專ら辯護士の業に從事す。國會恢復するに及び復た入京して衆議院議員と爲る。

民國之精華　（傳記）　陶保晉先生

Mr. Tao-hsun, sometimes called Pin-nan is a native of Tan-tu, Chiang-su province. He is a gentleman of sincere character and not guilty of any lies. While young, he was fond of reading books, and is known among his country men for his literary accomplishments. As he grew older, he was deeply interested in practical learning. In the previous Chinese regime, he was interested in education. In Nan-king he established a primary school. He occupied many important government posts, chiefly interested in military training. In 1910, when the industrial exhibition was held in Nan-king, he was appointed the head of the investigation office. When the first revolution broke out, he was keenly interested in the movement, occupying many important posts in his province. In the 2nd year of the Republic, he was appointed a member of the Senate. Because of the fact he belonged to the national party, the Yuanshi-kai government cancelled the certificate of his membership of the Parliament. However, he assisted in the independence of the Ho-Nau province, and when the Parliament was restored he was elected a member of the Senate.

陶　遜　字寶南

選舉地　江蘇省

籍　貫　江蘇省丹徒縣

住　址　北京西單武功衛二

君爲人誠實篤厚。生平不爲僞言。雖疾惡如仇。不疾以言屬色。人以非禮相加。但以理責之。不出惡聲。自幼聰穎好學。弱冠以詩文知于鄉里。及長尤銳志實學。造詣漸深。時不樂仕進以擔貧教育爲已任。創設民立思益兩等小學校于南京。是爲南京有小學之始。舉充江南學務處議紳。江督創練新軍。徵爲參謀處文案兼敎練處提調。幷兼充徵兵局提調。第九鎭新軍成立後。調充參謀處文案兼敎練處提調。宣統元年。充廣東參謀處文案。開會後。改外事科長。革命軍起。被推長江浙聯軍總兵站。嗣以南京政府交通部參事。調充津浦南段鐵路局長。被選參議院議員。因錄國民黨籍。被非法取消。同年靖武將軍軍聘充行署顧問。助成湖南獨立。國會恢復。仍就參議院議員之職。

君人と爲り誠實篤厚にして生平僞言を爲さず。幼より聰頴にして學を好み、弱冠詩文を以て鄉里に知らる。長するに及び、實學に志して造詣漸く深し。曾て南京に於て民立思益兩等小學校を創設す。庶で江南學務處提調となり、徵兵局提調を兼ね。參謀處文案兼敎練處提調を兼ねたり。宣統元年廣東參謀處文案に任じ、敎練處提調を兼ねたり。兩試蘇總督が新軍を編成するや、參謀處文案兼敎練處提調となり。第九師團編成後、廣東參謀處文案に任じ、敎練處提調を兼ねたり。宣統元年廣東參謀處文案に任じ、後も靖武將軍より聘せられて顧問となる。湖南の獨立を助成す。國會恢復して仍ほ參議院議員となる。

二年の頃、南京に於て勸業博覽督を開くに當り調査科長に任じ、開會の後ち外事科長に任ず。第一革命軍起りて長江浙聯軍總兵站に推さる。嗣で南京政府交通部參事を以て津浦南段鐵路局長に當る。民國二年參議院議員に當選す。國民黨員たるの故を以て袁政府の非法により議員證書を取消され、後も靖武將軍より聘せられて顧問となる。湖南の獨立を助成す。國會恢復して仍ほ參議院議員となる。

Mr. Tao Pao Chin, otherwise known as Hsi Sa, aged forty one, is a native of Chiang Ning, the Chiang Su Hsing. He was known for his natural gift of talents possessing clear brain. Early in life, he was fond of reading books, and was well posted up with classical teachings of scholars. He was full of high ideas, but regulated his conduct by strict systems of ettiquet. At the government expense he came to Japan, where he studied in the Hosei University from which he graduated. He occupied many important posts in his province, notably the member of the Chiang Su Local Assembly, that of the Chiang Su Bank, and the consulting lawyer to an important firms. In these possessions his new knowledge and ability came to be at once recognized. In the 2nd year of the Republic, when the Parliament was opened, he was returned for the House of Commons. At the same time he represented the Nanking firm to attend the federated meeting of the chambers of commerce. When the parliament was resolved he practiced law. Again, he became the member of the Parliament, when the regislative body resumed its function.

許峭嵩　字唐山　歳三十四

選舉地　廣東省
籍　貫　廣東省茂名縣人
住　址　北京潘家河沿高州會館

君賦性聰穎絕倫。然誠篤不欺。絕少浮誇氣習。自幼好讀能思。富於研究心。喜逐事逐物考求其所以。雖不已若者。不恥下向。弱冠即喜研求新學。旋入廣東高等工業學校預科肄業。畢業時。得優等。復習學日本。東京。入日本大學校法律專門部。畢業歸國。應中央第三屆知事試驗及格。取列乙等。分發黔省任用。歷署思南青谿縣知事。民國元年。當選為臨時縣會議員。二年當選為衆議院議員。國會解散後遂歸里閉戶讀書。絕不介懷政事。及國會復活。始應召來京。仍為議員。

君賦性聰穎にして然かも誠篤欺かす、絕へて浮誇の氣習なし。幼より讀書を好みて能く思索し、研究心に富み、事を逐ひ物を逐つて其の所以を考求する事を喜び、已に及ばざる者に對しても下問を恥ぢざる也。弱冠即ち努め新學を研究し、旋て廣東高等工業學校豫科に入り、優等を以て卒業す。繼で日本に留學し、日本大學法律科を卒業す。歸國後、中央政府の知事試驗に及第して、貴州省に分ちて補用さる。思南青谿各縣知事を歷署す。民國元年臨時縣議會議員に當選す。二年正式國會衆議院議員に當選す。國會解散後、遂に鄉里に歸りて、戶を閉ぢて書を讀み、絕て懷を政事に介せず。五年國會復活するに及び、始めて其の召集にじ應じて入京し、仍ほ衆議院議員と爲る。

民國之精華　（傳記）許峭嵩先生

二百七十五

Mr. Hsu Chiao-kao, otherwise called Tang-shan, aged thirty four, is a native of Mao-ming, Kuang-tung province. He is man of sincere temperament and free from any vain thoughts. While young, he was interested in the study of books, being naturally a man of studious turn of mind. He was always open to ask questions when he turned his direction towards the acquisition of new learning. He came to Japan, and studied law in the Nippon University. On returning to his home, he passed the examination successfully. In the 1st year of the Republic, he was elected a member of the special local assembly, and in the 2nd year of the Republic he was returned for the House of Commons. With the dissolution of the Parliament, he returned to his home where he devoted himself to the promotion of local interests and in self-culture. When the Parliament was restored he went to Peking and became a member of the Parliament.

郭廣恩 字澤田 歲四十二

選舉地　山東省

籍貫　山東益都縣

住址　北京鮑家街雅集公寓

君賦性清高。言動舉止。皆迥異凡流。然爲人勤謹耐勞。人有所託。輒喜爲盡力。不以功自居。以故里人皆極愛敬之。偶有糾紛。得君出一言。無不立即解釋。自幼天資極高。悟性敏捷。讀書能探究精義。不爲成見所局。故思想豐富。見解新穎。人但見其居常規規自守。不知其精神固異常活潑也。海內維新後。銳志新學。於前清廩貢生。分發奉天任用縣知事。留學日本。東京警監學校畢業。歷充奉天高等巡警學堂教員。財政廳清文局委員。山東法政學校教員。警監學校教務長。民國二年當選衆議院議員。

君賦性清高にして言動舉止皆な過に凡流に異る。然かも人と為く恪謹にして勞に耐へ、人若し託ずる所あれば輒ち喜んで力を盡し、功を以て自ら居らず、故に郷黨皆な君を推重し、偶ま紛糾あれば君が一言を得て立どころに解決す。幼より天資極めて高く悟性敏捷なり。書を讀みて其の義を攻め其の精を究めて思想豐見解新穎なり。海內維新に及び新舉に志して天下有用の材たる以て自任す。前清の廩貢生を以て縣知事に任用し、奉天省に分たる。君尚ほ大成を志して笈を負ふて日本に留學し、車京警察監獄學校に學びて業を畢へ、歸國して後ち、奉天高等巡警學校教員、財政廳清丈局委員、山東法政學校教員、警監學校教務長等の職に歷任したり。君は民國二年當選の正式國會衆議院議員にして、國會解散後、鄉里に在りたるも國會復活するや、其の名集に應じて再び入京し、仍ほ衆議院議員たり。

Mr. Kuo Kuang En, otherwise called Tse Tien, age forty two, is a native of I Tu, Shan-tung province. His character stands very high, and his words differ from the men of common heads. He is open to any suggestion and is far from claiming the merit to himself for any service rendered. Whenever there is trouble in his province, his one word is quite sufficient to put a stop thereto. He was a thorough reader of books and rich in thought and progressive in view. He was deeply interested in the new learning and gave his words to grow to be a useful man for his country. He became the governor of Feng-tien province. He went to Japan to complete his education and studied in the Tokyo police and prison school. On returning to his country, he was appointed to various important posts such as the instructor of the high police school, that of Shan-tung law college and the head master of the prison and police school in his province. In the 2nd year of the Republic, he was elected for the House of Commons, but, with the desolution of the Parliament, he returned to his home where he waited for the opportunity. When the Parliament revived, he entered Peking and was returned for the House of Commons.

郭寶慈　字少雲　歲三十九

選舉地　廣東省四區

籍　貫　廣東英德縣

住　地　北京東草廠、二條韶州館

君秉性誠厚。篤實不欺。然爲人精敏活
潑善辯。且長於辦事才。以前清附生。
容送日本。畢業于東京帝國大學農科。
庚戌歸國。應學部試驗。列優等。賞給
農科舉人。辛亥。殿試。列一等。授主事。
簽分農商工部。派農務司宣防科辦事。
是年改革事起。遂遄粵。創辦南韶連共
進會。以翊贊共和。居無何。被舉爲同
會總會長。民國成立。任廣東農業教員
講習所所長。旋被選爲衆議院議員。同
院第一期常會。選充實業委員。二期常
會。選充財政委員。國會解散後。歸里
獨居。不談政事。及國會復活。始來京
仍爲衆議院議員。

民國之精華　（傳記）郭寶慈先生

君秉性誠厚にして篤實なり、然かも人と爲り明敏にして活潑、
能辨にして事務の才あり。前清附生を以て日本に留學せ
しめられ、東京帝國大學農科を卒業す。庚戌の歲歸國し
て學部の試驗に應じ、優等に列して農科舉人を授けらる。
辛亥の歲殿試の一等に列して主事を授け農商工部に分た
れ、農務司宣防科の事務に任す。是年革命の事起るや廣
東に歸り、南韶連共進會を組織して以て共和を翊贊す。
辛亥の歲殿試の一等に列して主事を授け農商工部に分た
れ、農務司宣防科の事務に任す。是年革命の事起るや廣
舉げられて同會總會長と爲る、既にして民國成立するや
廣東農業教員講習所々長に任じ、地方農事教育の開發に
盡力する所ありたり。正式國會成立に際し選ばれて衆議
院議員となり、同院實業委員に舉げられ、また財政委員
に推さる。國會解散して後ち歸里に歸りて農事改良に徒
事して政事を談せず。國會復活するに及びて重ねて北京
に抵り、仍ほ衆議院議員たり。

Mr. Kuo Pao Tzu, otherwise known as Hsiao Yun, age thirty nine, is a native of Ying Te Hsien, the Kuangtung province. He manifested his ability as a wonderfully eloquent speaker when quite young. He was sincere, bright, and active minded in all his dealings. Under the previous Chinese government, he was sent to Japan, where he was graduated from the Agricultural College of the Imperial University of Tokyo. In 1910, he returned to his country, where he passed with honors the civil examination, and became an official of the agricultural, commercial and technical department. When the Revolution took place, he returned to Kuangtung, where he organized a society with a view to assist the Republican movement, of which he became the head. When the Republic was established, he was extensively interested in the agricultural education of his district. When the Parliament was opened, he was elected a member of the House of Commons, in which he was on the industrial commity as well as the commity of ways and means. When the Parliament was suppressed he returned to his home, where he was interested in the agricultural development and cared nothing about politics. He went up to Peking as soon as the Parliament was re-opened, and he became the member of the House of Commons.

郭光麟　字伯庸　歲三十七

選舉地　河南省

籍　貫　河南省陝縣人

住　址　北京驛馬市大街嵩陽別業

君天資絕高。悟性敏捷。而頭腦周密。其言論思想。皆秩序并然。絕無顛倒錯亂之弊。自幼讀書。即喜探索精義。不以文字自拘。故其於學問。雖歷未深。然每有所讀。必大有進益。以其能精思深入。抉其竅要。故其見解思想。皆極明瞭切實。且洞悉事情。明察物理。長於幹濟之才。前清廩貢生。專門法政畢業。夙抱經世濟民之志。籌畫地方公益。不遺餘力。光復後。被選爲本省臨時省議會議員。民國二平正式國會成立。被選衆議院議員。國會解散後。歸里讀書不問時事。及國會重開。遂應召入京。現仍爲衆議院議員。

君天資絕高にして悟性敏捷、而かも頭腦周密なり。其の言論思想皆な秩序并然として絕て顛倒紊亂の弊なし。幼より書を讀みて精義を探索して文學を以て自ら拘はらす。深く思索して其の竅要を抉す、故に其の見解思想皆な極めて明瞭切實なり。且つ事情を洞察して物理を明知し、幹濟の才を長す。前清廩貢生を以て、地方公益の事を籌畫し、經世濟民の志を抱きて、法政の學を卒して餘力を遺さす。辛亥の歲民國樹立して共和の新政を試るに當り、民國元年選ばれて河南省臨時省議會議員と爲る。二年正式國會成立に際し、推されて衆議院議員に當選す。國會解散後、鄉里に歸省して讀書自ら娛み、ま た時事を問はす。五年國會復活するや、遂に召集に應じて入京し、現に仍ほ衆議院議員と爲る。

Mr. Heng-kuang-lin, otherwise known as Pai-yung, age thirty seven, is a native of Hsia, Ho-nan province. Being naturally bright in character and quick of understanding, he is a shrewd student having clear brains. There prevails always order in his expressions and thoughts, so that he never grows confused. While young, he was a great admirer of books, the meaning of whiche he always fully appreciated. He was a deep thinker, and naturally his interpretation was always clear, scrutinizing to the point. Besides, he was a man of practical ability. He was graduated from a law school in China, and later he spared no efforts in the building up of local interests. When the Republic was formed, he was elected a member of the local assembly. In the 2nd year of the Republic, he was elected for the House of Commons. However, with the disolution of the parliament, he returned to his country, where he interested himself in study and kept aloof from politics. When the parliament was restored, he responded immediately to the summons of the new president, and went up to Peking where he was elected a member of the House of Commons.

郭 涵 字芳五 歳三十四

選舉地　河南省

籍　貫　河南省孟津縣

住　址　北京驛馬市大街嵩陽別業

君秉性聰慧敏捷。為人剛正不阿。思想
活潑。頭腦明晰。讀書不執成見。不拘
字句。故皆能得其眞義。與人交。常喜
為規勸。辭直而婉懇切而不數。以故人
多為所感動。夙抱濟世安民之志。以天
下有用之人才自任。辛亥革命宣布憲
政共和。中華民國肇造。正式國會成
立。君荷衆望。當選衆議院議員。國會
解散。歸里讀書。唯隨時提唱地方公益
之事。不問中央政治。此次及至國會重
行召集。遂又入京。仍為衆議院議員。

民國之精華　（傳記）　郭涵先生

君秉性聰慧にして、敏捷人と為り剛正にして阿らず。思
想活潑にして頭腦明晰、書を讀みて成見に囚れず字句に
拘らず、皆な能く其の眞義を究む。人と交りて常に規勸を
喜び辭直にして婉、懇切にして數々せず、故に人多く感
動す。夙に濟生安民の志を抱き、天下有用の人才を以て
自ら任ず。辛亥の歳、命を革めて憲政共和を宣布し、中
華民國の奠を擧めて正式國會成立するや君衆望を荷つて
衆議院議員に當選す。國會解散して、君鄉里に歸りて讀
書自ら娯み、唯だ時に隨つて地方公益の事を提唱し、中
央の政治如何を問はず。此次國會重ねて召集を行ふに及
び、遂に又た入京して仍は衆議院議員と為る。

Mr, Kuo-han, age thirty four, is a native of Meng-chin, Ho-nan province. He is a gentleman
of strong will, quick wit, and of active thought. Since he had a clear brain, he was interetsed in
the intelligent reading of books. In associating with his friends, he was very kind and often inspired
others. He claimed himself to be a useful man for his country. In 1911, when the revolutionary
movement accomplished its oblect and the Republic was established, he became a member of the Parliament. However, when the Parliament was dissolved, he went back to his native country and was greatly interested in the promotion of public welfare. When the Parliament was re-opened, he went to Peking
and was returned for the House of Commons.

郭相維　字雍賡　歲三十三

選舉地　黑龍江省

籍貫　黑龍江省慶城縣

住址　北京西單堂子胡同東口外寬街

君爲人勤勉好學。然性慧善悟。讀書能深思細玩。每畢一書。必能歷舉其發奧之所在。弱冠有文名。頗自矜滿。及長閱書愈多。始覺所得極淺。乃力去虛驕。不恥下問。中年。銳意新學。於前清光緒三十二年。由黑龍江初級師範學校畢業。三十三年充省城初等小學校教員。三十四年充海倫縣視學。四月調充呼蘭縣勸學員。兼初等工業學校教員。宣統元年八月。調充慶城縣高等小學校長。二年七月。調充海倫縣視學兼勸學員。擴充公立小學校十九處。三年九月。調充省城學務公所議紳。民國元年四月。兼省城南路農業中學校監督。十月兼省農會副會長。十二月被選爲省議會議員。二年二月。被選爲參議院議員。國會解散後。歸里杜門不出。五年五月赴上海。與同志等組織國會議員團。及國會復活遂仍就參議院議員。

君人と爲り勤勉にして學を好み、弱冠早くも文名あり。中年意を新學を傾けて研磋倦まず、造詣漸く深し。前清先緒三十二年黑龍江初級師範學校を卒業し、三十三年同省々城初等小學校教員となり、三十四年海倫縣視學に任じ、四月呼蘭縣勸學員に轉じ、初等工業學校教員となり、二年七月また海倫縣視學兼勸學員となり、公立小學校十九箇所を擴張し、三年九月省城學務公所義紳となり、民國元年四月

省城南路農業中學校監督を兼ね、十月黑龍江省農會副會長に舉げらる。多年銳意教育の普及と民智の開發に從して功勞あり。十二月選ばれて省議會議員となり、二年二月正式國會參議院議員に當選す。國會解散されて後も郷里に歸り、五年五月上海に赴き同志等と國會議員團を組織す。國會復活するに及び、遂にまた入京して仍ほ參議院議員と爲る。

Mr. Kuo Hsiang Wei, otherwise called Yung-keng, age thirty three, is a nature of Ching Cheng, Hei Lung Chiang. When young, he was fond of books, being quite an industrious students so that, even early in life, his literary fame stood high. He devoted himself to the acquisition of the new learning, in which he made a considerable progress. In 1907, he was graduated from the normal school in his province, and became the teacher of the primary school. In the following year, he was the educational inspector of the province aud the president of the elementary artisan school. Through his instrumentality as many as 19 paimary schools were establish. In the 1st year of the Republic, he was the vice-president of the Agricultural Society of his province. He was thus deeply interested in the promotion of education among his own people. He was returned for the Local Assembly, while in the 2nd year of the Republic, he was elected a member of the Senate. On the dissolution of the Parliament he returned to his home, and was constantly working for the interests of the Republic, When the legislative body was re-opened, he became a member of the Senate.

郭人漳 字葆生

選舉地　湖南省
籍貫　湖南省
住址　北京賈家胡同芳盛園一號

君為人慷慨好義。富於感情。然居恒以
謹行自持。絕小囂張氣習。且秉性篤實
不事浮華。生平極尚信義。重然諾。雖
好義舉。而人有所託。不輕于承諾。既
允諾。邁進果行。事成。不復望報與人
交。喜相責以善。人告以過。輒大喜。自
幼好讀。喜博覽群籍。純以主觀判斷是
非。而不同于習俗之成見。故其文采風
貌。亦超出儕輩。弱冠時。即以名儒自
期。及長。立志棄舊從新。遍購新書讀
之。尤注意於政治之學。以天下有用之
人材自任。所歷既多。功勢亦不尠。名
聲藉甚。民國二年。遂荷眾望。當選為
眾議院議員。此次國會恢復。再應召集
仍就議員舊職。

君人と為り慷慨義を好みて感情に富む。然かも居常謹約
を以て自ら持し、絕へて倨傲の習氣なし、且つ秉性篤實
にして浮華を事とせず、生平極めて信義を尚び然諾を重
んず、義舉を好むと雖も、人託する所あれば輕々しく承
諾せざるも、既に允諾すれば邁進して敢行し、事成るも
復た報を望まざる也。幼より讀を好み、喜んで群籍を涉
獵し、主觀を以て是非を判斷して習俗の成見に囚れず、
故に其の文采亦た迥かに儕業を援ぐ。弱冠の時、即ち名
儒を以て自ら期し、長するに及びて、志を立てゝ舊を棄
て新に從ひ、遍ねく新書を購讀し、尤も意を政法の學に
注ぎて、天下有用の人材を以て自ら任じたり。經歷既に
多く功勢亦た尠なからずして名籍甚なり。民國二年遂に
眾望を荷つて眾議院議員に當選す。此次國會恢復す、再
び召集にとて現に仍ち眾議院議員たり。

Mr. Fu Jen-chang is a native of Hu-nan province. Naturally heroic in temperament, he was
very sensitive and refined. He was very humble in dealing with others, and had no trace of arrogance
in him. He is faithful to his promise. Although heroic in temperament, he was not careless to under-
take anything, but as soon as he makes up his mind to accomplish any thing, nothing would prevent him
While young, he was reading books and not subjected to any local tradition. While young, he proposed
himself to be the leader among Chinese scholars, but he later begun to study new books particular by
those on law, and devoted himself to the acquisition of useful learning. His fame stored high among his
own countrymen. In the second year of the Parliament, he was elected a member of the Parliament
with a large majority. Under the new president, when the Parliament was re-opened, he was elected to
a member of the House of Commons.

郭生榮

選舉地　山西省

籍　貫　山西平遙縣

住　址　北京前門外冰窖胡同

君天性沈靜謹默。富有實業思想。居恒
以爲中國歷史流傳。自三代以還。素以
農立國。迄今海禁太開。列國莫不以謀
農工商業之發達爲富强之要素。偷中
國能舉國一心。從事於重農主義。以求
發展工商事業。潛滋暗長。則百年之
後。以難與美洲合衆國並駕齊驅。以故
研究農商諸學。不遺餘力。生平熱心教
育。聆君之議論風采。發聲振贖能發人
深省。青年即潛心學理。汎濫古今。與
君交遊者。莫不深相稱許。以爲今世之
有心人也。君以前清癸卯科舉人。在地
方辦理學務。提倡實業。贊助自治歷年
多。現充衆議院議員。

君天性沈靜謙默にして實業思想に富む。居常恪謹自ら持
し、凩に國利民福を以て念と爲す。唐虞三代以來の歴史
に稽へ、其の古き國策たる重農主義に加ふるに、現代世
界の大勢に鑑みて商工業の振興發展を企圖するを以て富
國强兵の要道なりとす。故を以て農商諸學を研究して餘
力を遺さず、且つ生平教育の普及を心を計る。君の議論風采、
藝實にして穩健、精緻にして明晰、世の覽を發し贖を振
はし、能く人をして三省反思せしむ。青年即ち心を學理
に潛め、識古今に通ず。君と交游する者、深く相稱許せ
ざるなし。蓋し支那近代に於ける時艱を匡敕するに最も
適任なる一人なり。前清癸卯科の舉人にして、地方に在
りて舉務を處理し、地方自治を勸助すること年あり。民
國二年當選の正式國會衆議院議員にして、此次約法復活
して國會重ねて開くるや、再び召集に應じ仍ほ衆議院議
員たり。

Mr. Heng-sheng-jung is a native of Pin-yao, Shan-hsi province. He is gentleman of deep thought and few words, being chiefly interested in industrial enterprises. He always bears in mind the promotion of the interests and well being of the people. By studying the history of China carefully, he came to the conclusion that much weight should be attached to agriculture, while the consideration of the modern world's tendency brought a conviction to his mind that commercial and industrial uprising is the most important method of enriching and strengthing the nation. Therefore, he devoted himself to the study of science concerning agriculture and commerce. His personal presence, national arguments, and clear reasoning are combined to make his ordience quite reflective. Any acquaintance would at once observe these qualities in this rising man of China. In the previous Chinese regime, he passed the civil service examination, and interested in the promotion of education in local districts. I the 2nd year of the Republic he was returned for the House of Commons, but when the Parliament was re-opened, after it was shut up by Yuanshi-kai, he went up to Peking, and was returned for the House of Commons, the position of honour he now enjoys.

常恒芳　字藩候　歳三十五

選舉地　安徽省

籍　貫　安徽省壽州縣

住　址　北京達智橋松筠庵

君自幼好學。及長。尤立志大成。中日戰後。慨然有澄清天下之懷。遂發憤攻新學。以縣學生員。先後肄業於安徽騎兵學校。日本同文書院。日本大學法科專門部。畢業後。值辛亥革命軍起。歷任滬軍參謀。南京臨時參議院議員。中央臨時教育會會議員。南京民生報記者。安慶國民黨皖支部長。民國二年。被選爲衆議院議員。主持正論。對抗袁氏。八月。以附亂嫌疑被捕下獄。即袁氏違法逮捕八議員之一也。後開皖禁錮二年有半。至袁氏死後。於民國五年六月二十五日始釋出。旅滬皖議員曾致電歡迎。中有公昔志共和國死。今幸與共和國生。國之福。皖之光處語。旋由滬來京。復爲衆議院議員。

君幼より學を好み、長ずるに及び志を立て〻大成を期す。日清役後、慨然として天下を澄清するの懷を抱き、發憤努力を以て新學を攻究す。縣學生員を以て、安徽騎兵學校、日本同文書院、日本大學法科を前後卒業したり。適ま辛亥革命起る、上海軍參謀、南京臨時參議院議員、中央臨時教育會々議員、南京民生報記者、安慶國民黨皖支部長等の職に歷充す。民國二年選ばれて衆議院議員と爲る。正論を主持して袁氏に對抗し、八月亂徒の嫌疑を被りて、獄に下る、即ち袁氏違法逮捕議員八名中の一人なり。即ち安徽に押送されて禁錮二年有半、袁氏の死後、民國五年六月二十五日始めて釋放せらる。在上海の議員同人、打電して歡迎す。直ちに上海に赴きて同志と會し、後ち國會の召集に應じ入京し、復た衆議院議員と爲る。

民國之精華　（傳記）　常恒芳先生

二百八十三

Mr. Chang-heng-tang, otherwise called Fan-hou, age thirty five, is a native of Shon, An-hin province. While quite young, he has been a lover of learning, and as he grew older he was filled with ambitions and turned his attention towards new learning. He graduated from the law course in the Nippon University. When the first revolution took place in China, he most jealously participated in the movement. In the 2nd year of the Republic, he was elected to a member of the Parliament. On account of his opposition, he was arrested and imprisoned by Yuanshi-kai. He was sent to An-hui where he was confined for two years or more. With the death of Yuanhshi-kai, he was released and went to Shanghai, where together with his fellow thinkers he went to Peking and became a member of the House of Commons.

崔懷灝　字香波。歲三十六

選舉地
　　　直隸

籍　貫
　　　直隸省晋縣

住　址
　　　北京二龍坑北貴人關十五

君少好學。稚齡讀經。日誦數千言。過目成誦。能一一領會其意。弱冠時。即工於詩文。吐屬華貴。氣勢雄俊。鄉里皆驚爲神童。然天稟雖高。而賦性篤實誠厚。絕無虛驕氣習。及長。尤謙虛好問。愈益奮勉求進。讀書博而能約。喜深思而能闕疑。其爲文取法漢魏。然生平推崇宋學。不以考据詞章爲能。蓋於漢宋二派皆已窺堂奧。故以宋學爲本。而於漢學亦能得其資助也。前清時以廩生。入北洋師範專脩科。畢業後。歷充本縣高等小學校校長。河間深澤中學教員。直隸第四師範教員。民國元年。被選爲衆議院議員。國會解散後。閉戶讀書絕口不談政見。及共和再造。國會重開。始應召。仍就衆議院議員職。

君少にして學を好み、弱冠即ち詩文に工に、格調華雅、氣勢雄偉、鄉里目して神童と爲す。天稟高しと雖も賓性篤實にして絕へて虛驕の風無し。長ずるに及びて盆々研学に志し造詣漸く深し。前清時代、廩生を以て北洋師範學校專脩科に入りて卒業す、後ち晋縣高等小學校々長、河間深澤中學校教員、直隸第四師範學校教員等の職に歷任し、育英の業に從事して後進を誘掖し、地方教育の普及を計りて民智の開通に銳意努力したり。民國正式國會の成立に際し衆議院議員に當選す。國會解散して後ち、門を閉ぢて讀書自ら娛み、傍ら後進子弟を指導啓發す。共和克復して國會重ねて召集を行ふに及び、君再び出で、院に到り、仍ほ衆議院議員の舊職に就きたり。

Mr. Tsui Huai Hao, otherwise known as Hsiang Po, age thirty six, is a native of Chi Lin province. He was fond of study and excelled himself as a poet and essaist. He was full of ambition and aspiration, being held in high esteem by his country men. He is far from being arrogant and vain. He advanced far in his study, when he was admitted to the Pei Yang normal school, whence he was graduated. Since then, he was successively a teacher of middle and normal schools. He was keenly interested in the local education, developing the knowdlege of the people. When the Parliament was opened, he was elected as a member of the House of Commons. On the dissolution of the Parliament, he shut himself up, taking great pleasure in the perual of books and the instruction of the young. When the Republic was restored and the Parliament started, became a member of the House of Commons, resuming actively his own fuuction under this capacity.

康愼徽　字邇英　歲三十九

君天資聰慧にして人と爲り誠實なり。幼より書を好みて新舊の學識共に素養あり。前清光緒末年、山西大學校西學專科に學びて卒業す。旋て宣統元年山西諮議局議員に舉げらる。第一革命の事起るや、楡次縣に在りて國民公會を組織し、同々長に推さる。地方の安寧維持に盡瘁して功勞あり。民國成立して後も臨時縣議會會長に舉げられ、又た行政公所を創設して諸規則を議定し、以て官吏多年の積弊を革新したり。正式國會の組織に當り選ばれて衆議院議員と爲り、正論を把持して公議を主張し民國の健實なる建設を期待す。不幸にして袁政府の非法により國會解散さるゝに及び、君歸鄉して怏々として樂まず。五年國會復活して憲政の曙光克復するや、其の召集に應じて入京し、仍ほ衆議院議員の職に復す。

選舉地　山西省
籍　貫　山西省楡次縣
住　址　北京東北園九十八號

君天資聰慧。爲人誠篤。自幼喜讀書。學識優良。新舊有素養。素旨勤儉。熱心國事。於前清光緒末年。由山西大學校。西學專齋畢業。宣統元年。充山西諮議局議員。當辛亥改革時。在楡次本籍組織國民公會。被舉爲該會會長。維持地方。煞費苦心。民國元年。被舉爲楡次臨時縣議會議長。創設行政公所。議定章程。革去官吏多年積弊。二年。被舉爲衆議院議員。旋國會被非法解散後。君即歸隱。脫離政累關係。五年。國會回復。仍列席衆議院議員。

民國之精華　（傳記）康愼徽先生

Mr. Kang Chin Hui, otherwise known as Erh Chueh, age thirty nine, is a native of Yu Tzu, Shan Hsi. He was a favored child being intelligent and bright in his nature. Being fond of books, he was considerably advanced in both new and old learning. At the latterdays of the previous Chinese regime, he graduated from the Shan Hsi University. In 1909, he was appointed a member of the Shan Hsi Local Assembly. When the Revolution broke out, he organized the national party in Yu Tzu, of which he became the president and contributed a great deal for the the maintenance of order and peace in the province. With the establishment of the Republic, he was elected the president of the Local Assembly. It was through his efforts that the administlative office was created which drew up various laws and regulations, introducing reforms among the officials. When the Parliament was opened, he was returned for the House of Commons; and it was hoped that he would contribute much through his knowledge to the sound development of the Republic. Having been, however, through the illegal conduct of Yuanshi-kai, shut up the Parliament, he returned to his country. When the dawn of the constitutsional government became known, he went to Peking and resumed his function as a member of the Parliament.

康佩珩　字子韓　歲四十

選舉地　山西省
籍貫　山西省五臺縣
住址　北京兵部窪十二

君自八歲入學。資質魯鈍。日讀一二
句。苟不能記誦。十二三歲後。始稍解
文義。改苦十餘載。始入邑庠。入學堂
二年。復因貧廢學。旋以自費東渡。入
中國同盟會。並充民報社幹事。專從事
革命事業。即遂歸國入晉垣。聯絡軍
隊。同志十餘人。經投塞北。出雁門。越
陰山。曉河套。履沙漠。凡蒙古有人之
處。無不遍及。所至聯絡健兒。演說革
命。周流年餘。爲歸綏將軍所偵悉。派
兵被拿捕。不得已星夜返鄉。蟄伏半
載。次年春。公推爲勸學總董。旋改就
隣縣高等學校教員晉省反正委爲忻
代寧公團長。次年春。共和告成。任臨
時省議會議員。閉會後委任爲調查各
省政見全權委員正式國會成立。被選
爲衆議院議員。國會解散後。歸里。曾
被委調查晉北礦務。旋以嫌疑避禍津
門。是年冬。復被委爲晉北營務處長。
及共和再造。國會重開。遂入京。復爲
衆議院議員。

君八歲より文を學ぶ、資質魯鈍にして日に一二三句を讀み
て記誦する能はず、十二三歲後始めて稍や文義を解くに
至る。刻苦精勵十余年、始めて邑庠に入りて在學二年復
た貧に因て學を廢す。旋て日本に遊び同盟會に入りて民
報社幹事となり專ら革命に從事す。後ち歸省して山西軍
隊の聯絡を計り、同志十余人と塞北に抵り、蒙古を跋跡
して至る所健兒を聯絡す。歸綏將軍の偵知する所となり
兵を派して捕へんとす、君乃ち鄉里に歸りて蟄伏す。後

ち推されて勸學總董となる。第一革命當時山西獨立する
や忻代寧公團長となる。民國成立後、臨時省議會議員と
なり、閉會後、各省政見調查委員を委任せらる。二年正
式國會衆議院議員に當選す。國會解散後、鄉里に歸りて、
山西北方の礦務調查の委托を受け、旋て革命の嫌疑を以
て天津に難を避けたり。其の後復た晉北營務所長と爲り、
國會再び召集され、遂に京に入りて衆議院議員と爲る。

Mr. Kang Pei Yen, otherwise called Tsu Kan was born in Uu Tai, the Shan Hsi Hsing, and fourty aged at present. While young he was very slow in understanding, and had very bad memory, but at the age of twelve or thirteen, he began to appreciate what he learned to some extent. He studied in one of village schools. To make the matter worse, he was the son of penury, and had to give up his learning on account of poverty: He came oner to Japan, and attended to the revolutionary affairs. On return home, he planned the federation of military men, and for this purpose, he travelled very extensively throughout hilly districts of the country. The Government suspected his movement, and he was in danger of being arrested. He escaped the espionage, and returned to his home, but when the revolutionary movement proned itself to be a success, he left his local occupations, he was appointed on the committee of political investigation. of different provinces. He was returned for the House of Commons; When the Parliament was shut up, he returned to his home where he was interested in the mining investigation of the Shan-Hsi district, but being suspected of the revolutionary movement, he fled to Tientsin. Later he resumed once more his presidency in the local institute of learning, but when the National Assembly was summoned, he became the member thereof.

梅光遠　字斐漪　歲三十七

選舉地　江西省

籍貫　江西省南昌縣

住址　北京報子街東口

君爲前清光緒二十三年舉人。嗣以內閣中書。爲江蘇補用道。保加二品銜。特保人材。奉旨召見。交內閣存記。仍發往江蘇特用。兼民政部諮議官。歷充江蘇上海清文局總辦。江南師範學堂監督。江寧小學四十所總滙處總辦。南洋勸業會江西物產總會總理。江南四區模範小學總理。考察日本學務委員。南洋華僑暨南學堂監督。民國成立。獎授四等嘉禾勳章。充財政部清理官產處處長。明保交政事堂存記。兼充財政部清理大清銀行整理委員會委員。奉令嘉獎。給予一等金質單鶴章。曾經舉充江西南潯鐵路公司董事。前民主黨本部常務員。曾當選爲衆議院議員。此次國會復活。仍到院復充原職云。

君は前清光緒二十三年の舉人なり。內閣中書を以て江蘇補用道に任じ二品銜を授けらる。前清朝廷特に人材とて謁見を賜り內閣に命じて記錄せしめられたり。曾て江蘇上海清文局總辦、江南師範學堂監督、江寧小學校四十箇所總滙處總辦、南洋勸業會江西物產會總理、江南四區模範小學校總理、日本學務視察委員、南洋華僑暨南學堂監督等の職に從事して敎育の普及を計り功勞勘なからず、民國成立して後ち四等嘉禾章を授けられたり。又た財政部官產整理處々長、大淸銀行整理委員會委員等に任じ、一等金質單鶴章を授けられたり。又た曾て江西南潯鐵道會社理事に舉げられて地方交通の事に當り。前民主黨本部常務員として黨務を處理したる事あり。第一次正式國會衆議院議員に當選し。此次復た其の召集に應じて現に仍ほ衆議院議員たり。

民國之精華　（傳記）　梅光遠先生

Mr. Mei Kuang Yuan, otherwise known as Fei-i, age thirty seven, is a native of Nan Chang, the Chiang Hsi province. He was known for his ability, and was a secretary of the Cabinet during the previous Chinese regime. He occupied a series of very important educational posts in his province. His contribution in this line of activity is by no means to be ignored. He was a teacher of the Chiang Nan Normal School, the president of the South Sea Industrial Association and a Committee of Japanese Educational Observation. When the Republic was brought into existence he was also appointed to many important government services. He was on the committee of the government property examination etc. He was also interested in the local railway affairs, assisting the development of communication facilities. When the Parliament was opened, he was elected to a member thereof. However, with the dessolution of the diet, he waited for the opportunity which was in store for him. He is at present an active member of the House of Commons.

符鼎升 字九銘 歲三十八

選舉地　江西省

籍　貫　江西省宜黃縣

住　址　北京順治門外香爐營二條六號

君自幼好學深思.稚年讀書.即喜推求精義.不厭數問.塾師常為所窘.益契重之.弱冠即有文名.詩文策論.皆有名家風味.及長.尤廣覽群書.並喜涉獵周秦諸子.然不屑從事舉業.及海內維新.尤奮志新學.不以舊見自拘.遂東渡留學日本.普通畢業後.考入東京高等師範學校.數理化本科.畢業歸國.于民國元年任江西教育司司長.二年當選為參議院議員.國會解散後.任北京高等師範學校及工業專門學校教員.及國會恢復後.遂應召仍為參議院議員.

君幼より學を好み、少年嘗を讀みて其の義理を攻究するに勉め、長じて群籍を涉獵し、海內維新に及び、進んで新學に意を注ぎて研磋倦まず、遂に笈を負ひて東海を渡り、新進日本の學府に游びて先づ普通學を修め、素地既に成りて後ち、東京高等師範學校數理化本科に入りて其の業を畢へたり。歸國して後ち、民國元年江西教育司々長に任じ、一省の學政を處理して教育の振興を計り、聲望漸く著る。二年國會の組織に當り参議院議員に當選す。國會解散せられしによりは、北京高等師範學校及び工業專門學校に在りて教鞭を取り、以て後進子弟を誘掖養成す。本年國會恢復して重ねて召集を行ふに及び、復た身を政界に投じて仍は参議院議員と為る。

　　Mr. Fu Ting Sheng, otherwise named Chin Ming, age thirty eight, is a native of I Huang Hsien, the Chang Hsi Hsiug. In his youth, he was a great admirer of books and deep students. As he grew older, his attention was directed to the new learning. He went to rising Japan where he educated himself in liberal learning and graduated from the Higher Normal School of Tokyo. On hisr eturn home in the 1st year of the Republic, he was appointed the chief of the Educational Bureau of his province. His reputation rose high, because in his position he made efforts to improve the educational standing of the people. In the 2nd year of the Republic, with the summon of the parliament, he was elected to a member of the same. When the parliament was broken up he was an instructor of the Peking Higher Normal School as well as the Techinical College. When the Parliament resumed its function, he again became interested in politics and was appointed to a member of the Senate.

選舉地　吉林省

籍　貫　吉林省長春縣

住　址　北京宣武門內油房胡同

君少好學。不喜制藝。專精經術。尤致力於易。偶有所得。惟書之秘編。不以問世。為人慷慨好義。富于感情。見人不平。常忿忿不禁。过於身受。然其舉動極為慎重。不逞一時之意氣。以為從井救人之行為。故生平所為義舉極多。然未曾以此陷於絕境。以發卯科舉人。為內閣中書。居京五年。翻然思歸曰。不能建設於朝。寧不如施敎於鄉耶。遂歸長春。以敎育為己任。四年之中。創立各種學校三百餘處。為各縣之冠。民國二年。被選為衆議院議員。國會解散後。署奉天本溪縣知事。該縣內政外交。號稱難治。君履任一年之久。中外翕然。及國會復活。遂辭職來京。復就議員之職。

君少より學を好みて制藝を肯はず、專ら經義を究めて尤も力を易に致す、偶ま得る所あれば、芝を秘編に書して世に問ふを欲せず。人と為り慷慨義を好みて感情に富む。人の不平を見て常に忿々として自ら禁せず、然かも其の舉動極めて慎重、一時の意氣を逞ふして井に從つて人を救ふの行為なし。前清癸卯の歲舉人に科せられ、內閣中書を授けらる。北京に居ること五年翻然歸去來を思ひ、曰く朝に於て建設する能はずんば寧ろ鄉に於て既設する

に如かずと、遂に關を出でゝ長春に歸り、地方敎育の振興を以て已が任と為す。四年間の短時日に於て各種學校實に三百餘處を創立したり。民國二年正式國會衆議院議院に當選す、國會解散後、內治外交共に難治を以て稱せられたる奉天省本溪縣知事を署理し、治蹟大に舉り令名大に聞ゆ五年國會復活するや、遂に職を辭して召集に應じ仍は衆議院議員たり。

民國之精華　(傳記)　畢維垣先生

Mr. Pi Wei-Yuan, otherwise known as Futing, age forty five, is a native of Chun Chun, Chilin province. While young, he was almost a lover of reading and especially he put his efforts to the study of classics. His habit was to recall the points which impressed him most. Being heroic in character he always acted for other at his own expense. However, he was far from being guilty. He was sincere in his doing and devoted himself to the interest of his country. He was in Peking five years but his attention was directed towards the building up of the local interes's. He went to Chengchun and contributed his service to the education of the people in the local districts for a short space of four years, through his instrumentality as many as schools were established. In the 2nd year of the Republic he was elected for the Parliament. After the disolution of the Parliament, he was appointed the governor of Pen Chi which is known as the district most difficult to govern. When the Parliament was restored, he resigned the post and elected for the House of Commons.

寇遐 字勝浮 歲三十三

選舉地 陝西省

籍貫 陝西省

住址 陝西蒲城縣內府村

君爲人精明強幹。富於忍耐。長於幹濟才。然情性圓活。不固執己私。自幼好讀。博而能約識力均極高而又虛心好問。能受藎言。及海內維新。專求天下有用之學。攻究新書。造詣旣深。即立志興學。開通民智。以挽救危忘自任。曾陝西師範學校附屬優級選科畢業。銳意力圖教育之普及。熱心從事育英。誘掖後進。聲望大著。民國元年被選臨時省議會副議長。二年被選爲衆議院議員國會解散後。歸里專從事教育。及國會重開。遂來京復爲衆議院議員。

君人と爲り精明強幹、忍耐に富み、幹濟の才に長ず。然かも情性圓活にして己私を固執せず。幼より讀書を好み心を虛ふして人に問ひ、能く藎言を聞く。海內維漸に及びて專ら天下有用の學を求め、新書を繙きて研磋倦まず造詣旣に深くして迥かに凡流を超出す。即ち興學の志を抱き、民智を開通して、國家の頹勢を挽回する事を以て自ら任す。曾て陝西師範學校附屬優級選科を卒業し、爾來銳意教育の普及を圖り、育英の業に從事して、後進の誘掖に努め、聲望大に著る。民國元年臨時省議會成立するや臨時省議會副議長に舉げらる。二年正式國會衆議院議員に當選す。國會解散後鄉里に歸りて、依然興學の事を以て念とし、暫らく時事を問はず。五年國會重ねて開くるに及び遂に又た召集に應じて入京し、仍ち衆議院議員と爲る。

Mr. Kon-hsia, otherwise known as Shengfon, age thirty three, is a native of Hsiahsi province. He is a gentleman of bright character full of patience and forbearing. However, he is very practical and is not egoistic. While young, he was a great reader of books, and was ready to listen to others. He was a seeker of useful learning. Studying the new book, he is never tired of diving into the real depth of that he studies. He is convinced of his mission which is to encourage learning among the people so as to restore the country from the crisis. Having graduated from the eclectic course of Hsia hsi normal school, he was keenly interested in the dissimination of the knowledge among the people with whom he was always popular. In the first year of the Republic, he was the vice-president of the local assembly. After the disolution ot the Parliament, he returned to his native country where he was interested in the promotion of his own education, keeping himself from politics. When the Parliament was restored, he resumed his function as the member of the House of Commons.

莫德惠 字柳忱 歳三十四

選舉地　吉林省

籍　貫　吉林省雙城縣

住　址　北京中鐵匠胡同

君秉性剛正。不隨流俗浮沈。然居心仁厚。雖仇敵亦不忍窘迫之。與人交喜相責以善。人告以過。輒大喜。自幼性慧頴於悟。於舉業之術。已深有所造。然以傾心西學故。不復留意科名。遂入北洋高等巡警學堂正科。畢業後。歷充警察局長。雙城縣知事。民國元年。俄皇贈給斯托呢斯拉夫三等勳章。二年。被選爲衆議院議員。國會解散後。歸里獨居。不問時事。唯時盡力於地方自治及教育等事宜。及國會復活。始來京仍爲衆議院議員。

君秉性剛直にして幹才あり。幼より總慧にして學を好み、長じて新進有用の學に志し、遂に笈を負ふて關を入り、天津に抵りて北洋高等巡警學堂正科に學んで其の業を畢へたり。乃ち錦衣歸鄕して警察局長及び雙城縣知事に歷任し、地方の治安を保持し又た生民を安撫して治蹟大に著れ鄕黨之を推重す。民國元年露國皇帝よりストニ スラフ三等勳章を受らる。二年第一次正式國會の組織に當り衆望を荷つて衆議院議員に舉らる。旋て國會解散さるゝや、鄕里に歸來して復た時事を問ふを欲せず。時に出でゝ地方自治の刷新並に教育の振興に努力したり。既にして國會は復活して第二の召集を行ふに及び、重ねて北京に抵り、現に仍ほは衆議院議員に在り。

民國之精華　（傳記）莫德惠先生

Mo Te Hui, otherwise called Lien Shen, age thirty four, is a native of Shuang Cheng Hsien, the Chi Lin Hsing. He is straight-forward in character and a man of great ability. Early in life he was interested in learning in general and the new learning in particular. He went to Tientsin where he entered the Pei Yang Higher Police School from whence he was graduated. On returning home, he was the chief of the Police Bureau, and then the governor of Shuang Cheng Hsien, in which capacity, his distinguished abilities were recognized and respected by the people. In the 1st year of the Republic, he was decorated by the Zar of Russia. In the 2nd year of the Republic, he was returned for the House of Commons with a large majority. However, with the suppression of this assembly he returned to his province and never became interested of current topics. From time to time he was interested in the improvement and promotion of local education. When the second Parliament was opened, he visited Peking, resuming his Parliamentary function.

曾有翼 字子敬 歳四十五

選舉地　奉天省

籍　貫　奉天省瀋陽縣

住　址　北京象來街北銅幌子胡同

君秉性溫厚。待人以和。然喜樸質。不事浮華。舉止皆以禮自持。不苟言笑。故和藹之中。復寓有莊嚴可畏之氣象。稚齡讀書。即能深造有得。明于理義。年才弱冠。即已畢諸經旁及子史。及長。尤務求淵博廣覽羣書。其爲文崇歐蘇。而學派則調和漢宋之問。謂宜明義理以定訓釋之優劣。謂宜精考据以求古義之精微。二者兼重。不執一編。及海內維新。愈篤志研究學理。頗以改良敎育開通民智爲己任。以前淸丙午科優貢。京師大學堂師範科肄業。歷充中學堂歷史國文科敎員。蒙文學堂監督。奉天敎育總會正副會長。提學司學務議紳。奉天行省公署諮議局議員。軍署秘書。大總統府政治諮議。臨時參議院議員。民國二年被選爲衆議院議員。國會解散後。歸里從事敎育。及國會重開。始應召仍爲衆議院議員。

君秉性溫厚にして人を待つに和を以てす。然り朴實を旨として浮華を事とせず。言語舉動省な禮を以て自ら持す。故に和藹の中復た莊嚴の氣を含む。年少書を讀みて其の義理を求め、弱冠にして諸經及子史を讀過す。長ずるに及びて努めて群籍を涉獵し、其の文を作るも歐蘇を崇ぶ。海內維新に及び、益々志を立てゝ其の改良、民智の開通を以て己が任と爲したり。前淸丙午科優貢生として、京師大學師範科を修業し、中學校歷史國文科敎員、蒙文學堂監督、奉天敎育總會正副會長、提學司學務議紳、奉天省公署諮議局議廳、軍署秘書大總統府政治諮議臨時參議院議員等に任じたる事あり。民國二年當選の正式國會衆議院議員にして、國會解散後、郷里に歸臥し、約法恢復して國會重ねて開かるゝや、其の召集に應じて衆議院議員と爲る。

Mr. Tseng-Yu I, sometimes known as Tzu Chen, age forty five, is a native of Feng Tieng. He is gentle in dealing with others. Simplicity is his chief characteristic, hating the pomp and vain glory in life. He is extremely cautious. While young, he was fond of reading books and was conversant with the meaning of what he read. When things were moving in his country for the new he devoted himself for the acquisition of the up-to-date knowledge. He considered that it was his responsibility to introduce the improvement in the educational system and to developing the modern knowledge among the people. He studied in the Peking University where his speciality was in the Normal School Despartment. He occupied a series to importa t positions of which we may mention that he was a member of the adversory commitee to the president. In the 2nd year of the Republic he was returned for the House of Commons. He returned to his home when the Parliament was disolved. When it was anounced that the Parliament was to be re-opened, he went up to Peking to became a member of the House of Commons.

曾幹楨　字昭森　歲四十

選舉地　江西省

籍　貫　江西省會昌縣

住　址　北京喪家街十五號

君少慷慨有大志。童時即以天下爲己任。其先本豫章望族。文學科第。累世貴盛。年十八入庠。旋補廩貢生。分發廣東試用知縣。而君年少才美潛心學問。不樂仕也。清光緒二十七年攻入江西官立高等學校肄業。光緒三十年由江西高等學校考取。官費咨送日本留學。初入早稻田大學預科。繼入中央大學法律本科。卒業後。再入明治大學商科研究商業。武昌起義。遂回國辦理新聞事業。兼辦贛省法制專門學校。民國二年被選爲衆議院議員。

君少にして慷慨、夙に大志を抱き、即ち天下國家を以て己が任とす。其の先は豫章の望族にして文學科弟、世々盛なり。年十八庠に入り、旋て廩貢生に補せられ廣東省知縣試補と爲る。然かも年少にして才美、心を學問に潛めて致任を樂まず、光緒二十七年江西官立高等學校に入りて學び、三十年江西高等學校に於ける試驗に及第し官費を以て日本に留學す。初め早稻田大學預科に入り、繼いで中央大學法律本科を修めて卒業し、又た明治大學商科に入りて修業し、最新の學術を攻究して孜々として倦まず、造詣日に大に進み師友共に囑目して驚嘆す。時適ま武昌義を起して天下響應す。君乃ち鄉國の革命に際會して慨然として國に歸り奔走畫策す。曾て新聞事業を經營して世論を指導し、又た江西省法制專門學校を管理して後進を誘導したり。民國二年選ばれて衆議院議員と爲り。此次復た召集されて現に仍ち衆議院議員たり。

民國之精華　（傳記）曾幹楨先生

二百九十三

Mr. Tseng Kan Chen, otherwise called Chao Sen, forty years of age is a native of Hisr Chang Hsien, the Chiang Hsi Hsing. He has public mind and ambitions, and, early in life, considered it is his responsibility to work for the interest of the country. He is of a well known scholar family. At the age of eighteen he studied in the country school, but being a man of public spirit he did not care to confine himself to the government service only. In 1901, he studied in the Chiang Hsi government school, and after passing the examination he was sent to Japan at the government expense. He studied both in the Waseda and the Chuo Universities as well as in the Commercial course of the Meiji University. His progress was so striking that a great hope was attached to his future career both by his instructors and friends. As soon as the first Revolutionary movement broke out, he returned to his country. He employed the newspaper as an instrument of inspiring the public. Besides he had charge of the Chiang Hsi Hsiang law college. In the 2nd year of the Republic, he was the member of the Parliament, and when it was decided to summon the Parliament for the second time he was returned for the House of Commons, the membership of which he enjoys at present.

富 元 字惠宣 歲三十五

選舉地　奉天省
籍貫　奉天省
住址　北京打磨廠興順店

君爲人誠厚篤實。不喜浮華。生平以險約自持。痛惡奢侈。然唯自待歉薄。而厚於待人。且喜爲善舉。鄉里之困於貧者。無不曾受君惠。少年時。好爲詩詞。而不汲汲於科第。及長。遂改志求有用之學。於前清時。由優附生。入奉天省學堂修業。歷充奉天吉林師範學堂教員。入本省自治研究所肄業。得有最優等文憑。旋充鐵嶺自治研究所所長。兼充警務局科長。又充奉天北路防疫局坐辦。保爲縣丞。嗣被選爲本縣議事會議長。復選爲省議事會議員。國會成立後。由省選爲參議院議員。國會解散。歸里獨居。無所表見。及國會復活。始入都復爲議員之職。

君人と爲り誠實篤厚、浮華を喜ばず、平生勤儉自ら持して痛から奢侈淫逸を戒む。然かも人を待つに厚く、喜んで慈善を爲す。少時好んで詩文を作り、長するに及び志を改めて有用の學を求む。前清時代優附生を以て奉天省學堂に學び、後ち奉天吉林各師範學堂教師に歷充して青英の業に從事す。又た奉天省自治研究所に入りて修業し最優等の證書を授けられたり。旋て鐵嶺自治研究所々長に任ひ、警務局科長を兼ぬ。又た奉天北路防疫局事務に任ひ、縣丞の官を保薦さる。嗣で鐵嶺縣議事會議長に舉げられ、復た奉天省議事會議員に選ばる。正式國會成立に際し參議院議員に當選したり。國會解散さるヽや、鄉關に歸臥して時事を論せず、時に地方公益の事に從ふのみ。此次國會復活して重ねて召集を行ふに及び、復た北京に抵りに仍は參議院議員の職に就く。

Mr. Fu Yuan, otherwise called Hui Hsuan, thirty years of age, is a native of Tieh Shan Ling Hsien, the Feng Tieng. He is a gentleman of sincere character and high virtue. Himself being economical, he hated the life extravagance, but is ready to extend help to the sufferer. While young, he was fond of poetry, however, as he grew older, he turned his attention to more useful learning. He studied in the Feng Tieng School. Later on, he was an instructor in Chi Lin and Feng Tieng Normal Schools. Later on, he was a chief of the Police Bureau in his province, and was elected the chief of the Local Assembly. When the Parliament was summoned, he was elected a member of the Senate. On the desolution of the Parliament, he returned to his country and never talked of politics. He was only interested in local public works. When the Parliament was revived, he went up to Peking and resumed his senatorial function.

馮振驥 字遇伯 歳二十九

選舉地　湖北省

籍貫　湖北省施南府建始縣

住址　北京前門外謙安棧

君賦性溫厚和平。然又篤實不欺。動止以禮自持。為人精明強幹。當於忍耐。與人交。鯁直不阿。人有過。輒直斥不諱。人告以過、雖未盡當、必欣然謝之。少好義。喜為人鳴不平。里人有以金錢受窘者。輒解囊助之。不復望報。遠近爭稱其名。中年。慨然有志以挽回危亡自任。光緒三十二年以秀才。留學日本宏文學院。卒業後。即入明治大學法科專門肄業。宣統三年。卒業回國。學部考取法科舉人。至民國二年。湖北省第八區被選為眾議院議員。國會解散歸里不所表見。及國會重開。遂來京復為眾議院議員。

民國之精華　（傳記）　馮振驥先生

君賦性温厚和平にして篤實欺かず、言動擧止皆な禮を以て自ら持す。然かも人と爲り精明強幹にして忍耐に富む。人と交りて和藹親ひべく、仇敵と雖も疾言遽色を以て之に加へす。然かも質を尚び華を卑み、惡を憎んで善を好み、親しむべくして馴るべからざる也。幼より學を求め德を修め、長じて益々切磋琢磨の功を積みて、鄉黨之を推重す。前清の秀才を以て、光緒三十二年、日本に留學し、宏文學院に入り、卒業後ち明治大學法科に學びて宣統三年卒業す。歸國後學部の試に應じて法科舉人を授けらる。民國二年正式國會成立に際し湖北省第八區より選ばれて眾議院議員と爲る。國會解散後、鄉里に歸りて韜晦自重し、五年國會復活して再び召集を行ふに及び、遂に之に應じて上京し、復た仍は眾議院議員と爲る。

Mr. Feng Chen Chi, otherwise called Yu pai, twenty nine years of age, is a native of Chian shih, Shih Nan Fu, Hu Pei Province. In nature he is quiet and gentle, and can never be guilty of deceitfulness. He is a strict observer of etiquette either in words or deeds. Having clear brain and robust constitution, he is full of patience. Even toward the implacable enemy, he never shows any hasty words or anger. He prefers substance to men external. He hates the evil, but loves the good. He is friendly, but could not become too familier. While young, he was an ardent scholar, but as he grew older, he became fond of hard application and study. On these scores, he was highly respected by his friends. In 1906, he came to Japan to complete his education. He graduated from the Meiji University in 1911. In the second year of the Republic when the Parliament was formally summoned, he was elected a member of the House of Commons. When Yuanshi-kai crushed the Parliament, he returned to his home where he kept himself aloof from politics. When the Parliament was restored, he went to Peking where he was chosen again as the member of the House of Commons.

景耀月 字太昭 歲三十五

選舉地　山西省

籍貫　山西省芮城縣

住址　北京安定門大街餌胡同

君天資英邁。爲人仁厚。自幼好學聰穎。弱冠有文名。及長。智德兼修。遠近敬重之。光緒三十年。由山西大學堂派送日本留學。旋入同盟會。宣統元年留日學生全體組織中國財政研究會。爲正會長。宋敎仁副之。旋發刊國報雜誌。倡言國命。二年日本大學法科畢業。辛亥革命。曾任山西軍政府代表。被選爲各省代表聯合會議長。改任南京參議院議員。旋任敎育次長。政府北移。被任總府政治高等顧問。正式國會成立。被選爲衆議院議員。國民黨一部改組政友會。被舉爲理事長。國會解散後。即偕同志。開辦東邊墾地公司。餘暇兼著成景芮城詩集三十五卷。帝制發生。與同志致函張作霖。運動獨立。事洩不成。嗣又被新華宮暗殺案嫌疑。旋黎氏繼任。主張恢復約法國會。籌辦北京議員通信處。及至國會重開。仍就議員職。

君天資英邁にして氣宇豪爽、人と爲り仁厚にして品格絕高なり。幼より聰穎、弱冠文名あり。長じて智德兼備す、蓋し少壯政治家中の天才なり。光緒三十年、山西大學堂より選派されて日本に留學す。同盟會に入り、全部の留學生間に中國財政研究會の組織あるや、其の正會長に舉らる。自ら國報雜誌を發刊して革命を皷吹す。宣統二年日本大學法科を卒業して歸國す。第一革命當時、山西軍政府代表に任じ、南京代表會議長と爲り、又た南京參議院議員と爲り、旋て敎育次長に任ず。南北統一後、總統府高等顧問と爲る。後ち衆議院議員に當選す。國民黨の一部と政友會を組織し理事長と爲る。國會解散後、東邊墾地公司を創設し、餘暇成景芮城詩集三十五卷を著す。帝制問題發生するや、張作霖に密書を送りて獨立を謀り、嗣で又た袁世凱暗殺案の嫌疑に座したり。黎氏繼任後北京議員通信處を發起す。國會復活後、仍は衆議院議員たり。

Mr. Ching Yao Yueh, otherwise known as Tai Chao, thirty five years of age, is a native of Jui Cheng, Shan hsi province. He is a gentleman of heroic temperament and broadminded. When young, he won a certain literary fame. He is a most promising politician of the time. In 1897, he was sent to Japan from the Shan hsi University. While stayed in Japan he was deeply interested in inspiring his country men with revolutionary ideas. He was appointed the head of the Association formed with such an object in view. In 1910, he graduated from the Nihon Law University. At the time of the Revolution, he was the president of the assembly of the Nanking representatives, and also a member of the Senate. When the South and the North were united, he was appointed the high class adviser to the president, and was returned for the House of Commons. With a section of the National Party, he formed a party of the political friend, of which he became he tchief director. When the Parliament was suppressed, he was interested in public enterprise, and in his leisure, he published a collection of Chinese poems: When the movement for the Imperial regime took place, he was suspected of the high treason against the life of Yuanshi-kai. When the new president was elected, and the Parliament was restored, he became a member of the House of Commons.

程　鐸　字振之　歲三十二

選舉地　江西省

籍　貫　江西省都陽

住　址　北京爛熳胡同三十一號

君秉性惇篤。而意志堅強。不喜隨同流
俗。自幼聰穎善讀。弱冠有文名。前清
時。由江西巡撫考取。為出洋學生。派
送日本留學。由東京早稻田大學豫科。
入政治經濟科。畢業歸國。歷充江西官
立法政專門學校主任教員。兼學監。及
江西官立地方自治研究所教員。法官
養成所教員。高等巡警學校教員。復與
同學創辦江西私立法政專門學校。任
該校學監兼教員。辛亥。改建民國。任
江西軍政府外務局（後改為交涉局）局
長。民國元年。當選為江西臨時省議會
議員。閉會後。充江西法官考試襄校
官。選舉國會議員時。當選為衆議院議
員。國會解散後。復歸里擔任江西各
法政專門學校教員。兼充律師。被選為
南昌律師公會會長。及國會復活。遂入
京。仍就衆議院議員職。兼在京師地方

君秉性惇厚にして朴實、意志また強固にして流俗に同ず
るを喜ばず、幼より聰穎善く談じ弱冠文名あり。前清時
代江西巡撫より選拔されて日本に留學す。早稻田大學豫
科に修業して政治經濟科に入り業を畢へて歸國す。江西
官立法政專門學校主任教員兼學監及び江西官立地方自治
研究所教員、法官養成所教員、高等巡警學校教員等の職
に歷充す。復た同學と謀りて江西私立法政專門學校を創
設し、同校學監兼教員に任ず。辛亥の歲浙江獨立するや、

江西軍政府外務局々長に任す。民國成立するや江西臨時
省議會議員に舉げらる。閉會後、江西法官試驗委員と
なり。正式國會議員選舉に際し衆議院議員に當選す。國
會解散後、後た鄕里に歸りて江西各法政專門學校教員に
任じ、兼ねて辯護士を業とし南昌辯護士公會々長に推さ
る。國會復活するに及び遂に復た入京して仍は衆議院議

登錄執行律師職務。

民國之精華　（傳記）　程鐸先生

Mr. Cheng To, otherwise called Chen Chi, thirty two years of age, is a native of Chiang Hsi Hsing. He is a gentleman of simple life and strong will, always keeping above the men of ordinary caribre. While young, he was noted for his literary attainment. In the previous Chinese regime, he was sent to Japan by the government. He entered the Waseda University and took the course in political science and economy. On return home he occupied very important posts such as the professorship of the Chiang Hsi Government Law School as well as many other important schools. He established a private law college which he became the director. When the Revolution took place, he was appointed the chief of the Foreign Department of the Chiang Hsi military head quarter. On the establishment of the Republic he was a member of the Local Assembly and Committee of the Examination of Judges. He was elected a member of the House of Commons. When the regislative body was shut down, he went back to his native province and became an instructor of the law school, besides practising law. When the Parliament was re-opened, he was elected a member of the Parliament.

程塋度　字百高

選舉地　四川省

籍　貫　四川省

住　址　北京西罩奧隆大院

君秉性剛正。不隨俗好。然居心仁厚。常喜周急貧困。與人交。和婉可親。見人有過。恆于無人處規勸之。示以利害。故人多爲所感動。早歲篤志舊學。及長。改志求攻新學。遂東渡留學日本。光緒三十四年。由日本明治大學專門部畢業歸國。被選爲四川諮議局議員。歷任本省官私立法政學校敎員。民國元年。曾任四川都督府參贊。兼籌備國會省會事務所主任委員。旋由省議會。當選爲正成國會參議院議員。到院後。復被選爲憲法起草委員會委員。國會解散後歸里。閉門戶不出。及共和復活。國會重開。遂來京。仍爲參議院議員。

君秉性剛直にして然かも居心仁厚なり。少年好んで經史を讀み、長じて新學を攻究す。遂に笈を負ふて巴蜀の境を出で遠く東海を越へて日本に留學し、研磋幾春秋、光緒三十四年明治大學專門部を卒業して錦衣歸鄕す。選ばれて四川諮議局議員と爲り。又た四川省內宮私立法政各學校の敎員に歷充して育英の業に從事す。民國成立して共和の新政を肇むるや、民國元年四川都督府參事官に聘せられ、國會參議院議員に當選す。院に到りて後ち憲法起草委員會事務所主任委員を兼ねたり。旋て正式國會參議院議員に當選す。既にして袁民死し黎氏出で、約法を改正して國會重ねて召集を行ふに及び、君また出で〻北京に入り現に仍ほ參議院議員と爲る。國會解散さるゝや、鄕里に歸省して地方公盆の事に預る、

Mr. Cheng Ying To, otherwise known as Pai Kao is a native of Hsi Chuan. He was straight-foreward in character and full of humanity in dealing with others. While young, he took a great delight in studying the history, and as he grew older he was interested in new learning. He crossed the eastern sea and came over to Japan. In 1908 he graduated from the Meiji University and went back to his country. He was elected a member of the Hsi Chiang Adversary Board, besides teaching in the law schools of the province. When the Republican regime was commenced, he was appointed the adviser to the governor general of the Hsi Chiang and was on the Committee preparing for the opening up of the Parliament. Shortly after he was elected a member of the Senate and was on the committee of drafting the constitution. When the Parliament was shut down, he returned to his native country being keenly interested in public works of the province. With the death of Yuanshi-kai, the new president summoned the Parliament, there upon he entered the Peking and was elected a member of the Senate.

程崇信 字載傳

選舉地　湖南省
韓　貫　湖南省衡陽縣
住　址　北京珠巢街南頭第二家

君天資聰慧。爲人篤厚。長于幹濟之才
自幼好讀。受業王湘綺門下。通詩書三
禮公羊春秋之學。五十後號蚵鶯山民。
其文采風度。超出凡流。由前清府學廩
膳生。選授辰州瀘溪縣教諭。中癸已恩
科。本省鄉試舉人。甲午會試挑取謄錄
國史館。膽錄官分部學習郎中。歸官陝
西延安府知府。在任候補道。加二品
銜。軍機處存記。歸充陝西洋務局。善
後局。營務處。學務處。課吏館。督諫兵
備處。西潼鐵路局。禁烟調縂公所。各
提調總辦。　延長油督辦。　兩等師範學
校。法政學堂監督。國收商州三原釐稅
局務。民國二年被選爲眾議院議員。國
會解散後。三年簡任平政院肅政史。四
年因中日條約喪失國權。上書力爭。感
慣辭職。五年重開議會。遂又應召。仍
爲眾議院議員。

君天資聰慧にして人と爲り篤厚、幹濟の才に長す。幼よ
り讀を好み、業を王湘綺の門下に受け、詩書三禮公羊春
秋の學に通す。其の文采風度蚵鶯山民と號す。五十後
に凡流に超出す。前清府學廩膳生より辰州瀘溪縣教諭に
選拔され、癸已の科に及第し、湖南省鄉試の舉人となり、
甲午の會議に國史館に謄錄され、郎中と爲る。陝西延安
府知事、在任候補道臺に任じ二品銜を加へ、軍議處存記
に叙せらる。陝西洋務局、善後局、營務處、課吏館、督
諫兵備處、西潼鐵道局、禁烟檢査所等の各堤調總辦に歷
充し、延長石油督辦、兩等師範學校、法政學堂監督に歷
任し、商州三原釐稅局に務を監理したり。民國二年正式
國會衆議院議員に當還す。國會解散後、民國三年平政院
肅政史にに任せられ、四年日支交涉傺約の歸結に反對し
て上書して職を辭し。五年國會復活するに及び、遂に復
た召集に應じて衆議院議員と爲る。

Mr. Cheng chung hsin, otherwise known as Chi Chuan, is a native of Hu nan province. Bright in temperament and noble in personality, he distinguished himself in learning. When young, he verse well in classical teaching. His diction and style in writing are superior to any of his contemporaries. In the previous Chinese regime, he successfully passed the examination and occupied important government posts; He was an instructor of the normal school, the school of politics. He was also an official in the government taxation office and the opiam prohibiting institution. In the 2nd year of the Republic he was returned for the House of Commons. When the Parliament was disolved by Yuanshi-kai, he was an official in the goverment, but resigned it because he opposed to the terms of Japan China treaty. When the Parliament was restored he was returned for the House of Commons.

民國之精華　（傳記）　程崇信先生

賀廷桂　字馥階　歲三十八

運動地　安徽省

籍　貫　安徽省宿松縣

住　址　北京北極巷皖潛劉底

君于光緒三十年。以主事籤分戶部。入計學館肄業。歷充津海關報銷覆核員。司務廳收發員。三十二年。經巡警部奏調。補授外城警廳警官。歷充行政司法處股長。左四區區長。官統元年因功由民政部奏獎知府分發貴州。特旨隨帶加四級。二年四月。到貴州。歸充審檢廳籌辦處提調。提法司署總務科長。礦業學堂監督。查辦法政學堂特派員。貴陽發審局提調。籌辦法官考試處總辦。奏派法官考試提調官。提法司屬司考試襄校官。審檢廳書記官。考試主試官。十一月。奉旨簡放貴州高等檢察廳檢察長。辛亥。貴州起義時。貴州公推為該省都督。此即辭職回籍。民國元年。司法部派充稅務廳辦事員。旋經江西都督調充南昌檢察廳撿察長。二年正月。被選爲衆議院議員。國會解散後。歸田不聞時事。及此次共和復活。國會重開。遂來京仍供舊職云。

君光緒三十年主事を以て戶部に分れ、計學館に入り修業す。天津海關報銷覆核員、司務廳收發員に歷充し。三十二年巡警部より調せられて外城警察廳官となり、行政司法處各科長、左四區々長に歷任し。宣統元年功に因り、民政部より知府に保屬され貴州に分たる。二年四月貴州に到りて審檢廳籌辦處提調、提法司署總務科長。礦業學校監督、法政學校査辦特派員。貴陽發審局提調、提法司屬官、試驗襄校監督、法政學校查辦特派員。提法司屬官、試驗襄驗準備處總辦、法官試驗委員提調。提法司屬官、試驗襄校官、審檢廳書記官試驗委員等の職に當り、十一月旨を奉じ貴州高等檢察廳檢察長となる。辛亥革命に際し貴州義を起すの初め、推されて同省都督となり。旋て辭職して鄉里に歸る。民國元年司法部より總務廳事務官に命せられ、旋て江西都督より南昌檢察廳檢察長に聘せらる。二年正月衆議院議員に當選す。國會解散後、鄉里に歸りて時事を聞かず。國會復活後出でゝ仍は衆議院議員たり。

Mr. Chia Ting Kuei, otherwise known as Pan Chieh, is a native of Sung Hsien, An Hui Sheng. Under the previous Chinese regime, he was appointed to occupy comparatively important positions such as the police office as well as the customs house, while in 1909 he was recommended to the Civil Department. In his province he was the committee of various kinds—that of the examination of judges as well as the inspector of mining schools etc. He was also the chief of the public prosecutor of the province. In the first year of the Republic, he was an active member in the Justice Department. In the 2nd year he was elected a member of the House of Commons, in which capacity he contributed a great deal for the promotion of the interest of the country. When Yuanshi-kai shut down the Parliament he returned to his country, and showed no interest what ever in current topics. As soon as the Parliament was revive1 he was elected a member thereof, a position which he now holds.

賀昇平 字瑞宇 歲三十四

選舉地　河南省

籍貫　河南省許昌縣

住址　北京西河沿

君性嚴重寡言。博覽強識。工古文辭。通英日德三國文學。留學日本早稻田大學部政治經濟科。辛亥武昌起義返國。為滬軍都督府軍事科員。時滬上組織威武軍。調辦軍需事宜。軍隊出發。轉餉運械。往來上海燕湖等處。君皆具有苦力。民國元年。威武軍至貴州。清帝已退位。共和告成。遂辭去軍需職。旋豫督張聘為河南法政學校監督。未就。二年春。被選為眾議院議員。國會解散後。充新聞記者。以其暇。涉獵經史子集。勞及道藏禪悅之書。以自娛。五年。國會重開。仍為出席眾議院議員。

君性嚴格にして寡言、博覽強記にして古文辭に工に、日英獨の三國文に通曉す。曾て日本に留學して早稻田大學部政治經濟科に修業す。辛亥革命に際し歸國して上海に赴き、滬軍都督府軍事科員と爲る。時に上海に於て威武軍を組織するや君軍需事宜を處辦す。軍隊出發して粮餉を運び軍器を送り、上海燕湖間を往來して具さに勞苦を嘗む。民國元年貴州に至れば清帝既に位を退きて共和告

成る。遂に軍需の職を辭し、旋て張河南都督より河南法政學校監督に聘せられたるも未だ就かず。民國二年正式國會議員選舉に當りて眾議院議員と爲る。國會解散後は新聞記者として操觚の業に從事し。其の餘暇を以て經史及び諸子の書を涉獵し、旁た道藏禪悅の書をも讀みて自ら娛む。五年國會再び開院するに及び、遂に又た出でゝ眾議院議員たり。

Mr. Chia Sheng Ping, otherwise known as Jui Yu, is a native of Hsu Chang Hsien, the Ho Nan Hsieng. He is a man of strict temperament and spare of words. He has a wonderful memory and verses well in Japanese, English, and German. He came over to Japan where he studied law and political economy in the Waseda University. On the outbreak of the Revolution, he returned to Shanghai, where he attended to the military supplies of the Revolutionary Army. In the 1st year of the Republic, he had a pleasure of witnessing the abdication of the Emperor of China and the formation of the Republic. He resigned at once the military service, and the post of the directorship of the Ho Nan law school was offered to him. Before he accepted it, he was elected a member of the House of Commons. After the desolution of the assembly, he became a journalist, and any time at his desposal, he employed for his own education. When the Parliament was held for the second time he bceame a member of the House of Commons.

賀贊元 字爾翊

選舉地　江西省

籍　貫　江西省永新縣

住　址　北京棉花五條西頭路南

君性質明敏。氣宇開闊。自幼好學。過
目不忘。於書無所不讀。時人稱爲博學
多能之士。每憤國事日非。懷慨悲歌
無不激動左右。然接以爲徒托空談無
裨實際。於是勵志求學。曾前清舉人。
以保送會考。任郵傳部主事。在江西省
辦理公益歷充全省敎育總會會長。自
治研究會副會長。法政學堂庶務長諮
議局籌辦處選舉科科長。地方自治籌
辦法制科科長。諮議局成立。被選爲
議員。辛亥革命。民國元年任江西政事
部長。二年被選爲衆議院議員。國會
解散。仍奔滬上。留心國事。及國會重
開。遂來京。仍爲衆議院議員。

君性質明敏にして氣宇宏潤なり、幼より學を好みて過目
悉く忘れず、博覽にして强記なり。曾て前淸の舉人を以
て會試に送られ、郵傳部主事に任す。江西省に在りて公
益事業に盡瘁して功あり。江西全省の敎育總會々長、自
治研究會副會長、法政學校庶務長等の職に歷任す。又た
諮議局準備處の選舉科長に任じ、地方自治準備處の法制
科長に任じたる事あり。諮議局成立するや選ばれて諮議
局議員と爲る。　辛亥第一革命の事起りて民國の樹立に際
し、江西省都督府政事部長に任ず。民國二年正式國會衆議
院議員に當選す。國會解散されて仍ち上海に赴きて國事
に奔走し、同志と共に帝制に反對して大局の恢復を圖る。
五年雲南義を唱へて天下驟然として起り、袁氏死して黎
氏大總統を繼任し、約法を復して再び國會を召集するや、
即ち又た北京に抵りて現に衆議院議員の職に就きたり。

Mr. Chia Tsau Yuan, otherwise called Ni I, is a native of Chiang Hsi. He is a gentleman of broad and comprehensive views. He distinguished himself for his wonderful retentive faculty. In the previous Chinese regime, he passed the examination and was appointed the head of the Communication Bureau. In his province he was keenly interested in the execution of works of public nature. He was the president of the Seneral meeting of educators in his province, the vice-president of Selfrule Investigation Society and director of the Business Department of the Law College. He was also the chief of the Election Department of the Local Assembly. When that assembly was formed he, was appointed the member thereof. When the Republic was formed, subsequent to the Revolution, he was the chief of the Political Bureau of the Chiang Hsi Government Seneral. In the 2nd year of the Republic he was elected a member of the House of Commons. After the shutting up of the Parliament, he went to Shanghai and opposing the Imperial Movement he worked for the grand course. With the death of Yuanshi-kai the new president decided to summon the Parliament. Whereupon he at once resumed the Parliamentay function by going up to Peking.

溫雄飛　

選舉地　廣東省
籍　貫　廣東省廣州府臺山縣
住　址　北京前絲公園廣州呂邑館

君生長美洲。畢業於高等學校。方謀入嘉里寬厄州立大學。會革命論興。君遂輟業。首創同盟會於美洲。兼投身操觚。藉資倡導。未幾。應檀香山某報之聘為總編輯。尋又轉任自由新報總編輯。辛亥武昌首義。乃代表歸粵。駐寗滬間者兩月。遂歸粵。被舉為粵臨時省會代議士。尋被舉為副議長。民國二年。被選為參議院議員。時黨爭劇烈。君作「公論」以明志。停職後。閉戶讀書。專事纂述。究心平民生計。三年秋。供職全國煤油礦處。巡勘陝西礦場。來往秦晉隴豫間。藉察民生計。停職後。所著有「平民生計問題」「民生主義綱要」「儲蓄海」「印度亡國痛史」「英國植民政治改攷」諸書。均未刊行。稿藏於家。及西南起義。君間關歸粵。與同志等謀於廣州。擬以粵應。計畫甫定。即被逮旋脫險至香港。為再舉之謀。嗣因共和已復。遂來京仍為議員。

民國之精華　（傳記）　溫雄飛先生

君米國に生長し、高等學堂を卒業す。會ま革命の論興る。乃ち米國に任りて同盟會を創立し、同時に身を操觚に投じ、桑港某新聞社の聘に應じて編輯長と為り、又た自由新報編輯長に轉任す。辛亥の年、武昌義を首むるや、乃ち國に歸り南京上海の間に駐ること兩月、遂に廣東に歸り。舉げられて廣東臨時省曾代議士と為り、副議長と為る。民國二年、參議院議員と為る。時に黨爭激烈、君「公論」を作りて志を明にす。停職の後、戶を閉ぢて書を讀み、專ら著述に從事し、心を平民の生計に傾く。三年の秋、全國煤油礦處に奉職し。陝西礦場を巡勘し。陝西山西甘肅河南の間を來往し、平民 生計を視察す。徐眼「平民生計問題」「民生主義綱要」「儲蓄海」「印度亡國痛史」「英國植民政治攷」を著す。未だ刊行せず。同志等と廣州に謀り、廣東を以て應ぜんと欲す。計畫甫めて定り、直に逮捕せらる。險を脱して香港に至り、再舉の謀を為す。共和恢復の後。上京して又た議員と為る。

Mr. Wen Hsiung Fei, aged thirty four, is a native of Tai Shan, the Kuang Tung Hsing. He was educated in America being a graduated of a college there. When the revolutionary movement broken out, he joined the movement in America, and had charge of various news papers of which he became the editor. When Gang's movement was started in China, he returned to his home, and became the member of the Special Kuantung Assembly of which he became the Vice-president. In the 2nd year of the Republic he was elected a member of the House of Commons. He published a magazine in which he gave expression to his ordent and burning beelings. When this was closed, he spent his days in reading books and in his own education. He remained always the friends of the people. His main field of activity was Hsia Hsi Kan Tai districts. Among his numerous literary works we may mention such as the Life problem, the outlives of Democracy, the sea of Savings, the India and Its Decline " the British Colonial Policy " etc. In the Revolutionary movement, he was about to be arrested in Kuantung from which he saned himself running away to Hongkong. On the Restoration of peace, he went up to Peking, became the member of the Parliament.

溫世霖　字支英

選舉地　直隷省

籍貫　直隷省天津縣宜興埠村

住址　北京象坊橋路北二十號

君天資聰慧絕倫。而稟性剛直。爲同儕
所敬畏。年十六。投考北洋海軍駕駛學
堂。旋因腿疾退學。庚子。創辦兩等小
學。溫氏女學。時新書室。醒俗人鏡兩
服館。普育女學校。女子職業學校。女子
演談會。幼稚園。並與同志創辦直隷自
治研究總所。憲政討論會。實業公會。
國會請願同志會。曾被舉爲天津縣議
事會議員。歸充國會請願代表。宣統二
年四次國會請願。被舉爲全國學生會
會長。卒被清政府逮捕。謫戍新疆。到戍
所後。倡辦實業。并組織移民會。大遭
迪化官府之忌。擬改發西藏。適武漢革
命事起。君與同志約期起義。被舉爲都
督。因反機不密。失敗。旋由西伯利亞
鐵路逃歸。任同盟會天津交通部部長。
民國二年。被舉爲衆議院議員。國會解
散後避禍山東。及國會重開。遂入京
仍就議員職。

君天資聰慧にして稟性剛直、同儕の畏敬する所と爲る。十
六歳北洋海軍機關學校に入りしも疾を以て退學す。庚子
の歳兩等小學校、溫氏女學校、時新書室、醒俗人鏡兩服館、
普育女學校、女子職業學校、女子演說會、幼稚園等を創
設經營し、又た同志と商りて直隷自治研究總所、憲政討
論會、實業公會、國會請願同志會等を創設し、曾て天津
縣議事會議員に舉げられ、國會請願同志會の代表に推さる。宣統
二年四次國會請願運動に際し全國學生會々長となりし

が、清政府に逮捕されて新疆に謫せらる。戍所に在りて
實業の振興を圖り、移民會を組織す。又た迪化府官憲に
忌まれ、改めて西藏に謫せられんとす。適ま武漢革命の
事起り、君同志と獨立を計りて都督に推されたるが、事
洩れて敗れ、西比利亞鐵道によりて遁れ歸り、同盟會天
津交通部々長に任ず。民國二年衆議院議員に當選し。國
會解散後禍を山東に避け、今復た出でし衆議院議員た
り。

Mr. Wen Yeh Lin, otherwise known as Chih Ying is a native of Tientsin, Chi Lin Hsing.
He was known for his precious learning. At the age of 16, he entered the naval engineering college,
but on account of ill health he had to leave the school. He had charge of various schools
especially intended for the education of women and children. When the Revolutionary movement was
in the air, he was connected with various societies formed for the purpose of promoting the interests of
the Revolutionists. In the 1910, he became the president of the Students Association in China but being
arrested by the Chinese government he was sent as exile. However nothing daunted while in exile
he organized the colonization society. He was about to be transfered to Thibet when the Revolution
broke out. He worked for the independence of Tientsin but his plan was frustrated so that he escaped
by the Siberian railway. He was appointed the head of the Communication Department of Tientsin. In
the 2nd year of the Republic, he was returned for the House of Commons. When the Legislative body
was shut down, he went to Shangtung where he remained until he was elected a member of the Parliament, which was opened by the new president.

傅家銓 字可堂 歲五十五

選舉地　浙江省
籍貫　浙江鎮海縣
住址　北京小甜水井鎮海館

君爲前清附貢生。太常寺博士。自幼倜儻不羣。見地迥異流俗。然又平易近人。不故爲奇特。自幼好讀書。弱冠即有文名。藏書三萬卷。以少有其軒。及長。慷慨好行公益。潛靈巖支河。辦愈愚小學。俱出千金以爲創。宣統辛亥。被選爲地方自治副董。設借錢局以利民。又平糶米價。已貧不足。則求貸於人以充去。再選爲縣議會議員。不赴。民國元年冬。被選爲衆議院議員。癸丑解散後。歸隱山林不問世事唯日與交好飲酒賦詩。以自娛。著有結感百詠。鎮海王侍讀榮商近輯蛟川耆舊詩補十二卷。手爲校刊。並助資付印。流覽之餘。成少有軒近體詩三卷。國會恢復。君欲終與政治界脫離。將不應召。友朋强其出並責以大義。始北上仍就議員之職。

君は前清の附貢生を以て大常博士と爲る。幼より倜儻不羈、見地迥に流俗と異る。然又平易人に近づき、故らに奇を以て衒はず。幼より讀書を好み、弱冠即ち文名あり。長ずるに及びて慷慨好んで公益の事に力を致し、靈巖支河を疏通し、愈愚小學を創辦するや、倶に巨資を投じた り。宣統辛亥の歲、選ばれて地方自治會の副董と爲り、借錢局を設けて民を利し、又た米價を調節す。民國元年冬、衆議院議員會議員に選ばれたるも赴かず。再び縣議

民國之精華　（傳記）　傳家銓先生

Mr. Chuan Chia Chuan, otherwise called Ko Tang, fifty five years of age, is a native of Chin Hai Hsien, Chi Chiang. While young, he was full of independent spirit, and his views were above those of the common people. He was a copious reader of books and gained literary fame while young. He was keenly interested in public affairs. In building the canal or in establishing schools, he made a large investment. In 1911, he was appointed to the Vice-President of the Local Civic Association. He established the many lending bureau to the benefit of the people and adjusted the price of rice. In the 1st year of the Republic, he was appointed to a member of the House of Commons. When the regislative assembly was suppressed, he returned to his home where he quietly spent his time with his friends. At his leisure, he wrote many poems, some of which were published. He was desirous of giving up his political connection forever, but at the urgent request of his friends, he complied with the summon and was elected to a member of the House of Commons, the position he holds in the present moment.

傳諧 字友于 歲四十四

選舉地　西藏
籍貫　四川省華陽
住址　北京騾馬市大街泰安棧

君爲人厚重自持。不苟言笑。然心思活潑。富于經營之才。與人交。和婉可親。喜怒不形於色。以前清廣東補用知縣。於光緒二十六年游歷南洋各島。考查商務實業等事。前後共歷兩年之久。旋赴日本東西京調查商業鑛務。歸國後。至粵。組織宏厚鑛務公司。集資五十萬元。開辦廉州石頭埠煤鑛。均仿西法。開至井桶三十餘丈。適值土匪起事。以致中止。宣統元年。組織同興公司。承辦廣東省城長隄。建築工程馬路千餘丈。隄岸六百餘丈。兩年内。一律告成。民國成立由西藏選舉會。選爲參議院議員。國會解散後。仍從事於商業實業之經營。迄至國會重開。始來京復爲參議院議員。

君人と爲り厚重自ら持し、輕々しく言笑せず。然かも心思活溌にして經營の才に富む。人と交りて和婉親むべく喜怒色に形さざる也。前清時代廣東省の補用知縣にして光緒二十六年南洋各島を歷游し、商務及び實業等の事を調査すること二年、旋て日本に赴きて商業及び鑛業を調査す。歸國後、廣東に抵りて宏厚鑛務公司を組織し、資本金五十萬圓を以て廉州石頭埠の炭鑛を採掘したるも適ま土匪事を起して中止したり。宣統元年同興公司を組織して廣東省城の長隄工事を請負ひ、車馬路及び隄岸工事を竣りたり。民國二年正式國會成立に際し、北京に開かれたる西藏選舉會より舉げられて參議院議員に當選す。國會解散後、仍ほ實業に從事す。國會復活するに及びて又た召集に應じて入京し、參議院議員と爲る。

Mr. Fu hsieh, sometimes called Yu che, age forty four, is a native of Hua yang, Hsichuan province. He is a man of deep thoughts, few words, and yet full of practical ability. In 1900, he travelled through South Sea Islands with a purpose of investigating commercial and industrial condition in which he spent two years. Then he went to Japan and was interested in business and running. On return to his country, he organized a company with a capital of half a million yen for the purpose of working a coal mine, but it was suspended on account of the bandits trouble. In the 2nd year of the Republic, when the Parliament was summoned, he was elected to a member of the Senate. After the dissolution of the Parliament, he went back to his business career. When the Parliament was restored, he was again elected to a member of the Senate.

傅師說　字仲華　歲四十

選舉地　浙江省
籍貫　浙江省瑞安縣
住址　北京南橫街浙江會館

君賦性敦厚溫和。與人交。和靄可親。雖仇敵亦假以顏色。不出惡聲。然爲人篤實不欺。動止以禮自持。雖長於交際。而無形中自有不可侵越之界限。曾末嘗曲己從人。較之碌碌追隨俗者。自屬大相逕廷。自幼好讀。喜博覽羣書。任意所之以爲快。而不屑規規然從事于科擧之業。故其讀書。純以至主觀判斷是非。而不局于習俗之成見。曾前清以貢生浙江官立法政學校畢業。宣統二年。考取法官。民國四年第四屆知事試驗取列乙等。分發江蘇任用。現充衆議院議員。

君賦性敦厚溫和にして人と交りて和靄親むべし。人と爲り爲實欺かず、動止禮を以て自ら持し、交際に長ずと雖も無形の中侵越すべからざる限界あり。曾て未だ己を曲げて人に從はず。幼より學を好み、博く群書を閱して意の向ふ所に任せて快とす爲す。而して矩々然として科擧の業に從はざる也。故に其の讀書は主觀を以て是非を判斷し、習俗の成見に囚れず。曾て前清の貢生を以て浙江官立法政學校を卒業す。宣統二年法官登用試驗に合格したり。民國二年正式國會議員選擧に當選したり。國會解散後、民國四年縣知事登用試驗に及第して乙等に列し江蘇省に分たる。五年國會恢復するや、君仍ち其の召集に應じて入京し、現に衆議院議員の職に在り。

民國之精華　（傳記）傅師說〃先生

Mr. Fu Shih Shuo, otherwise known as Chung Hua, age forty, is a native of Juian hsien, Che Chiang hsing. In dealing with others he distinguished himself in his gentleness and sincerity. While he is sociable in every respect he has a sphere in which he is morally superior and inaccessible. He was fond of learning when young, and spent much of his time in reading books. He formed his own judgement and not subjected to any traditional influence. He graduated from the State Law College under the previous Chinese regime. In 1910 he successfully passed the public examination for judges and in the 2nd year of the Republic he was elected a member of the House of Commons, in which capacity he distinguished himself. However, when the Parliament was suppressed by Yuan shi-kai, he left Peking for his native province until the re-opening of the Parliament, recalled him to the resumption of his duty as the member of the House of Commons.

傅鴻銓　字幼宜　歲四十

選舉地　四川省

籍　貫　四川省萬縣

住　址　北京山西街藝府會館

君賦性敦厚溫和。與人交。和靄可親。雖仇敵亦假以顏色。不出惡聲。然爲人篤實不欺。動止以禮自持。雖長於交際。而無形中自有不可侵越之界限。曾未嘗曲已從人。較之碌碌追隨俗者。自屬大相逕庭。自幼好讀。喜博覽羣書。任意所之以爲快。故其讀書。純以至主規判之是非。而不局于習俗之成見。及海內維新。愈立志求有用之學。於新書無所不觀。以前清光緒壬寅科舉人。丁未科會考官吏部主事。是年肄業京師法政學堂別科。民國二年被選爲衆議院議員。國會解散後。歸里不談政事。及國會重開。始應召。仍爲衆議院議員。

傅鴻銓先生

君賦性敦厚にして溫和、人と交りて和靄親むに堪へたり。人と爲り篤實にして欺かず、言動舉止皆な禮を以て自ら持す。交際に長ずと雖も、無形の中自ら優越すべからざる限界あり、未だ曾て已を曲げて人に從はざる也。幼より學を好みて孜々として倦まず。博く群籍を涉獵して思想豐富見解新穎なり。前清光緒壬寅の歲舉人に及第し、丁未の歲會考に及第して東部主事の官を授けらる。同年京師法政學校別科を卒業す。民國二年正式國會の成立に際し選ばれて衆議院議員と爲る。正論を把持し、公議を主張し、立法府に列して國家建設の大業を翼贊する所ありたり。國會解散後、鄉里に韜晦して暫らく時事を談せず。國會復活するに及び、再び其の召集に應じて入京し仍ほ衆議院議員と爲る。

Mr. Fu Hung Chuan, otherwise known as Yui, age forty, is a native of Wan, Hsi Chuan hsing. He is a gentle and friendly in associating with others. He regulates himself with strict rules of ettiquet. Holding as he does above the men in common level, he never kotows any one at the expense of his own personality. While young, he had always been a copious reader, which contributed to the rich stock of his knowledge. In the previous Chinese regime, he successfully passed the civil service examination, in 1907 he was appointed to the government position of note. The year following, he was graduated from the law college of Peking. In the second year of the Republic, when the Parliament was opened, he was elected to a member of the House of Commons. With his just opinions and his efforts, the legislature assembly contributed a great deal to the state towards the execution of her duty. At the collapse of the Parliament, he returned to his native province, and talked as more of politics. When the Parliament resumed its duty, he was elected a member of the House of Commons, the position he now occupies.

湯

漍　字斐予　歳三十六

選舉地　江西省
籍貫　江西省
住址　北京順治門大街路東

君秉性孤介耿直。而天資聰慧。悟性敏
捷。少年讀書。即以大器自期。喜靜座
深思。探求眞義。而不屑規規然從事於
章句詞藻之學。居恒以嚴謹自持。言動
舉止。皆確有規則。前淸時。以癸卯科
舉人。留學日本。入慶應義塾。光緒三
十三年。復渡美。入墨西根大學。宣統
三年。卒業歸國。適辛亥革命。方當組
織臨時政府之際。君被推爲江西代表。
旋被選爲南京參議院議員。並主撰民
國報。正式國會成立。被選爲衆議院議
員。兼任憲法起草委員會委員長。先
是。民國元年。君曾與同盟派盡力于國
民黨之發起。及二次革命後。復聯合他
派優秀人物組織民憲黨。居無何。袁氏
以非法停止國會。君遂匿迹韜光靜觀
世變。及國會復活。遂應召仍爲議員。

民國之精華　（傳記）　湯漍先生

君秉性孤介にして耿直。天資聰慧にして敏捷なり。少年
書を讀みて即ち大器を以て自ら期す。尤も思索を喜びて
眞義を探求し、徒らに章句詞藻の形式に拘泥するを申ふ。
居常謹嚴самに自ら持し、言動舉止端正なり。前淸發卯科舉人
を以て日本に留學し、慶應大學に入りて修業す。光緒三
十三年米國に赴き、モスケン大學に入りて學び、宣統三
年其の業を畢へて歸國す。適ま第一革命起り方に臨時政
府組織の事あり、君推れて江西代表と爲り、後ち選ばれ
て南京參議院議員と爲り、民國報主筆を兼ぬ。正式國會
成立に際し參議院議員に當選す。推れて憲の起草委員會
委員長と爲る。君曾て同盟會派と國民黨の發起に盡力し
第二次革命の後ち復た他派の有力なる人物を聯合して民
憲黨を組織したり。旋て袁氏非法を以て國會を停止する
や、君遂に迹を匿くし光を韜まして靜に世變を觀望し、
國會復活するに及びて復た出で、仍ほ參議院議員たり。

Mr. Tang I, otherwise called Fei Yu, thirty six years of age, is a native of Chiang Hsi Hsing.
He is a gentleman of high and noble nimd, full of sagacity. While young he was an admirer of books
and had great ambition. He was a deep thinker not tramelled with outward forms and expressions.
He was a man of strict behavior. He was sent by the government to Japan and studied in the Keio
University. In 1907, he went to America, where he received a college education and returned
America 1911. When the Revolution took place, he was a representative of the Chiang Hsi Province.
He was later a member of the Nanking Advisory Assembly and a editor-in-chief of a paper. On the
formation of the Parliament he was elected to a member of the Senate, and the chief of the committee
drafting the constitution. At the time of the 2nd Revolution, he came into touch with leading men of
various parties and formed the People's Party. When Yuanshi-kai suppressed the National Party he
returned to his home and quietly watched the progress of the situation. As soon as the Parliament was revived, he became a member of the Senate.

彭允彝　字靜仁

選地　湖南省
籍貫　湖南省
住址　北京中鐵匠胡同

吾人と爲り温和誠篤なり。明德師範學校卒業生を以て日本に遊學し、警監學校を卒業し、繼で又た早稻田大學の政治經濟科を卒業すること前後六年、專心學を修め、一面清政の頽敗を慨して大志を抱く。第一革命の事起るや、歸國して力を兵事に盡し、軍政府外交顧問となり、旋て選ばれて南京臨時參議院議員となる。宋敎仁蔡元培等と統一共和黨を組織して常務幹事に任ず。統一共和黨が南北統一後、北京臨時參議院議員と爲る。

君爲人溫和誠篤。以明德師範畢業生。遊學日本。入警監學校。畢業後。旋入早稻田大學政治經濟科。三年。畢業。在東前後共六年。壹志修學。武漢首義。歸國效力兵間。被任爲軍政府外交顧問。南京參議院成立。被任爲參議員。與宋鈍初蔡松波諸君創立統一共和黨。和議成。北京組織政府。仍繼任參議院議員。後統一共和黨與同盟會合併爲國民黨。復被選爲本部文事部主任。民國二年。被選爲衆議院議員。及袁氏以非法解散國會。遂流亡海外。日吸引國內外各黨派。共謀一致倒袁。帝禍既發。舊滬上與同人創辦中華新報。以聲助民軍。及袁氏死。共和恢復。國會重行召集。遂入京乃爲議員。旋被選爲全院委員長。

同盟會と合併して國民黨を組織するや、本部文事部主任と爲る。民國二年衆議院議員に當選す。袁氏が非法を以て國會を解散するや、海外に亡命して、國內外各黨派志士と聯絡して倒袁の事を謀る。帝制の禍既に發するや、上海に歸りて同人と中華新報を創刊して民軍の聲援を爲す。袁氏死し、共和恢復し、國會重ねて開かるゝや、召集に應じて入京し、仍は議員と爲り、旋て全院委員長に舉られたり。

Mr. Peng yun i, is a native of Hu-nan province. After graduating from the normal school in his province, he came to Japan, where he studied both in the police prison school and the University of Waseda. He spent six years in Japan and devoted himself to study always bearing in mind the improvement of the administration in China. When the 1st Revolution broke out, he was interested in the movement, himself having been appointed the diplomat of the military government. Later, he was a member of the special assembly met in Nanking, When the North and the South were united, he became a member of the special assembly held in Peking. When the national party was formed, he became the chief secretary of the headquarter. In the 2nd year of the Republic, he was returned for the House of Commons. When Yuanshi-kai dissolved Parliament illegally, he returned to Shanghai where he published a newspaper assisting the cause of the peoples party. With the death of Yuanshi-kai and the Restoration of the Republic, he returned to Peking where he became a member of the Parliament and the chief of the general committees of the House of Commons.

彭運斌　字右文　歲四十九

選舉地　河南省
籍　貫　河南省鄧縣
住　址　北京石駙馬大街橋西大院

君天資絕高。悟性敏捷。而頭腦周密。其言論思想。皆秩序井然。無顛倒紊亂之。弊。自幼聰慧好讀。深思明辨。於古義多所領悟。及海內維新。愈肆力千西學。千新書無所不觀。前清甲辰進士。授官法部主事。貧笈東渡。游學日本。入法政大學法政班。畢業歸國。經河南奏調籌辦本省諮議局。選充資政院議員。兼充河南優級師範學堂監督。民國成立。被選爲河南臨時省議會議員。辭職。任商辦潼濟鐵路協理。兼河南衆議院覆選第三區覆選舉監督。旋當選正式國會衆議院議員。國會解散後。歸里讀書。不問時政。五年國會重開。遂又應召入京。仍爲衆議院議員。

民國之精華　（傳記）　彭運斌先生

君天資絕高、悟性敏捷にして頭腦周密なり。其の言論思想皆な秩序井然として絕て顛倒紊亂の弊無し。幼より聰慧にして學を好み、古義に於て領得する所あり。海內維新にして、両學に志して博く新書を涉獵して研究大に進境あり、前清甲辰及第の進士にして、法部主事を授けらる更に笈を負ふて日本に留學し、法政大學法政科を卒業して歸國す。河南より調せられて諮議局の事を籌辦し、選ばれて資政院議員と爲る。兼て河南優級師範學堂監督に充る。民國成立するや、河南臨時省議會議員と爲る。辭職して潼濟鐵路協理に任じ、兼て河南省衆議院覆選第三區選舉監督に任す。旋て正式國會衆議院議員に當選す。國會解散後、鄉里に歸りて讀書自ら娛み、時に隨つて地方公益の事を提倡し、また政事を談せず。五年國會復活するに及び、遂に又た召集に應じて入京し、仍ち衆議院議員と爲る。

三百十一

Mr. Peng Yu-pin, otherwise known as Yu wen, age forty nine, is a native of Teng, Ho nan province. He is noble in character, quick wit and thorough in intellectual acquirement. Consequently either in thought or words, he keeps strict order. With the introduction of the new trend of thought, he was interested in the acquisition of accidental learning, and to that effect, he read new books. He visited Japan where he was graduated from the Hosei University. He was elected a member of the local assembly of Hu-nan, and the director of the Hu-nan normal school. When the Republic was established, he was a member of the Mecial Local Assembly of Hu nan, and later was returned for the House of Commons. After the dissolution of the Parliament, here turned to his nature province, and opent his time in the promotion of the well-being of the people. When the Parliament was restored, he entered Peking, and returned for the House of Commons, the position of honour he now holds.

彭占元　字青岑　歲四十六

選舉地　山東省

籍貫　山東省濮縣人

住址　北京象坊橋

君天資英邁豪爽。慷慨好義。尚氣節。由優廩生。於光緒二十九年本省師範學堂畢業。旋留學日本法政大學。是年發起同盟會。推爲山東同盟會部長。捐欸創立民報社。畢業後。回國。創立普通中學堂。爲運動革命之基礎。担任運動山東革命事。隨聯絡北七省函信。宣統元年被選爲諮議局議員。二年被選爲資政院議員。辛亥武昌起義。在山東謀響應。與同志竭力光復各地。後由同志推爲南京組織政府代表。旋推爲南京臨時參議院議員。復被選爲北京臨時參議院議員。民國二年被選爲衆議院議員。被袁氏解散。五年赴上海。擬在蘇皖魯豫之界。號招舊部。爲北討之計。袁死而罷。八月來京。就議員之職。

君天資英邁豪爽にして慷慨義を好み氣節を尚ぶ。前清貢生を以て、光緒二十九年山東省師範學校に入る。同年同盟會を卒業す。旋て日本に留學して法政大學校に入る。又た同志と民報社を創立す。同盟會山東部長に推さる。卒業後、歸國して普通中學校を創立して、革命運動の基礎と爲し、山東革命の事を擔任して北支那七省の通信聯絡を司る。宣統元年諮議局議員となり、二年資政院議員と爲る。三年武昌義を起すや、山東に在りて響應を謀

り、同志と力を竭して各地を光復す。後ち山東代表として南京に赴き臨時政府組織の事を議し、旋て選ばれて南京臨時參議院議員と爲り、又た北京臨時參議院議員と爲る。民國二年正式國會衆議院議員に當選す。國會解散後、五年一月一日上海に赴さて江蘇安徽山東河南各地に於て舊部下を糾めて北伐の計を爲さんとす。既にして袁死し、國會復活す。遂に入京して仍ち衆議院議員の職に就く。

Mr. Peng Chan-yuan, otherwise known as Ching shen, forty six years of age, is native of On hsien, Shan-tung province. Heroic in temperament, and novle in character, he was highly respected by his own countrymen. In 1903, he was graduated from the Shan-tung normal school. He came to Japan when he studied law in the Hosei University. He was elected too the head of the Shan-tung branch of the federation association held among his fellow thinkers. On returning to his home, he established a middle school, while taking charge of revolutionary affaris of Santung province, he conducted the Communication among seven provinces of north China. In 1910, he became a member of the local assembly. When the trouble arose in Wu chung, he travelled all over the province, working in union with his fellow thinkers. When the emasgency cabinet was formed, he was a member of the special assembly in Nanking and a member of the Senate in Peking. In the second year of the Republic, he was returned for the House of Commons. After the disolution of the Parliament, he was planning for the attack on the Northerns, and with the death of Yuanshi-kai, the Parliament was restored, and he was returned for the House of Commons.

彭施滌 字心筌 歲四十六

選舉地 湖南省
籍貫 湖南省永順縣
住址 北京香爐營四條西頭二十四

君幼樸實、好讀書。氣宇軒昂。儼然有出類拔萃之慨。庚子之亂。國事日非。慨然曰。丈夫不能救國救民。專用此七尺之軀。爲於是奔走天下以求所以福國利民之術。而知順究心科學。必無以爲濟。以前清舉人。留學日本。習師範。歸國偕同志組織上海中國公學。回湘歷任實業專門學堂優級師範學堂。高等學堂及西路師範學堂教職員。旋被選爲湘南諮議局議員。民國成立被選爲衆議院議員。國會解散後。歸里從事教育。及共和復活。國會重開。始應召仍爲衆議院議員。

君幼にして樸實、讀書を好び。氣宇軒昂、儼然として顯を出で華を拔くの慨あり。庚子の亂、國事日に非なり。慨然として曰く、丈夫國を救ひ民を救ふ能はずんば專ら此七尺の軀を用ゐて天下に奔走して國利民福の術を求むべしと。即ち心を科學に潛め、專ら新學を攻究して奧學の志を抱くに至れり。前清舉人を以て日本に留學し、師範科を修めて歸國す。同志と上海に於て中國公學校を創設す。旋て湖南に歸りて、實業專門學校優級師範學校高等學校、西路師範學校等の教師職員に歷充す。民國二年正式國會衆議院議員に當選す。國會解散されて後ち、再び鄉里に歸りて育英の業に從事して地方教育の振興に努力したり。五年國會恢復するや其の召集に應じて入京し、仍ち衆議院議員の職に復す。

Mr. Peng Shih Ti, otherwise called Hsi Chuan, age forty six, is a native of Yung Shun, Hu nan hsing. He was in youth a lover of books, being very ambitious, and he was always interested in public affairs with a view to save the people from the evils of maladministration. He was an ardent student of new learning, being greatly interested in the uplifting of his country men. At the latter days of the previous Chinese Government, he went to Japan, where he graduated from the normal school. In Shanghai he established a school of which he became an instructor. Later, he returned to Hu Nan where he was appointed an instructor of the technical school, the normal school, and the high school. In the 2nd year of the Republic, he was returned for the House of Commons. With the decolation of the Parliament, he returned to his province where he employed himself for the education of his people. When the Parliament, resumed its function he was returned for the House of Commons, the position which he holds in the present moment.

彭建標 字策遐 歲三十六

選舉地　廣東省

籍貫　廣東省龍川縣

住址　北京騾馬市大街佛照樓

君爲人耿介不阿。生平以緘默自持。不苟言笑。不輕於舉動。持已以嚴而待人以和。與人交極重然諾。持已以嚴而待人之。必待事成而後告。居恆以消極自持。能堅忍耐勞。不爲意氣所動。迨宗旨既定。則又猛勇直前。不復觀望。自幼聰敏異人。讀書能深思明辨。探求直義。及長。尤喜研究法學。曾前清副貢畢業於法政專門學校。民國元年。在本省充當律師。被選爲省議會議員。二年。復被舉爲參議院議員。國會解散後。旋粵復充律師。君因醉心共和。厭惡帝政。故拾四年籌安會發生後。憤不自安。願拋棄律師職業。避居澳門香港。聯合同志力倡反對。及袁氏病死。國會重開。仍就參議院議員之職。

君人と爲り耿介にして阿らず。舉動せず。人と交るや極めて然諾を重んじ、人託する所あれば之を允すと雖も必ず事成るを待ちて後ち告ぐ。居常消極主義を持して堅忍以て勞に耐へ、意氣の動す所と爲らず。方針飢に定らば則ち又た勇猛邁進して觀望踟跼するなし。幼より聰敏人に異り讀書能く思ひ明に辨じて異義を探求す。而して尤も法學を研究する事を喜びたり。曾て前清副貢を以て法政專門學校を卒業す。民國元年廣東省に在りて辯護士を開業し、旋て選ばれて省議會議員と爲る。二年參議院議員に當選。國會解散後、復た廣東に歸りて辯護士を業とす。四年籌安會發起さるゝや慨然業を棄てゝ澳門香港各地に赴き同志を聯合して帝制に反對し共和復活を圖る。五年袁氏死して國會再び開院するに及び、君踴躍して其の召集に應じ、復た仍ほ參議院議員の職に就く。

Mr. Peng Chien Piao, thirty six years of age, is a native of Lung Chuan, the Kuang-tung Hsien. He is a gentleman of independent spirit. He is taciturn and thoughtful. In dealing with others he knows how to keep his words. When entrusted with any charge, he silently works until he accomplishes his object. He is patient and forebearing and strong-minded. Once he makes up his mind he will not stop until he attains his end. He was a copious reader and deep thinker, particulary interested in the study of law. He studied from a Chinese law school under the previous regime. In the 1st year of the Republic, he practised law in his province. He worked hard against the Imperial Movement in favor of the revival of the Republic together with his fellow thinkers. With the death of Yuanshi-kai and the opening of the Parliament he went up to Peking and became a member of the Senate.

覃壽公　字達方　歳四十二

遷舉地　湖北省
籍　貫　湖北省蒲圻縣
住　址　北京前牛肉灣

君前清法政科舉人。辛亥革命。君充今
總統黎公鄂都督府秘書。民國元年。君
主張漢口建築分爲二大公司。一地皮。
分甲乙丙丁四等。地券作定價格。發
與各地主收執。供買賣及抵押收租之
用。將地上之各界限一齊混合。以便於
新式建築。一房產。先由地主投資。不
足。再由各方面及華僑集資。以此二大
公司。爲漢口兵燹後改良。不幸此策爲
有力者反對送止。君勤於著述。已出
版者。有商業政策經濟政策要論。拯危
三策。其拯危三策中。主張改論。軍隊
使從事於鑛屯。兵工製造場也。君由日本
留學畢業返國後。歷充前清度支部財
政學堂教員。其官湘南省時。充湘省官
立法政學校教員。國立二年國會解散。
君充教育部國立法政專門學校教員。
籌安會主張帝制時。君與孫洪伊君密
約。爲各方面反對之運動。尤爲有力。
君現爲衆議院議員。

君は前清法政科舉人たり。辛亥武昌義起るや、君鄂軍都
督黎元洪の秘書に任ず。民國元年、君乃ち兵燹後の漢口
市街再興に關し、具體的の意見を具して建議する所ありし
も、故を以て實行さるゝに至らず、君また著述に勤め既
に出版せるもの商業政策、經濟政策要論、拯危三策の
書あり。其の拯危三策とは、軍隊の編成改良、鑛屯事業の
振興兵器製造場の擴張等にして、現時尙ほ急務とすべき
もの也。君曾て日本に留學して新進の學を修め、歸來前
清度支部財政學校の教員となり。嗣いで湖南に於て官立
法政學校教員として育英の事業に從事したる事あり。民
國二年兼議院議員に常選す。國會解散さるゝや、國立法
政專門學校教授として再び敎鞭を取り、籌安會發起され
て帝政を唱導するに及び、君慨然として孫洪伊等と密約
して各方面の反對運動に努力したり。國會既に恢復す、仍
ほ復た衆議院議員と爲る。

民國之精華　（傳記）　覃壽公先生

Mr. Tan Shou Kung, forty two years of age, is a native of Pu Chai, Hu Pe. He belonged to the previous chinese regime, having become an official by the civil examination. When in 1911 the trouble arose, he was the private secretary of general Leang. In the 1st year of the Republic, he addressed his opinion in a concrete form concerning the rebuilding of Hankow burned up by the battle, but owing to some reasons his plans were not carried into effect. He wrote several books of which the commercial policy, the outline of economic policy are noted. While he wrote another book regarding the improvement of the military composition and the expansion of the Arsenal which is of urgent importance even at present. He came to Japan where he acquired a stock of new knowledge. On returning to his home he was interested in the education and became an instructor of provincial law schools. In the 2nd year of the Republic, he was elected a member of the House of Commons. When the Parliament was closed, he returned to his scholary work. As soon as the Imperial Movement was started, he was one of the most vehement opponents. With the revival of the Parliament, he at once proceeded to Peking where he was returned for the House of Commons, the membership of which he now holds.

覃　超　字哲民　歲三十八

選舉地　廣西省

籍　貫　廣西省柳州府馬平縣

住　址　東南園廣西議員俱樂部

君秉性溫恭謙讓。待人以誠。生平以虛
己下問自喜。人告以過。卑詞謝其忠告
之厚意。然後細辦其是否合理。人言
當。固不吝即改。即有不當。亦絕不辯
釋。居常以退讓自持。人有與爭者。常
以柔制勝。不逞意氣而自甘於兩敗俱
傷。自幼即知苦讀求進。及長。愈益奮
勵。故天資雖非絕倫。而其所造。則茜
遠大著實。前清時曾充廣西法政專門學
校最優等畢業。辛亥年充雲南都督府
秘書所編修官。次年回籍。充柳州中學
校校長。是年被選爲衆議院議員。袁氏
解散國會後。回籍因黨事被逮瀕于死
者數次。本省起義之日。出獄現復任衆
議院議員之職。

君秉性溫良恭謙にして人を待つに誠を以てす。生平己を
虛ふして人に問ふを喜び、人若し過を以て告ぐれば詞を
卑ふして其の忠告を謝し、然る後ち其の是非を省察して
人言當らば改むるに憚らざる也。幼より剋苦精勵以て學
に進み、長ずるに及びて愈々益々切磋琢磨の功を積み、
天資敢て絕倫ならざるも其の造詣則ち深きものあり。前
清末季、廣西法政專門學校を最優等にて卒業す。第一革
命の後ち雲南都督府秘書廳編修に任じ、民國元年鄉里に
帰り、柳州中學校々長となりて育英の業に從事す。旋て
選ばれて衆議院議員と爲る。袁氏非法を以て國會を解散
するや、南旋歸鄉して大業の恢復を志し、政黨の事に座
して逮捕され、死に瀕するもの數回なり。第三革命の事
起りて廣西獨立するや、其の日漸く獄を出で、旋て約法
恢復して國會再び召集を行ふ、君仍ち北上して院に蒞み、
現に復た衆議院議員と爲る。

Mr. Tan Chao, known as Che Min Hsien, thirty eight years of age, is a native of Kar Hsi. He is humble and sincere being absolutely open minded to receive others. He is always ready to accept the advise given by others with the sense of appreciation. He studied hard while young and as grew older he kept on his study until he accumulated a stock of knowledge not easily obtained by others. At the later days of the previous chinese regime he was graduated with honours from the Kwang Hsi Law College. At the time of the Revolution he was appointed the private secretary of the Yun Nan governor general. In the 1st year of the Republic he returned to his home and appointed the head of the middle school in his province. Shortly after he was returned for the House of Commons. When Yuanshi-kai shut down the Parliament illigally, he went back to his home always being desirous of the reviving the Republic. He was arrested several times and narrowly escaped death. When the 3rd Revolution took place and the independence of Huang Hsi was secured, he was released from his prison and at once went up to Peking and became the member of the House of Commons, the position he holds at the present moment.

民國之精華　（傳記）　童杭時先生

童杭時　專萱甫　歲四十

選舉地　浙江省

籍貫　浙江省崤縣

住址　北京三眼井三十號

君幼寡嗜好。具大志。稍長。潛心科學。為徐烈士錫麟高足弟子。嗣入浙省公立法校。肄習年滿。游學日本。卒業于法政大學。得法學士學位。辛亥革命。君慷慨出橐金。退集同志。組織北伐隊。洎南北媾和。無意仕進。獨立創辦共和法校。充任校長。延美國法學博士亨倍克。教授憲法。欲以平民政治。牖啓後學。弟子千餘人。多傑出才美。因熱誠公益。鄉望允孚。初被選省議會議員。繼當選參議院議員君夙長財政學。院內卒為財政股常任委員。緣反對袁氏。被取消議員。出走東瀛。仍力謀倒袁。迫帝制發生。知時機已熟。歸遣厥弟濟時。密招鄉勇。復躬滋省恒。鼓吹軍隊起義獨立。為滇黔助。誠熱心共和健將也。國會恢復後。仍任參議院議員。

君幼より嗜好寡なく大志を具ふ。稍や長じて心を科學に潛め、徐錫麟の高足弟子たり。嗣で浙江公立法政學校に學び、旋て日本に游學して法政大學を卒業す。第一革命當時、君慨然として橐を傾けて同志を邀集し、北伐隊を組織す。南北媾和して後ち仕進に意無く、獨力を以て共和法政學校を創設して校長に任じ、米國人の博士を聘して憲法を教授し、平民政治を以て後學を啓導し弟子千餘人、皆な傑出したり。初め選ばれて省議會議員となり。繼いで參議院議員に當選し、財政常任委員に舉げらる。袁氏に反對せるにより議員を取消され、出で〻日本に走り、倒袁の策を謀る。帝制發生するに追び、時機既に熟するを知り、其弟濟時を遣はし歸して密に鄉里の健兒を招き、復た躬ら浙江省城に蒞みて軍隊の獨立を鼓吹して雲南貴州の助けと爲したり。國會恢復後、復た仍は參院議員に任じたり。

Mr. Tung hang shih, otherwise known as Hsu an fu, age forty, is a native of Che chiang province. While young, he was quite ambitious. As he grew older he studied in the public law school of his province, then at the Hosei University in Japan. When the 1st Revolution was started, he at his own expence organized a party to attack the northerns. However when peace was arrauged between North and South he established the republic law school of which he became the president. Inviting american scholars who gave lecture unconstitution. Students numbered over one thousand, all of whom were distinguished men. He was elected a member of the local assembly and then a member of the Senate, where he was elected a member of the financial standing committee. Because of his opposition to Yuanshi-kai his certificate of the membership was cancelled so that he went to Japan he planned for the downfall of Yuanshi-kai. When the Imperial Movement was started he at once knew that opportunity arrived the in dependence of his province. After the restoration of the Parliament he was appointed a member of the Senate.

揭曰訓　字友莘　歲三十五

選舉地　山東省

籍貫　山東省單縣

住址　北京象坊橋

君秉性剛直。不隨俗浮沈。然居心仁厚。雖仇敵。亦不忍窘迫之。與人交。喜相責以善。人告以過。輒大喜。蓋謂其能直言不欺。不以流俗相待也。以前清宣統元年。畢業於山東優級師範學堂。學部試驗以舉人出身。歸部銓選。武昌義起即商同彭占元君回籍聯合同志。光復豐沛渦陽等縣。共和宣布。被選為臨時省議會議員。是年蘇皖魯豫之交。土匪蜂起。卽協辦清鄉事宜。一時地方賴以安謐。復考察東省官吏之優劣。更治為之一清。民國貳年被選為參議院議員。解職後。卽赴黑龍江省。籌辦礦墾牧畜事宜。帝制發生。卽赴滬聯合同志。力倡反對。袁氏猝死。國會復活遂仍就參院議員之職。

君秉性剛直にして俗尚に隨はず、然かも居心仁厚にして仇敵と雖も、亦た之を窘迫するに忍びず。人と交りて相責むるに善を以てする事を喜ぶ。前清宣統元年、山東優級師範學校を卒業し、學部試驗に應じて舉人を授けらる辛亥革命の事起るや、彭占元と兵に歸鄉して同志と聯合し、豐沛渦陽等各縣の獨立を成就したり。共和宣布後臨時省議會議員に舉げらる。山東安徽河南の省境に於て土匪蜂起す。之が鎮壓事務を協同處理して地方安謐を得たり。復た東三省官吏の優劣を調査して、吏治爲めに一淸するを得たり。民國二年參議院議員に當選す。解職後即ち黑龍江省に赴き、礦業開墾牧畜事宜を處理す。帝制問題發生するや、即ち上海に赴きて同志と聯合して反對に力む。袁死猝に死して國會復活す、遂に仍は參議院議員の職に就く。

Mr. Chieh Yueh hsun, otherwise known as Yu hsin, is a native of Shan tung province. Being a gentleman of straight forward character, he is above the mediocre. Even towards the enemy and rival he is always gentle and considerate. In 1909 when he was graduated from the Shan tung Higher Normal School, he passed the civil service examination with a success. In 1911 when the Revolution broke out he assisted the whole movement in conjunction with his friends. After the declaration of the Republic he was appointed a member of the assembly then held. When in the frontiers of Shang tung, An lui and Ho nan bandit's troubles arose he attended to their pacification with success. He was also appointed an examiner authorized to look into the official condition of the province. In the 2nd year of the Republic he was elected a member of the Senate, but when he was relieved of his post he returned to Hei lung Cheng where he was interested in mining, posturage, and other occupation. When the Imperial movement took place, he returned to Shanghai where he worked in conjunction with his friends in the opposition of the Movement. However with the sudden death of Yuanshi-kai the Parliament was restored and he was appointed a member of the Senate.

焦易堂　字希孟　歲三十七

選舉地　陝西省

籍貫　陝西省武功縣

住址　北京棉花下三條十號

君爲人儻侗不羈。言論思想。皆極活
潑。然秉性誠篤無欺。華盛而實亦富。
少年讀書。喜爲詞章。其吐屬氣勢。備
極華貴俊秀。上擬古人。旣冠。漸讀宋
明學者之書。始自悔昔日之玩物喪志。
遂改志肆力于身心修養及經時濟世
之書。且絕意科第。旣入庠爲廩生。後
不復求進。及海內風氣旣開。遂立志彈
精新學。曾入本法政專門學校。未畢業
改入自治研究所。畢業後。歷任本縣勸
學總董暨教育會自治會會長。辛亥改
革時。任都督府參謀。嗣改充參議兼總
務科長。民國二年被選爲省議會議員。
由此被舉爲參議院議員。國會解散。留
學京師。不談時事。五年。畢業于北京
中國公學大學部。未幾。國會招集。遂
應召仍爲參議院議員。

民國之精華　（傳記）焦易堂先生

君人と爲り儻侗不羈、言論思想皆な極めて活潑なり、然
かも氣性誠實にして欺かず、華盛なるも實亦た富む。少
年書を讀みて詞章に親み、其の吐屬氣勢、極めて俊秀華
麗なり。稍や長じて漸く宋明學者の書を讀み、遂に志を
改めて身心の修養並に時務に有用なるの學を求む。旣に
庠に入りて廩生の爲に。再び科學の學を顧みずして專ら
新智識の涵養に勤む。陝西省法政專門學校に修業し、後
ち轉じて自治研究所に入りて業を畢ゆ。爾來鄕縣にあり
て縣勸學總董及び縣敎育會、自治會等の會長として地方
敎育の普及並に地方自治の振興に努力したり。民國二年
省議會議員に舉げられ、旋て選ばれて參議院議員と爲る
國會解散するや、京師に留りて學を求め、また時事を談
せず、五年北京中國公學大學部を卒業す。未だ幾くもな
く國會重ねて召集を行ふ。遂に出でゝ仍ほは參議院議員と
なれり。

Mr. Chiao i tang, otherwised named Hsi weng, age thirty seven, is a native of Wu Chiao,
Hsia Ssi. While young, he was full of independent spirit. He was very active both in words and
thought. He shunned anything superficial and adopted substantial. While young he read most
copiously and his diction has easy flow. As he grew older, he sought the study of new knowledge, and
studied law in Hsia Ssi Law School. He was graduated from the institution established for the purpose
of studying the self-rule. Thereupon, he was interested in the educational works in the local province,
when he made efforts to dissiminate the idea of civic body. In the 2nd year of the Republic, he was
appointed a member of the Senate. On the dissolution of the Parliament, he staid in Peking studying,
but not talking politics. He was graduated from the Peking University. When the Parliament was
re-opened, he became a member of the Senate.

三百十九

楊潤身 字雨亭 歲四十六

選舉地　甘肅省
籍貫　甘肅省
住址　天水縣北鄉三陽川石佛鎮

君為人精明強幹。富於忍耐。然鯁直好
義。人有過。輒直斥不諱。甚至聲色俱
厲。而賦性朴質。不喜浮華。讀書博而
能約。故所讀皆足以為經世濟物之資。
及有益于身心者。詞章之屬亦常隨意
涉獵。不專力於斯。故能為詩歌。而不
喜常作。每有所作。必極精妙。以大都
於感慨淋漓時。一寫其至性至情非尋
常雕蟲刻鏤者可比也。於前清光緒戊
戌科二甲進士。誥授中憲大夫法部主
事加四級。戊子舉人。癸未廩膳生。丙
子州庠生。民國二年被選眾議院議員。
國會解散後。歸里獨居不談政治。及國
會重開。仍為眾議院議員。

君人と為り精明強幹にして忍耐に富む。然も鯁直にして
義を好む。賦性朴實にして浮華を喜ばず。書を讀むこと
博くして能く約し、其の讀む所の者皆以て經世
濟物の資と為すに足る。其の身心に有益なる者は皆詞章の
類と雖も亦た隨意涉獵して、自ら常に詩歌を作るを喜び
ざるも、作れば必ず精妙を極めて感慨淋漓一に其の至性
至情を寫して、尋常雕蟲刻鏤を事とする者の比にあらざ
る也。前清丙子の歲州庠生に及第し、癸未の歲廩膳生に

及第し、戊子の歲及第して舉人を給せられ、光緒戊戌科
に及第して二甲進士となり、中憲大夫、法部主事を授け
四級を加へらる。民國二年正式國會眾議院議員に當選す
國會解散後、鄉里に歸にりて政治を談せず、時に地方の後
進を誘掖して地方公益事業に力を惜まず。國會重ねて開
かるゝに及び、再び出でゝ召集に應じ、仍は眾議院議員
と為る。

Mr. Yang Jun Shen, age sixty four, is a native of Ten Hsiao, the Kan Su hsing. He is a thorough gentleman, being gallant in spirit and simple in life. He read books most extensively, and what he read was digested for the interest of the public. It was not very often that he wrote poems, but what he write, is full of spirit and vivacity, being quite different from an ordinary and labourious study. In the previous chinese regime, he passed successfully a number of civil examination which brought him the government's position. In the second year of the Republic, he was returned for the House of Commons. On the disolution of the Parliament, he returned to his home rnd spent his days in the improvement of public works. On the re-opening of the Parliament, he was elected a member of the House of Commons.

楊榮春　字熙坪　歲六十一

選舉地　黑龍江省
籍貫　黑龍江省蘭西縣
住址　北京西單皮庫胡同二十二

君爲人篤實不欺。秉性朴魯。而好讀深
思。故其成就。較資質爲九大。及入仕
途。尤以循謹著名。於前清光緒二十年
曾充鎮軍馬隊統領營務處辦事官差
使。於三十一年。蘭西縣設治。充幫辦
委員。後辦理地方自治會。未及一年。
被選爲蘭西縣議會副議長。宣統三年
又被選爲省城臨時省議會議員。民國
二年正月被選爲衆議院議員。國會解
散。歸里隱居。絕口不談政事。旋開設
遠東報館分社。以期主持正義。開通民
智。及此次國會重行召集。遂來京仍爲
衆議院議員。

民國之精華　　（傳記）楊榮春先生

君人と爲り篤實欺かず、秉性朴實なり。審を讀みて深く
思索す。仕途に入るに及びて尤も恪謹循良を以て名あ
り。前清光緒二十年、鎮軍馬隊統領營務處辦事官の職に任
ず。三十一年、蘭西縣新設さるゝや、幫辦委任となり。後ち
地方自治會の事を處理し、旋て選ばれて蘭西縣議會副議
長と爲る。宣統三年又た選ばれて黑龍省臨時省議會議員
と爲る。民國二年正月第一次正式國會衆議院議員に當選
し、關を入りて京師に抵り立法府の人と爲りて大政を議
す。國會解散さるゝや、鄕里に歸臥して暫らく時事を議
せず。旋て遠東報分局を設けて正義を主持し民智の開通
を圖る。旣にして袁氏死し黎氏繼ぎ、約法復活して國會
再び召集を行ふ。君復た途に之に應じて立ち。現に仍は
入京して衆議院議員の舊職に就きり。

Mr. Yang Jung-chun, otherwise known as Î Ping, age sixty one, is a native of San Ssi, Hei Sung Chiang. Honest and simple life is his special mark. He digests and appropriates what he reads for the benefit of the public. In 1894, he was employed under the previous Chinese regime, while, ten years later, he was an official interested in the development of the civic body, himself being the Vice-President of San Ssi Local Assembly. In 1911, he became a member of the Local Assembly of his province. When the Parliament was opened under the Republic, he was elected to a member of the House of Commons, and going up to Peking under that capacity, he contributed his service to the legislative body. He returned home on the breaking up of the Parliament. On the death of Yuanshi-kai, however, he went up to Peking, and became a member of the House of Commons.

楊夢弼　字肯巖　歲五十四

還舉地　廣東省
籍　貫　廣東省韶州曲江縣
住　址　北京東草廠二條韶州會館

君為人正直耿介。不隨流俗沈浮。性喜
質樸。富於堅忍之力。自幼好為義舉。
然不肯輕于允諾之力。人有所託。必量其力
所能至者。應允之。既允後。雖赴湯燼。
亦所不辭。事成。絕無矜意。生平疾惡
如仇。見人不平。雖陷路。必奮身助之。
常以此自瀕于危。而不以告其人。故受
恩者。事後聞之。感戴愈摰。自幼讀書。
探求義理。年方弱冠。作為文。詞達義
明。脫盡彫刻之陋習。及長。尤博覽羣
書。頗以名儒自相期許。其為文喜獨樹
一幟。不踏襲古人之陳規。而學派則不
拘漢宋。考据義理。兼重不偏。清時。以
拔貢輟考中試。分發湖南試用知縣。民
國元年。曾倡辦馬壩圩育才高初兩等
學校。自為校長。隨被舉為曲江縣議事
會議長。二年被舉為衆議院議員。國會
解散後。歸里獨居。不復出問時事。及
共和復活後。始北上仍就今職。

君人と為り正直、性質朴にして堅忍の力に富む。幼より
義を好み、輕々しく允諾せざるも、己の力を量りて人の
託に應ぜば、幾多の艱難を辭せずして之を敢行し、事成
つて絕へて誇ること無し。幼より書を讀みて其の義理を
求め、弱冠早くも文名あり。長ずるに及びて群籍を涉獵
して頗る名儒を以て相許す。前淸時代拔貢生を以て朝試
に及第し、湖南試用知縣に補せらる。民國成立するや、

曾て馬壩圩育才高初兩等學校を發起經營して自ら其の校
長に任じ、以て地方教育の普及を講じて民智の開發を計
りたり。旋て舉げられて曲江縣議事會議長と為る。二年
正式國會成立に際し衆議院議員に當選す。國會解散後南
旋歸里、獨居して書を讀み、復た出で〻時事を問はず。共
和復活するに及び始めて北上して國會の召集に應じ、仍
ち衆議院議員たり。

Mr. Yang Weng-pi, otherwise known as Hsia Yen, fifty four years of age, is a native of Shao Chon. He is noted for the simplicity of life, being straight forward and honest in character. He may meet any difficulty in the execution of his work, but nothing daunted plans for the accomplishment of the same. While young, he distinguished himself for being an avaricious reader. In the previous Chinese regime, he was employed by the government, after successfully passing the examination. On the establishment of the Republic, he founded a school, of which he himself became the presidents. He made efforts in the development of the local education, and the diffusion of the popular knowledge. He was elected the president of the Local Assembly of his own native province. In the 2nd year of the Republic, he was returnd for the House of Commons. On the dissolution of the Parliament, he devoted himself to the study of books. When the Parliament was re-opened under new president, he went up to Peking, resuming the fuuction of the member of the legislative body.

楊式震 字東川 歲四十八

選舉地 直隸省

籍貫 直隸省滿城縣

住址 北京西單二條胡同

君賦性敦厚溫和。與人交。和靄可親。雖仇敵亦假以顏色。不出惡聲。然爲人篤實不欺。動止以禮自持。雖長於交際。而無形中自有不可侵越之界限。未嘗曲已從人。較之碌碌追隨俗者。自屬太相逕庭。自幼好讀。喜博覽羣書。任意所之以爲快。而不屑規然從事于科學之業。故其讀書。純至以主觀判斷是非。而不同于習俗之成見。及海內維新。愈立志求有用之學。於新書無所不觀。前淸舉人。法部候補主事。曾充本縣勸學所總董。高等小學校校長。民國元年被選爲衆議院議員。

民國之精華 （傳記）楊式震先生

君賦性敦厚溫和にして人と交る和靄親ひべし。仇敵と雖も亦屬色惡聲を加へす。然り人と爲り誠實欺かず、言勤擧作皆な禮を以自ら持し、交際に長ずると雖も無形の中自ら侵越すべからざるの限界を有し、未だ嘗て己を曲げて人に從ふこと無し。幼より學を好み、博く諸子百家の群書を涉獵して、意の往く所に任せて自ら娛み、矩々然として科學の業に從事する者と異る。故に其の讀書は專ら主觀を以て是非を判斷して習俗の成見に囚はれざるなり。海內維新に及び志を立て〻有用の學を求め新學に於て造詣既に深く、前淸時代擧人を以て法部主事候補を授けらる。曾て滿城縣の勸學所總董、高等小學校々長等の職に當り、奧學の志を抱きて地方敎育の普及を計り民智の開發に力を渡したり。民國正式國會成立に際し擧げられて衆議院議員と爲り。今ま國會再び召集を行ふに及び復た仍は衆議院議員たり。

Mr. Yang Shih-chen, known as Tung Chuan, age forty eight, is a native of the Wan Cheng, Chen Li hsing. He is gentle and sociable in character, being brood-minded enough to receive even his enemy without any show of anger and hatred. Although sociable, he has a sphere of his own, to which others are inaccessible. While young, he was a copious and industrious reader, never bothering himself with the government's appointment or the public examination. He enjoyed what he read, being a real student. He digests what he reads, and forms his own judgement upon things. In the previous Chinese regime, he was employed in the law office, and became the chief of the high primary school, and that of the learning encouragement institution. He was also interested in the propagation of the local education, and development of knowledge among the people. He was elected a member of the Parliament when the Republic was established, and now for the second time he holds the important position.

楊樹璜　字寶丞　歲四十七

選舉地　福建省

籍　貫　福建省連城縣

住　址　北京長巷下二條汀州館

君少愚魯。好學不輟。及壯。始由邑廩
生捷秋闈。博通經史。洞明世變。明清
兩朝掌故。尤能鈎深索隱。指陳得失。
民國國會初開。膺第一次國會議員之
選。其時袁氏野心勃勃。意圖推翻民
國。復行帝制。停止國會之令既下。籌
安勸進之舉隨生。君乃飄然遠引。謀與
實業於東南。二年以來。多所創設。成
積極多。潮州電燈公司之組成。其一端
也。當袁氏盛時。天下皆以操莽視袁
氏。君則以為袁之自尊自石虎石生實
不及操莽百倍。為能持久。時有雷生
者。欲為國民代表卒先勸進。君謂之
曰。君等前程。歌零琴瑟。幸勿踰牆相從受此終
身之玷。雷生首肯者再。未幾滇省首
義。四海土崩瓦解。袁氏斃命。民國恢
復。果如君之言。以故里人皆服其卓
見。國會重開。君遂來京復為衆議院議
員。

君少にして愚魯、學を好んで研磋懈まず、壯年に及んで
始めて邑廩生となる。經史に通じ世變を明にし、明清兩
朝の掌故に於て尤も深く研究する所あり。民國正式國會
成立に際し衆議院議員に當選す。當時袁氏野心勃々とし
て民國を覆へして帝制を恢復せん事を思ひ、國會を停止
し、籌安會の發起、勸進表奉呈等相繼ぐ。君乃ち飄然と
して南下し、潮州電燈公司の創設を始め、地方實業の振
與を圖り、袁氏の勢威久しくを保つ能はざるを豫言して
密に友朋の權勢に阿附せんとする者を戒め、心靜かに時
運の再變を觀望したり。旣にして雲南義を唱へて天下響
應し、海内鼎沸、袁氏の威望を以て收集する能はざるに至
り、袁氏焦灼痛憤遂に命を失ふに及びて其の罪業全く土
崩瓦解す。約法は恢復され國會は再び召集さる。君復た
出でゝ北上し仍は衆議院議員たり。

Mr. Yangshu-i, otherwise named Pao Cheng, age forty seven, is to native of Lien Cheng, the Fu-chien. Although in youth he was rather slow of understanding, he was a dilligent student. He versed well as he grew older in classic history of China. On the establishment of the Republic, he was elected a member of the House of Commons. Being ambitious, Yuanshi-kai put a stop to the progress of the Republic, and proposed the return of the restoration of the Imperial Regime. He went to the south and interested himself to the promotion of the electric light company and the industrial concerns. He foretold the future decline of Yuanshi-kai influence, and quietly waited for the return of the tide. With the collapse of Yuanshi-kai, the political basis built up by him tottered down like a pack of cards. When the Parliament was re-opened, he went up to Peking and was returned for the House of Commons.

楊士驄　字芝青　歲四十七

選舉地　安徽省

籍貫　安徽省泗縣

住址　北京後內外澤公府

君賦性清高。言動舉止。皆迥異凡流。
然爲人勤謹耐勞。人有所託。輒喜爲盡
力。不以功自居。以故里人皆極愛敬
之。偶有糾紛。得君出一言。無不立即
解釋。自幼天資極高。悟性敏捷。讀書
能深思探究精義。不爲成見所局。故思
想豐富。見解新穎。人但見其居常規規
自守不知其精神固異常活潑也。海內
維新後。銳志西學。前清時。曾任候補
三四品京堂。湖南財政監理官。山西鹽
使等職。民國二年正式國會成立。被選
爲衆議院議員。

君賦性淸高にして言動舉止皆な迥かに凡流と異る。然か
も人と爲り恪勤して勞に耐へ、人君し託する所あれば輒
ちて喜んで盡力し、功を以て自ら居らず、里人皆な君を
推重す。幼より天資極めて高く悟性敏捷なり、書を讀み
て深く思索して其の義理を探求し、成見の囚る〻所と爲
らず。故に思想豐富にして見解新穎なり。曾て前淸時代
三四品京堂候補を授けられ、湖南財政監理官、山西運鹽

使等の職に歷任して功あり。民國樹立して正式國會成立
するに及び、安徽省より選ばれて衆議院議員に當選す。
國會解散されてよりは鄉里に歸りて讀書自ら娛み、時に
出でて地方公益の事を圖り、また時事を論せず。五年約
法復活して國會重ねて開かるゝや、君其の召集に應じて
入京し、仍ほ衆議院議員と爲る。

民國之精華　（傳記）楊士驄先生

Mr. Yang Shih-tsung, age forty seven, is a native of Ssu hsien, An Hui h sing. He is noted for the purity of character and the nobleness of action. He sacrifices gladly his own interest for the benefit of others, for which he is highly respected of his country men. He is a comprehensive reader and deep scholar. His thoughts are rich and views are quite up-to-date. Under the previous Chinese regime he occupied several important posts. When the Republic was established, he was returned from his province for the House of Commons. With the dissolution of the Parliament he returned to his home where he was keenly interested in the development of local interests. In his retirement he talked very little of politics. As promised the Parliament was re-opened when he entered Peking and resumed his function as the member of the Parliament.

楊肇基　字啓周　歲四十一

選舉地　四川省

籍貫　四川省西昌縣

住址　北京西城北絡鮀灣四號

君爲人溫厚。然富于毅力。不隨和流俗。年少時。篤志經史。旁通羣書頗以名儒自期。海內維新後。忽改途趨向西學。以前清增生。考入四川東文學堂肄業。畢業後。由四川督學院咨送日本留學。先入宏文學院。習普通科。卒業後入日本大學高等師範科。兼入法律科。明治大學法律研究科。旋更入三年卒業。歸國。應學部試驗。考列優等。授法政科舉人。民國元年任上海中國公學法律科教員。民國二年。被選爲衆議院議員。國會解散後。任上海神州大學敎員。及至共和恢復。國會重開。遂入京復爲衆議院議員。

君人と爲り溫厚、然かも毅力に富みて流俗に附和雷同せざる也。少年時代志を經史に注ぎ、傍ら群書に通じ、頗る名儒を以て自ら期す。海內維新後、忽ち途を改めて西學に趨り、前清の增生を以て、四川督學院より選派されて日本に留學す。先づ宏文學院にて普通科を修め、後ち日本大學校高等師範科を卒業して同法律科に入り、後ち轉じて明治大學法律高等專攻科に入り、宣統三年卒業歸國す。學部の試驗に應じ、優等を以て法政科舉人を授けらる。民國元年上海中國公學法律科教授に任す。二年正式國會衆議院議員に當選す。國會解散後、上海神洲大學敎員に任じ、青英の業に從事して後進を誘掖啓導する所ありたり。五年共和恢復して國會重ねて開かるゝに及び、遂に入京して復た衆議院議員たり。

Mr. Yang Chao-chi, otherwise called Chi-chon, age forty one. is a native of Hsi Chang, Hsi Chuan province. He is a man of gentle character, strong will, and not influenced by any popular feeling. While young, he was interested in the study of Chinese classics, and ambition was to become a learned Chinese scholar. However, with the introduction of new thonghts he turned his attention to the study of the new learning. He went to Japan where he was graduated from the Meiji University, and returned to China in 1911. He passed a civil service examination with honours. In the first year of the Republic he entered law school, while, in the 2nd year of the Republic, he was returned for the House of Commons. After the dissolution of the Parliament, he was interested in the education of the young. When the new president descided to open the Parliament again, he entered Peking and became a member of the House of Commons.

楊福洲 字溶川 歲四十

選舉地　吉林省

籍貫　吉林省吉林縣

住址　北京西交民巷路南

君賦性惇篤。尚質惡文。不事無益之繁華。然富於學識。新舊皆有素養。故其見解氣慨。皆迴異凡流。曾歷充前清吉林籌餉局委員。兵備處科長。陸軍清理財政局科長。督練公所隨員。安徽督練公所科員。旋以勞力授分省補用知縣。民國成立。歷任吉林省農事試驗場監督。都督府實業顧問。清丈局科長。國會成立。被舉為參議院議員。國會解散後。歸里獨居。無所表見。及國會重開始入京。仍就參議院議員之職。

民國之精華　（傳記）　楊福洲先生

三百二十七

君賦性惇篤にして質を尚び文を惡み、無益の繁華を事とせず。然かも學識に富みて新舊皆な素養あり、其の見解氣慨皆な迴かに凡流と異るものあり、曾て前清時代、吉林籌餉局委員、兵備處科長、陸軍財政整理局科長、督練公所隨員、安徽督練公所科員等の職に歷任し、其の功を以て保薦せられて補用知縣を授けらる。民國成立してより後は、吉林省農事試驗處監督、吉林都督府實業顧問、清丈局科長等の職に任じたり。民國二年正式國會の成立に際し舉げられて參議院議員と爲る。國會解散さるるや、鄉里に歸臥して暫く政見を發表する事無く、讀書自ら娛む。斯くて民國五年約法恢復して國會重ねて召集を行ふに及び、復た出でゝ入京し、仍は參議院議員の舊職に就きたり。

Mr. Yang-fu Chon, otherwise called Hsu Chuan, forty years of age, is a native of Chilin, the Chilin province. Being a lover of something substantial by nature, he never coveted anything vain and pompous. He is well versed both in old and new learniug. In the previous Chinese regime, he was the heat of the Military Financial Bureau and occupied several other important positions with success. After the establishment of the Republic, he was an inspector of the Chilin agricultural experimental farm as well as an industrial adviser to the Chilin governor general. In the second year of the Republic, he was elected a member of the Senate. On the dissolution of the Parliament, he returned to his home, and never published his political views. However, as soon as the Parliament was re-opened under the new president, he resumed his senatorial function.

楊銘源 字西堂 歲三十九

選舉地 陝西省

籍貫 陝西省宜君縣

住址 北京教場六條七號

君賦性慷慨好義。見人不平。常忿忿不
自禁。過於自受。弱冠時嘗以是與人
爭。不顧己之利害。及長。修養漸積。
始稍趨平和。於前清光緒二十八年。東
渡留學日本。入明治大學。遂入革黨。
共從事運動。曾充同盟會陝支部長。卒
業歸國後。委身從事教育。時復暗中
鼓吹辛亥光復之際。充陝西東路軍司
令部參謀長。兼理軍需。以故潼關戰
禍。雖烈且久。而餉糧賴以不缺者。皆
君之力也。至民國元年。組織臨時省議
會。即被舉爲議長。指揮立法。監督行
政。多所建白。二年。又被選爲衆議院
議員。及至憲法起草委員會成立之際。
當選爲起草委員。國會解散後。復遊學
日本。直至帝制發生。辭歸。滬上與諸
同志奔走國事。袁氏既沒。國會重開。
遂來京。仍供舊職。

君賦性慷慨にして義を好む。前清光緒二十八年、笈を負
ふて東渡し、日本に留學して明治大學に入る、遂に革命
黨に加盟して運動に從事し、曾て同盟會陝西支部長に任
じたり。卒業歸國して後ち教育の業務に從事して暗中革
命思想を皷吹宣傳す。第一革命當時、陝西東路軍司令部
參謀長兼軍需長に任ず、潼關の戰爭激烈にして永きに涉
りたるも、民軍の餉糧缺くるに至らざりしもの君の力な
り。民國元年臨時省議會成立に際して議長に舉げられ、
地方行政を監督して所議建白する所多し。二年正式國會
衆議院議員に舉げらる。憲法起草委員會委員に舉げらる
、國會解散して後ち、復た日本に游學す。帝制問題發生する
に及びて上海に赴き、諸同志と奔走して大局を圖る、袁
氏旣に沒して國會重ねて開かる、や、其の召集に應じて
遂に北京に抵り、仍ほ衆議院議員の舊職に就きたり。

Mr. Yang Ming Yuan, known as Shi Tang, age thirty nine, is a native of Shan Ssi. He is a gentleman of heroic temperament, and in 1902, he went to Japan where he entered the Meiji University, took part in the revolutonary movement. He was appointed the head of th Shan Ssi branch of the revolutionary confederates. On returning his own country, he was interesed in education, thus inspiring the people in secret with revolutionary ideas. At the time of the Revolution, he was the chief of the staff of the Shan Ssi army, besides being interested as the Chief of the Commissariat Department, in which capacity he contributed a great deal to the cause of his own army, In the first year of the Republic, he was the president of the local assembly, while in the year following, he was returned as a member of the House of Commons, and was on the committee for the drafting of the Constitution. On the dissolution of the Parliament, he visited Japan. On the outbreak of the Imperial restoration problem, he went to Shang-hai to fight the cause of his fellow countrymen. With the death of Yuanshi-kai, when the Parliament was to be opened, he went to Peking, and resumed his function as a member of the House of Commons.

楊詩淅 字海清 歲三十八

選舉地　陝西省

籍　貫　陝西省山陽縣

住　址　北京外城椿樹上三條門牌六號

君秉性溫良恭謙。待人以誠。生平以虛
已下問自喜。人告以過。卑詞謝其忠告
之厚意。然後細辦其是否合理。人言
當。固不吝即改。即有不當。亦絕不辯
釋。居常以退讓自持。人有與爭者。常
以柔制勝。不遑意氣而自甘於兩敗俱
傷。自幼即知苦讀求進。及長。愈益奮
勵。故天資雖非絕倫。而其所造。則甚
遠大着實。前清時以廩生。于宣統元
年舉孝廉方正。曾充縣議會議長。及
諮議局議員。民國元年。當選爲候補衆
議員。旋任財政司科員。二年冬入四
川。任巫溪縣雲陽縣兩處場知事。五年
夏。及國會復活。以照章遞補。得充衆
議院議員。

民國之精華　（傳記）　楊詩淅先生

君秉性溫良にして人を待つに誠を以てす。生平己を
虛ふして下問自ら喜ぶ。人の過を以て告ぐるあれば詞を
卑ふして其の厚意を謝す。然る後ち其の是非を省察して
人言當るあらば改むるに憚らず、當らざるも亦之を省ひて辯
解せず。居常退讓を以て自ら持し、人と爭ふ事あれば柔
を以て勝を制し、意氣を逞ふして兩者俱に傷くことを爲
ざる也。幼より刻苦勉勵して學業の進步を志し、長じて
益々切磋琢磨す。故に天資必ずしも絕倫なりと云ふを得

ざるも、其の造詣旣に深くして思想着實なり。前淸時代
廩生を以て宣統二年孝廉方正に舉げらる。曾て山陽縣議
會議長に舉げられ、又た選ばれて陝西省諮議局議員と爲
る。民國元年正式國會議員選擧に際し衆議院議員補缺員
に當選す。旋て財政司科員に任じ、二年冬四川に入りて
巫溪縣雲陽縣兩處場知事に任じ、五年國會復活するや補
缺として召集に應じ、仍は衆議院議員と爲る。

Mr. Yang Shieh Che, otherwise known as Hai Ching, age thirty eight, is a native of Shan
Yung, Shan Ssi. Being gentle and humble in temperamets, he is not ashamed to get thei advrice of
his inferiors, and is always open to accept any advice emanating from the good intention. While young, he
was an ardent scholar, and as he grew older, he became so more than ever. While he may not be a
genuis, but in steadness and soundnes of his thoughts, he is beaten by none. In 1910, he was elected
the president of the Shan Yung local assembly. In the 1st year of the Republic, he was returned for
House of Commons. During the suspension of the Parliamentary work, he was the governor of certain
districts in Ssi Shun. When the Parliament was re-opend, he was returned for the House of Commons,
the position which he now occupies.

三百二十九

楊崇山 字簡齊 歲三十五

選舉地 黑龍江省

籍　貫 黑龍江省海倫縣

住　址 北京邸祖胡同內口袋胡同二十一

君天資聰穎明敏。富于幹濟之才。然性情恬淡。謙虛好問。自幼志學。弱冠有文名。及長。醉心西學。研磋不倦。深明其精。洞察其義。造詣既深。列居要差。毫無過滿之態。壯年負笈入關。肄業直隸法政學堂。畢業後。歸本省。曾任黑龍江省高等檢察廳檢察官。君尤留意於人民寬苦。故其側身檢察時。該省刑無濫用。獄無怨聲。皆此君之力居多。民國元年。被舉爲第一次司法會議會員。二年正式國會成立。被選爲參議院議員。國會解散後。歸里閉居。不問時政。及約法恢復。國會重開。君復應召入京。仍就參議院議員舊職。

もし時、刑に濫用無く、獄に怨聲無かりし。民國元年舉げられて第一次司法官會議々員と爲れり。二年正式國會成立參議院議員に當選したり。國會解散されて後ち再び鄉里に歸りて時事を談せず、讀書自ら娛む。五年約法恢復して國會重ねて開院するや、君復た其の召集に應じて入京し、仍は參議院議員の舊職に就く。

君天資聰穎明敏にして幹濟の才に富む。然かも性情恬淡にして謙虛問を好み、幼より學に志して弱冠文名あり。長するに及び西學に心醉して研磋倦まず。其の義理に通曉して造詣既に深し。斯くて要職に歷充したるも毫も倨傲の風なし。壯年笈を負ふて關を入り、直隸法政學堂に修業し、卒業後歸省して曾て黑龍江高等檢察廳檢察官に任す。君尤も人民の苦樂に注意するを以て、其の檢察た

Mr. Yang Chung-shan, thirty five years of age, is a native of Hei Lun, Hei Lung Chinang. He is a shrewd and practical man of business. He is open minded and ready to listen to others. Early in youth, he was deeply interested in study. As he grew up he studied the western learning, in which he made a great advance. While occupying an important position, he was feer of any arrogance. He studied in the Chilin law school, from which he was graduated and appointed the public procurater of his province. Since, he was a great sympathizer of the people, so that no grudge was held against him as to the application of law. In the 1st year of the Republic, he was the member of the Council of lawyers, and, in the 2nd year, he was elected a member of the Senate. When the regislative assmbly was suppressed, he returned to his home and held. Complete silence about current topics. When the Parliament assumed its function, he entered Peking and was appointed a member of the Senate.

選舉地　吉林省
籍　貫　吉林省
住　址　北京打磨廠第一賓館

君賦性清高。言動舉止。皆逈異凡流。
然為人勤謹耐勞。入有所託。輒喜為盡
力。不以功自居。以故里人皆極愛敬
之。偶有糾紛。得君出一言。無不立即
解釋。自幼天資極高。悟性敏捷。讀書
能深思探究精義。不為成見所局。故思
想豐富。見解新穎。人但見其居常規矩
自守。不知其精神固異常活潑也。海內
雜新後。銳意西學。旋於前清時。由國
立法政專門學校預科畢業。復入銀行
專門學校正科畢業。服銀行業務。民國
二年民國正式國會成立。當選為參議
院議員。五年及至國會恢復。再充參議
院議員。

君賦性清高にして言動舉止な迥に凡流と異る。然も人
と為り悟謹にして勞に耐へ丶人若し託する所あれば輒ち
喜んで助力し、功を以て自ら居らざるを以て郷黨之を愛
敬す、郷里偶ま紛糾あれば、君の一言を得て立ところに
解決するなり。幼より天資極めて高く悟性敏捷なり。書
を讀みて深く其の義を究め、成見に囚はる丶所と為ら
、思想豐富にして見解新穎なり。前清時代、曾て國立
法政專門學校預科に學びて卒業し、次で銀行專門學校正
科に入り其の業を畢ゆ。爾來銀行業務に從事したり。民
國二年正式國會成立に際し選ばれて參議院議員と為る。
國會解散後は、また舊業の銀行事業に從事して時事を談
せず、五年國會恢復して重ねて召集を行ふに及び、遂に
復た參議院議員と為る。

Mr. Yang Sheng Shu, otherwise known as I-sun, age thirty four, is a native of Chilin. He is naturally a man of high spirit aud both in deeds and words he is distinguished from others. He is industrious, and stands the pain of the labor. He willingly sacrifices his interests for the sake of the people, so that a word from him often settled most compricated problems. He was deeply interested in reading up-to-date publications. Not being bound up his own ideas, his information is quite liberal and extensive. In the previous Chinese regime, he was graduated from the state law college as well as the bankers school. He was even since interested in banking. In the 2nd year of the Republic when Parliament was opened, he was elected a member of the Senate. When the Parliament was suppressed, he resumed the old work of banking. However, under the new president, the parliament was re-opened, and he became a member of the Senate.

楊家驤　字韻笙　歲三十四

選舉地　福建省

籍　貫　福建省晉江縣

住　址　北京後孫公園泉郡會館

君賦性誠厚篤實。不喜浮華。然天資聰
穎。思想活潑。爲人精明幹練。明察事
理。言動舉止。皆有定則。自幼好讀書。
不事嬉戲。能深思明辨。弱冠即能悟古
人精義。及長。尤肆力求博。謙虛好問。
不以小成自畫。及海內維新。專求有用
之學。遂負笈東渡留學。入日本大學法
科。研磋有年。畢業歸國。熱心提倡興
學。竭力籌畫公益。聲望日旺。民國二
年正式國會成立。被選爲衆議院議員。
國會解散後。持消極主義。不問時政。
五年及約法恢復。國會重開。遂又應
召仍爲參議院議員。

君賦性誠厚篤實にして浮華を喜ばす。然かも天資聰穎に
して思想活潑。人と爲り精明幹練にして事理を明に
し、言動舉止皆な定則あり。幼より讀書を好みて嬉戲を
事とせず、弱冠即ち能く古人の精義を悟得して、長する
や尤も博を求め、恭謙以て問を好み、小成を以て自ら畫
せず。海內維新に及びて專ら有用の學を求め、遂に笈を
負ふて東渡留學し、日本大學法科に入りて研磋の功を積
み、卒業歸國す。熱心に興學の事を提唱し、力を竭して
公益の業を圖り、聲望日に旺なり。民國二年正式成立
に際し、選ばれて參議院議員となる。國會解散後、消極
主義を持ちて時事を論せず。五年約法恢復して國會重ね
て開かるゝに及び、遂に又た召集に應じて仍は參議院議
員と爲る。

Mr. Yang Chia-hsiang, otherwise known as Yun sheng, age thirty four, is a native of Chin chiang, Fu Chien province. He is sober-minded and sincerely hates anything vain and fleeting in the world. He was active and deep thinker. Both in words and action he was guided by fixed principles. While young, he was interested in the reading of books. As he grew older, he was full of ambition and ready to listen any suggestion made to him. He devoted himself to the useful new learning. He entered the law college of Japan whence he was graduated. On his return home, he was deeply interested in the promotion of learning among the people and the furtherance of public interests. In the 2nd year of the Republic, when the Parliament was brought into existence, he was elected a member of the Senate. When the Parliament was dissolved, he was a conservative thinker and never discussed current topics. When the Parliament was re-opened, he was elected a member of the Senate.

楊大實 字秀翹 歲三十三

選舉地　奉天省

籍　貫　奉天省開原縣

住　址　北京爛縵胡同門牌四十三號

君以奉天警察學校卒業。曾任奉省巡查部長。旋稟請自費遊學日本。入東京警監學校肄業。嗣改入東斌學校。學習警察憲兵專科。兩年卒業後。歸國到奉。創辦鄉鎮警察半年後。成效卓著。經奉督調升錦州復州各屬警察長之職。旋辭職回奉。邀集同志。創辦國民報社。辛亥革命。鼓吹甚力。當與張榕等組織聯合急進會君任會內總務部部長。嗣充關外民軍第一軍司令部總參謀兼執法。佔據莊復。與清軍戰爭兩閱月餘。屢獲勝利。共和宣布。民軍退駐烟台。乃辭職。遍遊滬甯鄂淮各處。民國元年冬旋奉。充民國新聞社社長。二年春。被選爲衆議院議員。旋以二次革命嫌疑。遁跡於大連長春哈爾濱及海山歲等處。三次革命。仍回奉天召集舊部。組織東三省護國軍。大局解決。乃將所部民軍一律解散及國會復活。遂來京仍供令職。

君は奉天警察學校出身の秀才なり。初め奉天省巡査部長に任す、旋して日本に留學して東京警察監獄學校に學び、後ち轉じて東斌學校に入り警察憲兵專科を卒業す。歸國後郷里の警察を創め、後ち錦州各地の警察長に任ず。前清末季其の職を辭して奉天に歸り同志を糾合して國民報社を創立經營し、第一革命の事起るや、皷吹甚だ力め、張榕等と聯合急進會を組織して其の總務部長に任じ。嗣で關外民軍第一軍司令部總參謀兼執法に任ひ、莊復を占領して清軍を激へ戰ふ。共和宣布して、民軍烟臺に退くや乃ち職を辭して長江一帶各地に遊歷し、民國元年奉天に歸りて民國新聞社長と爲る。第二革命に際し嫌疑を被りて大連長春哈爾賓及び浦鹽斯德等に遁れ、第三革命の事起るや、奉天に歸りて東三省護國軍を組織し、大局解決して之を解散し、恢復せる國會の召集に應じて北京に入り仍は衆議院議員たり。

民國之精華　（傳記）　楊大寶先生

Mr. Yang Tai-shih, otherwise known as Hsin Chiao, age thirty three, is a native of Kai yuan, Feng Tien hsing. He is one of the most successful graduates of the Feng Tien police school. As soon as he was graduated, he was appointed the head of the certain section of the police. He came to Japan, where he studied in the Tokyo police and prison school. On his return home, he was interested in the work of the police and was the chief of the police in a number of a place. On the later days of the previous Chinese regime, he returned to Feng tien and established the national news society. As soon as the 1st revolution broke out, he organized a political society, of which he became the chief. As soon as the Republic was established he returned to his home and became the president of the Ning kuo newspaper, while, in the 2nd year of the Republic he was elected a member of the chamber of commerce. At the outbreak of the 2nd revolution, he was placed under the government suspicion, so that he ran away to Tailen, Chengshun, Harbin, and Vladiostock. When the situation was settled, he came up to Peking responding to the call and was appointed a member of the House of Commons.

楊振春　字生吾　歲三十一

選舉地　吉林省

籍貫　吉林省雙城縣

住址　北京宣武門都城廟街

君自幼慷慨好義慕古任俠之言行。廿一歲。由黑龍江省考送。北京國立法政專門學校肄業。前清宣統元年。東三省發起。第四次請開國會團。曾充黑龍江省代表。上書清廷請開國會。旋被清帝諭令。看送回籍。時張之洞主全國學務。正嚴防學生干與政治之際。君幾被放校除名。至廿六歲卒業。值武昌起義。當即回籍。被選爲地方保安會會長。旋被都督府聘爲顧問官。次年正式國會召集。即當選爲衆議院議員。國會被袁總統解散。君以國民黨黨籍。同被驅逐。退當即回里門。閉戶讀書。三年未出里門一步。及國會復活。始入京。仍爲衆議院議員。

宣幼より慷慨義を好み、古任俠の言行を慕ふ。年二十一歳、黑龍江省より選拔されて北京國立法政專門學校に學び、前清宣統元年東三省に於て第四回國會請願團を組織する、黑龍江省代表として參加し、國會の速開を請願す。旋て清帝の上諭ありて一同原籍に歸遷を命ず。時恰かも張之洞が全國の學務を掌りて、學生の政治に干與するを嚴禁する際なりしを以て、君殆んど放校處分を受けんとす。二十六才に至りて漸く卒業するを得たり。時適ま武昌義を起す。君即ち郷里に歸り、選ばれて保安會々長となる。旋て黑龍江都督府より聘せられて顧問となり、民國二年正式國會衆議院議員に當選す。袁政府が國民黨員の議員證書を非法剝奪するや、君亦た國民黨員たるの故を以て逐はる。君即ち田園に歸臥し、杜門閉戶讀書自ら娯み、三年未だ里門を出でず。五年國會復活するに及び、出でゝ仍ほ衆議院議員の職に復したり。

Mr. Yan Chen-chun, otherwise known as Sheng Wu, age thirty one, is a native of Chilin hsing. Being naturally of heroic temperament, he was, when young, a lover of gallant deeds. At the age of twenty one he was sent to the peking state law school. In 1909, he organized the memorial representation society for the opening of the Parliament, to which he attended as a representative. It was at this time that the chinese statesman, Mr. Chou-tsi tow prohibited students to take part in politics, so that he was nearly on the point of being expelled from the school. At the age of twenty six he graduated from the school. When Wu-chun's trouble broke out he returned to his home and was elected the president of the peace preservation society. In the 2nd year of the Republic he was elected a member of the House of Commons. When Yuanshi-kai suppressed the Parliament, he was also driven away from Peking, so that he went back to his home and practically shut himself up for the space of three years. He was returned for the House of Commons, as soon as the Parliament resumed its function.

楊渡 字沖溪 歲三十一

選舉地　奉天省
籍　貫　奉天省海城縣
住　址　北京背陰胡同

君為人耿介不阿。生平以緘默自持。不苟言笑。不輕於舉動。持己以嚴而待人以和。與人交。極重然諾。人有所託雖允之。必待事成而後告。居恆以消極自持。堅忍耐勞。不為意氣所動。追宗旨既定。則又猛勇直前。不復觀望。自幼聰敏異人。讀書能深思明辨。探求真義。及長。尤奮勉求博。頗以大器自期。曾入奉天省立高等警察學校。畢業後。歷充黑龍江省城警官。奉天海龍府警務長。海城縣參事會參事。正式國會成立。被選為參議院議員。兼憲法起草委員會起委員。國會解散後。歸里蟄居。不求聞達。及國會復活。始應召就職。

民國之精華　（傳記）　楊渡先生

君人と為り耿介にして阿らず、生平緘默を以て自ら持し言語動作共に慎重なり。人と交りて極めて然諾を重んじ人若し託する所あれば、之を允すと雖も必ず事成るを待ちて後ち告ぐ。居常消極を以て自ら持し、堅忍以て勞に耐へ、意氣の為に輕々しく動かず、主義既に定まるに及び、勇往邁進して敢て撓まざる也。幼より聰敏人に異り讀書能く其の義理を探求す。長ずるに及び精勵以て博を求め研磋怠まず。曾て奉天省立高等警察學校に入りて業を畢ゆ。後ち出仕して黑龍江省城警察官、奉天海龍府警務長、海城縣參事會參事等の職に歷任して功勞あり。民式二年正式國會參議院議員に當選し、憲法起草委員會委員に舉げらる。國會解散後、鄉里に歸りて蟄居し、また聞達を求めず。國會復活するに及び、再び出でゝ召集に應じ、仍ほ參議院議員の舊職に就きたり。

Mr. Yang Tu, otherwise called Chi pan, age thirty one, is a native of Hai Cheng hsien. He is straight forward in character, and never subject himself to any flattery. Being tacitern, he is always serious as to his every movement. In dealing with others he always keeps his words, and is never guilty of any carless action. However, when he once, makes up his mind he steadfastly accomplishes his object in view. He was educated in the high police school of his province. Ever since, he occupied many important positions in that province, in which his talents were fully displayed. In the 2nd year of the Republic, he was elected a member of the Senate and was on the committee of drafting the constitution. With the dissolution of the Parliament he returned to his home, and showed no interest in politics. As soon as the Parliament was re-opened, he at once came up to Peking, and resumed his function as the member of the Senate.

賈鳴梧 字鳳樓 歲五十二

選舉地　山西省

籍　貫　山西省汾城縣

住　址　北京敎場三條

君賦性耿介。嚴取與。重然諾。喜爲人盡力。事成。絕不望報。讀書求精而不求博。故每畢一書。必有所得。西學輸入後。君立志棄舉。從事新學。以丁酉拔貢。於光緒三十三年。充縣視學學務總董。宣統元年。被舉爲本省諮議局議員。及本縣自治事務所正所長。民國改建。改爲縣議會正議長。民國二年正式國會成立。被選爲衆議院議員。二年十月。以藉隸國民黨。被袁氏以非法解散。君歸里讀書。不聞政事。五年及約法恢復。國會重開。始應召至京。仍爲衆議院議員。

君賦性耿介にして然諾を重んじ、人の爲に力を致すを喜び、事成つて絕へて報を望まず。其の舊を讀むや、精を求めて博を求めず。西學輸入されより、志を立て、科學の業を棄て新學に從事す。丁酉の拔貢生たり。光緒三十三年縣視學學務總董に任じ、宣統元年本省諮議局議員に舉げらる。又た汾城縣自治事務所正所長に推さる。民國樹立するや、改めて縣議會議長に舉げられる。民國二年正式國會成立に際し、衆望を荷つて衆議院議員に當選す。同年十月、君もた國民黨員たるの故を以て袁政府の非法干涉により、議員の職務を剝奪されて南旋す。爾來鄉里に韜晦して讀書自ら娛み、また政事を聞かず。五年袁氏死して約法復活し國會再蘇するに及び、君復た其の召集に應じ入京し、仍ち衆讓院議員と爲る。

Mr. Chia Ming, otherwise called Feng Yi, fifty two years of age, is a native of Feng Cheng, the Shan Ssi hsing. He is a gentleman who is interested in doing good at his own expense and always keeps his words if he gives them. He was a reader of books, but in doing so he always aimed at the through understanding. When the estern learning was introduced, he directed his attention towards the acquisition of the same. In 1907, he was the chief of school inspectors, while in 1909 he was appointed a member of the local assembly and the head of the institution investigating the civic system in Fen Cheng. With the establishment of the Republic he was appointed the president of the Local assembly. In the 2nd year of the Republic, when the parliament was brought into existence, he was returned for the House of Commons with a large majority. Under the pressure of Yuanshi-kai he was deprived of his office as a member of the legislative body. He returned to his home where he indulged himself in reading and cared very little about politics. When the Parliament was opened again, he entered Peking and resumed his function as the member of the Parliament, the position he holds at the present moment.

董耕雲 字話 年歲五十三

選舉地　吉林省

籍　貫　吉林省長春縣

住　址　北京西單牌樓英子胡同門牌四號

君秉性溫厚篤實。頭腦明晰。而心力堅強。雖待人以和。而疾惡如仇。無形中界限極嚴。絕不以小德之出入。而隨同俗尚。自幼讀書。即專心一志。不事嬉戲。年方弱冠。已能淡于物慾。不以尋常嗜好縈懷。及長。尤以菲薄自待。但以免於飢渴凍餒爲限。然爲公益起見。則又勇於出資。前清宣統元年春。曾瓣辦長春縣立女子學校。民國元年冬。被選爲衆議院議員。旋組織長春國民黨分部。民國二年十一月。袁世凱羅織罪狀。坐以助亂違法。取消君等八十餘名之議員職權。國會亦旋即解散。君遂隱伏里門。絕口不談時事。及至共和再造。國會重開。始應召入京。仍爲參議院議員。

君秉性溫厚篤實にして、頭腦明晰志強固なり。人を待つに和を以てし、惡を疾むこと仇の如く、無形の中限界極めて嚴重にして絕へて小人の出入を以てせず。幼より專心一意書を讀みて嬉戲を事とせず。年方に弱冠にして旣に物慾に淡く、尋常の嗜好を以て縈がれず。長ずるに及び尤も菲薄を以て自ら待つ。然かも公益の爲には則ち又た出資を惜まず、前清宣統元年春、曾て長春縣立女子學校を創立經營す。民國元年冬、選ばれて衆議院議員と爲る。旋て長春國民黨分部を組織し、地方黨勢の擴張に盡力したり。二年十一月袁政府が罪狀を羅織して亂黨員と爲して、君等八十餘名議員の職權を取消して、國會もた旋て解散さるるや、君遂に里門に韜晦して時事を談せず。國會重ねて開かるヽに及び、再び出でヽ其の召集に應じ、仍ほ參議院議員と爲る。

民國之精華　（傳記）　董耕雲先生

Mr. Tung Ken Yun called Huo Nien, age fifty two, a native of Cheng Chung, the Chi Lin hsing, is a gentleman of clear brain and strong will. He had a high moral conception to which men of ordinary calibre fail to have an access. Early in youth, he was interested in reading books, and was above the sentiment of the common people. For the public interests, he grudges neither money nor labour. In 1909, he was interested in founding the Cheng Chung Girl School, while in 1912, he was elected a member of the House of Commons. He organized the Cheng Chung National party, and made his efforts in the extention of the influence of the party. In 1912, the Yuanshi-kai government enumerated accusations against about 80 members of which he was one, and deprived then of their function which brought about the dissolution of the Parliament. Then, he returned to his home, and never troubled him about politics. At the re-opening of the Parliament, he was elected as a Member of the Senate.

虞廷愷 字拍頎 歲三十七

選舉地 浙江省

籍貫 浙江省瑞安縣

住址 北京未央胡同南口

君性質明敏。氣宇開闊。自幼好學。遇目不忘。於書無所不讀。時人稱爲博學多能之士。每憤國事日非。慷慨悲歌。無不激動左右。然接以爲徒托空談無裨實際。於是勵志求學。前清光緒丙午歲。游學日本。入東京法政大學。己酉歲畢業回國。任抗州官立法政學校。兼高等巡警學堂。全浙自治研究所敎員。庚戌歲兼任私立法政學校敎員。辛亥光復後。充浙江財政部支應科科長兼秘書。嗣改部爲司升任財政司僉事。兼都督府財政秘書。代理財政司長。民國元年五月。因病辭職回里。二年被選爲衆議院議員。三年奉令大總統薦請任命爲參政院僉事。國會恢復後。代理參議院秘書長。其稱職有足多云。

君性質明敏にして氣宇開濶なり。幼より學を好み、博覽强記なり。國事日に非なるを見て悲歌慷慨す。然かも空論遂に實際に神益なきを悟りて、銳意天下有用の學を求めて研磋倦まず、前淸光緒丙午の歲、日本に游學して東京法政大學校に入る、己酉の歲其の業を畢へて歸國し、抗州官立法政學校、高等巡警學校、全浙自治研究所等に敎鞭を執り、庚戌の歲私立法政學校敎員を兼ねたり。辛亥の歲、命を革めて民國を樹立するや、浙江財政部支應科々長兼秘書に任じ、嗣いで部を改めて司と爲すや、財政僉事兼都督府財政秘書に任じ、財政司長を兼ぬ。民國元年五月、病氣を以て辭職て國に歸る。民國二年正式國會衆議院議員に當選す。國會解散後三年大總統より參政院僉事に薦任さる。國會恢復さるゝに及び、再び其の召集に應じ、參議院秘書長を代理し、現に仍は衆議院議員たり。

Mr. Lu Ting-Kai, age thirty seven, is a native of Jui An, Che Chiang province. He is a man of aspiration when quite young. Seeing the state of the country growing worse every day he thought of the necessity of studying useful science, since he recognized that empty words have no practical benefit. In 1906, he went io Japan where he studied in the Tokyo law college and returned to his country in 1909. He was appointed an instructor of the government law school, the the institusion for the investigation of the civic system. When the Revolution was actualized, he became the private secretary to the financial and justice bureaus. In the 1st year of the Republic owing to illness he resigned his post while in the 1st year of the Parliament he was returned for the House of Commons. When Yuanshi-kai disolved the Parliament, he was appointed the secretary of the Senate. However, with the dissolution of the Parliament he was appointed a private secretary to the Senate, but as a matter of the fact he was again returned for the House of Commons.

葛　莊　字戀忱　歲四十四

選舉地　江西省

籍貫　江西省雩都

住址　北京達智橋七號

君賦性篤厚。素以急公尚義。見知于鄉里間。生平所爲社會盡力事蹟。以教育及地方自治事宜爲尤多。君家非素豐。然爲公益故。常不吝解囊。宣統元年。創辦葛坳高初兩等小學校。捐開辦費壹百元。籌集學校基金陸千餘元。並擔任該校義務校長三載。宣統三年。被選爲永鄉自治會議長。捐自治開辦費壹百元。募集自治基金三千餘元。民國元年。任尋鄔縣知事。二年。被選爲衆議院議員。辭歲費二千元。倡辦私立昌村中學校。損開辦費六百元。民國三年。擔任昌村中學校義務校長。與同志募集學校基金壹萬六千餘元。購地建築洋式學校一所。民國四年。應第四次知事試驗。取列申等。籤分雲南。國會復活。遂辭知事職。仍爲衆議員。

民國之精華　（傳記）　葛莊先生

君賦性篤厚にして、公に急ぎ義を尚ぶを以て鄉黨に知らる。生平社會の爲に力を盡して教育の普及及び地方自治の發展に對し功勞多し。宣統元年自ら巨費を投じて葛坳高初兩等小學校を創立し、並に同校の義務校長たること三年、選ばれて永鄉自治會議長となり、同會の創立費並に自治基金の多額をも捐助する所ありたり。民國元年尋鄔縣知事に任じ令名あり。二年正式國會衆議院議員に當選し特に其の歲額を辭す。又た私立昌村中學校を發起創設して創業費を捐助したり。三年昌村中學校義務校長を擔任し、同志と謀りて學校基金を募集し、地を購ひて洋風の學校一箇所を建築す。四年第四回の知事試驗に應じて甲等に列し雲南省に分たる。五年國會復活するに及び、遂に知事の職を辭して召集に應じ、仍ほ衆議院議員と爲る。

Mr. Ko Chuang, age forty four, is a native of Yutu, Chian Hsi province. On account of the virtues of honesty, sicerity, and high spirit of sacrifice, he is respected by his countrymen. He was keenly interested in the expansion of education and the development of local interests. In 1909, at his own expence, he established a primary school both high and elementary grade, of which he was the principal for three years. He contributed a great deal of funds for the promotion of the study of the civic institution. In the first year of the Republic, he executed his function as a local governer in one of the province, while in the second year of the Republic he was returned for the House of Commons, but would not receive any pay. He also promoted a middle school, of which he was appointed the principal. He went about among his friends, and bought the land to build a foreign styled school building. When the Parliament was re-opened, he was returned for the House of Commons, the honour he now enjoys.

褚輔成 字慧僧 歲四十四

選舉地 浙江省
籍 貫 浙江省嘉興縣
住 址 北京象坊橋

君秉性剛正。待人以誠。自幼篤實不
欺。尚質惡文。然資質聰敏。悟性極高。
讀書能精思深入。探求眞義。雖博及經
史。而不喜搞華飾藻。尋摘章句。與人
交。重然諾。尚信義。人有所託。雖擬爲
盡力。常於事前。陽爲拒絕。然後暗中
援助之事成。絕不望報。曾留學日本。
東洋大學高等警政科。畢業歸國。曾于
前清時歷任南湖學堂校長。嘉興中學
堂敎員。嘉秀兩邑禁烟局總董。嘉興府商
會總理。浙江諮議局議員。民國成立。
任浙軍政府政事部長。元年春。改任民
政司長。是年秋。被舉爲國民黨本部參
議。浙支部部長。旋被舉爲衆議院議
員。二年八月。以政治犯嫌疑被捕。直
至是政府傾倒。始放免出獄。及國會重
開。遂應召仍爲衆議院議員。

君秉性剛正にして人を待つに誠を以てす。幼より篤實に
して欺かず、質を尚びて文を惡む。然かも資質聰敏にし
て悟性極めて高く、書を讀みて其の精を究め其の義を明
にす。人と交りて然諾を重んじ信義を尚ぶ。曾て笈を負
ふて日本に游學し、東洋大學高等警政科に入りて卒業
す。歸國の後ち南湖學堂校長、嘉興府商會議長、浙江
諮議局議員、嘉秀兩
邑禁烟局總董、嘉興府商會總理、浙江諮議局議員等の職
に歷充し、即ち初め育英の業に從事し、後ち地方の公益
に歷充し。民國の成立に當り浙江軍政府政事
部長に任じ、元年春改めて民政司と爲る。後ち擧げられ
て國民黨本部叄議として浙江支部長を兼ぬ。二年正式國
會衆議院議員に當選す。同年八月政治犯の嫌疑を以て捕
へられて獄に下り、五年袁政府傾倒するに及び始めて釋
放さる。旣にして國會恢復す。遂に其の召集に應じて仍
は衆議院議員と爲る。

Mr. Chu Fu-cheng, otherwise known as Hui Seng, age forty four, is a native of Chia Hsing, Che Chiang hsing. He is known for the uprightness and sincerity of his chatacter. He prefers the substance to men external pomp. He is quick of understanding, and is well conversant with the spirit of the authors. In dealing with others, he is faithful to his words. He went over to Japan to complete his education. He entered the Oriental University, whence he was graduated. On returning to his home, he was appointed the head of various institutes. He was thus keenly interested in the promotion of local educational interests in diverse ways. When the Republic was established, he was appointed the chief of the political Bureau of the Military Government of Chia hsing. He was also an adviser to the Government, he was released. When the Parliament was re-opened, he was returned for the House of Commons.

鄒魯　字海濱　歲三十二

選舉地　廣東省

籍貫　廣東省潮州犬埔縣

住址　北京順治門內油房胡同東十二號

君性剛正負奇氣。在廣東法政學堂畢業。後創辦大埔樂羣中學。及潮嘉師範。歷任廣東自治研究所及兩廣方言學堂教授。年小奔走革命。廣東新軍之役。三月廿九之役。君咸與焉。辛亥、粵軍北伐。君任兵站總監。敗張勳于固鎮宿州。凱還後。代表粵督晉京。參議要政。事竟回粵。粵督胡漢民、軍統陳炯明。疊欲以瓊崖鎮守使潮梅綏靖處督辦任君。君力辭不就嗣被選爲衆議院議員。在國會。侃侃有聲。彈劾內閣。袁氏忌之。必欲得而甘心。君以計南下再圖粵事。不成。東渡日本留學。兼主民國雜誌筆政。洎歐戰發生。往返港滬南洋日本。謀改革。適袁氏稱帝。與同志在滬。創設中華新報中華雜誌等。抗之。此次革命成功。運動潮梅獨立。爲全粵倡。潮梅官紳欲舉君與陳炯明。爲護國軍總副司令。君不尤。國會回復。仍就議員之職。

君性剛正にして奇氣を負ふ。廣東法政學校を卒業して後ち、大埔樂羣中學校及び潮嘉師範學校を創設し、又た廣東省自治研究所及び兩廣方言學校教授に歷任す。年少革命の志々を抱く。廣東新軍の役、三月廿九の役、辛亥の役、君咸く與る。辛亥の歲、廣東軍北伐するや、君兵站總監として南京に抵り要政に參議す。後ち廣東都督代表として南京に抵り要政に參議す。潮梅綏靖處督辦に任せし軍統陳炯明は君を瓊崖鎮守便、潮梅綏靖處督辦に任せしも辭して就かず。施て選ばれて衆議院議員と爲る。正論讜議法を守りて屈せず、袁氏深く之を忌む。第二革命の事成らずして日本に留學し、民國雜誌主筆を兼ぬ。歐洲戰爭發生後、香港上海南洋日本間を往來して革命を計り、後ち上海に於て中華新報新中華雜誌の編輯に從事して帝制に反對す。第三革命の車起るや、潮海の官紳君と陳炯明とを舉げて護國軍總副司令とす、君允さず。國會恢復して仍は衆議院議員の職に就く。

民國之精華　（傳記）　鄒魯先生

Mr. Su Lu, sometimes Called Hai-pin, age thirty two, is a native of Tai-pu, Chao-chou, Kuang-tung province. After graduating from the law college in Kuang-tung he established a middle and normal schools in his province while he was interested in the education of the rising generation. In 1911 when the Kuang-tung army started on the northren expedition he was appointed a Chief of the Commissariat department. He represented the Kuangtung Governor General and went to Nanking where he occupied an important post. When the Parliament was opened for the House of Commons he was a great debator in the House of Commons and incurred the displeasure of Yuan-shi-kai. In the 2nd Revolution his attempts were failure so that he went to Japan, and interested himself in the publication of magazine. outbreak of the European war he staged in Hongkong, Shanghai and South sea islands to plan for the Revolution. When the Imperial movement of Yuanshi kai was started he was a great opponent of the same. With the Restoration of the Parliament he was elected for the House of Commons, the honor which he enjoys even in the present moment.

榮厚　字僕儕　歲四十三

選舉地　蒙古

籍貫　直隷省大與縣

住址　北京安定門大街棉花胡同中間路北

君氣度從容。性情和緩。與人交。溫良恭讓。不爲意氣之爭。雖有所忿恨。亦未嘗以疾言遽色加入。然意志極强。富於獨立之性。且喜聞忠告之言。勇於改過。人告人曰。聞過而改。既得無過之實。又居從善如流之名。利執大焉。年少讀書。即以遠大自期。稍長。愈益從事於學養。故天資雖非絕高。而明察事情。洞悉直理。初入仕途。即老成練達。措置動止輒得宜。於前清時。由更部驗。封司掌印郎中。欽選爲資政院議員。京察一等。放廣東瓊州府知府。民國二年。正式國會成立。被選爲參議院議員。國會停止後。君閑居都門。無意仕進。及國會重開。始應召仍爲議員。

君氣度從客にして性情和讓、人と交りて溫良恭讓、意氣の爭を爲さす。嚇怒する時と雖も亦た甞て疾言遽色を以て人に加へす。且つ人の忠言を喜びて過を改むるに勇あり。幼より書を讀みて孜々として研磋倦まず、自ら大成を以て期したり。稍や長じて益々學を求めて切磋琢磨の功を積み、天資必すしも聰慧絕倫なりと云ふを得ざるも、博く群籍を涉獵して遂に其の眞義を究む。初め仕途に入るや、即ち老成練達にして言動措置共に報ち宜しきを得た

り。前清時代吏部の試に及第して司掌印郎中に勅選されたり。又た京察一等を以て廣東省瓊州府知府に放たる。民國二年正式國會議員の選舉に當り參議院議員に當選す。國會停止後、君師に閑居して讀書自ら娛み又た致仕榮達に意なし。國會重て召集を行ふに及び、遂に出で丶仍は參議院議員の職に就きたり。

Mr. Jung Hou, sometimes known as Pu Chai, age forty three, is a native of Tai Hsiong, Chilin province. He is a gentleman of tranquil temperament and in dealing with others he never showed any anger. He was open to listen to the advise of others and rectify his mistakes. He was a copious reader of books and was quite ambitious. Through the reading of these books he accumulated. a stock of knowledge which was a great use to him. In the previous Chinese regime he passed the civil service examination, and was elected for the assembly then held in China. In the 2nd year of the Republic he was appointed a member of the Senate. When the Parliament was shut down he stayed in Peking, but only in retirement and took great delight in the perusal books. When the parliament was summond he became a member of the Senate.

趙　鯨　字漢池　歲四十六

選舉地　雲南省
籍　貫　雲南省洱源縣
住　址　北京敎場西條雲南館

君爲人誠厚篤實。痛惡浮華。與人交。
常硬直不阿。絕無世故之念。人告以
過。亦欣然謝之。然居心仁厚。喜救人
急難。故其接物。雖稍露鋒鋩。而人亦
罕恨之者。自幼好讀深思、喜研究眞
理。而不屑尋章摘句。以爲博取功名
計。故其所讀多用之書。及海內維新。
志西學遂肆于新書。無所不覩。而尤醉
心于法律之書。曾前淸丁未。保送考取
度支部主事。在籍辦學。光復後。被選
爲參議院議員。

民國之精華　（傳記）　趙鯨先生

君人と爲り誠厚篤實にして浮華を憎惡す。人と交るや常
に硬直阿らずして世故の念無し。人若し告ぐるに過を以
てすれば欣然之を謝す。居心仁厚にして人の急を救ふこ
とを喜ぶ幼より讀を好みて深く思索し、眞理を攻究して、
章句の末に拘泥せず。海內維新に及び志を立て、新智識
の涵養に勤め、廣く新書を涉獵し、尤も志を法律の書に心醉
したり。前淸丁未の歲、登用試驗に及第して度支部主事を
授けられたるも、鄕里に在りて銳意興學に志し、地方敎
育の普及、民智の開發に盡瘁する所ありたり。民國樹立
して正式國會を組織するや選ばれて參議院議員を爲る。
同會解散後、復た鄕里に歸りて育英の業に從つて後進を
誘掖するを念とす。帝政問題發生するや雲南先づ立ちて
義を起し、旋て約法復活して國會重ねて召集さる、君遂に
首義の地を出で、入京し、仍ほ衆議院議員と爲る。

Mr. Chao Ching, otherwise known as Han Chih, forty six year of age, is a native of Erh Yuan hsien, Yun nan province. He is a gentleman of high character and since temperament. In dealing with others, he is sociable, but not necessary obsequious, and he is ready to listen to the suggestions given by others. He is also deeply interested in saving others from their trouble. Early in life, his education was started, but besides being a comprehensive reader, he took delight in seeking deep truth; not being transmelled with mere words. With the introduction of new thoughts, he became interested in the acquisition of new thoughts, and to that effect, he read new books, and particularly devoted himself to the study of law. At the later days of the previous Chinese regime, he passed the civil service examination, and was appointed the government official. He was greatly interested in the diffusion of education in his native province. With the establishment of the Republic, the parliament was summoned, when he was appointed a member of the Senate. On the dissolution of the Parliament, he returned home, he was engaged in the education of the younger generation. When the Imperial Movement of Yuanshi-kai was started, he was one of the greatest opponents. However, when the Parliament was re-opened he was appointed a member of the Senate.

趙炳麟　字竺垣　歲四十

選舉地　廣西省
籍貫　廣西省全縣
住址　北京臨清宮

君天資聰慧敏捷。為人剛直不阿。自幼
篤學。弱冠有文名。及長。提倡道德。把
持正義。前清諫官。鑑中之錚錚者也。
翰林院編修。掌京畿道監察御史。前清
光緒末李因彈劾慶親王奕劻。及軍機
大臣袁世凱。政府忌之。開去御史底
缺。以四品京堂候補。回籍。民國二年
被選為衆議院議員。國會停止後。退居
歸里。提倡農礦。袁氏帝制發生。佐廣
西都督陸榮廷起義。出師湖南。袁氏物
故。民國再造。陸榮廷為代表。北上抵
京。約法恢復。國會重開。仍就衆議院
議員職務。

君天資聰慧敏捷にして人と爲り剛直阿らず。幼より學に
篤く、弱冠早くも文名あり。長ずるに及びて道德を提唱し
て正義を把持し、前清諫官として後ち畿中の錚々たる者なり、
曾て翰林院編修にして後ち京畿道監察御史に任ず。前清
光緒末年、慶親王及び袁世凱を彈劾す。爲に政府に忌まれ
て御史の職を奪ひ、四品京堂候補を以て郷里に歸らしむ。
清廷覆沒して民國樹立するや、二年正式國會衆議院議員
に當選す。國會停止後、再び退いて鄉里に歸り、農業礦
業の改良發展を唱導す。袁氏共和を破壞して帝制を企圖
するや、慨然蹶起して廣西都督陸榮廷を佐けて事を舉げ、
以て師を湖南に出だす。旣にして袁氏物故して再び民國
の建設時代となる。陸榮廷の代表として北京に抵る。旋
て約法恢復して國會重ねて開く、君仍ほ衆議院議員の職
に就きたり。

Mr. Chao Ping-lin, known as Chu Yuan, forty years of age, is a native of Chuan hsien, Kuang hsi province. When young, he was distinguished for his smartness, and strength of will. He was also a deep scholar, and attained even in youth considerable literay fame. As he grew older, he became a moral teacher, and advocate of justice. Among the officials of the previous Chinese regims, his name stood indeed conspicuous. At the later days of the previous Emperor of China, he impeached Prince Cheng and Yuan Shi-kai because of which he was deprived of his government office, so that he had to retire to his native home. With the downfall of the Chinese dynasty, and the establishment of the Republic, he was returned for the House of Commons. When the Parliament was suppressed by Yuan Shi-kai, went back to his home when he was interested in the improvement of agriculture and mining. When the Imperial Movement took place, he was one of the opponents. With the deach of Yuanshi-kai, the Parliament was restored, and he was elected a member of the House of Commons.

選舉地　四川省
籍　貫　四川省江安縣
住　址　北京順治門外前靑廠

君爲人誠厚篤實。不喜浮華。生平以儉
約自持。痛惡奢移。然唯自待歡薄。而
厚於待人。且喜爲善舉。鄕里之困於貧
者。無不曾受君惠。少年時。好爲詩詞。
而不汲汲於科弟。及長。遂改志求有用
之學。嘗謂詞章誤人之事功。而舉業則
錮人之情性。卽購譯本讀之。尤喜研究
政法之學。於新學造詣亦旣深。夙抱濟
生經民之志。竭力於地方自治之發展。
辛亥革命。民國肇造。宣布憲政共和。
民國二年被選爲正式國會參議院議
員。國會解散。君歸里讀書。不談時事。
及國會重開。始入京。仍復充參議院
議員。

君人と爲り誠厚篤實にして浮華を喜ばず、生平儉約を以
て自ら持し奢移を痛惡す。然り自ら待つに甚だ薄きも、人
を待つに厚くして且つ慈善を爲すを喜ぶ。少年時代、好ん
で詩賦を作り、長ずるに及びて志を改めて有用の學を求
め、卽ち遍ねく譯本を購入して之を讀み、尤も法政の學
を研究する事を喜び、新學の造詣亦た旣に深し。夙に濟
生經民の志を抱きて地方自治の發展に盡力したり。辛亥
の歲、命を革めて民國の奠を肇め、以て憲政共和を宣布
するや、民國二年當選して正式國會參議院議員と爲る。
國會解散されてより鄕里に歸臥して讀書自ら娛み逍遙自
適して時事を談せず。國會重ねて開かるゝ及び遂に又た
召集に應じて仍ち參議院議員の職に任じたり。

民國之精華　（傳記）趙時欽先生

Mr. Chao Shih-chin, sometimes known as Tzu lin age forty is a native of Chiang An, Hsi Chuan province. He is a gentleman of high virtue, hating anything pompous and vain. Being naturally of frugal and economical habit, he conceived dead hatred against extravagance. In dealing with others, he is kind and open-minded. Even while young, he was a considerable poet. As he grew older, he sought a useful learning and acquired the new knowledge through translated books. He was particularly interested in the study of law in which he attained considerable proficiency. Through the Revolution of 1911, when the Republic was formed, he was elected a member of the Senate. When the Parliament was shut down, he returned to his home where he was interested in reading books, but turned a deap ear to politics. When the Parliament was restored, he was again appointed a member of the Senate, the position of honour he holds in the present moment.

趙學良 字伊田 歲三十九

選舉地　吉林省

籍　貫　吉林長春縣

住　址　北京西城石駙馬大街憲法研究會

君原名學臣。前清附生中式癸卯順天鄉試舉人。充任內閣中書。光緒三十二年。考入北洋法政學堂。修習法律專科。宣統元年。選爲吉林諮議局副議長。君憤於官府之專制淫威。而人思有以制止之。藉以爲民權之張本。以故彈劾陳撫救火不力各案。皆君一人主張之。卒使官威爲之一戢。而民氣爲之一振。及辛亥武漢起義。君爲吉林代表。潛赴上海。代達北方贊成共和之意。與各省代表團聯合一致。卒使南北意見藉以疏通。早收統一共和之效果。對於共和前途。君實大有關係焉。民國元年。連任爲吉林臨時省議會副議長。民國二年由省議會選爲參議院議員。君見當時黨爭甚烈。深慮失極端主張必生共和之反動力。故所持政見。純以國家爲前提。不爲各黨所操縱。民國五年國會恢復。仍就參議院議員之職。

君原名學臣と云ふ。前清の附生により癸卯順天鄉試及第の舉人として內閣中書に任す。光緒三十二年に北洋法政學校に入り法律專科を修む。宣統元年選ばれて吉林諮議局副議長と爲る。君官府の專制淫威を憤ること久しく、即ち陳巡撫を彈劾して民權擴張の爲に大に氣を吐き卒に吉林政界の官威大に戢みたり。辛亥の歲武昌義を起すや、吉林代表として上海に赴き各省代表團と一致して南北意見の疏通を計り、以て共和統一を促成するに努めたり。民國元年又た吉林臨時省議會副議長に舉げられ、二年正式國會參議院議員に當選す。當時の政界黨爭激烈なるを見て、極端の主張は却つて必ず共和政反動の大勢を馴致せん事を慮り、君乃ち偏に國家を以て前提とし、其の政見敢て各黨派の操縱する所に囚はれざりし。五年國會恢復するや、復た其の召集に應じて仍は參議院議員の職に就く。

Mr. Chao Hsiao-liang, sometimes known as I Tien, age thirty nine is a native of Chung Chun, Chi-lin province. In 1906 he entered the Pei An law school whence he was graduated after taking the special course in the University. In 1909 he was appointed the Vice-president of the Chi-lin Assembly, while in Chi-lin he was always on the side of the people trying to extend their right which naturally incurred the opposition of the government. In 1911, when the trouble arose in Wu Chuang, he went to Shanghai and acting in conjunction with representatives of various provinces he made efforts to bring about harmonious understanding between North and Southe Parties. In the second year of the Republic, when he was elected a member of the Senate, he was of opinion that an extreme opinion as entertained by some would bring about the strong reaction to the Republic so that his views were not necessarily controlled by party feelings. As soon as the parliament was re-opened he was elected a member of the Senate, the position of honor, which holds in the present moment.

趙成恩 字義吾 歳三十四

選舉地　吉林省

籍貫　吉林省吉林縣

生址　北京順治門裏中鐵匠胡同路北

君自幼喜談新學。不屑從事於科舉之業。於西書譯本無所不閱。而尤喜研究法學。前清末年。偶以故至北洋。因投入北洋高等巡警學堂畢業後。歷充吉林省城巡警第五區區官。黑龍江巴彥縣巡警局提調。吉林同賓縣警務長。黑龍江省城巡警第一區區官。呼蘭縣稅捐征收局文牘兼辦事官。旋被舉爲吉林省議會議員。光復後復被選爲民國參議院議員。國會解散後。以縣知事候補於黑龍江。及此次國會重開。始應召來京。仍爲參議院議員。

君幼より喜んで新學を談じ科舉の業に從事するを屑しとせず、博く西書譯本を閲覽し尤も法學を研究す。前清末年偶々故を以て天津に至る。遂に北洋高等巡警學堂に入りて卒業し、吉林省城巡警第五區々官に任ず、次で黑龍江巴彥縣巡警局提調、吉林同賓縣警務長、黑龍江省城巡警第一區區官、呼蘭縣税捐徵收局文牘兼辦事官等の職に歷充したり。民國成立後舉げられて吉林省議會議員とな る。民國二年正式國會議員選舉に當り君吉林省よりして參議院議員に舉げられ、北京に抵りて國政を議す。其の國會解散後は、縣知事の候補を以て黑龍江省に分たる。此の次國會重ねて開かるゝや、君復た其の召集に應じて北京に抵り。仍ほ参議院議員の職に就きたり。

民國之精華　（傳記）　趙成恩先生

Mr. Chao Cheng-en, otherwise called Hsi Wu is a native of Chi Lin Hsing being thirty four years of age. He was from youth an ordent admirer of the new learning and studied law through translation. At the last days of the previous Chinese regime, he went to Tientsin where he was graduated from the Pei Yen High Police School, and since then he successively the posts connected with police affairs in Hei Lung Chiang Chi Yen, Tung Pao as well as Hu Lan' Taxation Bureau etc. in which capacity he enjoyed quite a success. After the formation of the Republic, he was elected a member of the Chi Lin Local Assembly. In the 2nd year of the Republic, he was returned from the Chilin Sheng, and appointed a member of the Senate, and as such participated in the government of the country. After the desolation of the Parliament, he was a candidate for the prefectural governorship for the Amur district. When the Parliament was opened, he went to Peking where he now discharges his duty as the member of the Senate.

趙金堂　字升齋　歲三十三

選舉地　直隸省

貫籍　直隸省南宮縣

住址　北京西城南闢市口西前百戶廟十四號

君自幼慷慨好義。不畏強禦。及長。見時事日非。朝貴皆不足有爲。遂慨然有澄渚天下之志。宣統三年。列入同盟會。糾合同志。力圖推翻清廷。庚戌由直隸北洋師範畢業。復入北京中國公學大學部法律科。辛亥武昌義旗旣舉。南方各省。相繼獨立。獨張懷芝握重兵於天津。反抗民軍最力。君乃與薛烈士承華。尹君油坊。謀炸張懷芝於津車站不中。薛君適難。君幸免。未幾。清室退位。共和告成。民國紀元。被選爲順直臨時省議會議員。二年被選爲衆議院議員。是年十一月。袁氏以威力驅逐國民黨籍議員。君乃經營商業於京津間。不與聞政事。直至希制發生。雲貴倡義。始赴上海。加入滬上國會議員團。國會恢復。遂入京。仍爲議員。

君幼より慷慨義を好み強を畏れず、長じて時事日に非なるを見て遂に慨然として天下を澄清するの志あり宣統三年同盟會に入り、同志を糾合して清廷を傾覆せんことを圖る。庚戌の歲北洋師範學校を卒業して、復た北京中國公學大學部法律科に入りて學ぶ。辛亥の歲武昌に於て義旗旣に舉るや南方各省相繼て獨立したるも、獨り張懷芝重兵を天津に擁して民軍に反抗す。君乃ち薛承華、尹油坊と爆烈爆を以て張懷芝を天津停車場に襲ふて中らず、薛難に殉し君幸に免る。後ち清帝退位して共和の新政を創むるや、選ばれて順直臨時省議會議員となる。民國二年衆議院議員に當選す。袁政府が威力を以て國民黨議員を驅逐するや、君亦去つて商業を京津間に營み、隱忍して暫らく政事に預らず。雲貴に於て帝制反對の義を唱ふるや、君上海に馳せて上海國會議員團に加入し、國會恢復後、再び北上して仍は衆議院議員と爲る。

Mr. Chao Chin Tang, otherwise called Chuan Chi is a native of Nan Kung, the Chih Lin Hsing being thirty three years old the present year. He was a man of heroic temperament and has no fear of the strong which is likely to dominate the weak. Seeing that the politics of the country was going from bad to worse, he made up his mind to bring about a reformation, and with that object in view, he gathered together men of the like temperament, and proposed to upset the Chinese court. He was graduate from the Pei Yang Normal School as well as from the Law College of the Peking University. When the revolutionary movement broker out, as a consequence of which several states declared independence. Chang Huan Chih in Tientsin opposed the people's party. Acting in league with Pi Cheng Hua and Yin Tien Fang, he made an attempt to bombshell Chang Huai Chih at the Tientsin station, but failed, and in this attempt, Pi Cheng Hua perished. When the abdication of the Chinese Emperor took place, and the new Republic was established, he was elected as a member of the Shun Chi Extraordinary Local Assembly. Under the pressure of Yuanshi-Kai he hid himself in Tientsin for the time being, and passed himself as a business man wean while for getting politics. When the Imperial restration movement was started, he went to Shanghai, and took part in the opposition movement. With the restoration of the National Assembly, he was elected a member of the House of Commons.

趙　舒　字舍予　歲三十二

選舉地　浙江省
籍　貫　浙江省縉雲縣
住　址　北京象坊桥浙江議員公廨

君賦性溫厚。氣宇潤大。與人交。和藹
可親。雖所素惡。亦假以顏色。不出惡
聲。然為人耿直不阿。言行以禮自持。
故雖以和婉待人。而無形中自有不可
侵越之界限。曾未嘗曲已狥人。扛尺直
尋之事。較之尋常無意識之同流合汙
者。自屬大相逕庭。自幼聰慧好讀。深
思明辨。故於古義多所領悟。然喜求有
用之學。不為舉業所拘。及海內維新。
慨肆力于西學。于新書無所不覩。尤喜
研究法政之學。識才具備焉。民國二年
正式國會成立。被選為眾議院議員。此
次及至約法恢復。國會重開。遂又應召
入京。仍復就眾議院議員職。

民國之精華　（傳記）趙舒先生

君賦性溫厚にして氣宇潤大なり。人と交りて和藹親びべ
く、平生憎惡する所と雖も、假すに顏色を以てし、惡聲
を加へす。然かも人と爲り耿直にして阿らす。言行共に
禮を以て自ら持し、和婉人を待つと雖も無形の中自から
侵すべからざる威嚴あり。未だ曾て已を曲げて人に狥は
す、之を尋常無意識者の流に同じ汙に合するものと大に
逕庭あり。幼より聰慧にして讀を好み、深く思索して古
義に於て悟得する所多し、然かも喜んで有用の學を求め、
科舉の業に囚れざりし。海內維新に及ぶや、力を西學に
傾倒して新書を涉獵し、尤も法政の學を研究する事を喜
び、識才共に具備したり。民國二年正式國會成立するや
眾議院議員に當選し、此次國會重ねて開かるゝに及び、
遂に又た召集に應じて入京し、仍ち復た眾議院議員の職
に就きたり。

Mr. Chao Shu, otherwise called She Yu, age thirty two, is a native of Chin Yun, Che Chiang province. He is a gentleman of refinement and comprehensive views. In associating with others he is reasonable even towards his enemy. Both in words and action he has something in him which is inaccessible to others. He never kotowed to others against his own conciousness. While quite young he has been a lover of books and was a deep thinker. As he grew older he became a student of useful learning. With the introduction of new ideas he was interested in western learning, particularly in law. In the 2nd year of the Republic he was returned for the House of Commons. When under the new president the Parliament was re-opened, he resumed the Parliamentary function as the member thereof.

熊成章 字斐然 歲三十一

選舉地 四川省

籍貫 四川省華陽縣

住址 北京西單牌樓與隆大院二十四號

君秉性聰慧。然虛心好問。不恃天資。故進步尤速。弱冠。即有文名。時海內亦盛倡西學。君遂棄科舉業。遍閱新書。慨然以挽救危亡為己任。以官費留學日本。入東京早稻田大學。宣統元年。畢業歸國。是年秋入都受學部試驗。給法政科舉人。次年廷試。授民政部小京官。由廣西巡撫張鳴岐。調任梧州地方審判廳推事。旋升任廣西高等檢察廳檢察官。民國元年。任孫大總統秘書。隨被選為臨時參議院議員。二年。被選為眾議院議員。國會解散後。歸里。任四川岷江法政專門學校校長兼教授。及國會復活。遂辭職入都復為參議院議員。

君秉性聰慧なるも、心を虛ふして問を好み、天資の顆達に恃まずして拮据勉勵するを以て其の學の進境頗る速にして弱冠即ち文名を負ふ。時に海內亦盛に西學を稱す、君遂に科舉の業を棄て、新書を讀み、慨然として國家の危亡を挽回するを以て己が任とす。官費を以て日本に留學し、早稻田大學に入りて宣統元年卒業歸國す。學部の試驗に及第して法政科舉人を授けられ、次年の廷試に於て民政部小京官に補せらる。廣西巡撫張鳴岐より調されて梧州地方審判廳推事に任じ、旋て廣西高等檢察廳檢察官に任す。民國元年臨時大總統孫文の秘書に任す。尋で臨時參議院議員に選ばれ、二年正式國會眾議院議員に當選す。國會解散されてより鄉里に歸り、四川岷江法政專門學校々長兼教授に任じて育英の業に從事す。國會復活するや、職を辭して召集に應じ、仍ほ參議院議員たり。

Mr. Hsiung Cheng-chang, otherwise known as Fei Jan, age thirty one, is a native of Ko Yang hsien, Hsi Chuan hsing. Being frank in his nature he is open to receive suggestions from others. He is extremely fond of study and even quite young he attained some literary fame. He was an ardent reader of new books and was convinced that it was his duty to save the country from the crisis. He came to Japan where he entered the Waseda University and in 1909 he was graduated thereof and returned home. He passed the civil service examination successfully and was appointed the public proculator of the local court. In the Ist year of the Republic he was a private secretary to president Sun-I-sen and in the 2nd year of the Republic he was returned for the House of Commons. When the parliament was dissolved he went back to his native province where he interested himself in the education of the rising generation. When the parliament was restored, he was elected a member of the Senate.

葉顯揚 字振聲 歲四十九

選舉地　內蒙卓索圖盟
籍貫　東土默特旗
住址　北京東四牌樓南演樂胡同

君為人誠實無華。性喜緘默。居恆勤儉質樸。以直待人。常喜以已過告人。以為快意。人有過。亦直言不諱。生平疾惡如仇。朋友有失德。則漸與絕交。而不為決絕於一時之舉。年少時。即好為俠義之行。喜為人鳴不平。然極重然諾。人有所託。必審慎再三。覺其確有把握。然後慨然應許之。故既承諾。未有不成者。於民國二年當選為臨時參議院議員。正式國會成立。又當選為眾議院議員。君原籍安徽毫縣。租居蒙古八代。遂隸蒙籍。君既被選于臨時參議院。乃隸國民黨籍。癸丑。國民黨失敗。蒙古議員皆脫黨籍。君獨留。人或勸之。君毅然拒之曰。吾蒙人最重信義。豈效中土偵薄之士為哉。國會解散。閑居都門。不聞政事。及國會重開。始仍出為眾議院議員。

民國之精華　（傳記）葉顯揚先生

君人と為り誠實にして華なく、性緘默を喜ぶ、居常勤儉質樸にして直を以て人を待つ。生平惡を疾むこと仇の如し。少年の時即ち好んで俠義の行を為し、喜んで人の為に不平を鳴らす。中年漸く老成持重して言動皆な本末あり。民國二年舉げられて臨時參議院議員となる。正式國會議員選舉に際して衆議院議員に當選したり。君の原籍は安徽毫縣なるも、其の先蒙古に移住し君に至りて八代を經て遂に蒙古に其の籍を置く。曾て君選ばれて臨時參議院議員となり乃ち國民黨に入る。癸丑の歲國民黨が政界に敗る〵や蒙古議員は決を連ねて國民黨を脫したるも君のみ獨り留る。人の脫黨を勸むるあれば君毅然として之を拒みて曰く、吾蒙古人は最も信義を重んず、豈に中土偵薄の士に效はんやと。國會解散するに迨び都門に閑臥して政事を聞かず、國會復活するや再ひ出て〵仍は衆議院議員となる。

Mr. Yeh Hsien Yang, otherwise called Chen Sheng is a native of Mongolia, aged forty nine. Honest and sincere in character, and not being subject to any vain ambition, he enjoys silence. He is open, frank and simple in dealing with others. He hates the evil, and would sacrifice himself for others. As a young man, he was a vehement malcontent, but became more genteel as he grew older. In the 2nd year of the Republic, he became a member of the Extraordinaly Council held then, and when the parliament was opened, he became the member thereof. He was originally of An Wei Huo, but eight generations before his family moved to Mongolia, and he became a member of the National party. When the party is cause was defeated in the last struggle, his friends left the party, but he remained behind, and stuck to his own party saying that fidelity is the motto of we Mongols. When the parliament was dissolved, he shut himself up to any political movement. He became the member of the Parliament when it was re-opened.

葉成玉 字振之 歳三十七

原籍地 黑龍江省

籍貫 黑龍江省龍江縣

住址 北京宣武門內手帕胡同

君賦性耿介。而又精敏異人。自幼喜留心時事。及海內維新。尤盡力研究新學。黑省素少文士。以故里人多奉君爲先覺。前淸光緒年間。由法政講習科畢業。歷充稅務荒務各差。曾由國監生选保以知縣分省補用。光緒三十二年。創辦齊昂輕便鐵路。君被選爲股東董事會董事。宣統元年。選爲地方城自治會議員。兼充龍江縣勸學員長。三年內。創設高初等小學三十餘處。於民國元年。經民政長請獎九等嘉禾章。是年秋。選爲臨時省議會議員。民國二年春由第一選舉區被選爲衆議院議員。入京供職。國會解散。復歸鄉里。爲主持教育者指導一切。及聞國會復活。來京。復爲衆議院議員。

君賦性耿介にして精敏なり。幼より心を時事に留め、海內維新に及び勉めて新學を研究す、黑龍江省素と文士少く、故を以て里人多く君を奉じて先覺とす。前淸光緒年間、法政講習科卒業生として稅務荒務等の職に歷充し曾て國監生に保せられし知縣を以て省の補用に分たる。光緒三十二年齊昂輕便鐵道を創立經營し、君株主董事會董事に選ばる。宣統元年地方自治會議員となり、龍江縣勸學員長を兼ぬ。三年間に高初等各小學校三十餘所を創設したり。民國元年に至り黑龍江省民政長の推薦により九等嘉禾章を授けられたり。其の秋選ばれて臨時省議會議員となる。二年春選ばれて衆議院議員と爲り、北京に抵りて大政を建議す。國會解散さるゝや鄉關に歸りて教育の振興を計る。國會復活するに及び再び京師に上りて復た衆議院議員となる。

Mr. Yeh Cheng-yn, otherwise called Chen-chih, is a native of Lung-chiang, the Hei-lung Chiang-hsing. He is thirty seven years of age the present year. He is a gentleman of bright and shrewed nature. While young, he devoted his attention to new learning, and was interested in politics. The distirct where he was born has very few men of literary fame so that his name stood most conspicuous among his colleagues in his native province. Under the present Chinese regime, he took the course in law, and was appointed an official in the Taxation Bureau of his province, and he acted as an assistant to the governor. In 1906, he was interested in the promotion of the Chuar-ang light railway company of which he was appointed the director while in 1909 he was a member of the local civic body, and also the chief of the educational committee in Lung-chiang. In the course of three years, he established over thirty primary as well as high schools. In 1912, at the recommendation of the civil administration of the Amur district, he was decorated by the government. He was also elected a member of the House of Commons, and in Peking he presented his memorial to the government. With the dissolution of the Parliament, he returned to his native home, and soon as the Parliament was re-opened, he was returned for the House of Commons.

葉夏聲 字競生 歲二十八

選舉地 廣東省
籍 貫 廣東省番禺縣
住 址 北京浮西城水河□一號

君性聰慧異人。漢學英文皆自稚年即具有根底。年十四五。即鼓吹革命。充香港廣東日報中國日報通信記者。十六歲遊學日本。曾從事於民報之撰述。十九歲返國。歷充廣東法政學堂兩廣方言學堂。高等醫察學堂教授。辛亥革命。遂投身民軍。奔走運動。屢瀕於危。軍政府成立。歷充廣東都督府參議。教育部長。司法部長等職。次年赴寧。奉命抵贛。是年四月返粵。仍任法政學堂教授。幷充國民黨政務主任。癸丑正月。被選爲衆議院議員。無何。贛寧事起。君以嫌疑倉卒南下。亡命日本者半載。即返居香港。謀三次革命。前後兩年。籌安會起。走南洋各埠籌集軍資者三度。君與呂志伊等約於廣東舉事。事敗。家族爲龍濟光所捕。及龍被迫獨立。君適先時至粵運動。知龍東舉事。袁氏既逝。乃去而赴滬。君代表孫中山北上。於南下復命。復于國會召集前數日到京。遂應召入院供職。

君資性聰慧にして眉目清秀の青年政治家なり。漢學英文共に幼時既に根底に根底あり。年十四五即ち革命を鼓吹して香港廣東日報中國日報通信記者となり、十六歳日本に遊學し、曾て民報の編輯に從事す、兩廣方言學堂、高等醫察學堂教授に歷充す。辛亥革命に際し民軍に投じて危を犯して運動し、廣東都督府參議、同教育部長、同司法部長等の職に歷任す。次年南京に赴き、命を奉じて江西に抵る。旋て廣東に歸りて法政學堂教授に任じ、並に國民黨政務主任と爲る。癸丑正月選ばれて衆議院議員と爲る。第二革命の變に處して嫌疑を受けて日本に亡命し、後ち香港に抵りて第三革命を企圖すること前後二年なり。籌安會起るや、志伊等と廣東に於て事を舉げんとして敗れ、其の家族は龍濟光の爲に捕はる。後ち上海に赴きて同志と共に大計を圖る。袁氏死して黎氏出るや、君は孫文の代表として北上す。國會恢復して再び衆議院議員となる。

民國之精華 (傳記) 葉夏聲先生

Mr. Yeh Hsia-sheng, is sometimes called Ching Sheng, is a native of Fan-yu, the Kuang-tung-shen. He is a bright and shrewed young politician in China. At the age of 14, he was already well versed in Chinese and English, and was an ardent advocate of the revolutionary ideas. He was a correspondent to many important newspapers and news agencies in China. It was only when he was sixteen years old that he went to Japan to complete education; on return to his home, he was an instructor of many important colleges in his province. Although young, his scope of learning is quite comprehensive including as it does law, languages and police affairs: In the revolutionary movement, he took the part of the people and ran many risks. He occupied many important posts such as relating to education and justice. He went to Nanking where he went to Chiang-hsi and again on returning to Kuan-tung he was an intstructor of the law college, and a director of the national party. In January, 1912, he was elected a member of the Parliament. At the time of the second revolution, he was in Japan as a political refuge, and spent two years trying to start the third revolution, but the attempt at Kungtung later proved failure. He went over to Shanghai, but with the death of Yuan-Shi-kai, he went to Peking, and became a member of the Parliament.

齊耀瑄 字式幹 歲三十六

選舉地 吉林省

籍 貫 吉林省伊通縣

住 址 北京西城兵馬司

君賦性篤實試愨。生平無戲言戲動。然天資極高。悟性敏捷。弱冠即著文名。及長。愈益奮勵求進。謙虛好問。喜出盡言。人告以過。必欣然謝之。然若為貧困者之譽。則反盛怒形諸顏色。常喜為貧困者助力。而不輕於允諾。既承諾。無不成者。以是人愈信用之。同輩中偶有糾紛。君出調停。無不立即解釋。自幼富于好奇之性。然其立身行巳。多厚重自持。蓋君之思想極放誕。而行為則極規則也。曾以前清附生。創辦伊通巡警數年。歷保至分省補用知府。宣統二年辭差家居。民國元年冬。被選為衆議院議員。

其の身を立て〻己を行ふ厚重自ら持す。蓋し君の思想極めて奔放なるも、其の行為は則ち極めて規則あり。前清附生を以て、曾て伊通縣に於ける警察を創設して處理すること數年、後ち省に分ちて補用知府に任せらる。宣統二年職を辭して家居す、民國元年正式國會衆議院議員に常選す。此次國會復活するや、復た其の召集に應じて入京し現に仍ほ衆議院議員たり。

君賦性篤實誠愨にして生平戲言戲動なくて高く悟性敏捷なり。弱冠即ち文名あり。長ずるに及び益々奮勵して進を求め、謙虛以て問を好み、喜んで盡言を開く。人告ぐるに過を以て、ゝれば必ず欣然として之を謝す。常に貧困者の為に助力するを喜ぶ。輕々しく承諾せざるも、承諾すれば成さゞる事なし。同輩中偶ま紛糾あれば君出で〻直に調停解決す。幼より好奇の性に富み、

Mr. Chi Yao-hsuan, sometimes known as Shih-hsien, age thirty six, is a native of I Tung, Chi lin province. He is a sober minded gentleman, not addicted to any frivolity. Being a man of high culture and understanding, his credit among the people stood very high. While young, he attained literary fame, and was ready to listen to the suggestions of others, making himself quite empty. If his faults are pointed out, he took them in good hearts. He is a great helper of the poor. While slow to accept any one's request, he is sound in keeping the same when once accepted. Should there be any trouble among his fellow men, he acted always an arbiter in settling it. While his ideas are quite broad and untrammelled, his conducts are very regular. He was interested a number of years in the police administration of his province, and then was promoted the governor. In the second year of the Parliament, he was returned for the House of Commons. With the suppression of the Parliament, he returned home, and showed us interest in politics. He entered Peking, and was a member of the House of Commons.

斐廷藩　宜丞　三十八

選舉地　陝西省

籍　貫　陝西省神木縣

住　址　北京宣武門外椿樹下頭條

君韶齡好學。穎悟絕倫。年方弱冠。睹清政之衰頹。慨然以澄清中原爲己任。光緒三十四年。以優等第一卒業於北京大學。旋任陝西高等工業學校英文敎員。反正時。充任陝北安撫使。統帶揄林巡防各隊。兼權揄林道事。內平劇盜。外撫蒙族。三邊人士。倚若長城。交卸後。被選爲衆議院議員。國會解散。君於里創辦神木女子學校。並添設兩等小學數處。旋經神木縣知事焦。揄林道道尹吳。先後詳請陝省長任用。而斐君矢志甚堅。不願再列身于政界。本年全陝土匪四起。蒙匪亦狡爲思逞。君遂出任警備隊長及保衛團團總。與羣寇轉戰數次。大敗之。陝北得以保全。旋應國會召集。方將促裝北上。聞蒙匪余堂僉卒犯邊。君猶復卒領鄉團。與悍賊接戰。追奔逐北。驅使出塞。然復入都。就職云。

君幼より學を好み、穎悟絕倫なり。年方に弱冠・清政の頹敗を賭て慨然として天下澄淸を以て己が任とす。光緒三十四年首席を以て北京大學を卒業し、陝西高等工業學校英文敎師と爲る。第一革命當時、陝北安撫使に任じ、揄林巡防各隊を統率し、揄林道蟲の事を兼ね、內に匪賊を平げ、外か蒙古人を撫したり。任終つて後ち、衆議院議員に當選す。國會解散するや、鄕里に於て神木女子學校を創設し、並に兩等小學校數箇所を添設す。旋て焦神木縣知事、吳揄林道道尹より陝西省長に屢々任用を請ひたるも、君志を矢つて專ら仕途に就く事を欲せす。本年陝西各地土匪蜂起して蒙匪亦た逞を思ふに及び、遂に出で、警備隊長及び保衛團團長に任じ、轉戰數次大に匪賊を敗り陝北爲に安寧を得たり。旋て國會の召集に應じて北上せんとす、蒙古馬賊の邊境を犯すものあり、鄕國を率ゐて悍賊を邀擊して塞外に潰走せしめ、然る後ち入京して議員の職に就きたり。

Mr. Pei Ting-fan, otherwise called I Cheng, age thirty eight, is a native of Shen Mu, Shan Hsi province. While young he was deeply interested in study and distinguished for his superior power of understanding. In his youth he felt the decline of the Chinese government. As soon as he graduated in 1908, from the Peking University he was appointed an instructor ot Hsia hsi technical school. At the time of the Revolution he occupied various important posts and particulary showed his merit by pacifying bandits. He was then returned for the House ot commons. With the disolution of the parliament he returned to his native country where he was interested in the establishment of schools. When the bandits trouble broke out in Hsia hsi, he was the leader of expedition against the mand after a series of brilliant victories restored p ace in his province. He was summoned to Peking when mounted bandits assaulted the frontier of the province. He fought against them and defeated them completely. Afterwards he entered Peking and was elected a member of the Parliament.

劉昭一 字曉峰 歲四十九

選舉地 山東省

籍　實 山東省章邱縣

住　址 北京牟截碑保安寺胡同二十二

君賦性溫厚。與人交。和藹可親。雖所
素惡。亦假以顏色。然又篤實不欺。動
止以禮自持。爲人勤謹耐勞。人有所
託。輒喜爲盡力。不以功自居。自幼聰
慧異人。及長。尤活潑自喜。富于好奇
之性。然其立身行己。多厚重自持。好
讀書。博覽羣籍。任意所之以爲快。雖
備通羣經。而未嘗心于於舉業之術及
海內維新。尤立志實用之學。復從事
學師範各學校教員。民國元年。被選爲
科名。曾由本省師範畢業。歷充高等中
省議會議員。值濟南兵變。被推爲救急
會會長。辦理一切善後事宜。二年。被
選爲衆議院議員。國會解散後。歸里辦
理本省膠東賑務。監修濰縣等。提防事
宜。此及次國會重開。遂入京。仍爲衆
議院議員。

君賦性溫厚にして人と交る和藹親ひべし。人と爲り恪謹
勞に耐へ人託する所われば輙ち喜んで盡力し、功を以て
自ら居らず。幼より聰慧人と異り、長ずるに及び尤も活
潑自ら喜び、好奇の性に富む。然かも其の身を立て己を
行ふ、厚重自ら持す。書を讀みて博覽强記なり。海內維
新に及び、尤も志を立て、實用の學を求め、輿學を以て
己が任とす。曾て本省師範學校を卒業し、高等中學校、
師範學校等の各教員に歷充したり。民國元年選ばれて省
議會議員と爲る。時適き濟南府兵士の暴動あり。君推さ
れて救急會長となり、一切の善後事宜を處理す。二年正
式國會衆議院議員に當選す。國會解散後、鄉里に歸りて
本省膠東の賑務を處理し、又た濰縣等の提防事宜を監修
したり。五年國會重ねて開院するに及び、遂に入京して
仍は衆議院議員と爲る。

Mr. Liu Chao-i, otherwise called Hsiao Feng, age forty nine, is a native of Chang Chin,
Shan Tung hsing. He is a gentleman of sociable and friendly temperament. He takes delight in helping
others. As he grew older he was very active in acquiring the new knowledge, while he was distinguished for his wonderful retaintive faculty. He sought practical learning. After having graduated the
normal school of his province, he was appointed an instructor of the high middle school and the normal
school. In the 1st year of the Republic, he was appointed a member of the local assembly. At this time
there was soldiery outbreak in this part of China, when he was appointed the head of the relief party.
In the 2nd year of the Republic, he was returned for the House of Commons, but when the legislative
assembly was shut down he, returned to his home where he was interested in the construction of dams
in his province. With the reopening of the parliament, he entered Peking and was returned for the
House of Commons.

劉映奎 <small>字幼蘇 歳四十四</small>

選舉地　福建省
籍貫　福建省寧化縣
住址　北京校場五條榕廬

君秉性敦篤朴實。不喜浮華。爲人嚴正
不阿。疾惡崇善。鄉里有不平之事。輒
喜爲弱者盡力。必辦其曲直而後已。自
幼聰穎過人。讀書輒過目成誦。並能
深入精微。洞悉義理。年少時。喜爲詩
詞。然不從事推砌。唯期有以寄其感
慨。寫其至性至情。故無意求工。而所
作無不佳妙。稍長。漸讀宋明學者之
書。始覺前此所尚。不免玩物喪志之
譏。乃決然棄去。專精力於有用之書。
前清時以舉人。官法部主事。補授京師
高等審判廳推事。旋充本省臨時省議
會副議長。民國二年。正式國會成立。
被選爲參議院議員。國會解散。歸里從
事學問。不問時事。及國會重開。始入
京。仍爲議員。

君秉性敦篤朴實にして浮華を喜ばず。人と爲り嚴正にし
て阿らざる也。惡を疾み善を崇びて、弱者の爲に助力を
客さず。幼より聰穎人に過ぎ、書を讀むや過目直ちに誦
を成し、並に能く深く其の精徴を究めて義理を明にす。
年少の時詩詞を喜び、稍や長じて宋明學者の書を讀む、
爾來志を決して天下有用の學を求め、尤も法政の書に於
て研磨の功を積み、造詣旣に深きものあり。前清時代、
舉人を授け法部主事に任じ、京師高等審判廳推事に補せ
らる。旋て福建省議會副議長に舉げらる。民國二年正式
國會成立するや、選ばれて參議院議員と爲る。國會解散
されてより鄉里に歸省して、學問に從事し、また時事を
問はず。五年約法復活して國會重ねて開かるゝや、君復
た出でゝ召集に應じ、北上入京して、仍は參議院議員と
爲る。

民國之精華　（傳記）　劉映奎　先生

Mr. Liu Ying-kuei, known as Yu Su, age forty four, is a native of Ning Hua, Fu-kien province. He is upright in character, and above the vice of flattery. Being a lover of simple life, he opposed to the life of pompousness and vain glory. He is also an ardent reader of looks, and would not be satisfied with anything short of thorough understanding. Therefore, he is well posted up is the study of classical writings of the Chinese, but when he once turned his attention to the study of useful leaning, he was deeply interested in law in which he went into very deep. After passing the required examination, he was appointed the judge of the Peking Higher Court, and shortly after the vice-president of the Fukieng Local Assembly. When the Parliament was summoned, in the second year of the Republic, he was elected a member of the Senate. However, with the dissolution of the Parliament, he returned to his native country, not troubling himself about politics. However, when the new order of thing was introduced, he came up to Peking, and resumed his senational function.

劉光旭　字曙初　歲四十二

選舉地　貴州省

籍貫　貴州省修文縣

住址　北京象來街路北八號

君家世業儒。前清修文貢生。當科舉時代。即致力於經史百家。與歐西政學說。邑明王文成講學故地也。自咸同年間。遭何逆之變。文敎廢弛者數十年。慨謂振持文敎。吾輩責任。爰創辦學堂於龍岡。改良敎育。以知行合一說。訓導後進。每論及政治。必歎專制之不良。思有以改革之。邑中少年。感起者不少。辛亥革命。民國紀元。被選貴州臨時省議會議員。政黨發生。列籍共和黨中。推任編輯黔風報。凡所主張。多中時而可行。二年。重選省議員。復當選參議員。國會被袁氏非法解散。旋當省長戴戡。勸入政界。助理地方。任以錦屛縣事。錦屛初改爲縣。劃撥區域。建設邑治。悉經其手。甫宰一年。地方各種行政。舉辦無遺。井井有條。且或較舊縣而有過者。帝制發生。免。到省運動反對。革命功成。約法恢復。國會召集。以議員之天職。尚多未盡。因仍就職。

君が家世々儒を業とす。前清修文貢生にして科舉時代即ち經史百家と西洋の政治學説とに力を致したり。邑は明の王文成講學の故地なるも咸同年間何逆の變に遭ひて文敎廢弛する者數十年、文敎の振興を以て自ら任じ、龍岡に學校を創説し、敎育を改良して知行合一の説を以て後進を誘掖す。常に政治を論せば必ず專制の不可を歎したり。辛亥い歳、命を革めて民國の元を紀すや、貴州臨時省議員に選ばる。共和黨に入黨して黔風報の編輯に任す。

民國二年正式省議會議員に再選し、旋て正式國會參議院議員に當選す。袁氏の非法により國會解散するや、貴州省長戴戡の勸告により錦屛縣知事に任じ、甫宰一年、地方各種の行政を處理して治蹟大に舉る。帝制問題發生する第三革命功成つて約法恢復し、國法再び召集を行ふに及び、冠を掛けて省城に至り、帝制反對運動を爲す。に及び、遂に上京して仍ほ參議院議員と爲る。

Mr. Liu Kuang hsu, otherwise called Tzu Shu-chu, age forty two, is a native of Hsin Wen hsien, Kuei Chou province. He is of a scholary family and when young he studied classics and history most extensively, but later he became interested in the study of accidental learning. He established a school of his own, and when the Revolution was accomplished he became a member of the Kuei Chon local assembly. He joined the Republican party, and in the 2nd year of the Republic he was appointed a member of the Senate. When the parliament was dissolved by the unlawful conduct of Yuanshi-kai he was appointed a governor of Chin Ping where his administrative ability was amply shown with great success. When the Imperial Movement of Yuanshi-kai took place, he was a strong opponent. With the success of the 3rd Revolution, he went up to Peking and appointed a member of the Senate, a position he holds in the present moment.

劉尚衡　字聘珊　歳四十二

選舉地　貴州省

籍貫　江西省

住址　北京象來街八號

君爲人誠篤無欺。言動皆確守古訓。不
稍縱肆。居常以厚道待人。秉性聰敏異
人。自幼即明察事理。思考敏捷。而意
志堅強。弱冠讀書。即能發微起伏。別
關新奇。不爲流俗之成見所局。及長。
尤深思明辨。勵行身心之修養。以前淸
副榜貢生。爲雲南補用知縣。原任本省
江口縣知事。歷充本籍學董暨師範學
校校長。民國元年。被選爲省議會議
員。繼被選爲衆議院議員。國會解散
後。歸里獨居。靜觀世變。及帝制發生。
滇黔首義。乃爲黔軍東路。擔任採辦糧
秣。國會復活。遂入都復充衆議院議
員。

君人と爲り誠篤欺かず、言語動作皆な右訓を確守す。居
帝厚道を以て人を待つ。秉性聰敏人に異り、幼より即ち
事理を明察す、思考敏捷にして意志堅強、弱冠書を讀みて
即ち其の蘊奧を究めて別に新奇を開き、流俗の成見に四
はるゝ所とならず。長じて尤も深く思索して身心の修養
を勵みたり。前淸時代副榜の貢生を以て雲南省補用知縣
と爲り、本省江口縣知事に任じ、鄕縣の學董及び師範學
校長に歷充す。民國元年選ばれて省議會議員となり、繼
いで正式國會衆議院議員に當選す。國會解散後、鄕里に
歸りて獨居し靜に世變を觀望す。雲南貴州義を始むるや、
貴州軍の東路に任じて糧秣の事を處理す。旣にして約法
恢復して國會復活するや、再び召集に應じて途に北京に
入り復た衆議院議員の職に就く。

民國之精華　（傳記）　劉尚衡先生

Mr. Liu Shang-heng, otherwise called Ping Shan, age forty three, is a native of Chiang Hsi hsien. He is a man of strict character, observing the rules of ettignet according to the classical teaching. In dealing with others he is always full of hospitable spirit. He is quick of understanding and of strong will. He is stricktly original and never is bound up with popular tradition. In the previous Chinese regime he became the governor of Chiang Kow and also the headmaster of the normal school of his province. With the formation of the Diet he was appointed a member thereof. When Yuanshikai dissolved the Parliament he was interested in the commissarit arrangement for the Kuei Chou Army. When the Parliament was revived he went to Peking, and was elected a member of the Parliament, the position of honor which he most actively occupies.

劉盥訓　字字若　歲四十一

選舉地　山西省

籍貫　山西省猗氏縣

住址　北京下斜街雲山別墅

君爲人勤勉好學。然性慈善能悟。讀書能深思細玩。每畢一書。必能歷舉其竅奧之所在。弱冠有文名。及長。閱書愈多。始覺所得極淺。乃力去虛驕。不恥下問。中年。銳意新學。遂負笈入都。肄業於北京大學校師範科。畢業。得優等。叙官內閣中書科中書。歷充山西省大學校教務長。河南省高等學校監督。北京大學校學監。兼博物實習學校校長。辛亥改革。力勸淸內閣。贊成共和速定及南京政府成立君以山西代表名義。南下。遂得爲臨時參議院議員。兼庶務股委員。南北統一。授四等嘉禾勳章。旋充政治諮議。嗣復當選爲衆議院議員。兼交通股理事。國會解散後。歸里讀書。五年在滬上謀改革。充旅滬國會議員團幹事。及國會復活。遂入都仍爲議員。

君人と爲り勤勉にして學を好み、性聰慈にして讀書思索す。弱冠早くも文名あり、長ずる及びて研磋倦まず、中年新學に志し、遂に笈を負ふて京師に入り、北京大學校師範科に學びて其の業を畢ゆ、成績優等なりしを以て官を内閣中書に叙せらる。山西省大學校教務長、河南省高等學校監督、北京大學校學監兼博物實習學校長等に歷充して育英の業に從事す。第一革命の事起るや、淸内閣に共和贊成を勸告し、南京臨時政府成立するに及び、山西代表として南下し、遂に臨時參議院議員となり、庶務科委員を兼ぬ。南北統一して四等嘉禾章を授けらる。旋で政治諮議に任じ、嗣で正式國會衆議院議員に當選す。交通科理事に舉げらる。國會解散後、鄕に歸りて讀書し。五年上海に至りて革命を謀り、在上海國會議員團の幹事と爲る。國會復活するに及び遂に都に入りて仍は衆議院議員たり。

Mr. Liu Kuan-hsun, otherwise known as Fu Yao, age forty one, is a native of I Shih, the Shan Hsi province. He is a laborious student, being a wide reader and deep scholar. While young, he attained some literary fame, and is never tired of study. Perceiving the necessity of new learning, he came up to Peking where he was graduated from the Normal School with honors, and was appointed one of the secretaries of the Cabinet. He occupied various important posts in connection with the Shan hi university, the Ho nan High, the Peking university. When the revolution broke out, he urged the previous Chinese government to come to term with the Revolutionists, and when the extraordinary Nanking government was formed, he attended to it as a member of the Senate. When the south and the north came to terms, he was an adviser to the government. When the Parliament was summoned, he became the member thereof, and appointed the director of the Communication Department. After the collapse of the Parliament, he returned to his native province, and came up to Shang-hai being appointed the director of the Shang-hai Parliamentary Movement. With the revival of the legislation assembly, he was elected a member thereof.

劉 濂 字仿叔 歳四十一

選舉地　江西省
籍貫　江西省零都縣
住址　北京順治門外江西會館

君爲人耿介剛直。不喜隨同流俗。生平
疾惡如仇。遇不平。輙爲弱者盡力。又
喜爲周濟貧困。然人有所求。又不肯輕
於允諾。既諾。未有不成者。自幼聰慧
善讀。悟性極高。讀書喜求眞義。不爲
擧業所拘。海內維新後。慨然有澄清天
下之志。遂以前清優附生。留學日本。
人早稻田大學專門法律科。畢業。旋入
中央大學法科研究科。專攻刑律。歸國
歷充江西公立法政學校教員有年。光
復初。任江西司法局局長。嗣任江西法
官試驗委員長。民國二年。被選爲江西
省議會議員。旋被選爲中華民國參議
院議員。兼充律師。國會解散後。歸里
專營律師業。頗負令譽。國會重開。遂
來京爲參議院議員。

君人と爲り耿介剛直、流俗に隨ふを欲せず。生平惡を疾
ひこと仇の如く、弱者の爲に助力を惜まず、喜んで貧困
者を周濟す。幼より聰慧にして學を好み、書を讀みて其
の精を攻め其の義を究めて、科擧の業に拘泥せず。海內
維新に及び、慨然として天下有用の材を以て自ら任じ、
前清優附生を以て、志を立てゝ日本に留學し、早稻田大
學專門法律科に擧びて卒業し。尚ほ進んで法律の蘊奥を
研磋攻究すべく、中央大學法科研究科に入りて刑法を專
攻す。歸國後、江西公立法政學校に敎鞭を取り、民國樹
立の初め江西省司法局長に任す。嗣で江西法官試驗委員
長に任す。民國二年江西省議會議員に選ばれ、旋て正式
國會參議院議員に當選す。兼て辯護士の業とす。國會解
散後、郷里に歸りて專ら辯護士の業を營みて令名あり。
五年國會恢復して君復た其の召集に應じ、遂に來京して
復た參議院議員と爲る。

Mr. Liu Lien, known as Fan shu, age forty one, is a native of Yun tu, the Chiang-hsi province. He is a friend of the weak and rich, and a hater of the evil. He is far above running after the vulgar fashion. Being an admirer of books, his thoughts were comprehensive. Being deeply interested in public affairs, he studied in Japan where he was graduated from the Waseda University. With a view to persue his study, he entered the Chuo university where he took speciality in the study of the penal code. On returning to his native country, he taught in the law school. When the Republic was established, he was the chief of the juridical office, and the chief of the Committee appointed for the examination of the candidate for judges. In the second year of the Republic, he was elected a member of the Senate and practiced law, which occupation he continued after the dissolution of the Parliament. He went up to Peking with the re-opening of the Parliament, and was elected a member of the Senate.

劉正堃　字至元　歲四十一

選舉地　黑龍江省
籍　貫　黑龍江省綏化縣
住　址　北京窰子胡同東口外寬街九號

君賦性朴質。篤實不欺。與人交。常鯁
直不阿。人有過失。無不逕情詰責。不
稍存世故之念。然爲人慷慨尙義。喜爲
貧困者助力。而不輕於允諾。既承諾。
無不成者。以是人愈信用之。自幼聰頴
好讀。然非有益於身心及足以爲經世
濟物之資者。輒不終篇即棄擲之。故雖
曾殫精舉業。然經史之外。大都擇其富
於義理讀之。不喜拘章句。效彫蟲刻鏤
者之所爲。於淸季以優貢生朝考一等。
得授知縣。籖分奉天補用。歷充科員稅
務各職。民國二年。由省議會議員。被
選爲參議院議員。國會解散後。歸里讀
書。不復發表政見。及共和復活。始入
都仍供舊職。

君賦性篤實にして人と爲り、鯁直阿らず。義を伺ぶて然
諾を重んず。幼より聰頴讀を好みて、長ずるに及びて身
心の修養並に經世濟物の資とするに足る實學を求めて、
切磋琢磨の功を積み、其の章句の末に囚るゝことを喜は
すして、直ちに其の義を攻め其の精を究め、造詣日に深
し。前淸末季、優貢生を以て朝考一等に列し、知縣の官
を授けて奉天省の補用に分たる。爾來奉天省の各科員若

くは稅務の各職に歷充して事務の才幹を發揮す。民國二
年奉天省議會より選ばれて、正式國會參議院議員に當選
したり。北京に抵りて民國建設の大政に參議したるも、
旋て國會解散せらる。即ち鄕里に歸りて讀書自ら娯み、
復た政見を發表するなし。共和克復して國會重ねて召集
さるゝや、再び閭門を出でゝ入京し、仍は參議院議員の
舊職に就く。

Mr. Liu Cheng-ho, otherwise called Chi Yuan, age forty one, is a native of An Ka, Hei Lung Chiang province. He is man of faithful temperament who sticktly attaches great importance to the idea of justice and straight forewardness. While young, he was fond of reading books, and, as he grew older he sought a useful learning. In studying books he attached greater importance to the study of the real meaning rather than mere outward forms. At the later days of the Chinese regime he passed the examination successfuly and was appointed the governor of Fengtien province. In every position he occupied his ability was recognized by the public. Therefore, in the 2nd year of the Republic, he was elected a member of the Senate. He went up to Peking and took part in building up the Republic. However, when the Parliament was dissolved, he returned his home where he indulged himself in study and never gave publicity to his political views. However, when it came to pass to hold the Parliament he was appointed a member of the Senate.

劉景烈　字曉愚　歳三十八

選舉地　江西省
籍貫　江西省嶺南道頡縣
住址　北京達智橋路北

君二十歳にして江南陸軍學校に學び、廿二歳日本に留學
し、成城學校を經て士官學校に入る。肺患に罹りて中途
退學歸國す。江西常備中軍第二營々官、江南陸師學校學
生隊長、下士養成所監督、陸軍第九鎮正執法官等の職に
歷任す。嗣で又た現職のまゝ北京法律學校に入り、卒業
後原職に兼ぬるに太湖秋操審判官と爲る。三十歳病を以
て辭職休養し、嗣で江西諮議局議員に舉げられ、復た國
會請願代表に推され、遂に資政院議員に選ばる。後ち又

君于廿歳入江南陸師學堂。廿二歳
留學日本。入成城學校。卒業後入日本
士官學校。因患肺疾。遂廢學歸國。歷
充江西常備中軍第二營々官。江南陸
師學堂學生隊長。弁目養成所監督。陸
軍第九鎮正執法官。嗣又帶職來京。入
法律學堂。卒業後。仍供原職。兼充太
湖秋操審判官。卅歳以病辭職旋里。嗣
被舉爲江西諮議局議員。復推充爲國
會請願代表。資政院議員。後又兼充永
平秋操辦事官。武漢起義。君回省以圖
響應。時嶺省已先後獨立。惟各据一
方。君至。乃疏通意見。次年君被選爲
嶺省臨時議會議長。嗣以會匪蠢動嶺
省大局動搖。君與同志籌力謀挽救。派
人密告孫黎兩公。設法維持。次年君被
選衆議院議員。國會解散後。少所表
見。及此次共和復活。遂入京仍供今職
云。

た永平秋操辦事官を兼ぬ。第一革命の事起るや、歸郷し
て響應を志し、前後獨立せる江西各地を聯絡して統一を
圖る。翌年臨時省議會議長に舉げらる。嗣で會匪蠢動し
て江西の大局動搖するや、君同志と挽救を謀り、孫文黎
元洪兩氏に密告し法を設けて治安を維持したり。民國二
年正式國會衆議院議員に常選す。國會解散後、表見する
所少なく、國會復活するに及びて遂に入京して仍は衆議
院議員たり。

民國之精華　（傳記）　劉景烈先生

三百六十三

Mr. L'u Ching-Lich, known as Hsio Yu, age thirty eight, is a native of Nan Tao, the Chiang Hsi. At the age of twenty five, he studied at the Military school of his province, and entered the staff college. Falling into illness, he had to quit his work, and return his country where his service was welcomed in connection of military training. Even during the leisure of his office, he entered the Peking law school, and on graduating thereof, he was appointed the judge of one of the court. In 1904, owing to health, he resigned his post, and was elected a member of the local assembly, and the representative committee asking for the opening of the Parliament. As soon as the revolution broke out, he was in constant touch with the native province which declared its independence. In the second year of the Republic he was elected a member of the House of Commons, but when Yuanshi-kai dissolved the Parliament, he had to retire, and when the Parliament was revived, he was appointed a member of the House of Commons.

劉　緯　字鴻岷　歲三十八

選舉地　四川省

籍　貫　四川省建昌道榮縣

住　址　北京西單北後英子胡同九

君爲人誠厚篤實。痛惡浮華。與人交。常硬直不阿。絕無世故之念。人告以過。亦欣然謝之。然居心仁厚。喜救人急難。故其接物雖稍露鋒鋩。而人亦罕忌恨之者。自幼好讀深思。喜研求眞理。而不屑尋章摘句。以爲博取功名計。故其所讀多有用之書。及海內維新。志西學。遂肆于新書。無所不覩。而尤醉心于敎育之書。曾入四川高等學堂。畢業後。任榮縣縣立高等小學校校長四年。視學一年。前淸之末。被選爲四川諮議局議員。繼被選爲資政院議員。民國國會成立。被選爲衆議院議員。國會解散後。歸里不向政事。及國會復活。始入京復爲衆議院議員。

君人と爲り誠厚篤實にして浮華を痛惡す。人と交りて常に硬直阿らず、絕えて世故の念なし。人告ぐるに過を以てすれば欣然として之を謝す。然かも居心仁厚にして人の急を救ふを喜ぶ。幼より學を好み深く思索して其の義理を明にす。海內維新に及びて西學に志し、博く新書を涉獵して尤も敎育の書を攻究し、夙に興學の志を抱きて民智の開發を以て己が任ど爲す。曾て四川高等學校を卒業し、榮縣々立高等小學校長に任ずること四年、縣視學に任ずること一年なり。嗣で資政院議員に擧げらる。民國二年正式國會成立するや、當選して衆議院議員と爲る。國會解散後、鄉里に歸りて地方敎育の振興を計りて政事を談せす。五年國會復活するに及びて其の召集に應じ、遂に入京して復た衆議院議員の職に就く。

Mr. Liu I, otherwise known as Hung Min, age thirty eight, is a native of Tao Jung hsien, the Ssi Chuan province. Being naturally honest, frank and straight, he is opposed to anything pompous and vain. He is by no means an affable society man, but is always ready to listen to any advice given him.. He takes a keen delight in helping the poor and oppressed. He took up the western learning, and was greatly interested in books on education. After graduating from the high school in his native province, he was deeply interested in the local education sometimes acting as the head master of the primary school and sometimes as the inspector of learning. He was elected a member of the local assembly. When the Republic was established, he was returned for the House of Commons. When the Parliament was shut down he returned to his home, and was interested in local education. With the resumption of the Parliamentary work by the new president, he was elected for the House of Commons.

劉積學 字羣士 歲三十七

選舉地 河南省
籍貫 河南省新祭縣
住址 北京宣武門內頭髮胡同劉底

君天資聰穎。頭腦細密。自幼讀書。即以博及爲懷。故學無專業。義理考據以外。尤肆力於辭章之學。及冠。應科帆售。已而棄去。專治古代算術。方程勾股。盡窺其竅。甲辰之秋。聞豫省設立武備學堂。忽起投筆從戎之念。遂入堂肄習。二年畢業。丙午。由豫省派往日本留學。初入日語專門學校。嗣入東京小石川區實科學校理化專修班。二年半畢業。又入東京麴町區法政大學專門部政治科。三年畢業。辛亥返國。時適武昌起義。各省饗應。豫省以北兵歷境。事不可爲。遂携同志南行。組織河南北伐隊。民國元年。被舉爲臨時參議院議員二年正式國會選舉。又被舉爲參議院議員。國會解散。歸里讀書自遣。不復干與政治。及共和恢復。始入京仍爲參議院議員。

君天資聰穎にして頭腦周密なり。幼より書を讀みて博く群籍を涉獵し。長ずるに及びて古代算術を修めて方程勾股盡く其の竅を窺ふ。甲辰の秋、河南省武備學堂に入學して修業すること二年、丙午の歲、河南省より選派されて日本に留學し、日語專門學校を經て實科學校理化專修部に入りて卒業す。又た法政大學專門部政治科に學びて其の業を畢ゆ。辛亥の歲歸國して適ま第一革命の事起るに遭ふ。武昌早くも義を起して各省旣に饗應するも、河南省は北兵其の境を壓するを以て事偹に舉ぐべからず。」遂に同志と共に南行して、河南北伐隊を組織したり。南北統一するや民國元年舉られて臨時參議院議員となり。民國二年正式國會參議院議員に當選す。國會解散されてよりは鄉里に歸臥して讀書自ら娛み、復た政治に干與せや。共和恢復するや再び北京に入り、國會開院さるゝに及び、召集に應じて仍ほ參議院議員たり。

民國之精華 （傳記） 劉積學先生

Mr. Liu Chi-hsio, known as Chun Shih, age thirty seven, is a native of Hsin chi, the Hunan province. He is naturally a shrewed thinker. When young, he was fond of reading books. As he grew older, he was interested in the study of ancient mathematical study. In 1996, he came to Japan where he was graduated from the Japanese language school as well as the political course of the Hosei University. When he returned to his country, he was confronted the first revolutionary movement. In this war, he with his fellow thinkers took a keen delight. In the first year of the Republic, he was appointed a member of the local assembly, and in the second year, he was appointed a member of the Senate. When the Parliament was dissolved, he went back to his native country where he spent more of his time reading books rather than talking politics. When the Parliament was re-opened, however, he was appointed a member of the Senate.

劉 英 字聊述 歲三十五

選舉地　湖北省

籍　貫　湖北省京山縣

住　址　北京旗守墳牛圈

君少好義。喜爲人鳴不平。里人有以金
錢受窘者。輒解囊助之。不復望報。遠
近爭稱甚名。中年。慨然有志以挽回免
亡自任。遂決志以私費遊學東京。畢
業。師範。又入鐵道學校。旋又入明治
大學政治經濟科。乙巳夏孫中山倡三
民主義於東京。提倡種族革命。君極意
賛同。遂入黨共圖大事。丁未返國。赴
武漢。與孫武鄧玉麟蔡大輔劉公王守
愚等。運動軍學各界革命。醞釀四年。
機會既熟。辛亥武昌舉義。孫中山委任
君爲湖北第二鎮副都督。乃與其第劉
鐵率重兵。扼襄樊。克復南陽重鎮。南
北統一。君返鄂。充副總統府高等顧
問政府授以陸軍少將。及勳五位。壬
子。被選爲衆議院議員。國會解散後。
仍常居都中。萬事持消極態度。國會復
活。始入院。仍供舊職。

君より義を好み、喜んで人の爲に不平を鳴らし、人若
し金錢を以て窮困する者あれば、輒ち囊を解いて之を助
け復むを報を望まず。中年に至り慨然として國家の頹勢を
挽回するを以て自任し、遂に志を決し私費を以て日本に
留學し、師範學校を卒業して鐵道學校に入り、旋って又た
明治大學政治經濟科に學ぶ。丁未の歲歸國して孫武、鄧王
麟、蔡大輔、劉公、王守愚等と軍人及び學生間に革命を
吹吹して雲燕龍變の機を待つ。斯くて辛亥の秋、武昌義を
起すや、君は湖北第二鎮副都督を以て、弟劉鐵と重兵を
辛んて襄樊の地を扼し、南陽を克復す。南北統一して君
湖北に歸り、副總統府高等顧問と爲る。陸軍少將に任じ
勳五位を授けらる。民國二年正式國會衆議院議員に常選
す。國會解散後、依然北京に客寓して消極的態度を持し、
五年國會復活するに及び召集に應じて仍は衆議院議員と
爲る。

孫文が革命を唱道するを聞
きて遂に同盟會に加入す。

Mr. Liu Ying, age thirty five, is a native of King-shan, the Hu Pe. Naturally being gallant and heroic in temperament, he never grudged anything to help the poor and the oppressed. Perceiving the necessity of rescuing his country from its precarious fate, he came to Japan at his own expense. He studied in the normal school, the railway school and then the Meiji University. Being appraised of the revolutionary movement of Sun Yat-sen, he joined the movement. In 1904, he returned to his country where he inspired his people with revolutionary ideas acting in union with leaders of the movement. As soon as Wu Chung's trouble broke out, he with his brother restored Nan Yan after hard fight. When the terms between the North and the South were declared, he went to Hupei, he was appointed the highest adviser to the vice-president, and was promoted to the rank of vice-general. In the second year of the Republic, he has returned for the House of Commons. On the dissolution of the Parliament, he staid in Peking, always taking conservative steps. When the Parliament was reopened, he was elected a member of the Parliament.

劉治洲 字定五 歳三十五

選舉地　陝西省
籍　貫　陝西省鳳翔縣
住　址　北京校場六條

君賦性仁厚。待人以誠。然爲人剛直不
阿。慷慨好義。居恆疾惡如仇。人有過
失。輒當面痛斥。人以過相詰。恆自陳
不稍隱諱見人爲強暴所厄。常忿忿不
自禁。過于身受。弱冠時。嘗以是與人
奮爭。不計己身之利害。故其接物雖鋒
鋩过露。昧于社交之術。然以其萬事出
以至誠。故人亦弇忌恨之者。自幼好
讀。能深思不倦。喜推求眞義。不拘拘
于文詞。維新後至上海。入理化學校。
畢業歸里。充鳳翔府中學校教員。宣統
三年九月。倡辦民團。十月。佐民軍禦
清軍於鳳翔。民國元年。被選爲省議會
議員。兼充三秦公學教員。二年被選爲
衆議院議員。國會解散後。經理中部宜
君等縣勘礦事宜。不與政事。及國會重
開。始入京仍充議員。

民國之精華

（傳記）

劉治洲先生

君賦性仁厚にして人を待つに誠を以てす。然かも人と爲り剛直にして阿らす、慷慨義を好みて、居常惡を憎ひて仇の如し。其の物に接し事に當りて鋒鋩を露はして社交の術に昧しと雖も、萬事悉く至誠に出づるを以て人之を恨む者稀れなり。幼より學を好みて研磋倦まず。書を讀みて深く思索し、其の義理を推求する事を喜び、文字の末に拘泥せず。曾て笈を負ふて上海に抵り、理化學校に學びて業を畢り。後ち鳳翔府中學校に敎鞭を執ること三年、宣統三年九月地方民團を組織し、十月革命軍を佐けて清軍を鳳翔に禦ぐ、民國元年選ばれて省議會議員と爲り、三秦公學校敎員を兼ねたり。二年正式國會衆議院議員に當選す。國會解散後、中部宜君等各縣の勘礦事務を經理して政事に與らず。國會復活するに及びて再び其の召集に應じて入京し、仍は衆議院議員と爲る。

Mr. Liu Chih-chou, otherwise known as Ting Uu, age thirty five, is a native of Shan Hsi hsing. Whatever he does, he is sincere at all. Bearing strong animosity against anything evil, he is blunt and unconcealed, but none thinks worse of him on that account. When young, he has been a lover of books, and sober and earnest student. He went to Shanghai where he was graduated from the school of physics and chemistry, and taught over three years in the middle school. When the revolution was started, he tood an active cause of the revolutionists. In the second year of the Republic, he was elected a member of the House of Commons. When this assembly was suppressed, he was interested in mining while himself keeping aloof from politics. When the parliament was restored he went up to Peking, and became a member thereof.

劉星楠　字雲平　歲三十五

選舉地　山東省

籍貫　山東省清平縣

住址　北京西城小沙鍋琉璃胡同二號

君賦性清高。言動舉止。皆迥異凡流。然爲人勤謹耐勞。人有所託。輒喜爲盡力。不以功自居。以故里人皆極愛敬之。偶有糾紛。得君出一言。無不立即解釋。自幼天資極高。悟性敏捷。讀書能深思探究精義。不爲成見所局。故思想豐富。見解新穎。人但見其居常規規自守。不知其精神固異常活潑也。海內維新後。銳志西學。旋於前清入北京法政大學。未及畢業。適民國成立。遂南下爲南京臨時參議院議員。繼充北京臨時參議院議員。正式國會成立。仍爲參議院議員。兼任總統府諮議及內務部顧問。國會解散後。無所表見。及國會重開。遂仍供舊職爲參議院議員。

君賦性情高にして言動舉止皆な迥に風流に異る。然も人と爲り恪勤にして勢に耐へ、人若し託す所われば輒ち喜んで盡力し、功を以て自ら居らず。幼より天資極めて高く書を讀みて深く其の義を攻究して成見の局する所とならず、思想豐富にして見解新穎なり。海内維新後、西學に志し、博く新書を涉獵して、天下有用の實學を求む。曾て前清末季に於て北京法政大學校に學ぶ。未だ其の業を卒へざるに及ばずして第一革命の事あり、君即ち南下して南京臨時參議院議員に任じ、民國建設の大業を翼贊したり。南北統一して政府北京に移るや、北上して北京臨時參議院議員たり。民國二年正式國會參議院議員に常選す。總統府諮議及び內務部顧問を兼任す。國會解散して後ち表見する所無く、國會復活するに及び、其の召集に應じて遂に再び參議院議員の職に就く。

Mr. Lin Hsing-nan otherwise called Yung Ping, age thirty five, is a native of Ching-pin hsien Shan-tung province. In Both deeds and words, he is different from the men of common order. In, associating with others, he takes the responsibility of doing anything for others and never attribute the merit to himself. He is a copious reader and hard student. He is full of rich ideas and had wide scope. He was keenly interested in the western learning, and devoted himself to the useful learning. At the latter days of the previous Chinese regime, he studied in the Peking University. When the revolution took place, he went to the south, and worked for the interest of the country. He was a member of the Special Assembly held in Peking. In the second year of the Republic, he was elected a member of the Senate, and adviser to the President. With the dissolution of the Parliament, he held his peace and was appointed a member of the Senate, when the new President summoned the Parliament.

選舉地 河南省
籍　貫 河南省安陽縣
住　址 北京順治門內翠花街路西

君少負英名。讀書能抉其關鍵不執字句。應童子試輒列前茅。旋輟科舉業。覓笈北上。研究教育學科。居無何。見中國外患日迫。遂赴保陽從戎。勤勞耐苦。於行伍者不及也。清之末造。政益不綱。乃隻身赴日本。擬入陸軍校。以爲功令所格。遂肆業警監學校。同盟會成立後。有力者問題君名。極意聯絡。劉君遂慨然加入。擘畫經營。厥推中堅。宣統元年冬。回國。潛歸彰郡。物色同志。時復往來大江以北。皷吹改革主義。不遺餘力。辛亥起義。君星夜赴滬。與同志組織威武北伐軍。接應楚師。南北統一。被選爲衆議員。湖口之役。署名質問。深爲袁氏所忌。坐以祖護李烈鈞罪。追徹議員徽章。君遂歷迹深山。以避傾陷。客歲帝制發生。君間道至秦。佐成陝之獨立。又赴滬上解決諸大問題。直至約法恢復。始來京。就議員職。

民國之精華　（傳記）　劉峯一先生

君少りよ英名を負ひ、讀書能く其の關鍵を抉りて字句に囚れず。童子の試驗に應じて前茅に列したるも、旋て科舉の業を勵め、笈を負ふて北上し、敎育の學を研究す。適々外患日に迫るを見て慨然蹶起して保陽に赴きて戎に從ふ。後ち日本に赴きて警察監獄學校に學ぶ。同盟會組織さるや。遂に之に加盟す。宣統元年の冬、國に歸りて潛に彰郡に歸りて同志を物色す。時に復た大江以北を往來して革命を皷吹す。辛亥の秋、第一革命の事起るや、君星夜上海に赴き、同志と威武北伐軍を組織して湖北軍に應す。南北統一して後ち正式國會衆議院議員となる。第二革命に際し議院に在りて政府に質問し、深く袁氏忌む所となり、李烈鈞庇護の故を以て議員徽章を剝奪され、君遂に深山に韜晦す。帝制問題發生するや、君間道より秦に至り、陝西の獨立を助く。又上海に赴きて諸問題を解決す。直に約法恢復するに及び復た出でて衆議院議員と爲る。

Mr. Liu Feng-i, otherwise known as Peng shan, is a native of An Yung, Ho-nan province. While young, he was very extensively informed, and passed the examination with honours. However he gave up the old chinese study for the new learning and devoted himself to the study of pedagogy. Perceiving the precarious situation in China he went to Japan where he studied in the police school. When the Revolutionists' society was formed he became a member thereof, and in 1909 he returned to his country and acting in conjunction with others he inspired the public with revolutionary ideas. In 1911, when the 1st Revolution took place, he went to Shanghai where he orgainzed an army which worked in union with the Hu Pe army. When the Parliament was formed, he entered the House of Commons as its member. In the 2nd Revolution he became an object of hatred of Yuanshi-kai. The budge and certificate of the membership was taken away from him. When the Imperial Movement took place he went to Shanghai in order to settle various problems. When the Parliament was formed for the second time he became its member.

劉恩格 字鯉門 歲二十九

選舉地　奉天省

籍貫　奉天省遼陽縣

住址　北京西城鬭才胡同內掄鉸胡同

君天資聰穎絕倫、富於理想、然爲人誠實不欺。雖年少氣盛。而無虛驕氣習。少時肄業於東三省法政學校。畢業後。遍游長江一帶。嗣留宦於黔南三年。襄辦清理財政。兼充官立各法政學校敎習。武昌起義。歸奉省親。民國元年。在本省提法司助理司法行政。遂爲奉天司法代表。應中央司法會議召集來京。旅京兩月。事竣回省。民國二年。當選爲衆議院議員。國會開幕議制憲法。又當選爲憲法起草員。嶺皖事敗後。以民黨關係。于八月二十七日。被逮入京師軍政執法處。旋寄押於警察廳署。國會解散後。因病保釋。同逮者七人。即所謂八議員案者是也。民國五年。第三次革命告成。國會續集。遂來京仍爲議員。

君天資聰穎絕倫にして理想に富む。然かも人と爲り誠實欺かず、年少氣銳なりと雖も虛驕人を凌ぐの能無し。少時東三省法政學校に學び、卒業後長江一帶を游歷し、嗣で雲南に抵つて致仕すること三年財政整理を襄理し、官公立各法政學校の敎習を兼ねたり。第一革命の事起るや歸鄕して親を省る。民國元年奉天省提法司科員となり、途に奉天司法官代表として北京に抵り中央司法會議に臨席したり。民國二年正式國會衆議院議員に當選す。第二革命の事敗れて後ち、國民黨たるの故を以て、京師軍政執法處に捕はれ京師警察廳に抑留さる。國會解散後、病に因つて保釋さる。同時に捕はれたる者七人、即ち所謂八議員案なる者是れ也。民國五年第三革命の事成りて、國會復活すや、復た出でて仍は衆議院議員と爲る。

Mr. Liu Wen-ko, otherwise called Li Men, age twenty nine is a native of Liao Yang hsien, Feng Tien hsing. He is unique in his power of understanding and rich in his ideas. Although young and active he is never arrogant. In his youth he was graduated from the law school in his province. Upon graduation he went to Yun Nan where he was employed as an instructor of the government law school and had charge of the work putting finances of the province in order. When the 1st revolution broke out he returned to native district. In the 1st year of the Republic he represented judges of his native province at the central meeting of judges held in Peking. In the 2nd year of the Republic he was elected a member of the House of Commons and was on the committee for drafting the constitution. On the outbreak of the 2nd Revolution he was arrested by the Peking police and was held in custody. After the dissolution of the Diet he was baled out owing to illness. Besides him seven other members were arrested. With the re-opening of the parliament he was again returned for the House of Commons after going up to Peking.

劉振生 字慰齋 歲二十九

選舉地 黑龍江省
籍　貫 黑龍江省肇州縣
住　址 北京順治門內未央胡同口袋胡同二十

君秉性誠厚篤實。尚質惡文。不事無益之繁華。居恆謹約自持。絕少囂張氣習。雖好義舉。而人有所託。不輕于承諾。既經允諾。必無不爲。事成不復望報。自幼聰慧好讀。悟性敏捷。遇目爲誦。弱冠即有文名。鄉里以神童目之。及長。博覽群籍。闡明精義。洞察事理。然其立身行己。多厚重自持。不效時髦青年之浮薄淺躁。故思想見解。極明瞭切實。先輩即推重之。民國二年正式國會成立。被選爲衆議院議員。此次約法恢復。及國會再行召集。遂又入京。仍就衆議院議員舊職。

君秉性誠厚篤實、質を尚び文を惡みて無益の繁華に事へす。居常謹約自ら持して絕て傲慢の氣風無し。義擧を好むと雖も、人託する所あれば、輕々しく承諾せす、旣に承諾すれば必ず爲さゝる無く、而して事成つて其の報を望まさる也。幼より聰慧にして學を好み、弱冠文名あり、鄉里神童を以て之を目す。長ずるに及びて博く群籍を涉獵して精義を闡明して事理を洞察す。然かも其の身を立てゝ己を行ふ、厚重自ら持して時流青年の浮薄淺躁なるに效はざる也。故に思想見解極めて明瞭切實にして先輩即ち之を推重す。民國二年正式國會成立に當り、選ばれて衆議院議員と爲る。此の次約法恢復して國會再び召集を行ふに及び、遂に又た入京して、仍は衆議院議員の舊職に就きたり。

Mr. Liu Chen-sheng, sometimes known as Wei-chi, twenty nine years of age, is a native of Chao Chuan, Hei Lung Chiang. He is a man of sincere and sound principle. He is an enemy of idle and vain thoughts. When he says " yes," he means it and therefore he never neglected his study. While young he acquired already a certain literary fame. As he grew older he read books most extensively with the meaning of which he became quite conversant. In both the nationality of his thought and interpretation he was respected by his friends. In the 2nd year of the Republic when the Parliament was held, he was returned for the House of Commons. With the re-opening of the Parliament he was elected to a member of the House of Commons.

劉芷芬

選舉地　華僑

籍貫　廣東省梅縣

住址　北京西單、安福胡同

君襟懷高遠。生平以排除強暴爲第一事業。當前清光緒末年。革命黨人組織同盟會。時君年甫弱冠。即其黨員。後以參與黃岡革命軍事。逃于南洋。爲瓜哇同盟會支部長。辛亥湖北起義。君與黃興宋敎仁等。入武昌黃興統率義軍。爲總司令。駐紮漢陽。君爲參謀。南京臨時政府成立。君爲總統府秘書。民國二年第一次國會成立。當選爲參議院議員。癸丑贛寧之役。君留南京。爲總司令部秘書。參與其事。國會停職後。君乃奔走日本南洋香港各處。謀第三次革命。歐戰初起時。君欲乘人心紛擾。聯絡廣州軍隊起事。爲龍濟光偵知設陷被捕。入香港獄中。數月始得釋出。帝制發生後。君留上海。與各處黨人相策應。迄袁氏病殂。約法恢復。國會重開。君始來京就職焉。

君襟懷高遠にして生平強暴を排除するを以て念とす。前清光緒末年、同盟會の組織あるや、君弱冠にして其の黨員に列す。後ち廣京黃岡の義擧に參加し、事敗れて南洋に逃れ、同盟會爪哇支部長となる。第一革命の事起るや、君黃興宗敎仁等と武昌に赴き、黃興が民軍總司令として漢陽に駐紮するや、君其の參謀と爲る。南京臨時政府成立して、臨時大總統府秘書に任ず。南北統一して民國二年正式國會組織さるゝに及び、參議院議員に當選す。第二革命に際し君南京に在りて民軍總司令部秘書となる。國會停職後、日本南洋香港各地を奔走し、歐洲戰爭勃發して人心の動搖せるに乘じて廣洲軍隊と聯絡して事を擧げんとせしも、龍濟光の探偵に偵知され、香港に捕はれて獄中に在ること數ヶ月、漸く釋放さる。帝制發生後、上海に在りて各地の同志と策應す。袁氏病死して約法復活し國會再蘇するや、君即ち北上して參議院議員と爲る。

Mr. Liu Chi-fen, is a native of Mei Hsien, Kwang Tung hsing. He is a man of high and noble spirit. At the later days of the previous Chinese regime when the revolutionary ideas were germinating, he took a keen delight in them, but being suspected by the government, he went to the South Seas, and made Java his headquarter. In the outbreak of the first revolution he was one of the staff to the Revolutionists. After the establishment of the Nanking Government, he was appointed the secretary of the president. In this second year of the Republic, when the Parliament was formed, he was appointed a member of the Senate. When the Parliament was dissolved, he went to Japan, South Seas, Hongkong, and other places. Taking the advantage of the European war, he was about to carry out his grand work, but was arrested by the government, and spent several months in prison. When the movement for the Imperial System was started, he worked and planned against it in conjunction with others. With the death of Yuan Shi-kai, the Parliamentary work was revived, and he was appointed to a member of the Senate.

劉志詹 字蘇佛

選舉地　山西省

籍貫　山西省晋城縣人

住址　北京西斜街豆芽菜胡同

君爲浙中崇祀名官彝聽先生之次子。幼生抗州。弱冠得選拔貢生。遍游燕豫楚晋。以利濟民生爲已任。光緒癸卯辭晋省校長。赴日本。入法政大學。歲內午。內招爲山西諮議局籌辦處課長。歷充全省自治研究所敎務長。憲政研究會敎員。教育總會會長。諮議局議員。資政院議員。與諸名流會合立憲公會於滬上。時晋人以高等警校無人主持。函請返晋。長高等警校敎務兼辦監督事宜。辛亥正在京師。國民軍起。遍返晋南。倡練民團。保護民生。次年赴省。因政黨請求。剙立共和黨支部。與省垣國民黨對峙。遂於敵黨群撓力阻之中。被選爲衆議院議員。湖口變作。晋地動搖。又分函布告各地。以國家民人爲前提。國會解散。返里伏處。憤慨時事。耽翫泉石。丙辰國會復活。重入京師。仍爲衆議院議員。

君は浙中に祀られたる名官彝聽先生の次子にして杭州に生る。弱冠の時、選抜貢生を得たり。燕豫楚晋の故地を遍游して濟生利民の志を抱きたり。光緒癸卯山西の小學校長を辭して日本に赴き、法政大學に學ぶ。丙午の歲、招かれて山西諮議局準備處課長と爲る。爾來全省自治研究所敎務長、憲政研究會敎員、教育總會々長、諮議局議員、資政院議員等の職に歷任す。後ち諸名士と會合して立憲公會を上海に開く。時に山西高等警察學校に主持者なく、君を招きて敎校長たらしむ。第一革命當時、北京に在りて其の報を聞き、急ぎ山西南方に歸りて民國を組織す。次年山西省城に至り、共和黨支部を設け、旋て正式國會衆議院議員に當選す。第二革命に際し山西また動搖す。君乃ち國家民人の休戚を說きて輕舉を戒む。國會解散後、鄉に歸り、時事を憤慨して泉石を樂む。國會復活するや重ねて入京して衆議院議員と爲る。

Mr. Liu Chih-chan, otherwise known as Su Fo, is a native of Chin Cheng hsien, Shan Hsi hsing. He is an offspring of a wellknown scholarly family. When young he travelled through out the country. In 1903 he came to Japan and studied in the law college, while in 1906 he was appointed to the head of the bureau preparing for the local assembly of Shan hsi. Ever since, he occupied a series of important posts especially regarding the study of the civic institution, that of the constitution besides being a member of the local assembly. In the high police school in Shan hsi he was the president. At the time of the 1st Revolution, he went to Peking and organized the peoples party in Shan hsi. Later he formed the branch offices of the Republic in his native province. When the 2nd Revolution broke out he went about his province preaching the necessity of refraining from any rush conduct. On the dissolution of the Parliament he returned to his country and remained as one of the malcontents. However, as soon as the Parliament resumed its function, he was returned for the House of Commons, the position he holds in the present moment.

劉祖堯 字子欽 歲三十三

選舉地　山西省

籍貫　山西省長治縣

住址　北京西單牌樓報子街

君爲人勤謹耐勞。自待極薄而喜爲人盡力。人有所託。雖所不能。亦必勉爲助力。事成。決不受人酬報。故里人皆敬愛之。偶有糾紛得君一言無不立釋。自幼聰頴好讀。喜聞讜言。故其進益猛。年十五即補縣學生員。海內維新後。考入山西大學堂中齊。肆業二年。改入山西法政專門學校。於光緒三十四年畢業。曾充本縣勸學所總董兼縣視學。民國元年春。本縣匪擾兵變。曾以縣參事會會長。總辦團練事務。夏五月。並兼縣財政科長。民國二年一月。當選爲衆議院議員。國會解散後。無所表見。及國會復活。始來京。仍爲衆議院議員。

君人と爲り恪謹にして勞に耐へ、自ら待つに極めて薄くして而かも喜んで人の爲に盡力す。幼より聰頴にして學を求め弱冠早くも文名あり。然かも心を虚ふして聞を好み、讜言を聞くを喜ぶ。故に其の進境日に著して、年十五即ち縣學生に補せらる。海內維新後、山西大學堂中齊に入りて修業し、後ち山西法政專門學校に學び、光緒三十四年其の業を畢ゆ。曾て鄉縣の勸學所總董に任じ縣視學を兼ぬ。民國元年、長治縣に於て匪徒兵に混じて譁變す。君即ち縣參事會長を以て團練事務を總理して地方の秩序を恢復したり。同年五月縣財政科々長を兼任す。民國二年正式國會成立に際し、衆望を荷つて衆議院議員に當選す。國會解散後、韜晦して政見を發表せず。國會復活して重ねて召集を行ふに及び、君復た出でゝ入京し、仍は衆議院議員と爲る。

Mr. Lin Tsu-yao, otherwise known as Tzu Chin, age thirty three, is a native of Chang Chih, Shan Hsi hsing. He takes a keen delight to help others even at his own expense. Early in life, he acquired a certain literary fame. As he is open to listen to others, his progress has been indeed striking so that at the age of fifteen, he already enjoyed the scholarship of the prefecture. Since he turned his attention to the new learning he studied at the law school of his province. In 1908 he was graduated from the school and appointed the inspector of learning. In 1912 he was appointed to the head of the local council, and by his influence the order in his province was preserved. In the 2nd year of the Republic when the Parliament was opened he was returned for the House of Commons in a large majority. After the dissolution of the Parliament he never expressed his views on politics. When the Parliament was re-opened, he entered Peking and was elected to a member of the House of Commons.

鄧　鎔　字守瑕　歲四十五

選舉地　蒙古

籍　貫　四川成都縣

住　址　北京賈家胡同北頭路西

君爲人剛正不阿。而秉性聰慧。思想活潑。頭腦明晰。讀書不執成見。不拘字句。故皆能得眞義。弱冠即負文名。及長。尤廣覽羣書。自以遠大相期許。及海內維新。遂改志殫精西學。遍閱新書。慨然以挽弱爲强自任。以前清丁酉科優貢。咨送日本留學。畢業于明治大學專門部法律科。歸國後。入都應學部留學生試。授內閣中書。民國元年。由四川省議會選充臨時參議院議員。二年。正式國會成立。被選爲外蒙古科布多等處衆議院議員。國會解散後。無所表見。五年及國會重開。遂來京復爲議員。

民國之精華　（傳記）鄧鎔先生

君人と爲り剛正にして阿らず、秉性聰慧にして思想活潑頭腦明晰なり。書を讀みて成見に囚れず字句に拘泥せず。皆其の眞義を究むるを得たり。弱冠早くも文名を負ひ、長ずるに及びて尤も廣く群書を閲して遠大を以て相許す。海內維新に及び遂に西學に志し遍く新書を涉獵し、慨然として國運の挽回を以て自ら任ず。前清丁酉科優貢を以て官費として日本に留學し、明治大學專門部法律科を卒業す。歸國後、學部の試驗に及第して內閣中書を授けらる。民國元年四川省議會より選ばれて臨時參議院議員となり、民國建設の大業を翼贊したり。二年正式國會の成立に際し、外蒙古科布多等各地より選擧されて衆議院議員と爲る。國會解散されてより閑臥悠々韜晦して政見を表示せず。國會復活して再び召集を行ふに及び、遂に出でヽ復た衆議院議員の職に就きたり。

Mr. Teng Jung, otherwise called Shou Hsia, age forty five is a native of Cheng Tu hsien, Ssu Chuan province. He is a gentleman of active thoughts and clear brains. Being straight forward in character he is above the vice of flattery. In reading books he is never bound up with the traditional influence not with mere forms of expressions. He studies and attains the true import over what he reads. While young he secured literary fame and as he grew older his scope of reading has been enlarged more than ever. He was keenly interested in the promotion of the interest of his own country. He went to Japan where he studied in the Meiji University. On returning to his home he passed the civil service examination successfully. In the 1st year of the Republic he was elected to a member of the Local Assembly and contributed his service towards the establishment of full-fledged Republic. In the 2nd year of the Republic thus formed, he was elected to a member of the House of Commons representing ultra Mongolia. When under the pressure of Yuanshi-kai the Parliament was dissolved, he refrained from expressing his views on politics and mostly he kept them to himself. However when the Parliament was re-opened, he was returned for the House of Commons.

鄧峻德　字天乙　歲三十

選舉地　山東省

籍　貫　山東省樂安縣

住　址　北京東珠市口路北三十號

君秉性溫厚。待人以和。雖盛怒。無疾言遽色。然持己甚嚴。言動不苟。自幼讀書。喜推求義理。不拘拘於章句詞藻。曾肄業于登州文會館。畢業後。歷辦膠州安邱濰縣烟臺各學校。以提倡革命創造共和為宗旨。辛亥革命。充山東民軍參謀長。共和告成。被選為衆議院議員候補當選人。政界多欲以祿位致之。不就。惟一意辦理學校。嘗謂人曰。教育未普。民智未開。徒號稱共和。究何益耶。二次革命之際。君奔走山東各地謀響應。不遂。遂亡命海外。乙卯帝制亂興。乃偕山東同人等。組織護國軍。佔據山東東部各要地。親率軍隊攻擊濟南。及至國會重行召集。因循例提補。得為衆議院議員。

君秉性溫厚にして人を待つに和を以てし。盛怒すと雖も疾言遽色なし。然かも己を持すること甚だ嚴正なり。幼より書を讀み、喜んで義理を攻究し、章句詞藻に拘泥せず。曾て登州文會館に學びて卒業し、膠州安邱濰縣烟臺等各地の各學校に敎鞭を取り、革命を提唱して共和を創造する事を以て主義とせり。第一革命當時は山東民軍參謀長に任じ、民國成立後第一次正式國會衆議院議員補缺に當選す。爾來專ら學校を經營して育英の業に從事す。

曾て人に謂つて曰く、敎育未だ普及せず、徒らに共和を叫ぶも何の益わらん耶と。第二次革命に際し、山東各地に奔走して響應を謀りしも遂げず、山東の同志等と護國軍を組織し、山東東部の各要地を占領す、君親ら軍隊を率ゐて濟南を攻擊す。國會重ねて召集を行ふに及び、例に因りて缺員を補し現に衆議院議員と爲る。

Mr. Teng Hsun-te otherwise called Tien-i, age thirty, a native of Yo-an, Shan Tung hsing, is a gentleman full of consideration for others, but severe for himself. He seldom shows anger in his countenance. After graduating from the Tao Chow Literary school, he was an instructor in various parts of his province. He was an ardent supporter of the cause of the Revolutionists. He was on the staff of the Shanting military headquarters. After the establishment of the Republic, he was returned for the House of Commons. He has always been interested in education. As long as the people remained ignorant, and the diffusion of knowledge is not sufficiently extended, there is little necessity of talking about the Republic. Such was the trend of his thought. In the 2nd revolution, his efforts proved little so that he fled abroad. When the movement for the restoration of the Imperial government was talked about, he returned to Shang tung, and stood up against the movement. At the head of an army, he himself attacked Chi nan. He was elected to a member of the House of Commons by way of filling the gap left by his predecessor.

樂　山　字靜亭　歲四十九

選舉地　蒙古
籍貫　昭烏達盟克什克薩克鎮國公旗人
住址　北京後門內椅子胡同

君賦性清高。言動舉止。皆迴異凡流。
然爲人寡默而富決斷。尙義節。重道
義。自幼慷慨好義。喜救人急難。及長。
尤在任俠之風。遠近部落爭稱其名。盖
蒙古華胄界之雋傑也。君蒙古昭盟克
旗。前淸以頭品頂戴。花翎和碩總管。
都統銜。膺充繙譯官有年。民國成立
後。曾充蒙藏院諮議。贊勤五大民族
共和之建設。以功授三等嘉禾章。民國
二年正式國會成立。被選爲衆議院議
員。君與葉顯揚張樹桐。均稱國民黨三
中堅。癸丑國民黨失敗。被解散國會之
際。君爲各方面所勸迫令其脫黨。君決
然拒之。拂袖歸蒙。當時盛傳。樂君將
舉蒙兵討袁者。具見君爲袁氏所注意
矣。五年袁氏死。國會復活。遂又應召
入京。仍任衆議院議員。

君賦性清高にして言動舉止皆な逈に凡流に異る。然かも
人と爲り寡默にして決斷に富み。義節を尙び道義を重ん
す。蓋し蒙古華胄界の雋傑なり。君蒙古昭盟克旗人とし
て、前淸頭品頂戴花翎和碩總管都統銜として繙譯官に任ず
ること年あり。民國成立後、曾て蒙藏院諮議に任じ、五
大民族共和の建設を贊勤して功あり三等嘉禾章を授けら
る。民國二年正式國會成立して衆議院議員と爲る。君葉
顯揚張樹桐と國民黨の三中堅と稱せらる。癸丑の歲國民
黨失敗して國會解散さるゝや、各方面より其の脫黨を迫
る。君決然之を拒け袖を拂つて蒙古に歸る。當時君將に
蒙古兵を率ゐて討袁の軍を舉ぐべしと盛んに宣傳され袁
氏の爲に一敵國の感ありたり。五年袁世凱死して國會復
活す。遂に其の召集に應じて入京し、仍は衆議院議員と
爲る。

民國之精華　（傳記）樂　山　先　生

Mr. Yo Shan, otherwise called Ching Ting, age forty nine, is a native of Mongolia. In words, thoughts, and natural gifts, he differs from others. He is a man of few words and strong determination attaching great importance to moral virtues. He is one of the foremost man among the nobles in Mongolia. When the Republic was established, he was elected to a member the Mongolian local assembly and, in the 2nd year of the Republic when the formation of the parliament was actualized, he was returned for the House of Commons. In 1913 when the national party was deprived its privilege by Yuan Shi-kai and the Parliament was dissolved his friends urged him to leave the party. Turning a deaf ear to such request he returned to Mongolia. It was then rumoured that he would attack Yuanshi-kai with the help of Mongolian soldiers. However, with the death of Yuan Shi-kai, the Parliament was restored. He entered Peking and resumed function as a member of the Parliament.

鄭斗南 字曉江 歲五十四

籍址 北京

籍貫 江蘇省江都

選舉地 江蘇省

君秉性嚴正剛直。不隨流俗轉移。然居心仁厚。雖所疾惡。但遠不與交。決不乘隙相仇。與人交。尙信義。重然諾。人有所託。常爲拒却之詞。而暗中爲之竭力。事成。亦不以告。故人之受其恩惠者。常至數年後始知之。以故感恩者。益爲懇切。自幼即能攻苦讀書。不喜嬉游。年方弱冠。已負文名。然不以是自畫。及長愈益奮勉求進。輒能深造精微。不徒拘于章句。壯年入仕途。以舉人歷官山東臨淄縣知縣。調署歷城縣知縣。旋保升知府。歷充山東撫院文案。藩司新政文案。學務處總稽核。泉府讞局發審。並曾歷辦湖北沙市洋關稅務。兼通商交涉員。民國成立後。被選爲江蘇省議會議員。復被選爲國會參議院議員。國會解散後。歸里獨以詩酒自娛。不介懷時事。及此次國會復活。遂入京仍供舊職。

君秉性嚴正剛直にして流俗に隨はず、然かも居心仁厚にして憎惡する所と雖、決して隙に乘じて相仇せず、人と交りて信義を尙び然諾を重んず。幼より刻苦して書を讀み嬉戲を喜ばず、年方に弱冠既に文名を負ふ。長じて益々奮勉して進を求め、造詣愈々深し。壯年仕途に就き、舉人を以て山東臨淄縣知縣、歷城縣知縣署理に歷任し、旋て知府に升りて山東巡撫衙門文案、藩司新政文案、學務處讞稽核、泉府讞局發審等の職に歷充す。曾て湖北沙市海關稅務を處理し、通商交涉委員を兼ぬ。民國成立後、選ばれて江蘇省議會議員と爲り、次て正式國會議員選舉に際して參議院議員に當選し、北上して國政を議す。國會解散後、乃ち鄕關に歸臥して詩酒自ら娛み敢て時事を介せず。國會復活するや、君復た召集に應じて北京に抵り、再び參議院議員の舊職に就く。

Mr. Chung Ton-nan, a native of Chiang-tsu, Chiang-su-sheng, aged fifty four, is a gentleman of strict behaviour and strong will, and never runs after the vulgar fashion. He is gentle and humane, detesting wickedness. His words are always good. With him, "yes" is always "yes," no matter under what circumstance he may be placed. He was an ardent book reader, and even young, his literary fame rose quite high. He passed the civil service examination, and occupied various important positions in the government notably, the custom house officer in Lu-pei and Sha-hsi in which capacity, his ability was remarkably manifested. After the formation of the Cabinet, he became a member of the Chiang-su assembly. When the National Assembly was formerly opened, he was elected to a senator, and in Peking, participated in the government work. After the dissolution of the Parliament, he returned to his native province where he kept himself aloof from politics. After the reopening of the Parliament, he went to Peking where he resumed the senatorship as on the former occasion.

鄭懋修 字梅仙 歲五十三

選舉地　廣東省
籍　貫　廣東省潮陽縣
住　址　北京丞相胡同潮州館

君自幼好學深思。稚年讀書。即喜推求
精義。不厭數問。塾師常爲所窘。益契
重之。弱冠即有文名。詩文策論。皆有
名家風味。及長。尤廣覽羣書。並喜涉
獵周秦諸子。於前清光緒朝以主事籤
分戶部廣西司。旋任湖廣司主稿遂朝
旨改組度支以事分司。君任制用司庶
務科科長。旋任京餉科科長。辛亥革軍
起義。君棄官南歸。民國二年。被選爲
衆議院議員。旋因袁氏肆虐解散國會。
君仍歸里。學界同人舉君任縣教育會
正會長。潮陽經兵燹後學務退化幾有
一落千丈之勢。君力爲提倡頗有起色。
四年部令改組商會衆舉。君兼任縣商
會正會長。今國會恢復。遂仍就衆議院
議員之職。

民國之精華　（傳記）鄭懋修先生

君幼より學を好みて深く思索し、少年書を讀みて義理を
探求するを喜び、弱冠即ち文名ありて、詩文策論皆な名
家の風味あり。長するに及び、尤も廣く群書を閲して、
並に周秦諸子の書を渉獵する事を喜びたり。前清光緒時
代、主事を以て戸部廣西司に任せらる。旋て湖廣司主稿
に任す。度支部に改められてより、制用司庶務科科長に任
じ、旋て京餉科々長に任す。辛亥の歳革命の軍起るや君
官を棄てゝ南下し、民國二年選ばれて正式國會衆議院議
員と爲る。旋て袁氏擅まに國會を解散したるに因り、郷
里に歸臥す。學界の同人より舉げられて縣教育會正會
長に任す。兵燹後潮陽縣の學務衰退して幾んど一落千丈
の勢あり、君力めて奨學の事を主張して起色あり。四年
舉げられて縣商會正會長を兼任す。五年國會恢復して遂
に召集に應じて復た衆議院議員と爲る。

Mr. Cheng Men-hsiu, otherwise known as Mei Hsien, age fifty three, is a native of Chung Yang, Kwangtung province. Early in life he proved himself to be a student of books and deep thinker. While young he already attained some literary fame; as he grew older he studied Chinese classics most extensively. At the later days of the previous Chinese regime, he occupied an importance post in his province. In 1911 when the Revolution broke out, he disconnected himself with the government and went to the south. In the 2nd year of the Republic, he was returned for the House of Commons when Yuan Shi-kai disolved the Parliament he returned to his home where he was appointed the president of the prefectural educational association. When he undertook to discharge his function in this capacity there was marked improvement in the educational tone of the whole province. When the Parliament was restored, he went to Peking where he was returned for the House of Commons, the membership of which he occupies at present.

鄭際平 字平甫 歲四十四

選舉地 浙江省

籍貫 浙江省黃巖縣

住址 北京象坊橋浙江議員公廨

君秉性篤實無華。而精明強幹。與人交。常戇直不阿。人有過失。無不遽情詰責。不稍存世故之念。然居心仁厚。喜救人急難。故其接物。雖鋒芒過露昧于社交之術。然以其萬事出于至誠。故人亦罕忌恨之者。自幼聰敏過人。於舉業已深有所造。然以傾心新學。故但以一衿自足。不復從事舉業。日惟遍讀新書。銳意研究科學。旋以自費東渡。入日本明治大學。畢業。授政治學士位。歸國後。歷充浙江諮議局議員。諮議會代表。資政院議員。民國二年。被選為國會參議院議員。國會解散後。鄉里獨居修養。時復赴滬上。與諸同志為會。謀大局挽回之謀。及國會復活。遂入京。仍為議員。恢復大同之謀。

君秉性篤實にして華無く、人と交るや硬直にして阿らず。人若し過失あれば情を遽にして詰責し、稍も世故の念を有せず。然かも居心仁厚にして喜んで人の急を救ふ。其の世に處するや鋒鋩を露して社交の術に昧しと雖、其の萬事至誠に出るを以て之を恨む者罕れなり。幼より聰慧人に過ぎ、科舉の業に於て造詣する所ありしが、心を新學に傾注して科舉の業に從はず、新書を涉獵して銳意科學を研究す。旋て自費を以て東渡し、日本明治大學校に游び卒業す。歸國の後ち次込浙江諮議局議員、諮願會代表、資政院議員と為る。國會解散さるゝや、京師を去つて鄉關に歸臥し、韜晦して德を養ふ。時に復た上海に馳せて諸同志と會し、大局挽回の謀を講じたり。旣にして國會再蘇すや、君蹶躍して其の召集に應じ、北京に抵りて現に參議院議員の職に在り。

Mr. Chung Chi-ping, a native of Huang-yen, the Che-chiang-shen, aged forty four, is a gentleman of sincerity and sobriety. While he is straightforward in his dealings with others, he is full of merciful spirit, and takes pleasure in helping his friends in need. He is by no means compromising, but the people take no grudge against him. He turned his attention to the study of the new learning and particularly to science. At his own expense, he was graduated from the Meiji University. After his having returned home, he was appointed to many important posts in Che-chiang which he most ably filled. On the formation of the Republic, he was elected to a member of the Senate. When the Parliament was dissolved, he left Peking and has been spending peaceful time. He went to Shanghai, and joined with his friends to accomplish the grand object they had in common. When the Parliament was reopened, he went to Peking, and was elected to a member of the Senate.

鄭江灝　字南溪　歲三十五

選舉地　湖北省

籍　貫　湖北省襄陽縣

住　址　北京東城八棵槐蒙院後大平境一號

君爲人誠厚篤實。不尚浮華。前清時。
曾肄業于日新中學堂。轉入湖北武普
通學堂。又改入文普通學堂。丙午。游
學日本。東斌學校。旋歸國創辦湖北日
報于漢口。由湖北鐵路協會員。被推爲
報界代表。辛亥。以德育會幹事。共進
會參議部長偕湖南都督焦達峯。起義
長沙。復歸鄂。任總監察署顧問官。南
北休戰。君被派爲赴上海南方議和代
表。返鄂。民國元年。被舉爲民社幹事。
府副官。任縣知事考試師。湖北都督
民社改組共和黨。被舉爲鄂支部主任
幹事。二年由湖北省議會被選爲參議
院議員。任共和黨院內幹事。暨本部幹
事。國會停職。入川。任縣知事。及巡按
使公署秘書。帝制發生。川師長兼清鄉
軍司令官劉存厚起兵時。以清鄉軍法
官在納溪。成都獨立。任四川都督府秘
書。約法恢復。仍就議員職。

事試驗官に任じ、湖北都督府副官となり。民國元年民社
幹事となり、共和黨湖北支部主任幹事となる。二年參議
院議員となり、共和黨院內幹事及び本部幹事となる。國
會停止後、四川に抵りて縣知事及び巡按使公署秘書に任
す。帝制問題發生して劉存厚が兵を起すの時、其の清鄉
軍法官として納溪にあり、成都獨立して四川都督府秘書
に任す、國會復活して復た參議院議員と爲る。

君人と爲り誠厚篤實にして浮華を喜はず。前清時代、日
新中學校に學び、轉じて湖北武普通學堂に入り、又た文
普通學堂に入る。丙午の歲日本に游學して東斌學校に入
る。旋て歸國して湖北日報を漢口に創設す。湖北鐵道協
會に於て新聞界の代表に推さる。辛亥の歲、德育會幹事、
共進會參議部長を以て湖南都督焦達峯と義を長沙に起
し、復た湖北に歸り總監察署顧問官に任す、南北休戰す
るや君上海に赴きて和議の事に參し、後ち歸省して縣知

民國之精華　（傳記）　鄭江灝先生

Mr. Chung Chiang-hos, a native of Hsing-yang hsien, the Lu-pei-sheng, aged thirty five, is a gentleman of honest and sincere character. In the previous Chinese regime, he studied in various schools of China. In 1906, he visited Japan where he entered the Tung-wu school; On return to his country, he established in Han-Saw a newspaper called the Lu-pei Daily, and as a matter of fact, he was elected to a sort of leader among journalists. In 1911, he was appointed various important posts in Lu-pei, notably, the adviser to the governor general of Lu-pei. When trouble was concluded between the South and the North, he was interested to bring about peaceful negotiation between both parties in Shanghai, returned home. He was a staff to the governor general of Lu-pei, and in 1912, he was the director of the Lu-pei branch of the democratic party. In 1912, he was appointed to a senator, and the whip of the Republican party. After the dissolution of the Parliament, he went to Sei-chang, and was appointed to the secretary of the governor. With the reopening of the Parliament, he was returned for the House of Commons.

鄭林皋 字鳴九 歲三十四

選舉地　黑龍江省議會

籍　貫　黑龍江省拜泉縣

住　址　北京堂子胡同東口外寬街九號

君賦性溫和。與物無忤。少好讀。博覽
羣書。務期淹博。然不屑拘拘焉從事于
科舉之業。故其讀書純以研究眞理爲
主要。而不局于習俗之成見。及海內維
新。愈力求有用之學。而尤醉心于敎育
之書。清末。肄業于黑龍江初級師範。
卒業後以提倡敎育爲己任。從事敎育
者。六年。歷充敎習。校長學務公所議
員縣視學。省視學。勸學所所長。各職。
民國元年。被選爲臨時省議會議員。旋
被選爲敎育總會會長。民國二年。被選
爲參議院議員。國會解散後。杜門勤
學。不復與聞政事。及國會重開。始入
京爲參議院議員。

君賦性溫和にして物と忤ふ無し、少にして讀を好み博く
羣書を涉獵す、然かも其の讀書は義理を研究するを主と
し、科舉の業に從事するを屑しとせざりし。海內維新に及
び愈々力めて有用の學を求め、尤も敎育の書に心醉す。
前清末季、黑龍江初級師範學校を卒業して後ち、敎育の
振興を以て己が任とし、敎員、校長、學務公所議員、縣
視學、省視學、勸學所々長等の各職に歷充銳意地方敎育
の刷新に努力して貢獻する所尠少ならず。民國元年臨時
省議會議員に選ばれ、旋て同省敎育總會々長に推さる。
民國二年正式國會議員選舉に際して參議院議員に當選し
たり。國會解散後、田園に歸去來を賦し、杜門學に勤め
復た政事に預らず。國會重ねて開かるゝに及び、再び晉
京して國政の議に干與すべく現に仍ち參議院議員と爲
る。

Mr. Cheng Lin-pao, is a gentleman of gentle character, and studious turn of mind. He was quite different in his mode of study from other Chinese. When the new ideas were introduced to China, he devoted himself to the new leaning, and interested in education. As the later days of the previous Chinese regime, he was graduated from the Hei Lun-chieng primary Normal school, and was appointed to a series of educational posts in his province, making great efforts to improve the educational condition of the province. In the first year of the Republic, he was elected a member of the local assembly, and the head of the Educational Association. In the second year of the Republic, he was elected to a member of the Parliament, and a member of the Senate. After the dissolution of the Parliament, he returned to his native home, and is very interested in politics. However, with the re-opening of the Parliament, he was appointed to a member of the Senate.

鄭人康 字馭紛 歳三十二

選舉地 湖南省第二區

籍貫 湖南省衡山縣

住址 北京眾議院西次道十八號

君爲人忠厚誠懇。言動以禮自持。不喜
矜奇立異。居常老成持重。言笑不苟。
然熱忱愛國。勇於奉公。少時讀書。即
慨然有挽救危亡之志。及長。見國事日
非。愈立志捨身殉國。每次政變。君皆
奔走經營。不避危險。不計個人之利
害。曾於前清時畢業於湖南高等警察
學校。光緒宣統間。曾任衡山警察局局
長。主新寧廻龍書院講席。辛亥九月一
日。與焦達峯光復湖南。任都督府高等
政治顧問。旋任郴宜安撫使。民國元
年。任稽勳局湘調查會會長。兼北京
稽勳局評議。二年二月。當選爲眾議
院議員。國會解散。仍奔走江湖。留心
國事。及國會重開。遂來京仍爲眾議院
議員。

君人と爲り忠厚誠懇にして言動共に禮あり、居常老成持
重にして言笑苟もせず、熱心國を愛し、奉公に勇なり。
少時書を讀みて慨然として時艱を挽救するの志あり。長
ずるに及び、國事日に非なるに見て、身を捨てゝ國に殉
せん事を志し、政變ある每に、君皆な奔走經營して危險
を避けず個人の利害を計らず。曾て前淸時代湖南高等警
察學校を卒業し、光緒宣統間、曾て衡山警察局々長に任

じ、新寧廻龍書院講席を主りたり。辛亥九月一日焦達峯
と湖南の獨立を圖り、事就つて後ち都督府高等政治顧問
に任ず。旋て郴安撫使に任じたり。民國元年稽勳局湖南
調查會々長に任じ、北京稽勳局評議員を兼ね。二年二月
眾議院議員に當選す。國會解散の後ち仍ら江湖に奔走し
て心を國事に留め。國會の再開と共に出京して仍ら眾議
院議員の職に復したり。

民國之精華 （傳記） 鄭人康先生

三百八十三

Mr. Cheng Jen-kang. He is sincere and true in his every movement and conducts himself
in strict accordance with the forms of ettiquett. As he grew older he perceived that his country was
suffering from the results of maladministration. He became keenly interested in public affairs and ever
ran many risks in his life for the interest of the public. In 1909 he was appointed to the head of the
police office in his province. When the revolution broke out and all the provinces declared their independence, he was keenly interested in declaring the independence of Ho-nan. In the 1st year of the
Republic he was appointed to the president of the Ho-nan investigation association. In the 2nd year of the
Republic he was returned for the House of Commons. When the Parliament shut down, he was still
interested in politics, actively working for the restoration of the true Republic. When the Parliament
was reopened he was returned for the House of Commons.

蔡汝霖　字雨香　歳四十四

選舉地　浙江省

籍貫　浙江省東陽

住址　北京石燈庵西口

君爲人精敏多能。然富於感情。見人悲苦事。常爲之潛然下涙。若身受者然。戊戌以丁酉拔貢舉人北上會試。目覩政變慘狀。大受激刺。從此棄科舉業。專任地方公益事宜。癸卯。自備資斧東瀛。考察學務一年。歸國遂從事教育事業。曾任新昌縣渼西學堂堂長一年。金華府中學堂監督二年。金衢嚴處四府旅省公學監督二年。東陽縣教育會會長一年。又勸學所總董一年。浙省公推爲立憲請願代表。清季立憲議起。浙省諮議會幹事一年。全浙教育會公推爲諮議局議員。辛亥。浙軍政府成立。旋被選爲諮議局議員。辛亥。浙軍政府成立。特任爲金鄉宣慰使。旋被選爲臨時省議會議員。南北統一後。籌備國會。特任君爲浙江第四區衆選監督。旋被選爲衆議院議員。今年四月。浙省加入護國軍。組織軍政府。特任君爲政治顧問。及大局底定。國會重行召集。遂來京。仍爲衆議院議員。

君人と爲り精敏にして多能、また感情に富み、人の悲を見て自ら受くる者の如く潛然流涕す。戊戌の歳丁酉拔貢の舉人を以て北上して試に會す。目に政變の慘狀の舉人を以て北上して試に會す。目に政變の慘狀を受け、科舉の業を棄てゝ專ら地方の公益事業に任す。癸卯の歳自費を以て日本に渡り學務を視察し、歸國後教育事業に從事す。曾て新昌縣渼西學堂監督、金衢嚴處四府旅省公學監督、東陽縣教育會々長に歷任し、又た勸學所總董、全浙教育會ひ、金華府中學堂監督に歷任し、金衢嚴處四府旅省公學監督・東陽縣教育會に任歸國後教育事業に從事す。曾て新昌縣渼西學堂校長に任大に刺戟を受け、科舉の業を棄てゝ專ら地方の公益事業の舉人を以て北上して試に會す。目に政變の慘狀を見て自ら受くる者の如く潛然流涕す。戊戌の歳丁酉拔貢君人と爲り精敏にして多能、また感情に富み、人の悲を

幹事に歷充したり。前清末季立憲の議起るや浙江省立憲請願代表者に推され、旋て同省諮議局議員となる。辛亥の歳浙江軍政府成立するや特に金鄉宣慰使に任ず。旋て臨時省議會議員に選ばれ、南北統一後、國會の準備に際し浙江省第四區復選監督となり、旋て衆議院議員に舉げらる。第三革命に際し、浙江省獨立するや、其の軍政府政治顧問に任ず。大局既に定りて國會復活し、君復た召集されて衆議院議員たり。

Mr. Tsai Ju-lin, otherwise called Yu-hsiang, aged forty four, is a native of Tung-yang hsien, the Che-chuang-sheng. He is a gentleman of versatile ability, and is quite sympathetic. In 1898, he went up to Peking for examination. Seeing the evils of the political change, he gave up the official career, and devoted himself to the promotion of local interests. In 1903, he went to Japan for the observation of education, and after having returned to his home, he was interested in education. He was the headmaster of the Wu-hsi school, Hsin-chang hsien, as well as the Chin-hua-middle school. He was also appointed to the president of the Tung-yang-hsien Educational Society. Besides he was closely related with educational institutions of his districts. At the later days of the previous Chinese regime, he was appointed to a committee for presenting a memorial for the adoption of the constitutional government. It was elected a member of the extraordinary session of the local assembly, and after the unification of the south and the north, he was returned for the House of Commons. At the outbreak of the 3rd revolution, he was a political adviser to the military government. After the reopening of the Parliament, he was returned for the House of Commons.

蔡果忱 字興周 歲四十

籍貫 黑龍江省肇州縣
住址 北京宋央胡同內口袋胡同
蔽華地 黑龍江省

君為人老成厚重。言動有則。然頭腦明晰。思想放達。與人交。淡而不慢。喜怒不形於色。且意極強。萬事皆由主觀操縱。絕不為外誘或感情所動搖。然又謙虛好問。無我執。無偏私。從善如流。不文已過。年少讀書。即以清高廉潔自勵。及長。尤嚴謹自持一介不苟。生平富於獨立之性。雖喜利用他人之知識。而絕不盲從。曾肄業于直隸法政學堂。畢業後。于宣統二年。曾充呼。蘭縣視學員。兼教育會會長。宣統三年。調充海倫縣高等小學堂校長。復充中學堂法律經濟教員。民國元年。被選為臨時省議會議員。二年。被舉為正式省議會議員。復被舉為參議院議員。國會既停。君歸里獨居不問時事。及國會復活。始來京就職。

君人と為り老成厚重にして言動共に則あり。頭腦明晰にして思想放達なるも、人と交るに淡として慢らず、喜怒また其の色に形さざるなり。年少書を讀み、即ち清高廉潔を以て自ら勵み、長ずるに及びて謹言自ら持して一介も苟もせず、生平獨立の性に富み、喜んで他人の知識を利用すると雖、而かも絕へて盲從せざるなり。曾て直隸法政學堂に學びて卒業す。宣統二年曾て呼蘭縣視學員兼教育會々長に任ず。三年海倫縣高等小學校々長に補せられ、復た中學堂法律經濟教員に任ず。民國元年選ばれて臨時省議會議員となり。二年舉げられて正式省議會議員となり、復た正式國會議員選舉に際して參議院議員に當選す。國會既に停止さるゝや、君歸省して獨居時事を問はず。國會復活するに及びて君亦た召されて北上し、參議院議員の職に就く。

民國之精華 （傳記） 蔡果忱 先生

Mr. Tsai Kuo-shen, otherwise called Hsing-Chou, aged forty, is a native of Chao-chou hsing, the Hei-lung-chiang. He is a gentleman of mature thought and clear head. In associating with others he is never arrogant and does not show his feelings so easily upon matters he is concerned. He was a great reader of books when young, and as he grew older he was fond of cultivating the spirit of independence and yet gladly ultilized the knowledge of others. He studied law in one of the colleges in China. Since then, he occupied many important educational posts, particularly that relating to the education of law and political economy. In 1912, he was elected to a member of the local assembly, and then to a senator. On the dissolution of the Parliament, he went back to his province, and kept himself aloof from politics. On the re-opening of the Parliament he went to Peking, where he was appointed to a senator, an important position which he now enjoys.

三百八十五

蔡突靈　字少黃　歲三十六

選舉地　江西省

籍　貫　江西省新昌縣

住　址　北京正陽門外長巷四條上新會館

君自幼喜談革命。及長。全家皆加入同盟會。乃盡售祖業。運動革命。辛亥起義。舉充瑞州民軍總司令。旋任贛軍政府參謀長。調江西教育司長。後當選為參議院議員。袁世凱以其弟蔡銳霆擁重兵於湖口。憚之。乃使人以高官厚祿要君。君掉頭不顧。遂潛回江西。主張獨立。久敗後。兄弟同亡日本。甲寅秋。聯袂回滬。創設新華社。以上海為根據。發展於大江南北。皖北全贛。聲勢大振。袁恐。乃計捕銳霆。就義於九江。君復竄日本。袁乃藉沒其家。驅散康國被禁四月。六旬老父判禁十年。三弟蔡匡為獨立團長。妹蔡蕙為九江赤十字會長。皆通令嚴緝。君以全家罹此未曾有之奇慘。智窮力竭。神經恍惚。不問世事。同志舉任江西革命軍總司令。亦不就。迨國會再行召集。始回國。復供參議院議員舊職。

蔡突靈先生

君幼より革命を談ずるを喜び、長じて全家皆な同盟會に入り產を盡して革命を運動す。辛亥義を起すや瑞州民軍總司令となり、旋て贛軍政府參謀長となり、江西教育司長となる。後ち參議院議員に當選す。袁世凱は君の弟蔡銳霆が重兵を湖口に擁するを以て君を憚り、高官厚祿を以て招くも君順せして江西に去り獨立を主張す。敗れて兄弟共に日本に亡命し、後ちまた上海に返り新華社を創立す。袁乃ち計つて銳霆を捕へて九江に斬す、君復た日本に遁る。袁乃ち其の家を沒收して老幼を逐ひ、小弟良育捕はれて逃亡して殘す、四弟庚國禁獄四ヶ月に處せられ、六十の老父は禁獄十年の判決を受く。三弟蔡匡は獨立團長、妹蔡蕙は九江赤十字會長なりしを以て皆な逮捕の嚴命あり、全家離散して悽慘を極む。君智窮りて力竭き、後ち江西革命軍總司令に舉げられしも就かず、國會恢復し、始めて歸國し仍ほ參議院議員の職に就く。

Mr. Tsai Tu-ling, otherwise known as Shao-huang, aged thirty six, a native of Sin-chang hsien, was very much interested in stories of revolution. As he grew older, he took a keen interest in the revolutionary movement at the expense of his own property. During the revolutionary movement, he was appointed to the commander-in-general of Jui-chou militia, and the head of the staff of the Jui-chou military government as well as the educational head of the Chiang-hsi district. His brother Tsai-jui-lung occupied Lu-ku so that Yuanshi-kai offered him high rank and liberal payment to induce him to come up to Peking, but he refused and declared his independence at Chiang-hsi. Both brothers were defeated and came to Japan as the political refuges. On returning to Shanghai, he established a society called Hsin-hua. His brother was arrested by Yuanshi-kai by a clever strategem and was put to death, and his father was sentenced to ten years imprisonment. All the members of his family were subjected to rigorous persecution. He was placed under hard circumstances but, when the Parliament was opened, he was appointed to a member of the Senate.

蔣可成　字用甫　歲四十八

選舉地　廣西省
籍　貫　廣西省賓陽縣
住　址　北京賈家胡同廣西南館

君爲人精明幹練。富於常識。然篤實不欺。能耐勞苦。於前清。由訓導保舉雲南知州。歷辦剝隘威遠等處釐務。並歷充廣南府屬鹽務督辦。寶華錫鑛公司坐辦。維新後。入雲南法政學堂官學速成科。畢業後。歷任清普洱府屬營田。署威遠思茅等處同知。會辦迤南三點會匪。旋以功保舉知府。督辦猛遮等處善後改流事宜。兼管普防巡防隊第五營。督帶第四六兩營。南防副營務處。反正後。以原帶各營改爲國民軍。兼南防副統領。民國元年。因病辭職。九月回籍。即被選爲衆議院議員。國會解散後。歸籍讀書。不談政事。及國會復活。始入京。仍爲議員。

君人と爲り精明幹練にして常識に富み、然かも篤實にして欺かざる也。前清時代訓導を以て補せられ剝隘威遠等各地の釐務を歷辦し、並に廣南府管下の鹽務督辦、寶華錫鑛公司庫辦等に展充す。維新後、雲南法政學堂官學速成科に入り、卒業後、普洱府管下の營田を清查し、又た威遠思茅等各地の同知に署せられ、三點會匪を勦辦し、旋て其の功を以て知府に保薦せるら。猛遮等各地の改流善後事宜を處理し、普防巡防隊第五營管帶、第四、第六の兩營管帶、南防副營務處等を兼任す。第一革命後、其の率ゐる各營を改めて國民軍と爲し、南防副統領を兼ねたるも、民國元年病に因りて其の職を辭して歸郷したり。後ち選ばれて衆議院議員と爲る。國會解散後、郷里に韜晦して書卷と親み、また政事を談せず。其の國會重ねて復活するに及び、再び出で〻北京に入り、仍は衆議院議員たり。

民國之精華　（傳記）蔣可成先生

Mr. Chiang Ko-cheng, sometimes known as Yung-fu, aged forty eighty, a native of Pin-yau-hsien, the Kuang-hsi hsing, is a gentleman of commonsense and clear judgement. Under the previous Chinese regime, he was the governor of the Yun-nan. Once he was interested in salt and sugar business of the province under the government order. After the restoration of the new regime, he took the special course in the Yun-nan political institution. Then he was interested in the government of the district under various capacity in which he distinguished himself. His merits were recognized, which brought about a rapid promotion for him. After the 1st revolution, he organized the army under the new system, and was appointed the vice-governor of the southern defence. Owing to illness in 1912, he returned his home resigning his position. He was later returned from his province for the House of Commons. When the Parliament was dissolved he went back to his home when he was interested in the reading of books, but kept himself aloof from politics. He went up to Peking when the Parliament was re-opened, and became a member of the House of Commons.

蔣著鄉 字著卿 歲四十

選舉地　浙江省

籍貫　浙江省奉化縣

住址　北京象坊橋浙江議員公寓

君賦性嚴正。疾惡如仇。生平無妄言妄
動。然居心仁厚。富於惻隱之心。見人
不平。常思爲報復。過於身受。然以其
謹嚴成性。具頭腦明晰。洞悉利害。故
雖好爲義舉。卒未嘗試險境。及海內維
新。君遍覽新者大受刺擊。於是思想大
變。立志以革命爲天職。不復以危險介
懷。盖深知非此則不足以言改革也。遂
入舊同盟會。爲同會浙江總務主任。辛
亥光復後。充任浙江軍事參議。旋被選
爲衆議院議員。國會解散後。君被袁政
府通緝查拿。遂匿跡窮郷。日以詩酒自
娛。不問時事。迨及帝制發生。西南倡
義。遂與滬上諸同志組織民軍。共圖恢
復。及至國會重行召集。遂入京。仍爲
衆議院議員。

（右列日文）

君賦性嚴正にして惡むこと仇の如く生平妄言妄動な
し。然も居心仁厚にして惻隱の心に富み、人の不平を
見て常に報復を思ふ。明晰の頭腦を具へ利害を洞悉す。
故に好んで義擧を爲すと雖、卒に未だ嘗て險を犯さず。
海內維新に及び、遍く新著を閱して大に刺戟を受け、思
想大に變ず。志を立て、革命を以て天職と爲す。遂に舊
同盟會に入り、同會浙江總務主任と爲る。辛亥の歲第一
革命の事起るや君出で、奔走盡力し、浙江軍事參議に任

す。民國成立後、選ばれて衆議院議員と爲り、大政に建議
する所あり。國會解散後、袁政府の壓迫を受け、遂に漸
く其の跡を匿くして郷里に潛み、日に詩酒を以て自ら娛
み、深く大志を藏して暫らく時事を問はず。帝制問題發
生して西南義を倡ふるや、遂に上海の諸同志と民軍を組
織して民國の恢復を圖る、國會重ねて召集を行ふや、北
上して仍ほ民國の衆議院議員と爲る。

Mr. Chiang Chao-ching, aged forty three year, is a native of the Feng-hua hsien the Che-
chiang hsing. Being sincere in character, hates evil but full of sympathy towards others. His foresight
saved him from many dangers. Being clear-sighted he never runs the risk from which he could not
extricate himself. With the change of the regime, he spent his time in the perusal of new books which
transformed his thoughts. He thought that he had the heavenly call for the revolution. He was appointed
to the director of the Che-chiang branch of the National party. In 1911 when revolution took place, he
was appointed to the staff of the Che-chiang military council. With the first opening of the Parliament,
he became a member thereof, and participated in the government. After the dissolution of the Parliament,
he suffered from various forms of oppression under Yuanshi-kai but escaped to his native home where
cherishing ambitious hopes but never talking politics, he spent his time in poetry and drinks. When the
Imperial Movement broke out, acting in conjunction with his fellow-men in Shanghai, he repeated
attempt of restoring the Republic; when his hopes were realized, he went up to Peking and was chosen
to a member of the Parliament.

蔣義明　字石阜　歳三十九

選舉地　湖北省

籍　貫　湖北省潛江縣

住　址　北京西單牌樓都城隍廟街

君秉性篤實。自幼勤學。不事嬉遊。弱冠即廣通經史。長於詩文。旋以郡試第一補邑庠生。送入兩湖師範學堂肄業。由湖廣總督張之洞資送日本留學。入早稻田大學政治經濟科。宣統二年。畢業回國。受學部試。考取法政科舉人。三年。廷試。授七品小京官。簽分郵傳部路政司行走。民國元年。被選爲鄂省臨時省議會議員。旋辭職。充鄂軍政府財政司參議官。嗣由湖北都督以學識優長保送財政部。由部派充銀行籌辦員。兼充陸軍需學校教官。二年。被選爲省議會議員。復被選爲參議院議員。國會解散後。消極自持。無所表白。及國會重開。始入都。仍供今職。

君秉性篤實溫厚なり。幼より學を好み弱冠即ち歷史に通じ詩文に長じたり。旋て郡試第一に及第して邑庠生に補せられ、兩湖師範學堂に送りて修業しむ。嗣で湖廣總督張之洞より選拔されて日本に留學し、早稻田大學政治科に入り、宣統二年卒業歸國す。學部の試驗に及第して法政科舉人と爲り、三年廷試に於て七品小京官を授け、郵傳部路政司行走に分たる。民國元年選ばれて湖北臨時省議院議員と爲り、旋て職を辭して湖北軍政府財政司參議官に任す。湖北都督は君に命じ銀行籌辦員とし、兼て陸軍々需學校教官たり。二年選ばれて省議會議員と爲り、旋て復た舉げられて參議院議員と爲る。國會解散後、消極主義を以て自ら持し、緘晦して政見を發表せず。國會重ねて開かるヽに及び、再び召集に應じて仍ち參議院議員と爲る。

民國之精華　（傳記）蔣義明先生

Mr. Chiang Hsi-ming, otherwise called Shih Fou, age thirty nine, is a native of Chien Chiang hsien, Hu Pei province. While young he was already conversant with classics and poetry. He passed successfully the local civil service examination and was sent to Lian hu normal school. He was then sent to Japan by Chon shi tow where he entered the Waseda University. In 1910 he was graduated from the University and returned to his country. In the 1st year of the Republic he was elected to a member of the Special Assembly of Hu pei and then he was the financial advisor to the Hu pei military government. His service was highly admired by the governor general of Hu pei. He was also an instructor of military supply school. He was elected to a member of the Senate. On the dissolution of the Parliament he adopted the conversative principle and never gave publicity to his views. When the Parliament was reopened he was elected to a member of a Senate.

熙凌阿 字子捷

選擧地 蒙古喀拉沁東旗
籍　貫 蒙古喀拉沁東旗
住　址 北京東城燈市口

君秉性清高明敏。爲人誠厚篤實。尚質惡文。不事浮華。重然諾。自幼聰慧好讀。富于進取之氣象。弱冠於華文有進境。巧于詩詞歌賦。格調新俊。及長。博覽群籍。深思明辨。能精眞義。洞察事理。遂立志尤喜攻究有用之學。獨得風氣之先。以經世濟民挽救危亡自任。君即世襲內蒙古扎薩克親王銜郡王。蓋蒙古貴胄界之雋傑也。辛亥革命。民國肇造。宣布五大民族共和。君被選爲臨時參議院議員。把持正論。提倡讜議。翼贊建設之偉業。民國二年正式國會成立。被選爲參議院議員。國會停止後。兼充大總統府翊衞使。五年國會重開。遂又應召現充參議院議員。

君秉性清高明敏にして、人と爲り誠厚篤實にして質を尚び文を惡み、浮華を事とせず。品行端正にして氣宇雍容、人と交りて信義を崇び然諾を重んず。幼より聰慧にして讀を好み、進取の氣象に富む。弱冠既に漢文に於て進境頻しく、詩詞歌賦に巧に格調新俊なり。長ずるに及びて群書を渉獵して其眞義を究め事理を洞察す。君即ち内蒙古禮薩克親王衡郡王にして、て、有用の學を求め、獨り風氣の先を爲して、經世濟民を以て自ら任ず。君即ち内蒙古禮薩克親王衡郡王にして、蓋し蒙古貴胄界の俊傑なり。辛亥の歳、命を革めて民國を樹立し、五大民族の共和を宣布するや、選ばれて臨時參議院議員となり、正論讜議を以て、國家建設の偉業を翼贊す。民國二年選ばれて正式國會參議院議員と爲す。五年國會重ねて開くるや、遂に又た召集に應じて、現に參議院議員と爲る。

Mr. Hsi Ling-a; called by other name Tsu Chieh, is a native of Mongolia. He is a man of lofty spirit, prefering sincerity to pompousness by his nature. In his boyhood he already was fond of a learning and showed his great attainment of Chinese classics. When the Republic was established, he a Prince of Mongolia, was elected to a special member of the Senate, and contributed a great deal for the State. In the 2nd year of the Republic, he was officially elected to a member of the Senate. After suspension of the Parliament he was appointed to the Chamberlain to the ruler. When the Parliament was re-opened, he was again elected to a member of the Senate, which post he now holds.

潘學海 字會東 歲四十四

選舉地　江西省
籍貫　江西省上高縣
住址　北京長巷四條上新館

君爲人深沈厚重。言行不苟。居常以勤儉自持。而勇于濟公。少時讀書。游心詞章。及長。始力求有用之學。海內維新後。篤志研求西學。前清時。以優廩生。由江西巡撫考取。派赴日本留學。入早稻田大學政治經濟科。宣統二年畢業。復入中央大學研究科。提出論文。授與法學士證書。曾譯述日本帝國憲法論一書。刊行於世。歸國後。適武昌起義。江西隨之。被選爲省議會議員。嗣任都督府法制課課長。制定本省約法官制。暨各種暫行法律。民國二年被選爲衆議院議員。迄二次革命事起。因籍隸國民黨故。議員橫被取消。四年。在本省爲律師。及此次革命既起。遂赴滬。聯君同志。組織國會。以爲滇軍應援。及國會重開。遂入京。仍爲衆議院議員。

君人と爲り深沈厚重にして言行苟もせず、居常勤儉自ら持すも公事を濟ふに勇なり。少時書を讀みて心を詞章に游したるも、長ずるに及びて有用の學を求め、海内維新後、志を立てゝ西學を攻究す。前清時代、優廩生を以て江西巡撫より選拔され、日本に留學す。宣統二年早稻田大學政治經濟科を卒業し、中央大學研究科に入りて法學を專攻す。曾て日本帝國憲法論を譯述刊行す。歸國して乃ち第一命に會す、選ばれて江西省議會議員となる。嗣で

江西都督府法制課長の職に任じ、同省の官制其の他各種律例等を制定したり。民國二年正式國會衆議院議員に當選す。第二革命時代は國民黨員なりしを以て、議員の職を剝奪され、爾來江西省に在りて辯護士を業とせり。五年第三革命起るや上海に赴きて同志と共に議員團を組織して雲南軍の應援を試み。國會恢復するに及びて、石集に應じて入京し、仍は衆議院議員の職に復す。

民國之精華　（傳記）　潘學海先生

Mr. Pan Hsiao-hai, known as Hui tung, age forty four, is a native of Chiang Hsi province. Both in words and action, he is a gentleman of taciturn temperament, and courageous to fight against to save the situation. While young, he was interested in reading books, as he grew older, he was interested in western learning which is of practical nature. Under the previous Chinese regime, he went to Japan at the government's expense to couple his education. He studied in both Waseda and Chu-o Universities from which was graduated. He translated and published, the Explanation of the Japanese Constitution. returning to his country, the first revolution was going on, when he was elected to a member of the local council. He was the chief of the Bureau of Legislation, and as such, he contributes his service toward codification. In the second revolution, he was deprived of his certificate of the membership, because he was a member of the national party. When the third revolution broke out, he went to Shanghai where with his fellow men formed the society for facilitating the opening of the Parliament, and he was returned for the House of Commons.

潘祖彝 字竹孫 歳三十四

選舉地　福建省

籍　貫　福建省崇安縣

住　址　現住北京内城西單牌樓白廟胡同
大同公寓

君秉性誠篤朴實。脱盡浮華。生平極尚信義。言動舉止。確有本末。與人有約。雖遇意外危險。亦必捨身踐履前言。若以實際上無可排除之障碍。致末克如約以行。則引爲絶大恥辱。以故人有所託。常不肯輕於承諾。有時或先詞拒絶。然後暗中爲之盡力。事不成。可不負責事成。亦不望報。蓋生性使然。非有意造作以博學名也。少年讀書極喜研究宋明儒者之學。故於事理無所不明。見解亦異常穩健。及長。愈益洞察世情。敏於感覺工於辭令。其處理事務。曾留學日本。岩倉鐵道學校建設科畢業生。歸國後。充歷京奉鐵路局員。福建臨時省議會議員。福建正式省議會議員。現任參議院議員。

君秉性隱慧にして誠厚、浮華の態を脱盡して、生平信義を伺び、言動舉止共に後進の模範とするに足る。少年嘗て宋明儒者の學を了得して、事理二つながら闡明し、見解焦俊にして、幹濟の才あり曾て笈を負ふて日本に游學し、岩倉鐵道舉校に入りて其の業を畢ふ歸。國して後ち曾て京奉鐵道局員たりし事あり。第一革命の事起るや、君は福建省の代表として南京に赴き、南京臨時參議院に列して、臨時政府組織の事を議し、民國建設の偉業を賛勤したる事あり。又た福建省臨時省議會議員、正式省議會議員に選ばれて地方自治の刷新に盡瘁したり。民國二年正式國會成立に際し、參議院議員に當選す。國會解散後は南旋して鄉里に歸臥し、地方公益の事に從ひ、有無兩方面の功勞尠少ならず。約法恢復して國會再蘇するに及び、其の召集に應じて北上入京し、現に仍ち參議院議員の職に在り。

Mr. Pan Tsu-i, otherwise known as Chu Sun, age thirty four, is a native of Chung An, Fu Chien. He is sincere and honest in dealing with others. In both words and action, he is a worthy guide of the younger generation. When young, the was versd in the classical learning of the Chinese, which made his views quite comprehensive. He went to Japan a 1 was graduated rom the Iwakura railway school. On returning to his country, he was connected with the King-fien Railway Co. When the first revolutionary movement broke out, he went to Nanking representing the Fukien province. As a member of the special Nankin Assembly, he was interested in the formation of the Cabinet, and was interests in the establishment of the Republic. He was also a member of the Fu-kien local province, and was interested in the promotion of local interests. In the second year of the Republic, he was elected to a member of the Senate. When the Parliament was dissolved he contributed his efforts being interestes in public affairs. Under the new regime, when the Parliament was summoned, he was appointed to a member of the Senate.

選舉地　直隸省
籍貫　直隸省青縣
住址　北京宣武門內南岡市口回同眥門牌九號

君為人慷慨好義。喜鳴不平。然氣慨深沈。喜怒不形于辭色。自幼即以能文見知於世。及長大。博覽羣書。兼涉漢宋。然志在有用之學。不屑從事科舉。戊戌變法後。遂棄舊從新。輝精西學。旋入北洋大學堂肄業。畢業後。歷充北京高等實業學校。北京譯學館。陸軍第三中學校教員。復歸奉天。辦理新民府屬及遼陽州學務。辛亥革命。充北軍總會團參謀。民國二年河東鹽務稽核分所稽核科主任。奉天鹽務稽核分所征稅科主任。廣寧鹽稅局局長。及國會重開。遂來京。復為眾議院議員。

君人と爲り慷慨義を好みて喜んで不平を鳴らず。然かも氣慨深沈にして喜怒色に形さず。幼より即ち能文を以て世に知らる。長ずるに及びて博く群書を閲し、兼て漢宋を涉獵し、志は有用の學に在りて科舉の業を改究す。旋て北洋大學校に學びて業を畢へ、北京高等實業學校、北京譯學館、陸軍第三中學校教員に歷充し、復た奉天に歸りて新民府屬及び遼陽州の學務を處理して功勞尠少ならず。民國二年選ばれて衆議院議員と爲る。國會解散後、河東鹽務稽核分所稽核科主任、奉天鹽務稽核分所征稅科主任、廣寧鹽稅局々長等の職に歷任したり。五年約法復活して國會重ねて開かるゝに及び、遂に復た其の召集に應じて入京し、仍は衆議院議員たり。

民國之精華　(傳記) 錢崇塏先生

Mr. Chien Chung Kai, otherwise called Hsiang Chen, age thirty six, is a native of Ching hsien, Chi Lin Province. Being impulsive in character he is often guilty of being a malcontent, but he is very thoughtful and shows neither anger nor joy in his countenance. When young he is known for his proficiency in writing. As he grew older he read books quite extensively and particulary his attention was drawn to the perusal learning. Having graduated from the Peiyang University he was appointed to an instructor of the Peking higher industrial school and the third military academy. On returning to Feng-tien he was interested in the educational improvement of the district. When the Republic was securely established he was elected a member of the parliament. When Yuanshi-kai dissolved the Parliament he was in the government service of his province, having filled the post of salt office etc.

閻光耀　字連城　歲四十

選舉地　新疆省

籍　貫　新疆省烏蘇縣

住　址　北京順治門大街憲政討論會內

君爲人誠厚篤實。不喜浮華。生平以儉約自持。痛惡奢侈。然睢自待歉薄。而厚於待人。且喜爲善舉。鄉里之困於貧者。無不曾受君惠。少年時。好爲詩詞之學。嘗謂詞世誤人之事功。而舉業則錮人之情性。曾前清附貢生。畢業。諮議局自治研究所講員。充塔城參贊文案處委員。民國二年。被選爲參議院議員。國會解散後。歸里獨居不所表見。及共和恢復。國會重開。始來京。復爲參議院議員。

君人と爲り誠厚篤實にして浮華を喜ばず、生平儉約を以て自ら持し奢侈を痛惡す。然り自ら待つこと甚だ薄きも、人を待つに厚く、且つ慈善の事を爲すを喜ぶこと甚だ薄きも、好んで詩賦を作り、科弟に汲々たらず。長ずるに及び途に志を改めて有用の學を求め、曾て詞章の事功を誤り、舉業の情性を錮するを謂ふ。前清の附貢生を以て、諮議局附屬の自治研究所を卒業し、塔城參贊文案處委員に充りたり。辛亥の革命を革めて憲政共和と宣布するや、民國二年選ばれて正式國會參議院議員と爲る。國會解散後、鄉里に歸臥して門を鎖ぢて出でず、何等華々しき活動を爲さず。共和恢復して國會重ねて開かるゝに及び、其の召集に應じて始めて入京し、復た仍は參議院議員と爲る。

Mr. Yen Kuang-yao, otherwise called Lien-cheng, aged forty, is a native of Wu su, Hsin Chiang province. Being a man of strict living and fulgal turn of mind, he was very friendly and liberal to others. While young he was very much interested in the Chinese study, and for that purpose he devoted his interest. However, as he grew older he sought the useful learning, and for that purpose he took special training. In the 2nd year of the Republic he was elected to a member of the Senate, and when the Parliament was closed, he returned to his country where he kept aloof from any active step. However, when the Parliament was re-opened, he became a member of the Senate, the position which he holds even now.

閻鴻舉 字遇唐 歲三十八

選舉地　山西省

籍　貫　山西省山陰縣人

住　址　北京兵部窪門、牌十二號

君賦性高潔。言動舉止。皆逈異凡流。然爲人勤謹耐勞。人有所託輒喜爲盡力。不以功自居。以故里人皆極愛敬之。偶有糾紛。得君出一言。無不立即解釋。以廩生。於光緒二十八年。入山西大學堂中學專齋中等科。卒業後升第二類理化專科。肄業期滿。學部覆試。給獎舉人。籤分禮部司務。宣統三年。山西巡撫委充爲大同實業學校敎員。民國元年。充山西民政署選舉事務所事務員。二年一月被選爲衆議院議員。國會解散。君回藉發起富山水利股有限公司。自充工程科經理及國會份有限公司。自充工程科經理及國會復活。遂來京復爲議員。

（傳記）　閻鴻舉先生

民國之精華

君賦性高潔、言動舉止、皆過逈に凡流に異る。然も人と爲り勤謹勞に耐へ、人の託する所あれば力を以て自ら居らず。功を以て自ら居らず。故を以て里人皆めて之を敬愛し、偶ま紛料あれば君一言を出して立ち所に解決す。廩生を以て光緒二十八年山西大學堂中學專齋中學科を經て理化專科に入りて卒業す。學部の試に應じて舉人を給せられ、禮部司務に任す。宣統三年、山西巡撫より招かれて大同實業學校敎員と爲る。民國元年山西民政署選舉事務所事務員となる。二年一月選ばれて正式國會衆議院議員に常選す。國會解散さるや、鄕里に歸りて富山水利股有限公司を發起し、自ら工程科經理に任じたり。五年國會復活するに及び、再び其の召集に應じて上京し、遂に來京して復た衆議院議員と爲る。

Mr. Yen Huug-chu, sometimes known as Yu tang, aged thirty eight is a native of Shan In, Shan Hsi province. Being a gentleman of noble character, his action and words differ from those of others. He takes keen delight in doing things for others, but never claims any compensation thereof. He is therefore highly respected by his own countrymen. In 1902, he was graduated from the middle course of the Shan hsi university. He successfully passed the civil service examination and was appointed the official in the ceremorial Bureau. In 1909, he was appointed an instructor of the industrial school, and in the first year of the Republic, he was an official of the civil administration election Bureau. In the second year of the Republic he was returned for the House of Commons. On the dissolution of the Parliament, he was interested in industrial undertaking at his home. When the Parliament was restored, he came up to Peking where he was returned for the House of Commons.

歐陽鈞　字麓賓　歲三十五

選舉地　福建省
籍　貫　福建省長樂縣
住　址　北京化石橋七十號盧宅

君天資絕高。悟性敏捷。而頭腦周密。其言論思想。皆秩序井然。絕無顛倒紊亂之弊。自幼讀書。即喜探索精義。不以文字自拘。故其於學問。雖所歷未深。然每有所讀。必大有進益。以其能精思深入。抉其竅要。故其見解思想。皆極明瞭切實。且洞悉事情。明察物理。曾入北京法律學堂。畢業。銳意提倡興學。竭力從事公益。民國二年正式國會成立。被選為衆議院議員。國會解散。歸里讀書。絕口不談時政。惟隨時誘掖後進。開通民智。及至國會再行召集。遂入京。仍為衆議院議員。

君天資絕高にして悟性敏捷、加ふるに頭腦周密なり。其の言論思想皆な秩序井然として、絕べて顛倒紊亂の弊なり。幼より書を讀みて其の義理を探求し、文字の末に拘泥せず。故に其の學問、歷る所末だ深からざるも讀過する每に必ず大に進益あり。其の能く思索して竅要を抉きしを以て、見解思想皆な極めて明瞭切實にして、且つ事情を洞察し物理を明知す。曾て北京法政學校を卒業して、銳意興學を提倡して、熱心公益の事に盡瘁す。民議二年正式國會衆議院議員に當選す。國會解散されてより、鄕里に歸臥して讀書自ら娛み、口を絕ちて政事を談せず、時に臨みて後進を誘掖啓導するのみ。五年國會再び召集を行ふに及び遂に入京して仍ほ衆議院議員と為る。

Mr. Ou-yang Chun, otherwise called Lu pin, age thirty five, is a native of Chang Yo-chien province. He is a man of noble aspiration and deep logical thoughts. When young he was greatly interested in reading books, the meaning of which he understood thoroughly. Whatever he reads he intelligently digest and applies it to practical purposes. He is a graduate of the Peking law school and devoted himself to the promotion of public interest. In the 2nd year of the Republic he was elected to a member of the House of Commons, but when Yuanshi-kai dissolved the Parliament, he went back to his native country where he himself took to reading, never showing any interest in politics. He went to Peking and resumed his Parliamentary function when the new president declared it to re-open.

歐陽成 字集甫 歲三十八

選舉地　江西省

籍貫　江西省吉水縣

住址　北京潘家河沿吉安館

君為人朴質無華。言行誠篤。然慷慨好義。喜為俠義之舉。見人不平。常拾身赴之。有困于金錢者。雖路人輒解囊相助。不告以姓名。以故遠近爭稱其名。自幼天資聰慧。博覽群籍。及長。尤闇中外。頗有名儒之風。於丁卯壬寅二科。中副車二次。癸卯科。始中試為舉人。時適海內維新。遂改志研究西學。慨然以澄清天下為己任。旋以自費於光緒三十二年。留學日本。始入經緯學堂。習普通。畢業後。升入中央大學英法本科。校長菊地博士。以成績優異。拔為特待生。民國元年。畢業歸國。前江西都督李烈鈞聘充顧問二年。被選為衆院議員。國會解散時。君脫離政界。不談時非者二年有餘。及國會復活。遂來京仍為議員。

君人と為り朴實にして華なく、言行誠篤なり。然がも慷慨義を好み、俠義の擧を喜ぶ。幼より天資聰慧にして博く群籍を渉獵し、長ずるに及びて、ふと闊く外に明にして顔る名儒の風あり。丁卯壬寅二回の試に應じて副車中り、發卯の試に及第して擧人と為る。時適ま海內維新るを以て己が任と為す。旋て光緒三十二年、自費を以て日本に留學し、經緯學校普通科を經て中央大學英法本科に學ぶ、校長菊池博士其の成績優等なるを賞し、特に君を抜きて特待生とす。民國元年卒業して歸國す。江西都督李烈鈞より聘せられて顧問となる。二年正式國會衆議院議員に常選す。國會解散せらるや、君政界を脱して時事を談せざること二年有餘なり。五年國會復活するに及びて、復た出でゝ召集に應じ、遂に入京して仍は衆議院議員と為る。

Mr. On-yang Cheng, otherwise called Chi Fu, age forty one, is a native of Chi Shui hsien. In both words and deeds he was sober and service minded. Being heroic in nature he was fond of doing service to others. As he grew older he was interested in foreign affairs. When the new trend of thought was introduced to Japan he was extremely fond of western learning and was convinced that his duty was to purify his own country. Therefore, in 1906, with his own expense he went to Japan and studied in the Chu-o University. Dr. Kikuchi, the president of the University, gave him a scholarship fully appreciating superior results in his study. In the 1st year of the Republic he returned to his country and in the 2nd year he was elected to a member of the House of Commons. With the dissolution of the Parliament, he kept aloof from politics for more than two years. With the Restoration of the Parliament, however, he was elected to a member of the House of Commons, the position he enjoys in the present moment.

歐陽振聲　字駿民　歳三十五

選舉地　湖南省

籍貫　湖南省寧遠縣

住址　此京中華新報館

君賦性機警，寡言笑，胸中萬里，蓋奮人也。前清以附生。入湖北文普通中學。與宋教仁等。蓄謀革命。甲辰湖南之變。致仁亡走日本。獨留鄂。司同志通訊事。中學畢業後。游學日本。入早稻田大學政治經濟科。畢業回國。武昌起義游說同志甚廣。旋建臨時政府於南京。湘派宋教仁為代表。會有他事。君乃代之。旋為臨時參議院議員，政府北遷。仍為參議員。正式國會成立。被選眾議院議員。宋案起。激成贛寧之役。適湘省取消獨立。以議員團代表回湘。維持湘局。無何。國會解散。留滯天津。旋脫去之上海。與谷鍾秀等。創設泰東圖書局。坿設正誼雜誌。籌安會發生。乃與同志。發起共和維持會。叛辦中華新報任總理。雲南起義常往來港滬間。主治護國軍機要事宜。黎氏繼任。軍務院推為政治代表。政府擬任以農商次長辭不就。及國會重開。仍為眾議院議員。

君賦性機警にして寡言、蓋し闘士なり。前清附生を以て湖北文普通中學校に入り、宋教仁等と革命の志を抱く。甲辰湖南の變、宋は日本に亡命し、君は湖北に在りて同志の通信を司る。中學卒業後、日本に留學して早稻田大學政治經濟科を卒業す。歸國適ま第一革命の起る、即ち四ゞに游説し、湖南代表宋教仁の代理として南京臨時政府組織に予與し、旋て臨時參議院議員と爲る。嗣で正式國會衆議院議員に當選す。第二革命に際し君議員團の代表として湖南に歸り大局を計る。事敗れて上海に遁れ、谷鍾秀等と泰東圖書局を創設し、正誼雜誌を發行す。籌安會發起さる〳〵や、乃ち同志と共和維持會を發起して反對し、中華新報を發刊して總理に任す。雲南起義以來香港上海間を往復して、護國軍の要機に干預す。黎氏繼任するや、軍務院より政治代表に推され、政府より農商次長を擬せられたるも就かず。國會恢復後、仍は衆議院議員と爲る。

Mr. On-yang Chen-sheng, otherwise known as Chun Nui, thirty five years of age, is a native of Ning Yuan hsieng, the Hu Nan province. He is a gentleman of taciturn and pugilistic turn of mind. In the previous Chinese period as early as 1904, he was interested in the revolutionary movement, and on failure of his plans he stayed at Hu pei wheer he attempted to form a connection among his fellow thinkers. He came to Japan when he was educated in the Waseda University. On returning to his home, the first revolution took place, he attended the special assembly representing Mr. Sun, the representative of Hu Nan. When the Republic was established, he was returned for the House of Commons, but in the second revolutionary movement, he was fustrated in his attempts so that he fled to Shanghai when he was interested in the journalistic work. With his fellow thinkers, he established a society for the preservation of the Republic. Under the new president, the chair of the Vice-president of the Department of Agricultnre and Commerce was offered to him, but he declined the same. When the Parliament was restored, he was returned for the House of Commons.

盧 信 字信公

選舉地　華僑

籍貫　廣東省順德縣

住址　北京虎坊橋金星保險公司

君自弱冠讀書。即抱大志。少時嘗從事於詩古文詞諸文藝。嗣覽世界之趨勢。知非有用之學。遂決然棄舊從新。前清遊學美國。曾充香港中國日報編輯主任。廣東省議會議長。民國成立。被選爲臨時參議院議員。兼院內財政委員。正式國會被舉爲參議院議員。兼院內外交委員長。國會解散後歸里。與唐紹儀創辦金星人壽保險公司。於上海資本壹百萬元。唐被舉爲董事會主席。君爲董事會副主席。民國三年冬。又組織金星水火保險公司。資本一百二十萬元。唐紹儀爲董事會主席。君即由董事會公舉爲總理。五年八月。共和復活。國會重開。始應召復爲參議院議員。

君弱冠より書を讀みて大志を抱き、少時曾て詩古文詞諸文藝に従事し、嗣で世界の趨勢に覽て志を改めて天下有用の學を求む。即ち米國に游學して、歸來曾て香港の中國日報編輯主任に任す。民國成立するや、選ばれて廣東省議會議長と爲る。又た臨時參議院議員に選ばれ、院内財政委員に舉げらる。民國二年正式國會參議院議員に當選し、院内外交委員長に舉げらる。國會解散後、南旋して、唐紹儀等と金星人壽保險公司を上海に創立經營す、資本金一百萬圓にして、唐紹儀を理事會主席とし、君を副主席とす。民國三年の冬、又た金星水火保險公司を組織す、資本金百二十萬圓にして、唐紹儀を理事會主席とし、君を總理に公舉す。五年八月約法復活して再び國の開院式を舉ぐるや、君復た其の召集に應じて北上し、仍は參議院議員と爲る。

民國之精華　（傳記）　盧信先生

Mr. Lu Hsin, otherwise called Hsin Kung, is a native of Shun Te, the Kwangtung province. While young he was a great reader of books and full of aspiration. He was, in youth, well posted up in the study of poetry and classics. Perceiving the change in the tendency of the world he went to America to continue his study. On return to his home he was appointed to the editor-in-chief of the paper in Hongkong. When the Republic was formed, he was appointed to the president of the Kwangtung provincial assembly. In the 2nd year of the Republic he was elected to a member of the Senate and the chief of the diplomatic committee. With the disolution of the Diet he started a Life Insurance Company acting in conjunction with Tun-Show-i with capital of 10000 yen. He also established a Fire Insurance Company with a capital of 1200.000 yen. When the Republic was restored and the Parliament was again opened, he became a member of the Senate.

盧天游　字雲村　歲三十八

選舉地　廣西省
籍　貫　廣西省桂平縣
住　址　北京後青廠廣西三館

君幼樸實。好讀書。氣宇軒昂。儼然有出類拔萃之慨。庚子之亂。國事日非。慨然曰丈夫不能救國救民。專用此七尺之軀。爲於是奔走天下。以求所以福國利民之術。即知究心科學。必無以爲濟。遂留學日本。入法政大學畢業。歷辦本省法政財政自治各學。清季選充廣西諮議局議員。民國元年任廣西都督府法制局長。二年被選爲參議院議員。由院選充憲法起草委員會委員。此次西南起義。軍務院成立。任軍務院秘書。護國軍兩廣都司令部秘書。國會復活。現仍供參議員本職。遇事敢言。議論風生。明辨可誦。其乃鐵中錚錚。庸中佼佼。足以動衆。

君幼より樸實にして讀書を好み、氣宇軒昂、儼然として群を拔ぐ。庚子の亂、國事日に非なるを見て慨然として曰く、丈夫國を救ひ民を救ふ能はずんば、七尺の軀を提げて天下に奔走し、國利民福の術を求むべしと。即ち科學に志し、遂に日本に留學して法政大學を卒業す。廣西省法政財政自治各學校を歷辦し、選ばれて廣西諮議局議員と爲る。民國元年廣西都督府法制局長に任ず。二年正式國會參議院議員と爲り、憲法起草委員會委員に舉げらる。五年西南義を起して軍務院を組織するや、軍務院秘書に任じ護國軍兩廣都司令部秘書に任す。棄と是れ事に過ふて敢て言ひ、議論風生、蓋し鐵中の錚々、庸中の佼々たるもの。此次國會復活するや、欣然召集に應じて上京し、現に仍ほ參議院議員の職に就く。

Mr. Lu Ten-Yu, otherwise called Yun Tsun, age thirty eight, is a native of Kuei Ping hsien, Kuang Hsi hsing. While young he was fond of books and simple life. His ambition distinguished him from others. When China was greatly troubled in 1900, he declared that it was once' duty to save his country from the mind to promote the interests of the people. He came over Japan to complete his education and was graduated from the law college. He was appointed to a number of important posts among which we may mention the membership of the local assembly. In the 1st year of the Republic he was the chief to the legislative office and in the 2nd year of the Republic he was appointed to a member of the Senate and was on the committee for drafting the constitution. He was a man of strong will and his argument was solid. When the Parliament was re-opened, he came up to Pekin and elected to a member of the Senate.

盧鍾嶽 字臨先 歲三十二

選舉地 浙江省

籍貫 浙江省

住址 北京象坊橋浙江議員公寓

君賦性慷慨好義。弱冠即喜談革命。然不肯輕舉妄動以自輕其生。故論極激烈。而卒未罹於禍。年二十入紹興府中學堂。卒業後。遊學日本。由東京警監學校畢業後。復入明治大學。畢業回國。歷充浙江巡警學校教員。東湖法學堂教員旋以與徐錫麟同謀起義。事敗以嫌疑陷獄中數月。出獄後至奉天創辦微言報館。光復後。充上海閘北巡警局長。旋任爲浙江省會警察所長。民國二年被選爲衆議院議員。國會解散後。君南歸讀書。不復與聞政事。及國會復活。始來京復爲衆議院議員。

民國之精華 （傳記） 盧鍾嶽先生

君賦性慷慨義を好み、弱冠即ち喜んで革命を談ず。然かも輕舉妄動を戒むるを以て、議論激烈なるも、卒に未だ大禍に罹らざる也。年二十八、紹興府中學校を卒業し、日本に游學して東京警察監獄學校を卒業す。復た明治大學に入り、卒業して歸國す。浙江巡警學校教員、東湖法政學校教員の職に歷充し、旋て徐錫義と起義を謀り、事敗れて獄中に在ること數月、獄を出で、復た奉天に赴き、微言報社を創立經營す。第一革命後、上海閘北巡警察長に任ず。旋て浙江省會警察所長と爲る。民國二年正式國會衆議院議員に當選す。國會解散されて後、南に蹻りて書を讀み學に親み、復た政事を預り開かす。約法復活して國會再び開かる丶に、及び、復た其の召集に應じて入京し、仍ほ衆議院議員たり。

Mr. Lu Chung-yo, otherwise called Lin Hsien, age thirty two, is a native of Che Chiang-hsing. He is a gentleman of heroic and impulsive temperament, so that, when still young he took a great delight in discussing revolutionary affairs. Although his arguments are strong, he never is guilty of careless conduct. At the age of twenty eight he was graduated from a middles school in his province, and then came to Japan where he was graduated from the Tokyo Police and Prison School. Later he was graduated from the Meiji University. After returned to his home he was appointed to an instructior of law colleges. In the Revolutionary attempt with his fellow thinkers his plans were defeated and he was imprisoned for several months. After being released from the prison he went to Feng-tien and established a company for the publication of his views. After the 1st Revolution he was appointed the chief of the police in his native province, while in the 2nd year of the Republic he was elected to a member to the House of Commons.

賴慶暉 字紮平 歲三十五

選舉地　江西省

籍貫　江西省龍南縣

住址　北京官菜園上街五號

君爲國民黨最忠黨員。迭經他黨動搖。終不肯脱籍改入他黨。於前清宣統三年。由日本法政大學專門部法律正科卒業歸國。應學部留學生試驗。考取優等。授法政科舉人。辛亥革命。後任贛省總撿察分廳廳長。未幾辭職。獻身敎育。歷充公立法政學校。高等巡警學校。監獄專修科。法官養成所。及私立法政學校。贛省公學等處敎員。旋任本省高等審判廳民庭長。及內務司科長等職。民國元年。第一次國會選舉。由本省第二區復選爲衆議院議員二年。第一次本院常會。被選爲法典審查委員。國會解散後。無所表見。及此次國會重開。始來京供職。被選爲豫算審查委員。

君爲國民黨内最も忠實なる黨員なり。曾て笈を負ふて日本に游學し、前清宣統三年東京法政大學校專門部法律正科を卒業して歸國し、學部の留學生試驗に應じて優等を以て法政科舉人となる。第一革命の事成りて後、江西省總撿察分廳々長に任じたることあるも、旋て辭職して敎育に從事し、公立法政學校、高等巡警學校、監獄專修科、法官養成所、私立法政學校、江西省立公學等の各敎員に歷充し後進を誘掖する所ありたり。後ち又た江西省高等審判廳民事部長及び內務司科長等の要職に歷任したり。民國二年正式國會衆議院議員に當選し、院內に於て法典審査委員に舉げらる。國會解散後表見する所無く、五年約法恢復して國會再蘇するや、再び出で丶其の召集に應じ、遂に北京に抵りて仍は衆議院議員たり。

Mr. Lai Ching-hui, age thirty five, is a native of Lun-nan, Chen-hsi province. He is one of the most faithful members of the National Party. In 1912, he came to Japan when he studied in the Ho-sei University of Tokyo. After returned to his home, he passed the civil service examination with honour. When the first revolutionary movement was a success, he was appointed to the head of the branch office of the public procurator, but on resigning he was appointed to instructor of a number of law schools both public and private. He occupied also such important [posts as head of the civil section of the provincial court and the head of the Board of Justice, the Home Department. In the third year of the Republic, he was elected to the House of Commons where he was appointed to the committee of investigation of laws. When the Parliament was dissolved, he did not appear on the political stage for sometime, but with the re-opening of the Parliament, he was returned for the House of Commons.

駱繼漢 字墨蓀 歲三十二

選舉地　湖北省

籍貫　湖北省棗陽縣

住址　北京潘家河沿中間路東六十七

君為人倜儻不凡。處事精敏活潑。勇於決斷。居常持己以嚴。不隨同流俗。與人交。直而不黨。有所規勤。聽者無不為所動。好讀書。然喜探求真義。不以博聞強記。尋摘章句為懷。少時。好為詩歌。及長。因得宋儒學說之訓。斥為玩物喪志。遂棄不復為。專肆力於有用之學。及海內風氣開通。復改志殫精西學。遍讀新書。於西人郅治保邦之要。均確有把握。旋又東渡留學。入早稻田大學政治經濟科。畢業歸國後。歷任行政司法各要職。民國成立專充京滬各新聞撰述。正式國會成立。被選為眾議院議員。國會解散後。仍秉筆新聞。及國會復活。始入京。仍為議員。

民國之精華　（傳記）駱繼漢先生

君人と為り倜儻不羈、事を處して精敏活潑、殊に決斷に勇なり。居常己を持すること嚴正にして流俗に雷同せず。讀書を好みて然かも其の直義探求して倦まず。宋儒學說の訓を知得して、專ら治國平天下の學を求め、海內風氣の開通するに及びて、遍ねく新書を閱して西人郅治保邦の要道を攻究す。選に笠を負ふて新途の隣強日本に遊び、早稻田大學政治經濟科を卒業したり。歸國の後ち、行政司法の各要職に歷任して幹濟の才大に著る、辛亥革命を革めて民國を樹立し、共和の新政を布くや、君專ら筆を載せて北京上海各地の諸新聞の編輯に從事し、文章を以て天下を指導す。民國二年正式國會眾議院員に當選す。國會解散後、再び去つて操觚界の人と為る。五年國會復活するや、召集に應じて北京に抵り、仍ほ眾議院議員と為る。

Mr. Lo-chi-han, otherwise known as Mo Sun, age thirty three, is a native of Su Yang, Hu I . He is impartial, but courageous and full of determination. He is never influenced by the popular belief. He is fond of reading books, and is never tired of being an ardent seeker of the truth. He was deeply interested in the science of politics. When the new trend of thought was introduced to China, he became interested in the perusal of new works. He went over to Japan where he was graduated from the University of Waseda. On returning to his country, he occupied many posts of importance in the Department of Justice where his ability has come to be recognized. When the Republic was established, he engaged in the editorship of various papers of Peking and Shanghai. In the second year of the Republic, he was elected for the House of Commons. With the dissolution of the Parliament, he was again interested in a learning. Under the new president, when the Parliament was re-opened, he went to Peking, and was returned for the House of Commons.

蕭鳳翥　字仙渠　歲五十六

選舉地　廣東省
籍貫　廣東省潮陽縣
住址　北京丞相胡同潮州會館

君才高學博。急公好義。前清時拔貢舉人。授江西直隸州知州升用知府到省候補。痛官僚腐敗。國勢日非。非從根本上解決。不足以救危亡。不就。遂向上峰請咨赴日本東京。游歷凡八閱月回國。著有東游攷察政學紀略。自是絕意仕進。銳意興學。旋充本縣學務公所所長。改勸學所總董。兼充烟會會長。創辦官立東山高等小學堂。文昌第一官立小學堂。本族四序兩等小學堂。勸辦城鎮鄉小學堂。不下數十所。民國元年。充縣會議長。教育會會長。二年被選衆議院議員。國會橫被解散後。回家。創辦縣立中學校。推任校長。國會回復。仍到衆議院供職。

君や才高く學博く公に急ぎ義を好む。前清の時舉人を以て江西直隸州知州升用知府を授けられ、省に到つて候補す。官僚腐敗して國勢日に非なるを痛み、根本的の解決に非ざれば危亡を救ふに足らずとして官に就かず途に請ふて日本に遊び、歸國して後ち東游攷察政學紀略の著あり。是より意を官に絶ち、銳意學を興すを思び、旋て本縣學務公所々長となり、改めて勸學所總董兼衆戒烟會々長となり。官立東山高等小學校、文昌第一官立小學校、本族四序兩等小學校を創立經營し、城鎮各地方に於て小校の創設を勸誘指導したるもの數十箇所に下らざるなり。民國元年本縣の縣議會議長に舉げられ、又た同教育會々長に推さる。二年衆議院議員に當選したり。國會が横まに解散せらる、や歸省して縣立中學校を創立經營したり。國會恢復後召集に應じて再び出で、仍ほ衆議院議員の職に就きたり。

Mr. Hsiao Feng-chu, aged fifty six, a native of the Chao-yang hsing, Kuangtung hsing, is a gentleman of comprehensive information, and deeply interested in public affairs. In the previous Chinese regime, he was nominated as the governor of the Chiang-hsi Chih-lin. However, seeing the rotten condition of the government, and perceiving also the fact that the radical measure was the necessity to save his country from its doom, he refused to accept an offer of the government. He came over to Japan and after returned home, he wrote a book on administration. He was appointed to the head of the educational institution of his district. Naturally he was appointed to the president of the Educational Society as well as that of the local assembly when the Republic was established. In 1913, he was elected to a member of the House of Commons. He founded a middle school after the dissolution of the Parliament. However, he was again returned for the House of Commons when the Parliament was reopened.

蕭承弼 字右鄉 歲四十三

選舉地　山東省

籍貫　山東省長清縣

住址　北京魆家街雅集公寓

君賦性朴實にして浮華を喜ばず、讀書を好みて經世濟物に資すべきものは輙ち篇を終らずんば之を棄てず。また詩歌を能くして其の作多くは慷慨激越の調を帶ぶ。海內維新に及び君極めて西洋の文明を慕ひ、遂に京師に入りて北京大學校師範館理化科に入りて修業し、最優等を以て業を畢り。即ち例に從ひて內閣中書を授けらる。旋て山東に歸りて本省提學司署の試驗校閱委員、優級師範選科學校主任敎師、工業學校庶務長兼敎務長、地方自治局參議、財政公所科長等の職に歷任したり。民國成立して後ち復た北京に至り、財政部會計司行走、京兆地方自治調查員正式國會議員の選舉に會して參議院議員に當選したり。國會の解散後は縣知事候補を以て河南に分たれ、再び國會召集さるゝに及び、行政官を辭して北京に抵り、立法府の職に就き、仍は參議院議員たり。

君賦性朴實。不喜浮華。好讀書。雖非有益於身心。及足以爲經世濟物之資者。輙不終篇即棄擲之。能爲詩歌。而不常作。故每有所作。必極精妙。以大都於感慨淋漓時。一寫甚至性情。非尋常雕蟲刻鏤者可比也。及海內維新君極羨慕西洋之物質文明。遂入都。投入北京大學堂師範館理化科肄業。逾三年以最優等畢業。循例授前內閣中書。旋歸山東。歷充本省提學司署考驗校閱委員。優級師範選科學校主任敎習。工業學校庶務長兼敎務長。地方自治局參議。財政公所科長。民國成立。復至北京充財政部會計司行走。京兆地方自治調查員。正式國會成立君當選爲參議院議員。國會解散。以縣知事候補河南。及國會重開。始辭職來京。仍爲參議院議員。

民國之精華　（傳記）蕭承弼先生

Mr. Hsiao Cheng-pi, aged forty three, otherwise called Yu Ching, is a native of Chang-ching hsien. Simplicity and free of vanity were his motto. Naturally a profound reader of books, which he literary devoured, particularly if these related to the interest of the country. He was a great poet, and composed fine many poems. He was fond of the western learning. Consequently, he went to Peking where he studied in the Peking university whence he was graduated with honours. He was the secretary to the cabinet, an instructor in the normal school, an adviser of the local civic body, as well as the head of the local financial bureau. After the establishment of the Republic, he went up to Peking where he was committee of the local civic body and the Boad of Audit. He was elected to a member of the Senate. After the suppression of the Paliament, he was sent to Ho-nan as a candidate for the governorship. After reopening of the Parliament, he went up to Peking where he was interested in the state affairs, and became a member of the Parliament.

蕭文彬 字郁宜 歲三十三

選舉地　吉林省

籍　貫　吉林省五常縣

住　址　北京中鐵匠胡同

君自幼聰慧異人。及長。尤活潑自喜。
富于好奇之性。然其立身行己。多厚重
自持。不效時髦青年之浮薄踐燥。蓋君
之思想極放誕。而行爲則極規則也。清
末。以吉林高等巡警學堂畢業學員。歷
充警務局長。及五常縣參事會參事員。
光復後。由臨時省議會議員。得爲正式
省議會議員。旋復被選爲參議院議員。
國會解散後。吉林磐石銅鑛局局長。擘
畫經營。不遺餘力。至今辦理斯鑛者。
猶奉爲楷模。及帝制亂成。西南起義。
君遂赴上海。與諸同志共謀大計。及國
會恢復。始來京。復充議員。

君幼より聰慧人に異り、長じて活潑自ら喜び、好奇の性
に富む、蓋し君の思想は放誕なるも其の行爲は則ち極め
て規則に叶ふ。前清末季に於て吉林高等巡警學校卒業生
として、同地警務局長、五常縣參事會參事員等の職に歷
充したることあり。第一革命の事竣りて後、選ばれて臨
時省議會議員となり、後また正式省議會議員に舉げられ
たり。民國正式國會議員の選舉に會して參議院議員に當
選す。國會解散さるヽや、鄉里に歸りて後ち吉林磐石銅
鑛局々長となり、餘力を遺さずして擘畫經營今に到る。
而して現に本鑛は猶は奉じて模範と爲すなり。帝制の事
起りて西南義を舉ぐるや、君馳せて上海に赴き諸同志と
會して大計を謀る。約法恢復して國會復活するに及び、
君乃ち召集に應じて北京に入り、現に復た參議院議員の
職に就きてあり。

Mr. Hsiao Wen-sin, aged thirty three, a native of the Un-chang, Chi-iin, proved in youth himself to be sagacious and active. He has rather bold ideas, but his action was in accordance with strict regularity. At the later days of the Chinese regime, he was graduated from the Chi-lin High Police School, and after graduation, he was appointed to the Head of the Police Bureau and Councellor to the Un-chang prefecture. When the Revolution was accomplished, he elected to a member of the local assembly as well as the House of Commons. He was also chosen to a member of the national assembly. After the suppression of the Parliament, he was appointed to the head of the Chilin mining office, for the management of which he grudged no effort. As a matter of fact, thanks to his able management, this mine is now an example of mining success. When Yuanshi-Kai Imperial Movement was taking place, he went to Shanghai and worked against it with his friends. When the Parliament was opened for the second time, he was chosen to a member of the Senate, an honour which he enjoys at the present moment.

選舉地　江西省

籍貫　江西省永計縣

住址　北京花五條

君爲人精明幹練。頭腦明晰。而意志堅
强。清時以擧人。創辦本縣高等小學
堂。暨初級師範學校。並充當校長。兼
國文歷史地理敎員。己酉。被選爲本省
諮議局議員。創辦自治日報。庚戌。考
取法官。充京師地方審判廳民三庭推
事。時清政不綱。各省聯合請願。連開
國會。實行立憲政體。君由江西省敎育
總會電擧爲請願代表。辛亥革命軍起。
君至滬上。接贛政府電促回省。擔任政
事部祕書長。及省城外總稅局局長並
充江西國民黨支部文事科主任。創辦
預章日報。癸丑。被擧爲參議院議員。因
國會解散後。避禍出京。乙卯四月。因
新華社黨案。被捕於南昌。直至共和再
造。始得釋放。復適當國會復活。遂應
召。復充參議院議員。

君人と爲り精明幹練にして頭腦明晰意志鞏固なり。前清
時代擧人を以て永新縣高等小學校及び初級師範學校を創
設經營して校長となり、國文地理敎員を兼ねたり。己酉
の歲江西本省諮議局議員に選ばれ、又た自治日報を創立
經營す。庚戌の歲司法官試驗を受けて京師地方審判廳民
事第三庭推事に任す。時に淸政府紀綱紊れ、各省聯合し
て速に國會を開きて立憲政體を實行せん事を請願する
や、君は江西省敎育總會より推されて請願代表となる。

辛亥革命の際、君上海に至る、江西省政府の電報によりて
歸省し、政事部祕書長及び省城外總稅局々長に任じ、並
に江西國民黨支部文事科主任となり、又た預章日報を創
立經營す。癸丑の歲參議院議員に擧げられ、國會解散後
禍を避けて京を出で、乙卯四月新華社の黨案に因りて南
昌に捕はれ、民國復活の曉に及びて始て釋放さる。適ま
國會重ねて召集さるしや、之に應じて北上し、仍は參議
院議員の職に復したり。

民 國 之 精 華　（傳 記）　蕭 輝 錦 先 生

　　　Mr. Hsiao Hin-chin, otherwise known as Shih-chung, a native of Pin-hsing hsien, the
Chiang-hsi hsing is a gentlemen of clear head and strong will.　Under the previous Chinese regime, he
was interested in his province in the establishment of high and primary schools, and primary normal
school where he himselt taught literature and geography.　In 1910, he passed the examination and was
appointed to the public prosecutor of the Local Court.　At that time, the maladministration of the
Chinese government became so striking that representations were made from various parts of China for
introduction of the constitutional government.　He was one of the committees representing his own
province.　At the time of the revolution, he was in Shanghai, but he was recalled by the local government
to be the chief administrative secretary.　Simultaneously he had charge of the literary department of the
national party.　When the Parliament was opened, he was appointed to a member of the Senate.　After the
suppression of the assembly, he was arrested in Nan-chang, but with the restoration of the Republic, he
was acquitted and restored to his former position of the senatorial member.

君人と為り慷慨義を好み、幼にして大志あり。長じて尤も實學を攻究して造詣旣に深く、國政改革を以て自ら期す。民國二年當選の正式國會衆議院議員にして、第二革命に際し、衆議院議員伍漢、袁世凱を彈劾し、袁氏之を殺せしより、君即ち中華雜誌を創刊して丁世嶧を聘して主事とす、筆禍を買ひて發行を停止さる。君乃ち廣西に赴

蕭晉榮　字曜海

選舉地　廣西省
籍貫　廣西省富川縣
住址　北京西城貴人關

君為人慷慨好義。自幼夙抱大志。及長。充銳意攻求實學。博覽群籍。造詣既深。以國政改革自期。民國二年被選衆議院議員。讚寧之役。衆議院議員伍漢。持彈劾袁世凱謀叛。袁藉端殺之。時袁勢正盛議會莫敢誰何。君獨以伍之犯于非法。質問政府及國會被非法解散。君乃創設中華雜誌。聘丁世嶧主其事。攻擊政府甚力。政府迫令停版。君乃出走廣西。以袁將為帝說。將軍陸榮廷討之。陸不信。時陸方出巡。君尾之。逾月說。凡十餘次。卒與陸訂討袁之約。籌安會起。君走上海。與孫洪伊等。大張討袁之旗。並聯合十三省議員。致電各國公使。聲袁罪狀。袁死君乃入北京。說政府。以恢復約法。續開國會。嗣政府欲徵為內務次長。不就。現供衆議院議員職。被選為法典股委員長。

き、將軍陸榮廷を說きて密に討袁の約を結ぶ。籌安會發起されてより、君上海に赴きて孫洪伊等と圖りて大局を謀り十三省議負を聯合して各國公使に打電して袁の罪狀を訴ふ。袁死して後ち君乃ち北京に入り、政府に談ぜる約法の恢復、國會の續開を以てす。嗣て政府は君を調して內務次長に擬したるも就かず。國會の召集に應じて院に到り、現に仍は衆議院議員たり。

Mr. Hsiao Chin Jung, otherwise known as Yao-kai, is a native of Fu-chuan, Kuan-hoi province. While young, he was quite ambitious, and when grown up, he was deeply interested in the study of classics. In the second year of the Revolution, he was elected to a member of the House of Commons. At the time of the second revolution, Wu han, a member of the House of Commons, was killed by Yuanshi-kai for attacking him in the Parliament. He was vehement in starting an enquiry about this procedure. When the Parliament was dissoled, he published a paper which was suppressed. All the time he was working against Yuanshi-kai, in conjunction with members of thirteen provinces he sent telegrams to ministers of various countries, stating the crimes of Yuanshi-kai. After the death of Yuanshi-kai, he pressed the government to open the Parliament: When this was accomplished, he was elected to a member of the House of Commons.

鐘才宏　字百毅　歲三十七

選舉地　湖南省
籍　貫　湖南省藍山縣
住　址　北京香爐營四條

君爲人慷慨好義。自幼夙抱大志。於前
清壬寅科舉於卿。時方與學議起君獨
力創辦兩等小學堂。爲湘邊私立學校
之權輿。歷充勸學所董。自治所長。教
育會長。旋當選爲諮議局議員互選第
一次常駐議員。掌辦全省預算案。辛亥
改革。推爲藍山事務所長。旋任財產保
管處長。明年。湘督譚聘爲政治顧問。
國會選舉。被選爲眾議院議員會員先
議要案意見書。凡選舉總統。製定憲
法。釐正中央官制。地方制度。鹽政計
畫。預算案。確定幣制。劃分國稅省稅。
都爲八事。國會解散。君歸籍韜養。雲
南起義。君聞永州獨立遂以藍山首先
響應。及長沙宣布獨立。組成臨時參議
會。推君爲參議員。及至國會恢復。遂
入京。仍充眾議院議員。

君人と爲り慷慨義を好み、幼より夙に大志を抱く。前清
壬寅鄉試に舉げらる。時方に興學の議起る。君獨力を以
て兩等小學校を創立經營す。勸學所學董、自治所長、教
育會長に歷充し、旋て諮議局議員に當選し、第一次常駐
議員に舉げられ、全省の豫算案を處理す。第一革命當時、
藍山事務所長に推され、旋て財產保管處長に任ず。民國
元年湘南督譚延闓より聘せられて政治顧問と爲る。二
年正式國會衆議院議員に當選す。國會解散するや、君鄉
里に歸りて韜晦自ら養ふ。雲南義を起して帝制に反對す
るや、永州の獨立を聞き君遂に蹶起して藍山を以て最先
に響應す。既にして長沙獨立を宣布するや臨時參議會を
組織し、推されて參議員と爲る。旋て約法恢復して國會
再び召集を行ふに及び、遂に入京して復た衆議院議員に
任じたり。

民國之精華　（傳記）　鐘才宏先生

Mr. Chung-tsai-hung, age thirty seven, is a native of Lan-shan, Hu-nan province. Being heroic in temperament, he was full of ambition. In the previous Chinese regime, he successfully passed the civil service examination and established a primary school at his own expense. Later he was appointed to the president of the Educatinal Association and a member of the Advisory Assembly of his province, where he interested himself in the drawing up the budget of the province. In the 1st year of the Republic he was appointed to a political adviser to the Hu-nan province. In the 2nd year of the Republic he was returned for the House of Commons. When the Parliament was dissolved by Yuanshi-kai he went back to his home where he devoted himself to self-culture. When the Imperial Movement was caused by Yuan Shi-kai he opposed to it most strongly. When the independence of Chen-hsia was declared, he became a member of the assembly then summoned. When the Parliament was opened he entered Peking where he was elected to a member of the House of Commons.

謝鵬翰 字蔭南 歲四十五

選舉地　河南省

籍　貫　河南省商邱縣

住　址　北京賈家胡同歸德會館

君天資聰慧。性喜風雅。五歲即解吟
詠。有硯凹齋詩鈔一卷。十二歲。通十
三經。應童子試。不第。退而習拳捧術
七年。故身雖文弱。而力可敵數人。高
屋峭壁。不能阻其行也。十九入邑庠。
旋以歲試第一食廩。然屢科不第。戊戌
變政後。遂醉心西學。入本省法政學校
肄業三年。辛亥光復。君嘗親與戰事。
屢瀕于危。民國成立。被推爲縣議會議
長。兼本縣團練會會長。元年六月。土
匪蜂起。匪首率大股匪徒三千餘詔大
孔。衆進鏡歸郡。君鄉團百餘巡防兩營
督勦。身先士卒。激戰六時餘。身中數
十彈。體無完布。辛乃克之。又前後拿
獲土匪數十名。鄉里賴以安全。民國二
年。被舉爲參議院議員。大黨派嫌疑爲
袁政府。奪其職權遂歸隱於農。籌辦森
林一處。農務試驗場一處。及國會復
活。遂應召入京。就參議院議員之職。

君天資聰慧にして性風雅を喜ぶ、五歲にして吟咏を解し、
硯凹齋詩鈔一卷あり。十二歲にして十三經に通じ、童子
の試に應じて落第す。退て拳捧の術を習ふ。戊戌政變後遂に西學
に心醉し、河南法學校に入りて修業すること三年。十九にして
邑庠に入り、屢々科して及第せず。辛亥
革命の事起るや、君親しく戰事に預りて屢々危に瀕す。
民國成立後、推されて縣議會議長と爲り、縣團練會長を兼
ぬ。元年六月土匪蜂起し、三千餘匪敲躁して大孔を陷れ、

進んで歸郡を覘ふ。君乃ち鄉團百餘名、巡防兩營を率ゐ
て之を勘討し、躬ら士卒に先ちて激戰六時間、身に十數彈
を被りて體に完布なく、辛ふじて之に克ち、前後に土匪數
十名を捕へ、鄉里賴つて以て安全なるを得たり。民國二
年參議院議員に舉げられ、後ち國民黨員の故を以て袁政
府より其職を剝奪され、歸省して農に隱れ、森林一箇所
農事試驗場一箇所を經營す。國會復活と共に復た召集さ
れて參議院議員となる。

Mr. Hsieh Hung-han, otherwise called Yui-nan, aged forty five, a native of Ho-nan hsing, was fond
of classic of his own country from youth. He was a precautious child, and as a boy, he was well versed
in poetry and classics. As he grew older, he indulged in the study of western learning. In the law
school of his province, he studied law for three years. He participated in the revolutionary war of 1911,
and frequently ran the risk of losing his life. When the Republic was established, he was elected to the
president of the local assembly. In 1912, the bandits as numbering over three thousands assaulted his
province, but he, with about hundred of men, met them and after severe battle, himself being
wounded seriously, repeled them out and saved to his country men from further trouble. In 1913,
he was appointed to a senator, but being a member of the National Party, he was dismissed from
his office. On returning to his home, he was interested in agriculture, but with the reopening of the
Parliament, he was appointed to a member of the Senate.

謝 持　字慧生　歳四十一

選舉地　四川省
籍　貫　四川省富順縣
住　址　北京香爐營四條胡同

君於前清畢業于四川川南師範學校。曾任四川學務處委員。官私各學校教員。剻辦縣立高等小學校。自任校長。乙巳創設團練學校。丁未。投身同盟會員。是年秋。赴成都。任四川商務總局文牘主任。與黨人密謀起革命軍。襲據成都。事洩亡命。至上海。任中國新公學學監。旋入陝西。聯絡川陝同志。躬自牧羊鳳翔北山中。辛亥十月。與同志等起兵據重慶。建蜀軍政府。君為總政處長。旋遷四川政務處副理。改民政長署參事。民國二年。被選為參議院議員。其年五月袁世凱以君與黃復生趙鐵橋數人。阻其帝制逆謀遂誣以血光黨。儼造左證。投之於獄。袁之逮捕國會議員蓋自君始。旋出獄。東渡居日本東京仍時與黨人共謀大事。國會恢復。始來京供職。

君前清時代四川省の川南師範學校を卒業し、曾て四川學務處委員、官私立各學校教員に歷任し、縣立高等小學校を創立經營して自ら校長に任ず。乙巳の歳團練學校を創設す。丁未の歳同盟會員となり、成都に赴きて四川商務總局文牘主任となる。黨人と密に革命を謀り、事洩れて亡命し、上海に至りて中國新公學々監に任じ、旋て陝西に入りて四川陝西同志の聯絡を計り、躬ら羊を鳳翔北山中に牧す。辛亥十月同志等と兵を起して重慶に據り四川軍政府を建て、總政局長と為る。次で四川政務處副理となり、改めて民政署參事と為る。民國二年選ばれて參議院議員と為る。其の年五月袁政府は君と黃復生、趙鐵橋數人を謀るに血光黨の陰謀團と為し證據を偽造して獄に投ず、蓋し袁政府が國會議員を逮捕せること君より始る。後ち漸く獄を出で、日本東京に走り、在留の同志と共に大事を謀る。此次國會再開するに及び君また召集に應じて仍は參議院議員の職に就く。

民國之精華　(傳記)　謝持先生

Mr. Hsieh Chih, known as Hui-sheng, aged forty one, a native of Fu-shun hsien, the Ssu-chuan hsing, was graduated from the Chuan-nan normal school under the Chinese regime, and ever since he was interested in educational work, having several primary schools under his control. In 1907, he became a member of the revolutionist's association, but his plans having been divulged, he fled to Shanghai where he was appointed to an inspector of the Chinese school. He then entered Hsia-hsi whence in order to form connection with his friends he looked after the sheep disguising himself as a shepherd in Feng-hsiang mountains. He had his military headquarter in Chung-ching at the time of the revolution, and established an independent government in Ssi-shen in which he was appointed to the chief administration. In 1913, he was chosen a senatorial member. He was put into prison under a false charge by Yuanshi-Kai which was the first arrest of the member of the House of Commons. He came to Tokyo, and worked out his plans with his fellow-men. After the reopening of the Parliament, he was appointed to a member of the Senate.

謝書林 字東府 歲四十一

選舉地　奉天省

籍　貫　奉天省柳河縣

住　址　北京六部口西後水泡子三十二

君秉性溫厚篤實。而氣宇深沈。然居恆以緘默自持。不輕于言論。與人交和藹可親。雖所疾惡。亦假以顏色。生平未嘗以私隙仇人。人有失德。或以橫逆相加。唯踈遠之。不復與近。而不露絕交之痕迹。自幼聰穎好讀。不事嬉戲。弱冠時。即抱大志。誓爲天下第一人。讀古人書。唯注重義理。不尚詞藻。及長博覽羣書。益銳志實學。不以科第介意。及海內維新。復殫心西學。頗以開通民智。改良教育爲己任。於前以優附生。先後卒業於奉天師範傳習所及自治研究所。自治養成會。曾充本縣勸學員長。自治研究所所長。及奉天臨時省議會議員。民國二年。當選爲奉天正式省議會議員。旋當選爲參議院議員。國會解散後。歸里獨居。不問時政。及國會重開。始來京供職。

君秉性溫厚篤實にして氣宇深沈なり。居常緘默自ら持して言論を輕々しくせず。人と交りて和藹親むべし。幼より聰穎にして讀を好み嬉戲を事とせず。弱冠にして既に大志あり。天下第一人たらんことを誓ふ。古人の書を讀むや唯い義理を重んじて詞藻を尚はず。長ずるに及びて群書を涉獵し、銳意實學を攻究し、科舉及第を以て意に介せず。海內維新に及び心を西學に留めて顧る民智を開通して教育を改良する事を以て己が任と爲す。前清の優附生を以て前後して奉天師範傳習所及び自治研究所、自治養成會を卒業し、曾て柳化縣勸學員長、自治研究所長に歷充し、奉天臨時省議會議員に選ばる。民國二年正式奉天省議會議員に舉げらる。旋で選ばれて參議院議員と爲る。國會解散して後、鄉里に隱退し閉居して時事を問はず、國會重ねて召集さるゝに及び、君また之に應じて北京に抵り、現に參議院議員となる。

Mr. Hsieh Shu-lin, otherwise called Tung-fu, forty one years old, a native of I-ho hsien, the Feng-tien hsing is a gentlemen of deep thought and great ambition. Personally he is gentle and taciturn. He was a great reader of books from youth. His ambition distinguished himself. He was greatly fond of science, disregarding the civil examination then in vogue in China. He took it to himself that the education of the people to be his mission. Therefore, with this object in view he entered the normal school in Feng-tien; and was also graduated from the civic institute. Later, he was the head of the society intended for the study of civic bodies. Before the suppression of the Parliament, he was a member of the Senate, but this event made him to retire to his native home, and kept him away from politics until the Parliament was reopened. He is now a member of the Senate in Peking,

謝良牧 字叔野 歳三十三

選擧地　華僑
籍　貫　廣東省梅縣
住　址　北京延壽寺街三眼井三號

君少にして堅任剛毅、世に阿らす。其の伯父謝春生南洋
の巨富なり、其の子姪を日英兩國に遊學せしむ、君乃ち
兄逸橋、弟適祥と共に日本に留學す。是れ光緒甲辰乙卯
の時にして孫文黃興等前後して東渡し同盟會を主唱す。

君兄弟之を賛助し、君尤も激烈にして同盟會計晝の革命
事業悉く預り、為に清官吏の偵捕顏る急にして各地に亡
命數年、又た其の伯父に累を及ぼすを恐て自ら家と絕ち、
時に窮困に處し凜然志を易へざる也。辛亥の革命に廣州

獨立して提督李準全軍を以て降る、君の力多しとなす。
後ち廣東都督府と南京臨時政府に在りて謀畫に參預し、
民國元年冬々華僑選擧會より擧られて參議院議員と爲る。
後ち袁氏種々の違法あるや、上海に去りて、新開社を創
設して猛烈に袁政府を攻擊す。本年廣東に在りて民軍の
北伐隊を組織したるも、袁死するや解散して北上し、國
會の召集に應じて參議院議員の職に就く。

君少堅忍剛毅不阿。弱冠留學日本。其
伯父謝春生南洋巨富也。春生積貲産
千數百萬。嘗銳意使其子姪游學英日
各國、君與乃兄逸橋弟適祥。故留日。
時方清光緒甲辰乙巳之度。孫中山黃
克强。先後東渡。有同盟會之倡。君兄
弟首力贊助而左右之。而君尤激烈。自
是凡同盟會所擧排滿革命之役。無一
不與。中間聲名漸露。清官吏偵捕急。
乃展轉亡命數年。已不容於國。而又恐
累其伯父。亦自絕於家。有時倫受窘
困。或勸稍易志節。即席豊履厚。家庭
之福已靡盡。顧君凜然。不爲動。辛亥
廣州獨立提督李準以全軍降。實君力
爲多。功成不居。僅於粤都督府與南京
臨時政府中參領謀畫。民國元年冬。遂
由華僑選擧會擧爲參議院議員。二年
在院。見袁氏種種違法。立出京。曾在
滬創報館。痛斥政府本年在廣東組織
民軍北伐。袁死。始解散回京。今院內
擧爲請願股委員。

民國之精華　（傳記）　謝良牧先生

Mr. Hsieh Liang-mu, or Shu-yeh, aged thirty three, a native of Mei-hsien, Kuan-tung hsing
is a gentleman of high principle and strong will. His uncle Hsieh-ohun-sheng is a millionair of the
south sea islands. It was about the time 1903-1904 that together I-chiao and Shih-chun he came to
Tokyo: It was at the very time that Sun-yat-sen and others visited Japan to prepare for the
revolutionary movement. He was one of the staunch advocate of the revolution, and was chased by the
Chinese official who looked after him to arrest. To keep his uncle free from the trouble, he broke away
from his family plunging himself into the depth of great difficulty and trouble. In the revolutionary war,
it was chiefly through his instrumentality that the independence of Kuang-chan and the surrender of the
admiral Li Chun were obtained. In 1912, the 1st year of the Republic, he was returned for the House
of Commons. Seeing the illegal conduct of Yuan Shi-kai, he published a newspaper to attack him. He
was in Kuantung this year and was about to form anti-northern expedition. But after the death of
Yuansh-kai he went up to Peking and became a member of the Senate.

謝翊元 字筱現 歲三十

選舉地 江蘇省

籍 貫 江蘇省東海縣

住 址 北京前門外虎坊橋聚魁店

君秉性誠篤不欺。與人交。剛正不阿。然謙虛好問。喜聞讜言。人告以過。未盡當。必欣然謝之。然使譽過其實。則反盛怒形諸顏色。蓋謂言等之欺我也。少好讀書。然非有益於身心及足以為經世濟物之資者。輒不終篇即棄擲之。能為詩歌而不常作。故每有所作。必極精妙。以大都於感慨淋漓時。一寫其至性至情。非尋常雕蟲刻鏤者可及也。清末。以法部主事畢業于京師法政學堂。民國元年。被舉為共和黨東海分部部長。二年。當選為衆議院議員。兼充進步黨本部交際幹事。國會解散。君南歸不問時事。唯時至滬上與黨人通聲氣。並密圖恢復大業。及國會復活。遂現在復為議員。

君秉性誠篤にして欺かず、人と交りて剛正にして阿らず、然かも謙虛を以て問を好み、喜んで讜言を聞く。少にして讀書を好み、身心に有益にして經世濟物の資ある者は輒ち篇を終らずんば之を棄てず、詩歌を能くするも常に作らず、作れば必ず精妙を極め、多くは感慨淋漓として其の至性至情を寫す、尋常彫蟲刻鏤を能とする者の及ぶ所に非るなり。前清末季法部主事を以て京師法政學堂を卒業し、民國二年舉げられて共和黨東海分部々長となる。旋て正式國會議員選擧に際して衆議院議員に當選し、進步黨に籍を置き同黨本部交際部幹事に推さる。國會解散後、君南旋して鄉關に閑居しまた時事を談せず。唯だ時に上海に赴きて黨人と勢氣を通ひ、密に大業の恢復を念とす。飽にして國會復活するに及び、遂に召集に應じて北上し、現に復た衆議院議員と爲る。

Mr. Hsieh I-yuan, aged thirty, a native of Tung-hai, the Chang-su hsing is a gentleman of high and noble character. Being humble, he is open to listen others. He is an ardent reader of books. When he is inspired to composes, he expresses his ideas in such a wonderful way that none addicted to mere study of phrases and turn of sentence etc. can be favorably compared with his literary production. He was graduated from the Peking law college, and in 1912 he was returned to the House of Commons. He belongs to the progressive party. When the assembly was suppressed, he beguiled his time in study. From time to time, he went to Shanghai to hold consultation with his fellow thinkers. Having been accomplished the grand work of the revolution he is at present a member of the House of Commons.

韓玉辰 字達齊 歲三十二

選舉地　湖北省
籍　貫　湖北省松滋縣
住　址　北京西城後鬧胡同

君秉性誠篤朴實。脫盡浮華。生平極尚
信義。言動舉止。確有本末。與人有約。
雖遇意外危險。亦必拾身踐履。前言。
若以實際上無可排除之障碍。致未克
如約以行。則引爲絕大恥辱。以故人有
所託。常不肯輕於承諾。有時或先託詞
拒絕。然後暗中爲之盡力。事不成可
不頁責。事成亦不望報。蓋生性使然。
非有意造作以博浮名也。少年讀書。極
喜研究宋明儒者之學。故於事理無所
不明。見解亦異常穩健。及長愈益洞察
世情。敏於感覺。工於辭令。且文思敏
捷。其處理事務。亦機警異常。實爲民
黨中最有力之分子。曾入武昌法政學
校畢業。民國二年。被選爲參議院議
員。國會解散。仍奔走滬上。留心國事。
及國會重開。遂來京仍爲參議院議員。

民國之精華　（傳記）　韓玉辰先生

君秉性誠篤にして浮華の態なし。生平極めて信義を
尚び、言動舉作一進一退確に本末あり。少年書を讀み學を
求めて尤も宋明の學を研究す。故に深く事理を明かにし。
見解亦た穩健にして周到なり。長ずるに及びて益々世情
を洞察して感覺敏俊なり。社會に出で〳事務を處理す、
亦た機警人に異りて精透明敏なり。蓋し民黨中最も有力
なる分子なり。曾て志を抱きて新智識の涵養に怠らず。

武昌法政學校に入り研究の功を積みて卒業す。民國二年
正式國會選擧に際し選ばれて參議院議員と爲る。國
會解散するや、鄉に歸つて靜養し、後ち復た走せて上海
に赴き、諸同志と偕に心を國事に留め大業の恢復を念ふと
す。約法恢復して國會重ねて開かるゝに及び、遂に又た
其の召集に應じて入京し、仍は參議院議員と爲る。

Mr. Han Yu-chen, otherwise known as Ta chi, age thirty two, is a native of Sung Tzu, Hu nan. Simple in the mode of living and hating the life of extravagance, he is faithful to his promis, while his every movement is regulated by principles. He is an ardent reader of books, and highly conversant with classical teachings. Therefore his views are rational, and comprehensive. He is well acquainted with the conditions of the society at large, and conducts himself accordingly. He is the ablest and sound element of the peoples' parts. He was an earnest seeker of the new knowedge, and was graduater from the Wu-chun law college. In the second year of the Republic, he was elected to a member of the Senate. With the dissolution of the Parliament, he returned to his home when he quietly spent his days. Later, however, he went to Shanghai where with his fellow thinkers he made great efforts to restore the Parliament. Under the new president, the Parliament was summoned when he became a member of the Senate.

魏鴻翼 字可莊 歲四十五

選舉地　甘肅省
籍貫　甘肅省伏羌縣
住址　北京官菜園上街甘肅南館

君爲人淸高閑雅。長于詩文。於前淸光緒辛卯。擧于鄉試。戊戌成進士。隨入翰林院鹿吉士。癸卯。散館。改四川南江縣知縣。適値荒年。君奔走四鄉。設法救恤。民間詞訟。亦於鄉間了之。長官前應行之種種手續。未嘗硏究。以是失川督錫良歡。甫滿一年。即交卸。後丁母憂扶柩回籍安葬。大事畢後。方擬閉門讀書。不問世事。民國改建。初行正式選舉。被選爲參議院議員。遂北上就職。在院僅七月。即被袁政府用暴力解散國會。又偵探四出。槍斃日聞。踤威之下。不敢久住。乃復跟蹌出京。不問世事者。二年有餘。民國五年。帝制推倒。共和復活。以滬上友人函促於前。黎犬總統電召於後。遂仍北上就議員職之。

君人となり淸高閑雅にして詩文に長ず。前淸光緒辛卯鄉試に擧げられ、戊戌進士に及第して翰林院庶吉士となる。癸卯出でて四川南江縣知事に任ず、時適ま凶年なるを以て君四鄉に奔走し法を設けて救恤す。然かも官界遊泳の術に慣れざるを以て四川總督錫良の歡を失ひ一年にして任を解く。後ち母の喪に遭ひ鄉に歸りて葬を修む。爾來家鄉に閉居して閑臥悠々書に親しみてまた時事を問はず。民國成立して第一次國會議員の選擧を行ふに至り、君選ばれて參議院議員となり、家門を出て其の職に就く。在院僅に七ヶ月、袁政府壓迫して國會を解散し、偵探四出して銃殺日に聞ゆるや、君乃ち積威の下久しく住むに堪へずとなし、復た北京を去りて鄉關に雌伏す。民國五年袁氏の帝制を推倒して共和制復活するや、上海の友人亦た君の出山を促し、次で黎大總統の電召に遭ひ、仍ほ復た入京して參議院議員と爲る。

Mr. Wei Hung-i, otherwise named Ho-chuang, aged forty five, a native of Kan-su hsing, is a great scholar of classic. Having successfully passed the government examination, he was appointed to the governor of the Ssi-chuan. At the famine then prevailed in that district, he did an excellent work of helping the poor, but he retained this position only a year; on the death of his mother, he was in mourning about one year at his home entirely separating himself from politics. When the Republic was established, he was elected to a member of the Senate which post he occupied about seven months. Finding that the oppression of Yuanshi-kai was unbearable, he quitted Peking for his home. After the death of Yuanshi-kai, he went up to Peking, and again assumed the Senatorial function.

魏丹書　字吉卿　歳四十二

選舉地　山東省

籍　貫　山東省鉅野縣

住　址　北京頭髮胡同

君爲人方正嚴明。不苟言笑。不輕然諾。然居心仁厚。喜周濟貧乏。雖自處窘中。亦不以已事而緩人之急。勤謹耐勞。長于事務。人有所託。雖陋路亦允爲盡力。却事成不以功自居雖有大德于人決不肯受人一介之報。以故里人威愛威戴如父母。自幼聰慧絕倫弱冠爲文。即下筆數千言。頃刻立就。及長。尤工說理之文。不復從事推砌。海內維新。奮志求有用之學。而尤注意於政法之書。凡新出譯本。無不一購讀。曾肄業于法政大學。畢業後。歷充曹州鎮署文案。山東都督府軍事顧問。臨時省議會議員。民國二年。正式國會成立。被選爲衆議院議員。國會解散。復肆力研究法學。多所發明。及國會復活。始來京仍爲議員。

君人と爲り方正嚴明にして苟も言笑せず。居心仁厚にして貧家を周濟する事を喜ぶ。また勤謹にして勞に耐へ、事務の才あり、里人之を推重する。幼より聰慧にして、弱冠文を作るや下筆數千言頃刻にして就る。長ずるに及び、尤も說理の文に工にして復た推砌に從事せず。海內維新に及び奮つて有用の學を求め、尤も意を政治法律の書に注ぎ、凡そ新刊の譯本は一として購讀せざる無し。曾て法政大學に學び、卒業の後ち曹州鎮文案署理、山東都督府軍事顧問、臨時省議會議員等の職に歷任したり。民國二年正式國會議員選擧行はるゝや、君選ばれて衆議院議員と爲る。國會解散されし後は、復た勉めて法律の學を研究して發明する所多し。旣にして袁氏逝きて國會重ねて開かるゝに及び、君復た召集に應じて入京し、仍ほ衆議院議員となれり。

民國之精華　（傳記）　魏丹書先生

Mr. Wei Tan-shu, known as Chi-hsing, aged forty two, a native of Chu-yeh hsien, Shun-tung, is a strict disciplinarian, personally being full of sympathetic, and gentle sentiments. Added to these qualities, he is also highly practical. He is a profound and quick writer. He read very copiously books on law and politics, not missing any of new publication on the subject. He was an adviser to the governor-general of Shan-tun-fu after graduating from the law college. When Republic was established, he was elected to a member of the Parliament, but when it was suppressed, he turned his attention to the study of law. With the death of Yuanshi-kai, he resumed his function as the member of the House of Commons.

魏　毅　字文謙　歲三十三

選舉地　河南省

籍　貫　河南省武陟縣

住　址　北京宣武門內象牙胡同

君爲人謙虛退讓。以厚道待人。雖疾惡崇善。然責人薄而責己嚴。人有善行。喜爲之揄揚。務使得自然之酬報。有過則當面直言規勸。而對他人。則文爲之隱諱。居常以禮自持。言動舉止。皆極拘謹不放。然秉性聰慧。悟性敏捷。而思考力極強。弱冠讀書即能探求眞義。不從事于文詞。及長。尤力求有用之學。曾在安昌高等小學校及北京豫學校肄業。光緒三十一年。轉入天津北洋高等師範學校。宣統元年冬。畢業。歷充河南工業。中校覃懷中校。第二師各敎員。及武陟縣勸學員長。民國元年當選爲衆議院議員。國會解散後。快快歸里。不復求有表見。及國會復活。始入京仍爲衆議院議員。

君人と爲り溫良にして恭謙、惡を疾み善を樂ぶと雖、人を責むること薄くして己を責むること嚴なり。居常禮を以て自ら持じ言動舉止皆な極めて恪謹なり。然かも其の性聰慧にして思考力極めて強く、弱冠菁を讀みて眞義を究め、長じて尤も有用の學を求び。曾て安昌高等小學校及び北京豫學校に在りて修業す。光緒三十一年轉じて天津高等師範學校に入學し、宣統元年の冬其の業を畢へたり。爾れより出仕して河南工業中學校、覃懷中學校、第二師範學校等の各敎員及び武陟縣勸學員長等の職に歷充したり。民國二年選ばれて衆議院議員と爲り、入京して第一次正式國會の召集に應じ議を建て、大政に參與す。國會解散さるゝや、快々として田園に歸臥し、復た政見を發表することなし。國會復活するに及び、再び召集されて上京し、現に衆議院議員たり。

Mr. Wei Kin, otherwise named Wen-chen, is a native of Wu-chih hsien, the Ho-nan hsing. He is thirty three years of age. Gentleness of character, combined with that of a strict disciplinarian, is the very picture of our hero. He is a reader and thinker. After receiving education in primary and high schools, he was admitted to the higher normal school in Tien-tsin in 1905, and was graduated in 1909. Ever since, he was an instructor in various middle and normal schools. In the second year of the Republic, he was returned for the House of Commons, and thus participated in the government of the country. With the suppression of the Parliament, however, he returned to his home, and never had any more occasion to give publicity to his political views. With the reopening of the Parliament, however, he was invited to Peking and again resumed his function as a member of the legislative assembly.

魏肇文　字武伯　歳三十三

選擧地　湖南省

籍貫　湖南省寶慶縣

住址　北京象坊橋十一

君少負才名。尤善書法。光緒壬寅。留學日本。成城學校。甲辰。以父午莊尚書。前在陝西巡撫任。內得部議獎叙主事。遂歸國入都。簽分戸部雲南司。旋得獎候選郞中。又得獎候選道。入戸部計學館及財政部講習所。簿記講習所。聽講三年。充清理財政處雲南司主稿。戸部改組度支。充漕倉司京倉科科長。辛亥八月。革命事起。清廷起尚書公督湖廣。君聞旨下。馳書備陳時事。民國成立。尚書公亦不復出山矣。一年。君被選爲衆議院議員。國會解散後君以國民黨員關係亡避日本。逾年始歸。家居奉親。以書畫詩歌承懽堂上。不更問世事。唯留心實業。組織錦鑛公司十數處。及國會重行開幕。始來京。仍爲衆議院議員。

君少にして才名を負ひ尤も書法を善くす。光緒壬寅の歳日本に留學して成城學校に學ぶ。甲辰の歳父午莊尚書が前に陝西巡撫たりし時の獎により主事に叙せられ、遂に歸國して北京に入り戸部の雲南司に分たる。旋て候選郞中となり、又た候選道臺を獎せられ、戸部計學館及び財政部講習所簿記講習所に入りて講習三年の後、清理財政處雲南司副主稿となる。戸部が廢支部に改るや漕倉司京倉科々長に任ず。辛亥の歳八月革命の事起るや、君旨を聞きて南下し、書を馳せて時事を條陳したり。南北統一して民國成立するや、第一次國會議員選擧に際し選ばれて衆議院議員と爲る。國會解散後君は國民黨たるの故を以て袁政府の注目する所となりて日本に亡命す。年を逾へて歸國し、家居以て親を奉じ更に復た政事を問はず、專心實業を營みて錦鑛公司十數ヶ處を發起す。國會再び召集さるゝや、君出でゝ仍は衆議院議員たり。

民國之精華　（傳記）　魏肇文先生

Mr. Wei Chao-wen, otherwise called Wu-pai, aged thirty three, is a native of the Pos-ching hsien, the Hu-nan hsing. In 1904 he came to Japan, where he studied in the Seijo Gakko. On return home, he was appointed to one of the government function in Yun-nan-ssu. He studied the book keeping in one of the institute, and in this capacity, he served many important goverment function. In august 1911, when the revolutionary movement took place, he came down to the south, and had many opportunities of discussing politics. When the Republic was brought into existence he was appointed to a member of the House of Commons. On the ground that he was a member of the national party, he was so oppressed by Yuanshi-kai that he had to flee to Japan at the peril of his life. After one year, he returned home and never talked politics. He organized more than several times mining companies. With the reopening of the Parliament he was returned for the House of Commons.

譚煥文　字熙軒　歲三十九

選舉地　陝西省

籍　貫　陝西省長安縣

住　址　北京草帽胡同花園大院路北

君秉性聰慧。強於記憶。稚齡讀書。日誦數千言。詞義皆深入不忘。稍長。尤喜窮求理義。遂類旁通。不執於一隅。不同於文字。發微扶奧。於古書義理。常能獨出心裁。別創新解。年方弱冠。即以能文見稱於時。其為文雖專長於說理。不重詞藻。然氣勢雄奇。吐屬華貴。非尋常寒酸者所能幾其萬一。曾在本省法政學堂肄業。畢業後。即專力地方學務。手創初等小學貳百餘校。清宣統元年。赴津滬調查學務。辛亥九月。陝西光復。任省城督練民團總局幫辦。當時陝東陝西軍務異常吃緊。而省垣附近各地秩序絲毫未稍紊亂者。君之力也。民國二年被選為眾議院議員。國會既遭非法解散。乃奔走津漢。究心實業。及至國會重開。始入京。仍為眾議院議員。

君や秉性聰慧にして博覽強記なり。稍や長じて尤も窮理の學を喜び、一隅に執せず文字に局せずして深く古舊の義理に精通し、以て獨創の見解を立つ。年方に弱冠にして即ち能文を以て時に稱せられしが、其の文專ら說理に長じて詞藻を重せず、氣勢頗る雄奇なり。曾て陝西省に在りて法律學堂に學び、卒業後專ら地方の學務を處理し、省内に於ける初等小學二百餘校を創設したり。前清宣統元年天津及び上海に赴きて教育事務を調査す。卒亥の歲九月陝西獨立するや、省城督練民團總局幫辦に任ず、當時陝東陝西の軍勢頗る緊急なりしが、省城附近各地方の秩序は未だ絲毫も紊亂せざりしもの實に君が力なり。民國二年選ばれて眾議院議員と為る。國會既に非法解散に遭ふや、君乃ち天津漢口各地間を奔走して心を實業に傾注す。國會恢復するに及び、再び上京して眾議院議員となる。

Mr. Tan Huan-wen, aged thirty nine, a native of the Cheng-an hsien, the Shan-ssi. He is a thinker with remarkable memory. He is fond of reading of books and forms his own original views. He is strictly logical, but being trammeld with mere words and phrases. He studied law in one of the provincial schools. Through his insturmentality, as many as two hundred schools were established. In 1909, he visited Tien-tsin with a view to investigate educational affairs. When Soan-ssi claimed independence, he was the chief instrument in bringing about the order and regularity in the district of Hsingcheng. In the 2nd year of the Republic, he was elected to a member of the House of Commons. However, when the assembly was suppressed, he went over to Tsin-han district with a view of entering into commerce. With the reopening of the Parliament, he was elected to a member thereof.

譚瑞霖　字滌夏　歲三十一

選舉地　廣東省
籍　貫　廣東省廣州新會縣
住　址　北京永光寺西街新會新館

君性慧而勤學不倦。弱冠即有文名。然
能虛心納言。以故前輩皆樂於開導之。
於宣統二年。畢業於廣東師範完全科。
充新會中學附屬小學教員。後以清政
不綱朝廷不以教育爲重。拘守內地。終
無自由發展之精神。遂決計遍遊南洋
群嶋。以振興海外教育。開通華僑子弟
爲己任。曾在法屬安南。創辦海防華僑
時習兩等小學校。及武漢起義。投筆歸
國。時廣東方謀獨立。乃從黃明堂發難
江門。復與鄧統領漢榮據新會城以應
之。民國成立。被舉爲新會縣會議長。
元年冬。被任爲新會籌備選舉事務所
委員長。二年。被選爲衆議院議員。三
年充北京高等專門稅務學校學監。旋
以丁艱回里。值帝制發生。乃糾合舊同
志。屢倡義於岡州。遙爲護國軍之聲
援。國會恢復。始解散所部。入都復爲
議員。

君や性慧敏にして勤學倦まず、弱冠にして既に文名あり。
宣統二年廣東師範學校完全科を卒業して新會中學附屬小
學校教員となる。當時滿清朝廷が教育を重んぜざるを以
て、內地に在りて自由を延ばす能はざるを思ひ、
遂に出で〻南洋群島を遍歷し以て海外の教育を振興し華
僑の子弟を開導するを以て已が任とせり。佛領安南に在
りて海防華僑時習兩等小學校を創立經營し、第一革命に
際して歸國す。時に廣東獨立す、君乃ち黃明堂に從つ

て難を江門に發し、復た鄧統領と新會城に據りて之に應
す。民國成立して新會縣議長に舉げらる。民國元年新會
選舉籌備事務所委員長となり、二年衆議院議員に選ばる。
三年北京高等專門稅務學校學監に任じ、旋て喪に遭ふて
歸省す。帝制に反對して乃ち舊同志を糾合して義を岡州
に唱へ遂に護國軍の聲援を爲す。國會恢復後其の部下を
解散して北上し、再び衆議院議員と爲る。

民國之精華　（傳記）　譚瑞霖先生

Mr. Tan Jui Lin, otherwise known as Ti Hsia, aged thirty one, is a native of Hsin Hui Hsien Kang Chou, the Kantung Hsing. While quite young, he won literary fame to some extent. In 1910, he was graduated from the Kantung Normal Shool and since then, he worked as an instructor of the primary school. However, perceiving that the Manchu dynasty neglected education, and that in China, opportunities were not given him, he went to South Sea Islands and interested himself in the education of his own countrymen staying abroad. When Kantung claimed its independence on the outbreak of the Revolution, accompanning Huang Ming Tang, he reached Chang Men with a view to escape the trouble. When the Republic was established, he was elected to a member of the House of Commons in the 2nd year of the Republic; when the Imperial Question was mooted, he collected men around him to oppose the movement. When the Parliament was re-opened, he was returned for the House of Commons.

羅永慶　字善庭　歲五十三

選舉地　奉天省
籍貫　奉天省興京縣
住址　北京樹胡同二十三

君爲人精明強幹。長於事務才。維新後。極意留心時務。遍覽新書。雖公事旁午。每日必有一定讀書之時。故於各方面學識。皆畧有心得。以前清陝西候補知縣。歷充山東黃河工防汎監視。陝西督糧倉總辦各要差。至光緒二十四年。回籍創辦城鄉國民學校。並充勸學總董。嗣被選爲府參事會參事員。民國元年冬。國會選舉。被選爲衆議院議員。二年袁政府以暴力停止國會。君回籍經營實業。決計不聞時事。三次革命先期赴滬。與議院諸同人。組織國會議員團。及至袁死。大局底定。國會復活。乃於本年七月杪。由滬來京。仍爲衆議院議員。

君や人と爲り精明強幹にして事務の才あり。維新後心を時勢に留め遍ねく新書を閲し、公事旁午すと雖も日に必す一定讀書の時を有す、故に各方面の學識に於て略ば通曉する所あり。前清陝西候補知縣を以て山東黃河工防汎監視。陝西督糧倉總辦等の職に歷充し、光緒二十四年に至り歸鄉して城鄉國民學校を創立し、又た勸學總董となり、嗣で選ばれて府參事會參事員となる。民國元年の冬、第一次國會議員の選舉に際して衆議院議員に當選す。二年袁政府が國會を停止するや、君郷關に歸りて實業を經營し、暫らく時事を聞かず。第三革命の事起りて後ち、君乃ち馳せて上海に赴き、議員諸同人と國會議員團を組織す。袁世凱死して大局既に定り、國會また復活す、君再び北上して院に到り、仍ほ衆議院議員と爲る。

Mr. Lo Yung Ching, otherwise named Shan Ting, aged fifty three, a native of Hsing King Hsien, Ho Ten Hsing. He is a scholar of practical ability. He pursued with avidity new learning, and even in the busiest moments of his life, he had a definite time for reading which made him conversant with all sorts of information. As an acting governor of the Hsi Ssi Hou Hsien, he attend the riparian works of Chau Tung, Huang Ho. In 1898, he established the Cheng Hsing national school of which he became the director. In 1912, he was returned for the House of Commons, and in the year following when the constitution was suspended, he interested himself in business. When the third Revolution was talked about, he went to Shanghai and formed an association proposing to open the Parliament. With the death of Yuanshi-kai, the general situation was fixed, and when the Parliament was re-opened, he was returned for the House of Commons.

羅永紹　字儀陸　歲四十七

選舉地　衡州

籍　貫　湖南新化縣

住　址　北京西華門石板房新化羅店

君賦性篤實不欺。然天資聰敏。善讀穎
悟。弱冠即有文名。及長。遂以文學見
知于世。當中日戰後。中國方議變法。
君乃首創立實學堂於新化。一時之出洋
學習海陸軍法政及實業者。多出其門
下。旋又創立寶慶中學堂。成立後。東
渡留學。入法政大學。以最優等畢業。
歸國後。留省城創辦湖南遊學預備科。
湖南之科學界。實由此發展。居無何。
又至奉天舉行地方自治。武漢起義。與
藍天蔚等謀蔣駐遼軍隊直搗燕京。師
次灤州。謀未成。南走滬上。與諸民黨
同志組織軍事。民國元年。被選為眾議
院議員。國會解散後。奔走津滬。再渡
日本。以從事於民國之再造。及國會恢
復。遂入京仍為議員。

君賦性篤實欺かず。天資聰敏穎悟なり。弱冠文名あり、
長するに及び、遂に文學を以て世に知らる。日清戰後に
當り。中國力めて變法を議す。君乃ち實學堂を新化に創
立す。一時出洋して海陸軍法政及び實業を習ふ者、多く
其門下に出づ。又た寶慶中學堂を創立す。成立の後、日
本に渡りて留學し、法政大學に入り、最優等を以て卒業
す。國に歸るの後、省城に留り、湖南遊學豫備科を創設
す。湖南の科學界實に此れより發展す。幾くならずして
又た奉天に至り地方自治を圖る。武漢義を起すに當り、
藍天蔚等と謀り、駐遼軍隊を耕り、直ちに北京を搗かん
とす。師灤州に次ぐ。謀未だ成らざるに南のかた上海に
走り、諸民黨の同志と、軍事を組織す。民國元年選ばれ
て衆議院議員と爲る。國會解散後。天津上海間を奔走し
再び日本に渡り、民國の再造に從事す。國會恢復するや
遂に入京して仍ほ衆議院議員と爲る。

民國之精華（傳記）羅永紹先生

四百二十三

Mr. Lo Yung-shao, otherwise named I Lui, aged forty seven, a native of Hsin Hua Hsien, the
Hu Nan Hsing is a pure literary man, and as his name became widely known, he established a school
of his own, out of which many men noteworthy both in navy, army, and business were educated. He is
also the founder of Pao Ching middle school. He went to Japan where he completed his education
graduating from the Hosei University with honours. He stayed at Hsing Cheng where he was also
interrested in educational affairs. In Mukden or Hoten, he assisted in the promotion of the interest of
the civic body. He planned the attack of Peking with Lan Tien-wei, in which he was frustrated. He went
over to Shanghai where he organized an army. He was returned for the House of Commons. When Yuanshi-kai suspended this assembly, he went to Japan, and worked for the reconstruction of the Republic.
When the national assembly was restored, he became a member thereof.

選舉地　山西省
籍貫　山西省朔縣人
住址　北京兵部窪十二

羅繡　字子文　歲三十六

君秉性篤實。讀書喜求實學。不事浮
華。弱冠學爲八股文。即以考求身心性
命以眞義爲前提。不專視此等博取科
甲之手段。故所爲文多菅稿天崇氣慨。
及海內維新。遂決志棄舉業。以廩生入
山西優級師範學校肄業。宣統元年十
二月卒業。派充山西大同府師範學校
教員。二年。由學部審定卒業試恭。奏
獎舉人。以司務籤分學部。三年。到部
供職。民國元年。充山西朔縣教育財政
兩科科長。二年一月。當選爲衆議院
議員。十一月被袁政府追繳議員證書。
遂回籍充廣裕墾牧有限公司經理。自
此絕口不談政治。至國會復活。始入都
就議員職。

君秉性篤實、書を讀みて實學を求め、浮華を事とせず。
弱冠にして八股文を學びしも、即ち身心性命を事とせず。
を眞義として專ら試驗及び弟を念とせず、故に其の文稿氣
慨あり。海內維新するに及び遂に志を決し舉業を棄てて廩
生を以て山西優級師範學校に入り宣統元年十二月其の業
を畢ゆ。山西大同府師範學校敎員となり、二年舉部の檢
定試驗に及第して舉人に奏獎せられ、司務を以て學部に
分たれ、三年舉部に到て職に就く。民國元年に至り山西
省朔縣敎育財政兩科の科長に任す。二年一月選ばれて衆
議院議員となる。旋て袁敎府の壓迫によりて議員證書を
剝奪さるや。遂に田園に歸去來を賦して、廣裕墾牧有限
公司の經理に當り、農事を經營して、暫らく政事を談せ
す、國會重ねて復活するに及び、君亦た召集に應じして
晋京し、再び衆議院議員の職に就く。

Mr. Lo Chie, otherwise called Tzu Wen, aged thirty six, a native of Shao Hsien, the Shan Ssi Hsing is a solid man of self-education. He is far from being trammeled with the ideas possessed by those who go up for the government examination. Therefore what he writes is full of spirit. He gave up the idea of entering the Government service by passing though the examination, he entered the Shan Ssi Normal School, where he was graduated in December 1909. After occupying the Chair of an instructor in th Shan Ssi Yai Tung Normal School, he passed the government examination, and entered into the service of the Government. In 1913, he became the members of the Parliament, but when he was deprived the membership certificated by Yuanshi-kai, he returned to his home where he was interested in agriculture. With the reopening of the Parliament, he was elected to a member thereof.

羅家衡 字象平 歳三十三

選舉地　江西省
籍貫　江西省吉安縣
住址　北京爛縵胡同七聖廟側羅宅

君資質聰穎絕倫。幼讀書。常日誦萬言。及周秦諸子之書。及海內維新尤有文名。然不喜從事舉業。惟殫精經史。詞句意義。皆能備憶不忘。弱冠即銳意西學。慨然以挽救危亡自任。旋以官費留學日本。畢業于早稻田大學政治經濟科。回國後。於江西省垣。發起創設私立江西法政專門學校。並充該校校長及教員。辛亥九月。武昌首義。清軍以全力攻鄂急。君與諸同學謀光復江西。以爲武昌應援。旋任江西內務司長。兵不血双。秩序井然。生靈未遭塗炭民國賴以促成君與有賢大焉。民國元年。被舉爲衆議院議員。國會解散。歸里讀書。不問時事。及國會復活。始來京復出席議院。

民國之精華　（傳記）羅家衡先生

君や資質聰穎絕倫にして博賢強記なり。弱冠にして即ち文名あり。海內維新に及び尤も意を西學に注ぎ、慨然として國家の危急を挽回するを以て自ら任じたり。旋て官費を以て日本に游學し、早稻田大學政治經濟科を卒業す歸國後、江西省城に於て私立江西法政專門學校を發起創設して該校々長及び教員となる。卒亥の歲九月、武昌義を起し、清軍全力を以て武漢の地を攻む、君乃ち同學の諸士と共に江西の獨立を謀りて武昌の應援を爲す。旋て江西內務司長に任じ、及に血ぬらずして秩序井然たり。生靈未だ塗炭に遭はずして、民國賴りて以て促成するを得たるは、君の力預かつて大なり。民國二年舉げられて衆議院議員となり、國會解散されて後ち、田園に歸臥して筆硯に親しみ、燈下書冊を繙きてまだ時事を問はず。第三革命の事成つて國會復活するに及び、君再び出でゝ衆議院議員たり。

Mr. Lo Chia-wu, otherwise called Hsiang Ping, age thirty three, a native of Chi-an Hseng, the Chang Sai Hsiung, is quite celebrated for his ability. He paid his attention to the useful learning, and took it upon himself as his mission to save the country from its fatal situation. He went to Japan when he entered the Waseda University to complete his education. On return to his home, he established the law school in Chang Ssi of which he became the headmaster and instructor. In the trouble of Wu Chung he assisted him in every way, planning for the independence of Chang Ssi. He was appointed to the chief of the Chang Ssi Home Department, and was enabled to restore the order without taking to any blood shed and other radical measures. In 1912, he was elected to a member of the Parliament, but on the dissolution of this assembly, he returned to his native district when he spent his days in scholarly pursuits. With the success of the third Revolution, he was again returned for the House of Commons.

羅增麒 字祥徵 歲三十五

選舉地　廣南省

籍貫　廣西省凌雲縣

住址　北京賈家胡同廣西南館

君爲人精明強幹。洞察事理。思想活
潑。而行動謹嚴。生平不苟言笑。不輕
然諾。居常以緘默自持。然一有發揮。
則又娓娓動人。聽者無不感之應化常
訓其晚輩曰。求工辯。須自少說話起。
求幹練。須自少做事起。與人交。淡而
能久。以其能以恕道待人。雖疾惡崇
善。而未嘗稍露鋒鋩也。前清巳酉拔
貢。法政畢業。充泗鎮邑中學校校長。
民國二年正式國會成立。被選爲衆議
院議員。國會解散後。歸里從事教育。
不談政事。及共和復活。國會重開。遂
來京復爲衆議院議員。

君人と爲り精明強幹にして事理を洞察し思想活潑なり。
而して行動謹嚴。生平苟くも言笑せず然諾を輕々しくせ
ず。居常して人を動かし、聽く者感激して敬服す。常に其の
々として人を動かし、聽く者感激して敬服す。常に其の
後輩を訓して曰く、工辯を求む、多く說くべからず、幹
練を求む、多く爲すべからずと。人と交りて淡として能
く久しく、其の能く寬恕を以て人を待ち、惡を疾み善を
崇ぶと雖も、未だ甞て稍も鋒鋩を露さゐる也、前淸己酉
の拔貢生にして法政學校を卒業し、泗鎮邑中學校長に充
つ、民國二年正式國會成立に際し選ばれて衆議院議員と
爲る。國會解散後、鄉里に歸省して教育に從事し、また
政事を談せず、共和復活して國會重ねて開くるに及び遂
に入京して復た衆議院議員と爲る。

Mr. La Tseng-chi, otherwise called Hsiang Cheng, age thirty five, is a native of Ling-yun, Kuang-hsi province. He is a gentleman of clear understanding and active thoughts. Being naturally of taciturn temperament he appears to be unsociable but when he once starts on talking, what he says is indeed inspiring. He warned his students not to be verbose but to be practical. He is open and large minded to others. In the previous Chinese period he was selected by the government to study law and after graduation of the law college he was appointed to the president of the middle school. In the 2nd year of the Republic he was elected to a member of the Parliament, but when the Parliament was dissolved he went back to his home and was interested in education. With the restoration of the Republic he went to Peking, and resumed his Parliamentary function.

選舉地　西藏
籍　貫　土默特旗人
住　址　北京羅和宮北大門

君賦性篤實誠懇、生平無戲言戲動。然
天賦極高。悟性敏捷。弱冠即著文名。
及長。愈益奮勵求進。謙虛好問。喜聞
藎言。人告以過。必欣然謝之。然若為
過實之譽。則反盛怒形諸顏色。常喜為
貧困者助力。而不輕於允諾。既承諸。
無不成者。以是人愈信用之。同輩中偶
有糾紛。君出調停。無不立即解釋。自
幼富于好奇之性。然其立身行已。多厚
重自持。蓋君之思想極放誕。而行為則
極規則也。在西藏商上。曾當仲及繙
譯員各差。於光緒三十四年。來京。由
達賴喇嘛奏留駐京當差。歷充殖邊學
堂及唐古忒學藏文教員。國會成
立。被選為眾議院議員。正式國會解散後、
鬱鬱獨居。不談時事。及國會復活。始
應召。仍為眾議院議員。

民國之精華　（傳記）　羅桑班覺先生

君賦性篤實にして誠厚、生平戲言妄動なし。天賦極めて
高く悟性亦た敏捷なり。西藏人にして籍を土默旗人に列
す。幼より勵精以て學に志し、長ずるに及びて益々奮勉
して研磋琢磨の功を積み、然かも謙虛自ら持して問を好
み藎言を聞くを喜ぶ。故に其の學に於て其の德に於て顏
る境遇あり。蓋し支那西域を代表せる新進秀才なり。曾
て西藏にありて仔仲及び繙譯員等の職に任じ、前清光緒

三十四年入京し、西藏達賴喇嘛の奏派により北京駐在西
藏派遣員の任に就き。兼て殖邊學校及び唐古忒學藏文教
員等の職に歷充したり。民國樹立して五大民族共和の新
政を賛むるや、二年西藏より推されて正式國會眾議院議
員に當選す。國會解散後、快々として閑居し、また時事
を談せず。國會復活するや、再び其の召集に應じて仍ほ
眾議院議員と為る。

（傳記）羅桑班覺先生

Mr. Lo Sang Pan Chiao, otherwise known as Lu Ting, aged thirty five, is a native of Thibet. Noble in character and quick of understanding, he was deeply interested in his study. As he grew older, he was ready to listen statement of others. His humble attitude in all things were for him a high respect. Among the Thibetans, he is one of the most progressive men. In his own country, he was interested as a translator. In 1908, he entered Peking when he made his stay as a sort of representative of his country. He was at the same time an instructor of the colonial school. At the establishment of the Republic, he was returned for the House of Commons from Thibet. On the suppression of the diet he retired to his native place and never talked of politics. However, with the revival of the Parliament he was again elected to a member of the House of Commons.

羅潤業 字德堂 歲三十

選舉地　新疆省
籍　貫　甘肅鎮番縣
住　址　北京順治門外集成公司舊址

君賦性溫厚。與人交。和藹可親。雖所
素疾惡亦假以顏色。不出惡聲。然爲人
耿直不阿。言行以禮自持。故雖以和婉
待人。而無形中自有不可侵越之界限。
曾未嘗曲巳徇人。枉尺直尋之事。較之
尋常無意識之同流合汚者。自屬大相
逕庭。自幼聰慧好讀。深思明辨。故於
古義之多所領悟。然喜求有用之學。及
海內維新。愈肆力于西學。于新書無所
不覩。前清時選貢。新疆自治研究所畢
業。民國成立後。被選爲衆議院議員。

君賦性溫厚にして人と交るや和藹親むべし。平生憎惡す
る者に對しても顏色を和げて惡聲を加へす。然かも人と
爲り耿直にして阿らす、言行共に禮を以て自ら持す。故
に和婉以て人を待つと雖も、無形の中自から侵すべから
さる限界あり。未だ曾て己を曲げて人に從ひ尺を枉げて
尋を直とするの事を爲さず、之を尋常無意識者の流に
同じて汚に合する者と、自から大に逕庭あり。幼より聰
慧讀を好み深く思索して古義に於て悟得する所多し。然
り而して有用の學を求め、海內維新に及びて、力を西學
に傾け、新書覩ざる所無し。曾て前清時代の選貢生を以
て、新疆自治研究所を卒業す。辛亥革命を革めて憲政共和を
宣布して民國を肇造し、正式國會を成立するや、選ばれ
て衆議院議員と爲る。此次國會復活す、再び出で〻召集
に應じ、現に仍は衆議院議員たり。

Mr. Lo Jun-yeh, sometimes known as Tetang, aged thirty, is a native of Chin-pan, Kan-su province. Naturally being the man of gentle character he was very sociable. He is never obsequious being strong minded he could never bend himself against his own consiousness. He is no time severe. While young he was fond of reading books and studying a useful learning. With the introduction of new civilization he devoted his interests to western learning. In 1911 he was interested in the establishment of the Republic, and, when the Parliament was brought into existence, he was elected to a member of the House of Commons. With the restoration of the Parliament he was summoned to Peking and resumed the parliamentary function.

關文鐸 字振之 歲三十七

選舉地　黑龍江省
籍　貫　黑龍江省綏化縣
住　址　北京後門外鼓樓大街小石橋

君秉性誠篤。不喜浮華。居恆恭謙自持待人以和。然其言動舉止皆確有本末。與人交。和藹可親。而無形中自有不可侵越之界限。自幼好學深思。稚年讀書。即喜推求精義不厭數問。塾師常爲所窘。益契重之。弱冠即有文名。詩文策論。皆有名家風味。年十六。即補弟子員。已酉科取。補拔貢生。時值海內新學勃興。君遂立志棄舉子業。專求有用之學。以應于時勢之人材自任。曾歷充勸學員暨勸學所總董等差。力圖地方教育之普及。旋被選爲諮議局議員。嗣民國告成。被舉爲臨時參議院議員、民國二年正式國會成立。又被選爲衆議院議員。國會解散。歸里讀書。不問時政。五年及國會再行召集。遂又入京。就衆議院議員舊職。

民國之精華　（傳記）　關文鐸先生

君秉性誠篤にして浮華を喜ばず。居常恭謙自ら持し、人を待つに和を以てす。然かも其の言動舉止皆な確として本末あり、人と交りて和藹親むべきも、無形の中自から侵すべからざる威嚴ありて存す。幼より學を好みて深く思索し、少年書を讀みて即ち義理を推求する事を喜ぶ。弱冠早くも文名ありて詩文策論省な名家の風味あり。年十六。即ち弟子員に補し、己酉の試驗に拔貢生に補せらる。時會ま新舉勃興の際、君遂に志を立て、科舉の業を棄て、専ら有用の學を求め時勢に應ずるの人材を以て自ら任す。曾て勸舉員及び勸學所總董等の職に厯充ぶ。旋て選れて諮議局議員と爲る。民國の樹立に嘗り臨時參議院議員に舉げられ。正式國會成立するや、衆議院議員に常選す。國會解散後、鄉里に閑臥して時事を問はず。五年國會再び召集を行ふに及び、遂に又た入京して衆議院議員と爲る。

Mr. Kuan Wen-to, sometimes called Chen chih, a ge thirty seven, is a native of Anka, H ilung Chaina. He is a gentleman of humble character and is always gentle in his manners and quite sociable in every respect, but there is something in him which makes him quite inaccessible to others. While young he was fond of reading and early in life he already attained literary fame. At the age of sixteen he passed the government examination, but shortly after he turned his attention to new learning. He was elected to a member of the local assembly and in the 2nd year of the Republic he was elected to a member of the House of Commons. When the Parliament was opened, he went to Peking and resumed his parliamentary function.

賣應昌　字瑞卿　歲四十五

君秉性溫厚にして人を待つて和を以てす。然かも朴質を喜び浮華に事へず。舉止皆な禮を以て自ら持し、言笑を衒もせず。故に和靄の中復た莊嚴畏るべきの氣象あり。少年書を讀みて能く理義を明にし、年方に弱冠にして旣に經書を畢りて子史の書に及び。長ずるに及びて尤も努めて淵博を求め、廣く群書を繙さて、其の文を作るや、歐蘇を摹び、學派則ち漢宋の間を調和す。海內維新に及ぶや、愈々學理を研究し、頗る敎育を改良し民智を開通

選舉地　陝西省

籍貫　陝西省鳳翔縣。

住址　北京校場六條胡同路北劉宅

君秉性溫厚。待人以和。然喜朴質。不事浮華。舉止皆以禮自持。不苟言笑。故和靄之中。復寓有莊嚴可畏之氣象。稚齡讀書。即能深造有得。明于理義。年方弱冠。即已畢諸經。旁及子史。及長。尤務求淵博。廣覽羣書。其爲文崇歐蘇。而學派則調和漢宋之間。謂宜明義理以定訓釋之優劣。宜精考据以求古義之精微。二者兼重。不執一偏。及海內維新。愈篤志研究學理。頗以改良敎育開通民志爲己任。以前淸舉人主講正誼書院。歷任鳳翔縣高等小學校校長。兼敎員。敎育會會長。勸學所總董鳳翔府中學校兼師範傳習所敎員。民國元年被舉爲陝西省諮議會議員。二年被舉爲參議院議員。國會解散後。歸里任陝西省立第二中學校敎員。及鳳翔縣學務局學董。及國會重開。始入都仍任參議院議員。

するを以て己が任とす。前淸舉人を以て正誼書院の主講となり、鳳翔縣高等小學校長兼敎員、敎育會長、勸學所總董、鳳翔府中學校兼師範傳習所敎員等の職に歷任す。民國元年陝西省諮議會議員となり。國會解散後、鄉里に歸りて陝西省立第二中學校敎員及び、鳳翔縣學務局學董に任す。五年國會復活するに及び、再び其の召集に應じて上京し、仍ほ參議院議員に任す。

Mr. Chia Ying-chang, otherwise known as Jui Chiang, age forty five, is a native of Feng hsiang, Hsia hsi province. He is gentle and sociable in his character. Being simple in his habit he is deadly opposed to anything vain and pompous. He regulated himself by strict code of ettiquett. In the midst of geniality there is something austere in his personality. He was an intelligent reader of books and was well posted up in historical writings. As he grew older, he distinguished himself for his diction which bore similality to well known classial writers. When the new trend of thought was introduced to the country, he directed his attention to the new study, and made it point to improve the intellectual condition of his country men. In the previous chinese regime, he passed the civil service examination with success, and was appointed to the heads of educational institutions of his province. In the 1st year of the Republic he was elected to a member of the Hsia hsia Assembly. When the Parliament was officially summoned he was elected to a member of the House of Commons. However, with the dissolution of the Parliament he returned to his country, and interested himself in the education of the young men of his province. When the Parliament was restored, he went up to Peking and became a member of the Senate.

嚴天駿 字仲良 歲四十六

選舉地　雲南省

籍貫　雲南省新興縣

住址　北京新簾子胡同四十七

君為人恪勤耐勞。自待極薄而喜為人盡力。人有所託。雖所不能。亦必勉為助力。事成決不受人酬報。故里人皆敬愛之。偶有糾紛得君一言無不立釋。自幼聰穎好讀。弱冠即有文名。然虛心好問。喜出讜言。故其進益猛。曾前清光緒辛卯舉人。乙巳留學日本。東京弘文學院師範畢業。歸滇為徵江府師範傳習所教長。己酉官湖北長陽知縣。民國初年。被選舉為眾議院議員。著有玉湖詩文集各六卷。日京參觀瑣錄一卷。行政隨錄二卷。五年八月及國會重開。始來京仍為眾議院議員。

民國之精華　（傳記）嚴天駿先生

君人と為り恪勤にして勞に耐へ、自ら待つこと極めて薄きも、人の為に力を致すを喜ぶ。人若し託する所あれば難事と雖も亦た必ず勉めて助力し、事成つて決して人の報酬を受けず、里人皆な之を敬愛し、偶ま紛糾あるも君の一言を得て立どころに解決せざる無し。幼より聰穎にして學を好み、弱冠即ち文名あり。然かも心を虛ふして問を好み、讜言を聞くを及ぶ。故に其の進步益々著しきものありたり。前清光緒辛卯の學人にして乙巳の歲日本に留學し、宏文學院師範科を卒業す。歸國後、雲南徵江府師範傳習所教長と爲る。己酉の歲、湖北省長陽縣知事に任ず。民國二年正式國會眾議院議員に當選す。業餘著作に親み、玉湖詩文集各六卷、日京參觀瑣錄一卷、行政隨錄二卷等の著あり。五年國會復活さるゝに及び、再び起きて其の召集に應じ、現に仍は眾議院議員たり。

Mr. Yen Tien-chun, otherwise known as Chung liang, age forty six, is a native of Hsin yu, Yun nan province. He is a laborious and hard working student. He takes great delight in doing for the benefit of others even in his own expense. He would, if asked by others, face even the most difficult matter, and extend him helping hands, never even for a moment dreaming of compensation. In these respects, he is highly respected by his own countrymen. Even if there are troubles, his one word is enough to settle all. Even when quite young, he obtained a certain literary fame. He is open-minded and ready to listen to the advice of others. This fact alone helps him in making progress in any line of work proposed by him. He came to Japan when he was educated in the normal school department of the Kobun Gaku-in. On returning to his home, he was appointed to the headmaster of the normal school in the Yun Nan Province. In 1909, he was appointed to the governor of the province. In the second year of the Republic, he was elected to a member of the House of Commons, while in this capacity, he wrote many books on poetry. When the Parliament was restored, he responded to the summon, and was returned for the House of Commons.

蘇祐慈 字子和 歲五十

選舉地　廣東省
籍　貫　廣東省順德縣碧江卿
住　址　北京珠巢街南四門牌十號

君爲人精明強幹。富於忍耐。然鯁直好義人有過。輒直斥不諱。甚至聲色俱厲。而賦性朴質。不喜浮華。讀書博而能約。故所讀皆足以爲經世濟物之資及有益于身心者。詞章之屬亦常隨意涉獵。不專力於斯。故能爲詩歌。而不喜常作。每有所作。必極其妙。以大都於感慨淋漓時。一寫其至性至情。非尋常雕蟲刻鏤者可比也。於前清以附貢生出身。至花翎候選道。歷充廣東地方自治研究社社員。順德地方自治會會長。順德第三區地方自治會正會長。順德碧江卿蘇姓地方自治會正會長。順德第三區紅十字會正會長。西淋都八十一卿公立高等小學校校長。旅京廣東兩等小學校校長。順德縣議會代議士。國會成立。被選爲衆議院議員。國會解散。歸里從事公益事業。及國會復活。始入都仍充議員。

君人と爲り精明強幹にして忍耐に富む。然も鯁直義を好み、人過あれば輒ち直斥して諱まず。甚だしきに至つては聲色俱に厲し。而して賦性朴質にして浮華を喜ばず、其の讀書は博くして能く約し、經世濟物の資料となり、或は身心の修養に益ある者は、詞章詩歌の類と雖も隨意之を涉獵す。前清附貢生のを出身以て、花翎候選道臺に至る。廣東地方自治研究社々員、地方自治會々長、順德地方自治會正會長、順德第三區地方自治會正會長、順德第三區紅十字會正會長、西淋都八十一鄉公立高等小學校々長、旅京廣東等小學校々長等の職に歷任し。選ばれて順德縣議會議員と爲る。民國二年正式國會衆議院議員に常選す。國會解散後、鄉里に歸りて、地方公益事業に從事したり。五年國會復活するや、再び其の召集に應じて入京し。仍は衆議院議員の職に就く。

Mr. Su Yu-tzu, sometimes known as Tzu Hai, age fifty, is a native of Shin-te, Kuang tung province. He is a gentleman of intelligence and ability, being rich in that enviable quality of patience. He is earnest and loves justice. Simple in nature, he hates vain pomp. He is a copious reader of books which he uses as the materials for his statesmanship. He is keenly interested in self-culture, and any book relative to that is fully appreciated by him. He is the head of various civic associations in his province, and at the same time, he is a member of the local assembly. In the second year of the Republic, he was elected for the House of Commons. On the dissolution of the Parliament, he returned to his native country where he was interested in enterprises calculated to the benefit of the public. With the dissolution of the Parliament, he went to Peking where he was returned for the House of Commons.

饒芙裳　字芙裳　歲六十一

選舉地　廣東省
籍　貫　廣東省梅縣
住　址　北京延壽寺三眼井三號謝宅

君早年以文學知名。中年旁研西學。於新書無所不讀。前清以舉人選知縣。見朝政日非。隱不仕。嘗與溫仲和。丘逢甲黃遵憲。在潮州汕頭梅縣各地。倡辦新學。所成嶺東同文學校。梅縣師範學校。體育傳習所。及各初高小學校。凡十數所。造就人材甚眾。後為梅縣勸學所總董。更提挈督率。自梅縣中學以下小學。專門工藝暨女學等。增設至二百餘校。民氣益為丕變。時溫丘黃三君先後謝世。潮梅學界獨尊之如泰斗先季氏。因革命黨嫌疑。避地南洋。遍歷馬來半島蘇門答臘諸埠。所至復鼓吹華僑興學。尤得各大資本家信服。手創庇能時中學校。而於出入海外黨人多庇能之。辛亥光復。回國。任廣東全省教育司長。民國元年冬辭職。遂由第三選舉區與為眾議院議員。二年。國會為袁氏蹂躪。復走南洋。今國會重開。乃回京在院仍教育股委員。

民國之精華　（傳記）　饒芙裳先生

君早年文學を以て名あり、中年傍ら西學を研究す。前清舉人を以て知縣に選用さる。朝政日に非なるを以て隱れて仕を欲せず。曾て溫仲和、丘逢甲、黃遵憲と潮州汕頭梅縣各地に薪學を興し、嶺東同文學校、梅縣師範學校、體育傳習所及び十數箇の初高各小學校を創設したり。後ち梅縣勸學所總董に任じ、梅縣中學校下小學校、專門工藝學校女學校等增設して二百餘校に至る。光緒末年、革命黨の嫌疑により南洋に避けて各地を歷游し、至る所の華僑に興學の事を鼓吹し、庇能時中學校を創立經營し、又た海外に出入する黨人を庇護したり。辛亥の歲、漢土光復するや、歸國して廣東全省の教育司長に任す。民國元年冬、職を辭して正式國會衆議院議員に當選す。旋り國會が袁氏の蹂躪する所となるや、復た南洋に走す。五年國會重ねて開く、乃ち召集に應じて入京し、現に衆議院議員たり。

Mr. Jao Fu-shang, is a native of Mei-hsien, Kuang-tung hsing. Early in life he studied literature and as he grew older he turned his attention to the study of the western learning. In the previous Chinese regime he was elected to the governor, but observing the decline of the government he never accepted the appointment. He established schools of new learning in different parts of his province, numbering in all over 200 previous. At the last days of the Chinese government having suspected as a Revolutionist he went to South Sea islands where he taught where he inspired many of the Chinese staying there. He established schools for the purpose of educating his own country men. In 1911 when Revolution succeeded he returned to his country where he was chiefly interested in educational works. He was then elected to a member of the House of Commons. When the Parliament was trampled down by Yuan Shi-kai he went to South Sea Islands. However, with the election of the new president, he went to Peking and again entered the Parliament.

饒應銘 字鼎三 三十八

選舉地 四川省
籍貫 四川省越嶲縣
住址 北京未市胡同延賓館

君賦性敦厚溫和。與人交。和靄可親。雖仇敵亦假以顏色。不出惡聲。然爲人篤實不欺。動止以禮自持。雖長於交際。而無形中自有不可侵越之界限。曾未嘗曲己從人。較之碌碌追隨俗者。自屬大相逕廷。自幼好讀。喜博覽羣書。任意所之以爲快。而不屑規規然從事于科舉之業。故其讀書。純以至主觀判斷之是非。而不局于習俗之成見。及海內維新。慾立志求有用之學。於新書無所不覩。旋肄業于四川高等學校。畢業後。曾充本省正式省會議員。歷任本省將軍署巡按使公署顧問。正式國會成立。當選爲參議院議員。兼憲法起草會委員。國會解散後。恆以沉極自持。無所表見。及國會復活。始來京仍爲參議院議員。

君賦性敦厚にして溫和、人と爲りて和藹親むべし。然も人と爲り誠實にして欺かず、動止共に體を以て自ら持し交際に巧みなりと雖も、無形の中自から侵越すべからざるの限界を有し、未だ曾て己を曲げて人に從ひたること無し。幼より學を好み、群籍を涉獵し、其の書を誠むや主觀を以て是非を判斷す。海內維新に及び志を立てゝ新學を攻究し、即ち四川高等學校に學びて其の業を畢へた

り。辛亥命を革めて民國成立するや、選ばれて四川省正式省議書議員となり。次で四川將軍衙門及び間巡接使衙門の顧問に歷任したり。民國二年正式國會參議院議員に當選し、憲法起草委員に舉げらる。國會解散後は常に消極的態度を持して政治上何等の表見を敢てせざりし、五年約法恢活して、國會再蘇するに及び、再び出でゝ名集に應じ、仍は參議員議員の職に就く。

Mr. Jao Ying-ming, known as Tsing Sa, is a native of Yueh Sui, the Ssi Churu province. He is sociable and gentle, and quite charming in his ways. Although sociable, he does not fall into the state of flatterer. In a certain respect, he is a gentleman possessing high virtues which distinguish him from others. He never realise himself against conscience. He was a copious reader of books, and a good judge of what he read. He was interested in the new learning, and was graduated from Ssi Shang High school then the republic was established, he was elected to a member of the Local Assembly, and was adviser to the Governor General of the Ssi Chuan province. In the second year of the Republic, he was elected to a member of the Senate and was on the committee for drafting the constitution. On the dissolution of the Parliament by Yuanshi-kai, he never gave publicity to his views; when the Parliament was re-opened, however, he was appointed to a member of the Senate.

龔煥辰　字北居　歲三十七

選舉地　西藏
籍　貫　四川省江津縣
住　址　北京西單牌樓東鐵匠胡同西口

君秉性嚴正。疾惡如仇。久于新聞事業。常以痛惡時下自號名流者。率以權謀術數相尙。恆攻擊無稍隱諱。以是于京中新聞界頗有直聲。又長于文學。喜為詩歌。存稿甚多。人或勸其發刊。則曰。吾尙未敢自信也。君雖非由革命起家。而饒有民黨氣質。其為國人所欽仰。自辛亥武漢起義以前。蓋四川鐵路風潮。以君爭之為最力。迭次幾陷于險。則關數千里。呼號于各省南至廣東。所亡感動。厥功甚偉。民國二年經西藏選舉會選為參議院議員。國會解散後。仍從事新聞事業。為暫避專制淫威故。稍歛其筆鋒。國會復活。復就議員職。仍就執事新聞。為醒華報主任。

民○之精華　（傳記）　龔煥辰先生

君秉性嚴正にして惡を疾むこと仇の如し。久しく新聞事業に從事し、所謂名士なる者相率ゐて權謀術數を尙ぶを痛惡して、常に之に筆誅を加ふ。君文學に長じて詩歌を善し、存稿甚だ多し。君革命の先輩にあらざるも、民黨的の氣質に富む。辛亥第一革命勃發以前、鐵道國有問題反對の風潮洶湧たるや、君最も大聲疾呼するに努め、幾度が危地に陷りたるも、屈せず撓まずして民論を喚起した

り旋て革命の事成りて民國を樹立し、漢滿蒙回藏の五大民族共和の新政を創むるや、民國二年西藏選舉會より推されて、正式國會參議院議員に當選したり。國會解散後は專ら新聞事業に從事して暫らく專制の淫威を避け、暫らく稍や其の筆鋒を和げ、以て時運の到來を待ちたり。斯くて再び約法復活して國會再蘇するに及び、召集に應じて仍ほ參議院議員の職に就き、兼て醒華報を主宰す。

Mr. Kong Huan-chen, otherwise known as Pe Chu, age thirty seven, is a native of Chiang Chin, Ssi Chuan province. He is a gentleman of straight forward character, and great hater of evils. He was interested in the journalism, and vehemently attacked crafty politicians who are always guilty of political intrigues. Although not the leader of revolutionists, he is in favour of the People's Party. When the nationalization of railways was a public question, before the outbreak of the war, he was one of the strongest advocate of the people's party. When the Revolution came to be the fact, he was elected to a member of the Senate from the constituency of Thibet in the second year of the Republic. After the shutting up of the Parliament, he was interested in journalism, quiety waiting for his oportunity. As soon as the Parliament was re-opened, he was elected to a member of the Senate, the position he holds even in the present moment.

金鼎勳 字叔奮 歲三十八

選舉地　吉林省
籍　貫　直隸省
住　址　北京後居子大園

君秉性誠厚篤實。尚質惡文。爲人精明
強幹。與人交。崇節義。重然諾。然天資
絶高。悟性敏捷。而頭腦細密。其言論
思想。皆秩序井然。絶無顛倒紊亂之
弊。自幼讀書。即喜探索精義。及長。博
覽羣書。尤注意經世之學。深思明辨。
洞悉事理。夙以天下棟梁之材自任以
挽救危亡自期。曾貢笈東渡。留學日
本。入東斌學校。嗣畢業明治大學校。
辛亥年。充吉林民軍司令。頗有功勳。
民國元年。被選爲參議院議員。翼贊民
國建設之偉業。二年正式國會成立。被
選爲參議院議員。把持正義。提倡讜
議。院內外推重之。國會停止後。赴湖
北。本年簡充江漢道道尹。現值國會再
開。辭去道尹及內務部參事。遂應召。
仍充參議院議員。

君秉性誠厚篤實にして質を尚ぶ文を惡み。人と爲り精明
強幹にして、人と交りて節義を崇び然諾を重んず。然か
も天資絶高にして悟性敏捷、頭腦周密、其の言論思想皆な
秩序井然として、絶へて顛倒紊亂の弊なし。幼より書を讚
みて精義を探究するを喜び、長じて博覽強記、尤も經世
の學に注意し、深く思索して事理を明察す。夙に天下棟
梁の材を以て自ら任じ、國家の危亡を挽回するを以て自
ら期したり。曾て日本に留學し、東斌學校を經て明治大
學校を卒業す。辛亥の歲、吉林民軍司令に任じて功勳あ
り。民國元年臨時參議院議員に選ばれ、二年正式國會參
議院議員に常選す。國會停止するや湖北に赴き、後ち任
せられて江漢道道尹と爲り。又た內務部參事官に任す。
此次國會復活して再び召集を行ふに及び、行政の要職を
辭して立法府の人となり、現に仍は參議院議員たり。

Mr. Chin Ting-hsun, another name Shu Fen, a native of Chi-liu hsing, is a man of sincerity and generous mind. He used to render his service at any cost for others, if once entrusted with something. Having a quick perception caused by his clear brain, his arguments are so systematical that there is not a least disturbance in them at any time. He is a man of wide reading and strong memory and convinced it to be his mission to save his country from its fatal condition. He once visited Japan and graduated from Meiji University. After return to his country he was appointed to the Commander of Chilin militia. In the 1rst year of the Republic he was elected to a member of the Senate, and next year he was formally elected to the same. After the suspension of the Parliament he was appointed to the Governor of Chiang-han tao, and subsequently to the Councillors of the Home Department. As soon as the Parliament is restored, he was again elected to a member of the Senate, which post he now holds.

馬文煥　字化封　歲六十一

選舉地　直隸省

籍　貫　直隸省香河縣

住　址　北京西交民巷前紅井

君賦性仁厚。喜周濟貧困。常傾囊無吝色。然平時自奉甚薄。不知者見其計及錙銖莫能辦其爲慨慷好義之人也。以前清貢生。光緒三十二年。直隸初創警察。群情疑沮。君在籍任警務總董。毅然倡辦。規畫嚴整。故彼時香河警察爲各屬之冠。三十三年。由直督調入北洋法政專門學校紳班肄業卒業。回籍辦理地方自治。宣統二年舉貢會考取中。簽分山西補用知縣。歷任要差。三年九月。赴大同辦公。適值太原兵變。路梗不通。遂由京張鐵路回籍。民國元年。改歸直隸補用知縣。曾任本縣高小學校校長。勸學所長。理財所長。保衛局長。兼任保衛局長時。值大局初定。境內盜匪蜂起君遂購備槍械。創辦民團。閭閻安枕。旋被選衆議院議員。

君性仁厚にして貧困を周濟する事を喜ぶ。常に愛を傾けて客ひ色無し。然も平時自ら奉すること甚だ薄し。前清の貢生を以て、光緒三十二年直隸省に於て初めて新警察を創設するや、君警務總董に任じ、規畫嚴整にして香河縣警察は省內各州縣に冠たり。三十三年直隸總督より選拔されて北洋法政專門學校紳士部に入りて學び、卒業後歸縣して地方自治を處理す。宣統二年會考に及第して山西補用知縣となり、各要職に歷任す。三年九月大同に赴く。適ま太原の兵變に際し、道路極塞して通せず、遂に京張鐵道により歸鄉す。民國元年直隸補用知縣に改められ、香河縣高等小學校長、勸學所長、現財所長、保衛局長に任す。其の保衛局長に兼任せる時、管內匪賊蜂起す銃器を購入して民團を創設して閭閻を安んじたり。旋て正式國會衆議院議員に當選し、此頃復た再び召集されて議員の職に在り。

Mr. Ma Wen-huan, otherwise known as Hu Feng is a native of Hsiang Ho, Chi Lin province. Being naturally a man of charity he is keenly interested in helping the poor. He never grudges in doing this work. In 1906, when the new police system was adopted in Chi lin province, he was appointed to the head of the police. In 1907 he was appointed to the governor-general of Chi Lin when he studied law in the Pe Yang law school. After graduating from the institution he went back to his province where he was interested in the development of local civic institute. In 1910 he passed the civil examination and occupied vasious posts of great importance. In the 1st year of the Republic he was appointed to the head of the high school, the chief of the financial office as well as that of the sanitary bureau. In the latter capacity he assisted the formation of the militia to guard against the rise of bandits by making the purchase of riffles. When the Parliament was summoned he was elected to a member of the House of Commons. With the dissolution of the Parliament, however, he was again appointed to a member of the House of Commons.

民國之精華　（傳記）　馬文煥先生

萬鈞 字舉之 歲四十一

選舉地　貴州省

籍　貫　貴州省鎮遠縣

住　址　北京宣武門內象來街八號

君秉性耿介不阿。不隨俗尚。然爲人溫恭謙讓。待人以和。雖仇敵。亦不加以惡聲。自幼讀書。喜求有用之學。不拘守舉業。前清時。以貢生。入法政講習所。畢業後。歷充鎮遠勸學員長。兩等學校校長。自治研究所所長。勸業員長。旋創辦農事試驗場自充場長。宣統三年被選爲城議會議員。因反正辦團著有功績。核明存記錄用。民國元年。被選爲省議會議員。閉會後。充森林警察講習所所長。旋選爲省農會副會長。民國二年。被選爲衆議院議員。國會解散後。黔巡按使電調晉省。任爲修文縣知事。經前巡按使龍。電請中央獎給七等嘉禾章。此次國會重開。乃由修文縣解職。入京仍爲衆議院議員。

君性耿介にして阿らず、俗尚に隨はず。然かも人と爲り温良恭謙にして人を待つに和を以てす。幼より書を讀みて尤も有用の學を求め、長じて興學に志す。前清時代貢生を以て法政講習所に入りて業を畢ゆ。鎮遠縣勸學員長兩等學校長、自治研究所長、勸業員長等の職に歷充し、旋て農業試驗場を創設して場長と爲る。宣統三年縣議會議員に選ばれ、民國元年選ばれて省議會議員と爲る。省議會閉會後、森林警察講習所長に任じ、旋て選ばれて省農會副長となる。民國二年正式國會衆議院議員に當選す國會解散後は、貴州巡按使の招きにより貴州に歸り、修文縣知事に任す。地方行政官として治蹟大に著れ、巡按使の保管により七等嘉禾章を授けらる。五年國會復活するに及び、修文縣知事の職を辭して召集に應じ、現に入京して仍は衆議院議員たり。

Mr. Wan Chun, age forty one, is a native of Chin Yuan, Kuei Chou hsing. He is a gentleman of independent spirit keeping aloof from the ordinary channel of the people. In dealing with others he is gentle and honest. While young he sought a youthful learning. He studied the law and occupied a series of important post in his province. He was the head of industrial encouragement bureau. He also established the agricultural experimental farm at his own expence of which he became the president. In the 1st year of the Republic he became the member of the Local Assembly. He was also appointed to the Vice-president of the Agricultured Society. In the 2nd year of the Republic he was returned for the House of Commons, but when the Parliament was closed by Yuanshi-Kai he was appointed to one of the local governors, in which capacity his merits have appeared. When the Parliament was revived, he entered Peking and became a member of the House of Commons.

婁鴻聲　字醒園　歲四十四

選舉地　吉林省

籍貫　吉林省賓縣

住址　北京中鐵匠胡同五號

君性慷慨。少具大志。且敦品勵學。顏賈時譽。因鑒清廷失政。大局日非。故於登庸後。淡情仕進。專以提倡學校。振興實業爲已任。宣統三年。籌辦地方自治。被選爲吉林賓州府議會議長之職。地方興革。多賴擘畫。民國元年。公推爲吉林臨時省議會議員。是時陳昭常督吉。弊端叢生。財政紊亂。省議會提案彈劾君實力主其議。正式省議會成立時。復又被選爲省議會議員。民國二年國會成立。被選爲參議院議員。君因挂名國民黨籍。於是年十月取消國民黨議員時。亦橫遭蹂躪。迨國會停止。君知時局日非國事難。爲逡携眷旋里。往吉省東邊綏遠縣。領荒招墾。藉避強暴。自帝制發生。滇南首義。兩院議員均集滬上。君膺眞奉嚴命。亦潛行赴滬。追隨諸同志之後。迨共和復活。國會重開。仍來京。就參議院議員之職。

君性慷慨にして幼より大志あり、品に敦く學に勵み、顏る聲譽を荷ふ。清廷政を失して國政日に非なるに鑒み、學界を擧へて後ち仕官を思はず、專ら教育の普及と實業の振興を以て己が任と爲す。宣統三年吉林賓州府議會議長に擧げらる。民國元年吉林臨時省議會議員に擧げらる。二年正式國會の組織に際し參議院議員に常選す。

君國民黨員たるの故を以て袁氏の非法命令によりて議員職を剝奪され、次で國會停止するや、君昨局の非を慨し、て遂に鄕里に歸り、吉林省東邊の綏遠縣に赴きて開墾に從事し、以て袁氏の橫暴を避く。帝制問題發生して雲南義を首め、兩院議員の多く上海に集るや、君亦た潛に上海に赴き參加す。共和復活して國會重ねて開くるに及び仍ほ入京して參議院議員たり。

民國之精華　（傳記）　婁鴻聲先生

Mr. Lu Hung-sheng, otherwise known as Hsing Yuan, forty four years of age, is a native of Pin Hsien, Chi Lin province While young, he was ambitions, and deeply interested in study, Perceiving the maladministration at the later days of the Chinese government, he gave up the idea of serving the government, but was chiefly interested in the diffusion of education and building up of the industry. In 1911, he was elected to the president of the Pin-hsieng Assembly of Chi Lin, and in the first year of the Republic, he was a member of the Special Assembly in Chi Lin. When the Parliament was summoned, he was returned for the Provincial Assembly, and in the second year of the Republic, he was elected to a member of the Senate. Because he is a member of the National party, he was deprived of his Parliamentary priviledge and the Parliamant itself was shut up, so that he went back to Chili, and was engaged in farming in his province. When Yuanshi-kai's Imperial Movement took place, he came up to Shanghai together with representatives of other province. When the Republic was restored, he came up to Peking, and became a member of the Senate.

翟富文　字麗軒　歲五十一

選舉地　廣西省

籍貫　廣西省來賓縣

住址　北京賈家胡同柳州會館

君爲人莊重篤厚。不苟言笑。年少即博覽羣書。頗以大器自期。前清時以廩膳生舉于鄉。戊戌會試。報罷歸里。主講雷江書院。甲辰。投學兩廣學務處練習所。旣畢業。在本籍聯合同人創設橋濟兩等小學校。次年。代表縣父老至粵會議廣西鐵路。旋充旅穗廣西師範傳習所監學。是冬。歸州籌辦柳州中學。奉委充監督。居無何。轉廣西提學司學務公所議紳。民國元年。被選爲廣西臨時省議會議員。二年一月。被選爲衆議院議員。國會解散。歸里獨居不問世事。及至共和恢復。國會續開。始至京。仍供舊職。

君人と爲り莊重篤厚なり。幼より學を求めて博覽強記、長じて益々刻苦精勵研磋倦まず、其の業頗る進境あり。

前清時代、廩膳生を以て郷に舉げられ、戊戌の會試に應じて歸郷し、雷江書院の講師となる。甲辰の歲、兩廣學務處練習所に學び、卒業して後ち郷里に往りて同人と共に橋濟兩等小學校を創設す。次年縣の父老を代表して廣東に至り廣西鐵道問題を議す。旋て族穗廣西師範傳習所監學に任じ、後ち柳州中學校を創立し託せられて其の監督と爲る。居ること幾くも無く、轉じて廣西提學司學務公所議紳と爲る。民國元年選ばれて廣西臨時省議會議員と爲り、二年正式國會衆議院議員に當選す。國會解散するや郷里に歸りて時事を問はず、時に出でゝ地方興學する所あるのみ。共和恢復して國會再び開院さるゝに及び、遂に入京して仍は衆議院議員と爲る。

Mr. Chui Fu Wen, known as Li Hsien, age fifty one, is a native of Lei Pin hsien, Kuang-hsi hsing. He distinguished himself among his fellowmen for his wonderful memory. As he grew older he proved himself to be a dilligent student. During the previous Chinese regime, in 1898 he passed the civil examination successfully and was appointed to an instructor in one of the schools. In 1904 he established a primary school in his province. In the year following he went to Kuangtung to discuss the railway question on behalf of the people of his native town. He was also a fonder of Lieu Chou middle school of which he became the inspector. In the 1st year of the Republic he was elected to a member of the special local assembly of Kuang-hsi while in the 2nd year he became a member of the House of Commons. When the Parliament was disolved he returned to his native province and showed no interest in politics. From time to time he was interested in the education of the local people. When the Republic was restored and the Parliament was re-opened he appointed to a member thereof.

孫　鐘　字震東　歲二十八

選舉地　蒙古

籍貫　河南省祥符縣

住址　北京西太平街

君秉性聰穎敏捷。為人才氣縱橫。頭腦明晰。辨舌流暢。雖國學之所造不深。於新學能精通員義。光緒二十八年肄業于北洋大學露語本科。三十一年遂以自費留學日本。初入航海學校。肆業。後入中央大學經濟本科。以成績優良。為特待生。宣統二年以優等畢業。歸國後。應學部試。為舉人。授財政部主事。充陸軍測量學校。豫學校各教員。民國元年被選為臨時參議院議員。國會成立。由蒙古被選為衆議院議員。被舉為憲法起草委員。任國民黨幹事。後與一部同志改組政友會。被舉為政務討論會長。曾在國民黨時。與白逾恒景定成。創辦國風日報。皷吹共和。謳歌袁氏。及國會重開。遂又應召。仍為衆議院議員。

君秉性聰慧敏捷、才氣縱橫なり。頭腦明晰にして辨舌流暢、議政壇上稀有の雄辨家なり。國學の造詣未だしと雖も新學の素養深し。光緒二十八年北洋大學露語本科を修し、三十一年遂に自費を以て日本に留學し、初め航海學校に入り、後ち中大央經濟本科に學びて特待生となり、宣統二年優等を以て卒業す。歸國後學部試驗に應じて擧人と爲り、財政部主事を授けらる。陸軍測量學校、豫學校等の敎鞭を執る。民國元年臨時參議院議員と爲り、二年蒙古より選ばれて衆議院議員となり、憲法起草委員に舉げらる。曾て國民黨幹事に任じ、後ち政友會の組織に盡力して政務討論會長に任す。曾て國民黨に在る時、白逾恒景定成等と國風日報を發刊して共和を皷吹し、帝政發生後上海神州日報社長に任じて袁氏を謳歌せり。國會再び召集を行ふに及び、復た衆議院議員の職に就く。

民國之精華　（傳記）　孫鐘先生

Mr. Sun Chung, sometimes called Chen Tung, as a native of Hsiang-fu, Ho Nan province. He is the possessor of clear head and eloquent tongue. In the Parliament he was one of the most powerful debators. In 1902 he entered the Peyan University and in 1898 he went to Japan at his own expense where he was a student of the Chuo-University and given a scholarship. In 1912 he was graduated with honours. On returning to his country he was appointed to an instructors of the military surveying school and the chief of the Financial Bureau. In the 1st year of the Republic, he was elected to a member of the local Assembly and in the 2nd year of the Republic he was elected from Mongolia and was returned for the House of Commons and subsequently was appointed to the Committee for the drifting of the constitution. He was interested in the cause of Yuanshi-kai when the Imperial Movement took place. Under the new president when the Parliament was summoned he was returned for the House of Commons.

廖宗北 字灑川

選舉地　湖北省

籍貫　湖北省荊門縣

住址　北京都城隍廟街三

君賦性仁厚。自幼以孝行見知于鄉里。
為人精明強幹。洞察事理。少年讀書。
慕古任俠之所其。其為詩文。多激昂悲
壯之詞。能使人感發興奮。稍長。喜為
義舉。見人不平。常奮不顧身。欲捨身
為之報復。唯一念及身體髮膚之訓。則
又自給其不孝。遂專從事於周濟貧乏。
不復為從井救人之舉。人有困於資者。
常典鬻所有助之。不自為緩急之計以
定鄉里皆奉若神仙。里中偶有爭報常
求取決於君。君出一言。無不立即解
釋。曾日本法政大學專門部政治科畢
業。民國二年。正式國會成立。被選為
眾議院議員。國會解散後。遇事持消極
主義。絕無表見。及國會復活。遂復為
眾議院議員。

君賦性仁厚にして幼より孝行を以て鄉里に知らる。人と
為り精明強幹にして事理を洞察す。少年書を讀みて古任
俠の所為を慕ひ、其の詩文多くは激越の調あり。稍や長
じて義舉を喜び、人の不平を見て常に奮つて身を願みず、
唯だ一たび身體髮膚の訓を念ふに及び、自ら其の不孝を
答めて、遂に專ら貧乏を周濟する事に從事し、復た井に
從つて人を救ふの舉を為さゞる也。曾て笠を負ふて東海

を渡り、新進の隆強たる日本に留學して法政大學專門部
政法科を卒業したり。歸國後、民國二年正式國會の成立
に際し、選ばれて眾議院議員と為る國會解散して後ち、
事每に消極主義を持し、絕て華々しき活動を為さず。五
年國會復活して召集を行ふや、遂に復た出でゝ之に應じ、
北上入京して現に仍は眾議院議員たり。

Mr. Liao Tsung-pe, otherwise called Hui chuan, is a native of Ching-men, Hu-pei province. While quite young, he was known to his own countymen for his filial obedvince. He had a profound insight. While young, he was a great admirer of books, and proved himself to be one of the most progressive poet. He would go to the help of his friends at the peril of his life, a many occassions, he refrained from taking bold steps of endanghing his life, simply because of the consideration of the duty toward his parents. His impulsive spirit made him to direct his attention towards helping the needy. He went to Japan, and was graduated from the Hosei university. In the second year of the Republic, when the Parliament was brought into existence, he was returned for the House of Commons. However, when the Parliament was shut down, he adopted conservative policy, and never showed any sign of activity. When the Parliament was summoned under the name of the Republic, he entered Peking responding to the call, and was returned for the House of Commons.

廖希賢　字勁伯　歲三十一

選舉地　四川省

籍貫　四川省合江縣

住址　北京宣武門內西斜街北駱陀灣

君少慧好談。年十六。補博士弟子員。翌年。考入四川官立東文學堂肄業。畢業後。以官費派赴日本留學。在早稻田大學豫科及中央大學本科畢業。宣統三年。歸國。部試攷列優等。會武昌起義。遂南還與同志等組織中華民國聯合會于上海。民國元年。返川。授重慶軍政府實業分司司長。成渝合併。回籍辦理邑中公務。未幾。赴成都。主持四川日報報務。由四川第二選舉區復選爲衆議院議員,國會解散後,就中國公學大學部長聘。從事教育。民國三年九月。赴上海。任四川官銀行上海分行行長職。自是遂寄居海上。迨國會復活。始來京就職。

君少にして慧、談を好む。翌年、試に應じて四川官立東文學堂に入る、卒業の後、官費を以て日本に留學し、早稻田大學預科及び中央大學預科大學本科の業を畢ふ。宣統三年歸國し、部試に及第して優等に列す。會ま武昌義を起す、遂に南に還り、重慶軍政府實業分司司長を授けらる。民國元年、四川に歸り、重慶軍政府實業分司司長を授けらる。民國元年、四川に歸り、同志と中華民國聯合會を上海に組織す。民國元年、四川に歸り、重慶合併せらるヽや、鄉里に歸り邑中の公務を處理す。未だ幾くならずして成都に赴き、四川日報の事務を宰り。未だ幾くならずして成都に赴き、四川日報の事務を宰り。未四川第二選舉區より復選せられて衆議院議員となる。國會解散後、中國公學大學大學部長の聘に就き教育に從事す。民國三年九月上海に赴き、四川官銀行上海支店長に任せらる。是より遂に上海に寄居す。國會復活に及び、始めて北京に來りて議員の職に就く。

民國之精華　（傳記）廖希賢先生

Mr. Liao Hsi-hsen, otherwise called Chin-pai, is a native of Ho-chiang, Ssi-chuan-hsing, aged thirty one. He munifested early in youth his propensity for learning, and at the age of 16, a certain literaly honour was gained by him. He studied at the Ssi-chuang government school and after graduation, he went to Japan at the goverment expense, where he studied in the Waseda University and also at the Chu-o University from which he was graduated. In 1911, he returned to China where he passed the civil service examiuation with honour. When the revolutionary movement took place, he formed the Chinese federated popular society in Shanghai, and in 1912, he returned to Ssu chuan where he was appinted to the sectional head of the Chung ching military government. At the event of the combination of Chung-ching and Cheng-tu, he returned to his native country and attended the official bussiness of that district. Shortly after, he went to Ssi-chuan where he had charge of a news paper; He was returned for the House of Commons from the Ssi-chuan constituency. On the dissolution of the Parliament, he was appoiuted to the head of the university of China. In September, 1914, he went to Shanghai as the head of the branch of the Ssi-chun Goverment Bank where he remained until now. After the re-opening of the Parliament, he went to Peking wherer he was elected to a member of the House of Commons.

訥謨圖　字作霖歲三十九

選舉地　外蒙古

籍貫　原籍外蒙、嗣入京旗

住址　北京東四牌樓北汪家胡同路北

君爲人精明強幹。富於忍耐。然鯁直好義。人有過。輒直斥不諱。甚至聲色俱厲。而賦性朴質。不喜浮華。讀書博而能約。故所讀皆足以爲經世濟物之資。及有益于身心者。詞章之屬亦常隨意涉獵。不專力於斯。曾同文館俄文畢業。兼習醫學算術。嗣往遊俄法兩國遊學。有清之季。在外交部辦理電報。歷保花翎三品銜員外郞。候選知府。補充京師審判廳推事。署理縣知事。辦理歸綏蒙墾事宜。民國成立慞被選爲烏盟參議院議員國會解散後不談政事。五年八月。及國會重開。復爲衆議院議員之舊職。

君人と爲り精明強幹にして忍耐に富み、然かも鯁直にして義を好み、人過あれば輒ち直斥して諱まず。賦性朴直にして浮華を喜ばず、其の讀書博くして能く約す。故に讀む所皆な經世濟物の資と爲すに足り、身心に有益なる者は詞章の屬亦た常に隨意涉獵す。曾て同文館に入りて露語を學び、兼て算術を修む。嗣で露佛兩國に游學し。前清末季に於て、外務部電報課の職に任じ、花翎三品衙員外郞に補せられたり。また候選知府に補し、京師審判廳推事に任じ、嗣で縣知事理署理となり、歸化綏遠の開墾事宜を處理したり。民國成立後外蒙古烏蘭察布盟より推されて正式國會參議院議員に當選す。國會散解後暫らく政事を談せず。五年八月國會重ねて開院するに及び、君また其の召集に應じて院に到り、現に仍ほ參議院議員と爲る。

Mr. Nomoto, otherwise known as Tso Lin, age thirty nine, is a native of Ulta Mongolia. He is a man of shrewed and exact temperament but rich in the virtue of patience. Being simple in life he is a hater of any vain glory and pompousness. He has always been a copious reader of books and applied what he read to practice. He studied the Russian and was an expert in medical science and mathematics. He went to Russia and France for the purpose of accomplishing his study. At the later days of the previous Chinese regime he was employed by the Telegraph Bureau of the Foreign Department. His promotion was very rapid and occupied many posts of inportance. When the Republic was established he was elected to a member of the Senate. On the dissolution of the Parliament he talked no more of politics. However, when the Parliament resumed its function he was appointed to a member of the Senate.

諾們達賚　字恆山　歲三十三

選舉地　外蒙古

籍　貫　蒙古卓索圖盟喀喇沁右旗

住　址　北京地安門外福祥寺廊年

君秉性剛正嚴明。不隨俗好。為人精明
強幹。好質惡文。與人交。尚義節。重然
諾。居心仁厚。常喜周濟貧困。自幼勤
學。不事嬉遊。弱冠即廣通經史。長於
詩文。及長。博覽群籍。能精思深入。扶
其竅要。故其見解思想。皆極明瞭切
實。且洞悉事情。明察物理。長於幹濟
之才。君素在籍蒙古卓索圖盟喀喇沁
右旗。蓋蒙古華胄新進之雋傑也。辛亥
革命。宣布五大民族共和。肇造民國。
二年正式國會成立。君由外蒙古科布
多。被選為衆議院議員。議政壇上。代
表蒙族。把持正義。贊勤共和。此次及
共和再造。國會重開。再應召集。仍為
衆議院議員。

民國之精華　（傳記）　諾們達賚先生

君秉性剛正嚴明にして俗尚に隨はず、人と為り精明强幹
にして質を好み文を惡む。人と交りて義節を佾びて然諾
を重んす。幼より學に廳みて嬉遊を事とせず。弱冠即ち廣
く經史に通じて詩文に長す。長するに及びて群書を涉獵
して能く其の精義を思索して其の竅要を抉き、其の見解
思想皆な極めて切實明瞭にして、且つ事理と洞察明知し
て幹濟の才に長す。辛亥命を革めて五大民族の共和を宣布し中華民
國の奠を創むるに及び、外蒙古科布多より選れて民國二
年正式國會衆議院議員に當選し、議政檀上蒙古民族を代
表し正義を把持して共和して共和新の政を贊勤したり。
此次共和の憲政復活して、國會重ねて召集を行ふや、君
復た出でゝ衆議院議員と為る。

蓋し蒙古華冑界新進の雋傑なりと謂ふべし。

Mr. Nomentalai, otherwise called Heng Shan, thirty three years of age, is a native of Mongolia. He is gentleman of noble and straight foreward character. In associating with others he attached great importance in keeping promises. He was also deeply interested in helping the poor. Early in life he was fond of reading classical history and poems. As he grew older he proved himself to be a copious reader of books and practical interpreter of the thoughts contained in these writings. He is one of the eminent man among the Mongls. In the 2nd year of the Republic he was returned for the House of Commons representing his own race. When the Parliament was summoned for the second time under the new president, he was again returned for the Parliament, the position of honour which he now holds.

穆　郁　字晉卿　歲

選舉地　山西省

籍　實　山西省渾源縣

住　址　北京兵部窪十二

君天資聰穎。悟性敏捷。尤富理想。然
爲人誠實不欺。與人交。喜勸善規過。
相其人必能納練者。始規正之。否則惟
漸與疏遠。以示意。及其改悔。則愈善
律之。人告以過。則直認不諱。自幼好
讀。弱冠文采風流。已超出儕輩。及海
內維新之後。君慨然棄舊從新。銳意西
學。專心實學。夙抱治國安民之志。曾
以前清附生。光緒二十八年。肄業本省
大學堂中學專齋。三十三年遊歷日本。
宣統三年本縣舉孝廉方正。民國成立
後。被選爲衆議院議員。國會解散後。
南施歸里。盡力維持地方公安。及國會
重開。遂復入京。仍爲衆議院議員。

君天資聰穎にして悟性敏捷、尤も理想に富む。然かも人
と爲り誠實にして欺かず。人と交りて善を勸め過を規す
る事を喜び、其人を相して必す能く諫を納る〻者にして
始めて之を規正し、然らざれば則ち唯だ漸く之を疎遠し
て意を示し、其の悔ゆるに及びて、則ち愈々之を律す。
幼より讀書を好み、弱冠にして〻文采風流既に儕輩を超出
す。海內維新の後、慨然として舊を棄て新に從ひ、意を
西學に傾けて專ら實學に志し夙に治國安民の志を抱きた
り。曾て前清附生を以て光緒二十八年山西省大學校中學
專科に學び、三十三年日本に遊歷す。宣統三年渾源縣よ
り孝廉方正に保獎さる。民國二年選れて衆議院議員と爲
る。國會解散後、南旋して鄕里に歸り、地方公安の維持
に盡力する所ありたり。國會重ねて開かる〻や、遂に復
た入京して仍ほ衆議院議員と爲る。

Mr. Mu Hsun, otherwise called Chin Hsi-ang, is a native of Hun-yuan, Shan-hsi province.
He is a gentleman of high-ideals and genuine ambition. He is fond of making friends and ready to
give advice to others. While young he was fond of reading books. His personal presence distinguishes
him from others. When the new regime was introduced in China he became a student of western learning, and in 1902 he studied in the middle course of university in his province. In 1907 he visited Japan,
and after return to his country he was awarded a certificate of recognition for his filial obedience.
In the 2nd year of the Republic he was returned for the House of Commons. When the Parliament
was dissolved he returned to his home where he was interested in the improvement of local interest.
Under the new president when the Parliament was opened he again entered the House of Commons.

戴書雲　字紀白　歲四十五

選舉地　江西省
籍貫　江西省餘干縣
住址　北京棉花下六條

君秉性誠篤朴實，痛惡流俗之浮華。與
人交。常覯直不阿。人有過失。無不逕
情詰責。不稍存世故之念。然居心仁
厚。喜救人急難。故其接物。雖鋒鋩過
露。昧于在交之術。然以其萬事出以
至誠。故人亦罕忌恨之者。於前清光
緒間。中丁酉卿試副榜。及審備立憲。
被選爲諮議局議員。初次革命時。君駐
局翊贊本省之光復。功績㕘多。民國元
年冬。袁氏解散國會。並以國民黨籍收
消證書。君遂回籍。從事教育。並創辦
墾植。人與談及時政。輒持消極態度。
絕不爲可否之辭。及共和復活。國會重
開。始入都。仍就衆議院議員之職。

民國之精華　（傳記）戴書雲先生

君秉性誠篤朴實にして流俗の浮華を痛察す。人と交りて
常に硬直阿らず、人過先あれば直言以て之を詰責して世
故の念を有せず。然かも居心仁厚にして人の急難を救ふ
を喜ぶ。故に物に接して餘りに鋒鋩を露はして社交の術
に昧しと雖も、萬事至誠に出るを以て、人の之を恨む者
罕れなり。前清光緒年間、丁酉郷試副榜に及第し、立憲
準備に際し、諮議局議員に選ばる。第一革命當時、君局
に駐りて江西獨立を翼贊して功績多大なり。民國元年冬、
遲れて衆議院議員に常選す。二年冬、袁氏が國會を解散
するや、國民黨籍に在るを以て議員證書を剝奪され、遂
に鄕里に歸省して教育に從事し、並に開墾事業を經營し、
談時事に及べば輒ち消極態度を持し、絕へて可否の辭を
爲さず。共和復活して國會重ねて開くに及び、入京して
仍は衆議院議員の職に就く。

Mr. Tai Shu-yun, otherwise called Chi-pai, age forty five, is a native of Yu-che, Chiang-hsi province. He is a gentleman of simple and straightforward character. In associating with others he is quite honest and do not hesitate to give warnings to others without reserves. Although he is not a master in the art of social intercourse but since his action is actuated by sincere motive, so that none has grudges against him. During the previous Chinese regime he passed an examination successfully and became a member of the Local Assembly. In the movement for the first revolution he rendered great service bringing about the independence of Chiang-hsi province. In the 2nd year of the Republic, when Parliament was dissolved, his Parliamentary certificate was taken away by the Yuanshi-kai government. He went back to his home where he was interested in education and some exploitation work but kept aloof from current politics. When the Republic was restored and Parliament opened he entered Peking and became a member of the House of Commons.

戰雲霽 字林晴 歲四十四

選舉地 黑龍省

籍貫 黑龍江省木蘭縣

住址 北京西單鮑家街稚集公廨

君爲人深沈厚重。言動謹嚴。與人交。淡而不疎。有所規勸。必先豫量其人能納言者。然後慷慨矯正之。自幼聰慧善談。不事嬉遊弱冠。即能爲詩文。及長。尤銳意求博。然喜求義理之所在不沾滯於章句文詞。曾於前清被任爲黑龍江省諮議局副議長。宣統己酉。以拔貢籤分郵傳部小京官。調黑龍江省巡撫公署參事。歷保主事知府。民國元年。被選爲臨時參議院議員。及任滿解職歷充財政部國稅籌議員。清史館名譽協修。五年八月。國會重開。遞補爲參議院議員。

黑龍江省諮議局副議長と爲る。宣統己酉の歲。拔貢生を以て郵傳部小京官に叙せられ、黑龍江省巡撫衙門參事に調せられ、主事知府に歷保す。民國元年選ばれて北京臨時參議院議員となる。民國二年正式國會參議院議員補缺員に當選す。北京臨時參議院閉會後、財政部國稅籌議員となり、清史館名譽協修に任ず。五年八月國會重ね て開かるゝに及び、乃ち缺を補して召集され、參議院議

戰雲霽 先生

君人と爲り深沈厚重にして言動謹嚴なり。人と交りて淡として疎ならず。勸告する所あれば、必す先づ豫め其の人の言を納るゝ者なるや否やを量りて後らす。幼より聰慧善く談じ、嬉遊を事とせす。弱冠にして即ち能く詩文を作る。長するに及びて尤も銳意博を求め、然も義理の所在を求めて、章句文詞の末に拘泥せす。曾て前清時代、

員と爲る。

Mr. Chan Yun-chi, otherwise called Lin Ching, forty four years of age, is a native of Mu-lan Hei Lung Chiang province. He is a gentleman of deep thought and strict behaviour. In giving any advice, he always makes sure if his words are likely to be weighed at all or not. While young, he was a reader of books, and fond of versification. As he grew older, he was the seeker of the truth and nationality, but cared very little about mere external phrases. In the previous Chinese regime, he was the vice-president of the Local Assembly of Hei Lung-chiang, and also occupied many ports of importance. In the first year of the Republic, he was elected to a member of the Senate specially met in Peking. In the second year of the Republic, he was returned for the House of Commons. With the shutting down of the Parliament, he was an official in the financial department. When the Parliament was re-opened, he was appointed to a member of the Senate.

冀鼎鉉 字葆忱

選舉地 山西省
籍貫 山西省平遙縣
住址 北京前門外永光菴胡同二十三

君賦性敦厚溫和。與人交。和藹可親。雖仇敵亦假以顏色。不出惡聲。然爲人篤實不欺。勤止以禮自持。雖長於交際。而無形中自有不可侵越之界限。曾未嘗曲己從人。較之碌碌追隨俗者。自屬大相逕廷。自幼好讀。喜博覽羣書。于科擧之業。故其讀書。純以至主觀判斷之是非。而不局于習俗之成見。及海內維新。慨立志求有用之學。遂留學日本明治大學商科畢業。應前清學部考試。賞給商科擧人。歷充山西商業法政學校教員。現充衆議院議員。

君賦性敦厚にして溫和、人と交りて和藹親びべし。仇敵と雖も疾言厲色を以て之に加へず。人と爲り篤實欺かず。言動擧止禮を以て自ら持す。交際に長ずと雖も無形の中自ら優越すべからざる限界あり、未だ曾て己を曲げて人に從はず、之を碌々として俗に追隨するに較べて自ら大に逕庭あり。幼より讀書を好み群籍を涉獵して意の向ふ所に任せて快を呼ふ。海內維新に及び志を立て〈有用の學を求め、遂に笈を負ふて日本に留學し、明治大學校商科に入りて研磋の功を積み卒業して歸國するや、學部の試驗に及第して商科擧人を授けらる。山西商業學校、同法政學校教員に歷充し、育英の業に從事して後進青年の誘掖に努めたり。君は民國二年當選の正式國會衆議院議員にして、五年國會復活さるや、再び其の召集に應じて現に仍ほ衆議院議員たり。

民國之精華 （傳記） 冀鼎鉉先生

Mr. Chi Ting-yin, otherwise known as Pao Shen, is a native of Ping Yao, the Shan-ssi province. He is gentle and sociable, but always is able to keep up his own self-possession. He has in himself that nobleness of character that outsiders fail to grasp. He never bents himself against his own conscience. He was a copious reader of books, and as such he has grown to be a gentleman of very wide information. He went to Japan to complete his study in new learning. He was graduated from the Meiji University. Having successfully passed the civil service examination, he was appointed an instructor of the Shan-ssi Commercial School and Law College, where he was deeply interested in the education of the young. When the Parliament was re-opened, he was returned for the House of Commons.

四百四十九

廉炳華　字汲容　歲三十四

選舉地　新疆省
籍貫　山西省萬泉縣
住址　北京宣武門外永光寺西街門牌六號

君自少年即好義舉。見人不平。雖陷路
亦欲爲之報復。鄉里有困於資者。或求
助於君。君雖自在窘中。亦必勉爲盡
力。事成。絕不望報。尤喜獎勵善行。凡
鄰近有一德之長。如孝友信義廉介等
者。君必設法濟助之。使自知爲善行之
報。君於前清以附生。肄業于山西河東
中學堂。期滿畢業。得獎貢生。隨升入
北京法政大學。肄業二年。宣統二年八
月。因事赴新疆。即充新疆學務公所專
門科科員。兼普通科科員。後改充省視
學學員。民國元年。被選爲臨時省議會
議員。後又被選爲參議院議員。國會解
散。君歸里不問時事。及至共和再造。
始入京仍供舊職。

廉炳華　先生

君少より義舉を好み、人の不平を見るや、險を犯して之
が爲に報復を思ひ、鄉里若し貧に困るものあれば、亦た
必ず力を盡して之を助け、事成つて絕へて報を望まず。
尤も善行を獎勵する事を喜び、凡そ鄉近にして一德の長
ありて、孝友信義廉介等の賞すべきものは、君必ず法を
設けて之を救濟す。前清時代、附生を以て山西河東中學
校に學び、卒業後貢生となる。闆で北京法政大學校に入

りて修業す。宣統二年八月、事を以て新疆省に赴く。新

疆學務公所專門科々員に任じ、普通科々員を兼ぬ。後ち
改めて省視學員と爲る。民國元年選ばれて臨時省議會議
員と爲る。二年正式國會議院議員に當選す。國會解散
さるや、都里に歸りて、時事を問はず。約法復活して
國會重ねて開くに及び、及び其の召集に應じて入京し、
仍は參議院議員の舊職に就く。

Mr. Lien Ping Hun, otherwise called Se Jung, age thirty four, is a native of Wan Chuan, Shan Hsi-hsing. While young he was fond of heroic deeds. On seeing men suffer he at the peril of his life went to there rescue. He gave relief to the poor in his province without any thought of reward. His virtue became widely known and he was particularly interested in helping young men, who is known for virtues praise worthy such as felial obedience etc. At the government expence he studied in the law college of Peking. In 1910 he was appointed instructor of technical college and became an inspector of learning in his province. In the 1st year of the Republic he was elected a member of the local assembly, while in the 2nd year he was chosen a member of the Senate. With the desolution of the Diet he returned to his country where he held peace regarding current topics. With the Restoration of the Parliament he entered Peking and resumed the senatorial function as before.

張士才 字越鐘 歲四十五

選舉地　直隸省
籍　貫　直隸省獲鹿縣
住址　北京象坊橋

君自幼好讀。弱冠。廣通經史。間亦涉
獵諸子之書。年少時。頗以名儒自勵。
及壯。見國力愈益貧弱。遂改習實業。
歷辦本邑各頂公益事業。並曾充石家
莊商會總理。辛亥革命之際。吳祿貞駐
節石家莊。君協助糧餉。奔走經營。頗
著勞績。嗣後大軍雲集。商業恐慌。君
各方接洽。日夜馳驅。地方秩序。賴以
安全。未幾。被選爲臨時省議會議員
朋滿。入被選爲衆議院議員迨及國會
解散。遂歸里蟄居。不談政事。至帝制
發生。始潛赴滬上。與諸同志主持大
計。以圖恢復約法。重開國會。所志既
達。遂來京復供今職。

君幼より讀書を好み、弱冠にして廣く經史に通や。亦た
諸子百家の書を涉獵す。少年時代名儒を以て自ら勵み、
壯年に及びて國力益々貧弱なるを見て遂に改めて實業を
習ひ、地方の公益事業に盡瘁して、右家莊商會總理と爲
る。辛亥革命の際、吳祿貞が石家莊に駐るや、君は糧餉
の事を處理して功あり。嗣で大軍雲集して市面恐慌する
や、君各方面と接洽して地方の秩序を維持したり。未だ
幾くならすして臨時省議會議員に選ばれ、正式國會の成
立に際し衆議院議員に當選す。國會解散さるゝに及び、
遂に鄉里に歸りて杜門蟄居し、また政事を談せすして讀
書自ら娛む。帝制問題發生するや、潛に出でゝ上海に走
り、諸同志と計りて約法の恢復と國會の召集を主張す。目
的既に達するや、再び北上して入京し、現に仍は衆議院
議員たり。

(傳記) 張士才先生

Mr. Ma Pan-chun, otherwise known as Hsu Sheng, age fifty four, is a native of Fu-hsien, Eeng-tien Tin. He is a gentleman of strong will and full of patients. Being straight forward in character he does not hesitate to give warning to others in fault without any using language of circumspection. He is a lover of simplicity and hates vanity with strong dislike. Whatever he reads he digest the same for his own benefits as well as for the interests of the country. During the previous chinese period he was educated in the civic institute of his province and on the committee of investigating the particulars relating to the civic body statistical bureau and similar associations. At the same time he was the president of the forestry association. He was also on the committee of the financial investigation of his province. When the Republic was established he was the vice president of the provincial assembly. In the 2nd year of the Republic when the parliament was opened he became a member thereof. With the dissolution of the Diet he held his peace for the time being but when the parliament was reopened he was returned for the House of Commons.

焉沣春　字旭升　歲五十四

選舉地　奉天省

籍貫　奉天府復縣城東北焉家嶺村

住址　北京大城東六舖口西後水泡
子三十二號

君爲人精明強幹。富於忍耐。然而鯁直好
義。人有過。輒直斥不諱。甚至聲色俱
厲。而賦性朴實。不喜浮華。讀書博而
能約。故所讀皆足以爲經世濟物之資。
及有益于身心者。詞章之屬亦常隨意
涉獵。不專力於斯。故能爲詩歌。而不
喜常作。每有所作。必極精妙。而
於感慨淋漓時。一寫其至性至情。非尋
常雕蟲刻鏤者可比也。於前清以廩貢
生。委用訓導。奉天自治局養成會畢
業。歷充自治局。諮議局。統計處。自治
期成會。各調查員。地方團練會會首。
森林會會長辦理選舉事務。奉天省城
各機關財政調查員。被選諮議員。臨時
省議會副議長。並充復縣五湖咀煤礦
正經理。現充衆議院議員。

君人と爲り精明強幹にして忍耐に富み、然かも鯁直義を
好み、人過あれば輒ち直言排斥して諱まず、甚だしきに至
つては聲色俱に勵し、賦性朴實にして浮華を喜ばず。書
を讀みて博く且つ約す。故に其の讀みし所は皆な以て經
世濟物の資となすに足る。身心に有益なる者は詞章の類
亦た常に隨意涉獵す。前清廩貢生を以て訓導に委せらる。
奉天自治局養成會を卒業す。自治局、諮議局、統計處、
自治期成會等の各調查員と爲る。又た地方團練會々長、
森林會々長に推された。選舉事務を處理し、又奉天省
城各機關財政調查員と爲る。選ばれて諮議局議員と爲
る。並に復縣五湖咀煤礦正經理に任じたり、民國二年當
選の正式國會兼議院議員にして、此大國會するや、再び
出でゝ名集に應じ仍ほ兼議院議員の舊職に就く。

Mr. Chang Shih-ko, otherwise called Yueh-ching, age forty five, is a native of Chi-lin province. While young, he was fond of reading books, and particularly, he was well versed with classical teaching. As he grew older, however, he perceived the necessity of enriching the country, by the study of useful learning. At the time of the revolution, his service was really very great because he atttended the commissariat service. He also exerted his influence in keeping order in local districts. When the Parliament was formed, he was returned for the House of Commons. With the breaking up of the Parliament, he went back to his home, and kept himself out of the politics. However, when the imperial movement of Yuanshi-kai was started, he went to Shanghai, and planned for the downfall of the ambitious Politician. As soon as the Parliament was formed, he entered Peking, and was returned for the House of Commons.

中國政黨史

井上一葉

第一章　清朝時代の政黨

中國政黨の起因は康有爲、梁啓超等が變法自強を説き保皇黨なるものを組織せると孫文、黃興等が廣東に興中會、湖南湖北に華興會なるものを組織せると章炳麟が浙江に光復會を組織せるとに始る、保皇黨は帝制立憲を希望し興中會、華興會は民主共和を希望し、光復會は後者に近きも多少其趣を異にせり

保皇黨は戊戌政變後西太后の震怒と當道の嫌忌を恐れ黨籍に列する者の内より脱退者を多く出し其脱黨せざる者も亦保皇黨の名を口にせざるに至り殆ど自然消滅に歸せり其後同じく保皇黨に屬せし佛國天主教の神甫たる江蘇省丹徒縣人馬良（字湘伯）が政聞社なるものを組織したるあり又福建閩縣人鄭孝胥（字蘇戡）が預備立憲公會なるものを組織したるあり又湖北省武昌人湯化龍等の帝國統一黨なるものを組織したるありしも何等直接政治上に勢力を有するに至らざりき

宣統年間に至り資政院設置せられて議院政治の端は啓かれたり曩に光緒三十四年國會開設準備詔勅に基き各省に諮議局設置せられ地方自治の緒を爲す乃ち該詔勅に基き憲政編査館が規定したる順序は宣統八年に至り籌備完成以て國會を正式に開會する筈なりき然るに當時國民の憲政希望熱は非常に旺盛にして宣統八年迄空しく期限の至るを待たず江蘇諮議局發起と成り各省諮議局に通電し聯合以て目

の速開を請願せんことを協議し各省皆是に贊同し遂に再三請願を爲したる結果九年の準備期間を短縮して五年と爲すに至れり而して是等國體運動が效果を奏するや政客中には漸く政黨組織の必要を感じ來れり卽ち宣統三年に於て北京に在る各政客は政黨設立を唱道し同志を糾合して追々小團體を組織するに至り先づ左の諸黨を現出せり

政學會	汪榮寶	曹汝霖	章宗祥	陸宗輿 等
憲政實進會	陳寶琛	勞乃宣 等
辛亥俱樂部	易宗夔	羅傑 等
憲友會	湯化龍	孫洪伊 等

當時政學會は資政院に於ける新刑律編成問題に對し贊成を表するを以て白票黨と稱せられ會員は法政留學生等にして資政院に議員たる者のみに限り其數約二十餘人を算せり

憲政實進會は新刑律に反對なるを以て藍票黨と稱せられ保守派に屬す其會員約五十餘人多くは資政院議員なりき

辛亥俱樂部は是又資政院議員によりて發起せられたるも其會員は約六十人程にて議員と院外者と相半ばせり而して其系統より云へば度支部尙書澤公を中心とせる度支部派の人物多し

憲友會は全國諮議局聯合會中の湯化龍、孫洪伊等が發起せしを以て諮議局代表等の人多し卽ち前の帝國統一黨の後身にして國民經濟及び地方分權等に重きを置けり全國諮議局聯合會が國會速開の請願を爲し其の第一回請願却下せられ更に第二第三の運動を爲すに及びて全國諮議局代表は自然憲友會と行動を共にせるを以て憲友會は當時輿論の最も勢力ある代表たらんとせり前記第二次請願の代表は左の如し

直隷　孫洪伊　谷芝瑞　張銘勳　王法勤

奉天　永貞　劉興甲

吉林　李芳

江蘇　方還　于定一

江西　閻荷生

安徽　陶鎔　潘祖光　吳廣廷

浙江　鄭際平　應貽誥　吳榮華

福建　劉崇佑　連賢基

湖北　陳登山

湖南　羅傑　劉善渥

山東　周樹標　朱承恩

山西　陳熙朝　楊治清

河南　

廣東　沈秉仁

廣西　吳錫齡　劉篤敏　李素　劉懋賞

敍上の代表等中には憲友會と同一行動を取りたる者少からざりしが辛亥革命の勃發するに及びて是等の政黨は一時全然消滅し革命後に於て更に頻りに與りたれども其系統は全く一變し曩日の同志が或は反對と成り反對敵視したる者が却て互に提携握手せる等の事其類に乏しからざりき

革命派側に在りては左の團體興れり

廣　東　興中會……孫文派

兩　湖　興華會……黃興派

浙　江　光復會……章炳麟派

敍上の各派は均しく革命思想を有する者の會合にて或は事實の上に革命を企て失敗し或は文章の上に革命を鼓吹して逮捕せられんとし爲に海外に亡命して以て時機の來るを待てり乃ち此三派は日本に集り東京に於て聯合して同盟會なるものを組織したり初め同會は一種の祕密結社なりしが辛亥革命勃發南京政府成立し孫文歸國の上臨時大總統と成るに及んで同會は公然たる政黨となり其政綱等を發表するに至れり

今玆に光緒年間より宣統年間に亙る政黨系統概略を圖を以て示せば左の如し

光緒年間

宣統年間

憲政黨

保皇黨（康有爲　梁啓超）

政聞社（馬良）

帝國統一黨

革命黨

浙江光復會（章炳麟）

湖南華興會（黃興）

廣東興中會（孫文）

同盟會（孫文　黃興）

憲政實進會（陳寶琛）

憲政友會（湯化龍）

辛亥俱樂部（羅傑）

政學會（汪榮實）

尚志會（藉忠寅）

預備立憲公會（鄭孝胥）

第二章　辛亥革命以後の政黨

第一節　民國初期の政黨―同盟會、共和黨、統一共和黨の鼎立

辛亥革命以後從來革命黨の祕密結社たりし同盟會は南京に於て公然其政綱を發布して政黨と成れり其政綱左の如し

政　綱

一、行政統一を完成し地方自治を促進す

二、種族同化を實行す

三、國家社會政策を採用す

四、義務敎育を普及す

五、男女平權を主張す

六、徵兵制度を勵行す

七、財政を整理し稅制を釐定す

八、力めて國際平等を謀る

九、移民開墾事業に重きを置く

而して中華民國を鞏固にして民主主義を實行するを以て宗旨とす

是と同時に南北各地に於て政黨の續出するもの殆ご枚擧するに遑あらず今其重なる者を擧ぐれば

黨　名	領　袖
民　社　黨	黎元洪
統一黨	章炳麟
國民黨	溫宗堯

民國公會　　　張國維

國民共進會　　范源廉

國民協進會　　藉忠寅

同盟會　　　　孫文　黃興

統一共和黨

國民公黨　　　谷鍾秀

國民共進會　　岑春煊

共和實進會　　伍廷芳　王寵惠

共和建設討論會　湯化龍　孫洪伊

政群社

斯の如く團體の多きこと旣に枚擧す可らざるに又一人にて二黨若しくは三黨に籍を置く者あるを以て其實際の系統を確かむること甚だ困難なりき

民國元年の參議院時代に在りては同盟會多數なりしを以て同盟會に歡焉たりし左の六政黨は合同を謀り協議成立して茲に新團體を組織し共和黨と命名せり

國民協進會

統一黨

國民共進會　　　共和黨

民國公會

國民黨

國民協進會は素と日本留學生中の一部に依りて組織せられ居たる尚志會の革命後改名せし者にして其
重要分子は

憲念益　劉頌虞　邵義　陳懋鼎　陳敬第　藉忠寅

李渠長　福　黃遠庸　周大烈　黃群　熊範輿

等にて梁啓超系統に屬せり

統一黨は前同盟會員にして往年東京にて發行せる同會機關雜誌民報の主筆なりし章炳麟の組織せしも
のに係り章炳麟は始め光復會を組織し後に同盟會に加はり居たるが革命後孫文、黃興等と意見の衝突
より遂に同盟會を脱して統一黨を組織し江蘇、浙江、安徽等の有力者を糾合し前清時代の預備立憲公
會員多く之に加はれり

國民共進會（北部派）　范源廉、陸定等の設立する所なるが其會員甚だ多からず

民國公會は張國維、鄒福祥等が蘇州に於て組織せる小政團なり

國民黨は上海に於て潘鴻鼎、陸鴻儀、沈彭年等の組織せるものなり

民社は湖北の孫武、張振武等が黎元洪を擁し項驤、汪彭年、孫發緒、何雯、劉成禹等と結合し更に柏
文蔚、朱瑞等を加へたるものなり

以上六政團合同して共和黨と成りし後の政綱は

一、全國を統一して國家主義を執る

二、國家の權力を固め國民の進步を保持す

三、世界の大勢に感じ平和實利を以て國を立つ

而して其重なる者は

理事長　　黎　元　洪

理　事　　張　　謇　　伍　廷　芳　　那　彥　圖

會員重要分子　　熊　希　齡　　程　德　全　　湯　壽　潛　孫　武　孫　發　緒

周　大　烈　　藉　忠　寅　　阿穆爾靈奎

統一共和黨は南京政府時代に發生せしものにして同盟會と共和黨との間に在りて一鼎足を持し當時の參議院は此黨の向背に由りて勝敗を決するを得たり其政綱は左の如し

　政綱

一、行政區域を劃定し以て中央統一を謀る

二、稅制を釐定し以て負擔の公平を期す

三、民生に注意し社會の政策を採用す

四、國民經濟を發達し保護貿易政策を採用す

五、幣制を劃一し金本位制を採用す

六、金融機關を整頓し國家銀行制度を採用す

七、交通を振興し鐵道幹線を速成す

八、軍國民敎育を實行し專門學術を促進す

九、海陸軍備を振刷し徵兵制度を採用す

十、海外移民を保護し實邊開墾を勵行す

十一、文化を普及し國內民族を融合す

十二、外交に注意し國家對等權利を保持す

以上十二項にして蔡鍔、王芝祥を以て總幹事と爲し彭允彝、殷汝驪、歐陽振聲等常務幹事たり

當時參議院に於ける議員總數は百四十名なりしが蒙古、西藏等の議員至らざりしを以て實際約百名位

に過ぎざりき今其議員黨派別を擧れば

同盟會所屬

劉積學　熊成章　盧信　阮慶瀾　茹欲可　盧士模
王湘　　江辛　　劉盟訓　黃樹中　宋汝梅　顧視高
俞道暄　杜潛　　孫澄　　司徒頴　彭古元　張耀曾
劉星楠　陳鴻鈞　王慶雲　徐傅霖　李肇甫　殷宇清
覃振　　景志傅　曾彥　　李述膺　席聘臣　曹玉德
楊永泰

共和黨所屬

博廸蘇　劉崇佑　陳國祥　鄭萬膽　張伯烈　谷芝瑞
田駿豐　李渠　　郭同　　劉成禹　李國珍　王家襄
王文慶　祺誠武　汪榮寶　藉忠寅　姚華　　侯延爽
陳廷策　宋振聲　劉顯治　曾有瀾　陳時夏　王振堯
連賢基　周樹標　秦瑞玠　吳廷棟　王凌阿　秦望瀾
丁世嶧　張鶴弟　時功玖　楊廷棟　熙凌阿　湯化龍
達賚　　唐古色　那彥圖　阿穆爾靈奎　德色賚託布　鄂多台

統一共和黨所屬

劉興甲　李素　何裕康　王赤卿　關文鐸　殷汝驪
戰雲霽　趙世鈺　陳景南　李芳　王樹聲　胡璧城
谷鍾秀　彭允彜　孫孝宗　歐陽振聲　金鼎勳　高家驥
周珏　張聯魁　楊策　曾有翼　吳景濂　李秉恕
劉彥　王鑫潤

其餘は無所屬にて行動一定せざりしが唯湯化龍は籍を共和黨に置くも共和討論建設會として一八一旗を擁し居たり

第二節　共和黨の分裂及國民黨の組織

幾くもなくして六政團合併の共和黨中舊國民協進會派は舊民社派と常に相融和せず遂に左の諸政團合併して民主黨を組織する事に至れり

國民協進會
共和建設討論會
政群社
共和俱進會

民主黨は參議院に於て共和黨と行動を共にせり卽ち當時の參議院議員中同盟會に屬する者は三十餘人にて共和黨は民主黨と行動を共にせる爲め四十餘人を得統一共和黨は二十餘人を有し三黨鼎足の情況を呈せり

唐紹儀內閣瓦解後陸徵祥が超然內閣を組織するに當り其內閣員推薦中國民共和兩黨の人なりしが統一

共和黨中より一人も採用せざりしかば統一共和黨は小數黨なりとて侮蔑せられたるものなりとなし憤慨して一致反對したるを以て過半數を得るに至らずして否決せられたり。袁世凱は之を見て直に趙秉鈞に命じ軍界を煽動して大に脅迫を行はしめたるが爲め同盟會及統一共和黨の議員は甚しき壓迫を加へられたり

同盟會は革命の元勳を以て自任するも參議院に多數議員を有せざるを以て常に舊官僚與黨等の爲に左右せらるゝを憤慨したれども奈何ともすべからざるを以て大に黨勢擴張の必要を感じ居たる際軍警が共和黨を援け統一共和黨は同盟會を壓迫したるを憤慨し統一主義主張の相近き同盟會を援け以て政府及共和黨に當らざる可らずと爲し居たれば茲に同盟會と統一共和黨との合同成り同時に又同主義なる三小團體も亦之に加入し乃ち五政團の合併と成り名を國民黨と命名し時恰も（民國元年八月）孫文、黃興等の來京せしを以て八月十八日宣言書を發表し二十五日湖廣會館に發會式を擧げたり參會者約三千餘名張繼主席にて同黨成立の經過を報告し張耀曾合併の情況を演述し孫文の演說あり次に役員を選擧せり

國民黨役員

理事

孫文　黃興　王人文　王芝祥　宋敎仁

參議

張鳳翽　吳景濂　王寵惠　貢桑諾爾布
胡瑛　溫宗堯　陳錦濤　張繼　柏文蔚
沈秉堃　孫毓筠　譚延闓　于右任　馬君武
田桐　景耀月　閻錫山　胡漢民　趙炳麟
李烈鈞　蔣翊武　姚錫光　褚輔成　楊增新
尹昌衡　陳陶怡　徐謙　張琴　松毓

支那政黨史

王善荃　張培爵　唐文治、英永貞　唐紹儀

同盟會が統一共和黨及び其他の三政團と合併して國民黨と成るや參議院に於ける議員六十餘人と成り共和黨は四十餘名、民主黨十餘名にて國民黨絕對多數を占め政府黨たる共和黨は非常なる苦境に陷れり此時恰も梁啓超日本より歸來し大に袁世凱に持て囃されたるが共和黨にも民主黨にも其の知人舊識少からざりしを以て直に此兩黨を合せて一團と爲し自ら之を率ゐて以て袁世凱を援け大に自己の抱負を遂行せんこの野心を起し來れり然るに一方共和黨は國民黨に壓迫せらるゝ苦しさに由り頻に民主黨に秋波を送り以て相提携せんと試みつゝある時なりしかば梁啓超は機逸す可らずと爲し直に共和黨と民主黨の幹部連中に合同の必要を說きたり

參議院は初め同盟會、共和黨、統一共和黨の鼎立を爲したるが同盟會統一共和黨と合併して國民黨を組織し對共和黨と成るや又民主黨現れて國民黨、共和黨、民主黨の鼎立と成れり而して其間に於て統一黨（元と章炳麟の組織せし者なるも其後章炳麟去りて王賡之を牽ゆ）は參議院に議員を有せざるを以て何等活動する能はざりしも共和民主兩黨合併するに至らば統一黨も其中に加入して以て政府に忠勤を效さんと期し機の至るを待てり

露蒙協約問題の發生するや國民、共和、民主、統一の四黨は聯合行動の必要を認め四黨代表相會して當局に對時局方針を建議せし事ありしも此政團聯合は民主黨先づ脫會したるに由りて瓦解せり民主黨一部の者は露蒙協約に關する袁世凱の十大罪を數へて發表せしを以て黨內に內訌を起し共和統一黨會員二千八百餘名は一時に反對脫會するに至り此共和統一黨脫會者は彼の章炳麟の去りたる後王賡の代表せる統一黨に合したる者多し茲に於て梁啓超は共和黨、民主黨、統一黨の三派を合併して以て一大政黨を造り是を基礎として活動すべく竊に其聯絡に著手せり然るに參議院が國會組織法及議員選擧法

を議定し政府が是を發布するや参議院議員は各自其選擧區に運動の爲め歸りたるを以て自然に開會す

る能はざるに至れり隨て此三派合併問題は一時其進行を見ざりき

民國二年三月に至り全國議員選擧の結果は國民黨非常に多數にして兩院を通じて約八百の議員中國民

黨約五百を占め居れりと稱せられ共和、統一、民主の三黨が如何に合同結束するも到底奈何とも爲し

得べからざるに至れり

第三節・共和、統一、民主三黨の合併―進步黨の出顯

茲に於て袁世凱は己も政黨を組織し其援助に由らざる可らざるを感じ稍其意思を漏したりしに人意迎

合に最も長ぜる楊度は好機來れりと爲し國民、共和、統一、民主の四黨間を奔走して先づ共和、統一、

民主の三黨合併を交渉し更に國民黨中の穩健派（實は軟派）を拉し來り茲に四黨合併の一大政黨組織の

準備を爲したり而して其黨綱は中央集權に由りて鞏固なる政黨を組織し茲に領土の統一を完全にして國家

主義を實行するにあり此黨綱主旨に由りて察するに先に江蘇都督程德全の提唱し雲南都督蔡鍔等九都

督の贊成を得て袁世凱に打電し袁世凱又是を各省都督に頒電して意向を徵したる憲法制定に關する大

綱の主旨と相符合するに見れば或は此黨綱なるものは袁世凱の意を受けたるに非ざるかを疑はしむ

其政黨組織の重要人物左の如し

總　　理　　　袁　世　凱

協　　理　　　黎　元　洪

参　　事　　　楊　　度　　梁　啓　超　　蔡　鍔

　　　　　　　熊　希　齢　　張　　謇　　王　　慶　　岑　春　煊

　　　　　　　湯　化　龍

其他知名の士甚だ多し聯合運動者の豫測に據れば三派合同の上に國民黨中の穩健派を拉し來りて是に

加へ更に無所屬の新議員を吸集せば衆議院に於て優に三分の二を占め得べく國民黨中の舊同盟會派た
る激烈分子は僅に三分の一に足らざる少數黨と化し去るべしと思惟したり然るに恰も此運動に著手せ
る時彼の宋敎仁暗殺問題發生し而も其敎唆者が內閣總理兼內務總長趙秉鈞なりと云ふに至り袁世凱と
國民黨との感情は急に杆格するに至り此新政黨組織問題は此に全く頓挫せり
民國二年四月八日新議會は其成立式を舉げたり當時の議員所屬は左の如し

衆議院　　　　議員總數　五百九十六名
國民黨　　　　二百六十九名
共和黨　　　　百二十名
統一黨　　　　十八名
民主黨　　　　十六名
跨黨者　　　　百四十七名
不明者　　　　十六名
未選擧　　　　十名

參議院　　　　議員總數　二百七十四名
國民黨　　　　百二十二名
共和黨　　　　五十五名
統一黨　　　　六名
民主黨　　　　八名
跨黨者　　　　三十八名

斯の如く國民黨は兩院共に多數を占め三黨合併するも到底及ぶ所に非ず若し三黨合併し尚跨黨者も悉く拉して其内に入るゝを得ば衆議院にして僅に國民黨を壓し得けんも參議院は尚是を抑ふる能はず

茲に於て三黨の合併は勿論尚夫以外に脅迫買收等を行はざる可らざるに至れり

袁世凱は三黨を合併せしむるには黎元洪を味方に引入れ置くの利益なるを以て先づ其意を黎元洪に通じ黎元洪は孫武に意を含めて直に上京三黨合併に斡旋せしめたり孫武黎元洪の命を含みて來京し頻に三黨の間を斡旋し三黨員を迎賓館に招待し席上統一黨の理事王廳より三黨結合の必要を說き梁啓超は

三黨の結合が主義主張の同じきより來る自然の結果なりと說き湯化龍は三黨合同は國家問題にて政黨問題に非ずと說き茲に漸く合同の議成りたり

三黨合倂談は愈成立せしも當時衆議院議長選擧競爭にて多忙の爲め三派は一致の行動を取りしも未だ結黨式を擧るに至らざりき斯く袁世凱は三黨を合倂せしも未だ以て國民黨に對するに足らざるを以て

國民黨中の軟骨漢孫毓筠、王芝祥等を籠絡敎唆して國事維持會を組織せしめ專ら國家主義を標榜し縱令何黨たりとも國家を忘れて黨爭に陷らんとする者あらば直に干涉せんとするものにして多く軍人を會員とし以て國民黨を脅赫し又梁士詒を通じ民主黨の李慶芳を籠絡して國會同志會なるものを組織し

一、大總統は經驗ある人を選擧する事

二、憲法制定は國家主義を取る事

の二項を主旨とし入會資格を議員に限り唯此二項の目的を達せば足れりとする極めて簡單なる方法を取り以て入會に便ならしめ合せて被買收議員の足を置くに便ならしめ其他袁世凱は統一黨を純御用黨

とし是に巨額の買收費を與へて國民黨の田舍議員を買收し若しくは軟骨漢を墮落變節せしめたり

斯の如く所有る手段と黄白を使用したる結果國民黨は大に蠶食せられ衆議院の議長には國民黨の吳景

濂當選したるにも拘らず種々なる故障を設け其間に惡辣手段を運らし其結果遂に合同派の勝利に歸し

湯化龍の當選を見るに至れり

三黨は既に衆議院に於て議長副議長を自黨に贏ち得たるを以て五月二十九日愈三黨の結黨式を擧げ進

步黨と命名して左の如き政綱を發表せり

　　　　進步黨政綱

一、國家主義を執り强善なる政府を組織す

二、人民の公意を尊び法賦の自由を擁護す

三、世界の大勢に應じ平和の實利を增進す

理事長　　黎　元　洪

理　事　　湯化龍　王　賡　蒲殿俊　王印川

　　　　梁啓超　張　謇　伍廷芳　孫　武　那彦圖

而して同黨所屬兩院議員及び幹部等は特別聯合會を開き討議したる上理事梁啓超をして公然同黨の政

見を發表せしめたり其大要は

一、正式總統候補者は袁世凱を推す

二、內閣は此際改造の必要あり

三、內閣改造に對する態度は本黨にて組織の必要あらば起つて組織するの覺悟を要す

四、憲法制定後總統を選擧す

五、宋敎仁案は法律にて解決す

六、借款は用途を嚴重に監督す

進步黨斯の如くして漸く結黨式を擧げ同黨幹部の人選に就ては以後理事等熟議の上舊三黨中より夫々振合を計りて之を定め理事長黎元洪の承認を求めたり其顏振左の如し

政務部

部　　長	林長民	副部長	時功玖	王蔭棠
法制科主任	汪榮寶	副主任	汪有齡	饒孟任
財政科主任	吳鼎昌	同	解樹強	褚克翔
外交科主任	林志鈞	同	趙管侯	克希克圖
軍政科主任	羅倫	同	王傅炯	管雲臣
敎育科主任	耿瓛顯	同	陳廷策	蕭湘
實業科主任	張善與	同	李素	王湘
地方自治科主任	汪彭年	同	于元芳	董昆瀛
庶政科主任	張嘉璈	同	胡源漼	戴聲敎

黨務部

部　長	丁世嶧	副部長	孫洪伊	胡汝麟
文牘科主任	王家襄	副主任	凌文淵	郭桂芬
會計科主任	金還	同	胡瑞霖	張開屏
交際科主任	黃爲基	同	李文熙	李俊

地方科主任　　梁善濟　　副主任　　鄭萬膽　孫熙澤

庶務科主任　　張協燦　　同　　　　虞廷愷　于邦華

然るに役員問題より內訌を生じ舊共和黨なる湖北議員張伯烈、鄭萬膽、胡鄂公、彭介石等十二名は少數黨なる民主黨が合併原約に違背して多數の役員を得んと要挾し共和黨が最後の合併討論會を開きたる際出席者少數なりしに拘はらず獨斷的に合併を可決し又共和黨に於て黎元洪及び湖北共和黨支部より合併原約の如く履行せん事を求めたる電報を隱匿したりとの理由の下に脫黨の宣言書を發表し再び共和黨を復活したり

第四節　小黨簇出

共和、民主、統一の三黨が不完全ながらも合同して進步黨を組織し兎も角も政界は二大政黨に統一せられ互に相對峙するに似たるも其實支那人の性質として極めて團結力に乏しく且又各自佔名熱獵官慾の旺盛なる爲め大政黨の下に陣笠として追隨するを欲せず共和黨が分離せしを始めとして各自に小黨派を組織して別箇の旗幟を張らんとし二大政黨の時代は極めて短かく再び小黨簇出の時代となり左の諸黨を現出せり

共　和　黨
政　友　會
相　友　會
民　憲　黨
癸　丑　同　志　會
超　然　社

集益會

政友倶樂部

平民黨

議員同志會

是等團體以外に尚種々なる小團體ありたり勿論是等團體所屬の大部分は或は國民黨に若しくは進步黨に屬し居りて全く獨立せるには非ずと雖其母黨たる國民黨及び進步黨の指揮統一は毫も行はれざりき斯く小黨の簇出を見たるが其口實とする所は進步、國民の二大政黨が專橫を爲すの虞あるを以て第三黨の地位に在りて牽制を行はんとするに在りと雖も其實袁世凱の國民黨切崩策に使用せられたるに過ぎず今其各小團體の性質を揭ぐれば

共和黨　は張百烈、鄭萬膽等湖北人が中心となりて組織せられたるものにて進步黨に合併せしも當時常に湯化龍、梁啓超等と相容れざる所あり合併當時民主黨の湯化龍が衆議院議長となり同黨の陳國祥が又副議長となり各役員中にも民主黨多數の地位を占めたるを以て大に不平を鳴らし遂に脫黨、分離するに至りたるなり

政友會　は國民黨の景燿月、王用賓等の組織する所にして會長に景燿月副會長に于右任、彭占元を舉げ會員は兩院內にて百名近くを有したり國民黨に籠絡せられて其藥籠中に入りたるものなり

相友會　は劉揆一の組織せし所にして劉は舊同盟會員なるが民國元年政黨內閣問題に就て國民黨各總長が連袂辭職せし際南北融和の目的を以て同黨を脫して後繼內閣に入閣せしも意の如くならず殊に宋敎仁案發生の際調停せんとして南下せるも南方側よりは北方の廻し者の如く思はれ歸來すれば

又北方より重用せられず止むを得ず黨爭調和の名の下に同會を組織して自己の立場を造らんとせり

民憲黨　は孫毓筠の發起する所にて孫は舊同盟會員たるも安徽都督を罷めて上京し總統府の顧問となりてより以來漸次袁世凱に籠絡せられ國事維持會を組織して唯管袁世凱の爲めに奔走せんとせしが案外國民黨の重要人物多く入會するに至りて己の意の如く自由に左右し能はざる事情となりたるを以て茲に又民憲黨を組織して第三黨の地位と爲し專ら袁世凱の御用を勤めんとするに在りたり

癸丑同志會　は民國黨の陳家鼎が組織せし所にて陳は衆議院議長選擧の際國民黨が己を議長に推薦せざりしを不滿として國民黨を脫黨し本會を組織するに至り二年六月十二日宣言書を發表し役員を選擧したり其顏振左の如し

正會長　劉公
副會長　張我華　王湘
總務部長　胡祖舜
副部長　禹瀛　耿毓英
政務部長　陳家鼎
同　趙時欽　高仲和
交際部長　胡鄂公
同　王國祜　席綏
文事部長　馬小進
同　韓玉辰　邵瑞彭
評議部長　高旭
同　李載賡　鄭江瀨

超然社　は元と國民黨の郭人漳、彭介石等牛耳を取り社員としては兩院に議員四十餘名を有し居りしが漸次軟化の色を現はせり

集益會　は朱兆莘、周廷勵等廣東一部の人の會合にて會員は僅に三十名位なるも結合は非常に堅く、伍朝樞、司徒穎等其中に在り均しく獵官熱を有す

政友倶樂部　は國民黨の恒士豐及び進步黨の藍公武等が主動者にて專ら進國二黨の調和を計るに在

りたり

平民黨　は民國元年發生したる五族聯合會の後身にして同會は趙秉鈞、段芝貴、烏珍等の組織せしものなれば其系統を汲む官僚黨の會合なり六月二十九日愈北京西單牌樓石虎胡同同事務所に於て成立式を擧行し宣言書を發表すると共に政綱を發表したり

平民黨の政綱

一、種族同化を促進す

二、自治の能力を發展す

三、經濟政策を勵行す

四、軍國主義を採用す

五、國民外交に重きを置く

六、固有の領土を完全にす

其の役員は左の如し

理事　　　陸建章　段祺瑞　程德全　黃雲招　徐紹楨

　　　　　那彥圖　彭士勛

此內專ら牛耳を取り居る者は趙秉鈞、陸建章なるを以て同黨の行動略推知し得べし

議員同志會　は舊民主黨の李慶芳等が主唱せる所にして專ら議員を會員として進步黨の分身なるも實は梁士詒の頤使を受け居るものなり

叙上各小黨の簇出は殆ど御用黨と民黨との區別を混亂し腐敗、軟骨、野心、狡獪の徒は皆此中に出沒縱橫せり然し當時進步黨系も國民黨系も倶に其母黨との聯絡を有し居りしが故に小黨は恰も出先の活

勤隊の如き有樣なりき

第五節　進歩黨と共和黨との交渉

進歩黨は共和黨を中心とし統一黨と民主黨を招きて合同し之に加ふるに袁世凱の黄金政策にて極力國民黨切崩策を行ひたる結果漸く國民黨と相拮抗し得るに至りたるに役員問題により端なく共和黨の脱黨分立となり而も其勢ひ侮る可らざるものあり成行の儘に放置せば進步の本黨何時瓦解するに至るやも知る可らざりしを以て直に臨時總會を開き共和黨復黨策を講じ委員を設け交渉せしめたるに共和黨にては決心甚だ固く左の要求條件を提出せり

一、黄群、孟森、楊廷棟、寔念益、陳敬弟、孫發緒の六名は種々の奸策を弄し或は黎理事長の電報を隱匿したる者なれば之を除名する事

二、蒲殿俊及び王印川等二名の理事は原合併條件になき者なれば之を取消す事

三、孫洪伊、林長民、梁善濟、胡瑞霖等の如き民主黨出身者の部長及び主任を更迭する事

四、進步黨を共和黨と改稱する事

五、幹事は凡て大會の席上投票を以て公擧する事

進步黨にては共和黨の脱黨を非常に苦痛とする所なるも此條件を容るゝ事は不可能なるを以て交渉遂に破裂して共和黨は斷然分立せり

共和黨の脱退問題は張伯烈、鄭萬膽、劉成禹、胡鄂公及び湖北代表高振霄、梅寶璣の極力主張せし所にして直に同黨本部を置き左の如く役員を選擧せり

黨務科　黄雲鵬

文書科　賀孝齊

交際科　　　　　陳紹唐

庶務科　　　　　邱志岳

會計科　　　　　黎宗嶽

衆議院交際員　　何　雯　吳宗慈

參議院交際員　　王　湘　鄭江瀛

合併せる三黨は僅に國民黨を制し得るに至れる際又々進歩黨の分裂により國民黨に制せらるゝに至る

べく消長の關係最も切なる所なれば百方共和黨引留めに盡力したるも何等の效を奏せざるのみならず

種々引戻運動を試みたる結果は却て益反撥の氣勢を增し遂には單に進步黨より脫退して中立的行動を

取るに止らず進んで國民黨と提携せんとするに至り國民黨の張繼は共和黨を國民黨側に引寄すべく好

機逸す可らずと爲し自ら進で共和黨に加入し遂に兩黨大に接近するに至れり

第六節　憲法起草問題

憲法起草機關を設けて憲法を編成せしめ其脫稿を待ちて議會の決議に付せんとは袁世凱の希望せる所

なりしが國民黨側にては約法及び國會組織法に由り兩院議員にて制定すべきが當然なりと主張せりさ

れば政府は前參議院當時旣に憲法起草機關設置案を提出せしに前參議院は一擊の下に是を斥け違法な

りとして取合はざりき

然れ共當時買收に由りて袁世凱の頤使に服從し暴威の脅迫に由りて其主張を變更し或は籠絡の時機を

以て擧附の機會と爲す者等尠からざりしかば憲法が果して如何なる機關に由りて起草制定せらるゝに

至るべきや遽かに知る能はざる情態に在りたり然るに共和黨が進步黨より脫退して國民黨に連合する

に及んで憲法起草問題に大々的促進を與へ衆議院に於て憲法起草委員選擧問題起れり此問題愈事實と

成り委員選舉となるや國民黨は景耀月等の牽ゆる相友會竝に新に進歩黨より脱出せし共和黨と互に連衡して進歩黨に當りたるを以て進歩黨は到底敵す可らず其結果兩院選出憲法起草委員は左の如し

衆議院選出三十名

國民黨（十四名）
張耀曾　李肇甫　伍朝樞　易宗夔　褚輔成
劉恩格　彭允彝　陳景南　徐秀鈞　孫潤宇
孫鍾　李芳　谷鍾秀　楊銘源

進步黨（九名）
汪榮寶　劉崇佑　王印川　李國珍　王敬芳
李慶芳　孟森　張國溶　汪彭年

共和黨（五名）
何雯　黃璋　黃雲鵬　吳宗慈　王紹鏊

政友會（一名）
史澤咸

超然社（一名）
夏同龢

參議院選出三十名

國民黨（十四名）
湯漪　楊永泰　宗淵源　朱兆辛　高家驥
蔣曾煥　殷世垣　金永昌　張成華　蔣舉清
呂志伊　向乃祺　金把椄　王鑫潤

進步黨（十名）
王家襄　丁世嶧　藍公武　曹汝霖　陸宗輿
王虞　解樹強　陳銘鑑　阿穆爾靈奎　陳善

政友會（四名）
趙世鈺　王用賓　石德純　金鼎勳

共和黨（二名）
饒應銘　東林桑多布

即ち衆議院部分の内にて

政府黨（進歩黨　　　　十一人）超然社　　　一人

民　黨（國民黨　　　　十四人）共和黨　　　五人
　　（三十人）政友會　　　一人

參議院部分の内にて

政府黨（十人）進歩黨　　　　十人

民　黨（國民黨　　　　十四人）政友會　　　四人
　　（三十人）共和黨　　　二人

憲法起草委員は參衆兩院を通じて民黨多數なり是に加ふるに墺國スコダ借款質問に對する六月二十五日衆議院に於ける財政次長梁士詒の爲したる答辯説明が甚だ國會を侮辱したるを以て反對派と御用派たるとを問はず均しく憤慨し期せずして政府彈劾案提出に一致し國民黨、共和黨、進歩黨、皆各彈劾案（其内彈劾論旨には輕重あり）を提出したるあり江西にては李烈鈞愈討袁の師を舉ぐるに至りたるを以て袁世凱は最早政黨を相手として云爲すべき時に非ずとの決心を爲したり當時御用黨たる進歩黨の彈劾案は唯世間に對する形式にして政府の急處を衝きたるものに非ざるも内心此際政府を改造し熊希齡を總理としして内閣を組織せしめんとの野心を有せり袁世凱は臨時政府期間中成るべく現政府（趙秉鈞政府）を維持する意見なりしも南方數省既に獨立を宣言するに至り其怨府た

る趙秉鈞内閣を維持するは不利なるを以て是が改造を為すは止むを得ざる事とし之が後繼者には徐世昌に囑望せり然れ共徐世昌が是を引受くるを承認せざるのみならず進歩黨が徐世昌に反對して熊希齡の辭職を許可して熊内閣の同意を衆議院に求めたり衆議院は熊希齡總理の同意案を議事日程に上しに際全然進歩黨の希望を斥くる能はず遂に熊希齡を國務總理に推薦するに決し趙秉鈞の辭職を許可して熊内閣の同意を衆議院に求めたり衆議院は熊希齡總理の同意案を議事日程に上したるが當初袁世凱は此問題を以て僅に進步黨の二三重要者にのみて國民黨は勿論共和黨にも何等協議せざりしが共和黨は凡そ斯の如き問題を豫め各黨に協議し互に意見を交換したる上にて決すべきものなるに事茲に出でざりしは他黨を蔑視したるものなりと大に憤慨し代表を國民黨に送つて當日缺席の交涉を為さしめ國民黨既に熊希齡の總理に反對決議を為したる程なれば早速其交涉に應じ當日二黨議員は出席せざりし爲め法定數に達する能はず遂に流會に終り熊希齡は當時來京せしも議會の形勢不利なるを見て倉皇熱河に歸れり

袁世凱は議會が益々邪魔者なる感を深くし之に威壓を加へて畏服せしめざる可らずと為し二年七月一日北京に戒嚴令を布き又同時に新任步軍統領趙秉鈞を北京警備地域司令官に京畿軍政執法所長陸建章を副司令官に任命し更に又言論機關に對し高壓手段を取り國民黨系に屬する新聞は續々發行を禁止し民黨側の議員には軍警を尾行せしめ以て震慄せしめたり斯くて熊希齡の總理問題は更に日程に上されたるに參衆兩院とも軍警の脅迫に止むを是に同意を與へたり

茲に於て國民黨所屬の參議院議員韓玉辰は此次江西の獨立は政府の種々なる違法失政が激成したるものにて然も總統が國憲を紊亂し宵小を信用し閣員を傀儡にし國會を玩弄したると為し其罪狀を舉げて袁總統に辭職勸告の建議案を議會に提出したり又上海に在る蔡元培、汪兆銘及び唐紹儀等は此次江西事件爆發南北衝突せしは國家重大の損害にて此衝突を止むるには此際袁世凱の退職を求むるに如かず

と爲し又電報を發して辭職を勸告せり

袁世凱は戒嚴令を楯にし軍政執法所に命じ國民黨議員にて多少疑はしき所あれば犯證の有無に拘らず直に之を拘引し後より罪跡を構成するが如き暴擧に出でしが爲め議員等は到底危險にして國事を議する能はずとなし天津若しくは南方に避難する者多く議會は議員數不足の爲め遂に開會する能はざるに至れり議會既に法定議員數を缺き開會する能はず袁世凱は直に議員を塵殺するより寧ろ漸次餓死せしむるの策を採り議員等の體給支出を停止せり又江西獨立事件は起事の人物が國民黨に籍を有せるを以て北京に殘れる國民黨國會議員を壓迫破壞するに極めて好口實を與へたれば袁世凱は更に檢察廳に命じて壓迫檢束手段を取らしめたり依て總檢察廳にては先づ國民黨理事長代理吳景濂を召喚して左の嚴命を下せり

各國政黨の例を見るに皆其黨の首領に由て左右せらる然るに今國民黨の首領株なる黃興、柏文蔚、陳其美、陳烱明等南方に於て民國に反抗する叛逆行動を執りつゝあり國民黨は彼等の行動を默認する者なるや否や若し認め居らば黨員を其一味として處罰するの外なく然ざれば此際彼等を除名すべし

吳景濂は此言渡を受けたるも自分一己の意見にて卽答する能はざれば黨員會議の上囘答すべしと謂ひ引下りたり然るに黨員の大半は江西事件發し、後天津若しくは上海に避難せる現狀とて直に會議決定するに至らざりしに袁世凱は更に重ねて左の敎令を發して三日間に同黨の態度を決すべく然らざれば內亂助成機關と看做し假借せざるべしと威壓的手段に出でたり

（民國二年七月三十一日敎令）

政黨の行動は首として法律を重んず近來江西、湖北、上海、南京等の兇徒亂を構へ其逆首たる黃興陳其美、李烈鈞、陳烱明、柏文蔚等は皆國民黨の重要人物にて其他の逆徒者も亦多く國民黨員なり

究竟該黨は通謀するものなるや將た僅に黃興、李烈鈞等の私人行動なるや態度明ならずして人言藉
藉たり今戒嚴時代に當る警備地域總司令をして該黨幹部人員を傳詢せしめ若し果して逆謀に預らず
ば三日內に自ら是を宣布し並に該黨に隷する叛黨を一律除名すべく政府は當然常の如く保護すべき
も若し聲言亂を助け或は詞を藉りて搪塞せば是政黨の名義を以て內亂機關を爲すものにして法律の
許さゞる所決して該黨の爲めに假借せず

國民黨は止むを得ず殘留黨員幹部會を開き凝議の結果警備司令部に對し左の回答を爲したり

江西、南京等の事變は全く個人の行動にして本黨に何等關係なし故に其宣言せり尙本黨理事若し
くは參議たる黃興、陳其美、李烈鈞、陳烱明、柏文蔚の五名に對しては大會を開きて公決すべき筈
なるも時日なき爲め取敢へず幹部會に於て敎令通り除名したり此旨報告す

第七節　南方新政府の豫想

當時南軍には疾くも新政府設立の計畫あり其內閣の顏觸左の如し

國務總理　　　　　　汪　兆　銘

內務總長　　　　　　程　德　全

外務總長　　　　　　王　寵　惠

交通總長　　　　　　溫　宗　堯

陸軍總長　　　　　　李　烈　鈞

海軍總長　　　　　　湯　薌　銘

農林總長　　　　　　王　正　廷　或は　毛　仲　芳

敎育總長　　　　　　蔡　元　培

財政總長　　　陳錦濤

司法總長　　　張耀曾

參謀總長　　　李烈鈞

參謀次長　　　鈕永建

警視總監　　　陳其美

參議院議長　　張繼

衆議院議長　　谷鍾秀

日本公使　　　胡瑛

露國公使　　　胡漢民

英國公使　　　未定

米國公使　　　伍廷芳

佛國公使　　　魏宸組

獨逸公使　　　馬君武

然るに一時衝天の勢を以て組織せられたる南方諸省の討袁軍も僅か一箇月ならざるに全然失敗に歸し首領連多く亡命するに至れり袁軍が斯く優勢にして南軍遂に失敗に至りたるは全く左の理由に由る

三、統一したる行政機關を有したる事

二、訓練あり且つ統一したる軍隊を有したる事

一、五國借款成立に依て是を軍費に流用するを得たる點

北軍の優勢なりし點

支那政黨史

四、鐵道、電信、汽船其他交通及び輸送の機關を有したる事

五、軍費豐富なりしを以て平常よりも將士に多額の給料及び手當を與へ得たる事

六、動員に際し又は戰場に臨むに當り將士等の榮譽とし希望する勳位勳章を與へたる事

七、支那人一般が平和を好む性質より南北を通じて動亂を恐怖嫌忌したる事

八、袁世凱は外交に巧にして且つ列國に多少信用ありし爲め種々の便宜を得たる事

九、軍器及軍需品を外國より容易に供給せらるゝの利便を得たる事

南軍の不振なりし點

一、軍資に缺乏したるのみならず一般支那人は勿論軍人等も南軍發行の軍票を授受することを欲せず十元の軍票よりも一元の銀貨を好みたる事

二、統一的中心人物を有せず又省と省との間に完全なる聯絡を缺きたる事

三、南軍に加擔して若し戰爭敗北せんか皆嚴刑に處せられんことを恐れたるを以て南方各省軍隊は二心を抱き躊躇して容易に立たず爲めに時機を失したる事

四、前項三、四、五、八及九に列擧したる如き機關及び條件を缺如したる事

第八節　第二次革命後の險象

第二次革命は遂に其目的を達する能はずして壓伏せられ大局は鎭定に歸したり然れ共此鎭定たる單に一時的のものにして換言すれば五國團の借款ありたる爲め金力にて纔に贏ち得たるなり隨て其後には尚左の危險を有せり

一、北方は全く袁世凱を中心とするを以て袁の生命及び勢力維持の如何は治亂の岐るゝ所なり

二、南方は主義目的に依つて集合したる團體なるを以て二三有力者を失ふも其主義目的を拋棄せず

将來種々の形式に於て現はるべし

三、北方の袁世凱系及接近者は道義の觀念に乏しきに反し南方人士は正義派をして漸次內外人の同情を得るに至るべし

四、支那の新聞雜誌著作物に益袁世凱反對の言論を見るに至るべし

五、此次の革命に失敗したる志士は各國に亡命して益革命思想を鼓吹すべし

六、人心險惡に陷り漸次反亂を好むに傾くと共に功名心の熾なるもの每に革命を企圖し冒險性增大すべし

七、袁世凱の內治外交にして失敗せんか直に革命黨に益攻擊の絕好機會を與ふべし

八、世人は一般に北强南弱を惟思するも決して然らざるは明朝朱元章及洪秀全を見て知るべし

第九節　進步黨及國民黨の衰滅

袁世凱を援け議會に於て或は新聞雜誌に因りて國民黨と抗爭戰鬪したるものは進步黨なり兵力を動かし戰爭に訴へて討平鎭壓したる者は袁世凱なり卽ち袁世凱は進步黨の擁護を得て國民黨に當り進步黨は袁世凱の使嗾を受けて國民黨を排し所謂敵を同ふする者意氣相合し兩々相幇助して以て最終の勝利を得此に創設に對し一致の行動を取るべく期したるものゝ如きも國民黨が武力的打擊に由りて其首領連を失ひ餘黨の勢力も亦大に振はざるに至りたるや袁世凱と進步黨との間に於ける兩々幇助の態度は甚だ冷々淡々たるのみならず進步黨は袁世凱より所謂狡兔死して走狗烹られ飛鳥落ちて良弓藏められんとするの取扱を受くるに至れり

國民黨は同黨に密接なる關係を有せる首領連が南方に事を擧ぐると共に多數の同黨議員南下したる爲め當時在京する者は僅に二百名前後に過ぎざりしが政府の同黨に對する態度は恰も黨員全部を以て南

支那政黨史

軍加擔者の如く思惟し種々の壓迫を加ふる爲め在京議員にして脫黨して他黨に轉入する者尠からざるに至り結局同黨は如何なる方針を取るべきかは世人一般の注意する所なりしが在京同黨所屬兩院議員等百數十名は民國二年八月七日同黨本部に會合凝議の結果政黨として同黨が今囘の事件に關係なきは過般宣言したる如くなれば敢て組織を變更する必要を認めず依然現狀を維持し正々堂々法律の範圍內に於て行動するに決定し追つて戰爭平定の後大會を開き理事を改選する事とせり

第十節　小黨の離合

一時二大政黨對立の觀を呈したる政界も政府の國民黨分裂策效を奏し種々の小政黨出顯するに至り又湖北選出の舊共和黨議員の進步黨より分離するあり憲政公會の發生するあり議會の形勢は是等小黨の向背離合に由つて左右せられつゝ有るが此次南北衝突は國民黨に與へ同黨は僅に消極なる現狀維持に屛息せざるを得ず尙黨員中には政府壓迫を恐れて他黨に轉籍する者あり其影響少からざるより同黨の易宗夔、趙炳麟、恒鈞及楊永泰等は寧此際進步黨の如く純然たる政府擁護にも非ず又國民黨の如く政府に反對にも非ずして共和を鞏固にし政府を監督する目的を以て左の諸小黨を合倂せんとしたり

一、相友會　前農工商總長劉揆一の組織したるものにて國民、進步兩黨の議員を羅致し成立以來僅に二箇月なるも議員中に一頭角を顯し陳懿宸等之を主持せり曩に劉揆一が工商部借欵問題にて輿論の攻擊を受け會務に影響する所尠からざりしを以て會務一切を舉げて楊度に委し楊の左右する所なりしが楊は大に合同に贊成せり

二、集益會　約一箇月前重に廣東選出國民黨議員等の組織したるものなるも他省國民黨議員の加入する者も亦少からず朱兆莘、周廷勵等之を左右す

三、大同會　素と西北實業協會と稱せしものにして既に成立後一年餘なるも一向活動せず朱得裳
　李濆丞等是を主持す

四、潛社　司徒穎、黄霄九等が組織し國會成立後間もなく成立せしものなり

五、憲政公會　蒙古王公及び許世英、恩華、張國溶等の組織したるものにて蒙藏選出議員等を網
　羅す

六、超然社　國會開會後夏同龢、郭人章、李增及び黄懋等の組織せるものにて所屬兩院議員數十
　名を有す

七、政學社　蕭瑞鱗等の組織せるものなり

然れども該小黨中には純然たる官僚分子存在し居るを以て遂に其合同を見る能はざりき

第十一節　大中黨の成立

袁世凱の横暴威力は既に各政黨を畏伏したるを以て漸く其包藏せる野心を露出し來り先づ憲法を制定
する以前に正式大總統の地位に就き其地位既に確固となりたる後徐ろに時勢の趨向を卜し帝制可なら
ば帝制を取り憲法は欽定に由りて施行し共和可なれば大總統の權限は皇帝と同一にし以て憲法の拘束
を受けざらん事を企圖するに至れり茲に於て梁士詒は其慧眼能く袁世凱が帝冠を戴かんとする野心あ
るを看破し直に大總統の選擧及び憲法制定の二問題に對し大に忠勤を效さんとし竊に潛社を通じて集
益社、相友會、超然社、憲政公會、政德會の各小政團を操縱するの策を取りたり而して此操縱策は首
尾克く效を奏し總統先選憲法後定も澁滯なく進行し遂に憲法の一部即ち總統、副總統の選擧法のみを
制定し先づ是に由りて總統を選擧し袁世凱は臨時總統より選ばれて正式總統に當選したり

今其大總統選擧に關する憲法の一部及大總統選擧の情況を示せば左の如し

大總統選舉法（民國二年十月四日憲法會議通過五日公布）

中華民國憲法會議謹で大總統選舉法を制定し並に之を宣布す

第一條　中華民國人民にして完全に公權を享有し年齡四十歳以上にして滿十年以上國內に居住する者は大總統に選擧せらる〻ことを得

第二條　大總統は國會議員にて總統選擧會を組織し之を選擧す

前項の選擧は選擧人總數三分の二以上の列席を以て之を行ひ得票が投票人數の四分の三に滿つる者を以て當選とす但し二囘投票するも當選人なきときは第二囘の得票の比較的多き者に就て決選し得票が投票人數の半に過ぐる者を以て當選とす

第三條　大總統の任期は五年とし若し再選さるれば一囘連任するを得

大總統の任滿つる三箇月前に國會議員は自ら集會を行ひ總統選擧會を組織して次任大總統の選擧を行ふべし

第四條　大總統就職するときは須く左記の宣誓を爲すべし

余は誓つて至誠を以て憲法の職を行ふ謹で誓ふ

第五條　大總統缺位するときは副總統之を繼任し本任大總統の任期滿つるの日に至て止む

大總統事故ありて職務を執行すること能はざるときは副總統を以て之を代理す

副總統同時に缺位するときは國務院に於て其職を攝行し同時に國會議員は三箇月內に自ら集會を行ひ總統選擧會を組織して次任大總統の選擧を行ふ

第六條　大總統已に任滿つるの日解職するも若し期に至り次任大總統未だ選出せられざるか或は選出後未だ就職せず次任副總統亦未だ代理する能はざるときは國務院に於て其職務を攝行す

第七條　副總統の選擧は大總統選擧の規定に依り大總統の選擧と同時に之を行ふ但し副總統缺位する

ときは是を補選すべし

　附則　大總統の職權は憲法の未だ制定せられざる以前に在りては暫く臨時約法の臨時大總統に關す

る規定に依る

斯くの如く憲法の一部を制定し直ちに十月六日正式總統の選擧を行ひたるに其の結果初選、再選等しく

法定數の投票を得る能はず決選投票に由り漸く袁世凱の當選を見翌日又副總統を選擧し黎元洪當選せ

り而して袁世凱の當選に就ては梁士詒の操縱する六政團與て大に力ありたり

總統の選擧終るや此六政團は尚袁世凱に忠勤を致さんが爲め合併することゝなり黨名を大中黨と稱し

國家主義を採り政治を立憲の軌道に導き共和を鞏固にし統一を保持するを政綱として標榜せり其臨時

職員は左の如し

文　牘　林紉武　張樹森

庶　務　林紉武　張樹森　楊增炳　辛漢梁義

黨約起草　江天鐸　張樹森　張國溶　朱兆莘

第十二節　民憲黨成立

袁世凱の政黨壓迫愈激烈と成るに隨ひ國民黨中の穩健分子と進步黨中の民權分子とは漸く接近し來り

遂に兩分子より一の民憲黨なるものを組織せり黨中重要人物は國民黨の谷鍾秀、孫潤于、沈鈞儒、張

治祥、曹玉德、鍾才宏、張耀曾、湯漪、楊永泰、進步黨の劉崇佑、汪彭年、解樹強、李國珍、丁世嶧、

藍公武等にして民主精神を貫徹し立憲政治を勵行するを以て趣旨とせり

袁世凱は江西事件に由りて國民黨に大打擊を與へ己れ既に正式總統と成りたるに由りて資格の鞏固を

加へ茲に勃々包藏せる野心を發露し來り先づ總統選擧法の公布權に對し憲法會議に反對を唱へ次に臨
時約法の修正增加五箇條を議會に提出し次いで憲法草案の起草發表せらるべや憲法制定に干涉して自
己の欲する如き憲法を制定せしめんが爲め左の意味の通牒を議會に送り挑戰の端を啓けり

大總統の職に居り將來民國議會の擬する憲法を執行する責任を有す隨て苟も執行困難及び國家の興
亡治亂に影響するものは勢ひ一言せざる可らず云々

斯の如く漸く起草せられんとする憲法が袁世凱の攪亂に由り危險に瀕せしを以て國民進步兩黨中の隱
健分子は其起草したる憲法維持の爲に兩黨を融和せしめざる可らずとして此民憲黨を組織したるなり

第十三節　袁世凱の憲法破壞

袁世凱は憲法起草委員會が憲法の大綱を擬定し將に條項の編成を爲さんとするに當り突然左の如き通
牒を送り破壞的妨害を試みたり

大總統の職に居り將來民國議會の擬する憲法を執行する責を負ふ以上苟も見て執行困難とし及び國
家の治亂興亡に影響を及ぼす所あらば勢ひ一言なき能はず況や共和成立し本大總統幸に其間に周旋
する事を得今や國民の推擧を受けて此重任を負ふ民國根本組織の憲法大典に對し若し知る所ありて
言はず或は言て盡さざるは殊に民國に忠なるの素志に非ざるに於てをや茲に本總統は至誠を以て民
國憲法に對し陳述するあらんとし特に國務院に命じて委員施愚、顧鼇、饒孟任、黎淵、方樞、程樹
源、孔昭薪、余棨昌を派遣し本總統の意見を代表せしむ爾後貴會或は憲法起草委員會或は憲法審議
會を開くときは豫め國務院に通知して該委員等の出席陳述に便せられたし

憲法起草委員會は此通牒に接するや直に左の通りの意味の書面を送りて之を拒絕せり

憲法會議の性質は兩院と異り大總統は憲法會議に議案を提出するの權なければ當然委員を出席せし

め說明せしめらるゝ必要なし云々

然るに袁世凱は當時開會せる憲法起草會に八人の該委員を派遣し該委員は突然政府委員と稱して同會
會場に至り出席說明の任に當らんことを申込みたり
起草委員は政府委員が本委員會に出席するは法律上何等の根據なく且つ憲法起草規則に據れば兩院議
員以外の人員の出席する能はざるのみならず傍聽も禁ぜる所なり隨て其入場を許さずとて是を拒絕し
政府委員等は強ひて入場したるを以て守衞に命じ引出さしめたり
袁世凱は憲法起草干與策が斯の如く失敗に歸したるを以て更に其方法を替へ從來問題ある每に慣用せ
る各省都督及び民政長を動かし憲法會議に向ひ一大警告を爲さしむる策を執り各省都督に左の電報を
發したり

今囘起稿せる憲法草案は行政部に對する束縛甚しく卽ち第十一條に總理の任命は衆議院の同意を經
べしと言ひ第四十三條に衆議院は國務員に對し不信任の決議を爲すことを得と言ひ第八十三條には
不信任の決議を受けたる者は須らく其職を免ずべしと言ふ此規定あれば議員は任意不信任の投票を
投じ隨時行政權を推倒することを得て國會の專制と成らん今約法を按ずるに別に平政院を設け行政
訴訟をして亦平政院に隸せしむるは行政官に行政處分の權なく法院は行政の掣肘を爲す國會委員會
は少數を以て專制す而して閉會期間內の總理を行政官に任命すると緊急命令及財政緊急處分を發布すること
は須らく此委員會にて決議すとは最も立法を侮蔑す審計院は院より選任又は事前に監督する法を用
ひ政府をして運用の餘地なからしむ斯の如く重々束縛を行ふは皆立法部議員の
下に隸屬せしむるものにて是れ無政府と同じ大總統本と憲法に與聞する先例あり特派員を國會に赴
かしめ一面中外法家を集合して公同討論すべし各該文武官は共に國民の一分子にして且つ各治安を

支那政黨史

保衞するの任務あれば詳細研究の上電報到著後五日內に返電し各其議論を述べ以て採擇に便せよ云云

袁世凱が此電報を發するや直隷都督馮國璋先づ袁の意に迎合して左の返電を爲し來れり

憲法起草委員會の議せる草案の種々背謬なるは枚擧に遑あらず今同會の議せる草案の行政權に對する一方面を見るに箝制剝奪至らざるなく甚しきに至つては國會閉會後國務員を國會委員十數名にて否決するを得べきが如き是れ行政官の一擧一動を槪して少數人の手に操縱するもの議會專制此に至りて極まれり尙政務の進行を言ひ得べきか今三權分立を圖らず政府を束縛するを先務と爲し行政權をして立法權司法權の下に奴隷たらしめんとす故に一般輿論皆曰く起草委員會は乃ち是れ國民黨連の主持する所にして其破壞行爲は南方に志を肆にするより憲法に毒を肆にせんとするなりと余の考にては此次の憲法草案中行政權の各條に對しては竭力研究して改修を加へ政府をして克く力を盡さむるを良とす若し破壞主張者が己れの意見を固持して肯せずば是れ區々たる數十名の起草委員を以て國家の公意に反する者は蠹賊なり大總統は南北旣に統一し列國旣に承認した

る今日縱ひ曲げて蠹賊を容さんも四億の人民の爲に計り國家の前途の爲めに計れば勢必ず起草委員の故を以て激動し擧國紛爭し或は意外の變生じて憲法をして永く告成するの日なからしめ國家は遂に傾覆するの虞有らん云云

其他各省都督の返電亦大略皆此電報と大同小異にして袁の意を迎合するに非ざるはなかりき

袁世凱は飽迄憲法上自己の權力を大ならしめんとし場合に由りては非常手段にも出で兼まじき注意を爲し居り御用黨の結束に著手すると同時に慣用得意の手段なる議員買收を始めたり當時各政黨の態度を見るに大中黨、公民黨、政友會の如きは勿論其他進步黨の過牛及び國民黨の一部は忠勤を擢んと

各提携を企て幹部連は頻に奔走運動に従事せり

是に對し民憲黨、國民黨の大部分、進步黨の一部は成るべく民主黨的の法を制定せんことを力め相一致

して如上の連合黨に當れり然れども買收日々に盛なる爲め日頃強硬說を唱へ居たる者にして漸次態度

曖昧となる者あり幹部連が是を防止するに努むるも奈何せん金力と權力の迫る所は到底敵し能はざる

を以て此際總統選舉のときの如く各自の自由に委する方を寧ろ得策と爲し遂に一切放任せり

第十四節　國民黨本部の封鎖

袁世凱は機關新聞及び軍警界をして行政權を立法權又は司法權の下に奴隷たらしめんとする憲法案を起

草したるは畢竟國民黨議員等の跋扈する結果なりと呼號せしめ而して各省都督等の返電も亦省の意

を迎合して雷同するや袁は機熟せりと爲し十一月四日午後四時軍警三百餘名を新儀門大街なる國民黨

本部に派遣し適同部に在りたる同黨首領なる吳景濂、王正延等數名を監視せしめたる上家宅捜索を行

ひ荷馬車數輛に滿載する多數の書類を押收し同本部を封鎖せしむると共に國民黨の罪狀を宣布し特に

全國に對し（一）國民黨本支部の閉鎖及同黨所屬國會議員の資格を剝奪し其補充を行ふべきこと（二）各

省地方長官及知事に對し國民黨員に報復す可らざることの二命令を發したり此結果四日よ

り五日にかけ三百六十五名の國會議員が資格を剝奪せられ又四日國民黨本部より書類を押收調査した

る結果當て同黨に籍を置きたること判明したる參議院議員二十二名、衆議院議員七十一名合計九十三

名は七日に至り更に其の資格を剝奪せられたり是に於て前後四百五十八名は一片の命令を以て資格を

剝奪せられ國會は事實上解散と同一に歸せり

參議院議長王家襄、衆議院議長湯化龍は議會維持に關し袁世凱に協議する所ありしも要領を得ざるを

以て殘留議員を招集して結局政府は國議を維持する意思なければ最早開會する望なきが如しと報告し

支那政黨史

但法律上未だ解散せざるものなれば今後も亦平常の如く議事日程を配付なすべきや如何と謀りしに自由解散を主張する者ありしも牟琳、王乃昌、蕭晋榮等は政府が國民黨議員の資格を剝奪したるは國會を解散するの意なるや明にして唯其名に由らずして其實を取りたるのみなれば今若し自由に解散せば其責議員に歸し政府過失なきに至らんされば何を以て國民に對し一時休會すると共に一面國會の開會する能はざる理由を全國に電告して一般人民をして議會の今日に至りたるは議員の罪に非ざる事を知らしむべしと主張し黃雲鵬は更に一步を進めて曰く議會が今日活動する能はざるは唯機關が停止したるのみにて議員に異狀なし議員は約法に據り質問提出權を有するを以て一面其事情を全國に電告するを同時に一面全部連署にて政府に質問書を提出せんと主張し御用黨の陸宗輿は曰く政府の今囘の行動は文字にて能く解決し得る所に非ず前年武漢の起義は人民の爲めに政府の命を革めたるものにして今日政府が議員の資格を取消したるは卽ち政府の爲めに人民の命を革めたるものなり既に革命問題なれば政府に質問書を提出するも政府は顧みざるべし故に質問書提出の如きは見合して唯休會すれば可ならんと揶揄せり參議院議員丁世嶧奮然起つて曰く陸議員が此擧を以て政府の爲めの革命を爲したるは確論にして亦休會の主張も道理あるが如きも唯だ議會は革命的に非ず又政府と武力的對峙を爲す能はず現在人數不足の爲め議決する能はず且一旦議決せば此次休會の後千秋萬世を經るも亦長く法律上開會するの日なきを恐る余の所見を以てすれば唯一同辭職するのみ但し其時機は必ず質問の結果を待つべし質問書も亦效力ありや否やを望むに非ず四日の命令發布後國會は未だ是に對する意思を表示せざれば一般國民是を知ずして政府の行動を以て合法と誤解するやも計り難し吾人は此質問書を藉り命令に對し相當に辯論を爲し決して一人の手を以て天下の耳目を掩はざらしむるに過ぎず若し政府が囘答せざれば是れ理に屈したるものと謂ふべし假令囘答するも若し其當を得ざれば

國民に自ら公論あるべし吾人此時に於て辭職するは最も適當の時機に非ずやと主張したり茲に於て衆論は議員にして若し果して内亂行爲あらば約法に依り逮捕して可なり政府は如何なる法律に依據し命令を以て議員の資格を取消したるやとの意味の質問書を提出せり然れども政府は是に對し何等の回答をも與へざりき

第十五節　憲法起草委員會解散及進步黨の最後

民國二年十一月四日突然國會議員中國民黨に關係ある者の資格剝奪命令を發したるが爲め憲法起草委員會の委員六十名中にも該命令にて資格を取消されたる者二十八名あり殘る三十二名にては會議を催す能ざるに至れり當時憲法案は旣に議了せられて憲法會議に送付濟なりしも其理由書の起草未了なりしが殘留委員の議員會を開きたるも殘務整理委員に理事李國珍を擧げ書記二名を殘したるのみにて自ら解散を決議し是を通知せり

進步黨は十一月三十日議員會を開き國會維持に關し強硬なる態度に出で尙同黨所屬の國務員を訪問して其意向を質したるが十二月六日に至り再び議員會を開き梁啓超、汪大燮及び張謇の三國務員は出席し梁啓超は席上從來自己の意見として世上に流布せらるゝ點に誤報ありとて國會に對する意見を發表したり是は梁一箇の意見に非ずして進步黨所屬國務員は勿論國務員全體の意見と思惟せらるゝ節あり卽ち左の如し

國會問題の發生以來屢々來塲して應酬せんと欲したりしも他務の爲め遺憾ながら今日迄遲延したるが此次の國會問題に對し大總統は初めより國會を打消さなどの意思なく國會を維持するを熱望し居り國務院は殊に國會維持を主張しつゝあり大總統が今囘の手段に出でたるは嚴格なる法律より見れば固より違法なり然れども湖口の起事後著名の亂黨員にして國會に籍を置ける者多かりしに兩院

支那政黨史

は亂黨に通じたる議員の資格を取消すの提議を爲したることもなく國會の威嚴を損ずるを免れざる
に由り袁總統は亂黨に對しては既に法に依り懲治したるも議院が亂黨員を刪除するを肯せざるを以
て袁總統は國會の尊嚴を維持する爲め故らに此舉に出でたる次第にして政治方面より見れば實に諒
すべき所あり殊に今囘は決して議員を除名せるに非ずして唯議員證書は乃ち行政官なれば證書を取戻すことも仍ほ行政上の作用
書は選擧監督より受くるものにて選擧監督は乃ち行政官なれば證書を取戻すことも仍ほ行政上の作用
と視るを得べし政府の爲めに辯ぜざれば已むも若し政府の爲めに辯ずれば固より振々として辭有る
なり去月四日命令の發せられたる後余は國務院に於て最も多く發言し且つ最も激切なりしに外間多
く是を知らず甚しきに至りては余が五年間國會を要せずと主張したりとか或は國會解散を主張した
りとか新聞に報ずるに至れり尤も該起事が盡く不確實なりと稱するに非ずとも唯だ余の談片を取ら
んとして其眞意を失したるなり當初余の主張は若し總統及び國務院が五年間能く責任を負ひ得て國
會を不用とする氣力あらば一時國會を停止するとも解散するとも可なる可きも若し如上の決心なく
んば速に維持法を講ずべく國會をして不死不生ならしむるは卽ち余の敢て贊成する所に非ずと云ふ
に在りしなり袁總統は曾て國民黨を以て議院中少數を占むと爲し一部分の議員を取消さしむるとも
必ず開會不能に至らざるべしと思惟し居りしに命令を下したる後豈料らんや遂に國會をして支持す
る能はざるに至らしめたり是實に袁總統の意想外なりしなり今日國會を維持せんとする先決問題は
卽ち去月四日の命令を承認し仍ほ命令の範圍外に出でざるを要するに在り唯如何に進行
すべきに關しては諸君の討議を望む
是に由りて觀れば國會が此境遇に陷りたるは袁總統の豫定か違算かは暫く措き兔に角梁啓超は袁の走
狗と成りて國民黨を倒し其國民黨の大打擊を受けたる爲め進步黨も兔死狐悲の地位に陷りたるを懺悔

するものにて己の罪を袁に負はせて黨員に對する自己の言譯を爲し尙黨員をして袁の不法命令を承認して其下に哀を乞はしめんとするに在り如何に軟骨被買收著多き進步黨と雖是に盲從する能はず兎に

角理事長黎元洪の訓示を仰ぐことゝせり

袁世凱は國民黨を驅逐し國會を摧殘したる後黎元洪の進步黨理事長たり共和黨に推戴せらるゝを好まず軍人にして政黨に關係するは禁令なりとて强て脫黨せしめたれば黎元洪は止むを得ず脫黨を宣言して進步黨に何等の援助を與ふるを得ざるを聲明せり進步黨は國會維持の說を固執し種々運動する所ありたるも政府は單に莊嚴神聖の國會を破壞せずと稱するのみにて何等維持の方法を講ぜざるのみならず曖昧なる政治會議なるものを組織して國會の處分約法の修正を講ぜしめ或は憲法會議を組織せんとする爲め國會固有の權限を剝奪し盡くし國會維持全く絕望に歸したるに由り二年十二月二十五日悲慘なる留別會を開き來會議員三百餘名皆萬斛の恨を含み悲憤の演說を爲して散會し翌三年一月五日更に殘留國會議員最後の會議を開き國會に對する懺悔として左の二項を議決せり

一、本年は必ず國會を召集すべきこと

二、憲法は必ず民選機關にて制定すること

國民黨を倒さん爲め袁の走狗と成りて狂噪せし進步黨も僅に半年を經ざる內に狡兎死して走狗煮らるゝ境遇と成り最後の悲鳴として前二項を議決し玆に全く雲散霧消せり而して同月十二日袁世凱は政治會議の上申に因り國會を斷然解散せり玆に至りて共和民國は純然たる袁專制と成り過去の政黨は到る所の空屋軒頭に其黨名の看板を存せるのみ

第十六節　政治會議の組織

袁世凱は國會を不死不生の境遇に陷るゝと共に直に中央行政會議なる名稱の下に中央及び各省の代表

者を召集し之に依りて一時彌縫せんとしたりしが該會議は其名稱の範圍を越え立法權に迄立入らんとするの形勢ありしかば國會議員及一部政治家間に反對の聲囂々として起り流石の袁世凱も持て餘し氣味なりしに十一月二十六日に至り政治會議を特設する左の如き命令を出したり

共和の精義は衆思を集め忠益を廣くし國利民福を謀り實事求是を期するに在り現在正式政府既に成立し本總統は國務院を督同し業に大政方針を次第に議決せり但だ建設の始め萬端理を待ち根本大計に關しては討論最も精詳を貴ぶが故に前に電報にて各省に命じ人を擧げて上京せしめ特に政治會議を開きて内外の隔關を去り共に時艱を濟ふを得せしむるを以てせり現に各省派遣の人員不日齊集するに由り國務總理より二名を擧派し各部總長は毎部一人を擧派し法官二人蒙藏事務局は酌量の上數人を擧派すべし本總統は李經義、梁敦彥、樊增祥、蔡鍔、寶熈、馬良、楊度、趙惟熈を特派し合せて政治會議の機關を組織して各々知る所を竭し共和政治を襄け邦基を盤石に奠め以て全國喁々待治の心を慰せんこと本總統の望む所なり

政治會議の性質は唯袁世凱が專制獨裁にして各方面の集議に由りて政治を進行すると云ふ世間に對する言譯に過ぎず隨て其範圍甚不明瞭なり

其委員の顏振左の如し

總統府特派八名　　李　經　義　　梁　敦　彥　　樊　增　祥　　蔡　鍔　　寶　熈

國務總理擧派二名　　方　　樞　　吳　貫　因

馬　良　　趙　惟　熈　　楊　度

外交部擧派一名　　陳　懋　鼎

內務部擧派一名　　顧　鼇

財政部舉派一名　　　　　吳乃琛

陸軍部舉派一名　　　　　徐樹錚

海軍部舉派一名　　　　　王崇文

司法部舉派一名　　　　　余紹宋

教育部舉派一名　　　　　許壽裳

工商部舉派一名　　　　　夏敬觀

農林部舉派一名　　　　　劉夢馥

交通部舉派一名　　　　　陸夢熊

法　官二名　　　　　汪羲芝　姚震

蒙藏事務局舉派七名

內　蒙　　　貢桑諾爾布　阿穆爾靈圭

外　蒙　　　那彥圖　　　塔旺布魯克

前　藏　　　江贊桑布

後　藏　　　廈仲阿旺益喜

青　海　　　札勒根頓丹增諾爾布

直　隸　　　梁建章　　　劉彭壽

湖　北　　　劉邦驥　　　夏壽康

奉　天　　　陳瀛海　　　張國淦

吉　林　　　徐鼎康　　　齊忠甲

省	氏名
山東	王丕煦
山西	邢殿元
陝西	王恒晉
甘肅	秦望蘭
江蘇	張一麐
浙江	孫世偉
黑龍江	張志潭
江西	梅光遠
福建	方熬
湖南	貝昕
河南	沈兆昌
廣東	周允易
廣西	朱銘潮
四川	胡爲亮
安徽	孫忠筠
雲南	朱毓寶
貴州	王家撲
新疆	王學曾
川邊	嚴崇徑

此政治會議は開會第一に國會の改組を請願し袁世凱は是を藉つて國會殘留議員に職務停止布告を發し
次で又袁世凱が約法增修に關する造法機關の組織方法等に就き諮詢する所ありたるに對し約法會議を
組織するの可なるを議決覆申し以て約法改刪の端を啓けり

第十七節　約法會議の組織

民國三年一月二十六日袁世凱は約法會議組織條例二十二箇條及約法會議議員選舉順序施行細則等を公
布すると共に左の如き約法會議組織の命令を下せり

造法機關は民國國家の根本法を改造する爲めに設け其職權範圍及び其組織方法は均しく重要に關す
前に一再政治會議に諮詢し決議申覆せしむ茲に該會議の上申に據れば此種の造法機關は旣に約法增
修案及約法に附屬する重要なる法案を議決するを以て其職權となすものなれば約法會議と稱すべく
此項の約法會議を組織する議員に就ては選擧方法を酌用し其選擧區劃は都會集中主義を取り選擧資
格は人材標準主義を取らば旣に吾國が賢能を選ぶの遺意に符し復た各國の制限選擧の良規に合す云
云と查するに臨時約法は南京臨時參議院に成り其時該院議員は十四省より原と派遣せる代表を改組
せる所に係り約法制定後統一政府成立するに及びては約法に稱する所の參議院は旣に最初組織せる
參議院とは同じからず然も該院を組織せる議員も亦僅に約法に定むる所の選派方法に按照して處理
せる者に係れば均しく鄭重を昭かにするに足らず今囘政治會議の議決せる約法會議組織條例及び議
員選擧法は均しく折衷矯計せるものにて約法を制定せる前參議院の其議員が純乎たる選派にて來れ
る者と比すれば惟だ顯かに指派、選擧の各々殊なるあるのみならず之れ法理事實に準據して妥當な
り綜するに該會議の議定せる大綱は一として造法機關を尊重する爲めならざる無く上申の約法會議
組織條例は別に公布を行ふは勿論其外望むらくは各選擧監督は一に選擧手續に關する施行細則の訂

支那政黨史

定頒布の後務めて切實に進行し此次特設の造法機關をして期を定め成立せしめ我國民が亂極り治を思ふの公心を慰めよ

約法會議議員左の如し

北京	鄧鎔 寶熙 黎淵 程德樹
直隸	王劭廉 李榘
奉天	袁金鎧 陳瀛洲
吉林	齊耀珊 徐鼎霖
黑龍江	施愚 秋桐豫
江蘇	莊緼寛 馬揖良
安徽	孫毓筠 王揖唐
江西	李盛鐸 趙惟熙
浙江	朱文劭 蔣尊簋
福建	嚴復 王蓋
湖南	夏壽田 舒禮鑑
湖北	劉心源 張國溶
山東	柯劭志 王丕煦
河南	王祖同 王印川
山西	賈耕 田應璜
陝西	汪涵 王恒晋

甘肅　顧鰲　秦望瀾

四川　傅增湘　曾彝進

新疆　王學曾　王樹枬

廣東　梁士詒　張蔭棠

廣西　張其鍠　關冕鈞

雲南　朱家寶　嚴天駿

貴州　任可澄　陳國祥

蒙藏青海　那彦圖　齊默特散皮勒　阿旺根敦　棍布扎布　噶拉增

全國商會　馮麟霈　向端琨　李湛陽　張振勳

江曲達結　許世英　錢能訓

約法會議は舊約法を袁世凱の希望する如く增修改删し五月一日公布せられたり而して該約法中には參政院組織の規定あり

第十八節　參政院の組織

民國三年六月二十日參政院開院式擧行せられたり正副院長は總統の任命する所にして其餘の參政約七十名も殆ど指定にて全く自家藥籠中の者のみを集めたり

參政院院長　黎元洪

同　副院長　汪大燮

參政　胡鈞　徐紹楨　楊守敬　汪大燮　馮麟霈

孫多森　姚錫光　蔣尊簋　劉若曾　汪有齡

袁世凱は此參政院を以て恰も日本の樞密院の如き機關とする目的にて約法會議にては尚立法院組織法案を議定せしむる筈なりしも既に內閣制を改めて總統制と爲し全然獨裁の權を握りたるを以て立法院を組織する如きは希望せざる所なりしが故に六月二十九日命令を以て參政院は立法院の代行を爲す事を公布せり

王世澂　李盛鐸　程樹德　梁士詒　陳漢弟

趙爾巽　梁啓超　王家襄　李經義　熊希齡

呂海寰　孫毓筠　趙惟熙　寶熙　陳國祥

鄧鎔　朱文劭　王印川　饒漢祥　那彥圖

李國杰　李士偉　聯芳　黎淵　王揖唐

王樹枏　蔭昌　王闓運　嚴復　王良

施愚　李湛陽　馬其昶　蔡鍔　宋煒臣

袁樹勛　阿穆爾靈奎　塔旺佈理理甲抗　其他未定

約法第六十七條立法院未成立以前は參政院其職權を代行すとあるに基き現在參政院は開院せるに及び尚約法所定の立法院未成立に付き茲に其職權を參政院に於て代行を命ず

斯くて政治會議は國會を解散せしめ約法會議を組織せしめ內閣制を總統制に改むるの議決を爲し又約法會議は約法の總統を檢束せる條項を改刪し總統の權力を增大する條項を加へて總統萬能たらしめ參政院は更に一步を進め共和政體を改めて帝制となし遂に袁世凱に勸進表を奉じて帝位に卽かん事を請願し袁世凱をして外に對しては民國總統內に對しては洪憲皇帝なる珍劇を演ぜしむるに至れり

第十九節　第三次革命

民國四年十二月十九日蔡鍔、唐繼堯等帝制反對共和維持の義旗を雲南に舉げて以來五年六月六日袁世
凱が死亡する迄約六箇月間は帝制反對派も共に其行動を一にして袁政府に當りしが袁の死
後黎元洪總統となりて舊約法を復活し舊國會を招集するに及び初め敵を同ふせしときは聯絡行動を取
りし者も敵亡びたる曉は各自の權利競爭の爲め又々黨同伐異を爲すに至れり
第三次革命の起義中心人物は蔡鍔、唐繼堯、李烈鈞なりしが蔡、唐は進歩黨に屬し李烈鈞は國民黨な
り上海にて帝制に反對し極力革命に援助を與へたる者は唐紹儀、孫洪伊、谷鍾秀、殷汝驪等なり其所
屬を問へば唐紹儀は國民黨にして孫洪伊は進歩黨に屬し谷鍾秀、殷汝驪は舊共和統一黨にて後國民黨
に合せし者なり天津にて帝制反對を唱へ袁をして脚下に鳥の立つ思ひあらしめたるは梁啓超、湯化龍
なり同じく進歩黨に籍を置くも梁は共和黨にして湯は民主黨なり斯の如く極めて複雜なる聯合にして
僅に帝制反對若しくは袁世凱反對と云ふ一點に於て相一致し居たるも其他に在りては個々別々なり袁
の死後は是等反對者は直に自己の勢力攫取に熱中し過去の共同一致の情に移れり
抑も第一次革命は中途妥協に終り革命の目的を貫徹したるに非ず第二次革命は未だ革命と命名するに
及ばずして消滅したるものなり第三次革命に至りては前二囘の失敗に懲り稍持續貫徹的態度に出で少
くとも第一次革命に於ける當時の遺留的舊勢力を根絶せんとせしに袁世凱斃れたるを以て中途其の目
的を失ひ矢は滿を引きたる弓の敵の射るべき無きに至りたるなり
然らば第三次革命は其功を何人に歸すべきか頗る斷定し難き問題にて先づ共同に分配せざる可らず共
同の分配は乃ち競爭の生ずる所、競爭の結果は黨同伐異の由て起る所、黨同伐異は乃ち陰謀陷擠の止
むを得ざる所なり斯くの如くして初めは堂々たる帝制反對共和維持の大革命が終には革命起義の元勳
が帝制走狗の殘孽と相提携し極端なる民主論者が絶對なる帝制論者と相結託するに至れり卽ち中央政

支那政黨史

府が統一力を喪失せる結果第一次革命の結果國民の服從心を喪失し、國民の服
從心を喪失したる結果第二次革命を誘起し、第二次革命の勃發したる結果國民の
民の破壊心を養成したる結果第三次革命を見るに至り、第三次革命を見たる結果
でて支配するに非ざれば何人にも委託する能はざる感念を各個人の頭腦に深刻し己の欲する所に非ざ
れば直に囂々反對し又國家の利害得失を顧みず所謂る兄弟鬩牆の境遇に陥り大局より支持を計る者な
きに至り表面より見れば干戈銃聲の響くなきも實際に於ては群雄割據し攻伐侵略春秋戰國と異ならざ
る混亂狀態に陥れり

第二章　第三次革命後の政黨

第一節　梁啓超の劃策

袁世凱の死するや革命を囂々せし者唯狂喜して其後に處する策を講ずる者なし獨り其間に在りて早く
も自己の立場を造らん爲め竊に計劃を運らせしは梁啓超なり梁啓超は民國二年袁世凱が國會を解散せ
し時の命令に署名せる閣員なり故に此次帝制に反對したる革命の一元動たるに拘らず革命を呼號せし
者梁啓超を排斥せり梁啓超自ら之を以て必ず革命黨中に一の標榜を有する歸著點を設け其標榜
の反面に在りて劃策し漸次に己の勢力を作らざる可らずと爲し遂に岑春煊を擔ぎて肇慶に軍務院を組
織し自ら總參謀長兼民政總長と成り南北講和等の事あるに至れば（此時既に段內閣成り講和休戰中な
り）己先づ交渉の局に當り以て政海の一大重要地位を占めんことを期せり
然れ共肇慶政府の設立は廣東の龍濟光との交渉豫定の如く進行せざりしを以て甚だ持て餘し居る際袁
世凱死せしを以て梁啓超は茲に態度を一變し徒に革命黨と提携せば其功は遂に唐紹儀等に奪はるゝ虞

あり寧ろ北方の勢力を把握する段祺瑞と提携し以て民黨と稱する唐紹儀、孫洪伊等の黨派を牽制せん

と企圖し是に於て湯化龍に意を授け行動を共にせり

梁啓超は前議會の解散署名者として所屬進步黨中の人も皆彼を恨み眞の部下は參衆兩院に於て五六十

人に過ず故に梁啓超は袁死し黎元洪總統と成りたるとき舊約法を復活し舊國會を召集するには極力反

對したり然れども大勢の赴く所如何共爲し難く遂に舊約法も舊國會も共に復活したるを以て己の希望

悉く相違し自派及び湯化龍派を合するも其勢力甚だ微々たるを以て茲に不黨主義なるものを提唱し以

て他黨の聯合團結するを妨げ竊に段祺瑞との提携を極力運動せり然し無黨主義なる空漠なる拘束が能

く何時迄も持續し得べきに非ず議會が憲法を議するに及んで梁啓超、湯化龍の派は第一に黨派を造り

是を端緒として各派とも皆夫々同志を集めて政團を作り茲に始めて政黨の叢出時代を見るに至れり

第二節　政團の叢出

梁啓超、湯化龍派が暗々裏に政黨の準備を爲し梁派は憲法研究會を組織し湯派は憲法討論會を組織す

然して兩者の主張甚だ相近きを以て遂に合併して憲法研究會となり是より各派は續々不黨主義を破つ

て政黨を組織せり

○憲法研究會

簡章

第一條　本會は憲法及其他重要政務を研究するを以て宗旨とす

第二條　凡そ國會議員にして本會宗旨と相一致し入會を願ふ者は本會員たるを得

第三條　國會議員に非ざる者にして本會と宗旨を同ふし入會を願ふ者は本會會員三人以上の紹介に由

り入會するを得

支那政黨史

第四條　本會は毎日曜日に一次開會す若し重要問題あるときは臨時開會するを得主席は臨時推舉す

第五條　一問題討論終了後は表決に付し以て會內多數の意見を覘ふを得

第六條　多數表決後は本會議員は憲法會議或は國會に於て一致之を主張す

但表決案自己の意思と絕對に相反する者は亦自由主張すべし

第七條　本會は會員中より公推する編輯員八人を以て各研究案を擔任整理す

第八條　本會員中より交際員若干人を公推し交際事務を擔任す

第九條　本會は會員中より幹事十五人を公推し文書會計庶務等を分掌す

第十條　本會事務所を石駙馬大街に設く

辨事員の雇用は幹事より之を定む

第十一條　本會の經費は會員より籌出し臨時出納を報告す

第十二條　本章程未だ悉さゞる所あれば臨時提議修改す

同會の役員左の如し

　編輯員

　　藍公武　陳光燾　林長民　陳　善　賈庸熙

　　孫光圻　彭運斌　吳日清

　幹事員

　　王家襄　陳銘鑑　曾有翼　陳光譜　陳景烈

　　梁善濟　周大烈　虞廷愷　郭涵　王錫泉

　　凌文淵　劉星楠　胡源滙　張樹森　杜成鎔

　文書科

　會計科

　庶務科

一般會員

但し其內にて他黨に跨る者或は實際反對の者もあり今之等を一併概舉すれば左の如し

張雲閣	張宏銓	胡源滙	陳銘鑑	莫德惠	張雅南
范殿棟	王湛塵	郭涵	劉雲屏	陳瀛州	張樹森
范樵	張蔭亭	何昌阿	陳善	沈河清	李耀忠
蔣鳳梧	陳義	姚文枡	汪秉忠	張烈	王戈忠
李兆年	鄧毓怡	周祖瀾	陳秉善	張還	李耀忠
林長民	陸大坊	閻與可	姚文梅	郭廣璋	王廣坼
王之籤	李元亮	王謝可家	杜師業	常埠息	王光坼
魏丹書	周祖瀾	張玉鈺	劉不元	金還	孫凱之
王鑾聲	閻與可	吳蔭淵	祺誠武	曹蔭瀛	王廣圻
陳洪道	董毓梅	熙阿	楊繩祖	馬蔭榮	杜光坼
趙成息	虞文愷	郭廣榮	楊振州	王廣璋	孫光坼
陳士髦	蕭廷增	張玉鈺	布爾格特	金還	王廣圻
陳允中	謝可均	熙鈺	徐希之	孫還	王凱之
劉興毅	劉翊元	吳蔭淵	榮熙厚	杜光坼	李耀忠
陳嗣申	張嗣良	熙阿	榮熙阿	王廣坼	孫世杰
陳光壽	姚守先	岳雲韜	杜凌阿	馬良弼	陳金鑑
許植材	譚煥文	王鴻慶	白常潔	程崇信	周學源
孫世杰	陳光譜	劉鴻慶	彭昌福	姚華	王卓甫

支那政黨史

谷鍾堂　賈洞元　張則林　韓增慶　耿北棟　呂沴林

張恩級　張敬之　崔懷灝　張滋大　劉士三　宋槙

張其密　劉尚衞　謝書林　唐士行　藍公武　張敬弟

林輅存　高登鯉　黃荃　連賢基　王敬芳　胡汝霖

籍忠寅　唐鄉懷　唐瑞銅　金承新　佈霖　王敬瑄

吳涑　朱繼之　李文治　翁恩裕　葛恩銘　齊耀瑄

李增穆　侯効儒　楊廷棟　嚴天駿　張聯芳　陳經鎔

唐理淮　王多輔　恒詩峯　黃鏡人　吳作棻　吳文淵

李景濂　李保邦　王文芹　汪震東　孟昭漢　呂金鏞

田美峯　　　　　　　　　　　　　　　　　　金桂山

○憲法商榷會

商榷會は民國五年九月孫洪伊、谷鍾秀、張繼、王正廷、田桐、白逾桓、劉成禹、王湘等各方面の民黨相約し團城に大會を開きて組織したるものに係り名は憲法に對する商榷會なるに過ぎざるも其目的は一大政黨を組織せんとするに在りき然れども成立後其網羅せる範圍が甚だ廣大複雜にて相一致する能はず間もなく分裂を生ぜり卽ち國民黨中にても舊同盟會に屬する分子は相寄り丙辰俱樂部を組織し張繼、王正廷等は益友社を組織し孫洪伊等は韜園を組織し谷鍾秀、張耀曾等は政學會を組織し殆ご四分五裂と成れり然れども此內にて谷鍾秀、張耀曾の政學會一派を除くの外は依然商榷會を民黨の總括的團體と爲す

更に商榷會が斯く分立する理由を詳論せんに政學會派の谷鍾秀、張耀曾は韜園派の孫洪伊を喜ばず丙辰倶樂部派は谷鍾秀、張耀曾を喜ばず故に政學會派が谷鍾秀、張耀曾を除き韜園派が孫洪伊を除かば四派完全に合同し得べきが如しと雖事實は必ずしも然らざるものあり乃ち丙辰倶樂部派は舊同盟會員を限りたる團體にて舊同盟會員なれば景耀月の如き帝制派にても復黨せしめ他派の人は一切之を拒絕す是が爲め同じ商榷會中に在るも他系の人は是を喜ばざるの有樣にして尙此外に憲友會なるもの存す

憲友會は一時商榷會中に加入せし者にて商榷會分裂後益友社に屬し更に益友社より分離したる舊共和黨員の組織する所に係り張伯烈、何雯、駱繼漢等其主なる者なり

今假りに黎總統を民黨の首領とし段總理を官僚海の首領として相爭ふ問題に對しては左の聯合を見るべし

商榷會

舊同盟會系
丙辰倶樂部
舊國民黨系
益友社系
舊進步黨系
韜園系
舊統一共和黨系
政學會

（田桐、白逾桓等）

（張繼、王正廷、吳景濂等）

（孫洪伊、丁世嶧、汪彭年、郭同等）

（谷鍾秀、張耀曾、彭允彝等）

丙辰倶樂部
益友社

商榷會卽民黨韜

政　學　會　（此中張耀曾、谷鍾秀、段汝驪を除く）

憲　友　會　（此中張伯烈、何雯を除く）

（但し張伯烈、何雯、駱繼漢は段祺瑞より買收され居るを以て將來憲友會は漸々研究會派に接近すべし）

〇丙辰倶樂部　（部員約七十人）

丙辰倶樂部は舊同盟會員田桐、白逾桓、馬君武等の組織する所にして其倶樂部員は皆舊同盟會員に限らる此會員は同じく商榷會中に在るも谷鍾秀、張耀曾等と相容れず故に商榷會を脱して一團體を爲したるなり部員は參衆兩院を通じ約七十八を有す事務所は米市胡同に在り

〇益　友　社　（社員約二百人）

益友社は舊國民黨員にして張繼、王正廷、吳景濂等其牛耳を執る此派は激烈派の丙辰倶樂部と多少相容れざる所あるも全く相反撥するに至らず故に大體に於ては互に相一致す其會員の如きも兩派に跨り居る者多し會員約二百を有し事務所は石駙馬大街に在り

同社の役員左の如し

政務處　　　　　吳景濂　　張　繼　　林　森　褚輔成　王正廷

文牘處主任　　　徐傅霖　　趙其相

會計科主任　　　李肇甫　　陳鴻鈞

庶務處主任　　　周珏　　　宋淵源

交際處主任　　　王有蘭　　金兆棪

○韜園（會員約八十人）

韜園は舊進步黨員中孫洪伊派に屬する者を以て組織す固より孫洪伊派なるものありしに非ざるを帝制問題發生以來進步黨中の或部分は帝制に贊成して袁の走狗と成り或部分は共和維持を主張し國民黨と相通じて反袁を呼號せり其際進步黨反袁派中率先討袁の主張を全國に移檄發表せし者は孫洪伊なり故に進步黨中に帝政反對者の郭同、汪彭年、王乃昌、蕭晉榮、牟琳等は皆相寄りて上海に集合せる國民黨と聯絡せり初め帝制問題の起りし時は反對派國民黨と進步黨との別なく殆ど相一致せる所ありしも袁死後國民黨と進步黨とが分離せるのみならず國民黨中にも舊同盟會は丙辰俱樂部となり舊國民黨は益友社となりたる如く進步黨中にも梁湯派（梁啓超及湯化龍派）と非梁湯派を生じ所謂孫洪伊一派の如きは非梁湯派にて梁湯等を疾視する結果國民黨と相提携するに至り此派が最も黎總統に接近せり此派會員は約八十人あり孫洪伊、丁世嶧、汪彭年、郭同、王乃昌、蕭晉榮等其中堅なり事務所は安福胡園に在り

○政　學　會

政學會は舊共和統一黨にして谷鍾秀、張耀曾等其牛耳を取る共和統一黨は民國二年既に國民黨に合併したるも其舊團體は依然存在し舊同盟會員と融和せず殊に袁死後谷鍾秀、殷汝驪等舊共和統一黨員は獵官に熱狂し就官後國民黨を捨てゝ段祺瑞の藥籠中に入り純官僚となりたるを以て丙辰俱樂部派の國民黨員の攻擊甚しく就めに谷鍾秀、張耀曾等は茲に政學會を組織したるなり

此の政學會員は約四十人と稱し居るも皆益友社に籍を有する者の跨黨にして本會純粹なる會員と認むべき者は左の如し

谷鍾秀　張耀曾　李根源　彭允彝　歐陽振聲　殷汝驪

文　群　王　侃　李肇甫　童士釗　李述膺　徐傳霖
韓玉辰　高冲和　其他二名

○平　社　（會員約五十人）

平社は早稻田學生派の組織せる所にて黃雲鵬、向乃琪等國民黨員、進步黨員及中立黨員ありて極めて平等的なりしに會員由宗龍の兄が雲南督軍唐繼堯の祕書長たるを以て漸次聯絡を取り一種の關係を造れり又劉榮澤は竊に背面に在りて是を利用操縱せる形跡あり近頃衡社の梅光遠が此平社を衡社と合併せしめ陸宗興、楊士驄等と共に結合して徐世昌の下に投ぜんとするあり尤も會員中にて約十八程の國民黨系の者ありて其計劃に贊成せず乃ち衡社と合併の時は該國民黨系分子は益友社若しくは丙辰倶樂部に復歸すべし現今の會員は約五十人を有し事務所を後孫公園に置く

○蘇　園　（會員約二千人）

蘇園は元政友會員孫鍾、狄樓海等の組織する所なり其系統を詳にせば舊國民黨員にして民國二年國民黨に背き政友會に入りたる者なり然るに同じ政友會の反國民黨中にても景耀月の如きは丙辰倶樂部に復歸し蘇園一派の者と分離せり此派は其系統上將來如何なる方面に阿附するや知る可らず會員は約二十人を有し事務所を芝麻街に置く

○憲政討論會　（會員約七十人）

憲政討論會は大中黨の系統にして江天鐸、恒鈞、孫潤宇、恩華、黃贊元、張國溶、夏同龢、張樹森、朱兆莘、陶遜、袁榮叜、陳㲄宸等の發起組織せし所にて會員系統は甚だ複雜なり同會は商推會と研究會との二大政黨の間に立ち第三黨として調和を取らんことを主旨とせり其簡章左の如し

憲政討論會簡章

第一條　本會は憲法及其他一切の法案を討論するを以て主旨とす

第二條　凡そ本會に同情を表する者は會員の紹介を經て本會會員と爲す

第三條　本會の辨事員は會員より輪選す

第四條　本會は毎週少くとも一回開會す

第五條　本會討論の議題は會員より豫め擬定し本會幹事員に交付し編列通告す

但し緊急問題發生の時は臨時提議す

第六條　本會毎囘開會の時は會員より一人を推擧して主席とす

第七條　凡そ一議題討論終了せば多數を以て之を決するを得

第八條　凡そ多數決定の意見は憲法會議及び兩院會議に於て是を一致主張す

但し本會討論のとき絶對反對の意見を發表せし者は拘束を受けざるを得

第九條　本會經費は會員より自由捐助す

第十條　本簡章不備の所は隨時提議修正す

本會は其主旨に第三黨的調和主義を表明し飽迄騎牆態度を以て風向きに由つて向背せんとする曖昧黨たれば其集合分子も極めて複雜にて結合甚だ堅からざる觀あり卽ち其中にて孫潤宇等の一派は全然研究會に近く唐寶鍔等の一派は益友社に近く江天鐸、朱兆莘等の廣東一派は自然廣東團を成し該討論會中又第三黨たらんとするの狀況なり

會員約七十名を有し事務所を順治門大街に置く

會員の主要分子は左の如し

　辛　漢　　孫潤宇　　江天鐸　　溫雄飛　　克希克圖　　夏同龢

張國溶　黃贊元　朱兆莘　唐寶鍔　楊福州　黃宵九

恩華　于寶軒　林繩武　吳榮華　王立延　譚瑞霖

可徒頴　黃錫銓等

○憲法協議會（會員約二十八）

憲法協議會は蒙古議員を以て組織せらる蒙古議員と云ふも純粹蒙古人に非らずして袁世凱が北京にて選舉し己の用を爲す王廕、曹汝霖等を外蒙西藏等の選出額數丈指定し曖昧なる代理選舉機關を作りて選舉したるものなれば一種の勅選議員にして蒙藏議員と稱し曖昧議員の團體なり其中の主要分子は陸宗輿、曹汝霖、王廕、王文芹、王振堯、李芳、王顯等にて會員約二十名を有し主なる顏觸は陸宗輿、張滋大等にして事務所を後水泡子に置く

○衡　　社　（會員約十五人）

衡社は帝制派梅光遠等の組織せる處にして其背後には平社と同じく劉榮澤關係を有す梅光遠は近頃民德社なる者を組織し平社と衡社とを合併せんと企圖せり元來梅光遠は舊公民黨員なれば其組織せんとする民德社なるものは帝制派系、梁士詒系たるや言を待たず從て平社中の國民黨系及び四川省の共和黨系分子は分離するを免れず梅光遠は又近頃徐世昌の麾下に奔らんとす即ち衡社と平社は何れも背後に劉榮澤の有るによりて既に關係あり而も梅光遠が陸宗輿の如き徐世昌派と接近し衡社と平社を合併して以て其の旗下に馳參せんとすれば將來衡社と平社と憲法協議會とは當然合併すべき性質を有す目下衡社としては會員僅に十數人を有するに過ぎざるも漸次擴張さるべき見込あり事務所を舊刑部街に置く會員の主なる者は黃佩蘭、梅光遠、陸宗輿、楊士驄等なりとす

○靜　　廬　（會員約十人）

憲法中に省制を加入すると否とに就き憲法研究會は其不加入を主張し益友社、丙辰倶樂部は加入を主張し兩大政黨共に堅く執つて相下らず憲法討論會の一部及び憲法協議會等は憲法研究會主張の不加入を賛成す其結果憲法審議會が常に兩院を通じて約六百人の出席中益友社派の加入主張は三百七十を占め研究會派の不加入主張は二百二三十を占む爲めに何れも法定の三分の二の數を得るを得ず種々協商する所と成る然れども居中調停者に資格制限等あるに非ず唯一政團より一代表を出し各政團聯合にて調停を爲す其結果一意見を提出せんとせば一政團を組織するの必要あり其組織内容は如何に貧弱なるにせよ將た勢力あるにもせよ一政團と云へば一代表を出し得るなり靜廬は全く此目的より出でたるものにして憲法研究會及び憲政討論會の一部卽ち陶遜等の組織する所にて會員僅に十人を有するに過ぎず事務所は西北園北口一號に置く

○潛　　　　園（會員約十五人）

潛園は謝書林等の組織する所にて其主旨目的は靜廬と同じ會員約十五人程にて名聲ある政客の加入せるを聞かず憲法研究會派が居中調停の政團に自黨多からしめんが爲め特に出店的小政團を造らしめたるなり事務所は臨清宮東口張宅に置く兎に角憲法問題に對する一時の小結合たるに過ぎず

○憲　　友　　會（會員約十五人）

憲友會は共和黨の湖北派たる張伯烈及び何雯、駱繼漢等の組織する所にて民社系統に屬するを以て初めは黎總統派に歸し居りしも段祺瑞が徐樹錚をして籠絡せしめ尙金鼎勳をして買收せしめたるを以て漸々段派と成り殊に最近に於ける張伯烈、何雯、駱繼漢等は段の爲めに盡力すること甚しく彼の段總理彈劾案の提出せらるゝや駱繼漢は動議を提出して曰く彈劾案は議員總數四分の三以上出席するに非

支那政黨史

ざれば議するを得ず最近議員の出席は殆ど四分の三を超過する事稀なり故に常に議事日程に上すも議するの時なし議する能はざるに常に日程に彈劾案を載せ置くは甚だ體面に關す宜しく是を日程に載する事を止め法定數の出席を得たる時緊急動議として提議すべしと主張し遂に段及び谷鍾秀、陳錦濤等の彈劾案を日程に記載せざることゝなれり是等は最も段に盡したるものゝ段も亦甚だ德とする所なり

會員は

○淵　　廬　（會員約二十人）

張　伯　烈　　何　　雯　　駱　繼　漢　　陳　邦　變　　蕭　承　彌　　尹　宏　慶

辛　際　唐　　盧　元　弼　　歌　陽　成　　陳　子　斌　　查　季　華　　胡　祖　舜

席　　綬　　禹　　瀜　　鄭　樹　槐　　鄭　衡　之　　黃　攻　素　　潘　子　海

邱　冠　棻　　載　書　雲　　劉　　濂　　梁　系　登　　蔣　羲　明　　廖　宗　北

鄭　江　灝　　金　承　新　　馮　振　驥

紋上の如く二十七人の名を列するも其內には跨黨の者あり實際贊成し居らざる者あり眞の本會員と認むべき者は約十五人に過ぎず事務所を櫻姚斜街に置く本會員は素と湖北民社に屬し最近に於ては憲法商推會に屬し商推會分裂するに及びて益友社に屬せし者なれば當然黎派に屬すべき者なるに買收の爲め段派となれり然れ共段に盡す所あるも是が爲め直に梁湯派に配和混同する者には非ざるなり

○憲　政　會　（會員約二十人）

淵廬は研究會中の舊派乃ち吳文翰、阮毓崧等の組織する所にて其主旨目的は彼の靜廬、潛園等と同一にて同じく憲法研究會派の支派なり會員は約二十名を有し事務所を米市胡同に置く

憲政會は帝政派の楊士驄、胡璧城、湯松年等の組織する所にて憲法協議會蒙古議員康士鐸、烏澤聲等

も又此中に入會す此會亦憲法研究會の別働隊と看做すべき者なるが兎に角帝制に熱狂奔走せし徒輩の
みなれば研究會中に在りても常に面恥かしき所あるを以て別に此一政團を組織せし者なり然し此會は
將來平社、衝社等の徒と合併すべき系統及び性質を有す烏澤聲、康士鐸の如きは梁士詒の部下にして
楊士聰は楊士琦の弟なり卽ち本會と憲法協議會、平社及衝社は何れも親類筋にして同意氣者なり何れ
も權勢に走るに拔目なき徒のみなれば漸々相率ゐて徐世昌の下に投ぜん會員は楊士聰、胡璧城、湯松
年、烏澤聲、康士鐸を始めとし約二十人を有し事務所を半壁街に置く

○民　彜　社（會員數未詳）

民彜社は前參政院參政李盛鐸等の組織せるものにして熊希齡、汪大燮、胡鈞、汪有齡等前參政を網羅
す熊希齡、汪大燮等は他に尚一の政社を組織する計劃を有するも目下取敢へず李盛鐸等と事を共にせ
るなり李盛鐸、熊希齡等の目的は前參政院參政等を集めて基礎と爲し參衆兩院無所屬及び小政團を吸
集せんとするに在り目下會員數は未だ知るを得ざるも策士等の團體にして背後に資本家との聯絡ある
樣子なれば一勢力を爲すに至るべし

第三節　參議院議員三分の一改選後に於ける豫想

參議院は民國五年十二月十八日其議員三分の一を改選したるが該三分の一の退職者約九十一人中國民
黨員約六十人あり而して目下選擧確定せる十三省の當選者を見るに四十八人中國民黨二十人に過ぎず然
らば此率を以て推せば全部選擧終了後民黨は四十八人乃至四十五人に過ぎず然らば民黨は現在より二三
十人の勢力を減じ官僚黨は其反比例に二三十人の增勢となるべし若し民黨と無所屬を除きたる殘餘悉
く集りて官僚大團結を造ることありとせば其數は約三百三十前後となり民黨は三百七十前後となる則
ち無所屬百人の向背は其優劣を決する所となり甚しき取合運動を惹起すべし（今日迄の政團情況斯の

如くなるも變遷極りなき風向政客多きと特に煽動攪亂する者多き政界なれば如何なる變化を爲すも知る可らず）

現在各政團勢力一覽表

政團	代表者	人數
商榷會　益友社	張繼　吳景濂　王正廷等	二百人
丙辰俱樂部	田桐　白逾桓　馬君武等	七十人
韜園	孫洪伊　丁世嶧　汪彭年等	八十人
政學會	張耀曾　谷鍾秀　彭允彝等	十六人
憲法研究會	陶遜　鍾允諧等　林長民等	五十人
憲友會	梁啓超　湯化龍　駱繼漢等	十五人
平社	張伯烈　何雯　向乃祺等	百二十人
靜廬	黃雲鵬　由宗龍等	十八人
潛園	謝書林等　阮毓崧等	二十人
淵廬	吳文翰　朱兆莘　江天鐸等	七十八人
憲政討論會	孫潤宇　康士鐸　烏澤聲等	二十人
憲法協議會	李芳　狄樓海等	二十人
藐園	孫鍾　陸宗輿等	十五人
衡社	梅光遠　胡璧城　湯松年等	二十八人
憲政會	楊士驄　陸宗興等	二十五人
民彝社	李盛鐸　熊希齡　汪大燮等	未詳

現在各政團所屬一覽表

無所屬
　○民黨（黎元洪派）　二百人
商榷會
　益友社　七十人
　丙辰俱樂部　八十人
　韜園　十五人
政學會　二十人
合計　三分の一　約四百人
平社　五十人
憲法討論會　三分の一　七十人
○更黨（段祺瑞派）
憲法研究會
　梁啓超派
　湯化龍派　二十人
憲法討論會　三分の一　十人
静盧園　十五人
潛盧園　十五人
憲友會　十五人
淵盧園　二十人
穭園　二十人

百人

憲政會　　　　　　　　　　約二百四十人

○中立協議會（徐世昌派）　　二十人

憲法協議會　　　　　　　　三十人

平社　　　　　　　　　　　十五人

衡社・三分の二　　　　　　二十人

憲政合計會　　　　　　　　約八十五人

○中立派（無所屬）

無所屬　　　　　　　　　　約百人

附北京發刊新聞一覽表

名稱	黨派別	經營者
大國民日報	民黨	景耀月
大聲報	同	白逾桓 景定成
國風日報	同	李烈鈞 李安陸
亞東日報	同	張我華
民生報	同	周亮三
醒華報	同	王君武 龔煥辰
民主報	同	馬彥聲
中央日報	同	葉夏聲
新震旦日報	皖派	馬仲權
大中華日報		張仲錦
國是報	同	光雲錦
危言日刊	皖孫派少侯系	汪彭年
新民報	民黨	向瑞彝 彭希民
國民公報	研究會	藍公武 孫光圻
晨鐘報	同	湯化龍 梁秋水

大 中 報	研 究 會	范 源 濂
北 京 中 華 新 報	牛 官 牛 民	谷 鍾 秀
民 國 新 報	同	張 耀 曾
北 京 公 民 日 報	同	劉 揆 一
法 言 報	同（政學會に稍關係あり）	
北 京 日 日 新 報	憲 法 討 論 會	克 希 克 圖 周 需 三
新 中 國 報	憲 友 會	何 雯
尊 聞 報	同	何 雯 張 扔 人
北 京 日 報	中 立	朱 小 祺
北 京 時 報	同	楊 小 歐
公 言 報	帝 制 派	汪 有 齡 林 萬 里
京 津 時 報	同	汪 立 元
民 視 報	同	康 士 鐸
亞 細 亞 日 報	同	袁 乃 寬 出 資
璇 宇 日 報	同	袁 乃 寬
大 興 日 報	交 通 銀 行 系	
日 知 報	同	王 伯 謙
每 日 新 聞 報	帝 制 派	烏 澤 聲
大 信 報	政 府 黨	

新聞名	系統	主筆
北京民強報	同	王河屏
陸海軍日報	同	羅澤煒
興中報	同	劉文錦
眞共和日報	中立	黃雲鵬
京華日報	陳樹藩機關	
覺報	政府黨	張伯烈
二十世記	尹昌衡機關	
大陸報	天主教	杜竹軒
益世言		
民言		
忠言		

血歷史30　PC0249

新銳文創
INDEPENDENT & UNIQUE

中華民國珍貴史料：
民初議員列傳
——附民初政黨及議會史

作　　者	井上一葉、佐藤三郎
主　　編	蔡登山
責任編輯	王奕文
圖文排版	彭君浩
封面設計	王嵩賀

出版策劃	新銳文創
發 行 人	宋政坤
法律顧問	毛國樑　律師
製作發行	秀威資訊科技股份有限公司
	114 台北市內湖區瑞光路76巷65號1樓
	電話：+886-2-2796-3638　傳真：+886-2-2796-1377
	服務信箱：service@showwe.com.tw
	http://www.showwe.com.tw
郵政劃撥	19563868　戶名：秀威資訊科技股份有限公司
展售門市	國家書店【松江門市】
	104 台北市中山區松江路209號1樓
	電話：+886-2-2518-0207　傳真：+886-2-2518-0778
網路訂購	秀威網路書店：http://www.bodbooks.com.tw
	國家網路書店：http://www.govbooks.com.tw

出版日期	2012年09月　初版
定　　價	760元

國家圖書館出版品預行編目

中華民國珍貴史料：民初議員列傳：附民初政黨及議會史 /
佐藤三郎, 井上一葉編著. -- 初版. -- 臺北市：新銳文
創, 2012. 09
　面；　公分
ISBN 978-986-5915-09-4 (平裝)

1. 參議員　2. 傳記　3. 中華民國史　4.議會制度

782.218　　　　　　　　　　　　　　　101015410

讀者回函卡

感謝您購買本書，為提升服務品質，請填妥以下資料，將讀者回函卡直接寄回或傳真本公司，收到您的寶貴意見後，我們會收藏記錄及檢討，謝謝！
如您需要了解本公司最新出版書目、購書優惠或企劃活動，歡迎您上網查詢或下載相關資料：http:// www.showwe.com.tw

您購買的書名：_____

出生日期：_____年_____月_____日

學歷：□高中 (含) 以下　　□大專　　□研究所 (含) 以上

職業：□製造業　□金融業　□資訊業　□軍警　□傳播業　□自由業
　　　□服務業　□公務員　□教職　　□學生　□家管　　□其它_____

購書地點：□網路書店　□實體書店　□書展　□郵購　□贈閱　□其他

您從何得知本書的消息？

　□網路書店　□實體書店　□網路搜尋　□電子報　□書訊　□雜誌

　□傳播媒體　□親友推薦　□網站推薦　□部落格　□其他_____

您對本書的評價：（請填代號　1.非常滿意　2.滿意　3.尚可　4.再改進）

　封面設計____　版面編排____　內容____　文／譯筆____　價格____

讀完書後您覺得：

　□很有收穫　□有收穫　□收穫不多　□沒收穫

對我們的建議：_____

_____

_____

_____

11466
台北市內湖區瑞光路 76 巷 65 號 1 樓

秀威資訊科技股份有限公司 　　收

BOD 數位出版事業部

....

（請沿線對折寄回，謝謝！）

姓　　名：＿＿＿＿＿＿＿＿＿　年齡：＿＿＿＿　性別：□女　□男

郵遞區號：□□□□□

地　　址：＿＿＿＿＿＿＿＿＿＿＿＿＿＿＿＿＿＿＿＿

聯絡電話：(日) ＿＿＿＿＿＿＿＿＿＿　(夜) ＿＿＿＿＿＿＿＿＿＿

E-mail：＿＿＿＿＿＿＿＿＿＿＿＿＿＿＿＿＿＿＿